Instruction Shall Go Forth

Instruction Shall Go Forth
Studies in Micah and Isaiah

JOHN T. WILLIS

edited by
TIMOTHY M. WILLIS
and MARK W. HAMILTON

☙PICKWICK *Publications* • Eugene, Oregon

INSTRUCTION SHALL GO FORTH
Studies in Micah and Isaiah

Copyright © 2014 John T. Willis. All rights reserved. Except for brief quotations in critical publications or reviews, no part of this book may be reproduced in any manner without prior written permission from the publisher. Write: Permissions, Wipf and Stock Publishers, 199 W. 8th Ave., Suite 3, Eugene, OR 97401.

Pickwick Publications
An Imprint of Wipf and Stock Publishers
199 W. 8th Av.e, Suite 3
Eugene, OR 97401

www.wipfandstock.com

ISBN 13: 978-1-62032-989-4

Cataloging-in-Publication data:

Willis, John T.

    Instruction shall go forth : studies in Micah and Isaiah / John T. Willis ; edited by Timothy M. Willis and Mark W. Hamilton.

    xx + 348 p. ; 23 cm. Includes bibliographical references.

    ISBN 13: 978-1-62032-989-4

    1. Bible. Micah—Criticism, interpretation, etc. 2. Bible. Isaiah—Criticism, interpretation, etc. 3. Bible. Prophets—Criticism, interpretation, etc. I. Willis, Timothy M. II. Hamilton, Mark W. III. Title.

BS1615.53 W55 2014

Manufactured in the U.S.A.

Contents

Introduction | vii

Abbreviations | xv

Part One: The Book of Micah

1. The Structure of the Book of Micah | 3
2. Thoughts on a Redactional Analysis of the Book of Micah | 36
3. Fundamental Issues in Contemporary Micah Studies | 55
4. The Structure of Micah 3–5 and the Function of Micah 5:9–14 in the Book | 66
5. Micah 4:14—5:5—A Unit | 92
6. Some Suggestions on the Interpretation of Micah 1:2 | 111
7. On the Text of Micah 2:1aα-β | 118
8. Micah 2:6-8 and the "People of God" in Micah | 126
9. A Note on ואמר in Micah 3:1 | 144
10. ממך לי יצא in Micah 5:1 | 150
11. The Authenticity and Meaning of Micah 5:9–14 | 156

Part Two: The Book of Isaiah

12. The First Pericope in the Book of Isaiah | 175
13. An Important Passage for Determining the Historical Setting of a Prophetic Oracle—Isaiah 1:7-8 | 191

14	On the Interpretation of Isaiah 1:18	210
15	Lament Reversed—Isaiah 1:21ff	230
16	The Genre of Isaiah 5:1–7	244
17	Textual and Linguistic Issues in Isaiah 22:15–25	277
18	An Interpretation of Isaiah 22:15–25 and Its Function in the New Testament	303

Acknowledgments | 319

Bibliography | 321

Introduction

THE FIRST REDACTOR OF the book of Qoheleth describes the work's author as someone who "was wise and moreover taught the people knowledge by hearing, considering, and arranging proverbs. . . . Finding pleasing words, and accurately writing reliable words" (Eccl 12:9–10). Such a description fits our honorand, John T. Willis, perhaps with less irony than its original subject. While his métier has not been the proverb, John has distinguished himself over many years as one who takes the Hebrew Bible with the utmost seriousness and unaffectedly seeks to make it understandable, believable, and livable to a modern audience. As a master teacher over many decades, as an expert in the Hebrew prophets, and as an author of popular works (especially for his religious tradition), he has always distinguished himself—and we should by no means speak only in the past tense!—as a scholar whose life has been given to the worthy cause of educating a broad audience in the ways of Scripture.

As his former students and now colleagues, we are privileged to present to a larger scholarly audience a selection of Willis's work on the prophets. Written over a period of more than four decades and thus reflecting the changing habits and values of our guild over that time, the collection stands as a consistent witness to the contemporary search for coherence in the elegant jaggedness of the prophetic books. Seeking to study these texts *as texts*, but more than that as religious literary works that have been disseminated and passionately perused because they reflect not only the concerns of their own world, but the concerns of humankind writ large, Willis has tried to let the Bible be heard on its own terms.

In similar fashion John displays a remarkable willingness to honor the views of the scholars who preceded him, and those who walk alongside him. And if we might sometimes wish that he had been a little less deferential and a bit bolder in going his own way, this reticence reflects a view of scholarship that is all too rare in our own time. Willis's work, without stating the claim overtly, operates on the twin assumptions that knowledge is best advanced one careful step at a time and that this caution shows a respect for other practitioners of the discipline, a respect that in the long run will create a culture of learning that promotes genuine understanding more surely than a culture of agonistic strife. Rather than making sweeping claims that disintegrate with the passing of the next-to-last fashion, he has preferred a kind of scholarly craftsmanship that finds reliable results, however small, so that the community of scholars may grow in its understanding. Perhaps such an approach deserves wider practice than it sometimes enjoys.

Before describing the collection that follows, we do well to say a few words about John Willis the human being. He has been famous at his home institutions, first David Lipscomb College and then primarily Abilene Christian University, as the professor who knows the names and birthdays of hundreds of undergraduate students and remembers them years after they graduate and turn gray-haired. This phenomenal memory, fueled by a genuine care for others, has combined with an extraordinary generosity to make his classes and his home oases for young people far away from home. Generations of graduate students have experienced John as rigorous but fair, thorough but expansive of thought, and willing to work hard with those who share that drive. For the editors in particular, he has modeled the old Roman ideal of the *vir bonus*, the good man who carries out his profession well. And for one of us, he has succeeded masterfully in coupling the task of academic mentor to his personal role of *paterfamilias*.

The essays collected in this volume constitute the bulk of John's published work on Micah and Isaiah. All the entries save one—an essay on the structure of Isaiah 1–5—have appeared in print previously. The editors explored the possibility of including several other unpublished papers investigating the prophets, but space considerations and Willis's own unease with putting into print that with which he is not yet satisfied compelled us to limit this work to the selected items. We gave similar thought to the inclusion of both published and unpublished works on various psalms and other sections of the Hebrew Bible, but a desire to bring focus to the collection likewise precluded further expansion of the volume. What follows is a brief summary of the main theses of Willis's works on Micah and Isaiah, with some minor speculation on its place in the scholarly conversation.

Overview of Contributions to Micah Studies

John T. Willis entered into his scholarly career with his doctoral dissertation, "The Structure, Setting, and Interrelationships of the Pericopes in the Book of Micah," which he successfully defended before the faculty of Vanderbilt Divinity School in 1966. He proceeded to disseminate his conclusions further in a series of ten articles published in peer-reviewed journals between 1967 and 1970, and a Seminar Paper in the Proceedings of the 1978 meeting of the Society of Biblical Literature. The articles provide a mix of thorough treatments of the structure of the book of Micah and detailed analyses of selected crucial passages among its contents (e.g., 2:1; 2:6–8; 4:14—5:5).

The approach that Willis adopts primarily revolves around the redaction history of the book. He begins by outlining some of the typical examples of this approach produced over the preceding decades. Most involved the positing of certain assumptions about what an eighth-century prophet like Micah would or would not have said, identifying the passages that confirmed those assumptions and labeling them as the original pieces, and then reconstructing how the book was redacted from those original pieces through various expansions and alterations in response to historical and theological developments in Israel/Judah until it reached its final form somewhere between the fall of Jerusalem in the early sixth century and the early stages of the canonization of the Hebrew Bible in the late Hellenistic period. The standard proposal, formulated by Stade and championed more recently by commentators like Wolff, limits the contributions of the eighth century prophet to the first three chapters, with two or more epigones expanding the book in subsequent centuries with blocks of oracles during times of national crisis.[1] A common alternative regards the contents as more fragmented groups of oracles gradually brought together into a single, loosely-arranged book through a long process of transmission.

Willis enters into this field of study dominated by proposals of fragmentation and offers a very different reconstruction. He argues that one should start with the final form of the book and seek to discern its overall structure and flow. Once a structure and flow are established, the redaction critic can then work backwards from the final redaction and attempt to reconstruct the book's preceding redactional layers. Like others before

---

1. Stade, "Bemerkungen über das Buch Micha"; Wolff, *Micah*.

him, Willis identifies as main guideposts the location of the summons, "Hear!" in Mic 1:2; 3:1; and 6:1. These guideposts suggest three blocks of oracles in the book: chapters 1–2, 3–5, and 6–7. Willis breaks some new ground in the way he sees a common progression in each section, a progression from doom oracles to hope oracles (1:2—2:11 + 2:12-13; 3:1-12 + 4:1—5:15; 6:1—7:6 + 7:7-20). Having established a possible structure, Willis then identifies verbal and thematic linkages that run both "horizontally" and "vertically" throughout the sections of the book. In other words, he finds significant similarities between the language (catchwords, etc.) and message of the doom oracles in all three sections, and significant similarities between the language and message of the hope oracles in all three sections. Moreover, one can show that the descriptions and justifications for the punishments in the doom oracles of each section indicate that the punishments are the necessary prerequisites for the promised times of restoration given in each corresponding set of hope oracles.

Willis attributes the structure to a compiler(s) living during the Babylonian crisis, when the longstanding signs of Israel's covenant relationship with Yahweh were swept away. A redactor presents the prophet's message anew to a generation of believers that shared many of the same attitudes and experiences of Micah's original audience during the Assyrian crisis. Willis contends that the contents of the individual oracles need not have changed much in the process of being redacted for later audiences, and the primary difference is in refinements to the repeated doom-hope structure of the book.

The most profound element of the analysis, though, comes in the theological rationale Willis proposes for the doom-hope structure. Source and redaction critics often assume that it would be unlikely for a single author to place doom and hope oracles side by side, as one would seem to undermine the other. Many redaction critics thus regard hope oracles in Micah as secondary additions to a prophetic collection of doom oracles. Willis proposes that the repeated juxtaposition of doom oracles and hope oracles was essential to the message that Micah presented to his original audience, and that it was a primary reason for redactors to reuse and expand Micah's work to later generations. The juxtaposition illustrates the principle of *jus talionis*—Yahweh sends punishments that befit the offenses. Moreover, he does this within the larger context of a long-term relationship between Yahweh and the people of Israel. Careful comparisons of the language and imagery of the doom and hope oracles in each section demonstrate the thematic elements they share in common. These common elements show that Yahweh is responsible for both destruction and restoration, for death and life. If it were not so, then the people could conclude that their collective suffering came from a source that existed outside the realm of Yahweh's power and authority, which would make it truly frightening. And if Yahweh were to act solely with wrath, he would be untrue to his divine character. Because both destruction and restoration come from Yahweh, the people can be reassured that the devastation endured by Israel and Judah will not be the final word. It is in hope and anticipation of the future restoration that the people can endure the present punishment, but only if they understand that the one promising future restoration has authority over the forces of the present punishment. In fact, both destruction and restoration result from the same premise—that Yahweh is in covenant relationship with Israel. The same motivation—the desire of a righteous and loving God to dwell among and exist in intimate relationship with His chosen people—prompts both actions, destruction as a response to willful sin and reconstruction as a response to genuine repentance and obedience.

There is a real beauty to this analysis that imitates the beauty it proposes for the book of Micah itself. Not only does it show a balanced literary structure, that structure is employed in the service of the prophet's theological message, which gives an equally balanced portrayal of Yahweh's character (see, for example, Exod 34:6–7 and related passages; Ps 78:32–39). It would be inaccurate to assert that this analysis of the book's structure has won widespread acceptance. Some subsequent commentaries on Micah follow this proposal in its main contours, but others maintain the more fragmented reconstruction formulated by Stade.[2] It would be more appropriate to say that Willis represents an early voice among several recent studies that attribute a well-developed and balanced theological perspective to Israel's eighth-century prophets, rather than postponing that until the days of the Exile.

2. Among English-speaking commentators of the recent past, the closest adherent to Willis's proposal would be Bruce K. Waltke (*A Commentary on Micah*), and Leslie C. Allen does not diverge greatly (*The Books of Joel, Obadiah, Jonah and Micah*). A couple of studies minimize the significance of 2:12–13 to the book's structure and see all of Micah 1–5 as a block (Hagstrom, *The Coherence of the Book of Micah*; Jacobs, *The Conceptual Coherence of the Book of Micah*). The basic outline of Bernhard Stade and Hans Walter Wolff holds sway with others, such as William McKane (*The Book of Micah*) and Philip Peter Jenson (*Obadiah, Jonah, Micah*).

The Book of Isaiah

If his extensive early work on Micah invited interpreters to see the book as a well-wrought theological whole, his ongoing research on Isaiah has done that and more. Over the past four decades he has published a commentary[3] and a series of articles on literary, historical, and theological issues, the chief of which are included in this volume. All of this work shows meticulous attention to detail in the biblical text, a preference for the MT but with thorough attention to alternative ancient versions, careful documentation of all scholarly views, and a suspicion of unnecessary emendation or fanciful readings. In every case, this work clears away much previous sloppy thinking and misuse of evidence and draws conclusions that deepen our understanding of the pericope in question, and thus of Isaiah as a whole.

Professor Willis has been a fixture in the long-running discussion of Isaiah at the Annual meeting of the Society of Biblical Literature, where he continues to be active. The years of his activity have coincided with a revolution in scholarship on the book, including publications of major commentaries by Childs, Beuken, Koole, Blenkinsopp, Paul, Baltzer, Sweeney, and others, all of which are well known. The revolution that has occurred over the past four decades has focused much greater attention on Isaiah as a book with both a long and rich interpretive history and an internal coherence and intricacy that reflects a very complex yet deliberate and artistically sophisticated process of creation over a period of generations. Far from being a loose collection of oracles from Isaiah of Jerusalem and anonymous epigones, the book has come to seem a great work of art singular in scope and focus. As Blenkinsopp puts it with characteristic sophistication, "Isaiah, a collection of many 'scraps' and several compilations differing in linguistic character and theme, therefore much closer to the *Dodekapropheton* than to Jeremiah and Ezekiel, is nevertheless presented as a unity, *a book*."[4] Professor Willis's work has played a role in the growth of such an understanding.

Collectively these essays address major aspects of the structure of Isaiah 1–39, sorting through the role of the book's opening(s) and a major transitional point in its overall structure. The first four essays address questions regarding the construction of chapter 1, which serves as more

---

3. Willis, *Isaiah*.
4. Blenkinsopp, *Opening the Sealed Book*, 6. Emphasis in the original.

than a précis of the First Isaiah's work, but rather as an introduction to the entire book. In a motif that echoes a main theme in Micah, the author(s)/redactor(s) set up the overall work's dialectic between doom and hope, and thus Isaiah 1 anticipates much that follows it. In a related vein, Willis shows that the placement of chapter 5 is deliberate and that the complex use of multiple literary genres in that pericope serves as a foretaste, again, of the book as a whole.

On the whole, these essays mark an advance, characteristic of recent Anglophone and to some extent European scholarship, in understanding Isaiah as a deliberately constructed artistic whole. Unlike the fragmenting approach of the previous generation of redaction critics, Willis's work thinks of Isaiah as a "book" that can be engaged (read, enacted) as a whole. This approach does not move into a purely synchronic reading, since the text does reveal evidence of its own disparate origins. Yet at the same time, by addressing the function of individual text units within the larger entity called "Isaiah," the articles collected here open the door to a richer understanding of the multiple affects and ideas that the prophetic book proposes.

Similarly, Willis's essays on chapter 22 do more than elucidate an interesting text. They illustrate how the development of that text, in the historical situation of the eighth century and later in the formation of the entire book of Isaiah, could shape its interpretation even centuries later. Some of Willis's conclusions in these essays might surprise some modern readers (particularly the Protestant ones, as when he concludes that Jesus' gift of the keys to Peter draws on a set of imagery suggesting Peter's role as his "major domo" in the heavenly kingdom). But such essays illustrate Willis's commitment to let the Bible be heard on its own terms rather than just those of later generations. In other words, they provide an example, one of several possible ones, of the very process of interpretation and reinterpretation that Brevard Childs, in his last book, felicitously called "the struggle to understand Isaiah as Christian Scripture."[5]

A Note on the Editing of This Work

To conclude this introduction, we should explain the editorial approach underlying it. With few exceptions, we have represented these essays as they originally appeared. Aside from obvious typographical errors in the

---

5. Childs, *The Struggle to Understand Isaiah as Christian Scripture*.

original published articles, changes are limited to a standardization of the footnotes in the contemporary SBL style. We have not updated the bibliography because doing so would have meant substantial rewriting in places. Nor have we eliminated various elements of the text that reflect older scholarly conventions (such as references to Canaanite Baalism or other constructions of the history of Israelite religion) or non-gender-inclusive language. In general, these items occur so rarely and are of so little consequence to the overall argument that we believed that change was unnecessary. We crave the reader's indulgence on the rare occasion when a sentence or two seems dated or ill-judged in view of subsequent scholarship. Our belief is that presenting the articles in their original form allows the reader to trace the development of Professor Willis's work and, more importantly perhaps, to recall the ways in which the studies of the prophets have evolved over the past few decades.

Finally, we thank a number of persons who have made this work possible. In addition to John Willis himself, we must thank his gracious and supportive wife Evelyn, whose partnership with John is a thing of beauty in its own right. We also thank our own universities for their support. A number of our students and staff colleagues also did significant work at various stages of the editing of this volume, especially Morgan Philpott and Matt Fredrickson at Abilene Christian University and Tiffany Ferguson at Pepperdine. Moreover, we are grateful to J. J. M. Roberts and Rick R. Marrs for their contributions to a recent seminar session on Professor Willis's contributions to the study of the eighth-century prophets. Their observations and support for the present project have been of incalculable value to the quality of the work.

Abbreviations

AB	Anchor Bible
AfO	*Archiv für Orientforschung*
AJSL	*American Journal of Semitic Languages and Literature*
AJT	*American Journal of Theology*
ANET	Ancient Near Eastern Texts Relating to the Old Testament
ANQ	Andover Newton Quarterly
AoF	*Altorientalische Forschungen*
ATD	Das Alte Testament Deutsch
ATR	*Anglican Theological Review*
BASOR	*Bulletin of the American Schools of Oriental Research*
BAT	Die Botschaft des Alten Testaments
BDB	Brown, Driver, and Briggs, eds., *A Hebrew and English Lexicon of the Old Testament*
BeO	Bibbia e oriente
BETL	Bibliotheca ephemeridum theologicarum lovaniensium
BH³	*Biblia Hebraica³*
Bib	*Biblica*
BibLeb	*Bibel und Leben*
BibOr	*Biblica et Orientalia*
BibS(N)	Biblische Studien (Neukirchen, 1951–)
BJRL	*Bulletin of the John Rylands Library*
BKAT	Biblischer Kommentar, Altes Testament
BR	*Biblical Research*
BRev	*Bible Review*
BW	*Biblical World*
BZ	*Biblische Zeitschrift*

BZAW	Beihefte zur Zeitschrift für die alttestamentliche Wissenschaft
CAT	Commentaire de l'Ancien Testament
CBC	Cambridge Bible Commentary
CBQ	*Catholic Biblical Quarterly*
CGTC	Cambridge Greek Testament Commentary
CMQ	*Canadian Methodist Quarterly*
ConBOT	Coniectanea biblica: Old Testament Series
CTQ	*Concordia Theological Quarterly*
DJD	Discoveries in the Judaean Desert
DOTT	*Documents from Old Testament Times*
DTT	*Dansk teologisk tidsskrift*
EB	Echter Bibel
EBib	*Etudes bibliques*
EHAT	Exegetisches Handbuch zum Alten Testament
EI	*Eretz-Israel*
Enc	*Encounter*
EstEcl	*Estudios Eclesiásticos*
EvT	*Evangelische Theologie*
ExpTim	*Expository Times*
FRLANT	Forschungen zur Religion und Literatur des Alten und Neuen
FT	*Folia Theologica*
HAR	*Hebrew Annual Review*
HAT	Handbuch zum Alten Testament
HBT	*Horizons in Biblical Theology*
HeyJ	*Heythrop Journal*
HKAT	Handkommentar zum Alten Testament
HSAT	Die Heilige Schrift des Alten Testaments
HTR	*Harvard Theological Review*
HUCA	*Hebrew Union College Annual*
ICC	International Critical Commentary
Int	*Interpretation*
ITC	International Theological Commentary
ITQ	*Irish Theological Quarterly*

JAOS	*Journal of the American Oriental Scoiety*
JBL	*Journal of Biblical Literature*
JCS	*Journal of Cuneiform Studies*
JETS	*Journal of the Evangelical Theological Society*
JNES	*Journal of Near Eastern Studies*
JNSL	*Journal of Northwest Semitic Languages*
JOTT	*Journal of Translation and Textlinguistics*
JPT	*Jahrbücher für Protestantische Theologie*
JQR	*Jewish Quarterly Review*
JR	*Journal of Religion*
JSOT	*Journal for the Study of the Old Testament*
JSOTSup	Journal for the Study of the Old Testament Supplement Series
JSS	*Journal of Semitic Studies*
JTS	*Journal of Theological Studies*
KAT	Kommentar zum Alten Testament
KHAT	Kurzgefasstes exegetisches Handbuch zum Alten Testament
KHC	Kurzer Hand-Commentar zum Alten Testament
KVHS	Korte verklaring der Heilige Schrift
LASBF	*Liber annuus Studii biblici franciscani*
LD	Lectio Divina
LQ	*Lutheran Quarterly*
MelT	*Melita Theologica*
NCB	New Century Bible
NICOT	New International Commentary on the Old Testament
NKZ	*Neue kirchliche Zeitschrift*
NTT	*Norsk Teologisk Tidsskrift*
OBT	Overtures to Biblical Theology
OIP	Oriental Institute Publications
OLZ	*Orientalistische Literaturzeitung*
OTE	*Old Testament Essays*
OTL	Old Testament Library
OtSt	Oudtestamentische Studiën
POut	De Prediking van het Oude Testament

	Proof	*Prooftexts*
	PSB	*Princeton Seminary Bulletin*
	PTMS	Pittsburgh Theological Monograph Series
	RB	*Revue biblique*
	ResQ	*Restoration Quarterly*
	RevExp	*Review and Expositor*
	RHB	Randglossen zur hebräischen Bibel
	RHR	*Revue de l'histoire des religions*
	RivB	*Rivista Biblica*
	RSém	*Revue de Sémitique*
	RSPT	*Revue des Sciences Philosophiques et Théologiques*
	RTP	*Revue de Théologie et de Philosophie*
	SB	Sources bibliques
	SBLDS	*Society of Biblical Literature Dissertation Series*
	SBLSP	*Society of Biblical Literature Seminar Papers*
	SBOT	Sacred Books of the Old Testament
	SBS	Stuttgarter Bibelstudien
	SBT	Studies in Biblical Theology
	Scr	*Scripture*
	ScrHier	Scripta Hierosolymitana
	SEÅ	*Svensk Exegetisk Årsbok*
	SJOT	*Scandinavian Journal of the Old Testament*
	SJT	*Scottish Journal of Theology*
	ST	*Studia Theologica*
	TBC	Torch Bible Commentaries
	TeU	Tekst en uitleg
	ThEv	*Theologia Evangelica*
	ThT	*Theologisch tijdschrift*
	TLZ	Theologische Literaturzeitung
	TNTC	Tyndale New Testament Commentaries
	TOTC	Tyndale Old Testament Commentaries
	TQ	*Theologische Quartalschrift*
	TRu	*Theologische Rundschau*
	TS	Theological Studies
	TThSt	Trierer Theologische Studien

TTZ	*Trierer theologische Zeitschrift*
TZ	*Theologische Zeitschrift*
UBL	Ugaritisch-biblische Literatur
UF	*Ugarit-Forschungen*
VD	*Verbum Domini*
VT	*Vetus Testamentum*
VTSup	Vetus Testamentum Supplements
WBC	Word Biblical Commentary
WD	*Wort und Dienst*
WMANT	Wissenschaftliche Monographien zum Alten und Neuen Testament
ZAW	*Zeitschrift für die alttestamentliche Wissenschaft*
ZBK	Züricher Bibelkommentare
ZDMG	*Zeitschrift der deutschen morgenländischen Gesellschaft*
ZDPV	*Zeitschrift des deutschen Palästina-Vereins*
ZS	*Zeitschrift für Semitistik und verwandte Gebiete*
ZTK	*Zeitschrift für Theologie und Kirche*

PART ONE

The Book of Micah

1

The Structure of the Book of Micah[1]

A Survey of Analytical Approaches to the Book of Micah

HAND IN HAND WITH the increasing persistence of form criticism and traditio-historical criticism, there has been a growing awareness that the scholar's first duty in approaching a piece of literature is to analyze it as it now stands to determine whether it has some sort of meaningful arrangement and if so to attempt to understand the purpose of the message which such a significant structure might exhibit. During the past century, five basic explanations of the present arrangement of the book of Micah have emerged, each differing in details in harmony with the particular interpretation of the individual critic.

(1) Several scholars find that the final form of the book of Micah is hopelessly incoherent as a result of accidental or intentional disarrangement of the original material in transmission. They seek to restore the original coherence by rearranging the pericopes in their original order. Haupt and Hanon[2] represent attempts to organize verses and pericopes in the order that they became a part of the book chronologically, while Elhorst and Halévy[3] represent attempts to organize the material logically by

---

1. Due to limitations of space, a lengthy defense of many statements in this paper is impossible. The reader is invited to examine my dissertation, "The Structure, Setting, and Interrelationships of the Pericopes in the Book of Micah," Vanderbilt Divinity School, 1966, and my other articles on various aspects of Micah studies alluded to in the notes below. The versification throughout this paper follows the MT.

2. Haupt, "The Book of Micah," 26:201–52; 27:1–62; Steinmann and Hanon, *Michée*, 12–14.

3. Elhorst, *De Prophetie van Micha*, 66–96; Halévy, "Le Livre de Michée," 12:97–117, 193–216, 289–312; 13:1–22.

grouping similar subject matter. The differences between the "original order" of the book as it is restored by each scholar who has advocated this approach is ample evidence of its inherent subjectivity.

(2) The most common explanation of the final form of the book of Micah (and especially of chs. 4–7) is that it is a collection of pericopes that arose at different times and in different situations, which came together in piecemeal fashion. Thus the book is composed of several disconnected incoherent pericopes, like Hosea and in fact all the prophetic books.[4] Budde has gone so far as to suggest that Micah 4–7, like Zechariah 9–14, served post-exilic editors of the prophetic corpus as a "catch-all" for late eschatological oracles.[5] Several scholars exhibit a modified form of this view when they explain the supposed incoherence of the book by arguing that it contains summaries of the prophet's message or perhaps oracles delivered by the prophet on different occasions, which were subsequently poorly arranged.[6] In my opinion, the "incoherence" which many critics find in the book of Micah is imaginary, and grows out of the propensity of modern man to judge the literature of ancient man according to his own rigid criteria.

(3) A number of critics think that the present book of Micah is a compilation of originally independent collections of prophetic oracles, although they do not agree as to their extent. Most scholars who offer this explanation find between two and four large groups of oracles in the book. Ewald and recently Kraeling[7] find two collections: chs. 1–5 and 6–7. W. R. Smith and T. H. Robinson discover three,[8] but the extent delineated by each scholar differs, Smith dividing the book into 1–5; 6:1—7:6, and 7:7–20, but Robinson dividing it into 1–3, 4–5, and 6–7. Baudissin and recently Pákozdy see four original collections,[9] the former suggesting 1–3, 4–5, 6:1—7:6, and 7:7–20, but the latter suggesting 1–3, 4:1—5:9, 5:10—7:7, and 7:8–20. However, if it can be demonstrated that there are

---

4. Cf. i.e., Wade, *The Books of the Prophets*, xx; Cheyne, *Micah*, 10; Sellin, *Das Zwölfprophetenbuch*, 328; and Gautier, *Introduction*, 502, 506.

5. Budde, "Verfasser," 157.

6. See Driver, *An Introduction*, 325–26.

7. Kraeling, *Commentary*, 325–26.

8. Smith, *The Prophets of Israel*, 365, 427 n. 3, 428 n. 5, 439 n. 13; Robinson, *Die zwölf kleinen Propheten*, 127–28.

9. Baudissin, *Einleitung*, 525–26, 529, 532–33. Pákozdy, "Michabuch," col. 1211.

interrelationships between the different parts of the book, it would be incredible to think that two or more different collectors, each working independent of the other, could produce two, three, or four separate works as similar in structure, contents, and sequence of thought, and as interdependent as the present form of the book of Micah seems to be.

(4) Another view which is somewhat related to this explanation maintains that while the present form of the book of Micah is not a compilation of originally independent collections, it is the end product of a long literary history. This began with a nucleus of original Mican oracles. As these were handed down, several redactors from different historical eras revised the original book and added new material to it, each in order to contemporize it for his own community, or to make it reflect his own theological biases, or for other reasons, some of which may not be discoverable.

At least four theories of how this process took place have been promulgated. (a) Principally in order to explain apparent contradictory teachings in the pericopes of chs. 4–5, Stade advanced what might be called the "two epigone" hypothesis.[10] He maintains that originally the book of Micah was composed of 1:1—2:11; 3. But since this work contained only doom oracles, it was in constant danger of being eliminated from the Jewish tradition, and would have been if Micah had not received such high commendation in Jer 26:17ff. In the post-Jeremian period, one epigone added 4:1-4; 4:11—5:3; 5:6-8, 9-14. "Der Grund, aus welchem jener Epigone seine Ausführungen hinter 3,12 einschaltete, war ohne Zweifel dieser, dass er an der Einseitigkeit des Inhalts von Kap. 1–3 einen nicht unberechtigten Anstoß nahm."[11] Later, a second epigone, thinking that the additions of the first epigone were Mican, added 4:5-10 and 5:4-5 to promote the view that Israel's enemies would be defeated. (b) Marti believes that the original material in the book of Micah is 1:5b, 6, 8, 9, 16; 2:1-3, 4(?), 6-11; 3:1, 2a, 3a, 4, 5a, 2b, 5b-8, 9-12. The rest of the material in the book (except for the additions in chs. 1–3) was grouped around two "poles" or "cores," viz., 4:1-4 and 6:6-8. About 500 BCE, 4:1-4 was added to the original corpus to modify the negative impact of 3:9-12. Shortly afterward, 6:6-8 was added to 4:1-4, the two pericopes being connected by the transitional verse 4:5.

---

10. Stade, "Bemerkungen," 161–72.
11. Ibid., 170.

Between the fifth and second centuries, the other passages in chs. 4–7 were added at different times and under various circumstances, some accruing to 4:1–4 and some to 6:6–8.[12] (c) The most common view of the gradual growth of the book of Micah outlines three stages through which the material passed: the period of collecting and writing down the genuine oracles, a rather long nebulous period in which various additions and changes were made, and the period in which the book reached its final form. G. B. Gray seems to have been the first scholar to advance this view,[13] and he has been followed by several outstanding critics. The original materials for Gray are 1:2–2:11; 3; 4:14; 5:9–13; 6:1—7:6.[14] They provide a summary of Micah's teaching and were possibly written down by the prophet himself. Jeremiah 26:17ff. indicates that it was this form of the book (containing only doom oracles) which was known in Jerusalem at the end of the seventh century BCE. Between that time and the third century BCE, the original material was re-edited, provided with an expanded title, and enlarged by a collection of prophetic pieces both of pre-exilic and post-exilic origin. The book of Micah reached its final form toward the end of the third century, when it was incorporated into the Book of the Twelve. (d) G. Hylmö offers a very complex reconstruction of the development of the book of Micah. He thinks the prophet himself edited chs. 1–3. Also Micah's friends and disciples preserved a few genuine oracles which were later incorporated into the book: 4:9–10a; 4:14—5:1; 5:9–12a, 13b. But Jer 26:18 shows that the book of Micah ended with 3:12 in the time of Jeremiah, indicating that these passages were inserted after that time. The person who added these verses to Micah's own edition also inserted 2:12–13 in its present position. Later, another redactor inserted 4:1–4, 5, 8. Near the Greek period, another redactor added 4:6–7, 11–13; 5:2–3, 4–5, 6–7, at the same time "retouching" 4:6–7, 10a, so that they would correspond to 4:1–4 and. 2:12–13. A later redactor had in his possession some early detached pericopes, viz., 6:1–4, 6–8, 9–15; 7:1–4, which he appended to 5:9–13. All of these earlier passages except 6:6–8 originated in the seventh century. They had probably already been connected by 6:5, 16; 7:5–6, before their insertion into the Mican corpus. Later, another redactor added

---

12. Marti, *Das Dodekapropheten*, 262–64.

13. Gray, "Micah, Book of," 614–15.

14. In his later work, *A Critical Introduction to the Old Testament*, 219, Gray rejects the authenticity of 4:14; 5:9–13; and 6:1—7:6.

7:7–10, 11–13, 14–20, and either he or still another redactor added 5:8, 14 to complete the book.[15]

Surely, it must be agreed that the present form of the book of Micah is the end product of a rather long and complex evolution. But, as is now becoming increasingly apparent with biblical literature in general, this evolution involves oral as well as written transmission,[16] and the abridgement of originally longer oracles as well as the expansion of earlier material.[17] It must also be kept in mind that some, if not much, of the material in the present book (and some possibly in its present order) shaped the thinking of the final redactor. Thus, while it is true that the theology of the "final redactor" must have determined the shape of the final form of the book, the material with which the redactor worked must have shaped his theology and made a determinative impression on him as he sought to make the traditional material in his possession relevant to the problems of his contemporary situation. Furthermore, it needs to be realized that as one attempts to reconstruct the history through which the materials passed from their original oral delivery to the final form of the book, the impression which the book as a whole makes on him influences his decisions with regard to the evolution of this material in its oral and written stages. Therefore, in my opinion, the proper method of approach to biblical literature in general (and to the book of Micah in particular) must begin with the final form of the literary piece and from this work back through the written and oral stages of transmission to the "original" form of its component parts, which was sometimes written and sometimes oral.[18]

(5) A few leading scholars defend the view that the book of Micah was put together on the basis of chronological considerations. Perhaps the most ingenious and certainly the most stimulating presentation of this analysis is that of A. van Hoonacker.[19] He argues that chs. 1–3 were writ-

15. Hylmö, *Kompositionen*, 286–88.

16. With regard to the book of Micah, we may call attention to the treatment of 4:1–5 by Ringgren, "Oral and Written Transmission," 34–59; and to the analysis of chs. 4–5 by Nielsen, *Oral Tradition*, 79–93.

17. Cf. e.g., Budde, "Eine folgenschwere Redaktion," 218–29; and Willis, "A Note on ואמר," 51–52.

18. See the important work by Koch, *Was ist Formgeschichte?* and on this point esp. 54.

19. Hoonacker, *Les douze petits prophètes*, 339–411.

ten in connection with Shalmaneser V's invasion of Palestine (725–722 B.C.E.). Jeremiah 26:18 assigns Mic 3:12 to the reign of Hezekiah, but 2 Kgs 18:9–10 indicate that Hezekiah's reign began in 727. Furthermore, the corrupt text in Mic 2:8 should be emended to *šlmnṣr*, "Shalmaneser."[20] The oracles in chs. 4–5 come from the period after the fall of Samaria. The Assyrians had left Palestine and the Judeans had occasion to rejoice because the threat was lifted. Since Judah had been spared from the invasion of Shalmaneser V, no promise would be too astonishing for the people to believe. Now Micah would not have spoken the things preserved in chs. 4–5 unless Judah has repented of the evils which he had condemned in chs. 1–3. Jeremiah 26:18–20 speaks of just such a repentance led by Hezekiah. It is logical to believe that chs. 4–5 represent encouragements that Micah gave those who participated in this reform. Van Hoonacker's treatment of chs. 6–7 is very complicated. This material is Mican and comes from the period after the fall of Samaria. It is composed of two parts: 6:1—7:6, 7:11b–13, and 7:7–11a, 14–20. The prophet's major concern here is with Samaria's spiritual response to the invasion of Shalmaneser V. Micah urges the city to interpret this disaster as Yahweh's chastisement intended to bring her to repentance. To accomplish this, he creates a dramatic fiction in which he identifies himself with Samaria. His own repentance and confession are a way of representing Samaria's repentance. His action is the action he hopes to evoke from Samaria. But this passage assumes that the overthrow of the Northern kingdom had already taken place. Now the two parts of chs. 6–7 are inseparable, so the entire section must be a prophetic fiction. Thus, the chastisements which seem to be in the present or immediate future are actually in the past. The past tense is used in 6:12–13 because the author forgot momentarily that he was presenting a fiction. 6:6–7 and 7:4ff. show that the writer knew the trials through which the people had passed. The fallen city had already resigned herself to her chastisement (7:9), although 6:9ff. and 7:4bff. present the chastisement as still in the future. 6:1ff. describes Yahweh's intervention as a present reality, but 7:7ff. as a coming event. The purpose of the whole section is to show Samaria that her punishment and humiliation were the result of her sins.

The view that the various sections of the book of Micah contain oracles grouped together because they belong to the same general

---

20. For an extensive treatment of the text of Mic 2:8, see my article, Willis, "Micah 2:6–8," 72–87.

chronological period is to be rejected. There is just not enough objective evidence in the individual pericopes with regard to date to justify such an analysis, and often unnatural explanations of the text are necessary to support it.

The Horizontal Coherence of the Book

Under the growing influence of form criticism and traditio-historical criticism, within the past fifteen years a number of scholars have called attention to the coherent structure of the book of Micah. We may mention such names as A. George,[21] A. Weiser,[22] von Ungern-Sternberg,[23] Kapelrud,[24] and Schilling.[25] But as far as I am able to learn, no critic has undertaken the task of providing an extensive demonstration of this coherence.[26] The purpose of this paper is to try to demonstrate that this book has a basic coherence, which would indicate that its arrangement is the result of a well devised purpose, and to invite dialogue to correct flaws in the presentation or to present a radically different alternative so as to further illuminate the nature and purpose of the present form of this prophetic work.

It seems most natural to divide the book of Micah into three major sections: 1–2 (I), 3–5 (II), 6–7 (III).[27] Each section then begins with *šim'û* (1:2; 3:1; 6:1), and we have three doom sections (1:2—2:11; 3; 6:1–7) followed by three hope sections (2:12–13; 4–5; 7:7–20). The symmetry of this analysis of the book may be demonstrated in broad outline by the following chart.

---

21. George, "Michée (Le Livre de)," cols. 1252–63; George, *La Sainte Bible*, 11–12.

22. Weiser, *Das Buch der zwölf Kleinen Propheten*, 231, 263, 267, 269; Weiser, *The Old Testament*, 255.

23. Ungern-Sternberg, *Der Rechtsstreit Gottes*, 24, 26, 84–85, 93–94, 118, 123, 133.

24. Kapelrud, "Mikas Bok," col. 106.

25. Schilling, "Michäas," col. 391.

26. Ladame, "Les chapitres IV et V," 446–61; Nielsen, *Oral Tradition*, 79–93; and Renaud, *Structure*, have provided rather extensive attempts to demonstrate the coherence of chs. 4–5.

27. In my essay, "The Structure of Micah 3–5," 191–214, there is a lengthy discussion of the various views of the major divisions of the book of Micah, and I have given my reasons for rejecting divisions other than chs. 1–2, 3–5, and 6–7. As pointed out in that essay, the two major problems are: (1) Should a major division be made between chs. 3 and 4 or between chs. 2 and 3? (2) At what point should a major division be made between chs. 5 and 6?

Structure of the Book of Micah

Type of Oracle	Part I Chs. 1–2	Part II Chs. 3–5	Part III Chs. 6–7
Doom	1:2—2:11 Extensive	Ch. 3 Brief	6:1—7:6 Extensive
Hope	2:12–13 Brief	Chs. 4–5 Extensive	7:7–20 Brief

Such an arrangement gives the impression of being the result of a well-conceived plan, and we may assume that the person (or persons) responsible for this structure had a specific purpose in mind when he produced this work. The general doom-hope arrangement as well as the passages in the book which exhibit a liturgical character (in my opinion, these are 2:12–13; 4:5; 5:8; 6:9b; and 7:7–20)[28] seem to justify the conjecture that its final form was intended to be used by a specific worshipping or cultic community which was struggling with a particular type of problem in its own historical situation.

Now if the book of Micah was purposefully arranged, we may expect to find striking parallels in form and ideology within the three sections of doom on the one hand and within the three sections of hope on the other. In other words, there should be a *horizontal* coherence in the book.

Affinities in the Doom Sections

All three doom sections begin with "Hear" (see above). Sections I and III begin with a covenant lawsuit (1:2–7; 6:1–8), and each contains a lament (1:8–16; 7:1–6) and an oracle giving the reasons for the impending doom (2:1–11; 6:9–16). Furthermore, the structures of the lawsuits in these two sections have interesting similarities. (a) Each begins with a summons to witnesses to hear Yahweh's accusation against his people. In the former, the summons is to the peoples and the earth (1:2a),[29] and in the latter to the mountains, hills, and foundations of the earth (6:1–2). (b) In both passages, Yahweh himself appears as Israel's accuser (1:2b–4; 6:3–5). (c) Both pericopes present general (rather than specific) accusa-

---

28. For a discussion of this point, see my dissertation, Willis, "The Structure, Setting, and Interrelationships," 123–35.

29. Cf. Willis, "Some Suggestions," 372–79.

tions which Yahweh brings against his people (1:5; 6:3–5). (d) In both lawsuits, Yahweh announces impending judgment on his hearers (1:6–7; 6:13–15).[30]

The central section of the book of Micah has a different structure. Whereas chs. 1–2 and 6–7 are predominantly oracles of doom, chs. 3–5 are primarily oracles of hope. Unlike the doom oracles in Sections I and III, ch. 3 is composed of three parallel pericopes of approximately equal length (vv. 1–4, 5–8, 9–12) and of similar structure.[31] Therefore, we seem driven to the conclusion that the book of Micah exhibits and A-B-A pattern. And the fact that the arrangement of ch. 3 is different from that of 1:2—2:11 and 6:1—7:6 argues *in favor of* a well-conceived plan in the book, *not against it*.

The three doom sections of the book all describe Yahweh's punishment of Israel's sins according to the principle of *jus talionis*. In section I, we are told that because Israel had heaped up riches for her sanctuaries by sacred prostitution, their riches would be carried into a foreign land to be used for sacred prostitution (1:7). And because the rich had "devised evil" against the poor, Yahweh will "devise evil" against them (2:1, 3). Just as the rich had seized the fields of the poor, so Yahweh will send an enemy to seize the promised land from them (2:2, 4–5). The rich had driven the poor out of their houses, therefore Yahweh will send an enemy to drive them out of their land (2:9–10). In section II, it is announced that since the leading classes in Israel had consumed the flesh of the poor, their flesh also would be consumed (3:2b–3). Again, because Israel's rulers had not hearkened to the cries of the poor, Yahweh will not hearken to them when they cry unto him (3:2–4). The popular prophets had not used the gift of prophecy with responsibility, therefore Yahweh will deprive them of this gift (3:5–6). The Judean leaders had built up Zion with blood and iniquity, so Zion shall be plowed as a field, Jerusalem will become heaps, and the temple mountain a forest sanctuary (3:10–12). In section III, the point is made that as the rich had deprived the poor of the necessities of life, they themselves will be deprived of prosperity, food, and security from the invader (6:10–15). There is a word play in 7:4 which seems to involve the principle of *jus talionis*. Since even the

---

30. I have offered a limited defense of the unity of Micah 6 in my "Review of *Micah 6, 6–8*," 273–78.

31. On the similarity of the structure of vv. 1–4 and 9–12, see Westermann, *Basic Forms*, 174–75.

most upright in Israel are as a thorn hedge (*mimměsûkkāh*), they will suffer perplexity (*měbûkātām*). It is significant that 7:9 (in the final section of hope) assumes that indignation is the natural consequence of sin.³²

The three doom sections emphasize the extreme severity of the impending punishment. Section I declares that Samaria will become as a heap of the field, as a place for planting vineyards. Her stones will be poured down into the valley, her foundations will be uncovered, her graven images will be beaten to pieces, her Asherim burned, her idols made desolate, and the rich ornamentation of her sanctuaries carried into captivity (1:6-7). Her punishment will be like an incurable wound inflicted by Yahweh that spreads as far as Jerusalem (1:9, 12). Yahweh brings the Assyrian army into the land to overthrow the fortified cities that had been built to protect Jerusalem. The enemy marches up to the gate of Jerusalem (1:9, 12), besieges the city, and carries away many of the inhabitants of the land into captivity (1:16). The destruction will be complete ("we are utterly ruined," 2:4), and the enemy will take over the land for its own possession and distribute it to its own people (2:4-5). The rich oppressors will be carried into exile, and Israel will suffer "a grievous destruction" (2:10). In section II, the prophet states that the rich oppressors will be treated shamefully because of their treatment of the poor (3:3). Yahweh will intentionally turn his face away when they cry to him for help (3:4). The popular prophets will be completely divested of their visions, and shamefully exposed before their clients (3:6-7). And like Samaria (1:6), Zion will be plowed as a field, Jerusalem will become heaps, and the temple mountain will be reduced to a forest sanctuary, presumably by an invading army (3.12). In section III, the impending punishment is compared with a grievous wound (6:13), as in 1:9. The enemy army will completely desolate the land (6:13, 16). That which the people attempt to save will be given over to the sword (6:14), and the enemy will enjoy the harvest of Israel's labor (6:15). The divine visitation will bring great perplexity to Israel (7:4), and a portion of the inhabitants of the land will be carried into captivity.³³ The following table

---

32. See Willis, "On the Text," 539–41.

33. A partial captivity is implied by *hašmeēm* (6:13) and *lěšammāh* (6:16). One thing involved in making a land desolate was carrying some of its inhabitants into captivity. See Isa 6:11–13; Mic 1:7 (in which it is implied that idols are made desolate by their ornamentation being carried away by the conqueror); Jer 6:8; 9:10; 34:22. *měbûkātām* (7:4) also seems to include a captivity of some of the inhabitants of the land, as a comparison with Isa 22:5 (with its surrounding context) would seem to suggest.

summarizes the striking similarities between the doom sections with regard to punishment.

Similarities in the Emphasis on Severe Punishment in Micah's Doom Sections

Description of Punishment	Section I	Section II	Section III
Principle of *jus talionis*	1:7; 2:1, 3; 2:2, 4–5; 2:9–10	3:2b–3; 3:2–4; 3:5–6; 3:10, 12	6:10–15; 7:4; 7:9
Type of Oracle	Part I Chs. 1–2	Part II Chs. 3–5	Part III Chs. 6–7
Doom	1:2–2:11 Extensive	Ch. 3 Brief	6:1—7:6 Extensive
Hope	2:12–13 Brief	Chs. 4–5 Extensive	7:7–20 Brief

The concept of sin is the same throughout the doom sections in Micah. *peša'* and *ḥaṭṭā't* occur together in all three sections (I—1:5, 13; II—3:8; III—6:7). The only place that either of those words occurs without the other in the doom sections is in 6:13.[34] Throughout the doom sections, sin is understood as failure to practice *mišpāṭ*, which is used in Micah as a summary for all the law, and has to do primarily with man's responsibility to man.[35] The word *mišpāṭ* itself appears in sections II (3:1, 8, 9) and III (6:8), but the specific sins condemned in all three sections indicate that this idea underlies what is said of sin in section I, even though the word itself does not occur there.

The specific sins condemned in the doom sections are so similar that they can be discussed together. The people are reproached because they feel no responsibility to treat one another justly. The "haves" mistreat the "have-nots" by seizing their fields, homes (2:2, 9), and clothing (2:8) and by oppressing the poor (2:2; 3:2–3; 6:12; 7:2), the orphans, and the widows (2:9). But these oppressors are religious people. They demand prophets after their own heart, who will declare Yahweh's mercies and mighty acts (2:6, 11), but without applying their meaning to them (6:3–5) or reproaching them in any way (2:6–7). They approach Yahweh willing to offer sacrifices of the greatest quantity and quality (6:6–7), but

---

34. These two words also occur together in the last hope section 7:18–19.
35. See Lindblom, *Micah*, 172.

unwilling to experience a real transformation of life (6:8). Their main concern is their own gain at any cost. They wrest possessions from the poor by practicing iniquity and bribery in the courts (3:9, 11; 7:8). They use false weights and measures to cheat their customers (6:10–11). No one can be trusted, not even the most intimate members of one's family (7:5–6). And yet, these very people expect Yahweh to intervene in their behalf whenever they wish. After all, they are God's people (2:7), and thus are worthy of his help in any time of distress (1:12; 3:4, 11).

All three sections of doom single out the capital as the center of corruption in Israel and Judah (I, 1:5, 6, 9, 12, 16; II, 3:10, 12; III, 6:9). This is implied in passages which single out leaders of the people as guilty of heinous crimes against society (I, 2:1–2, 8–9, 11; II, 3:1, 5, 9, 11; III, 6:10–12, 16; 7:3). The capitals, Samaria and Jerusalem, are apparently intended as representatives of the whole land.[36] With this in mind, it is especially significant that in all three doom sections, the people of the land are said to be as guilty as the capital for Judah's corruption. It is through Lachish that the corruption of North Israel has come into Judah (1:13). "This family" against whom Yahweh devises an evil (2:3) evidently refers to the people of Judah as a whole, and not to Jerusalem alone. The expression placed in the mouths of the people, "We are utterly ruined," (2:4) suggests a punishment of the whole land. The reason that the popular prophets are able to continue to proclaim their lies is because "this people" sanctions it (2:11). To be sure, these prophets are guilty because they cause the people to err, but still "the people" do err (3:5). Micah feels that his task is to declare to *Jacob* his transgression, and to Israel, his sin (3:8), and this includes more than the capital. Yahweh's controversy is with "his people," and not merely with the capital (6:2), for it is this same people that he brought up out of Egypt, not merely the people who lived in the large city (6:4). Surely, the leaders are guilty, and perhaps carry a greater responsibility than the common people for the impending disaster (7:3), but the people themselves are far from being free from guilt (7:2, 4–6).

All three doom sections in the book of Micah are connected by the fact that they trace "external" sins to "internal" corruption of the sinner.

---

36. "Wer sehen will, was Israels, was Judas Schuld ist, der muss nach Samaria oder nach Jerusalem blicken; diese Städte *repräsentieren* das" (italics mine). Ungern-Sternberg, *Der Rechtsstreit Gottes*, 29. Porteous, "Jerusalem-Zion," 235–52, points out that Jeremiah often uses "Jerusalem" in this way.

The wicked practice the evil they *devised* on their beds (2:1). They seize the fields they had *coveted* (2:2). The rich oppress the poor because in their hearts they *hate* the good and *love* the evil (3:2) and *abhor* justice (3:9). The rich mistreat the poor because of the evil *desire* of their soul (7:3). The best in Israel is as a brier and the most upright as a thorn hedge *inwardly* (7:4).

Now the concepts of sin and punishment are closely related to the representation of Yahweh and his activities in the doom sections of the book of Micah. The predominant name for the deity is "Yahweh" (I, 1:1, 2, 3, 12; 2:3, 5, 7; II, 3:4, 5, 8, 11 [twice]; III, 6:1, 2 [twice], 5, 6, 7, 8, 9). *ădōnāy* occurs only twice, and that in the same verse (1:2), and the first time it seems to be a later addition.[37] *ĕlōhîm* occurs only three times in the doom sections: once in synonymous parallelism with Yahweh (6:6, on the lips of the people), once to avoid using Yahweh repetitiously (6:8), and once in a phrase which seems to have been adapted from Canaanite religion (3:7).

The book of Micah does not describe Yahweh abstractly, but always in relationship, as a God who *acts* with *his* people[38] in mind. His activity is represented by verbs with Yahweh as subject (usually in the first person singular), and by verbs in the passive voice (where Yahweh is apparently the motivation). Two basic assertions are made concerning Yahweh's activity. First, he appears (1:2-4) to punish his people for sin. In section I, we find these statements "I will make (*wĕśamtî*) Samaria a heap of the field," "I will pour down (*wĕhiggartî*) her stones into the valley," "I will uncover (*ăgalleh*) her foundations" (1:6). All her graven images will be *beaten to pieces (yukattû)*," "all her hires shall be burned (*yiśśārĕpû*) with fire," "I will make desolate (*ʾāśîm šĕmāmāh*) all her idols" (1:7). "Evil is *come down (yārad)* from Yahweh" (1:12). "I will bring (*ʾābîʾ*) the possessor to you" (1:15). "I will *devise (ḥōšēb)* an evil against this people" (2:3). In section II, similar assertions occur. When the leaders of the people cry unto Yahweh, he will not *answer (yaʿăneh)* them (3:4). It is Yahweh who will bring night and darkness upon the popular prophets, and cause the sun to go down and the day to be black over them (3:6).

---

37. (a) It is omitted by the LXX and Aquila (according to Deissler, *Les petits prophètes*, 302). (b) By an eye mistake, a copyist may have accidentally inserted it here from the following line. (c) It may be a gloss on "Yahweh."

38. "This people"—2:11; "his people"—6:2; "my people"—1:9; 2:4, 8, 9; 3:3; 6:3, 5, 16.

It is he who causes the seers to be put to shame and the diviners to be confounded (3:7). It is by his power that Zion will be plowed as a field, that Jerusalem will become heaps, and that the temple will be reduced to a forest sanctuary (3:12).[39] Section III describes Yahweh's activity in a similar manner. "I have begun (*haḥillôtî*) to smite you." "I have *made* you *desolate* (*hāšēm*)" (6:13). "That which you save, I will *give up* (*'ettēn*) to the sword" (6:14). "I will make (*tittî*) you a desolation" (6:16). It is Yahweh who will be responsible for the day of visitation. It is he who will cause Israel to suffer perplexity (7:4). Secondly, the doom sections also assert that Yahweh interprets the meaning of and the reason for the approaching punishment to his people. Thus all three sections are concerned with what Yahweh says (אמר) (I, 2:3; II, 3:5; III, 6:1). Yahweh enters into a lawsuit with Israel and *strives* (*yitwakkāḥ*) with his people (6:2). He reminds them of his *righteous acts* (*ṣidqôt*) in their history: "I *brought* you up (*he'ĕlîtîkā*) out of the land of Egypt," "I *redeemed* you (*pĕdîtîkā*) from the house of bondage." "I *sent* (*wā'ešlaḥ*) before you Moses, Aaron, and Miriam" (6:4). It is Yahweh who turned Balaam's curse into a blessing for Israel, and who led them across the Jordan River from Shittim to Gilgal (6:5). When the people respond to this accusing appeal by asking what kind of sacrifices Yahweh would accept for appeasement of his wrath (6:6–7), the prophet declares that Yahweh had already shown (*higgîd*) them what was good, and that he requires (*dôrēš*) that they practice justice and faithful love and walking wisely with God (6:8). The voice of Yahweh calls unto (*yiqrā'*) the city to hear this proclamation (6:9).

These passages emphasize the vital connection between Yahweh and his people, in whose interest he acts. The idea of the "people of God" is essentially the same in all three doom sections. "Israel" occurs eight times in the doom sections. It means "all Israel" in 1:14, 15 (I); 3:1, 8, 9 (II); and 6:2 (III). In 1:13, it probably means the Northern tribes in a constitutional sense in contrast to "Judah" in 1:9. The idea here is that the sins of the Northern kingdom have infected the South. The meaning of "Israel" in 1:5b is debatable. But it seems most natural to consider lines a and b as parallel, and lines c and d as parallel. If so, "Jacob" and "Israel" in lines a and b are comprehensive terms for all Israel. "Jacob" occurs

---

39. In describing the fall of Samaria, the writer uses the first person singular (1:6), and in describing the fall of Jerusalem, the passive (3:12). But he also uses the passive of Samaria (1:7).

six times in the first two sections of doom. With the exception of 2:7, it always appears alongside "Israel." In 1:5a; 3:1, 8, 9, it is a comprehensive term for all Israel, but in 1:5c it refers to North Israel in distinction to the Southern kingdom, as the reference to Samaria shows.

'am occurs eleven times in the doom sections. In 2:4, 11; 3:5; 6:2, 3, 5, 16, it is a comprehensive term for all Israel. "His People" and "Israel" are used interchangeably in 6:2. In 1:9, "my people" refers to the Southern kingdom as distinguished from North Israel. The point is that the sin of the Northern kingdom had spread to Judah, and so the punishment which North Israel had suffered would also come upon the south. But the most significant thing about the use of "people" in the book of Micah is that sometimes it refers to only a part of Israel, i.e., it divides Israel into two groups: those who claim to be God's people but are not, and those who are genuinely God's people. This appears to be the significance of "my people" in 2:8. A similar distinction is made in 2:9. The same phrase is used for the oppressors in v. 8 and for the oppressed in v. 9. Its use in v. 8 is derived from the claims made by Micah's opponents and so is ironical, while its use in v. 9 is straightforward and represents Micah's own position. Verses 8 and 9 vividly distinguish between two groups in Israel. And the same distinction appears in 3:3, where "my people" is identical with the oppressed.[40] Now *gôy* occurs only in the hope sections of the book of Micah (4:2, 3 [three times], 7, 11; 5:7, 14; 7:16), and refers to Israel only once (4:7). Speiser argues that 'am is used in the Old Testament primarily in a subjective and personal sense, and is usually associated with a strong feeling of kinship, whereas *gôy* is used objectively and impersonally, and applies primarily to a loosely knit superorganization by which people are externally bound together.[41] Yahweh's deep concern for his "people" reflected in the book of Micah supports such a distinction. And the identification of "this people" (2:11) with "this family" (*mišpāḥāh*) (2:3) indicates that "people" conveys the concept of intimate relationship between Yahweh and Israel.

With the exception of 7:14, 'am occurs exclusively in the doom sections of the book of Micah. It means pan-Israel except in 2:8–9 and 3:3. But this word is not used to assure Israel of her inviolability as God's people. This was the view of Micah's opponents, and is explicitly rejected in 2:6–9; 3:4, 11 (cf. similarly Amos 3:1). Rather, the book of Micah calls

---

40. For an extensive treatment, see my article referred to in note 20.
41. Speiser, "'People' and 'Nation' of Israel," 157–63, especially 158–59.

Israel "God's people" in order to condemn her for being unfaithful to the divine covenant with her. Thus, it is most significant that this term is so prominent in the lawsuit in ch. 6 (vv. 2, 3, 5, 16). This lawsuit (and its companion piece in 1:2ff.) is crucial to an understanding of Micah's distinction between external Israel and genuine Israel. Micah seems to have felt that his work affected two types of people: Israel as a whole, which must be punished, and a few innocent sufferers whose cause Yahweh espoused. The prophetic message, with its strong emphasis on approaching punishment, inevitably produced a division between those that rejected it and those who accepted it.[42] So the intention of the theophany in the cultic recitation was the purification of the community,[43] and in the book of Micah the theophany is a vital part of Yahweh's lawsuit with his people.

The division within God's people (along with the fall of Samaria and the Assyrian threat to Palestine) seems to have enhanced the concept of the individual and of individual responsibility in prophetic thought. All three sections of doom reflect a concern for the individual. Micah 2:2 (*'îš*); 7:6; and apparently 3:2–3 denounce the oppression of the individual. 2:11; 7:2 (*'îš*), 3–4; and seemingly 3:1, 9 condemn individuals for oppressing the poor and for prophesying lies. Yahweh makes his demands on the individual (*'ādām*) in the Israelite community (6:8). Micah himself has a strong feeling of personal responsibility to Yahweh and of personal concern for the people (1:8–9; 3:8; 6:1; 7:1; and possibly 7:7).

Summarizing, the doom sections in the book of Micah seem to follow an A–B–A pattern. All three sections begin with "Hear." Sections I and III are composed of three pericopes each: a lawsuit, a lament, and a reason (*Begründung*) for the announced punishment. Section II is composed of three pericopes of similar length, structure, and content. These three sections exhibit striking parallels, often extending even to similarities in vocabulary and sequence of thought. They all emphasize the principle of *jus talionis*, and announce an extremely severe punishment. Their concept of sin is the same, including the specific sins condemned and their source in the inner man, as well as the groups condemned—

---

42. Eichrodt, *Theology*, 356, writes: "The prophetic preaching created a split within the nation which separated membership of the true people of God from the mere fact of belonging to Israel."

43. Cf. Weiser, "Zur Frage," 513–31, esp. 525.

both the leading classes and the nation as a whole. All three sections ascribe the punishment for sin to Yahweh's activity toward his people, which is represented in a similar manner in each, and the concept of the people who are condemned and soon to be punished is the same. In my opinion, these similarities are too numerous and interrelated to be explained as an accident. Rather, they indicate that the person (or persons) who gave the book of Micah its final form organized the book according to a specific pattern to meet the needs of a Jewish community in a certain historical situation.

Affinities in the Hope Sections

The first and third hope sections in the book of Micah consist of only one pericope each (I, 2:12–13; III, 7:7–20),[44] while the central section consists of seven pericopes (4:1–5, 6–8, 9–10, 11–13; 4:14—5:5; 5:6–8, 9–14). Two basic concepts intimately connect the hope sections with the doom sections. First, Yahweh is the "leading actor" in every section. And secondly, the punishment described in the doom sections is interpreted in the hope sections as a prerequisite to the execution of Yahweh's promises. The same God who acts in punishing his people will also act in delivering his people. It is very important to observe that *there is not a single oracle of hope in the entire book of Micah which does not assume a situation of extreme punishment*. Thus, it would be a mistake to separate the sections of doom from the sections of hope. Taken together, they convey a logical and coherent message. Israel has called forth Yahweh's severe punishment by turning away from him. But this punishment is intended to show Israel that it is by trusting in Yahweh alone that her hopes will ever be realized.

As in the doom sections, "Yahweh" is the predominant name of the deity, occurring in all hope sections (I—2:13; II—4:1, 2 [twice], 4, 5, 6, 7, 10, 12, 13; 5:3 [twice], 6, 9; III—7:7, 8, 9, 10, 17). "Elohim" occurs seven times in the hope sections, always in connection with "Yahweh"— twice in the phrase "Yahweh our God" (4:5; 7:17), twice in synonymous parallelism with "Yahweh" (4:2; 7:7), once each in the phrases "Yahweh his God" (5:3) and "Yahweh your God" (7:10), and once in a context in

---

44. Scholars are by no means agreed as to the number of pericopes in 7:7–20. I believe that these verses are to be taken as a unit following an *abab* pattern. See Gunkel, "The Close of Micah," 115–49; Reicke, "Liturgical Traditions," 349–67; and Willis, "The Structure, Setting, and Interrelationships," 134–35, 191.

which its connection with Yahweh is apparent (7:7). In the hope sections, Yahweh's activity is described by the use of verbs in the first person singular with Yahweh as the subject, by the passive voice with Yahweh as assumed subject, and by the third person singular with the prophet as speaker describing Yahweh's activity.

The hope sections announce that Yahweh's essential task will be that of *leading* his people, to give them victory over their enemies and to restore them to their former status as his covenant people. In contrast to the incompetent human leaders in whom the people trust in the doom sections (the princes, prophets, priests, and rich landowners), the hope sections announce that Yahweh is the only leader worthy of Israel's complete trust. The first oracle of hope (2:12-13) is very brief, but its emphasis on Yahweh's leadership of his people is very strong. "I will surely assemble (*'āsōp 'e'ĕsōp*) all Jacob." "I will surely gather (*qabbēṣ 'ăqabbēṣ*) the remnant of Israel." "I will put them together (*yaḥad 'ăśîmennû*) as sheep in a fold" (v. 12). "The breaker (Yahweh[45]) is gone up (*'ālāh*) before them." "Their king is passed on (*wayya'ăbōr*) before them, and Yahweh at their head" (v. 13). The synonymous parallelism in the last two lines of v. 13 shows that Yahweh's essential task is that of leadership. He is the king (מלך) and the head (ראש) over his people. The verbs אסף and קבץ may have special significance in this context. To be sure, they are used of a shepherd bringing his sheep together to protect them. But Mic 2:13 states that once the sheep are gathered, Yahweh will pass on before them as their *king*. "Shepherd" and "king" were interchangeable terms for the reigning monarch among many Ancient Near Eastern peoples. Thus אסף and קבץ may be military terms referring to a king gathering his army for battle.[46] W. Beyerlin has shown that the Davidic tradition had a great influence on the terminology used Mic 1:15 and 5:1-4a, 5b.[47] The same may be said of 2:12-13. The verbs אסף and קצף are used in several passages where David "gathers" all Israel to fight against an enemy. (See e.g., 2 Sam 10:7 = 1 Chr 19:7; 2 Sam 12:18-19). But it is most significant

---

45. The identity of the "breaker" or bellwether here is much debated. In my opinion, it refers to Yahweh because: (1) The figure seems to be based on the Davidic tradition in 2 Sam 5, where it is *Yahweh* who "breaks" Israel's enemies before David; (2) The "breaker" goes before the flock (the people, the army) in the first line of v. 13, and Yahweh is at their head in the last line.

46. See especially Josh 10:5 (אסף)-6 (קצף) and Mic 4:11 (אסף)-12 (קצף). There is a lengthy discussion of this involving many passages in my dissertation, 197-206.

47. Beyerlin, *Die Kulttraditionen Israels*, 75-85.

that in the Davidic tradition, David's leadership is explicitly understood as submissive to Yahweh's rule: "*By the hand of* my servant David I will save my people Israel" (2 Sam 3:18), apparently in contradistinction to Saul who by his disobedience virtually stifled Yahweh's rule. Thus, when Mic 2:12–13 announces that Yahweh will *gather* Israel, three things seem to be implied: (a) Israel will place herself completely under Yahweh's rule; (b) Israel will do this because she is not satisfied with the existing leadership; and (c) Yahweh will subsequently lead Israel in battle against her enemies. The shepherd-sheep motif which occurs here in Micah is also characteristic of the Davidic tradition (cf. 1 Sam 16:11; 2 Sam 5:1 = 1 Chr 11:2; Ps 78:70–21; etc.). J. J. Glück argues very convincingly that the term "shepherd" was used for leaders in the Old Testament primarily when the concept of ideal leadership was in mind.[48] This is supported by the book of Micah, which contrasts Yahweh's ideal rule through submissive leaders with that of leaders who rule according to their own dictates and ideals. The reference to "the breaker" in 2:13 also may be drawn from the Davidic tradition. Second Samuel 5 tells how David was anointed to be shepherd and prince over all Israel (v. 2). When the Philistines learn of this anointing, they go up against David, and he withdraws to "the stronghold" (v. 17), apparently to be identified with the Cave of Adullam (1 Sam 22:1–5). But instead of devising intricate military stratagem, David puts his trust wholly in Yahweh, who then orders David to go up and fight against the Philistines. "And David smote them there; and he said, Yahweh has broken (*pāraṣ*) my enemies before me, like the breach of waters. Therefore he called the name of that place *baʻal pĕrāṣîm*, "Baal-perazim" (2 Sam 5:20 = 1 Chr 14:11). The *happōrēṣ* may have been chosen intentionally to refer to this event in the Davidic tradition.

Micah 2:12–13 also alludes to Yahweh's purpose to restore Israel to her former status as his covenant people. He puts his people together as sheep in a fold, and as a flock in the midst of the pasture. The similarities between the three hope sections in the book make it likely that "fold" (and perhaps "pasture") here refers to Zion or Jerusalem.[49]

In the second hope section, again emphasis is placed on Yahweh's leadership. He will reign (*ûmālak*) over his people in Mount Zion (4:7). Israel's plight is desperate because she trusts in the earthly ruler(s) and

---

48. Glück, "Nagid-Shepherd," 144–50.
49. See Mic 4:8. Compare 7:14 ("dwell solitarily") with Isa 1:8.

not in Yahweh (4:9, 14), and thus Yahweh will raise up a ruler who will "come forth to me" (5:1), i.e., rule completely under submission to Yahweh's will.[50]

Each of the seven pericopes in chs. 4–5 is composed of two parts: a description of the present, hopeless situation, and an announcement of divine deliverance.[51] This material is held together by its announcements of the results of Yahweh's leadership. One result is that Yahweh will give Israel victory over her enemies. 4:6–8 (pericope II) describes Israel as lame, driven away, afflicted, cast far off, apparently without adequate leadership in Mount Zion, and Jerusalem as a desolate tower of the flock, hopelessly exposed to enemy assault (cf. Isa 1:7–8). But the prophet announces that Yahweh will intervene and reverse these circumstances. "I will *assemble* that which is lame, and I will *gather* that which is driven away." "I will *make* that which was lame a remnant." "Yahweh will *reign* over them in Mount Zion." 4:9–10 (pericope III) apparently assumes that Jerusalem is under siege to an invading army, and the king is helpless before the enemy's strength. The people must abandon the security of the fortified city, go out into the field in surrender to the enemy, and be carried to exile in Babylon. But again the writer declares that Yahweh will *rescue* them in Babylon and *redeem* them from their enemies. 4:11–13 (pericope IV) states that the nations have already assembled against Jerusalem to overthrow the city. But this is actually the work of Yahweh. He has *gathered* them as sheaves to the threshing floor. And he announces to his apparently helpless people, "I will make your horn iron, and I will make your hoofs brass." Thus, when her besiegers are routed, Israel is not to take the spoil for herself as if she had defeated them by her own strength, but according to the ancient law of *h*[dot below h]*erem* leave the booty on the battlefield in public acknowledgement that the victory is Yahweh's. 4:14—5:5 (pericope V) describes a situation in which the enemy has already besieged the city, and "they will smite the judge of Israel (the king) with a rod upon the cheek." But Yahweh will raise up a new David to deliver the people. He will come from the "little town of Bethlehem," hardly a suitable birthplace for a king, indicating

50. See my article, "*mimmĕkā lî yēṣēʾ* in Micah 5:1," 317–22.

51. The nature of the present article seems to necessitate a repetition of the pertinent material in my essay, "The Structure of Micah 3–5" (see note 27, above), in order to produce a well-balanced and complete analysis of the book. Here I will be as brief as possible, and refer the reader to the extensive documentation and explanation cited in that article.

that his rise to power is of divine origin. "And he shall stand and feed his flock *in the strength of the Lord, in the majesty of the name of the Lord his God*" (5:5).[52] 5:6–8 (pericope VI) depicts Israel as scattered among the nations as a hapless remnant. But Yahweh will multiply his people like dewdrops or raindrops in the lands of their captors and they will devour their enemies like a lion devours unprotected sheep. Thus Yahweh will *lift up* Israel's hand over her adversaries and *cut off* all her enemies. 5:9–14 (pericope VII) seems to reflect a situation in which Israel was being attacked by powerful foes, and had begun to retaliate futilely with horses and chariots, by taking refuge in her fortified cities, and by seeking help from various types of magical arts and idolatrous practices to thwart the enemy attack. But the prophet announces that Yahweh will destroy all these objects of Israel's trust, and then will declare: "*I* will take vengeance . . . on the nations."[53]

Another result of Yahweh's leadership is the restoration of Israel to her former status as his covenant people. 3:9—4:5 (pericope I) begins by stating that because of inadequate leadership, Zion will be plowed as a field, Jerusalem will become heaps, and the temple will be reduced to a forest height. But Yahweh will intervene and establish the temple as the highest of the mountains, the nations will stream to Zion seeking Yahweh's instruction, and Zion will enjoy security comparable with that which characterized her golden age under David and Solomon (compare especially 4:4 with I Kgs 4:25). 4:6–8 (pericope II) proclaims that the former dominion (i.e., the kingdom in its golden age under David and Solomon), "the kingdom of the daughter of *Jerusalem*," will be restored, and "Yahweh will reign over them *in Mount Zion* from henceforth even forever." 4:9–10 (pericope III) affirms that Zion will be rescued from Babylon and that Yahweh will redeem her from the hand of her enemies, in other words, he will reclaim her as his covenant people. 4:11–13 (pericope IV) announces that Yahweh's thoughts are wholly in Zion's behalf, and that he will deliver her from her besiegers. 4:14—5:5 (pericope V) declares that through Yahweh's power "the rest of his brethren shall return to the people of Israel," "they shall dwell secure," and shall be delivered from the Assyrian. Here this restoration is coupled with the promise of the re-establishment of responsible leadership in Israel.

---

52. See my essay, "Micah IV 14–V 5," 529–47.

53. For a full discussion of the meaning of this pericope, cf. my essay, "The Authenticity and Meaning," 353–68.

The pronominal suffixes -*ekā* and -*êkā* in 5:9–14 (pericope VII) seem to refer to Jerusalem. If so, this pericope also proclaims the restoration of a theocratic government to Zion, as the abolition of the objects of Israel's trust implies.

Like the first hope section in the book of Micah, the central hope section draws from the Davidic tradition. *Zion* will be the center of Israel's political and religious life, as it was under David (2 Sam 5–6). The coming king will rule like a good shepherd over his flock (see 4:6, 7, 8; 5:3, 4), as David did. His dominion will be as extensive as David's kingdom (see 4:4, 8; 5:4). Like David, he will give Israel rest from her enemies round about (cf. 4:3, 13; 5:4–5, 8, 14 with 2 Sam 5:17–27; 8:1ff.). When he defeats his enemies, Israel will devote the spoil to Yahweh (4:13) as David did (2 Sam 8:9–12).

In the third hope section of the book of Micah (7:7–20), Yahweh is again the main actor, although the first person singular is never used here to describe his activity. The address to the enemy (vv. 7–10) uses the divine name or the third person singular, the address to Zion (vv. 11–13) the passive, and the prayer to Yahweh and the hymn (vv. 14–20) the second person singular. The author of this pericope is apparently a prophet intentionally imitating the dramatic acts of the king or his representative in the cult in order to dramatize for his hearers the attitudes and actions which he desires for them to adopt (prosopopoeia).[54] As in the other hope sections, the emphasis here is on Yahweh's leadership. The fact that the speaker imitates the king is significant, because in contrast to the existing inadequate leadership (7:3), he subjects himself wholly to Yahweh, the real king, so that his rule is no alternative to Yahweh's (vv. 8–9). He beseeches Yahweh to feed (*rĕʿēh*) his flock, his people, and does not presume to do this without divine support (v. 14).

Yahweh's leadership involves giving his people victory over their enemies. He will plead Israel's cause, execute judgment for her, and bring her forth to the light (v. 9). Israel's enemies will be forced to retract their mocking words charging Yahweh with impotence, and will be trodden down (v. 10). They will be compelled to acknowledge publicly Yahweh's superiority and their own weakness (vv. 16–17). This divine leadership also involves restoring Israel to her former status as Yahweh's covenant people. This pericope assumes that Zion is under oppression by her en-

---

54. For an extensive defense of this view, cf. Reicke, "Liturgical Traditions." See also Mowinckel, *Det Gamle Testamente*, 672.

emies because of her sin. Her protective walls are useless, her territory is very small, she dwells alone and in despair. But Yahweh will intervene and forgive the sins of his penitent people (vv. 18–20). Their walls will be built and their borders extended (v. 11). Yahweh will gather all Israel to one place to prepare her for battle against her foes (v. 12). The nations will be made a desolation as divine retribution for their evil deeds (v. 13). The prophet entreats Yahweh to restore Israel to her former status as his flock as in the days of David, when her border extended even beyond Jordan (v. 14).

As in the other hope sections, there are striking affinities between 7:7–20 and the Davidic tradition. The king will rule in complete subjection to Yahweh as David did (vv. 7–9). He will give Israel rest from her adversaries through Yahweh's power as David did (vv. 8, 10, 16–17), Yahweh will rule through him as a shepherd guides his flock, as he ruled through David (vv. 11, 14).

Since the three hope sections in the book of Micah deal with Yahweh's activity in behalf of his people, we may expect that the concept of the people of God is the same throughout these sections. "Israel" occurs in the first two hope sections (I, 2:12; II, 4:14; 5:1, 2), apparently meaning all Israel understood in the context of the Jerusalem cult. "Jacob" occurs in all three hope sections (I, 2:12 [in parallelism with "Israel"]; II, 4:2; 5:6–7; III, 7:20), referring to all Israel. "Judah" (5:1) and "thy people" (7:14) occur only once each in the hope sections. Throughout this material, Israel is referred to as a "remnant" and as Yahweh's "flock." Her apparent defeat at the hand of her enemies is so complete that only a remnant is left (I, 2:12; II, 4:7; 5:6–7; II, 7:18). Like a flock of sheep that has been attacked by wild beasts, this remnant is lame, driven away, afflicted, and cast far off (4:6–7). Like a flock of scattered sheep, Israel is wholly at the mercy of her enemies (6:6–7). Her only hope is that Yahweh will intervene, and the hope oracles in the book of Micah declare that he will. He will gather all Israel (2:12) and make the remnant a strong nation (4:7). He will assemble his people and put them together as sheep in a fold, where they will be protected from the enemy. And when they leave the fold and go out into the pasture, they will have nothing to fear because their king will go out before them and Yahweh will be at their head (2:12–13). The present protection is very weak, like a tower of the flock, but Yahweh will restore the former kingdom (4:8). The coming ruler will feed his flock in the strength of Yahweh, and they will abide

(5:3). At present, Yahweh's flock is poorly protected because the walls of the sheepfold are filled with breaches or completely torn down, but the prophet announces that these walls will be rebuilt or repaired (7:11). He prays that Yahweh will feed his flock, guiding and protecting it with the shepherd's rod or staff, and that the pastureland will be increased to accommodate this flock (7:14).

The numerous and striking affinities which are found in the hope sections of the book of Micah are hardly accidental. Rather, they can best be explained by assuming that an individual (or "school") purposefully arranged these oracles within the larger framework of the whole book so as to achieve a type of horizontal coherence between them.

The Vertical Coherence of the Book

Not only does the book of Micah contain striking parallels in form and content between the three doom sections and the three hope sections, but there is also a progression of thought within each of the three divisions of the book, which is supplemented by catchwords, connectives, and contrasts. Due to the striking similarities in structure and thought, it seems most natural to deal first with sections I (1–2) and III (6–7).

Section I consists of four pericopes: a covenant lawsuit (1:2–7), a lament (1:8–16), an explanation (or reason, *Begründung*) for the impending catastrophe in the form of a reproach (2:1–11), and a hope oracle (2:12–13). 1:2–4 should not be separated from 1:5–7. 1:5a or 1:5b is not a good beginning for an oracle, and if we subdivide this material, vv. 2–4 announce an impending judgment which is not described and vv. 5 (or 5b)–7 describe a judgment that is not announced. 1:2–7 contains the basic elements of a lawsuit: summons to the peoples and the earth (v. 2), the theophany (vv. 3–4), the reason for the theophany, i.e., the sins of Samaria and Jerusalem (v. 5), and the description of the coming destruction (vv. 6–7). It is equally unsatisfactory to isolate 1:8–9 from 1:10–16. By doing this, vv. 8–9 announce a lament whose contents are not stated, and vv. 10–16 give the contents of a lament which is not announced. The "catch phrase" "the gate of Jerusalem" in vv. 9 and 12, and the idea that the sin (and resulting punishment) of Israel had spread into Judah in vv. 9, 12, and 13 compel us to look upon vv. 8–16 as a unit. Furthermore, no sharp division should be made between 1:2–7 and 1:8–16. It is more natural to interpret "For this" (*'al zō't*) in 1:8 as the connective between these two pericopes than to take it to refer to that which follows.[55] The view that the reference to Jerusalem and Judah in 1:5b is a later insertion because the description of punishment in vv. 6–7 concerns only Samaria is unnecessary. References to the sin and punishment of Samaria also occur in vv. 8–16, an oracle which deals primarily with the fate of Jerusalem. Verses 9 and 13 (and by implication v. 12) lament because the sin (and resulting punishment) of Samaria has infected Jerusalem. In light of this, it is striking that in 1:5b the writer mentions the sin of Samaria first, then the sin of Jerusalem. Thus one theme which seems to permeate the entire first chapter is that the fate of Samaria will be the fate of Jerusalem, because the sin of Samaria has become the sin of Jerusalem (so similarly Isa 7:14–17; 8:5–8). If so, v. 5b should not be severed from vv. 9, 12, and 13. Also, it is significant that vv. 2–7 and 8–16 both end with an announcement of impending captivity (vv. 7 and 16).

Again, it is a mistake to separate 2:1–5 and 2:6–11 into separate pericopes. Those who make such a separation argue that the allusion to prophecy (נטף) in vv. 6 and 11 indicates the beginning and conclusion of a pericope, and that v. 5 (or 4) is the natural conclusion of a pericope. But vv. 6–7 represent the reply of Micah's opponents to one of his doom oracles, and it seems very unlikely that a pericope would begin with the response of the prophet's opponents. The provocation for such an emotional reply would be expected to precede that reply, and vv. 1–5 offer just such a provocation. The prophet condemns the rich for oppressing the poor and announces that they will suffer severe punishment (vv. 1–5). They rejoinder by asserting that he is a false prophet whose message does not correspond to the divine nature and requirements (vv. 6–7). Then the prophet reinforces his charges of sin against his hearers and reiterates his announcement that they will be punished (vv. 8–11). It may be that v. 5 was the "end" of Micah's oracle in the sense that vv. 1–5 represent the entire message that the prophet originally intended to give on a particular occasion. But the vehement reply of the hearers in vv. 6–7 would naturally provoke a response from the prophet in which he would advance further evidence of their sin and reassert that they

---

55. E.g., Lindblom, *Micah*, 39, writes: "Müssen wir zu dem Resultat kommen, dass die Verse 8–16 eine selbständige Revelation bilden, die mit der vorhergehenden nichts gemeinsam hat," but on 38 he feels compelled to say: "Der Eindruck, dass sie [i.e., the words 'for this'] . . . noch den Inhalt von den Versen 2–7 aufnehmen sollten, beruht auf der formalin Verbindung mit einander, die einmal die beiden Revelationen durch den Sammler bekommen haben."

would be punished. This explains why captivity is threatened both in vv. 4–5 and in v. 10.

In addition, 1:2–16 and 2:1–11 are interrelated. The emphasis in 1:2–16 is on the punishment which is about to come on Samaria and Jerusalem, although broadly speaking it alludes to sins responsible for this judgment.[56] At the same time, the emphasis in 2:1–11 is on specific sins necessitating a severe desolation, although it does refer to the impending punishment (vv. 3–5, 10). 1:2–7, 8–16, and 2:1–11 all threaten an enemy invasion into the land (1:7, 10–15; 2:3–4), and each of these pericopes ends with a threat of captivity (1:7, 16; 2:10). It seems more reasonable to believe that these affinities are the result of a well conceived plan for the redaction of the book than that they are the result of accident.

The present position of the hope oracle in 2:12–13 can also be supported with good reasons. First, 2:10 threatens that the Israelites will be carried into captivity. 2:12–13 offers an interesting contrast to this in asserting that the exiles will be gathered together under the rule of Yahweh. Secondly, 3:1 begins the second doom section by denouncing the "heads" of Jacob (see also 3:9). In contrast to this, the first section of the book ends with a hope oracle which affirms that Yahweh will be "head" over his people (2:13).[57] Thirdly, if we are correct in interpreting 2:12–13 liturgically, its connection with 1:2—2:11 is even clearer. The execution of the punishment announced in the first doom section will leave Israel completely helpless, and yet this punishment is directly attributed to Yahweh (1:2–4, 6–7, 12 ["evil is come down from Yahweh"]; 2:3–5). Thus, either Yahweh has completely forsaken his people because of their sins, and Israel has no future, or else Yahweh is using the punishment of his people as a means of teaching them the seriousness of their apostasy and their need to trust in him alone. 2:12–13 is an affirmation of the latter.

Section III of the book of Micah also contains four pericopes: a covenant lawsuit (6:1–8), an explanation for the impending catastrophe in the form of a reproach (6:9–16), a lament (7:1–6), and a hope oracle

---

56. Verses 5 and 13 mention only the broadest kind of explanation for the coming destruction. It is true that v. 7 suggests some reasons for the destruction of Samaria, but the primary purpose of this verse is to announce the nature of the punishment which Yahweh will bring upon the city, and not to give the reasons for it.

57. For a lengthy discussion, see Willis, "A Note on ואמר," 50–54.

in the form of a liturgy (7:7–20). Like the lawsuit in 1:2ff., 6:1–8 contains a summons (to the mountains, hills, and foundations of the earth) (vv. 1a, 2), an accusation in the form of a question (v. 3), and an indictment, or rebuke for Israel's ingratitude toward Yahweh's mighty acts (vv. 4–5). But at first, one element indigenous to a lawsuit seems to be missing, viz., the sentence or announcement of punishment. J. M. P. Smith[58] and others maintain that a redactor replaced the original judicial sentence with the Torah Liturgy in 6:6–8. R. E. Wolfe suggests that the person who recorded the lawsuit beginning with 6:1 was unable to remember the sentence, so omitted it.[59] Basing his argument on Ancient Near Eastern suzerainty treaties dating about 2000–1700 BCE, J. Harvey contends that actually Mic 6:1–5 is an ultimatum from a powerful suzerain to his rebellious vassal, and such an ultimatum contains no sentence.[60] But in my opinion, the structural difficulty of the lawsuit in Mic 1:6ff. is due to the interruption of his hearers (similar to that found in 2:6–7). Apparently moved by Yahweh's lawsuit in vv. 1–5, they penitently urge the prophet to declare the sacrifices which Yahweh requires to forgive their obvious ingratitude (vv. 6–7). The prophet affirms that they already know what Yahweh demands—not sacrifice, but practicing justice and faithful love and walking wisely with God (v. 8). Then he resumes the explanation or reason for Yahweh's lawsuit that had been broken off at v. 5 by the hearers' interruption (vv. 9–12), and then declares the sentence or announcement of punishment (vv. 13–15), closing with a summary of the people's sin and the sentence (v. 16). The connection between vv. 1–8 and 9–16 is further indicated by the repetition of "hear" in v. 9 (cf. v. 1) after the continuity of thought had been broken, and by the marked contrast between Yahweh's demands (v. 8) and the people's activities (vv. 9–12).

It is also possible, although admittedly more difficult, to understand Micah 7 as a unit. The identity of the speaker in vv. 1–6 may assist in finding a key to this chapter. He cannot be Israel, because he refers to Israel in the third person plural several times.[61] Nor can he be Yahweh, because "woe is me" in v. 1 would be out of place in Yahweh's mouth.

---

58. Smith, *Critical and Exegetical Commentary*, 122.
59. Wolfe, "The Book of Micah," 938.
60. Harvey, "Le *Rîb*-pattern," 172–96.
61. Notice "they" in v. 2 (twice); "their" and "they" in v. 3; and "them" and "their" in v. 4. The same thing is indicated by the direct address to Israel in vv. 4–5.

So he must be the prophet, but his function in this context seems to be of a specific nature, corresponding in a striking way to the function of the king or his representative in the New Year Festival. There are several elements in ch. 7 which remind us of this festival.[62] First, 7:1 seems to indicate that the harvest season is present, and thus points to the Festival of Booths. Secondly, vv. 1–6, 8 are strikingly similar to a ritual of lament in which the king or his representative symbolically suffered and descended into Sheol, while vv. 9–10 appear to be a ritual of rejoicing, like that in which the king was symbolically raised up and restored to his former position. Thirdly, the speaker is not basically disturbed by the lack of food in the land (as a casual reading of v. 1 might lead one to believe), but by the threat of destruction by an enemy army (vv. 8, 10), and by corruption in Israelite society (vv. 2–4a, 5–6), both of which normally fall within the province of the king and reflect oft-recurring themes of the New Year Festival.[63]

Gunkel has offered convincing evidence of the unity of 7:7–20 by analyzing it as a liturgy. The alternations of dissimilar tunes, the oscillation between individual and collective, and the different speakers and audiences of these verses are all characteristics of liturgical texts in the Psalms. Verses 7–20 were used as a dirge or lament containing two essential elements: (a) the distressed suppliant who realizes that human or material aid cannot avail, and (b) the longing for Yahweh's intervention.[64] As is often the case, this liturgy begins with a Dirge (vv. 7–10; cf. Pss 7:1; 11:1; etc.), which has several parallels in Psalms in which the king urges Yahweh to appear to help and promises to wait for him in the certainty that he will hear (cf. Pss 68:2f., 12; 4:2–4, 6:7–10; etc.). Verses 11–13 are a Prophetic Oracle addressed to the city. "It was the practice in Israel, when the dirge had been chanted, for the priest or prophet to lift up his voice and communicate the divine answer to the praying people."[65] Verses 14–17 are a National Dirge, in which the prophet by empathy puts into the mouth and heart of the people what they should feel and

---

62. The points made here follow Reicke, "Liturgical Traditions."

63. For the cultic aspects of the king's concern with an enemy invasion, see Pss 2 and 110 and the comments of Bentzen, *King and Messiah*, 16–17, 23–24. The king's concern for corruption in society in reflected in several psalms of lament, as e.g., 4:3; 5:6f., 10; 10:3ff.; 12:2ff.

64. Gunkel, "The Close of Micah," 119.

65. Ibid., 132. See Isa 26:8–14a, 16–18, 19–21; 33:2, 3–6, 7–9, 10–12; Hos 6:1–3, 4–6.

say in order to lead them to trust in Yahweh alone in time of distress. Verses 18–20 are a Hymn of Praise to Yahweh for doing what the suppliant feels sure he will do. Thus, 7:7–20 is composed of two parallel sections:

A.	B.
1. Dirge of Zion (vv. 7–10) answered by	1. Dirge of Israel (vv. 14–17) continued by
2. Divine oracle (vv. 11–13)	2. Hymn of assurance of future deliverance (vv. 18–20)

While this arrangement may not seem logical or coherent to the modern western mind, it "was a favorite method in Hebrew poetry,"[66] as Pss 24; 95:1ff., 6f.; 100:1ff., etc., show.

Still further evidence favors interpreting ch. 7 as a unit. The "day" of vv. 11–12 presupposes the "day" of v. 4. Again in v. 4, the prophet declares that the punishment has come, but fails to explain to his hearers its nature and significance. Verses 7–20 supply this information. Israel is threatened by an invading army (vv. 8, 10, 16–17). This army has been sent by Yahweh to punish Israel for her sins (v. 9), and she must learn from this that Yahweh is her only reliable source of help (vv. 7–10, 14–20). Also, there is a contrast between Israel's behavior in vv. l–6 and the attitude expressed in vv. 7–20. It seems most natural to assume that vv. l–6 are a lament over Israel's attitude, and vv. 7–20 describe empathically what her attitude should be.

The lament in 7:1–6 belongs to the lawsuit of 6:1–8 and the reproach of 6:9–16 as naturally as the lament of 1:8–16 belongs to the lawsuit of 1:2–7 and the reproach of 2:1–11. When we compare the structure and contents of 6:9–16 and 7:1–6, we find that both oracles contain a description of Israel's corruption (6:10–12; 7:1–4a), then a description of punishment (6:13–15; 7:4b), then a summary description of corruption (6:16a; 7:5–6). In addition to this, there are several connections between the four pericopes in chs. 6–7. (a) The punishment in both 6:13–15 and 7:4b is by a foreign invader. (b) Yahweh's "righteous acts" in 6:5 correspond to his "marvelous things" in 7:15. (c) 6:4 and 7:15, 19 are based on the Exodus tradition. (d) The resolution to "bear" (*'eśśā'*) Yahweh's indignation in 7:9 is similar to the statement that the prophet's hearers would bear (*tiśśā'û*) the reproach of "my people" in 6:16. (e) The announcement of an impending "desolation" of Israel's enemies "for the

---

66. Gunkel, "The Close of Micah," 142.

fruit of their doings" in 7:13 is apparently an intentional contrast to the announcement of an impending "desolation" of Israel "because of thy sins" (6:13, 16). The interrelationships between the pericopes in Mic 6–7 are too numerous and too striking to be fortuitous. Instead, they indicate an attempt on the part of an individual or a "school" to produce a coherent literary piece.

A good case can also be made for the coherence of the central section of the book of Micah (chs. 3–5). Scholars generally agree that the doom section (ch. 3) is composed of three pericopes of similar length, form, and content. Verses 1–4 condemn Israel's rulers; vv. 5–8, the false prophets; and vv. 9–12, the rulers, priests, and false prophets in "summary" fashion. Westermann's analysis of the first and third pericopes[67] and the obvious similarity of the second pericope to them indicate the coherence of this chapter. Each pericope condemns Israelite leadership, each gives the reason for this condemnation (i.e., the failure of the particular leading class to discharge its responsibility), and each announces a coming judgment suitable to the crime.

Due to the somewhat extensive analysis of chs. 4–5 suggested above, only a few remarks need to be made here to demonstrate their vertical coherence. First, all the pericopes in these chapters assume the same sort of historical situation, viz., Israel is in desperate, seemingly hopeless, circumstances. Either she is threatened by an enemy (especially 4:6–8, 9–10, 11–13; 4:14—5:5; 5:9–14) or realizes that she has lost her former status as Yahweh's covenant people (especially 3:9—4:5; 5:6–8), both concepts being interrelated in most of the pericopes. Secondly, each pericope in chs. 4–5 contains a contrast between the present hopeless situation and the glorious future, so that while 3:9–12 is a vital part of ch. 3, it is also inseparably connected with 4:1–5 according to the contrast principle.[68] Thirdly, the contrast between the present and the future is set forth in three ways in the seven pericopes of Mic 4–5: a long section of doom followed by a short section of hope, a short section of doom followed by a long section of hope, and a section of hope containing references to the present hopeless situation.

In addition to this, it, is noteworthy that each pericope in chs. 4–5 is linked together with its adjoining pericope or pericopes by catchwords or catch phrases. (a) In 4:6–8, "in that day" in v. 6 is connected with "in

---

67. See note 31.

68. See my essay referred to in note 27.

the latter days" in v. 1; "Mount Zion" in v. 7 is related to "mountain of Yahweh's house" in v. 1 and "mountain of Yahweh," which is equated with "Zion," in v. 2; and "from henceforth even forever" in v. 7 joins onto "for ever and ever" in v. 5. (b) In 4:9–10, *'attāh* in v. 9 is similar in sound to *wĕ'attāh* in v. 8; and "daughter of Zion" in v. 10 also occurs in v. 8. (c) In 4:11–13, *wĕ'attāh* in v. 11 also appears in v. 9; "Zion" in v. 11 and "daughter of Zion" in v. 13 are linked with "daughter of Zion" in v. 10; and "counsel" in v. 12 may be an intentional connective with "counselor" in v. 9. (d) In 4:14—5:5, *'attāh* in 4:14 and 5:3 joins onto the same word in 4:11; *wĕ'attāh* in 5:1 has a similar sound; and "daughter of troops" in 4:14 seems to be a variation on "daughter of Zion" in 4:13. (e) In 5:6–8, *wĕhāyāh* in vv. 6 and 7 is connected with the same word in v. 4; "remnant of Jacob" in vv. 6–7 is linked with "residue of his brethren" in 5:2; "tread down" (*wĕrāmas*) and "deliver" in v. 7 join onto "tread" (*yidrōk*) in vv. 4–5 and "deliver" in v. 5. (f) In 5:9–14, *wĕhikrattî* in vv. 9–12 is connected with *yikkārētû* in 5:8; and *wĕhāyāh* in v. 9 joins onto the same word in vv. 6–7.

It is also striking that each large division of the book of Micah is connected to its adjoining section by the catchword principle. Sections I and II are connected by *bĕrōšām*, "at their head," in 2:13, and *rāšê ya'ăqōb*, "heads of Jacob," in 3:1. Sections II and III are linked together by *šāmē'û*, "that did not hear," in 5:1, and *šim'û*, "hear," in 6:1.

Concluding Remarks

The book of Micah falls into three large divisions (chs. 1–2, 3–5, 6–7) according to an A–B–A pattern. Analyzed horizontally, the doom sections and the hope sections exhibit striking similarities in structure, ideology, and phraseology. Analyzed vertically, the pericopes in each section have been joined together with that which precedes and/or with that which follows by a logical continuity of thought or by catchwords and catch phrases. And the major divisions themselves have been linked together by catchwords. The affinities in the book are so striking and numerous that they can hardly be accidental. It is more reasonable to believe that an individual (or a "school") arranged the materials which now compose the book of Micah according to a specific scheme in order to produce a message which he felt to be relevant to a certain Jewish community. "Det dreier sig her om en *virkelig sammensveisning*, ikke bare om en tilfeldig sidestilling innenfor den større samling Tolvprofetboken."[69]

Finally, a few remarks concerning the time and place that the book of Micah may have reached its "present form" seem to be in order. Scholars have suggested dates all the way from 700 to 100 BCE as the time that the book reached its final form.[70] In light of the historical situation which seems to be reflected in the book, I agree with those who place it in the exilic period. In the wake of Nebuchadrezzar's siege of Jerusalem in 597, Judah would have been impressed with the hopelessness of thwarting the onslaught of her enemies. The fall of the city in 586 would have been even more convincing. The popular view was that this catastrophe showed that Yahweh had completely abandoned his people (cf. Jer 7:3-4, etc.). Apparently the crisis which the community to which the book of Micah was addressed faced was a rather recent thing. This would help to explain the passionate nature of the hope oracles, the reflective character of 7:7-20, and some of the "radical" contrasts between the present situation and the future promises in chs. 4-5. The strong emphasis on the Davidic tradition may indicate that the Davidic dynasty had been dethroned only comparatively recently.

Furthermore, it seems to me that internal evidence favors a Palestinian provenance for the book of Micah. In the first place, the references to Zion and Jerusalem in the hope passages indicate that the writer is either in Jerusalem or near the city. In 4:8, 9, 10, 11, 13, 14; 7:11, 12, the speaker addresses the city as he would a person in close proximity. There are several references in the hope sections to the nations going to Zion. But they do not leave the speaker and go to Zion. Instead, they come from afar and assemble near Zion, in close proximity to the speaker. For example, in 4:14 the writer says: "they have besieged *us*." In 5:4-5, he states that the Assyrian comes into *our* land, and marches into *our* country and into *our* territory, and announces that *we* will raise up against him seven shepherds, etc. Similarly, the remnant comes from afar to assemble at Zion under Yahweh's leadership (2:12; 4:6-7; 7:12). Perhaps the strongest evidence for the Palestinian provenance appears in 4:9-10. Zion[71] will go forth out of the city and dwell in the field, and shall come to Babylon, and "there" (*šām*) she shall be rescued, and "there" (*šām*) Yahweh will redeem her from the hand of her enemies.

---

69. Mowinckel, *Det Gamle Testamente*, 672.
70. For the various views, see my dissertation, 302-3.
71. *Here* (where the speaker is) and *not there*, as the address "you" shows.

Secondly, the similarity between the Assyrian threat to Palestine and the captivity of Israel in the period extending from about 734 to about 700 BCE and the Babylonian threat to Palestine and the captivity of Judah in the period extending from about 605 to about 586 BCE would tend to make the material belonging to the Mican corpus take on new and significant meaning for the later community. It is likely that some of the Judean prophets of the sixth century BCE (perhaps including Jeremiah and some of his circle) considered themselves to be "disciples" of Micah, members of the Mican school. Attention may have been called to the similarities between Micah's message and Jeremiah's message.[72] This would explain why it was natural for the elders (who apparently had heard Jeremiah on several occasions) to recognize immediately the parallel between his announcement that the temple would be destroyed and Micah's threat which appears in 3:12 in the present form of the book (Jer 26:16–19).[73] It is among non-aristocratic groups such as those that the Babylonians left in Palestine after 586 that one would expect the type of promises as those found in the hope sections of the book of Micah to be cherished and preserved. The announcement of a leader to come forth from the insignificant village of Bethlehem (4:14—5:5) fits such a circumstance very well.

The identity of the coming ruler in the hope sections of the book of Micah is vague. The most that we are told is that he will be a new David. In contrast to the inadequate rulers that brought Israel to ruin because they failed to depend wholly on Yahweh, the coming ruler (like David) will submit himself wholly to Yahweh's rule. (See especially 5:1–5.) This vagueness may point to a time before some concrete individual like Zerubbabel appeared as a possible fulfillment of Israel's messianic hopes. W. Harrelson has argued that Isa 4:2–6; 13:1–22; 24–27; and 33–35 originated among "the disciples [of Isaiah] left in Judah after the city's fall in 586."[74] In my opinion, it is quite possible that a member of this same circle of disciples is responsible for the arrangement of redaction of the "final form" of the book of Micah.

72. I have listed thirty-one striking similarities in my dissertation, 307–10, and am convinced that there are many more, although admittedly less striking.

73. If we take the text in Jer 26 *prima facie*, we get the impression that the elders' response to the suggestion that Jeremiah's words demanded the death penalty (v. 16) was a quick natural reflex, not a well thought out reply. If so, it is highly unlikely that they hit on the similarity between Micah and Jeremiah on the spur of the moment.

74. Harrelson, *Interpreting the Old Testament*, 245.

2

Thoughts on a Redactional Analysis of the Book of Micah

REDAKTIONSGESCHICHTE OR REDACTION CRITICISM is still in its infancy. Attempts at a programmatic presentation of this methodology[1] have raised many questions as to definitions, scope of the task, and the applicability of Redaction Criticism to the biblical text. These efforts point to the need for painstaking work on specific biblical books or works. A major issue which surfaces repeatedly is the role the redactors of a particular biblical book played in the growth, arrangement, and theological tendency of that book. After sketching four major recent means of dealing with the redaction of prophetic books, March appropriately concluded his essay with this challenge: "It is our task now to begin to test the various assumptions and conceptions against the text to discover whether and how we may better define, describe, and understand the work of redaction and the formation of prophetic books."[2] The present paper represents a modest attempt to probe certain problems related to redactional activity in the book of Micah.[3]

---

1. See e.g., Budde, "Eine folgenschwere Redaktion," 218–29; Wolfe, "The Editing," 90–129; Eissfeldt, "Zur Überlieferungsgeschichte," cols. 529–34; Kraus, "Zur Geschichte," 371–87; Koch, *Was ist Formgeschichte?*; Ringgren, "Litterärkritik," 45–56; Rendtorff, "Litterarkritik," 138–53; Perrin, *What is Redaction Criticism?*, Stein, "What is Redaktionsgeschichte?," 45–56; Rast, *Tradition History*; Knight, *Rediscovering*; Wharton, "Redaction Criticism, OT," 729–32; Fortna, "Redaction Criticism, NT," 733–35; Coats and Long, *Canon and Authority*; Knight, *Tradition and Theology*; and March, "Redaction Criticism," 87–101.

2. March, "Redaction Criticism," 98.

3. A number of articles and books appeared in recent years dealing with the redaction of the book of Micah, among which may be mentioned Willis, "Structure

The Starting Point

A widely practiced scholarly approach to the prophetic books is (1) to attempt to determine the extent of each oracle or literary unit and to fix its setting and date so as to decide what is authentic and what is secondary; (2) to reconstruct the historical setting, life, and theology of the prophet from the authentic texts; and (3) to seek to understand the purposes of or reasons for the later additions so as to rediscover the theological emphases of the redactors.[4] It is typical of those who adopt this approach to affirm that hope oracles were inserted at strategic places in the text at later times to neutralize or soften or offset oracles of doom which were offensive to or inadequate for a generation living in suffering and poverty.[5] This approach inevitably leads to the conclusion that the prophetic books are disconnected or at best very loosely arranged. At the end of the nineteenth century and during the early decades of the twentieth, when this point of view was particularly prevalent in scholarly circles, "the task of the critic was seen primarily as one of separating the genuine words of the prophet form the handiwork of later annotators and edi-

---

of the Book," 5–42; Woude, "Micah in Dispute," 244–60; Jeremias, "Die Deutung," 330–54; Lescow, "Redaktionsgeschichtliche Analyse von Micha 1–5," 46–85; Lescow, "Redaktionsgeschichtliche Analyse von Micha 6–7," 182–212; Willis, "A Reapplied Prophetic Hope Oracle," 64–76; Mays, *Micah*; Woude, *Micha*; Mays, "The Theological Purpose," 276–87; Renaud, *La Formation*.

4. Speaking of Micah 4–7, Lindblom (*Micha*, 82) writes: "Sie sind aus sehr disparaten Elementen zusammengesetzt, von denen ein jedes mit Hinsicht auf den Inhalt. und die Entstehungszeit eine selbständige Behandlung verdient." He takes a consistent position on this point throughout his work. Similarly, Mowinckel (*Prophecy and Tradition*, 40) states that one of the exegete's tasks is to separate out the individual units within the larger traditional complex. "Only when he has succeeded in this can he attempt to make a satisfactory reply to the question why these originally independent units have been placed together in the tradition, and 'what the transmitters may have meant by it—if they have meant anything at all, apart from collecting in groups the sayings they felt had a certain affinity to each other.'"

5. "Wo nur immer eine scharfe Drohung in den alten Texten vorlag, fügten die Späteren gern sofort einzelne Worte oder Sätze hinzu, welche die Aufhebung der Drohung aussprechen sollten." Hölscher, *Die Profeten*, 457; Nowack (*Die Kleinen Propheten*, 197) suggests that the redactor of the book of Micah probably inserted 4:1–4 "um ein Gegengewicht gegen v. 3 12 mit seiner düsteren Perspektive zu bilden." With regard to 2:12–13, Lindblom (*Micha*, 67–68) writes: "Entweder wird eine Heilsweissagung an ein Gerichtswort angeknüpft, um in liturgischem Interesse das dunkle Zukunftsbild mit einem helleren zu ergänzen, oder werden die Vorstellungen von einer glücklichen, Zukunft, die auch bein den ältesten Propheten bisweilen hervorbrechen, vervollständigt und weiter ausgeführt."

tors. Since material was often excised with a high hand because it fitted poorly in its context, or because of allegedly inferior style, or because its ideas were conceived to be unworthy of, or too advanced for, the prophet in question, the result was not infrequently a shredding of the prophetic books."[6]

In recent years, however, scholars have become increasingly aware that by the very nature of the situation and the task one is forced (1) to begin with the final form of a biblical book or work, analyze its present arrangement, theological emphases, and intentions (or lack thereof); (2) proceed deliberately but cautiously to earlier redactional or traditio-historical stages which may be discernible; and (3) reconstruct, where possible, the original setting and event or oracle reflected in the present text.[7] While such an approach is destined to make the work of the biblical and ancient Near Eastern historian very difficult, the nature of the biblical books demands it.

The Nature of the Book of Micah

The works of modern critical scholars demonstrate that there is a high degree of subjectivity in the assessment of the nature of biblical books in their final form. The appraisal of the book of Micah is no exception. A great deal depends on the mind frame the evaluator brings to the text. There are four major views as to how the present final form of the book of Micah is to be explained.

First, the most widely held view is that the book of Micah (like other prophetic books) is an anthology of authentic and spurious oracles (or pieces of literature) of varying length from different periods of Old Testament history, which have been collected out of a desire to preserve material that the tradents or redactors deemed valuable or divinely motivated, and not according to any discernible scheme. Marti states emphatically that "einen einheitlichen Zusammenhang innerhalb

---

6. Bright, "Modern Study," 19.

7. Koch (*Growth*, 57) states succinctly: "The history of the transmission of traditions . . . takes the final form of a unit and investigates the various stages it has been through . . . in order to get back to the oldest ascertainable versions of it." Fortna ("Redaction Criticism, NT," 733) affirms that methodologically "we must go backward from his (the author's) finished work, using as far as possible the insights of form criticism." Very recently B. W. Anderson ("From Analysis to Synthesis," 25) wrote: "one is compelled to agree that the proper starting-point methodologically is with the text as given, not with the reconstruction of the prehistory of the text."

der Heilsweissagungen oder auch der Mahnworte aufzuweisen gelingt nicht."[8] Wade concurs: "The book as a whole lacks any systematic structure; . . . its contents comprise a number of sections of which many stand in no logical or orderly relation to one another; . . . various oracles included within it must have been delivered on distinct occasions."[9] Gautier compares the discontinuity of the book of Micah with that of Amos and Hosea: "Comme les livres d'Osée et d'Amos celui de Michée est une collection, non pas de discours à proprement parler, mais de morceaux oratories très brefs, souvent sans lien les uns avec les autres, et ce caractère fragmentaire est encore plus accentué ici."[10] Budde argues that Mic 4–7 and Zech 9–14 served as "catch-alls" for late eschatological oracles and thus consist of "fliegenden Blätter" which post-exilic editors wanted to incorporate into the prophetic corpus.[11]

Second, several scholars interpret the book of Micah as a compilation of previously existing collections of oracles, either 1–5 and 6–7[12] or 1–5; 6:1—7:6; and 7:7–20[13] or 1–3; 4–5; 6:1—7:6; and 7:7–20.[14] There may be some sort of coherence within the collections themselves, but not between the disparate collections. The adoption of either of these views is tantamount to a general skepticism about the possibility of discovering a meaningful creative contribution on the part of the redactors, and indeed about the possibility of discerning a coherent theological thrust in the whole of the book in its final form.

Third, some critics, convinced that the book of Micah as it· now stands is incoherent, rearrange the whole so as to restore the original coherence. Haupt, Hanon, and Scharbert[15] attempt this on chronological grounds, while Elhorst, Halévy, Schmidt,[16] and others follow what seems to them a logical scheme. Even if one adopted this solution, which actu-

8. Marti, *Das Dodekapropheton*, 262.

9. Wade, *The Books of the Prophets*, xx.

10. Gautier, *Introduction*, 502.

11. Budde, "Verfasser," 157.

12. This was the view of Ewald, *Commentary*, 325–26; and has been espoused most recently by Mays, *Micah*; and, "The Theological Purpose."

13. W. R. Smith, *The Prophets of Israel*, 427 n. 3; 428 n. 5.

14. Baudissin, *Einleitung*, 525–26, 529, 532–33.

15. Haupt, "The Book of Micah," 27:1–62; Steinmann and Hanon, *Michée*, 12–14; Scharbert, *Die Propheten Israels*, 310–35.

16. Elhorst, *De Prophetie van Micha*; Halévy, "Le Livre de Michée," 12:97–117, 193–216, 289–312; 13:1–22; Schmidt, *Die Grossen Propheten*, 130–53.

ally has to do with scribal activity rather than redactional activity, when the alleged original order is restored he is still faced with the problem of explaining the process by which the book of Micah reached that form.

Over against these appraisals, at least to some extent, stands the fundamental *redaktionsgeschichtliche* concept that the book of Micah (like most other prophetic and biblical books) is the end product of a rather long history of handing on, selecting, revising, updating, arranging, and expanding earlier traditional material. Generally speaking, four theories of the redactional growth of this book have emerged.

(1) Stade, Cornill, and Cheyne[17] find the hands of two or three epigones or redactors. Stade argues that the original book was composed of one prophecy, namely, 1:1—2:11; 3. This material survived only because Jer 26:17ff. gave it high commendation. After the time of Jeremiah one epigone added 4:1-4; 4:11—5:3; 5:6-8, 9-14. "Der Grund, aus welchem jener Epigone seine Ausführungen hinter 3,12 einschaltete, war ohne Zweifel dieser, dass er an der Einseitigkeit des Inhalts von Kap. 1-3 einen nicht unberechtigten Anstoss nahm."[18] Later a second epigone, assuming that this whole corpus was genuine, added 4:5-10 and 5:4-5 to incorporate the idea of an assault on Jerusalem by the nations and their defeat. This gave the work a balance of doom and hope which enabled it to be accepted into the canon.[19] Stade does not deal with 2:12-13 and chs. 6-7 in this discussion.

(2) Marti contends that the materials in the book of Micah were attracted to two poles or nuclei which were expanded gradually over a, period of approximately five centuries. The original corpus was 1:5b, 6, 8, 9, 16; 2:1-3, 4(?), 6-11; 3:1, 2a, 3a, 4, 5a, 2b, 5b-8, 9-12. About 500 BCE, a redactor added 4:1-4 to modify the negative thrust of 3:9-12. Shortly thereafter another redactor added 6:6-8 to 4:1-4, joining them by 4:5. 4:1-4 and 6:6-8 functioned as two nuclei around which the rest of the book was added by different redactors at different times from the fifth to the second centuries BCE. 5:1, 3 were among the earliest passages to be added, and 5:4-14 and 7:7-20 were some of the latest.[20]

17. Stade, "Bemerkungen," 161-72; Cornill, *Introduction*, 343-47; Cheyne, *Micah*; and "Micah (Book)," cols. 3072-73.

18. Stade, "Bemerkungen," 170.

19. Ibid., 169, 171.

20. Marti, *Das Dodekapropheton*, 262-64. Marti (263) states emphatically: "Man

(3) The most widely accepted view of the growth of this prophetic book is that it occurred, generally speaking, in three stages. (a) Genuine oracles were preserved, collected, and written down by the prophet or his disciples at some indeterminate period. (b) Over a rather long time span, additions, deletions, explanations, updates, and changes of various kinds were made as the earlier collection was reapplied and reinterpreted in light of new circumstances and needs. (c) At the end of this long transmission period, a redactor or redactors put the book in its present, final form. G. B. Gray seems to have been the first to champion this view. He thought that the original material consisted of 1:2—2:11; 3; 4:14; 5:9–13; 6:1—7:6 and may have been written by Micah himself as a kind of summary of his teaching. Jeremiah 26:17ff. shows that the book was known in this form at the end of the seventh century BCE. Between the time of Jeremiah and the end of the third century BCE this material was gradually enlarged by the addition of pre-exilic and post-exilic pieces, re-edited, and given an expanded title. Then, at the end· of the third century BCE it reached its final form and was incorporated into the Book of the Twelve.[21]

Similarly, Wolfe finds three stages in the development of the book. The original oracles are 1:5—2:11; 3; 6:1—7:4. Between 700 and 200 BCE many additions were made, and about 200 BCE the book reached its final form.[22] Wolfe remarks:

> It is gradually coming to be realized that in those days commentators did not make separate books of their productions but that a manuscript, such as the present text of Micah, consisted of the basic document plus the comments which accrued to it during the time it circulated as a living, growing book. In the case of Micah this period of growth lasted almost five centuries, from the time some collector edited what was available of the addresses into a manuscript shortly after 700 B.C. until the collection became regarded as sacred scripture at approximately 200

---

wird versuchen müssen, die Entstehung des jetzigen Buches aus einem allmählichen Anwachsen verschiedener fremder Bestandteile zu erklären."

21. Gray, "Micah, Book of," 614–15. Commenting on the growth of the book, Gray (615) writes: "It is impossible to determine through how many stages of editorial treatment the book passed, but some of these stages certainly fell within the post-exilic period." In his later work, *A Critical Introduction*, 219, Gray denies the authenticity of 4:14; 5:9–13; 6:1—7:6.

22. Wolfe, "The Book of Micah," 899–900.

B.C. ... Micah is a source book for observing the development of Hebrew thought from 714 B.C. to approximately 200 B.C.[23]

Marsh holds the same general view but is a bit more specific at certain points. For him, the original book consisted of 1:6, 8–16; 2:1–11; 3. Other oracles were added gradually over a period of time, but primarily during the Babylonian exile as the Jews were anxiously hoping to be able to return to Palestine (7:7–20) and after the return from exile when the Jews were expecting Yahweh to overthrow their enemies (4:9–13). The book reached its final form some time during the post-exilic period.[24] Jeremias (with cautious reservations in some cases) thinks the original oracles were 1:2–4, 6, 8–12, 14–16; 2:1–2, 5–9, 11; 3:1–3, 5–12; 4:9–10bα, 14; 5:1, 3, 4a; 6:9–13, 15; 7:1–7. These were updated in the early exilic period by the addition of 1:5, 7, 13; 2:4–5, 10; 3:4; 5:9–13; 6:14, 16, all of which were inserted by the same redactors, as is clear from their method of exposition, bias, and language. Other additions were made until the book reached its present form.[25]

(4) Other scholars have thought it possible to identify much more precisely the stages through which the Mican materials passed until the final form of the book was attained. Hylmö argues that Micah himself edited chs. 1–3 with the exception of 2:12–13, and that in the time of Jeremiah the book ended with 3:12, as Jer 26:17ff. shows. Micah's friends and followers preserved additional genuine Mican oracles, namely, 4:9–10a; 4:14—5:1; 5:9–12a, 13b, which they inserted after the time of Jeremiah along with the spurious 2:12–13. Next, a later redactor inserted 4:1–4, 5, 8. Near the Greek Period, still another redactor inserted 4:6–7, 11–13; 5:2–3, 4–5, 6–7, and retouched 4:6–7, 10a to make them correspond to 4:1–4 and 2:12–13. A later redactor had certain early detached pericopes in his possession, namely 6:1–4, 6–8, 9–15; 7:1–4 (all of which originated in the seventh century BCE, except 6:6–8), which he appended to 5:9–13. When these were inserted into the book, probably they had already been linked together by 6:5, 16; 7: 5–6. Later, another redactor added 7:7–10, 11–13, 14–20; and either he or another redactor added 5:8, 14 to complete the book.[26] Accordingly, the present book of Micah

---

23. Ibid., 900.
24. Marsh, *Amos and Micah*, 87ff., 106.
25. Jeremias, "Die Deutung," 330–54, especially 352–54.
26. Hylmö, *Kompositionen*, 286–88.

is "a conglomerate of oracles which come from different authors and from widely different times."²⁷ And yet, when each redactor completed his alterations, he left the book in a form which he felt suitable for the community for which it was intended.²⁸

Lescow also detects several stages in the growth of the book. The original material composed (with minor glosses here and there) 1:2–5a, 8–13a, 14–15; 2:1–11; 3. In the exilic period interpolations were made including 1:5bc, 13bc, 16; 2:12, songs concerning Zion were written and added to lament the fall of the temple, as 4:6–8, 9–10, 11–13, 14, and other passages were added including 5:1–3, 4–5, 6–8, 9–14. After the temple was rebuilt in 516 BCE, 4:1–2 was written as a part of the feast of the dedication of the temple, and by the beginning of the fourth century BCE, 4:3–5 and other minor additions were made, including 1:1, which originally had no reference to Samaria and so was inserted before the Samaritan Schism. The Samaritan Schism was the *Sitz im Leben* of the last redactional stage in the development of the book, for at that time 6:1–8, 9–16; 7:1–6, 7–20 were compiled and added to the work, and 1:6–7 was inserted as an anti-Samaritan polemic.²⁹

This survey points out (among other things) the wide divergence of opinion as to whether the book of Micah has a structure and whether its final redactor (or redactors) compiled and/or composed this book as a theological work designed to meet the needs of a certain audience or kind of audience.

Scholars are divided on the question whether the book of Micah has little or no structure at all, or some structure within the smaller individual collections, or a structure of the whole. Those who find a structure for the entire book usually follow one of these divisional patterns: (a) 1–5; 6–7; (b) 1–3; 4–5; 6–7; (c) 1–3; 4:1—5:8; 5:9—7:20; (d) 1–3; 4–5; 6:1—7:6; 7:7–20; (e) 1–2; 3–5; 6–7.³⁰

The modern critic should not expect to find a structure in biblical (or other kinds of ancient) literature corresponding to modern literary canons. But at the very outset it seems only fair to give ancient literary works the benefit of the doubt and to allow them the possibility of con-

27. Ibid., 286.
28. Ibid., 142.
29. Lescow, "Redaktionsgeschichtliche Analyse," 46–85, 182–212.
30. For a detailed discussion of these views, see Willis, "The Structure of Micah 3–5," 191–214.

taining coherent principles of organization. Koch affirms that "chiefly they (redactors) give the whole structure which close analysis reveals to consist of clearly defined parts."[31] Danell writes:

> Even for a convinced literary critic, it is interesting to try to interpret the content and tendency of an Old Testament book in its present form, for a redactor or reviser has of course had his motives for publication . . . In my opinion, the definite and essential aim of Old Testament study ought . . . to be to try to interpret *the Old Testament texts in their present form* . . . When one approaches the texts with this attitude of confidence, prepared to listen to what they have to say in their present form, one has of course a better chance of understanding and interpreting difficult passages than if one approaches them with distrust on principle. One's scholarly ideal is then not to find mistakes, contradictions, and inconsistencies in a book, in order to get back to the 'original text' on this basis, but by intuition to live oneself into the author's world of thought and into the texts in the form they now have . . . Books like Amos or Hosea, for instance, prove if investigated on these lines, to be on the whole a unit.[32]

Weiser says concerning the book of Micah: "In der heutigen Form der Sammlung ist ein gewisses Ordnungsprincip nicht zu verkennen."[33] And even Lindblom cautions that in breaking up the material into its original components "muss man natürlich zusehen, dass man nicht der wesentlichen Einheitlichkeit verlustig geht."[34] But the recent remarks of Mays deserve serious attention:

> When the book (of Micah) is studied carefully with an interest, not in what makes it come apart, but in what holds it together, then a variety of integrating features begin to appear. Catchwords and repeated motifs connect units which lie in sequence, and sometimes those set in different parts of the book. Units are arranged by style and subject in some segments. Passages are juxtaposed so that their contrasting or complimentary content is illuminated. Introductory rubrics are repeated to link units into larger complexes, and transitions lead from one to another. These features are the expressions of an understanding of the material which employs them in a movement of proclamation that

---

31. Koch, *Growth*, 59.
32. Danell, *Studies*, 13–14. Cf. similarly Hahn, *The Old Testament*, 155–56.
33. Weiser, *Das Buch der zwölf kleinen Propheten*, 231.
34. Lindblom, *Micha*, 142.

flows through the entire book. The form of the book does not, of course, have the clarity and coherence of an original composition where movement of thought creates the material itself. But there does seem to be a continuity present which is the result of an accumulative and sustained purpose to say something which incorporates all the parts into a larger message.[35]

Now while it cannot be expected that there will be any sort of general agreement on this point, March's remarks on Hessler's assessment of Isa 40–55 are worthy of careful consideration in approaching the book of Micah and indeed the entire prophetic corpus: "Unity may be present on the basis of a genre well-known in antiquity but not immediately recognized by later interpreters ... An initial assumption of unity should be advanced rather than the opposite notion of random growth so frequently assumed."[36]

The Redactors' Functions

If it can be assumed that redactors used earlier material with specific audiences or kinds of audiences in mind who had certain needs, and that these redactors attempted to deal with those needs by means of relevant theological concepts, then it is important to determine the functions or roles those redactors played in their own contemporary *Sitz im Leben*. Such an undertaking demands that one envision the kinds of situations to which redactors may have addressed themselves. These seem to fall naturally into at least four broad categories.

Personal

In certain instances redactors may have simply written words, lines, verses, and the like into the traditional material for their own benefit to clarify obscurities, for personal edification, and/or to update archaic terminology.

Hortatory

Frequently an earlier oracle, song, or record of a historical event was used in and (re)applied to a new situation because the circumstances surrounding the· past and the present were so similar that the redac-

---

35. Mays, "The Theological Purpose," 277.
36. March, "Redaction Criticism," 95.

tors felt the message from the earlier period was appropriate to the new setting. For example, it may be that Mic 1:2–5b, 6–7 was originally delivered against Samaria before 721 BCE and later reapplied to Jerusalem shortly before Sennacherib's invasion in 701 BCE.[37] Further, 7:7–20 in its original form could have been delivered in North Israel some time after the invasion of Tiglath-pileser III in 732 BCE or after Sargon II's overthrow of Samaria in 721 BCE, and later adapted to the situation following Sennacherib's invasion of Jerusalem in 701 BCE, then finally reapplied to the circumstances in which the Jews found themselves after the Babylonian destruction of Jerusalem in 587 BCE.[38]

Cultic

The preservation of the material now constituting the book of Micah may have involved a process connected with a cultic setting. Redactors arranged and edited the material so as to make it suitable for use in a liturgical setting with the laity in mind. Weiser reasons: "Das Interesse an der Erhaltung der Worte des Propheten ursprünglich nicht ein 'historisch-biographisches,' sondern ein praktisches gewesen ist, was wohl in der Verlesung der Prophetenschriften im Kultus seine Ursache hat."[39] L. P. Smith suggests: "The completed book was intended for the edification of the laity. The compilers (like the preachers of today) were not concerned with historical reconstruction but with the needs of the people of their own times." They "doubted the ability of untrained readers to understand without help the figurative and sometimes fragmentary sayings of the prophets, and they added explanation and amplification for increased clarity or emphasis."[40]

Didactic

The growing interest in the Wise Men or Sages of Israel in recent years is well known. Since much work is yet to be done in this area, one must at least explore the possibility the prophetic materials were preserved in

---

37. So Lindblom, *Micha*; George, "Michée (Le Livre de)," col. 1259; Weiser, *Das Buch der zwölf kleinen Propheten*, 237; and Beyerlin, *Die Kulttraditionen Israels*, 13.

38. Willis, "A Reapplied Prophetic Hope Oracle," 64–76.

39. Weiser, *Das Buch der zwölf kleinen Propheten*, 254.

40. L. P. Smith, "The Book of Micah," 210. Cf. similarly Ungern-Sternberg, *Der Rechtsstreit Gottes*, 11. Schilling, "Micháas," col. 391; and Grimm, *Euphemistic Liturgical Appendixes*, especially 1–8.

circles or schools of the Wise for the purpose of teaching their pupils. A text like 6:9 might indicate wisdom influence in the book of Micah. Some sort of orderly arrangement of traditional material would facilitate both the teaching and the learning process.

Keeping in mind these hypothetical kinds of situations, some of the functions of redactors in any given context may be surmised. They may have grouped oracles together because these contained material dealing with the same chronological period or similar subject matter. They may have arranged the material in such a way as to give a specific effect or exhibit a certain theology: attention has often been called to the woe-weal pattern in the book of Micah and to the key-word or catchword arrangement principle. Redactors may have retouched traditional material to clarify obscure terms or ideas or information, to provide the hearer or reader with chronological or other types of information needed to understand what was handed down, or to emphasize a particular item in the text. They may have inserted hope oracles at strategic places to soften or neutralize the harsh negative impact of oracles of doom for a later audience living in destitute circumstances, aware of their sins, and penitently desiring to return to Yahweh. Nowack suggests that Mic 4:1–4 was probably inserted "um ein Gegengewicht gegen v. 3 13 mit seiner düsteren Perspektive zu bilden."[41] Similarly Bloomhardt proposes that 2:12–13 "was inserted here so that later readers might not be left depressed by Micah's lament."[42] Further, redactors may have inserted their own reflections on a certain passage. They may 'have added brief statements to make the transition from one traditional piece to another smoother.[43] They may have summarized portions of the traditional material either in anticipation of what was to follow (Judg 2:6—3:6)[44] or in summation of what preceded (1 Sam 14:47–48) or in place of material at their disposal (cf. 2 Sam 8:1–14, and compare vv. 3–8 with 2 Sam 10).

Two other matters pertaining to the functions of redactors deserve studious attention. First, two explanations of apparent incompatible pericopes standing side by side or of rough or abrupt transitions from

---

41. Nowack, *Die Kleinen Propheten*, 197. Cf. also Grimm, *Euphemistic Liturgical Appendixes*, 82.

42. Bloomhardt, *Old Testament Commentary*, 845.

43. For rather extensive treatments of the work of redactors" see Condamin, "Interpolations?," 379: and particularly in the book of Micah, Lindblom, *Micha*, 160.

44. Cf. Willis, "The Function," 194–214.

one line or oracle to the next have come to be accepted. One is that the lack of smoothness is due to redactorial deletions of traditional material because it was offensive or did not suit the redactors' purposes. The other is that the incoherence is due to the lofty reverence in which redactors held their material. Now while each of these suggestions seems reasonable in itself, the two together, especially in dealing with the same book or work, tend toward convenient means of escaping difficult problems. To say the least, a new look at this issue would seem to be in order.

Second, if redactors (especially final redactors) intended to convey a theological message to a specific audience or kind of audience to meet their spiritual needs, it is important to seek to determine the source of their theology. It is often assumed that redactors brought their own theology to the traditions, a theology they had attained from sources other than the traditions they were passing on, and intermingled their viewpoint with the inherited material in such a way as to cause that position to prevail. For example, Wolfe finds thirteen editors (or editorial schools) who worked through the Book of the Twelve, each leaving his (or its) own theological biases at strategic places in the text.[45] Their work ranged from approximately 621 to 175 BCE and "can be traced almost as accurately as the various geological strata on a hillside slope."[46] The insertions of seven of these are discernible in the book of Micah: (a) 1:2–4; 2:12–13; 4:1–4; 5:6 by the Late Exilic Editor (540–500 BCE); (b) 5:1, 2b–3; 7:11–12 by the Messianist (520–445 BCE); (c) 4:9–14; 5:4–5, 7–8, 14 by the Nationalistic School of Editors (360–301 BCE); (d) 2:3e–5; 4:6–8; 5:9–11 by the Eschatologists (310–300 BCE); (e) 1:5ab, 6–7; 5:12–13 by the Anti-Idol Polemist (300–275 BCE); (f) 6:6–8; 7:1–10, 13–14, 16–20 by the Psalm Editor (275–250 BCE); and (g) 1:1; 4:5; 5:2a; 6:3–5, 16a–c; 7:15 by the Early Scribes who edited the Pentateuch. Of course, this view goes hand in hand with the idea that the prophetic books have no literary or logical pattern.

In contrast to this kind of approach, it seems justifiable to suggest the possibility that redactors of biblical materials had a great respect for the traditions they inherited, that their theology was shaped by those traditions, and that a major reason they passed those traditions on to their audiences was that they were convinced this material spoke meaningfully to the new situations in which they and their audiences found

---

45. Wolfe, "The Editing," 90–125.
46. Ibid., 125.

themselves. In the final analysis, the modern critic must, at some point, wrestle with the problem of relating the theology of the redactor to that of the traditions he edited.

Interpreting the Text

While it is valuable and necessary to deal generally with hypothetical explanations of the functions of redactors in the shaping of biblical books and works, the interpretation of the text is crucial to one's evaluation of the redactional process. This is true of one's appraisal of the book as a whole. For example, one evaluator sees the repetition of *šimʿû* in Micah 1:2; 3:1; and 6:1 along with the key words ראש in 2:13 and 3:1 and שמע in 5:14 and 6:1 as indications of a threefold division of the book into chs. 1–2, 3–5, 6–7.[47] Another contends that the repetition of שמע in 1:2 and 5:14 in conjunction with the *ʿammîm* and *gôyîm* shows that chs. 1–5 are to be taken together as "einer prophetischen Gerichtsliturgie."[48] The same problem exists with regard to the interpretation of specific texts within the completed corpus. Some of the most crucial relevant passages in the book of Micah include at least 1:1, 2–4, 5e-f, 6–7, 9c-d, 13c-f; 2:5, 12–13; 3:2b–3b; 4:1–5, 10e-h; 5:4a, d–e, 14; 6:6–7, 9, 16; 7:7, 11, 14; 20.

It is impossible to deal with each of these passages in this paper. The purpose here is to mention types of problems the critic faces as he attempts to reconstruct the development of the material that lies before him and the role of the redactors in that development and in the arrangement of the final form of the book.

Scope of the Superscription

The tendency is to assume that the superscription in 1:1 belongs to the final stage of the redactional process and was intended to cover the whole book. Some argue that all but the last line covers the entire book, and that the final redactor added that line to make the superscription apply only to what immediately followed.[49] Apart from the question of redactional stages within 1:1 itself, one must question the validity of an

---

47. Willis, "Structure of the Book," 12, 39–40.
48. Lescow, "Redaktionsgeschichtliche Analyse," 58.
49. Cf. Schmidt, *Die Grossen Propheten*, 131 n. 1; Robinson, *Die zwölf kleinen Propheten*, 130.

assumption that it was intended to cover the whole book.⁵⁰ The superscription of the book of Jeremiah (Jer 1:1–3) purports to cover a period from the thirteenth year of Josiah to the fall of Jerusalem in the eleventh year and fifth month of Zedekiah (627–587 BCE), yet there are several sections in that book dated after this time (e.g., chs. 40–44; 52:31–34).⁵¹ This superscription, then, does not cover the whole book in its present final form. The same could be true of the superscription of the book of Micah.

Nature of the Terminology.

Micah 5:4d–e speaks of God's people raising up against Assyrian invaders "seven shepherds and eight princes of men." Some interpret these as demonic or angelic powers to be used by the Messiah. Others think they are Israel's vassals who fight side by side with them in times of war. Others regard them as (inadequate or adequate) Jewish rulers. Among those who hold the view, some take the numbers literally (either eight or fifteen) and apply this text to the Maccabean leaders Mattathias, his five sons, and the two sons of Simon, or to an alliance of Jewish rulers summoned to stop the advance of Antiochus III (218–198 BCE), or to the Davidic dynasty; while some take them as indefinite and apply the passage to the messiah's subordinates or to a group of leaders sufficient or insufficient to the task. Still others interpret this phraseology as an idiomatic way of speaking of sufficiency.⁵²

One's interpretation of these two lines has a direct bearing on his understanding of the redaction of the book. If the passage is taken literally, it clashes with the promise of the coming of one ruler in vv 1–4a, indicating that 4b–5b comes from a different hand than 1–4a, 5c–e; and if the reference is to the Maccabean rulers, this might date the time of

---

50. Initially Mowinckel ("Mikaboken," 3, 20) argued that chs. 1–5 and 6–7 were two originally independent collections and that 1:1 was the superscription only for 1–5. Later, however (*Det Gamle Testamente*, 667, 670), he proposed that 1–3 perhaps should be separated from 4–5 and that 1:1 is the heading only of 1–3, since these are the only chapters in the book containing oracles against Samaria and Jerusalem.

51. Tucker ("Prophetic Superscriptions," 65) recognizes the problem with Jer 1:1–3, but does not discuss possible implications of this for other prophetic superscriptions.

52. For a full discussion of these positions with bibliography, see Willis, "Micah IV 14–V 5," 539–42. See also the more recent studies of Coppens ("Le Cadre Littéraire," 57–62) and Cathcart ("Micah 5,4–5," 38–48).

the final redaction of the book. However, if the expression is an idiom for adequate leadership, the pericope might include 4:14—5:5 and conceivably date from the period just after Sennacherib's invasion of Jerusalem. Then it would not be helpful in dating the final redaction of the book.

Identification of the Speaker.

Some consider Mic 6:6-7 to be rhetorical questions of the prophet used as a teaching device perhaps in a cultic setting (like Ps 15:1). Others think this text preserves a dialogue between one or two speakers in the audience and the prophet. The determination of this issue is related to one's understanding of the extent of the pericope including these verses, which is variously thought to range all the way from 6:6-8 to 6:1-16.[53] The conclusion pertains to the view of the structure of the entire book and to the date assigned to its final redaction depending on the perception of the period to which a Torah Liturgy of the type represented in vv. 6-8 belongs.

Micah 2:12-13 is often interpreted as a late post-exilic hope oracle directed to destitute Jewish exiles. However, van der Woude has offered a logical and intriguing proposal that this little passage contains the words of pseudo-prophets who opposed Micah, and that 2:6ff. contains a *Disputationswort* or dialogue between Micah and these prophets (cf. 2:7; 3:11; and the dialogue between Amaziah and Amos in Amos 7:10-17).[54] If one follows van der Woude, these verses belong to the time of Micah and have no direct bearing on the redaction of the final form of the book. On the other hand, if they are a late post-exilic hope oracle inserted into the text at this point for some theological purpose, they might contain important clues concerning the final redaction.

Identification of the Audience

The hope oracles in the book of Micah have long been a source of scholarly discussion. Many assume that these oracles were directed to the whole body of Jewish exiles in Babylon or their descendants and thus are exilic or post-exilic. Micah 4:1-3 (= Isa 2:2-4) is a case in point. The majority of scholars think later editors inserted the same oracle in two different places in the prophetic literature. Others contend that

---

53. On this problem, see Willis, "Review of *Micha 6, 6-8*," 273-78.
54. Van der Woude, "Micah in Dispute," 256-57; Van der Woude, *Micha*, 94-98.

Micah borrowed from Isaiah; others, that Isaiah borrowed from Micah.[55] Kapelrud, however, contends that this is a cultic text originating very early probably in connection with the great Autumn New Year Festival, and that Micah (and Isaiah) borrowed it from this setting.[56] It is striking that there are at least five links between 3:9-12 and 4:1-5: (1) both are concerned with the role of Zion and Jerusalem (3:10, 12; 4:2); (2) 3:12 announces the diminution of the "mountain of the house" of the Lord, whereas 4:1 declares its exaltation; (3) there is a contrast between the wickedness of the "heads" of the house of Jacob (3:9, 11) and the divine determination to establish the temple mountain as the "head" (in both instances the Hebrew word is *rōš*) of the mountains; (4) 3:10 speaks of building Zion with blood and wrong, whereas 4:1-2 speaks of establishing it as the center from which Yahweh's teaching or word can emanate; (5) 3:11 condemns the religious leaders of Jerusalem for "judging" and "teaching" for selfish purposes, while 4:2-3 proclaims that Yahweh will "teach" the nations his ways and "judge" between them justly (in both instances, the verb for "judge" is *šāpaṭ* and for "teach" *yārāh*). One cannot help but wonder how many links like this are necessary to support the view that the passages involved come from the same speaker or writer.[57] Assuming, for argument's sake, that 4:1-3 originated in the cult, it is conceivable that 4:1-5 is from Micah himself. His audience might have been his own disciples, and he might have delivered this oracle on a different occasion from that presupposed in 3:9-12. In fact, it might have been his response to questions or thoughts from his disciples arising from their having heard him deliver 3:9-12 to a larger Judean audience. On the other hand, it is not absolutely certain that 4:1-3 in its present context is a hope oracle. Verse 5 might reflect a situation in which Micah was addressing himself to a Judean audience that was trusting in foreign idols, and he used a familiar cultic song as a means of trying to persuade them to walk in the light of Yahweh.

Numerous other pertinent observations could be made on this much debated text. But enough has been said to emphasize that one's

---

55. On these three options, cf. Cannawurf, "Authenticity," 26-33, who takes the view that Isa 2:2-4 and Mic 4:1-4 were post-exilic insertions into these two prophetic works.

56. Kapelrud, "Eschatology," 395-96.

57. Nielsen (*Oral Tradition*, 92) goes so far as to say: "The thought forces itself upon us that these passages (i.e., 3:9-12 and 4:1-5) cannot even have originated independently of each other."

Circumstance

The situation to which Micah 1:6–7 (or portions thereof) has been assigned is much debated. At least five explanations have been proposed. (a) Jepsen contended, on the basis of linguistic considerations, that these verses originally belonged in Hosea 13; as the LXX testifies, in an early stage of the prophetic corpus the book of Hosea stood just before the book of Micah, and it is easy to see how a passage at the end of Hosea could have been transferred to the beginning of Micah.[58] (b) Haupt assigns it to the period after John Hyrcanus sacked the city of Samaria and sold the votive offerings (107 BCE).[59] (c) Lescow interprets it as an anti-Samaritan polemic perhaps connected with the Samaritan erection of a sanctuary when they received permission from Alexander the Great in the latter half of the fourth century BCE.[60] (d) Since this text predicts the destruction of Samaria and Samaria was not destroyed but only captured by Sargon II in 721 BCE, many scholars date this oracle after 721 and often connect it with Sennacherib's invasion of Jerusalem in 701 BCE.[61] (e) Many scholars think 1:5a–d, 6–7 were originally delivered in North Israel before the overthrow of Samaria in 721 BCE, and then later reapplied to Judah by Micah or some other Judean prophet perhaps in connection with Sennacherib's invasion in 701 BCE.[62]

The circumstance lying behind this passage had little significance for determining the period and setting if the more widely held scholarly position is correct (that is, either d or e). But Lescow insists that these verses were among the last inserted into the book and place the final redaction during the Samaritan Schism in the fourth century BCE.

---

58. Jepsen, "Kleine Beitrage," 96–99.
59. Haupt, "The Book of Micah," 26:239; 27:60; Haupt, "Micah's Capucinade," 95.
60. Lescow, "Redaktionsgeschichtliche Analyse," 82–83.
61. See Baudissin, *Einleitung*, 519; Clamer, "Michée," col. 1653; Marty, *L'Ancien Testament*, 769.
62. See Gray, *A Critical Introduction*, 218; Hylmö, *Kompositionen*, 31–34; Scharbert, *Die Propheten Israels*, 315.

Concluding Remarks

It is time for scholars to take a new look at Old Testament books in their present form in an attempt to discover clues as to the nature of their structure, the functions of redactors in their formation, and the theological emphases which they communicated to their intended audiences. While comprehensive statements are helpful, a major task now seems to be that of reexamining the text verse by verse and pericope by pericope with a *redaktionsgeschichtliche* assessment in mind.

3

Fundamental Issues in Contemporary Micah Studies

RESPONSIBLE CRITICAL TREATMENT OF the book of Micah was initiated a little over a hundred years ago in Germany by Ewald.[1] During the intervening period, this tiny prophetic work has been subjected to the same scientific approaches and dealt with on the basis of the same standards as the rest of the Old Testament. Therefore, it is imperative that one studying the book of Micah be aware of the nature and scope of these approaches. *Literary-historical criticism* is usually traced back to Julius Wellhausen, who saw reflected in the Old Testament literature an evolution of religious ideas which were finally petrified in a post-exilic priestly milieu. This view generally assumes that the present form of the Old Testament is the end product of a long process which was *literary* (written) from first to last.[2] One recent application of this approach to the book of Micah is that of T. H. Robinson, who contends that "the present book consists of three originally independent collections,"[3] and that the materials found here passed through two *literary* stages. First, three separate redactors in three indeterminate historical periods combined *portions* of originally longer oracles into three complete prophetic corpora, each independent of the other. Later, compilers combined these complexes in the following way: first, chs. 4–5 with 6:1—7:13; later, chs.

---

1. Ewald, *Jesaja*. English translation: *Commentary on the Prophets of the Old Testament*, II.
2. Wellhausen, *Geschichte Israels*, I.
3. Robinson, *Die zwölf Kleinen Propheten*, 127.

1–3 were added at the beginning; and at the same time or later, the same editor or a later editor added 7:14–20.[4]

It is usually agreed that form criticism originated with Hermann Gunkel, who emphasized that while the individual writer or speaker was important in the history of Old Testament literature, the type *(Gattung)* of speech form which his milieu thrust upon him was of infinitely greater importance. Gunkel outlined the task of the form-critic in this way: (a) determine the extent of the pericope under consideration, (b) determine the oral and written types of the material and categorize them, (c) ascertain the setting in life *(Sitz im Leben)* out of which a type originated and in which it was at home, and (d) trace the history of the pericope from its original (usually oral) form to its present position in the Old Testament. He believed that prophetic oracles passed through four stages: very brief ancient oracles *(Worte* or *Wortzusammenstellungen)*, brief oracles in metric form *(Sprüchen)*, longer oracles approximately the length of a chapter *(Reden)*, and whole books *(Büchern)*.[5] The first attempt to apply this method to the book of Micah was by Schmidt, who offers some useful suggestions,[6] but the classic work is that of J. Lindblom.[7] In the opinion of the present writer, however, Lindblom's treatment lacks equipoise. He contends that "as a rule the individual passages (of all the prophetic books including Micah) are connected with one another on the basis of very superficial and purely accidental characteristics,"[8] and thus the only suitable approach is to treat each pericope in isolation. "Each particular revelatory unit must be analyzed in isolation according to its own form and content, first of all without side-glances at the surrounding pericopes."[9] He insists that "how the different passages are related to each other is a relatively subordinate question for the analysis of the book of Micah."[10] Even so, Lindblom feels the need to reconstruct theoretically the manner in which the book reached its present form, and at one place states surprisingly: "of course, one must be careful not

---

4. Ibid., 127–28. See also pp. 133, 135, 143, 151.
5. Gunkel, "Die Propheten," xxxvi–lxxii.
6. Schmidt, "Micha," 130–53.
7. Lindblom, *Micha*.
8. Ibid., 9.
9. Ibid., 11.
10. Ibid., 133.

to forfeit the essential unity" of the book.[11] In essence, Deissler's commentary[12] represents a return to Lindblom's position. The form-critical treatments of Weiser, von Ungern-Sternberg, and Kapelrud[13] reflect a much greater respect for coherence in the final form of the book, and emphasize the *cultic* setting of all or portions of the book. Weiser, for example, speaks of "the present arrangement of the oracles, in which we cannot fail to recognize a certain attempt at order . . ."[14]

The *traditio-historical method* is still in the process of emerging and evolving. Different scholars interpret and use this method in different ways. Beyerlin uses "traditio-historical" to define his attempt to trace certain major Israelite traditions (Sinai-theophany, amphictyonic laws, Exodus-Conquest, Davidic) from their origin to their use by the prophet Micah. His purpose is to show that (contrary to the general tenets of literary historical criticism) Micah was steeped in the cultic traditions of the amphictyonic cult festivals in Jerusalem.[15] Tournay and Hammershaimb have generally accepted this thesis, but differ with Beyerlin as to the specific cult festival involved.[16] "Traditio-historical" is a term which many scholars use to describe the history of the growth of a book from the original spoken or written units to the final form of the book. Eissfeldt, Hahn, and Koch consider this discipline to be one phase of form criticism,[17] but Engnell and Kraus think of traditio-historical criticism as being the comprehensive method of which form criticism is but one facet.[18] The present writer has adopted the latter position with modifications and attempted to apply it to the book of Micah.[19] Within

---

11. Ibid., 142.

12. Deissler, *Les Petits Prophètes* 2, 293–359.

13. Weiser, *Das Buch der zwölf Kleinen Propheten*, 228–90; Ungern-Sternberg, *Der Rechtsstreit Gottes*; Kapelrud, "Eschatology," 392–405; Kapelrud, "Mikas bok," cols. 105–7.

14. Weiser, *The Old Testament*, 255.

15. Beyerlin, *Die Kulttraditionen Israels*. In summary form, "Kultische Tradition," 2–12.

16. Tournay, "Review," 438; Hammershaimb, "Einige Hauptgedanken," 11–34; English translation: "Some Leading Ideas," 29–50.

17. Eissfeldt, "Zur Überlieferungsgeschichte," cols. 529–34; Hahn, *The Old Testament*, 153–56; Koch, *Was Ist Formgeschichte?*, 45.

18. Engnell, "Methodological Aspects," 13–30, esp. p. 28; Kraus, "Zur Geschichte," 371–87, esp. pp. 380–81.

19. Willis, "The Structure of Micah 3–5," 191–214.

the larger framework of these critical approaches, Micah studies seem to have focused on three general problems: (1) the present arrangement of the book and the process by which it reached its final form, (2) the authenticity of the hope oracles (2:12–13; 4–5; 7:7–20), and (3) the nature and interpretation of difficult passages, especially 1:10–16; 2:6–11; 4:11–13; 4:14—5:5; 6:1–8; and 7:7–20.

The Present Arrangement of the Book of Micah

In order to comprehend the message of the book of Micah, it is necessary to try to determine the way in which it is arranged, and to reconstruct the historical process which produced this literary work. Five hypotheses have been advocated in an attempt to solve this difficult problem.

The Rearrangement Theory

Some critics argue that the book of Micah in its present form is incoherent because redactors have accidentally or intentionally obliterated the original order in the course of transmission, and they maintain that they can make the book coherent by rearranging the pericopes in the sequence which they once possessed. Haupt, Hanon, and Scharbert[20] attempt this on the basis of chronological order, while Elhorst and Halévy[21] employ an arrangement based on similar subject matter. It is significant, however, that the exponents of this solution are unable to agree in detail on the order the pericopes followed originally.

The Chronological Order Theory

G. A. Smith and A. van Hoonacker maintain that the book in its present form is arranged chronologically, i.e., that the pericopes which compose each large division of the book belong to the same general chronological period.[22] Smith, for example, assigns chs. 1–3 to the period between 722 and 705 BCE, chs. 4–5 to 701, 6:1—7:6 to the reign of Hezekiah, and 7:7–20 to the time of Tiglath-pileser III's invasion of Palestine in 734. But most scholars have rightly rejected this solution because the dating of most oracles in the book rests on very scanty evidence.

---

20. Haupt, "The Book of Micah," 26:201–52; 27:1–62; "Micha's Capucinade," 85–112; Steinmann and Hanon, *Michée*; and Scharbert, *Die Propheten Israels*, 310–35.

21. Elhorst, *De Prophétie*; Halévy, "Le Livre de Michée."

22. Smith, *The Book of the Twelve Prophets*; Hoonacker, *Les douze petits prophètes*.

The Compilation Theory

Many scholars conclude that the present book of Micah is a compilation of originally independent collections of prophetic oracles. Ewald and Kraeling find two collections: 1–5 and 6–7;[23] W. R. Smith and T. H. Robinson, three: Smith dividing the book into 1–5; 6:1—7:6; and 7:7–20, and Robinson into 1–3, 4–5, and 6–7;[24] and Baudissin and Pákozdy, four: the former separating into 1–3, 4–5, 6:1—7:6, and 7:7–20, and the latter into 1–3, 4:1—5:9, 5:10—7:7, and 7:8–20.[25] However, the demonstrable interrelationships which exist between the different parts of the book make it incredible to believe that two or more different collectors, each working independent of the other, could produce two, three, or four separate works as similar in structure, contents, and sequence of thought, and as interdependent as the present "sections" of the book of Micah seem to be. A somewhat different type of compilation theory is held by critics such as Beck and Brandenburg, who consider this prophetic work to be a compilation of three sermons which Micah delivered on three different occasions.[26]

The Disconnected Pericope Theory

The most widely held view of the present arrangement of the book is that it is a collection of pericopes that originated in different eras and under varying circumstances, and were thrown together in piecemeal fashion without any intention of achieving coherence. Scholars who hold this position often maintain that the same is true of all the prophetic books: Amos, Hosea, and "Deutero-Zechariah" (Zech 9–14) are favorite analogues.[27] But it may be that this evaluation reflects the tendency of modern Western man to impose his own standards of symmetry and literary unity on ancient Semitic writings.

---

23. Ewald, *Jesaja*, 325; Kraeling, *Commentary*, 204, 221.

24. W. R. Smith, *The Prophets of Israel*, 365; 427 n. 3; 428 n. 5; 439 n. 13; Robinson, *Die zwölf Kleinen Propheten*, 127–28.

25. Baudissin, *Einleitung*, 525–26, 529, 532–33; Pákozdy, "Michabuch," col. 1211.

26. Beck, *Erklärung*, 63–64, 133; Brandenburg, *Das Lebendige Wort*, 69–70, 102.

27. For an extensive bibliography, see Willis, "Structure, Setting, and Interrelationships," 56–65. Here we may mention Budde, "Verfasser und Stelle," 152–58, esp. 157; and Gautier, *Introduction*, 502, 506.

The Literary Development Theory

In reaction to the compilation theory, many scholars contend that there never was more than one collection composing the book of Micah, but the present form of the book is the end product of a long literary history. The original nucleus contained genuine Mican oracles. In the process of transmission, several redactors in different historical periods revised and added to the original nucleus in order to make it contemporary, each for his own community, or to make it reflect his own theology, or to clarify the meaning, or for some other reason. Scholars have set forth at least four theories as to the way in which this growth took place, which the present writer discusses elsewhere.[28] The present form of the book of Micah is the end product of some sort of evolutionary process. But as one attempts to unravel this process, several matters must be kept in mind. First, this development involves oral as well as written transmission.[29] Secondly, in this process, abridgement as well as expansion of earlier material took place.[30] Thirdly, the theology of the redactors including the final redactor was surely largely shaped by the material which was handed down to him. And finally, the impression which the present form of the book makes on the critic to a large extent determines his decisions as to the probable stages through which the material passed before it reached its present form. Recent studies indicate a growing appreciation for some type of coherence in the book of Micah. Renaud finds a chiastic arrangement in chs. 4–5.[31] A. S. van der Woude discovers a series of discussions (German *Streitgespräche, Diskussionswort, Disputationswort*) between Micah and his opponents, the false prophets, in chs. 2, 4, and 5.[32] The present writer defends an A–B–A arrangement in the book.[33]

---

28. Willis, "The Structure of the Book of Micah," 5–42.

29. Cf. Ringgren, "Oral and Written Transmission," 34–59; Nielsen, *Oral Tradition*, 79–93.

30. Cf. Budde, "Eine folgenschwere Redaktion," 218–29; Willis, "A Note on ויאמר," 50–54.

31. Renaud, *Structure*. See my extensive critical treatment of this work in Willis, "Review of *Structure*"; and Willis, "The Structure of Micah 3–5."

32. Woude, "Micah in Dispute," 244–60.

33. See the essays referred to in nn. 19 and 28.

The Authenticity of the Hope Oracles

An early dictum of literary historical criticism (which one still encounters in scholarly works) was that the pre-exilic prophets were altogether harbingers of doom, and thus all hope oracles contained in the prophetic books must be creations from a later age which were inserted into the genuine material in order to "neutralize," "soften," or "weaken" the passionate threats and reproaches to make them palatable to later Judaism. Applied specifically to the book of Micah, it has long and often been argued that a prophet of doom who condemns Samaria and Jerusalem with their leaders and people as vehemently as Micah does in chs. 1–3 (excluding 2:12–13) could not have uttered the oracles depicting the glorious future of Jerusalem and Judah in chs. 4–5 without wholly nullifying every reason to believe that he was sincere and/or consistent.[34] However, continuing study of ancient Near Eastern documents from the pre-exilic period (especially the Ras Shamra tablets) and rather revolutionary reevaluations of the canonical psalms from the form-critical and traditio-historical points of view make it increasingly clear that the doom-hope motif was prominent very early in Israelite cult centers, and particularly in Jerusalem.[35] In the opinion of the present writer, therefore, the time is ripe for a complete reexamination of *criteria* which have been used and may be used to determine the date and authenticity of Biblical materials, especially the prophets, in order to determine their relative validity.[36] An evaluation of the most impressive criteria alone is out of the question in the space allotted for this paper. Only a few suggestions may be offered. It is admittedly quite unlikely that Micah would have delivered the doom oracle in 3:9–12 and the hope oracle in 4:1–5 to the same audience on the same occasion, or even to the same audience on different occasions. But it is certain that (like his contemporary Isaiah, cf. Isa 8:16–18) Micah had disciples, i.e., men who accepted his oracles as God's word. The very fact that some of his genuine oracles have been preserved supports this assumption. Is it reasonable

---

34. Cf. i.e., Mowinckel, *Det Gamle Testamente, III*, 668–69; Wolfe, "The Editing," 90–129; Wolfe, "The Book of Micah," 921; and Renaud, *Structure*, 21, 24.

35. See the articles by Kapelrud mentioned in n. 13, and Gottlieb, "Den taerskende Kvie," 167–71.

36. The present writer attempts to deal with this problem in a modest way in an essay entitled, "The Authenticity," 353–68.

to believe that Micah ever spoke to this smaller group "away from the madding crowd"? And if so, is it likely that he condemned those who had subscribed to his message and threatened them with doom, or that he sought to encourage them with hopeful promises of a glorious future? Von Rad, e.g., makes this very point in dealing with Isaiah and Micah:

> These prophets increasingly wrote off the reigning members of the house of David of their own day, and . . . they regarded the whole history of the Monarchy from the time of David as a false development. If they did not, what meaning could there be in their expectation that Jahweh would once again make an entirely new beginning? Was it only amongst their intimate friends that die prophets talked about these matters? The literary form in which these prophecies are clothed might suggest that this is so; for they do not look like open proclamations designed for a wider public; there is never any sign of an audience whom the prophet addresses, nor are they formulated as divine oracles, revelations made by Jahweh. Their literary category is really unique.[37]

Another criterion which is vital in determining date and authenticity is that of deciding the *nature* of a pericope. Does the speaker intend to be straightforward, or is he ironically parroting the words of his opponents? Does the passage represent an oracle delivered on a certain occasion, or is it a summary of the prophet's message during a particular historical crisis or during his career? This general criterion seems to be applicable, e.g., to Mic 4:1–5 with its parallel in Isa 2:1–5. The possibilities are well known: this oracle originated with Micah and Isaiah or Isaiah's disciples adopted it; it originated with Isaiah and Micah or Micah's disciples adopted it; it is of late origin and was inserted into the Mican and Isaian material; it originated before Isaiah and Micah and they used it.[38] Von Rad removes the main aversion to accepting Isa 2:2–4 as authentic by demonstrating that the ideas contained in it are quite at home in the Psalms of Zion which are pre-exilic.[39] Wildberger accepts and further develops this thesis, but rejects the authenticity of Mic 4:1–5 while accepting the authenticity of Isa 2:2–4, primarily because

---

37. Rad, *Old Testament Theology,* 2:171.

38. In addition to the works mentioned in the next two notes on this problem, we may mention: Budde's article referred to in n. 27; Huddle, "Isaiah ii. 2–4," 272–73; Cannon, "The Disarmament Passage," 2–8; Fullerton, "Studies in Isaiah," 134–42; and Ackroyd, "A Note on Isaiah 2:1," 320–21.

39. Rad, "Die Stadt auf dem Berge," 214–24.

the contrast between Mic 3:9–12 and 4:1–5 is too great.⁴⁰ Could it be that another alternative has been overlooked? The similarity between these pericopes and the Zion Psalms indicates that the ideas expressed in the parallel lines reflect common cultic beliefs. But the conclusion in Mic 4:4–5 is quite different from the conclusion in Isa 2:5. Perhaps these conclusions indicate applications of an original cultic song by Isaiah and Micah at different times to different audiences under different circumstances. Finally, it is necessary to mention the repeatedly used criterion of determining whether a particular religious concept and/or historical situation are possible during the career of the prophet under consideration. Several hope oracles in the book of Micah, e.g., speak of the "remnant" (2:12–13; 4:6–8; 5:7–9 [Heb.]). This presents the scholar with many difficult questions. Does this term refer to a physical group left after foreign invasion, or to a spiritual group that has accepted the prophet's message? If the former, does it pertain to North Israelites after the fall of Samaria in 722 BCE, or to Judeans after the fall of Jerusalem in 586 BCE? In any given passage, does the promise that "a remnant shall return" (compare the pertinent passages in Isaiah) intend to encourage (a remnant *shall* return) or discourage *(only* a remnant shall return)?⁴¹ After these questions concerning the "remnant" have been answered, then one is faced with many other motifs in the book.

The Interpretation of Difficult Passages

Micah 1:10–16 is fraught with serious textual problems which are far from solution. Elliger and Schwantes conjecture that the right side of some early manuscript was torn off or mutilated in some way, thus destroying the first letter or so of each line in these verses. However, their "restored text" can be nothing more than purely subjective logic,⁴² and thus this solution is generally rejected, but as yet no one has been able to solve the problems involved in this pericope to the satisfaction of the majority.⁴³

---

40. Wildberger, "Die Völkerwallfahrt," 62–81. See also Cannawurf, "The Authenticity," 26–33.

41. On the "remnant" motif, cf. Vaux, "Le 'Reste d'Israël,'" 526–39; Campbell, "God's People," 78–85; Heaton, "The Root *shʾr*," 27–39; and Dreyfus, "La Doctrine," 361–86.

42. Elliger, "Die Heimat," 81–152; Schwantes, "A Critical Study," 32–52; this section of the dissertation is now published under the title, "Critical Notes," 454–61.

43. See the special studies of Graham, "Some Suggestions," 237–58; Donner, *Israel unter den Völkern*, 92–105; and Fohrer, "Micha 1," 65–80.

Micah 6:1-8 has been the subject of much discussion, not only because of the theological emphasis in verses 6-8 pertaining to the relationship between "cult and ethics," but also because verses 1-8 contain an interesting example of the "covenant lawsuit."[44] The present writer has recently maintained that the lawsuit does not terminate at verse 8, as is often assumed, but continues through verse 16.[45] Verses 6-8 and Mic 2:6-11 contain disputes between Micah and his opponents, which are ultimately important in determining the theology and position of "false prophets" in Israelite society and in the viewpoints of the classical prophets.[46]

Recent studies of Mic 7:7-20 by Burkitt, Reicke, Eissfeldt, and Dus maintain that this psalm is of North Israelite origin, primarily because of the allusion to Carmel, Bashan, and Gilead in verse 14.[47] Dus, apparently enamored with "ark studies," places the origin of this passage in the period, just after the battle of Ebenezer in which the Israelites lost the ark to the Philistines, i.e., about 1100 BCE. (!) The other scholars mentioned are more likely to gain disciples in suggesting a time near the siege and fall of Samaria in 722 BCE. The present writer is of the opinion that 6:1(or 9)-16 and 1:2-16 also originated in North Israel. The reference to Ahab and Omri in 6:16 would support this view in the former passage, and the announcement of the fall of Samaria in 1:6-7 would support it in the latter, to mention only one argument for each pericope. This would seem to indicate that the prophets sometimes took over an oracle which had been delivered (by them or others) on a previous occasion, expanded, revised, or edited it, and reapplied it to a new situation. This would account for apparent inconsistencies in the present form of the text, such as a reference to Judah and Jerusalem in 1:5c-d in a passage that clearly originally pertained to North Israel and Samaria alone.[48]

---

44. On Mic 6:1-8, we may mention G. W. Anderson, "A Study of Micah 6:1-8," 191-97; Hyatt, "On the Meaning," 232-39; Deissler, "Micha 6, 1-8," 229-34; Stoebe, "Und demütig," 180-94; Watson, "Form Criticism," 61-72; and Lescow, *Micha 6, 6-8*; and on the "covenant lawsuit," Würthwein, "Der Ursprung," 1-16; Huffmon, "The Covenant Lawsuit," 285-95; and Harvey, "Le 'Rib-Pattern,'" 172-96.

45. Willis, "A Review of *Micha 6,6-8*," 273-78.

46. Cf. Willis, "On the Text of Micah 2, 1a," 534-41; and Willis, "Micah 2:6-8," 72-87.

47. Burkitt, "Micah 6 and 7," 159-61; Reicke, "Liturgical Traditions," 349-67; Eissfeldt, "Ein Psalm," 259-68; and Dus, "Weiteres zum nordisraelitischen Psalm," 14-22.

48. Cf. Willis, "Some Suggestions," 372-79.

The meaning and unity of Mic 4:14—5:5 (Heb.) has been discussed by the present writer in recent articles which the reader may consult.[49] The increased interest in "the holy war" and the Old Testament ideas concerning the relationship between Israel and the nations has led to a number of studies on Mic 4:11-13, including those of Gottlieb, Wanke, Lutz, and Cazelles.[50] The problems are quite complex. Is the setting in life *(Sitz im Leben)* of this passage historical or cultic? Is the battle which is envisioned real or sham, imminent or eschatological and perhaps apocalyptic? Where does Mic 4:11-13 really stand theologically in relationship to other passages in the Old Testament which reflect similar themes? Perhaps the present survey of some of the problems encountered in Micah research may enhance the reader's anticipation for the publication of the volumes on Micah from H. W. Wolff in the *Biblischer Kommentar* series and from B. W. Anderson in The Anchor Bible series, to which the writer looks forward with great expectations.

---

49. Willis, "Micah IV 14-V 5," 529-47; Willis, "*mimmĕkā lî yēṣē*," 317-22.

50. Gottlieb, "Den taerskende Kvie"; Wanke, *Die Zionstheologie*, 81-83; Lutz, *Jahwe, Jerusalem und die Volker,* 91-97; and Cazelles, "Histoire et géographie, 87-89.

4

The Structure of Micah 3–5 and the Function of Micah 5:9–14 in the Book[1]

THE BOOK OF MICAH as it now stands (and especially chs. 3–5) has long posed very serious problems for critics. Scholars have found different ways of explaining the present form of the book of Micah, usually in light of their general explanation for the present form of prophetic books as a whole. The literary-historical critic thinks of the prophet himself as writing down in good literary form a coherent nucleus of material representing his genuine oracles.[2] He reasons that in the following centuries various scribes added pericopes here and there for one reason or another.[3]

---

1. The present essay is based (in part) on my unpublished PhD dissertation at Vanderbilt Divinity School: "The Structure, Setting, and Interrelationships," 1966. I am greatly indebted to Professors J. Ph. Hyatt and W. Harrelson for their guidance and suggestions in this work. The Hebrew versification is followed throughout this article.

2. Stade, "Bemerkungen," 162, e.g., argued that the original book of Micah was composed of 1:2–2:11; 3, which "bilden . . . eine Weissagung." Clamer, "Michée," 1655, argues that chs. 1–3 "constituent l'élement essentiel du livre dont les caractéristiques une fois bien établies pourront servir de pierre de touche pour admettre ou rejeter l'authenticité" des autres parties du recueil." Hylmö is so impressed by the symmetry of chs. 1–3 (except 2:12–13) that he maintains that they must have been written by the same author, Micah: "Varje ord, varje sats, varje utsaga har präglats av en och samma författarepersonlighet . . . Då 3 12 utgör slutordet i den av allt att döma enhetliga skriften 2 1–11 och 3 1–12, är frågan om författarens namn en gång för alla avgjord." Hylmö, *Kompositionen*, 95. With regard to chs. 1–3, D. Deden, *De Kleine Profeten*, 201, writes: "Zij vormen duidelijk een literaire eenheid."

3. Stade argued that since the original book of Micah contained only oracles of doom, it was in constant danger of being eliminated from the Jewish tradition. In fact, the only thing that saved it from obliteration was the high commendation given to the prophet Micah in Jer 26:17ff. In the post Jeremian period, an anonymous epig-

R. E. Wolfe summarizes this understanding of the prophetic material very well when he writes: "The great difference between the twelve prophets and the secondary editors is that, while the former issued their writings as unified collections on single scrolls, the latter, acting somewhat as commentators, inserted their writings here and there within the prophetic oracles."[4] Wolfe thinks that each redactor (or school of redactors) read through the prophetic material at his disposal with the intention of inserting his own theology at vulnerable places throughout the prophetic corpus. This would mean that they were not primarily concerned to make the prophetic books or individual pericopes which were handed down to them relevant to their contemporary situation. These redactors for the most part worked with prophetic corpora, and not with individual books. Over a period extending from about 621 to 175 BCE, at least thirteen redactors had a part in revising the Book of the Minor Prophets. Seven of these made significant contributions to the book of Micah. 1:2-4; 2:12-13; 4:1-4; 5:6 were added by the Late Exilic Editor, 540-500 BCE,[5] 5:1, 2b-3, 7:11-12, by the Messianist, 520-445,[6] 4:9-14; 5:4-5, 7-8, 14, by the Nationalistic School of Editors, 360-301,[7] 2:3e-5; 4:6-8; 5:9-11, by the Eschatologists, 310-300,[8] 1:5ab, 6-7; 5:12-

---

one added 4:1-4; 4:11—5:3; 5:6-8 and 5:9-14 to the original corpus. "Der Grund, aus welchem jener Epigone seine Ausführungen hinter 3:12 einschaltete, war ohne Zweifel dieser, daß er an der Einseitigkeit des Inhalts von c. 1-3 einen nicht unberechtigten Anstoß nahm." Stade, "Bemerkungen," 170. Even later, a second epigone, thinking (erroneously) that 4:1-4, etc. was genuinely Mican, added 4:5-10 and 5:4-5 in order to insert into this prophetic material the idea of the assault of the nations on Jerusalem and their defeat. "Bemerkungen," 169. Stade thinks that this reconstruction is important because it brings out the fact that the later additions to the book supplied the originally one-sided prophetic work with a balance adequate enough to permit its finding a place in the canon. And if this reconstruction is correct, it affords an important witness to the development of Messianic hopes in Israel. "Bemerkungen," 171. Stade does not attempt to explain when or why 2:12-13 and 6-7 were added to this work, nor does he suggest whether they were inserted by one of the two epigones who added the sections in chs. 4-5, by a third redactor, or by several other redactors. Stade's general literary historical approach to the book of Micah is adopted by Cornill, Cheyne, Marti, Gray, Riessler, Lindblom, Nötscher, Wolfe, Marsh, Eissfeldt, and Hylmö; cf. Willis, "The Structure, Setting, and Interrelationships," 75-83.

4. Wolfe, "The Editing," 90.
5. Ibid., 93.
6. Ibid., 98.
7. Ibid., 100.
8. Ibid., 105.

13, by the Anti-Idol Polemist, 300–275,⁹ 6:6–8 7:1–10, 13–14, 16–20, by the Psalm Editor, 275–250,¹⁰ and 1:1; 4:5; 5:2a; 6:3–5, 16a–c; 7:15, by the Early Scribes who edited the Pentateuch.¹¹ The end result of such a process could hardly be anything other than a series of disconnected, incoherent pericopes.

Another approach to the prophetic material is represented by one type of form critic, who insists that the present structure of the prophetic books forces us to conclude that these works are incoherent. E.g., Lindblom contends that the present arrangement of all the prophetic books is accidental,¹² and therefore, that it is inconceivable that the coherence of a prophetic book could be demonstrated.¹³

Thus, in dealing with the book of Micah, he insists that "jede gewonnene revelatorische Einheit muß allein fur sich, zunächst ohne Seitenblicke auf die Umgebung, der Form und dem Inhalte nach analysiert werden,"¹⁴ lest its surrounding context lead the exegete to interpret it in a way contrary to its original intention. This understanding of the prophetic material leads Lindblom to conclude that "wie sich die verschiedenen Stücke zueinander verhalten, ist für die Analyse des Michabuches eine relativ untergeordnete Frage,"¹⁵ and that the attempt to defend a coherence in the book leads to serious misunderstandings.¹⁶

In contrast to these two interpretations, it seems to me that there is ample evidence to warrant the affirmation that the book of Micah in its present form exhibits a type of coherence. The purpose of this paper is to attempt to demonstrate this coherence, especially in chs. 3–5, and to indicate the function of 5:9–14 in the book. In the following article, "The Authenticity and Meaning of Micah 5:9–14," we will discuss 5:9–14 from a traditio-historical perspective, considering the text and authenticity of this pericope.

The outline of the book of Micah is very important in dealing with the problem of coherence. This little prophetic work offers two prob-

---

9. Ibid., 110.
10. Ibid., 112.
11. Ibid., 115–16.
12. Lindblom, *Micha*, 9. Cf. also 67 and 153.
13. Ibid., 85 n. 1.
14. Ibid., 11.
15. Ibid., 133.
16. Ibid., 141. Cf. also 90 n. 1.

The Structure of Micah 3–5 and the Function of Micah 5:9–14 in the Book   69

lems with regard to the limits of its major divisions: (1) Should a major division be made between chs. 3 and 4 or between chs. 2 and 3? (2) At what point should a major division be made between chs. 5 and 6? The answers to these two questions are of utmost importance in interpreting 5:9–14. As a matter of fact, the answer to the latter has a direct bearing on its Interpretation.

Several scholars find a general threat-hope pattern in the book of Micah, and divide the book into four major parts: 1–3, 4–5, 6:1—7:6 (or 7), 7:7 (or 8)-20.[17] It must be admitted that these critics offer very strong arguments in defense of this division. (1) Chapters 1–3 contain the only undisputed authentic passages in the book. (2) The symmetry of chs. 1–3 is lost if a division is made between chs. 2 and 3, since both of these chapters are directed against Israel's ruling classes and condemn the same basic sins. This section begins with a threat that Samaria will become as a heap of the field (1:6) and ends with a threat that Jerusalem will become heaps (3:12).[18] (3) "And I said" in 3:1 connects ch. 1:2 with ch. 3.[19] (4) The occurrence of "hear" in 3:1 no more indicates the beginning of a major division in the book than does its occurrence in 3:9 or 6:9. (5) 2:12–13 has no connection with that which precedes or with that which follows. Its present "context" is not its original position, and so it must be transferred to another place in the book.[20] With a few insignificant modifications, the present writer's thesis that the "final form" of the book of Micah is coherent could fit this scheme very nicely. The final redactor of the book may have intentionally arranged it in two parallel sections, chs. 1–5 and chs. 6–7.[21] Later, possibly by accident, 2:12–13

---

17. Baudissin, *Einleitung*, 522, 532; Kent, *The Kings and Prophets*, 165; Steuernagel, *Lehrbuch*, 623; Sellin, *Introduction*, 175; Bentzen, *Introduction*, 148; Pfeiffer, *Introduction*, 589; Deden, *De Kleine Profeten*, 201; Fichtner, *Obadja, Jona, Micha*, 34; George, *La Sainte Bible*, 11; Kühl, *The Prophets of Israel*, 89; Kapelrud, "Eschatology," 393; Steinmann and Hanon, *Michée*, 371; Schilling, "Michäas," 391; Bright, "Micah," 666; Weiser, *Das Buch der zwölf Kleinen Propheten*, 231; and Deissler *Les Petits Prophètes*, 334.

18. See Kleinert, *The Minor Prophets*, 19; Nowack, "Bemerkungen," 288; Kuenen, *Historisch-Critisch Onderzoek*, 370 n. 2; Findlay, *The Books of the Prophets*, 266; Hoonacker, *Les douze petits Prophètes*, 341, 376, 380; Hölscher, *Die Profeten*, 439; and Ungern-Sternberg, *Der Rechtsstreit Gottes*, 155.

19. For a detailed study of this argument, see my article: Willis, "A Note on ואמר," 50–54.

20. Ibid., 53 n. 37.

21. As a matter of fact, several scholars outline the book in just this way. Thus Ewald, *Commentary*, 324; Kleinert, *The Minor Prophets*, 6; *Die Propheten Israels*, 61, 66; W.

was transferred from its original position to its present position in the book.²² Thus, when analyzed, the 1–3 (threat)—4–5 (hope); 6:1—7:6 (threat)—7:7–20 (hope) outline of the book actually amounts to a twofold division: chs. 1–5 and chs. 6–7.

Now this analysis of the book of Micah is significantly different from the widely held threefold division of the book: 1–3, 4–5, 6–7,²³ an outline which, in this writer's opinion, obscures the symmetry of the whole and tends to lead to serious misconceptions. This outline seems to be based on the assumption that the genuine Mican material is to be found only in the first three chapters, and that all of the authentic oracles must be arranged under one major heading in an analysis of the book. But granting for argument's sake that the prophet Micah is responsible for materials in chs. 1–3 alone, this would not preclude the possibility that a later redactor could have taken this material and for his own purposes divided it in his own arrangement of that larger corpus of prophetic oracles which forms the present composition of the book. Now the contrasts between 3:9–12 and 4:1–5 are so striking²⁴ that one is almost

---

R. Smith, *The Prophets of Israel*, 427 n. 3; Driver, *Introduction*, 326; Findlay, *The Books of the Prophets*, 247, 263; Hölscher, *Die Profeten*, 438; Burkitt, "Micah 6 and 7," 159; Mowinckel, "Mikaboken," 3; Mowinckel, *Det Gamle Testamente*, 666; *Prophecy and Tradition*, 51; Orelli, "Micah," 2046; G. W. Anderson, *A Critical Introduction*, 155; Kapelrud, "Mikas bok," 106; and Kraeling, *Commentary*, 204, 221.

22. Thus, 2:12–13 may be an illustration of a transposition which was made after the redactor had issued the "final form" of the book.

23. Thus Bellett, *The Minor Prophets*, 53; Orelli, *The Twelve Minor Prophets*, 188; Sellery, "The Book of Micah," 17; Beardslee, *Outlines*, 115f.; Marti, *Das Dodekapropheton*, 258; G. A. Smith, *The Book of the Twelve Prophets*, 530; Fairweather, *The Pre-Exilic Prophets*, 71–73; Cornill, *Introduction*, 348; Hoonacker, *Les douze petits Prophètes*, 339, 353; "Micheas," 278; Gray, "Micah, Book of," 614; *A Critical Introduction*, 217; J. M. P. Smith, *Critical and Exegetical Commentary*, 8; W. R. Smith, "Micah," 357; Stave, *Inledning*, 214; *Israels Profeter*, 11, 31, 41; Batten, *The Old Testament*, 227; Cheyne, *Micah*, 10; Wade, *The Books of the Prophets*, XIX; Clamer, "Michée," 1654; Gautier, *Introduction*, 502; Goldman, *The Twelve Prophets*, 153; Coppens, *Les douze petits prophètes*, 31; Lods, *Histoire*, 286, 289, 290; Schumpp, *Das Buch der zwölf Propheten*, 187; L. P. Smith, "The Book of Micah," 216; Clarke, *Concise Bible Commentary*, 606; Snaith, "Micah," 308; Henshaw, *The Latter Prophets*, 105; Gottwald, *A Light to the Nations*, 306–7; Robinson, "Micah," 407; Robinson, *Die Zwölf Kleinen Propheten*, 127.

24. 3:9ff. concerns the imminent future, while 4:1ff. concerns the far distant future; the former announces that Zion will be plowed as a field, the latter, that Zion will be exalted; the former declares that Zion will become just another forest or jungle sanctuary, the latter, that Zion will be exalted above the surrounding hills and will assume the enviable position of being a sanctuary for all nations; the former describes Jerusalem

compelled to conclude that the final redactor intended for chs. 3 and 4 to be taken together. By making a major division between these chapters, one destroys the full effectiveness of these contrasts. Furthermore, an analysis of the book composed of a section of doom, then a section of hope, then a section of doom-hope is not really as symmetrical as a doom, hope, doom, hope or a doom–hope, doom-hope pattern.

It seems most natural, therefore, to divide the book of Micah into three major sections: 1-2, 3-5, 6-7.[25] Each section begins with שמעו (1:2; 3:1; 6:1) and with oracles of doom (1:2—2:11; 3; 6:1—7:6) and ends with oracles of hope (2:12-13; 4-5; 7:7-20).

The general arrangement of the book seems to conform to an A (1-2)—B (3-5)—A (6-7) pattern. In the first and third divisions, the doom sections are much longer than the hope sections, whereas in the central division, the hope section is much longer than the doom section. It is striking that the first and third sections are composed of four pericopes each: (a) a covenant lawsuit (1:2-7 in I and 6:1-8 in III); (b) a lament (1:8-16 in I and 7:1-6 in III); (c) an explanation (*Begründung*) for the impending catastrophe in the form of a reproach (2:1-11 in I and

---

as a city built by violence and bloodshed, the latter announces that this city will be the place whence Yahweh's word will proceed; the former declares that Zion will become heaps, the latter describes her as the navel of the earth and as a city that attracts peoples. Both pericopes use the terms "Zion," "Jerusalem," and "the mountain of the house." Therefore, the present writer agrees with Beck, *Erklärung*, 64, when he says: "Der Schluß von Kap. 3 ... und der Anfang von Kap. 4 ... unverkennbar sich auf einander beziehen." Mowinckel, *Prophecy and Tradition*, 71, writes: "It is very possible, perhaps even probable, that, e.g., Isa 2:2-5 has always belonged to the tradition complex Isa 2-5, or that the identical Mic 4:1-5 from the beginning has been created in connection with the complex Mic 1-3," but he argues that the authenticity of 4:1-5 is another problem, in fact, that this pericope is late. *Prophecy and Tradition*, 67. Even Nielsen, *Oral Tradition*, 92, is probably not too radical when he says: "The thought forces itself upon us that these passages (i.e., 3:9-12 and 4:1-5) cannot even have originated independently of each other." Ackroyd, "A Note on Isaiah 2:1," 320, is quite justified in contending: "The opening words of Micah 4 are entirely appropriate, and provide, as has been noted in recent years, the strongest argument against the so popular division of the book into two distinct parts, 1-3 and 4-7." Weiser, *Das Buch der zwölf Kleinen Propheten*, 263 is undoubtedly correct when he writes: "Der Ernst der prophetischen Gerichtsdrohung wird durch das Wort der Verheißung *nicht aufgehoben, sondern vorausgesetzt*" (italics mine). Pákozdy, "Michabuch," 1211, calls this type of composition "Kontrastverfahren." See further, Halévy, "Le Livre de Michée," 213; Budde, "Verfasser," 153, 156; Sellin, *Das Zwölfprophetenbuch*, 328; Lippl, *Die Zwölf Kleinen Propheten*, 199; George, *La Sainte Bible*, 12; Renaud, *Structure*, 35.

25. A rather full bibliography is given in my article: "A Note on ואמר," 52 n. 34. To this may now be added Brandenburg, *Die Kleinen Propheten*, 69f.

6:9–16 in III); and (d) a hope oracle (2:12–13 in I and 7:7–20 in III).²⁶ To include ch. 3 as part of the first section, or portions of ch. 5 as part of the last would destroy this symmetry. A further thread of evidence which supports this division is the fact that the large divisions of the book are conjoined by catchwords (*Stichwort*). Sections II and III are linked together by *šāmēʻû* in 5:14 and *šimʻû* in 6:1. Sections I and II are connected by בראשם in 2:13 and ראשי יעקב in 3:1.²⁷

Now we must turn our attention to the structure of Section II (Mic 3–5) in order to lay the foundation for our remarks on 5:9–14. This division contains a relatively short doom section (ch. 3) and a relatively long hope section (chs. 4–5). Scholars are generally agreed that ch. 3 is composed of three pericopes similar in length, form, and content: vv. 1–4 (an oracle against Israel's rulers);²⁸ 5–8 (an oracle against false prophets); and 9–12 (a "summary" oracle against the rulers, priests, and false prophets of Israel). Westermann's analysis of the first and third pericopes in ch. 3²⁹ and the obvious similarity of the second to them show the coherence of this chapter. Each pericope condemns Israelite leadership, each gives the reason for this condemnation (i.e., the failure of the leading class in question to discharge the responsibility accruing to its particular office), and each announces a judgment suitable to the crime condemned. Furthermore, these pericopes are composed of "immer sich steigernden Anklagen und Drohungen."³⁰

Now chs. 4–5 are admittedly the most difficult chapters in the book of Micah in which to demonstrate coherence. As a matter of fact, most scholars flatly deny that any coherence is to be found here.³¹ In my opin-

---

26. The fact that the order of the lament and the reproach are reversed is, of course, of little consequence. Only these scant remarks can be made about sections I and III in this essay, since the main concern is with the structure of the central section of the book.

27. For further details, cf. my article: "A Note on ואמר."

28. Bruno, *Micha und der Herrscher*, 57–59, maintains that Mic 3:11 is a summary of condemnations against the leaders, priests, and prophets of Israel in 2:6—3:8. Since 2:6–11 is against the leaders and 3:5–8 is against the prophets, 3:1–4 must have been originally against the priests. Using similar reasoning, Hylmö, *Kompositionen*, 86–87, 92 argues that 2:6–11 is against the priests and 3:1–4 is against the leaders of the people. However, there appears to be little real justification for these views.

29. Westermann, *Basic Forms*, 124–25.

30. Budde, "Eine folgenschwere Redaktion," 223.

31. Cf. above 66 n. 3.

ion, however, B. Renaud's recent monograph[32] has opened the way to a possible defense of the coherence of these difficult chapters. Basing his thesis on Nielsen's earlier observations,[33] Renaud divides these chapters into six pericopes and attempts to show that their author arranged his material so that the first pericope (A—4:1-4) corresponds to the last (A'—5:8-14), the second (B—4:6-7) to the fifth (B'—5:6-7), and the third (C—4:8-14) to the fourth (C'—5:1-5).[34]

According to Renaud, 4:1-4 and 5:8-14 belong together because: (a) they have the same theme—the destiny of the nations in the eschatological age; (b) they form a striking detailed contrast according to the principle of antithetical parallelism:

A Salvation of the subject nations, 4:1-4
  a Exaltation and blessing of Zion, v. 1
    b Pilgrimage to the Temple, v. 2a
      c In order to seek the law and word there, v. 2b
        d Transformation of weapons into tools for agricultural work, v. 3
          e Happiness of the nations, v. 4
A' Chastisement of the unsubdued nations, 5:8-14
          e' Unhappiness of the nations, v. 8
        d' Destruction of weapons of war and fortified cities, vv. 9-10
      c' Destruction of sorcerers and diviners, v. 11
    b' Suppression of idols and the ungodly cult, vv. 12-13
  a' Curse against the nations, v. 14

and (c) they begin with the same verbal joint והיה (4:1; 5:9).[35] But as attractive as this line of argumentation may appear at first, several points in Renaud's presentation are not too convincing. (1) It is true that (according to the present MT) "the nations" are mentioned in both of these pericopes. But it does not necessarily follow that the theme of these two

---

32. Renaud, *Structure*, 35.

33. Nielsen, *Oral Tradition*, 79-93, especially 85-86.

34. A similar chiastic explanation for Old Testament books has been suggested for Habakkuk by Walker and Lund, "The Literary Structure," 365-70; and for Ruth by Bertman, "Symmetrical Design," 166-68.

35. Renaud, *Structure*, 13. Previously, Ladame, "Les chapitres IV et V," 459-60, had argued that 5:9-14 was the original continuation of 4:1-3, and had pointed out contrasts between the two pericopes.

oracles is the destiny of the nations in the eschatological age. 5:9ff. is devoted primarily to a description of the chastisement of Israel, not of the nations. The nations appear for the first time in v. 14 (assuming that v. 8 belongs together with vv. 6–7). This pericope seems to come from a time when the nations are threatening Israel's security and Israel intends to try to thwart their attack by the use of horses, chariots, fortified cities, etc. Since she depends on these things rather than on Yahweh, Yahweh declares that he will destroy all the objects of Israel's trust (vv. 9–13). This will leave Israel in a hopeless situation, apparently at the mercy of her adversaries. But at this point Yahweh will intervene and overthrow Israel's foes (v. 14). Thus, the purpose of this pericope is to encourage Israel to trust in Yahweh alone in this time of great distress. Furthermore, in this writer's opinion, it is a mistake to separate 4:1ff. from 3:9–12.[36] But if 3:9—4:5 is a unit, then the major concern of the pericope is Israel and not the nations.[37] The future of the nations is important only in relationship to Israel's future, as 4:4 seems to indicate.[38] Thus, one is hardly

---

36. See above, 70 n. 24.

37. On this point, see further my dissertation, 231–33.

38. This writer assumes that the interpretation of the emphasis intended in 4:1–5 must be determined by the contrasts with 3:9–11 and by the parallels with other pericopes in chs. 4–6. Thus, the idea of the nations coming to Jerusalem to hear the word of Yahweh in v. 1d–2 is understood as a secondary consideration of the redactor of the "final form" of the book, who placed the passage in its present position. These lines are included in contrast to the gathering of the nations to Jerusalem on other occasions (e.g., 4:11) to fight against her. The idea is retained because of this contrast and because this passage includes an oracle other than that represented by the "final form" of the book, as the parallel in Isa 2:2–4 shows. The emphasis in the second hope section of Micah is primarily on Yahweh's restoring Israel to her former status. The coming of the nations to Zion to hear Yahweh's law is a result of this restoration and thus secondary to it. This receives further support from the conclusion of the passage in v. 4, which does not occur in Isa 2. (a) Some scholars maintain that this verse promises peace to all nations. "Il semble que l'auteur ait intentionnellement étendu aux paiens ce retour à l'âge d'or davidique et salomonien que sera le royaume messianique." Renaud, *Structure*, 111. See also Halévy, "Le Livre de Michée," 216; G. A. Smith, *The Book of the Twelve Prophets*, 541 (possibly); Ridderbos, *De Kleine Profeten*, 83; and Wildberger, "Die Völkerwallfahrt," 81. (b) The present writer, however, thinks that v. 4a announces the effect that the cessation of war by Israel's enemies will have in Israel itself. The expression used here appears in 1 Kgs 4:25 and Zech 3:10 referring to Israelite prosperity and security. "Peace abroad brings peace at home." Horton, *The Minor Prophets*, 245. The purpose of v. 4 is to "show how the international peace prophesied in vv. 1–3 will redound especially to the advantage of Israelites." Fullerton, "Studies in Isaiah," 137. See also Wellhausen, *Die Kleinen Propheten*, 143; Marti, *Das Dodekapropheton*, 282; G. A. Smith, *The Book of the Twelve Prophets*, 541 (possibly); and Nowack, *Die Kleinen Propheten*, 218.

justified in concluding that the primary concern of this pericope is the destiny of the nations in the eschatological age. (2) Renaud's argument depends on including 5:8 as a part of 5:9ff. rather than as the conclusion of 5:6–7.[39] He recognizes the difficulty of such a position, but justifies his arrangement by contending that 5:8 overloads the figure in 5:6–7, and by pointing out that יכרתו in 5:8 joins this verse with והכרתי in 5:9ff.[40] However, the structure of 5:8 sharply disrupts the very striking arrangement of the Hebrew text in 5:9ff. Renaud himself argues that the verbal joint והיה occurs in 4:1 and 5:9 (not 5:8).[41] Moreover, apparently the function of *yikkarĕtû* and *wĕhikrattî* is to connect 5:6–8 with 5:9–14. If so, 5:8 is a part of vv. 6–7 rather than of vv. 9–14.

The only argument which Renaud advances to justify the combination of 4:6–7 with 5:6–7 is that they both have the same theme, i.e., the remnant in the Messianic Age.[42] It is true that the "remnant" functions significantly in the thought of both of these passages. But it also occupies an important place in Renaud's C' pericope (5:2), and yet Renaud does not feel compelled to combine C' with B'. Actually, the concept of the "remnant" is assumed in all of the pericopes in chs. 4–5, and with good reason. The author of these chapters wishes to emphasize that Israel's condition is hopeless, and that her future depends on complete trust in Yahweh. Renaud finds extensive parallels between 4:8–14 and 5:1–5. (a) He argues that the theme of both pericopes is the eschatological age, presented by means of contrast. C describes the final combat, while C' describes the peace of the Messianic Age.[43] But, admitting that the two pericopes speak of events to take place in the eschatological age, this does not mean that the eschatological age is the theme of these pericopes. This "theme" is a broad one, and might include many things. If this is the theme of the two middle pericopes of Mic 4–5, is there any reason why it cannot be the theme of the entire two chapters? Furthermore, it is not entirely accurate to state that the motif of C' is the peace of the Messianic age, for even if vv. 4b–5a are removed, v. 5b still speaks of the coming

---

39. Following George, *La Sainte Bible*, 13, 38.

40. So also Gailey, "Micah . . . Malachi," 29.

41. Mowinckel, *Prophecy and Tradition*, 102 n. 24, argues that "and it shall come to pass in that day, saith Yahweh, that" is a connective of the collectors of the originally independent prophetic oracles.

42. Renaud, *Structure*, 14.

43. Ibid., 16.

ruler delivering Israel from an enemy army.[44] (b) Renaud thinks that it is significant that each of these pericopes begins by referring to a city (4:8—Jerusalem; 5:1—Bethlehem),[45] although he is somewhat vague as to what implications he would deduce from this. Some scholars have suggested that these two passages may contain an intended contrast between Jerusalem, the capital despised by the country man Micah, and Bethlehem, a small town which a country man would tend to favor.[46] However, these pericopes draw heavily from the Davidic tradition.[47] But in that tradition, the fact that David was born at Bethlehem, and that Bethlehem played a significant part in the earlier phase of his career, was by no means inconsistent with his making Jerusalem his capital. Did Micah (or the redactor of the "final form" of the book of Micah) intend to cast disparagement on David's choice of Jerusalem and carrying the ark to Jerusalem, on Solomon's building the temple in Jerusalem, etc., when he announced the destruction of the Holy City (3:12)? In this writer's opinion—No! On the contrary, Micah condemned the city because its rulers, the avowed descendants of David, had not ruled as true sons of David. He saw no way of restoring the type of rule which David symbolized without completely removing the present authorities. Therefore, it seems most unlikely that 5:1ff. is intended to be a contrast to 4:8–13. Instead, it seems to be a contrast to 4:14. (c) Renaud calls attention to the similarity of ideas between the two sections: Yahweh's leadership, return to former days and the shepherd-sheep motif.[48] Of course, these parallels do exist, but it does not necessarily follow that Renaud's arrangement is the most logical explanation for them. (d) Renaud argues that 5:1 is the watershed between chs. 4 and 5.[49] Everything before this verse describes the situation which makes the appearance of the Messiah necessary, while everything after this verse describes the benefits which will result from the Messiah's coming.[50] Thus, there are several contrasts between

---

44. As a matter of fact, Renaud maintains that 5:4b–5a is originally earlier than the writing of Mic 4–5, and that the author of this midrash incorporated it into his work.

45. Renaud, *Structure*, 18.

46. E.g., Bruno, *Micha und der Herrscher*, 209, who reads "Beth-Ophrah" instead of "Bethlehem."

47. Cf. especially Beyerlin, *Die Kulttraditionen Israels*, 76–85.

48. Renaud, *Structure*, 18–19.

49. Ibid., 32.

50. Ibid., 34.

the two chapters, but more particularly between 4:8–14 and 5:1–6. 4:9 describes Yahweh's abandonment of his people, but 5:2 describes the return of the dispersed to Yahweh. 4:11–13 describes the heathen attack on Jerusalem, but 5:5 points to a time when all the nations will live in universal peace. 4:14 describes Assyria humiliating the leader of Judah, but 5:4–5 declares that Assyria will be destroyed by divine power.[51] But it seems to the present writer that Renaud has forced these passages into a pattern which is not supported by their contents. The "king" in 4:9 is not Yahweh, but the earthly king.[52] It is true that 4:11–13 describes the heathen attack on Jerusalem, but it also announces the complete overthrow of the heathen. It is not necessary to read as far as 5:1ff. to encounter the declaration of this victory. Again, 5:5 is not a description of universal peace, but of Israel's victory over Assyria. Even if Assyria is a collective term for Israel's enemies (which it undoubtedly was for the redactor of the "final form" of the book, although not necessarily for the original spokesman), and even if the difficult phrase והיה שלום זה (5:4) is interpreted as the beginning of the sentence,[53] still the "peace" of 5:4a

---

51. Ibid., 19.

52. For an extended discussion of this problem, cf. my dissertation 218–19 n. 1.

53. This phrase has been variously interpreted. (a) Bruno, *Micha und der Herrscher*, 95, emends the text to יהוה שלום, "Yahweh is salvation," because "kaum von einem Menschen, sondern nur von Gott gesagt werden konnte, Dan er Heil sei." He thinks that this is an inscription borne on a standard at an altar, which he identifies with "Yahweh-Shalom" in the Jerubbaal story (Judg 6:24). (b) At first Cheyne, "Gleanings," 580, emended the text to והיה ביום הזה, "and it shall happen on that day," and argued that "peace" was an intrusion into the text. Later in *Critica Biblica*, 160, and *The Two Religions of Israel*, 371, he reads זה ישמעאל "that is, Ishmael," as a gloss on Asshur. (c) Hylmö, *Kompositionen*, 213 deletes *zeh šālôm* as a gloss on *wĕyāšābû* in 5:3. (d) Marty, *L'Ancien Testament*, 777, regards this phrase as a redactional joint which was inserted to connect two originally independent oracles. (e) Allegro, "Uses of the Semitic Demonstrative Element," 311; Beyerlin, *Die Kulttraditionen Israels*, 35 (following Eerdmans); Hammershaimb, "Einige Hauptgedanken," 31; and Schwantes, "A Critical Study," 133, identify *zeh* with the Arabic *ḏu* and the Akkadian *šu*, and read "lord of peace." They cite Judg 5:5 and Ps 68:9, in which זה סיני means "lord of Sinai," and compare "prince of peace" in Isa 9:5. (f) Instead of *zeh*, Riessler, *Die Kleinen Propheten*, 120, reads *lazzeh*, "and peace will be to them," i.e., and they will have peace. (g) Ungern-Sternberg, *Der Rechtsstreit Gottes*, 111 argues that "this will be peace" refers to the result of the Messiah's reign described in vv. 1–3. (h) Ladame, "Les chapitres IV et V," 468; Halévy, "Le Livre de Michée," 211; Marti, *Das Dodekapropheton*, 288; Hoonacker, *Les douze petits Prophètes*, 391; Duhm, "Anmerkungen," 89; J. M. P. Smith, *Critical and Exegetical Commentary*, 108; Stave, *Israels Profeter*, 38; Nowack, *Die Kleinen Propheten*, 224; Schumpp, *Das Buch der zwölf Propheten*, 209; Deden, *De Kleine Profeten*, 221; Thomas, "Micah," 632; and Scharbert, *Die Propheten Israels*, 335, regard the phrase as

which most concerns the speaker is not universal peace among the nations, but peace for Israel, i.e., prosperity and rest from the fear of attack by enemies, as in 4:4. The present writer agrees with Renaud's suggestion that 4:14 describes Assyria's attack on Israel, and that in contrast to this 5:4–5 declares that Israel will defeat Assyria through Yahweh's power, and for this reason (along with others) believes that the pericope should extend from 4:14 through 5:5 instead of from 5:1 through 5:5, as Renaud insists.

Although several of the details in Renaud's argumentation seem to be untenable, the importance of his work must not be minimized. He has called attention to a large number of parallels in thought and vocabulary between the pericopes in Mic 4–5. But the present writer is unable to subscribe to Renaud's explanation, not simply because of disagreement in details, but more basically because of fundamental methodological differences. (a) Renaud examines the hope sections of the book without any significant attempt to explain their relationship to the doom sections. By way of contrast, the present writer maintains that in order to deal with the problem of coherence in the book of Micah, one must examine the book as a whole, and not limit his investigation to a "horizontal" analysis[54] of the hope sections. We cannot agree to the oft-repeated assertion that the hope passages in the book of Micah are attempts by later generations to "neutralize" or offset the severity of the doom oracles of the pre-exilic period.[55] If this is the case, why is it neces-

---

the introduction to a new thought, and argue that it should be followed by a colon to indicate that it refers to what follows, "And this shall be peace." (i) It seems most likely, however, that *zeh* should be interpreted as a demonstrative referring to the coming ruler in vv. 1–8: "And this one (man) shall be peace." The phrase probably means that the Messiah will inaugurate a period of peace and prosperity. This would form a good contrast to the present conditions described in 4:14. This is the view of Kleinert, *The Minor Prophets*, 37; Elhorst, *De Prophetie van Micha*, 166; Orelli, *The Twelve Minor Prophets*, 212; Horton, *The Minor Prophets*, 253; Haupt, "The Book of Micah," 26:238; 27:67 (the messiah is Zerubbabel); Ridderbos, *De Kleine Profeten*, 94; Shoot, "The Fertility Religions," 148; Brandenburg, *Die Kleinen Propheten*, 98; and Deissler, *Les Petits Prophètes*, 334.

54. I.e., an analysis which deals with the hope sections alone or the doom sections alone.

55. The following statements are representative. "Kann man sich doch des Eindrucks nicht erwehren, daß (Mi) 4:1ss . . . ein Pflaster auf die durch 3:12 gerissene Wunde sein soll." Wellhausen, *Die Kleinen Propheten*, 143. 4:1ff. "has been appended at the end of the first three chapters containing the genuine prophecies of Micah in order to blunt the edge of the too keen prediction in 3:12." Haupt, "The Book of Micah," 27:43.

sary for the later redactor to repeat the "atmosphere of doom" (as in 4:9–10a, 11, 14; 5:9–13) which is already so apparent in the doom sections of the book? (b) Renaud maintains that the affinities between 2:12–13; 4–5; and 7:7–20 compel one to conclude that these sections were all written by the same author. The present writer would agree if Renaud did not intend something very particular by the word "auteur." He means that the hope sections in the book of Micah for the most part *came into existence for the first time* when they were written by a Jerusalemite priestly-scribe of the fifth century.[56] Renaud explicitly denies the possibility that Mic 4–5 may be an attempt to arrange previously independent oracles into a coherent whole. "Une telle multiplicité de motifs littéraires aussi divers, s'imbriquant aussi étroitement les uns dans les autres, requière non pas un assemblage d'oracles indépendants, mais bien une oeuvre originale."[57] However, he himself concedes that 5:4b–5a and 5:8–14 originated before the author of chs. 4–5 incorporated them into his work.[58] Summarizing, Renaud's approach seems to grow out of a denial of the "liveliness" of prophetic oracles. In the present writer's opinion, however, traditio-historical critics have shown that oracles which once had an "original" *Sitz im Leben* in one historical situation were often applied to later similar circumstances, in the process of which they may have been expanded

---

The redactor inserted 4:1ff. "um ein Gegengewicht gegen v. 3:12 mit seiner düsteren Perspektive zu bilden." Nowack, *Die Kleinen Propheten* 197. 4:1ff. is "*a foil to offset* the dark picture of Jerusalem which had preceded." McFadyen, "Micah," 795. Micah 2:12–13 was "perhaps inserted in this position when the prophecies were collected, to *soften* the harshness of the doom which Micah had pronounced." Goldman, *The Twelve Prophets*, 164. 2:12–18 and 4:1ff. were added "*um die Wucht* der Unheilsdrohungen *aufzuheben*." Sellin, *Einleitung*, 130. 4:1ff. "diente . . . vermutlich dem Zweck, bei der liturgischen Verlesung in der jüdischen Gemeinde die vorausgehende Drohung gegen den Tempel 3:12 in ihrer Härte *abzuschwächen*." Weiser, *Das Buch der zwölf Kleinen Propheten*, 231. Speaking of the redactor's purpose in surrounding Mic 3 with 2:12–13 and 4–5, Renaud writes: "Il faillait *parer le coup, les neutraliser*. C'est ce qu'un redacteur a sans doute tenté de faire par cette insertion." Renaud, *Structure*, 21. See also 24, 36, 43, 69 (all italics mine). See also Stade, "Bemerkungen," 170; Cheyne, "Micah (Book)," 3072; Ladame, "Les chapitres IV et V," 450; Marti, *Das Dodekapropheton*, 280; Haller, "Michabuch," 367; Hölscher, *Die Profeten*, 457; Hylmö, *Kompositionen*, 80; Lindblom, *Micha*, 156; Pfeiffer, *Introduction*, 590; Fichtner, *Obadja, Jona, Micha*, 35; George, *La Sainte Bible*, 13; Gottwald, *A Light to the Nations*, 307; Deissler, *Les Petits Prophètes*, 299; and Kraeling, *Commentary*, 215.

56. Renaud, *Structure*, 108.
57. Ibid., 32.
58. Ibid., 20, and 20 n. 3.

or diminished or arranged with other similar oracles in order to meet the needs of the later situation. That the present book of Micah is the result of such a process is as reasonable as Renaud's thesis, if not more so.

Chapters 4–5 describe two basic goals or results of Yahweh's leadership—that of giving Israel victory over her enemies, and that of restoring Israel to her former status as Yahweh's covenant people. It is at this point that a recognition of the symmetrical structure of these chapters is helpful in exegesis. Each of the seven pericopes in these two chapters[59] is composed of two parts: a description of the present hopeless situation, and an announcement of divine deliverance, involving giving Israel victory over her enemies, or restoring her former status, or both. The idea that chs. 4–5 represent an attempt to soften the severity of the doom oracles in chs. 1–3 does not account for the fact that the real contrast lies within each pericope, and not between chs. 1–3 and chs. 4–5. Each pericope begins with a description of or a reference to the disastrous nature of the present situation. Then it announces the glorious future. *But there is no logical transition between these two contrasting pictures!*[60] One must attempt to discover how such a scheme is to be understood. (1) The reversal of ideas within each pericope leads the present writer to reject the idea of chs. 4–5 were intended to "nullify" or "neutralize" the effect of chs. 1–3.[61] E.g., 4:1–5 is not a purposeful contradiction or nullification of 3:9–12, but a purposeful contrast to it. 3:9—4:5 is one pericope! And 3:9–12 belongs to 4:1–5 as much as 4:9–10a to 4:10b, or 4:11 to 4:12–13, or 4:14 to 5:1–5, or 5:9–13 to 5:14, or as much as "lame, driven away, etc." belong to "I will assemble," "I will gather," etc. in 4:6–8, or "remnant" to "dew," "rain," and "lion" in 5:6–8. (2) Now these chapters might be taken to mean that Yahweh will redeem his people unconditionally. In this case, however, one is again driven to the previous position, and chs. 4–5 are understood to contradict chs. 1–3. In view of these interpretations, one gets the impression that often scholars mean that Micah thought that

---

59. 4:1–5, 6–8, 9–10, 11–13; 4:14—5:5, 6–8, 9–14.

60. Speaking of the abrupt transition from ch. 3 to ch. 4, Stave, *Israels Profeter*, 31, writes: "övergkången från domsförkunnelsen till frälsningsförkunnelsen är icke på något satt förmedlad; ingen motivering lämnas för frälsningsförkunnelsen, intet villkor för löftets förverkligande angives." Speaking of the pericopes in chs. 4–5, Brandenburg, *Die Kleinen Propheten*, 67 says: "Sind die Übergänge von der Drohung zur Verheißung, von der Verheißung zur Drohung oft vorbereitet."

61. This is based on the idea that once a word is released it has power, and that the only way to nullify the power of a doom oracle is to neutralize it by a hope oracle.

Yahweh would punish his people severely for their sins and he was correct. But a later editor (or editors) considered such an idea repulsive and so added chs. 4–5 to proclaim that ultimately Yahweh would deliver his people unconditionally because they were his people. (3) But in light of the affinities between the three hope sections, and the apparent progression of thought from first to last, it is the present writer's opinion that the first two hope sections must be interpreted in view of the last. 2:12–13 and chs. 4–5 describe the present condition and announce the future promise, but make no attempt to explain the reversal of circumstances. However, 7:7–20 offers just such an explanation. Yahweh punished Israel because of her sins. Israel acknowledges the righteousness of Yahweh in doing this (v. 9). Yahweh (by means of punishment) has stripped Israel of all people and things in which she had trusted, and now she realizes the necessity of trusting in Yahweh alone. The enemy threatens, yet Israel does not seek help in human or material means, but in Yahweh alone (vv. 8, 10, 14–17). Therefore, the transitional explanation from the deplorable present to the glorious future (which is absent in 2:12–13 and chs. 4–5) is supplied in the final hope section. The glorious future will come because Yahweh's severe punishment has brought about a change in Israel—a change to complete trust in Yahweh.[62]

If this analysis is correct, each of the seven pericopes in Mic 4–5 occupies a vital, meaningful position in relationship to the message and purpose of the book as a whole. The thread which holds this material together is the proclamation of the aims and results of the complete leadership of Yahweh in the coming age. One of the things which his leadership involves is giving Israel victory over her enemies—a victory which she cannot hope to achieve by human schemes or material strength. 4:6–8 (pericope II) describes Israel as lame, driven away, afflicted, cast far off. Apparently there is no adequate leadership "in mount Zion." Jerusalem is like a desolate tower of the flock (v. 8). The similarity between this expression and Isa 1:7–8 indicates that Jerusalem is in a hopeless situation. But the prophet declares that at some future time ("in that day") Yahweh

---

62. Although many scholars have called attention to the emphasis on the theme of complete trust in Yahweh in now one, now another, pericope in chs. 4–5, it is Barnes, "A Messianic Prophecy," 376–88, who has elaborated on this theme most extensively with regard to the entire two chapters. Barnes points out the purposeful contrast between the present hopeless situation of 3:9–12 and the future glory described in 4:1–7, and observes correctly that the text does not attempt to explain the transition. He thinks that 4:8—5:5 forms this explanation.

will intervene and completely reverse the present circumstances. First Yahweh speaks: "I will assemble that which is lame, and I will gather that which is driven away." "I will make that which was lame a remnant, etc." Then the prophet announces: "Yahweh will reign over them in mount Zion." The former kingdom, i.e., the kingdom as it was in the height of its glory during the reign of David (and Solomon), shall come to the daughter of Zion, Jerusalem. Apparently, the purpose of this oracle is to teach Israel to accept her present hopeless situation as just retribution for her infidelity and to encourage her to trust her future completely to Yahweh.[63] This pericope seems to assume that the hearers have (or should have) the attitude expressed in 7:7-20.

The situation presupposed in 4:9-10 (pericope III) is quite similar to that assumed in 4:6-8. The daughter of Zion is in distressing, even hopeless, circumstances. Evidently, Jerusalem is being besieged by an invading army. The king is powerless before the undaunted strength of the enemy. It is clear to all the people that they must abandon the security of the fortified city and go out into the field in open surrender to the foe, where they will be completely helpless before the natural elements and the adversary. According to the "final form" of the book of Micah, the enemy will carry the Judean captives into exile in Babylon, and it will be "there" that Yahweh will rescue them and redeem them from their enemies. Apparently, the purpose of this pericope (as in the case of 4:6-8) is to encourage Israel to acknowledge her own weakness and the impotence of human strength, and to trust in Yahweh completely in this dark hour.[64] Again, 7:7-20 illuminates the significance of the surprising and abrupt change from 4:10a to 4:10b.

---

63. "Aanvaardt Jahveh de koninklijke waardigheid (v. 7), dan begint er ook voor zijne residentie eene nieuwe periode van bloei (v. 8)." Kuenen, "De Koning uit Beth-Ephrath," 61. "The Remnant... is a group, *divinely spared and divinely guided*, destined to be the means by which the *Will of God* shall be maintained in a world gone wrong." Snaith, *Amos, Hosea and Micah*, 94. Marsh, *Amos and Micah*, 107, contends that 4:1–8 means that "by some change *impossible of achievement save by God*, the radically new age would be wholly of God's making" (italics mine in both quotations). See also Beck, *Erklärung*, 154–55; Barnes, "A Messianic Prophecy," 376; Cheyne, *Micah*, 37; Sellin, *Einleitung*, 330; Schumpp, *Das Buch der zwölf Propheten*, 207; Wolfe, "The Book of Micah," 926; Ungern-Sternberg, *Der Rechtsstreit Gottes*, 84–85; and Gailey, "Micah... Malachi," 24.

64. "Der tragende Grundgedanke der beiden Verse ist der des inneren Zusammenhangs von Not und Erlösung... Erst muß das Volk seiner ganzen Ohnmacht und Hilflosigkeit bewußt werden, muß erkennen und anerkennen, daß *allein Gott im-*

Micah 4:11–13 (pericope IV) also describes Israel's present situation as utterly hopeless. The nations have already assembled themselves in great military power around the city of Jerusalem. They justifiably assume that the city will fall under their might in a short time. But then, without warning (and seemingly without reason), the prophet declares that this gathering of foreigners is the work of Yahweh, and that the apparent victors will become the defeated. He charges the helpless Israelites to arise and thresh these sheaves that Yahweh has gathered. But they have nothing with which to fight the enemy! If they are to win the battle, they must trust completely in divine aid and power. Thus Yahweh declares: "I will make your horn iron, and I will make your hoofs brass." Furthermore, when the battle is finished and the victory secure, Israel is not to take the spoil for herself as if she had defeated her adversaries by her own strength, but must put the booty under the ban in public acknowledgment that the victory is Yahweh's. As with the two preceding oracles, the purpose of this pericope is to convince Israel of her own impotence and of the futility of confiding in material strength, and to persuade her to trust completely in Yahweh in spite of the apparent hopelessness of the present situation.[65]

A pitiable situation in Israel is assumed once again at the beginning of 4:14—5:5 (pericope V). The enemy has already besieged the city and there is no doubt in anyone's mind as to the outcome: "they will smite the judge of Israel (i.e., the king) with a rod upon the cheek." But at this point, without any congruous reason, the prophet announces that Yahweh will raise up a new David to deliver the people. It will be evident that his rise to power is of divine origin, because he will come from a "little," insignificant village—hardly suitable as the birthplace for a king.

---

stande ist, ihm zu helfen, ehe die Erlösung wirklich und wirksam werden kann" (italics mine) Weiser, *Das Buch der zwölf Kleinen Propheten,* 270. Cf. also, i.a., Cheyne, "Micah (Book)," 3070; Barnes, "A Messianic Prophecy," 379; Halévy, "Le Livre de Michée," 200; Margolis, *Micah,* 49; Lippl, *Die Zwölf Kleinen Propheten,* 204; Wolfe, "The Book of Micah," 915, 929; and Ungern-Sternberg, *Der Rechtsstreit Gottes,* 92f.

65. So Marsh, *Amos and Micah,* 112 argues that the speaker in 4:11–13 says that Israel will have to take up arms, "and he avows his belief that even there God would aid his people miraculously . . . The restored people of God who resorted to arms would not suppose that their own strength had won them victory, and therefore that they had a right to all the spoils of war . . . God would be acknowledged as the true victor." Thus similarly Wolfe, "The Book of Micah," 929; Ungern-Sternberg, *Der Rechtsstreit Gottes,* 99f.; Brandenburg, *Die Kleinen Propheten,* 94; and Weiser, *Das Buch der zwölf Kleinen Propheten,* 270f.

Now 4:14 indicates that the author of this pericope was dissatisfied with the existing ruler. He seems to be saying that the coming ruler will replace the present ruler as David replaced Saul. If this is the case, the fact that the coming ruler will arise from *Bethlehem* is not to be interpreted as an attempt to discredit the future Jerusalem as his capital and headquarters, any more than the fact that David came from Bethlehem made it incompatible for him to rule under Yahweh's sovereignty in Jerusalem. "Att framtidens ideal frusta säges skola utgå från Bet-Lehem, bör ice uppfattas som en blott geografisk notes utan (i enlighten med Jes 11:1) som eat uttryck för den tankan, att den närvarande dynasties skall störtas ouch Messiahs framträda ur samba slat ouch med samma ringa början som den förste David."[66] Thus, there is no necessary incoherence between the "Bethlehem" pericope and the pericopes in chs. 4–5 which announce an exalted Zion of the future. Now the purpose of this oracle is to persuade Israel (evidently in a time of great distress) to trust her future completely to Yahweh rather than to material strength or human ingenuity.[67]

5:6–8 (pericope VI) also originates in a situation of deep despair for Israel. Many of God's people are scattered among the nations. Numerically, Israel is but a remnant of her former aggregate. Her situation is obviously hopeless. But incongruently, the prophet announces that this helpless remnant will suddenly become as plentiful as dewdrops or raindrops in the lands of their captors, and that she will devour her enemies as a lion devours vulnerable sheep. The two lines at the end

---

66. Stave, *Inledning*, 215.

67. "While Jerusalem labors and has no strength to bring forth, God of his own strength sends the Messiah." Kleinert, *The Minor Prophets*, 35, see also 36. "Nous préférons y (i.e., in 5:1) reconnaître un tableau de l'abaissement d'Israel dans le temps présent, intentionnellement opposé" à la peinture lumineuse qui va suivre (52–54) du regne du Messie de l'avenir." Marty, *L'Ancien Testament*, 776. "The compiler-prophet means the postexilic Judaeans to believe that out of their contemporary chaos God would similarly raise up a new and great king." Marsh, *Amos and Micah*, 113. After the present disaster, "dann wird die Geschichte Israels und seines Königtums wieder von vorne in Bethlehem beginnen. Wie David aus Bethlehem gekommen war, so wird von dort, aus kleinen, bescheidenen Anfängen der zukünftigen Davidide, der Heilskönig kommen." Scharbert, *Die Propheten Israels*, 333. Similarly also Barnes, "A Messianic Prophecy," 383, 384, 386; Schmidt, "Micha," 150; Schumpp, *Das Buch der zwölf Propheten*, 210; Shoot, "The Fertility Religions," 146; George, "Michée (Le Livre de)," 1259; Kunstmann, "Der Prophet Micha," 184; Snaith, *Amos, Hosea and Micah*, 96; Ungern-Sternberg, *Der Rechtsstreit Gottes*, 113; Weiser, *Das Buch der zwölf Kleinen Propheten*, 274; and Brandenburg, *Die Kleinen Propheten*, 96f.

of v. 6: "that tarry not for man, nor wait for the sons of men," and the prayer in v. 8 reveal the purpose of this oracle, i.e., to encourage Israel to trust completely in Yahweh to deliver her from an apparently despairing situation.[68]

It is in light of this emphasis in the pericopes of Mic 4–5 that 5:9–14 (pericope VII) is to be interpreted. This oracle apparently comes from a time when Israel was being attacked by powerful foes. She retaliates with horses and chariots, takes refuge in her fortified cities, and seeks help from various types of magical arts and idolatrous practices to thwart the enemy attack. But the prophet announces that Yahweh will destroy all these objects of Israel's trust, leaving her in a desperate, hopeless condition. It is at this point that Yahweh (without any reasonable motivation) declares: "And *I* will take vengeance . . . on the nations." Once again, it seems that the purpose of this passage is to encourage Israel (faced with insurmountable obstacles) to trust completely in Yahweh.[69]

---

68. "Just as the dew and the rain are blessings from the Lord *which no human effort can bring about*, so the restored community, as it shall stand forth among the nations, *will be the direct result of the divine salvation coming spontaneously and when least expected*" (italics mine) Margolis, *Micah*, 56. "Zal Israel onder de natien zijn het volk, dat de HEERE zegent, en . . . *aan Hern genoeg heeft en zijn heil niet van mensen behoeft te verwachten*" (italics mine) Ridderbos, *De Kleine Profeten*, 96. "*This was not to come about by human effort, for it was in the purpose of God*, and as inevitable as the coming of the rains in springtime" (italics mine) Wolfe, "The Book of Micah," 934. Cf. also Kleinert, *The Minor Prophets*, 37; J. M. P. Smith, *Critical and Exegetical Commentary*, 112; Cheyne, *Micah*, 47; Sellin, *Einleitung*, 339; Lippl, *Die Zwölf Kleinen Propheten*, 209; Deden, *De Kleine Profeten*, 222; Marsh, *Amos and Micah*, 117; and Thomas, "Micah," 632.

69. "The purpose of the destruction of the horses and chariots, like the overthrow of the strongholds . . . is to deprive Israel of all support of fleshly confidence." Orelli, *The Twelve Minor Prophets*, 209. Verses 9–10 foretell "the destruction of the munitions of war in which Israel places confidence instead of trusting in Yahweh" and vv. 11–12 denounce "idolatrous practices which likewise lead Israel away from Yahweh." J. M. P. Smith, *Critical and Exegetical Commentary*, 113. "Though Yahweh will destroy all Israel's means of defence, it is not to leave her defenceless; he himself will be her strength and shield. But she must be brought to realize her absolute dependence upon him." Ibid., 115. "In the future here contemplated the people will no longer trust for security to military defences but to the protection of Jehovah." Wade, *The Books of the Prophets*, 45. "Les grands prophètes du VIIIe siècle condamnaient l'accumulation du matériel de guerre . . . parce que la confiance mise dans ces moyens de défense était à leurs yeux un manque de foi en Yahvé." Marty, *L'Ancien Testament*, 778. "Men merke . . . op, dat de opgesomde misbruiken all ingaan tegen het Godsvertrouwen." Deden, *De Kleine Profeten*, 222. "Horses and chariots were used for war and, along with fortified cities, implied a lack of faith in the Lord." Bewer, *The Prophets*, 527. "There will

This analysis of the central hope section of the book of Micah indicates that pericopes II–VII announce that Yahweh will lead his people in victory over her enemies, in spite of her present apparently hopeless situation. But there is another aspect of Yahweh's leadership which is presented in chs. 4–5—that of restoring Israel to her former status as Yahweh's covenant people. The doom oracles in chs. 3 present a suitable background for this emphasis by showing the lack of responsible leadership in Israel and by announcing the destruction of Zion (3:1–2, 5, 9, 11–12). For Israel, this loss is tantamount to Yahweh's abandonment of his people (3:11). As has already been suggested, each of the seven parallel pericopes in chs. 4–5 assumes or states that Israel's leadership is impotent and/or that Zion is hopelessly doomed or is about to be destroyed. But these oracles announce that these losses will be restored through the power of Yahweh.

Each of the pericopes in Mic 4 announces that Yahweh will restore Zion to her former status. In 3:9—4:5 (pericope I), the prophet declares that Zion will be plowed as a field, Jerusalem will become heaps, and the temple will be reduced to a forest height. He specifically states that all this will happen because of Judah's irresponsible leadership. Israel's condition will be absolutely hopeless. But then, wholly unexpectedly, Yahweh will intervene, and the temple shall be established as the highest of the mountains, and shall be exalted above the hills.[70] The nations

---

be disarmament . . . to obviate trust being placed improperly in arms . . . there will be a demilitarization with no more fortified towns to remove the false security they may evoke . . . occultism will be abolished and with it the pretense that any power other than God controls men's lives . . . Israel's life will rest solely in God, and derive wholly from him." Marsh, *Amos and Micah*, 118. "Die prophetische Predigt richtet sich gegen jene gottlose falsche Sicherheit, die sich nicht auf Gott, sondern auf die eigene Stärke verläßt." Ungern-Sternberg, *Der Rechtsstreit Gottes*, 127, see also 123, 130. Thus similarly, Sellery, "The Book of Micah," 22; Beck, *Erklärung*, 175; Halévy, "Le Livre de Michée," 212–13; Marti, *Das Dodekapropheton*, 271; Riessler, *Die Kleinen Propheten*, 121; Hylmö, *Kompositionen*, 251; Stave, *Israels Profeter*, 54; Binns, "Micah," 587; Mowinckel, *Det Gamle Testamente*, 669; Lippl, *Die Zwölf Kleinen Propheten*, 189; Ridderbos, *De Kleine Profeten*, 98; Schumpp, *Das Buch der zwölf Propheten*, 212; Fichtner, *Obadja, Jona, Micha*, 49; George, *La Sainte Bible*, 38; Kapelrud, "Eschatology," 403; Gailey, "Micah . . . Malachi," 30 (possibly); Brandenburg, *Die Kleinen Propheten*, 101; Weiser, *Das Buch der zwölf Kleinen Propheten*, 277–78; Deissler, *Les Petits Prophètes*, 339; Renaud, *Structure*, 111; Robinson, *Die Zwölf Kleinen Propheten*, 145; and Eissfeldt, *The Old Testament*, 408.

70. Note the use of the passives to indicate the divine activity. Wildberger, "Die Völkerwallfahrt," 69 points out several similarities between Ps 48 and Isa 2:2–4 (= Mic 4:1–3). It is interesting with regard to the point here being made that whereas Mic 4:1 states that Zion will be established (passive), Ps 48:9 declares that God יכוננה will establish it (i.e., Zion) forever.

will stream to Zion to seek Yahweh's instruction. Yahweh will judge between the peoples and decide concerning the nations. Invading armies will no longer threaten Zion, as is now the case. The nations will no longer scheme to overthrow her, because Yahweh will cause the nations to desire peace. Thus, Israel will be secure, without fear of enemy attack. Apparently the purpose of this pericope is to encourage Israel to trust completely in Yahweh even when the city of Jerusalem and the temple have been reduced to insignificance and even when it is obvious that the existing leadership has utterly failed.[71]

Pericope II (4:6–8) announces that the former dominion, i.e., the kingdom in its golden age under David (and Solomon), will be restored, and specifically identifies it with "the kingdom of the daughter of *Jerusalem*." Inseparable from this is the declaration that responsible divine leadership will be re-established in Jerusalem. "Yahweh will reign over them *in mount Zion* from henceforth even forever." The restoration of Zion to her former status is also a crucial interest in pericope III (4:9–10). When Zion goes out into the field and is carried into Babylon, she does not cease to be Zion! The writer indicates this by retaining the second person singular in speaking of Zion throughout this pericope. In Babylon, Zion will be rescued, and Yahweh will redeem her from the hand of her enemies, i.e., he will reclaim her as his covenant people. The proclamation of Zion's restoration to her previous status of favor with Yahweh is apparent once again in pericope IV (4:11–13). The prophet announces that Yahweh's thoughts and counsel will be wholly in Zion's behalf, and in turn that Zion will place the spoils of war under the ban in order to make clear to all that it is Yahweh alone, and not her own human strength or material power, that is responsible for such a victory. Pericope V (4:14—5:5) also declares Zion's future restoration, and (as in pericope II) couples this with the re-establishment of responsible leadership in Israel. Assuming that the MT of 4:14 offers the correct reading, "daughter of troops" undoubtedly refers to Zion, and is probably an intentional variation on the phrase "daughter of Zion" (4:8, 10, 13) or "daughter of Jerusalem" (4:8). The coming ruler will be a new David, whose government will be executed in the strength of Yahweh and in the majesty of the name of Yahweh. The pronominal suffixes -*ĕka* and –*êkā* in pericope VII (5:9–14) also seem to refer to Jerusalem. If so, this

---

71. "The future contemplated will be the work of God." Marsh, *Amos and Micah*, 106–7. Similarly also Beck, *Erklärung*, 144; Wolfe, "The Book of Micah," 923–24; Ungern-Sternberg, *Der Rechtsstreit Gottes*, 76, 78f.; and Gailey, "Micah . . . Malachi," 24.

pericope also announces the restoration of a theocratic government to Zion, as the abolition of the objects of Israel's trust implies.

Analysis of the Oracles in Micah 4–5

Oracles with Long Doom-Short Hope Pattern	Oracles with Short Doom-Long Hope Pattern	Oracles of Hope including References to Doom Pattern
3rd Oracle: 4:9–10a—Doom 4:10b—Hope	1st Oracle: 3:(9)–12—Doom 4:1–5—Hope	2nd Oracle: 4:6–8
7th Oracle: 5:9–13—Doom 5:14—Hope	4th Oracle: 4:11—Doom 4:12–13—Hope	6th Oracle: 5:6–8
	5th Oracle: 4:14—Doom 5:1–5—Hope	

Thus an examination of the seven pericopes in chs. 4–5 leads to the following conclusions. (1) All of the pericopes in these chapters seem to reflect a similar type of historical background. Israel is in desperate, seemingly hopeless, circumstances. She is threatened by a far superior enemy and/or feels that she has lost her former status as Yahweh's people. 3:9—4:5 and 5:6–8 deal more with the problem of Israel's loss of her former Status, and 4:6–8, 9–10, 11–13; 4:14—5:5; and 5:9–14 deal more with the problem of a threatening foe, although there is much interrelationship between these two concepts in most of the pericopes involved. (2) Each pericope in chs. 4–5 contains a contrast between the present hopeless situation and the glorious future, so that while 3:9–12 is a vital part of ch. 3, it is also inseparable from 4:1–5. (3) This contrast between the present and the future is set forth in three ways in the seven pericopes of Mic 4–5: (a) a long section of doom followed by a short section of hope, (b) a short section of doom followed by a long section of hope, and (c) a section of hope which includes references to the present hopeless situation. Accordingly, Marti seems to be correct when he writes: "Von einem Gedankengang ken im zweiten Toile (Mic 4–5) nicht die Rede sein, sondern nur von eine Grundgedanken, der in den verschiedensten Variationen durchgeführt wird."[72]

---

72. Marti, *Das Dodekapropheton*, 258–59. However, the present writer's analysis of

But there is still another indication that an attempt was made to combine these oracles into a well-arranged whole, i.e., the fact that each succeeding oracle is linked together with the oracle which precedes it by a catchword or a catch phrase. (a) In 4:6–8, "in that day" in v. 6 is connected with "in latter days" in v. 1;[73] "mount Zion" in v. 7 is related to "mountain of Yahweh's house" in 4:1 and "mountain of Yahweh," which is equated with "Zion" in v. 2; and "from henceforth even for ever" in v. 7 joins onto "for ever and ever" in v. 5. (b) In 4:9–10, עתה in v. 9 is similar in sound to ואתה in v. 8; and "daughter of Zion" in v. 10 is identical with the same phrase in v. 8. (c) In 4:11–13, ועתה in v. 11 is connected with the same word in v. 9; "Zion" in v. 11 and "daughter of Zion" in v. 13 are linked with "daughter of Zion" in v. 10; and "counsel" in v. 12 may be an intentional connective with "counsellor" in v. 9. (d) In 4:14—5:5, עתה in 4:14 and 5:3 joins onto the same word in 4:11; ואתה in 5:1 has a similar sound;[74] and "daughter of troops" in 4:14 seems to be a variation on "daughter of Zion" in 4:13. (e) In 5:6–8, והיה in vv. 6 and 7 is connected with the same word in v. 4;[75] "remnant of Jacob" in vv. 6 and 7 is linked with "residue of his brethren" in 5:2; "tread down" ורמס and "deliver" in v. 7 join onto "tread" ידרך in vv. 4–5 and "deliver" in v. 5. (f) In 5:9–14, הכרתי in vv. 9–12 is connected with יכרתי in 5:8; and והיה in 5:9 joins onto the same word in vv. 6–7.[76]

The seven originally independent pericopes in Mic 4–5 were for the most part (if not entirely) undoubtedly combined secondarily,[77] and

---

these chapters has few affinities with Marti's analysis.

73. So also Kuenen, "De Koning uit Beth-Ephrath," 60; Beck, *Erklärung*, 153; Hylmö, *Kompositionen*, 150; Nowack, *Die Kleinen Propheten*, 219; Ridderbos, *De Kleine Profeten*, 85; and Wolfe, "The Book of Micah," 934.

74. Elhorst, *De Prophetie van Micha*, 80; Beck, *Erklärung*, 156–57; Marti, *Das Dodekapropheton*, 284; Hylmö, *Kompositionen*, 177; Nowack, *Die Kleinen Propheten*, 220; Lindblom, *Micha*, 83f.; Deden, *De Kleine Profeten*, 219; Ungern-Sternberg, *Der Rechtsstreit Gottes*, 91, 96; Beyerlin, *Die Kulttraditionen Israels*, 18; Deissler, *Les Petits Prophètes*, 328; and Renaud, *Structure*, 32, 63, have already called attention to wĕʿattā as a catchword in 4:9ff.

75. Prof. Hyatt has suggested to me that the recurrence of והיה in these verses may be gratuitous, but in light of the fact that the other pericopes in chs. 4–5 have apparently been connected by catchwords, it seems to me likely that this is the case here.

76. Kraeling, *Commentary*, 220 argues that 5:4–5, 6–8 and 5:9–14 are three parallel passages of "supplementary predictions" each beginning with "and shall be."

77. "Too often it is obvious that the 'connection' established by the catch-words is merely the relatively outward means of association that the collecting tradition has em-

it is quite possible, as Mowinckel has pointed out,[78] that the original meaning of a prophetic oracle and its transmitted meaning may differ. However, it is equally possible that the collector or redactor of this section or of the final form of a prophetic work may have been strongly influenced by the materials (oral or written) which he inherited and included in his collection. Indeed, it seems to me that this is precisely what happened in the case of Mic 5:9-14. The redactor included this oracle in his work because he thought it spoke to the needs of the Jewish community of his day, which seemed to him to be similar to the circumstances which existed when the oracle was originally uttered. By way of summary, the evidence presented above strongly suggests that Mic 4–5 are not to be approached sequentially or chiastically, but as a group of parallel pericopes. "De onderscheidene pericopen van H. IV en V zieh niet met elkander laten rijmen, veelmin ordelijk op elkaar volgen."[79]

Now, let us turn to the problem of the proper major line of division between chs. 5 and 6. Within the past thirty years, Lippl,[80] Nötscher,[81] Fohrer,[82] Meyer,[83] Pákozdy,[84] Eissfeldt[85] and Scharbert[86] have advocated making this division between Mic 5:8 and 5:9. These scholars argue that 5:9-14 is an oracle of woe and thus belongs with the oracles of woe in 6:1—7:6 rather than with the oracles of weal in 4:1—5:8. Of course, this entire pericope is composed of threats; but in the present writer's opinion, there are several strong arguments against its belonging to chs. 6–7 as the first pericope in the last major division of the book, and for its belonging to chs. 3–5 as the last pericope of the second major division. (a) A lawsuit such as that found in 6:1ff. is a common beginning of a large section in a prophetic book.[87] (b) The structure of 5:9-14 is es-

---

ployed in order to bind independent units together in a bundle." Mowinckel, *Prophecy and Tradition*, 54.

78. Mowinckel, *Prophecy and Tradition*, 63.
79. Kuenen, *Historisch-Critisch Onderzoek*, 375.
80. Lippl, *Die Zwölf Kleinen Propheten*, 182.
81. Nötscher, *Zwölfprophetenbuch*, 90.
82. Fohrer, "Micha," 1327f.
83. Meyer, "Michabuch," 930.
84. Pákozdy, "Michabuch," 1211.
85. Eissfeldt, *The Old Testament*, 409.
86. Scharbert, *Die Propheten Israels*, 312.
87. Cf., e.g., Mic 1:2ff.; Isa 1:2ff.

sentially the same as that found in the other pericopes in chs. 4–5, and particularly as that found in 4:9–10. In both passages, Israel is stripped of all possible military power before her approaching enemies (4:9–10a and 5:9–13), and yet Yahweh intervenes and gives her the victory (4:10b and 5:14). "Al wat Jahwe mishaagt wordt uit haar midden weggedaan en de wraak aan hare tegenstanders voltrokken."[88] (c) 5:9–14 may be interpreted as an oracle of weal in spite of the fact that it contains nothing but threats.[89] Indeed, it is "en forjettelse i form av et truselsord."[90]

---

88. Kuenen, *Historisch-Critisch Onderzoek*, 371.

89. Thus, Kosters, "De Samenstelling," correctly points out: "De eerste vraag die beantwoord moet worden is deze: hebben wij hier belofte of bedreiging?"

90. Mowinckel, *Det Gamle Testamente*, 687.

5

Micah 4:14—5:5—A Unit

Frequently a scholar's interpretation of a prophetic pericope is intimately connected with his understanding of the extent of that pericope (its beginning, end, and progress of thought), of its function in the prophetic complex where it has been placed (i.e., its relationship to the pericopes surrounding it), and of the essential idea or ideas which it expresses. The celebrated "Bethlehem pericope" is no exception. Critics are by no means agreed as to where this pericope begins or where it ends; 4:14—5:5 is variously divided into two, three, or even four parts. The purpose of this paper is to offer some suggestions toward a solution of the problems just mentioned as they pertain to this pericope.

A number of exegetes have felt compelled to separate 4:14 from 5:1ff.[1] 4:14 is an oracle of doom in which the king of Israel (= Judah) is humiliated by an enemy, whereas 5:1–5 is an oracle of hope in which the prophet announces that the coming ruler of Israel will be victorious over his adversaries.[2] Furthermore, either 4:14 or 5:1ff. fits better at a place other than its present position in the book. J. M. P. Smith,[3] Bruno,[4] Mowinckel,[5] and Lindblom[6] think that inadvertently or purposely 4:14 was separated from its original position after 4:9 or 4:10a. This rearrangement makes the sequence of thought smooth, and the "original" text of 4:14 is in the Qinah measure, as is 4:9–10. However, Beyerlin

---

1. The versification of the MT is used throughout the article.
2. Cf., e.g., Lindblom, *Micha*, 156; and recently, Renaud, *Structure*, 16.
3. J. M. P. Smith, *Critical and Exegetical Commentary*, 100.
4. Bruno, *Micha*, 84.
5. Mowinckel, "Mikaboken," 34.
6. Lindblom, *Micha*, 84.

considers 4:14 to be the "original" continuation of 1:8-16, because the historical background, meter, thought, and style of the two passages are the same, and because the train of thought from 1:16 to 4:14 is logical.[7] And Halévy transfers 4:14 to a position between 6:12 and 6:13 because it breaks the logical sequence between 4:14 and 5:1 and restores the original line of thought in 6:12ff.[8] Elhorst conjectures that what is now the book of Micah was originally on four disconnected leaves. Chapters 4-5 were written in double columns, which may be reconstructed in this way.

Column II	Column I
B. 5:1-7	A. 4:1-4
	4:6-8
D. 5:8-14	C. 4:9-14

He maintains that the scribe who arranged the material in this way intended that pericope A in Col. I be read first, then pericope B in Col. II, etc. But unfortunately, copyists wrongly read the entire right column first in sequence, then the entire left column.[9] So 5:1-7 must be restored to its original place after 4:8, thus restoring the original sequence of thought: the kingdom of Jerusalem will be established (4:1-4, 6-8) and the house of David will be restored (5:1-7).[10] Horton[11] and Nowack[12] also regard 5:1ff. as the original continuation of 4:8, but consider 4:9-14 to be a later insertion designed to contrast the present (4:9-14) with the future (4:8 and 5:1ff.). Giesebrecht argues that 5:1ff. originally followed 3:12

---

7. Beyerlin, *Die Kulttraditionen Israels*, 18-19. Beyerlin's six arguments to support this are: (1) 1:16 refers to an old mourning custom of shaving the head bald, and 4:14 refers to an old mourning custom of making a cut. These two customs are mentioned together in Lev 19:27-28; 21:5; Deut 14:1. (2) Both 1:8-16 and 4:14 are in the Qinah meter. (3) Both passages contain word plays. (4) 1:16 and 4:14 both use feminine forms. (5) Both passages address Jerusalem, and the train of thought from 1:16 to 4:14 is logical. (6) The historical background of both passages is Sennacherib's invasion of Jerusalem in 701 B.C.E.

8. Halévy, "Le Livre de Michée," 300.

9. Elhorst, *De Prophétie van Micha*, 66-96, especially 72-73, 76-77, 86-87, 93.

10. Ibid., 81. Kosters, "De Samenstelling," 252, agrees with Elhorst that 5:1 was the original continuation of 4:8, but denies that 5:2-7 should be moved.

11. Horton, *The Minor Prophets*, 251.

12. Nowack, *Die Kleinen Propheten*, 223.

because this provides a contrast between proud Jerusalem (chs. 1–3) and humble Bethlehem (5:1ff.).[13]

Without attempting to deal with all the details involved in these suggested transmissions, it seems to me that there are several considerations which make such a solution to the difficult passages in Mic 4–5 very dubious. First, it assumes that the prophetic material must be read sequentially, and that when this cannot be done it must be rearranged in a "logical" manner. Secondly, it assumes that at various times and for various reasons redactors inserted words, lines, verses, and whole pericopes into original prophetic corpora to neutralize doom oracles with hope oracles in light of later historical developments, to inject their own theology into traditionally respected material, etc. However, a careful analysis of Mic 4–5 and of the suggested rearrangements of material in these chapters has led the present writer to have a much higher respect for the present arrangement as reflecting a coherent purpose. Wildeboer criticized Elhorst's rearrangement of the book of Micah by saying: "Man mag über Elhorst's Hypothese urteilen wie man wolle, das ist sicher, dass uns die überlieferte Schrift in der von ihm angenommenen Anordnung viel grösseren Genuss bereitet."[14] In my opinion, essentially the same thing is true when we compare the present arrangement of the book with any suggested rearrangement yet proposed (with one or two minor exceptions involving individual verses within pericopes). "A modern view of the prophetic books implies not only that these books may have formed combinations of larger or smaller separate collections, but also that every single collection consists of separate episodes and utterances, for the most part connected with each other *according to other principles than those that seem natural to us. Modern men require historical or, at any rate, logical coherence in what is related. The old collectors of the prophetic revelations had a different interest*" (italics mine).[15]

Thus, it is just possible that the redactor or redactors responsible for the present structure of the book of Micah arranged its oracles according to a certain pattern for a specific purpose. Stimulated by the earlier suggestions of Nielsen,[16] Renaud has recently attempted to dem-

---

13. Giesebrecht, "Review of B. Stade's 'Bemerkungen,'" col. 444.
14. Wildeboer, *Die Literatur*, 156.
15. Lindblom, *A Study*, 4.
16. Nielsen, *Oral Tradition*, 79–93, especially 85–86. Ladame, "Les chapitres IV et V," 459–60, had previously pointed out contrasts between 4:1–3 and 5:9–14, and had

onstrate a chiastic structure in Mic 4–5. He finds six pericopes in these chapters, each counterbalancing its correlate: A (4:1–4) and A' (5:8–14); B (4:6–7) and B' (5:6–7); C (4:8–14) and C' (5:1–5).[17] This attempt is a decided improvement over sequential explanations, but raises serious problems of its own. E.g., according to this structure, one pericope begins with a hopeful announcement of future glory, continues with a picture of present distress, and concludes with another announcement of future deliverance and glory (5:8–14). Another pericope follows this same pattern and then concludes with a description of the present hopeless situation (4:8–14)! It seems psychologically unlikely that such arrangements, and especially the latter, represent the original intention of Jewish redactors. Furthermore, the symmetrical structure of 5:9ff., in which every verse begins with the *waw conjunctivum* and the first person singular of the imperfect, and where *miqqirbekā* appears several times and the pronominal suffix *-ekā* is repeated in the middle of the line, and *-ekā* at the end of the line, argues strongly against including 5:8 in this pericope. As a matter of fact, 5:8 provides a good ending for the pericope beginning with 5:6.

As an alternative to Renaud's analysis, my own studies have led me to believe that Mic 4–5 consist of seven parallel pericopes, each with a description of the present hopeless situation and an announcement of divine deliverance containing a promise that Yahweh will give Israel victory over her enemies, or restore her to her former status, or both: 3:9 (or 12)—4:5; 4:6–8; 4:9–10; 4:11–13; 4:14—5:5; 5:6–8; and 5:9–14. Each of these passages has a contrast structure, which assumes three forms: (1) a long section of doom followed by a short section of hope, (2) a short section of doom followed by a long section of hope, and (3) a section of hope which includes allusions to the present hopeless situation, 4:14—5:5 belongs to the second group along with 3:9 (or 12)—4:5 and 4:11–13.[18]

In light of this analysis, 4:14 must not be separated from 5:1ff. The manner in which the elements in 4:14 are counterbalanced in 5:1ff. indicates that the contrasts in this pericope are intentional, and that at least

---

concluded that the latter was the original continuation of the former.

17. Renaud, *Structure*, 11ff. Cf. in particular the chart on p. 26.

18. In "The Structure of Micah 3–5," 191–214, I have given a rather extensive defense of this analysis, with a more detailed treatment of Renaud's view. For an earlier criticism of Renaud's position, cf. my "Review of B. Renaud's 'Structure,'" 400–403.

it is possible that those responsible for the final form of this prophetic book intended for them to be taken together. There are three striking contrasts between the doom and hope sections of this pericope. First, there is a contrast between the present "judge of Israel" who is smitten on the cheek with a rod (4:14) and the coming "ruler of Israel" who will deliver Israel from her enemies (5:1, 4–5). The "judge of Israel" is apparently the ruling king,[19] who is unable to defend Jerusalem successfully against enemy besiegers. It seems from the contrast between 4:14 and 5:1 that the prophet (and/or redactor) interpreted this failure to be due to his confidence in military power rather than in Yahweh. This is especially emphasized in the statement made concerning the coming ruler, ממך לי יצא, "from you (one) will come forth to me" (5:1), which (in light of 1 Sam 11:3, 10; 1 Kgs 20:31, 33; 2 Kgs 18:31 = Isa 36:16; and 2 Kgs 24:12) probably means that in contrast to the present ruler, the coming ruler will acknowledge his complete subjection to Yahweh, who is to be regarded as the real king of Israel who rules through him.[20]

It seems to me that this contrast, as well as the general tenor of the pericope, is obscured by emending תתגדדו בת גדוד to יתגדד תתגודד, "cut yourselves severely" (or something similar), and by interpreting this as a mourning rite.[21] Throughout the pericope military terminology is used. Even in the rest of 4:14, line b refers to the siege of the city, and line c to the humiliation of the reigning king by the enemy-military terminology. In line a, the Syriac *mkyl tpwyn blys' brt lys' 'šyn'*, "Now you shall go out in bands, O daughter of strong bands," basically agrees with the MT, and the Targum כען תסתעין במשרין קרתא דאשדין, "Now, you shall join in troops in the camps, O city of bloodsheds (?) (pourings out)," and

---

19. מלכים is parallel to שפטי ארץ in Ps 2:10. The king of Moab is called *šōpēṭ* in Amos 2:3. The king is often said to "judge" the people, as e.g., in 2 Sam 15:2, 6; 2 Kgs 15:5; Isa 16:5, etc. Cf. also 2 Sam 12:1ff and 14:2ff. It is highly probable that שפט was chosen in Mic 4:14 to form a wordplay with שבט, "rod." Cf., i.a., Beck, *Erklärung*, 161; Marti, *Das Dodekapropheton*, 286; Cheyne, *Micah*, 42; and recently Beyerlin, *Die Kulttraditionen Israels*, 19; Brandenburg, *Die Kleinen Propheten*, 96; and Weiser, *Das Buch der zwölf Kleinen Propheten*, 272 n. 1.

20. For a detailed study, cf. my dissertation, "The Structure, Setting, and Interrelationships," 207–13.

21. Thus Beck, *Erklärung*, 161; Wellhausen, *Die Kleinen Propheten*, 145; Marti, *Das Dodekapropheton*, 286; Duhm, "Anmerkungen," 88; Mowinckel, "Mikaboken," 16, 34; *Det Gamle Testamente*, 685; Lindblom, *A Study*, 84; Ungern-Sternberg, *Der Rechtsstreit Gottes*, 106; and Deissler, *Les Petits Prophètes*, 331; et al. For a brief analysis with references to passages involved, cf. BDB, 151.

the Vulgate *Nunc vastaberis filia latronis*, "Now you will be laid waste, O daughter of a thief," while varying in details from the MT, nevertheless retain the military terminology. Therefore, it seems best to respect the MT of line a and to translate:

> "Now gather together in troops, O daughter of troops,
> They[22] have besieged us,
> With the rod they will strike the judge of Israel upon the cheek."

The expression "daughter of troops" is apparently parallel to "daughter of Zion" in 4:8, 10, 13; and to "daughter of Jerusalem" in 4:8. In 4:14, this variant expression "daughter of troops" is possibly to be taken sarcastically as a mocking call to Zion to defend herself from her enemies by her own strength, thus representing the typical prophetic aversion to trust in military power rather than in Yahweh.

Secondly, there is a contrast between the great city of Jerusalem in 4:14 and the "little town of Bethlehem" in 5:1.[23] Now Bruno,[24] i.a., has suggested that there is an intended contrast between Jerusalem, the capital which the country man Micah naturally despises, and Bethlehem (emending the text to "Beth-Ophrah"), a small town which a man of the country would favor. However, in light of the fact that the prophet here is drawing heavily on the Davidic tradition, this view is hardly tenable. The fact that David was born at Bethlehem, and that Bethlehem played a significant role in the early part of his life, was by no means inconsistent with his making Jerusalem his capital. Did Micah (or the redactor of the "final form" of the book of Micah) intend to cast disparagement on David's choice of Jerusalem in his carrying the ark to Jerusalem, on Solomon's building the temple in Jerusalem, etc., when he announced the destruction of the Holy City? (3:12). In my opinion—No! On the contrary Micah condemns the city of his day because its rulers, the avowed descendants of David, were not ruling as true sons of David. To him there is no way to restore the type of rule which David symbolized without completely removing the present authorities. After this was done, he envisioned the coming of a new ruler like David who would

---

22. שמו is to be preferred above the שם of the MT, because this forms a parallel with יכו in line c. This emendation is supported by the Vulgate *posuerunt* and the Syriac *qmw*.

23. Cf. Marty, *Les Prophètes*, 776; George, *La Sainte Bible*, 35; Ungern-Sternberg, *Der Rechtsstreit Gottes*, 112; and Harrelson, "Non-Royal Motifs," 155.

24. Bruno, *Micha*, 209.

restore the kind of rule with which Israel had been blessed in the days of David (4:14—5:5).

Finally, there is a contrast between the reliance of the present king on military power and his subsequent defeat, and the reliance of the coming ruler on Yahweh and his subsequent success (cf. especially 5:3–5).

These considerations indicate that 4:14 is a good introduction to 5:1ff.,[25] and thus should not be separated from it. The contrast between Jerusalem and Bethlehem which Giesebrecht "achieves" by moving 5:1ff. immediately after 3:12 already exists in 4:14 and 5:1ff. Even Lindblom, who transfers 4:14 right after 4:9 or 4:10a, admits that 4:14 is "zwar . . . eine passende Einleitung zum Gedicht von neuen Herrscher in Kap. 5!"[26] And Mowinckel reverses his earlier opinion that 4:14 originally followed 4:9 with the view that the collector of chs. 4–5 wrote 5:1, deliberately modeling it after 4:9 to provide the gloomy background for 5:1ff.[27] There is really no valid reason for separating 4:14 from that which follows, and the diverse opinions of scholars as to where either 4:14 or 5:1ff. "originally" belonged in the book argues strongly against solving the problem in this way.

A second verse which many scholars have considered to disrupt this pericope is 5:2. They argue that it represents a type of "messianic" understanding of earlier prophetic oracles (in this case Isa 7:14) characteristic of post-exilic redactors or prophets. Furthermore, v. 3 is the natural continuation of v. 1.[28] A few critics have maintained that v. 2,

---

25. With regard to 4:14, Marty, *Les Prophètes*, 776 writes: "Nous préférons y reconnaître un tableau de l'abaissement d'Israël dans le temps présent, *intentionnellement* opposé à la peinture lumineuse qui va suivre (5,2–4 [= Heb. 5,1–3]) du regne du Messie de l'avenir" (italics mine). In an attempt to understand 4:14ff. sequentially, Goeje, "Ter verklaring," 283, and Bruno, *Micha*, 105, have identified the ruler in 4:14 with the ruler in 5:1. However, the more common interpretation that 4:14 and 5:1 form a contrast is undoubtedly correct. Cf. i.a., Oort, "Het Beth-Efraat," 504; Stave, *Israels Profeter*, 35, 54; Ridderbos, *De Kleine Profeten*, 91; Beyerlin, *Die Kulttraditionen Israels*, 18, 21; and Scharbert, *Die Propheten Israels*, 332–33.

26. Lindblom, *A Study*, 84.

27. *Det Gamle Testamente*, 669, 683, 685, where he also calls attention to the contrast between 4:14 and 5:1.

28. Among those who make either one or both of these arguments, we mention only Kosters, "De Samenstelling," 264; Ladame, "Les chapitres IV et V," 457; Welch, "Micah 5:1–3," 235; Marti, *Das Dodekapropheton*, 287; Duhm, "Anmerkungen," 89; J. M. P. Smith, *Critical and Exegetical Commentary*, 102, 104; Steuernagel, *Lehrbuch*, 627; Hylmö, *Kompositionen*, 199–200, 202–3; Lindblom, *A Study*, 95; Pfeiffer, *Introduction*,

unlike its poetic surroundings, is in prose. They also point out that there is a change of subject from the first person singular in v. 1 to the third person singular in v. 2, and that "them" in v. 2 has no antecedent.[29]

The question of the origin of v. 2 is irrelevant to the concern of the present paper, because whether v. 2 originated at the same time as its surrounding context or not, it is at least theoretically possible that the redactor who was responsible for the "final form" of the book of Micah may have combined prophetic oracles or parts of prophetic oracles which originated at different times and under different circumstances into what he considered to be a coherent whole. As a matter of fact, v. 2 seems to fit into its present context very well. The present situation looks very dark (4:14). But the prophet announces that a new ruler will arise in Israel (5:1). "Therefore,"[30] the present dismal situation is temporary, i.e., it will continue "only" until the "birth" (arrival or enthronement) of the coming ruler (v. 2), a ruler who (unlike the present monarch) will depend wholly on Yahweh for strength and victory (v. 3). In light of this interpretation, I concur with Mowinckel,[31] Ridderbos,[32] and Deden[33] in inserting the word "only" into the text. I would translate v. 2 in this way:

> "Therefore he will deliver them up *only* until the time
>   that the woman in birth-pains has brought forth,
> And *then* the remnant of his brothers will return to the children of Israel."

The change of subjects is a common occurrence in prophetic literature and does not justify separating adjoining verses. In light of our limited understanding of, and general lack of agreement with regard to, Hebrew poetry,[34] we can hardly justify severing v. 2 from its surrounding context

---

594 n. 21; Robinson, *Die zwölf Kleinen Propheten*, 143; and Deissler, *Les Petits Prophètes*, 334–35.

29. Cf., i.a., Welch, "Micah 5:1-3," 235; Marti, *Das Dodekapropheton*, 287; Riessler, *Die Kleinen Propheten*, 119; J. M. P. Smith, *Critical and Exegetical Commentary*, 102, 104; and Steuernagel, *Lehrbuch*, 627.

30. Lindblom, *A Study*, 95 n. 1, maintains that "therefore" refers to that which follows, not to that which precedes. Ladame, "Les chapitres IV et V," 457, is offended by "therefore" in its present position because it is difficult to see how the prophet could announce the coming of an ideal ruler (v. 1) as the background to God's "giving up" his people.

31. Mowinckel, *Det Gamle Testamente*, 686.

32. Ridderbos, *De Kleine Profeten*, 89.

33. Deden, *De Kleine Profeten*, 220.

34. Cf. Gottwald, "Poetry, Hebrew," 834–35.

on this basis. As far as the antecedent of "them" is concerned, it seems to me that there are two possibilities in v. 1. The "thousands of Judah" could be the antecedent. Or it is conceivable that "them" represents the plural correspondent to the comprehensive word "Israel" in v. 1. Thus v. 2 may well be regarded as a logical part of the pericope which begins at 4:14.

The way in which 5:4–5 is to be analyzed in relationship to its surrounding context is a most perplexing problem. At least four solutions have been suggested: 5:4–5 is a self-contained unit; 5:4a belongs to the preceding pericope and 5:4b–5 is a complete unit; 5:5c–e is the original continuation of the preceding pericope and 5:4–5b is a separate piece; 5:4a, 5c–e is the original conclusion of the preceding pericope and 5:4b–5b is a self-contained unit. Here we discuss only the first and last solutions, as they claim a large number of advocates and are supported by strong arguments.

Critics have given six reasons for regarding 5:4–5 as separate from the preceding passage. First, in 5:1–3 Yahweh Himself appoints the coming ruler and we are told what he will do, but in 5:4–5 the people appoint their own rulers and we are told what they will do.[35] However, the Old Testament reflects a concept of the intimate relationship between Yahweh and the king, who is Yahweh's representative to the people and in turn the people's representative to Yahweh—a concept which has its foundation in the idea of "corporate personality."[36] Thus, an interplay between the activities of Yahweh, the king, and the people indicates no more than a Jewish author's freedom to oscillate between these subjects which in his mind are inseparable, especially in a context where they are set at variance with a common foe. In fact, we encounter just this sort of oscillation in 4:14. Line b says: "They have besieged *us*," but line c (which apparently intends to further describe the same situation) says: "With the rod they will strike *the Judge of Israel* (i.e., the king) upon the cheek."

Secondly, it has been argued that the author of 4:14—5:3 trusts in Yahweh to give Israel victory over her enemies, while the author of 5:4–5

---

35. Cf. i.a., J. M. P. Smith, *Critical and Exegetical Commentary*, 107; Hylmö, *Kompositionen*, 220–21; Nötscher, *Zwölfprophetenbuch*, 100; and Kraeling, *Commentary*, 219.

36. Cf. Johnson, "The Role of the King," 73–75; *Sacral Kingship*, 2–4. See the stimulating criticism of the Myth and Ritual School by Noth, "God, King, Nation," 20–48. Noth also maintains the concept of an intimate relationship between Yahweh, the king, and the people, but regards the kingship as an innovation into the earlier *direct* relationship between Yahweh and the people. Cf. especially pp. 38ff.

trusts in Israel's superior military strength.[37] However, these two concepts are not necessarily incompatible in Jewish thought. E.g., the author of Exod 18 describes Israel's victory over Amalek in this way: *"And Joshua mowed down Amalek and his people with the edge of the sword"* (v. 13). But the present form of the text cannot be taken to mean that this author credits Joshua and Israel's military strength with the victory. On the contrary, vv. 9–11, 14–16 make it clear that Joshua's success was possible only because Yahweh gave him the victory. Again, the author of 2 Sam 8 describes David's victory over the Syrians in these words: *"David slew twenty-two thousand men of the Syrians"* (v. 5). Yet he does not mean to leave the impression that David and his military power are to receive credit for this success, because in the next verse he writes: "And the Lord gave victory to David wherever he went." In a similar way, the prophet and/or the redactor responsible for the present form of Mic 4–5 may mean that because Yahweh will be with His people (5:1, 3), they will defeat their enemies with the sword (5:5).

Thirdly, it is maintained that the phrase "to the ends of the earth" in 5:3 is a "resonant conclusion" of a pericope. Indeed, it seems strange that the author would announce that the power of the coming ruler will extend to the ends of the earth and then immediately declare that the Assyrians would invade Palestine and enjoy temporary success.[38] But the most natural explanation of ו, "and," at the beginning of v. 4 is that the final redactor intended for vv. 4–5 to be understood as the continuation of that which precedes. It is possible to interpret vv. 4–5 as an elaboration of the way in which the success of the coming ruler promised in 5:1ff. was to be realized. The expression, "And this shall be peace" (v. 4a), is a poor beginning for a pericope, even if it is interpreted as a promise of peaceful conditions to come, which are described in vv. 4b–5,[39] because this announcement itself seems to require some background.

Fourthly, it has been asserted that 5:4–5 does not allude to the new David which is the central theme of 4:14—5:3.[40] But the promise of "peace" (v. 4a) is an element which has a vital place in the Davidic tradi-

---

37. Cf., i.a., Hylmö, *Kompositionen*, 221.

38. Cf. Marti, *Das Dodekapropheton*, 288; J. M. P. Smith, *Critical and Exegetical Commentary*, 107; and recently Kraeling, *Commentary*, 219.

39. See below, 107–8.

40. Cf. Marti, *Das Dodekapropheton*, 288; J. M. P. Smith, *Critical and Exegetical Commentary*, 107; and Nowack, *Die Kleinen Propheten*, 225.

tion (cf. Isa 9:5; 1 Chr 22:9; 1 Kgs 4:24–25). Furthermore, the "shepherd-prince" terminology (v. 4) is also an integral element in this tradition (cf. 2 Sam 5:2; 7:7–8; also 1 Sam 16:1, 11–12; Ps 78:70–72).

Fifthly, since vv. 1–3 announce that *one* ruler will arise to deliver Israel, while vv. 4–5 declare that *seven/eight* rulers will deliver the people, it is often maintained that these verses cannot be parts of the same pericope.[41] And yet, someone felt no aversion to placing these passages side by side. Thus, it is theoretically possible that they belong together. Furthermore, the interpretation of the "seven shepherds and eight princes of men" in v. 4 is too ambiguous for us to be able to affirm unequivocally that the *one* ruler of vv. 1–3 is *incompatible* with the several rulers here. The different views may be conveniently grouped under four major categories.

(a) Some scholars think of the coming ruler in v. 1 as a supernatural being, and so interpret this phrase of supernatural beings. Riessler[42] and Sellin (possibly)[43] change *rōʿîm* "shepherds" to *raʿîm*, "wicked ones," and *nĕsîkê*, "princes" to *nĕśîkê*, "tormentors" (of men). They conceive of the Messiah using demonic powers to defeat the enemy. On the basis of texts in Jewish Apocalyptic literature, such as Dan 10:13; 12:1; Ben Sira 17:17; Enoch 89:59; 90:22, etc., a number of scholars argue that these shepherds and princes are angelic beings who execute the Messiah's vengeance on Israel's enemies.[44]

(b) Other critics apply this expression to Israel's allies and usually interpret these allies to be Israel's vassals. Most scholars who take this view do not attempt to identify these allies.[45] However, Peiser[46] reads "princes

---

41. Thus e.g., Stade, "Bemerkungen," 168; Ladame, "Les chapitres IV et V," 458; Marti, *Das Dodekapropheton*, 288; J. M. P. Smith, *Critical and Exegetical Commentary*, 107; Steuernagel, *Lehrbuch*, 627; Hylmö, *Kompositionen*, 220; and recently Gottwald, *A Light to the Nations*, 307.

42. Riessler, *Die Kleinen Propheten*, 120.

43. Sellin, *Das Zwölfprophetenbuch*, 338.

44. Thus Margolis, *Micah*, 90; Schmidt, *Die Schriften*, 151; Mowinckel, "Mikaboken," 18; Mowinckel, *Det Gamle Testamente*, 687; Sellin, *Das Zwölfprophetenbuch*, 338 (possibly); Lippl, *Die Zwölf Kleinen Propheten*, 208; and Weiser, *Das Buch der zwölf Kleinen Propheten*, 275.

45. Thus Elhorst, *De Prophétie van Micha*, 81–82; Halévy, "Le Livre de Michée," 211; Hoonacker, *Les douze petits prophètes*, 391; and Kapelrud, "Eschatology," 401 (possibly).

46. Peiser, "Micha 5," 365.

of Edom" instead of "princes of men," and Cheyne maintains that the seven princes of Jerahmeel are intended. Cheyne writes: "When the king of Asshur invades the land of Israel, the Israelites will instigate subject leaders of Jerahmeel and Edom to carry war into the Asshurite land, and so deliver the holy land from the presence of its once dreaded foe."[47]

(c) The largest number of scholars believe that this expression refers to Israelite rulers. Kleinert,[48] Stave,[49] Wade,[50] and Ridderbos[51] understand the coming ruler of v. 1 to be an earthly messiah, and regard the shepherds and princes to be his subordinates. Haupt and Duhm,[52] taking the numbers literally, contend that these rulers are the Maccabean leaders: Mattathias, his five sons, and the two sons of Simon. Wolfe[53] maintains that the shepherds and princes refer to a coalition of Jewish rulers who were called upon to thwart the advance of Antiochus III (218–198 BCE). Several scholars interpret the expression to mean an indefinite, but adequate, number of leaders—sufficient to defeat the enemy.[54]

In opposition to this view, Barnes and George understand the rulers in vv. 4–5 as inadequate Israelite leaders, whose failure to overthrow the enemy emphasizes even more vividly the necessity of trusting Yahweh alone, who will defeat the adversary through the king that He will choose. Barnes's translation of this passage is ingenious: "And this *man* shall be *our* peace, when the Assyrian shall come into our land, and when he shall tread in our palaces, (and we shall have raised against him *in vain* seven shepherds, and eight princes of men, that they might waste the land of Assyria with the sword, and the land of Nimrod through her open graves,) then he shall deliver us from the Assyrian, even when

---

47. Cheyne, *Critica Biblica*, 160.
48. Kleinert, *The Minor Prophets*, 37.
49. Stave, *Israels Profeter*, 38.
50. Wade, *The Books of the Prophets*, 43.
51. Ridderbos, *De Kleine Profeten*, 95.
52. Haupt, "The Book of Micah," 55; and Duhm, "Anmerkungen," 89; Duhm, *Die Zwölf Propheten*, xxxvi.
53. Wolfe, "The Book of Micah," 933.
54. "A number sufficient for the task." Binns, "Micah," 587. "Whatever the demand for leaders may be it will be met." Thomas, "Micah," 632. Similarly, Driver, *An Introduction*, 329; Ungern-Sternberg, *Der Rechtsstreit Gottes*, 114; Weiser, *Das Buch der zwölf Kleinen Propheten*, 275; Deissler, *Les Petits Prophètes*, 336; Harrelson, *Interpreting*, 369, Robinson, *Die zwölf Kleinen Propheten*, 143, and many others.

he cometh into our land, and when he treadeth within our border."[55] He remarks: "The contrast, I believe, is between fruitless human effort and Divine *fiat* executed without a struggle."[56] Similarly, George maintains that these words "peut rapporter des paroles des contemporains, condamnées par Michée, et mises en regard de l'espérance vraie."[57]

Gailey regards this expression as a reference to a succession of family leaders.[58] Similarly, and more specifically, Kapelrud (possibly)[59] suggests that this may be a way of speaking of the Davidic dynasty.

(d) Now in my opinion, *"seven* shepherds and *eight* princes of men" does not necessarily refer to a *plurality of persons*. Rather, this expression may be an idiomatic way of saying that the leadership will be *sufficient* and *adequate* to any situation that arises. "As three and four (Amos 1:3–11), four and five (Isa 17:6), six and seven (Job 5:19; Prov 6:16), so seven and eight here (also Eccl 11:2) *are not to be regarded mathematically*, but as rhetorical figures, used to express an indefinite number . . . *satis superque,* enough and more" (italics mine).[60] In his essay on "The numerical Sequence X/X +1 in the Old Testament," Roth concluded that when two lines are involved, with one number appearing in the first line and the next succeeding number in the second, the two numbers are parallel, and the second number is the one actually intended. But he also makes it clear that in such constructions (he lists twenty-one in the Old Testament) the context must determine whether the numbers are to be interpreted as definite or indefinite.[61] The small number of biblical and extra-biblical passages which use the 7/8 sequence[62] are of minimal assistance in reaching an unimpeachable verdict as to the interpretation of Mic 5:4. However, it is *possible* to interpret all of them "indefinitely," and Crook has suggested that Col. 1, lines 7–9 in The Legend of King Keret

---

55. Barnes, "A Messianic Prophecy," 385.

56. Ibid., 386.

57. George, *La Sainte Bible,* 36. Cf. also his "Michée (Le Livre de)," cols. 1258, 1259.

58. Gailey, "Micah . . . Malachi," 28.

59. Kapelrud, "Eschatology," 401.

60. Laetsch, *The Minor Prophets,* 274–75.

61. Roth, "The Numerical Sequence," 303–4, 310.

62. Ecclesiastes 11:2; the Legend of King Keret, Col. 1, lines 7–9; Aqhat 1,1, 42–44; and an Aramaic incantation from Nippur. On these texts, cf. Crook, "The Promise," 317; and Roth, "The Numerical Sequence," 305, 307.

must be interpreted in this way.⁶³ Thus if 5:4–5 is to be severed from 5:1–3, one must find a more valid reason than the alleged contradiction between the *one* ruler of vv. 1–3 and the *several* rulers of vv. 4–5.

Finally, it is asserted that 5:4–5 does not belong to 4:14—5:3 because these verses do not provide a logical sequence to or continuation of 4:14—5:3 and thus disrupt the context.⁶⁴ However, in light of what has been suggested above, it seems to me that there is a logical sequence extending from 4:14 through 5:5. 4:14 describes the present disastrous situation. Jerusalem is under siege (possibly Assyrian). The present leadership is inadequate because it depends on its military power rather than on Yahweh. But in 5:1–3 the prophet announces the coming of a "David redivivus" who will trust in Yahweh and let Yahweh rule through him, and thus deliver Israel from her plight. Then in 5:4–5 he summarizes: when Assyria attacks the "new regime" will be quite adequate to the task of successfully repelling and defeating her.

Now let us turn our attention briefly to a view which can be regarded as a modification of the position which we have just discussed, i.e., that 4:14—5:4a, 5c–e is a complete pericope and that 5:4b–5b is a self-contained unit which must have been inserted later. This view is based on some of the same arguments which are advanced to separate 4:14—5:3 from 5:4–5. But its advocates also point out that 5:4b–5b seems to be symmetrical,⁶⁵ that 5:5c–e is the natural continuation of 5:4a,⁶⁶ and that the subject in vv. 4a, 5c–e is singular while the subject in vv. 4b–5b is plural.⁶⁷ Of course, it must be admitted that these observations are true, but does this mean that vv. 4b–5b do not belong to this pericope? It is possible to interpret this section parenthetically. Furthermore, the obvious similarity between 5:4b–c and 5:5d–e both in structure and wording indicates that these two portions of vv. 4–5 must not be separated. Actually these verses seem to exhibit an ABA' structure.

---

63. Crook, "The Promise," 317.
64. Cf. i.e., Hoonacker, "Micheas," 278.
65. Thus Mowinckel, "Mikaboken," 19; Renaud, *Structure*, 20, 27; and Deissler, *Les Petits Prophètes*, 299.
66. Thus Mowinckel, "Mikaboken," 18, 35; George, "Michée (Le Livre de)," col. 1252; Beyerlin, *Die Kulttraditionen Israels*, 79; and Deissler, *Les Petits Prophètes*, 334.
67. Thus Sellin, *Das Zwölfprophetenbuch*, 337.

[A]   v. 4 – And this one will be peace, (1)
       When Assyria comes into our land, (2)
       And when he marches into our country. (3)⁶⁸
[B]   We will raise up against him seven shepherds
       And eight princes of men,
       v. 5 – And they will devastate the land of Assyria with the sword,
       And the land of Nimrod with the spear.⁶⁹
[A'] And he will deliver (us)⁷⁰ from Assyria (1)
       When he comes into our land, (2)
       And when he marches into our territory. (3)

If we adopt this structure, there emerges a previously overlooked interpretation of the difficult phrase והיה זה שלום, a phrase which has been variously interpreted. Bruno emends the text to יהוה שלום, "Yahweh is salvation," because "kaum von einem Menschen, sondern nur von Gott gesagt werden konnte, dass er Heil sei." He thinks that this is an inscription borne on a standard at an altar, which he identifies with "Yahweh-Shalom" in the Jerubbaal story (Judg 6:24).⁷¹ At first, Cheyne emended the text to והיה ביום הזה, "and it shall happen on that day," and argued that "peace" was an intrusion into the text.⁷² Later, he advocated an emendation to זה ישמעאל, "that is, Ishmael," as a gloss on Asshur.⁷³ Hylmö deletes *zeh šālôm* as a gloss on *wĕyāšābû* in 5:3.⁷⁴ Marty regards

---

68. The MT as it now stands destroys the parallelism. Several solutions have been offered. Cheyne, *Critica Biblica*, 160, reads בערינו, "in our cities," in line b to correspond to "in our citadels" in line c. In agreement with the LXX, Riessler, *Die Kleinen Propheten*, 120, reads בארצכם, "in your land," in line b, and באמדתכם, "in your district, region," in line c. Horton, *The Minor Prophets*, 253; Schmidt, *Die Schriften*, 149–50; and T. H. Robinson, *Die zwölf Kleinen Propheten*, 142, read באדמתינו, "in our fields," in line c. Taylor, *The Massoretic Text*, 119, retains the MT on the principle of *lectio difficilior*. I follow a large number of scholars in reading באדמתנו in order to preserve the parallelism with the previous line, in harmony with the LXX text adopted by Ziegler. But see Rahlfs's text.

69. The present MT destroys the parallelism with line a. In order to preserve the parallelism with the previous line, in harmony with Aquila, the Ethiopic Version, Ibn Ezra, and Ḳimḥi, and in part with the Vulgate and Quinta, the present writer follows the large majority of critics in conjecturing an original *bappĕtîḥāh* or (less probably) *biptîḥāh* here.

70. It is not necessary to add the pronominal suffix as a number of scholars do in order to get this meaning. The context suggests that "us" be understood.

71. Bruno, *Micha*, 95.

72. Cheyne, "Gleanings," 580.

73. Cheyne, *Critica Biblica*, 160; and *The Two Religions of Israel*, 371.

74. Hylmö, *Kompositionen*, 213.

this phrase as a redactional joint which was inserted to connect two originally independent oracles.[75] Several scholars identify *zeh* with the Arabic *ḏu* and the Akkadian *šu*, and read "lord of peace." They cite Judg 5:5 and Ps 68:9, where זה סיני means "lord of Sinai," and compare "prince of peace" in Isa 9:5b.[76] Instead of *zeh*, Riessler reads *lazzeh* "and peace will be to them," i.e., and they will have peace.[77] Von Ungern-Sternberg argues that "this will be peace" refers to the result of the Messiah's reign described in vv. 1-3.[78] A number of critics regard this phrase as the introduction to a new thought, and contend that it should be followed by a colon to indicate that it refers to what follows—"And this shall be peace:"[79] However, it seems most likely that *zeh* should be interpreted as a demonstrative referring to the coming ruler in vv. 1-3: "And this one (man) shall be peace." The phrase probably means that the Messiah will inaugurate a period of peace and prosperity. This would provide a good contrast to the present conditions described in 4:14.[80] In light of the translation and structure suggested above, since line 2 of A corresponds to line 2 of A' and since line 3 of A corresponds to line 3 of A', it seems most likely that והיה זה שלום in line 1 of A is intended to convey the same meaning as והציל in line 1 of A'. Thus, "to be peace" means to "give peace," i.e., by delivering Israel from her enemies.

On the basis of these considerations, we are convinced that the arguments which are often advanced against the coherence of Mic 4:14—5:5 are not conclusive. As a matter of fact, there are several indications that these verses are to be taken together as a unit. First, this passage seems to display a logical sequence of thought which is generally parallel to that which occurs in the other six pericopes of Mic 4-5.[81]

---

75. Marty, *Les Prophètes*, 777.

76. Allegro, "Uses of the Semitic Demonstrative," 311; Beyerlin, *Die Kulttraditionen Israels*, 35 (following Eerdmans); Hammershaimb, "Einige Hauptgedanken," 31; and Schwantes, "A Critical Study," 133.

77. Riessler, *Die Kleinen Propheten*, 120.

78. Ungern-Sternberg, *Der Rechtsstreit Gottes*, 111.

79. Halévy, "Le Livre de Michée," 211; Marti, *Das Dodekapropheton*, 288; Hoonacker, *Les douze petits prophètes*, 391; Duhm, "Anmerkungen," 89; J. M. P. Smith, *Critical and Exegetical Commentary*, 108; Deden, *De Kleine Profeten*, 221; Thomas, "Micah," 632, et al.

80. Cf. i.a., Kleinert, *The Minor Prophets*, 37; Elhorst, *De Prophétie van Micha*, 166; Mowinckel, *Det Gamle Testamente*, 687; Ridderbos, *De Kleine Profeten*, 94; and Deissler, *Les Petits Prophètes*, 334.

81. See above, 95-96, and 106.

Secondly, the historical background of this pericope seems to be an Assyrian invasion of Judah throughout, 4:14 probably refers to Sennacherib's invasion of Jerusalem in 701 BCE.[82] 5:4-5 actually name "Assyria" as the enemy. It is true that some critics argue that "Assyria" is not a geographic designation because the passage is "Messianic." Therefore, Assyria is simply an all-embracing term including all the enemies of Yahweh and His people,[83] or a term for Syria, i.e., the Seleucid dynasty about 200 BCE.[84] However, in light of 4:14, there is no reason to doubt that an actual siege of Jerusalem provided the original setting for this pericope.[85] Also, a number of leading Old Testament scholars have recently shown that it is most reasonable to believe that Mic 7:7(8)-20 is Mican and that "Assyria" in 7:12 actually means the geographical land of Assyria.[86] The coming ruler of 5:1 probably refers to a king who (unlike

---

82. Thus Lindblom, *A Study*, 86-88; Lippl, *Die Zwölf Kleinen Propheten*, 204; George, "Michée (Le Livre de)," cols. 1255, 1257; George, *La Sainte Bible*, 35; Beyerlin, *Die Kulttraditionen Israels*, 19; Weiser, *Das Buch der zwölf Kleinen Propheten*, 272; Scharbert, *Die Propheten Israels*, 312-13, 331, et al.

83. "Da nun hier der Prophet bis in die siegreiche Zukunft des Messias hinaussieht, und zwar bis dahin, wo sein Reich Universalreich sei, lässt sich Assyrien nicht auf seinen historisch begrenzten geographischen Begriff beschränken." Beck, *Erklärung*, 168. "Assur est envisagé ici, sans doute, comme *type* des peuples ennemis d'Israël, exactement comme Is. VIII, 8, 9ss." Hoonacker, *Les douze petits prophètes*, 392. Thus similarly many others. This position finds support in the fact that "Assyria" occurs in Lam 5:6; Ezra 6:22; and Zech 10:11 where it obviously cannot mean the "nation" of Assyria.

84. Thus Kosters, "De Samenstelling," 264; Marti, *Das Dodekapropheton*, 288; Duhm, "Anmerkungen," 89; Haupt, "The Book of Micah," 236; Nowack, *Die Kleinen Propheten*, 225; Wolfe, "The Book of Micah," 933; Marsh, *Amos and Micah*, 116; et al.

85. So also Cheyne, *Micah*, 42, 45; Danell, *Studies in the Name Israel*, 200-201; Crook, "The Promise," 317 (but she dates this pericope in 841 BCE!); Beyerlin, *Die Kulttraditionen Israels*, 78; et al.

86. Eissfeldt, "Ein Psalm aus Nord-Israel," 259-68, writes (265): "Wenn trotz aller in diese Richtung weisenden Kriterien die Herleitung des Psalms Micha, 7, 7-20 aus dem Nordstaat oder seinem Territorium, wie es scheint, bisher niemals erwogen worden ist, so liegt das daran, dass man herkömmlicherweise zu einseitig mit der Erhaltung so gut wie ausschliesslich judaisch-jerusalemischen Gutes gerechnet und in diesem Vorurteil die Gewichtigkeit der für Herleitung mancher Stücke des Alten Testaments aus dem Norden Israels sprechenden Argumente unterschätzt hat. Dabei kann es doch gar nicht anders gewesen sein, als dass die Katastrophen des Nordstaates von 732 und 722 v. Chr ähnliche Dichtungen hervorgebracht haben wie die auf Jerusalems Katastrophe von 586 v. Chr verfassten Klagelieder innerhalb und ausserhalb des Psalters." Similarly, Reicke, "Liturgie Traditions," 349-67, argues (354): "the names of Carmel, Bashan, and Gilead in v. 14 give the prophecy a northern perspective, and for good reasons it has been placed in the Northern kingdom," and again (363): "the idea of rebuilding the walls

the present ruler of Israel) would trust in Yahweh alone, and thus carry out faithfully his role in a theocratic government. Therefore, "Assyria" in 5:4–5 probably refers to the geographical land of Assyria or to Assyria as a nation.[87]

Thirdly, there is an emphasis on the Davidic tradition throughout this pericope. The present ruler is like Saul, and this Israel is destined for a defeat at the hand of her enemies (4:14). The promised ruler will come from Bethlehem in the province of Ephrathah like David (cf. Ruth 4:11–12, 17–22; 1 Sam 17:12). It will be evident that his rise to power is of divine origin, because he will come from a "little," insignificant village-hardly suitable as the birthplace for a king (5:1). Like David, this ruler will govern Israel in complete subjection to the will of Yahweh (5:1), and in a manner comparable to the skilful way in which a shepherd controls his flock (5:3). The use of pastoral terminology is characteristic of the Davidic tradition in speaking of the relationship between king and people, as is the "shepherd-prince" sequence in 5:4. The tribes of Israel recall that Yahweh had said to David: "You shall be *shepherd* of my people Israel, and you shall be prince over Israel" (2 Sam 5:2 = 1 Chr 11:2). Yahweh's word to David through Nathan the prophet included these words: "In all places where I have moved with all the people of Israel, did I speak a word with any of the judges[88] of Israel, whom I commanded to *shepherd* my people Israel, saying, 'Why have you not built me a house of cedar?' . . . I took you (i.e., David) from the pasture, from *following the sheep,* that you should be *prince* over my people Israel" (2 Sam 7:7–8). When Yahweh first called David, he was tending (*rō'eh*) his father's sheep (1 Sam 16:11). The Psalmist wrote:

He (Yahweh) chose David also his servant,

---

cannot be used as an argument for dating the Mican text in or after the Judean exile. It is geographically outside the Judean perspectives of Ezekiel and Nehemiah, and does not mention Babylon and Jerusalem, but Assyria in v. 12 and Carmel, Bashan and Gilead in v. 14. These names refer to the historical and geographical horizon of the Northern Kingdom." So similarly Kapelrud, "Eschatology," 405; Kapelrud, "Mikas Bok," col. 107; Dus, "Weiteres zum nordisraelitischen Psalm," 14–22; and Scharbert, *Die Propheten Israels,* 313, 324–25. Burkitt, "Micah 6 and 7," 159–61, held a similar view.

87. Cf. Pont, "Micha Studiën, II," 452–53; Stave, *Inledning,* 215; Haller, "Michabuch," col. 368; Mowinckel, "Mikaboken," 18; Mowinckel, *Det Gamle Testamente,* 669, 687; Bentzen, *Introduction,* 148; Weiser, *The Old Testament,* 254; Weiser, *Das Buch der Zwölf Kleinen Propheten,* 231, et al.

88. Following the parallel text in 1 Chr 17:6.

> And took him from the sheepfolds:
> From following the ewes that have their young he brought him,
> To be the *shepherd* of Jacob his people,
> and Israel his inheritance. (Ps 78:70–71)[89]

Thus, neither in the Davidic tradition nor in the final form of the book of Micah is the rule of David considered to jeopardize the rule of Yahweh. Rather, Yahweh rules by David. Glück's very convincing argument that the term "shepherd" was used for leaders in the Old Testament primarily when the concept of ideal leadership was in mind[90] lends strong support to this contention. Finally, the coming leader will rule a kingdom which extends "to the ends of the earth" (5:3),[91] and will lead Israel victoriously against her enemies (5:4–5),[92] as David did.

Finally, the interlocking catchwords and connecting words in 4:14—5:5 indicate that these verses should be taken as a unit. רעים in v. 4b and ורעו in v. 5a are "a clear allusion to ורעה in 3a."[93] עתה occurs at the beginning of 4:14 and in line c of 5:3, and this has the same sound as אתה at the beginning of 5:1. "Therefore" (לכן) in 5:2 is apparently intended to connect 5:1 with vv. 2ff.

All of these considerations seem to point to the same conclusion, that Mic 4:14—5:5 is a unit, essentially parallel in structure and sequence of thought to the other six pericopes in Mic 4–5. It begins with a description of the present hopeless situation, then announces future deliverance by the hand of Yahweh using terminology characteristic of the Davidic tradition. Each part of this pericope is vital to the understanding of the whole.

---

89. See also 1 Sam 16:19; 17:15, 20, 28, 34, 40; 2 Sam 29:17; 1 Chr 17:7–8.

90. Glück, "Nagid-Shepherd," 144–50, especially 149, where he cites 2 Sam 5:2 and 7:8.

91. Cf. 2 Sam 7:9; Pss 2:8; 72:8–11.

92. 2 Sam 5:17–25; 7:9, 11; and ch. 8, especially vv. 6 and 14.

93. Hylmö, *Kompositionen*, 226.

6

Some Suggestions on the Interpretation of Micah 1:2

MICAH 1:2 IS DIFFICULT to interpret because of the context to which it belongs. As the MT now stands, vv. 2-4 seem to be an oracle against all[1] the peoples and the earth, while vv. 5ff. clearly contain an oracle against Israel and Judah. This has led several scholars to conclude that the original beginning of the book of Micah was v. 5b, and that vv. 2-4 were added later by a post-exilic redactor who connected them with vv. 5bff. by inserting v. 5a.[2] However, this view has serious weaknesses. First of all, vv. 2-4 do not form a complete pericope since they announce an impending judgment which is not described. At the same time, vv. 5 (or 5b)-7 describe a judgment which is not announced, and explain the reason for the theophany in vv. 2-4.[3] Furthermore, neither v. 5a nor v. 5b is a good beginning of a pericope.[4] כל זאת in v. 5a refers back to the theophany in vv. 2-4, thereby connecting vv. 5ff. with what precedes.[5] Finally, there is really no valid reason for denying vv. 2-4 to

---

1. The LXX λόγους seems to imply an original *millîm*, and not *dĕbārîm*, contra Deissler, *Les Petits Prophètes*, 302. The MT is vindicated by the other versions, the parallel reading in 1 Kgs 22:28, and the parallelism with ארץ.

2. Thus Stade, "Streiflichter," 163; Marti, *Das Dodekapropheten*, 285, 266-67; Cheyne, *The Two Religions*, 366; Riessler, *Die Kleinen Propheten*, 104; Hölscher, *Die Propheten*, 438; Guthe, *Das Buch Jesaja*, 54; Pfeiffer, *Introduction*, 590, 593; Wolfe, "The Book of Micah," 902; and Marsh, *Amos and Micah*, 87.

3. Cf. Sellin, *Das Zwölfprophetenbuch*, 311; and Weiser, *Das Buch der zwölf Kleinen Propheten*, 236.

4. Cf. J. M. P. Smith, *Critical and Exegetical Commentary*, 34; Bruno, *Micha und der Herrscher*, 13; Wade, *The Books of the Prophets*, 3; and Lindblom, *Micha*, 24.

5. Thus Halévy, "Le Livre de Michée," 100; J. M. P. Smith, *Critical and Exegetical*

the prophet Micah. The argument that the meter or rhythm in vv. 2–4 is different from that of vv. 5–7[6] has by no means enjoyed unanimous agreement among experts. In fact, Duhm, J. M. P. Smith, Hylmö, and Lindblom contend that the meter throughout vv. 2–7 is basically the same, i.e., 3/3.[7] But even if this could not be determined to the satisfaction of all scholars, the present writer is very dubious that a pericope can be denied or attributed to a certain author on the basis of meter. Some critics deny that vv. 2–4 and vv. 5–7 can come from the same person because the speaker in vv. 2–4 is the prophet, whereas the speaker in vv. 5–7 is Yahweh.[8] However, this sort of transition is common in prophetic literature. Lindblom's explanation for it is suggestive.

> In der allgemeineren Schilderung der Theophanie spricht der Prophet selber; wenn aber vor dem Auge seiner Seele sich die Begebenheiten um Samaria her konzentrieren und sich bis zur vollständigen Vernichtung der Stadt steigern, dann, im Augenblick der höchsten Steigerung der Inspiration, verschwindet er selbst als Erzähler und Schilderer, und er wird nur ein Sprachrohr Jahves.[9]

Another objection to the Mican origin of vv. 2–4 is that the pre-exilic prophets delivered oracles concerning specific nations, while general oracles concerning all the nations are encountered first in the post-exilic period.[10] But this is hardly realistic. If Amos (chs. 1–2) could deliver oracles against a number of specific nations, there is no reason why his contemporary Micah could not have delivered an oracle against all the nations without naming them specifically.[11] Other scholars argue that vv. 2–4 cannot be Mican because the ideas expressed here, e.g., the Lord coming forth out of His place, treading on the high places of the

---

Commentary, 36; Hylmö, *Kompositionen*, 29; Lindblom, *Micha*, 23–24; and Sellin, *Das Zwölfprophetenbuch*, 311.

6. Stade, "Streiflichter," 163, and Marti, *Das Dodekapropheten*, 266.

7. Duhm, "Anmerkungen," 82; J. M. P. Smith, *Critical and Exegetical Commentary*, 32; Hylmö, *Kompositionen*, 14; and Lindblom, *Micha*, 29 n. 1.

8. Marti, *Das Dodekapropheten*, 266; Hölscher, *Die Propheten*, 438.

9. Lindblom, *Micha*, 26. Cf. also p. 25.

10. Stade, "Streiflichter," 163; Marti, *Das Dodekapropheten*, 266; Clamer, "Michée," col. 1655.

11. Thus also, i.a., Budde, "Das Rätsel," 86; Stave, *De Minore Profeterna*, 28; Beyerlin, *Die Kulttraditionen Israels*, 41; and Deissler, *Les Petits Prophètes*, 304.

earth, etc., are post-exilic.[12] However, there is no general agreement as to when these ideas originated. E.g., Watts maintains that Amos 4:13 (which also speaks of Yahweh's "treading on the high places of the earth") belongs to a hymn dating earlier than the time of Amos, which Amos used for his own purposes.[13] In addition, the fact that the covenant lawsuit *(Gerichtsrede)* was a common form used by the pre-exilic prophets (cf. Isa 1:2-9; Hos 4:1-3; Jer 2:4-13; Mic 6:1-8), and that the theophany (based on the Sinai theophany, Exod 19:18, 20) was an integral part of the pre-exilic Judean cult[14] also points to a pre-exilic date for Mic 1:2-4. At the same time, the evidence favoring the "Mican authorship" of these verses does not preclude the possibility that Micah may have taken over an earlier oracle (or part of an earlier oracle) which he or some other prophet had delivered in North Israel, and applied it to Judah. Perhaps the earlier oracle was composed of vv. 2-7 (with the exception to the reference to Jerusalem in v. 5b), and was actually delivered in Samaria. Later (possibly after the earlier oracle had been vindicated by the fall of Samaria in 721 BCE), Micah may have incorporated this oracle into a longer oracle against Jerusalem (vv. 2-16). The idea is: the fate of Samaria will be the fate of Jerusalem, because the sin of Samaria is the sin of Jerusalem. (Note especially vv. 5, 9, 13.) A similar type of reasoning occurs in other prophetic passages from the eighth century BCE, as, e.g., in Isa 8:5-8 and 10:5-11.

A second way in which scholars have dealt with the difficulties in Mic 1:2 is by transferring this verse to a position between vv. 4 and 5.[15] They argue that in its present position v. 2 announces an oracle of doom which is not delivered, and v. 5 is the beginning of an oracle of doom which is not announced, but when these two verses are put side by side they complement each other. Such a rearrangement apparently rests on the assumption that an announcement of an oracle of Yahweh

12. Stade, "Streiflichter," 163; and Wolfe, "The Book of Micah," 902-3.

13. Watts, *Vision and Prophecy*, 52-54. Halévy, "Le Livre de Michée," 100; and Budde, "Das Rätsel," 86, i.a. cite this expression in Amos 4:13 as an argument in favor of the authenticity of Mic 1:2-4. The same expression occurs in Deut 32:13, 14; 33:29; 2 Sam 22:34; Hab 3:19; and Isa 58:14. See the interesting study of this phrase by Devescovi, "Camminare sulle alture," 235-42.

14. Referring to Mic 1:2-4, Deden, *De Kleine Profeten*, 203, writes: "De klassieke gebeurtenis bij de Sinaï heeft deze denkwijze zonder twijfel beïnvloed." Cf. also Weiser, "Zur Frage," 513-33, especially 525; Weiser, *Das Buch der zwölf Kleinen Propheten*, 235-36; and Beyerlin, *Die Kulttraditionen Israels*, 29-34.

15. Budde, "Das Rätsel," 82, 83; and Nowack, *Die Kleinen Propheten*, 200, 201.

must be followed *immediately* by that oracle. But in Mic 1 this solution raises more problems than it solves, because in v. 3 Yahweh *descends* from heaven to earth, but by transferring v. 2 after v. 4, Yahweh would still be in heaven (v. 2) after He had descended from heaven (v. 3).[16] Furthermore, the description of the theophany in vv. 3-4 by no means disrupts the continuity of thought between vv. 2 and 5. On the contrary, the theophany enhances the importance of the speech in vv. 5ff. which v. 2 announces. There is no valid justification for the assertion that an announcement of an oracle must be followed immediately (without *any* intervention) by that oracle.

Some scholars solve the problem of Mic 1:2 by deleting lines c and d as a later addition.[17] But this does not explain the function of this portion of the verse in the "final form" of the book. If some valid explanation can be found for its significance in the present context, such is to be preferred to deleting the difficult passage. T. H. Robinson is able to avoid the difficulty by making v. 2 and vv. 3-6 two separate pericopes, each originating at different times and each wholly unrelated to the other.[18] However, such a division is hardly warranted by the context, or even necessary. Bruno resolves the problem by changing עמים "peoples," to עמי "my people," deleting lines c and d, and understanding vv. 2-7 as an oracle against North Israel from the very first.[19] But the Versions do not support this emendation, and as far as the present writer knows no scholar has accepted it. Furthermore, if the explanation suggested in this essay is defensible, there is no reason to emend the text here.

Other critics deal with the problem by contending that the LXX ἐν ὑμῖν represents the correct interpretation, and so take בכם to mean "among you," "before you," or "in your midst."[20] Marty even emends the text of לכם to obtain this idea.[21] According to this interpretation, the

---

16. Bruno, *Micha und der Herrscher*, 16.

17. Thus Lindblom, *Micha*, 22-23, 157, 171 n. 2; Sellin, *Das Zwölfprophetenbuch*, 310-11; Lippl, *Die zwölf Kleinen Propheten*, 185; Jepsen, "Kleine Beiträge," 96; and Kraeling, *Commentary*, 207.

18. Robinson, *Die zwölf Kleinen Propheten*, 131.

19. Bruno, *Micha und der Herrscher*, 14.

20. Thus Bliss in Kleinert, *The Minor Prophets*, 10; Beck, *Erklärung*, 70; G. A. Smith, *The Book of the Twelve Prophets*, 536, note *; Duhm, "Anmerkungen," 82; Nötscher, *Zwölfprophetenbuch*, 90; Weiser, *Das Buch der zwölf Kleinen Propheten*, 235; and Scharbert, *Die Propheten Israels*, 315.

21. Marty, *L'Ancien Testament*, 768.

peoples and the earth are witnesses who testify to the justification of Yahweh's punishment of Israel.²² Riessler avoids the difficulty altogether by pointing the text לְעַד, "it may be that the Lord will always be among you."²³ The Micah Pesher, as it is printed in the מגילות מדבר יהודה, points the text in just this way.²⁴ But this is an unpointed text, and the consonants are not even visible on the fragment! However, the LXX text at this point does not represent a different "interpretation" of the Hebrew text, but a good idiomatic rendering of the Hebrew phrase. I.e., ἐν ὑμῖν εἰς μαρτύριον *must be taken together* as an idiom meaning "for a witness *against* you," which is a good translation of the Hebrew בכם לעד, as is demonstrated below. μαρτύριον ἐν or its equivalent translates עד ב in Deut 31:19, 26; 1 Sam 12:5; and Jer 49:5 (= 42:5 in MT). Ignatius's *Epistle to the Trallians* 12:3 provides an interesting corroboration of this interpretation: ἔχομαι ὑμᾶς ἐν ἀγαπῇ ἀκοῦσαί μου, ἵνα μή εἰς μαρτύριον ᾧ ἐν ὑμῖν γράψας.²⁵

Another explanation which has been offered to solve the problem of Mic 1:2 is that lines a and b are addressed to the whole world, while lines c and d are addressed to Israel alone.²⁶ But this is not the natural meaning of the context. Others, comparing this verse with Deut 33:19 and Ezek 30:12, argue that "peoples" refers to the tribes of Israel, and "earth" to the land of Palestine.²⁷ Beyerlin tries to relieve the difficulty by reasoning that while the oracle appears to be directed against Israel, it is ultimately directed against foreign nations, whence idolatry (condemned in v. 7) came into Israel.²⁸

In my opinion, the "peoples" and the "earth" in Mic 1:2 are the defendants or the accused in the lawsuit. In other words, they do not perform the same function in the *Gerichtsrede* of Mic 1:2ff. as the "mountains," "hills," and "foundations of the earth" perform in Mic

---

22. So Nowack, "Bemerkungen," 288–89; Mowinckel, *Det Gamle Testamente*, 674; Gemser, "The Rîb- or Controversy-Pattern," 130; Delcor, "Les attaches littéraires," 24; and others.

23. Riessler, *Die Kleinen Propheten*, 102, 104.

24. Habermann, *Megillot Midbar Yehuda*, 151.

25. Page, *The Apostolic Fathers*, 222.

26. Orelli, *The Twelve Minor Prophets*, 190; and others.

27. I.a., Kleinert, *The Minor Prophets*, 11; Halévy, "Le Livre de Michée," 99; Hoonacker, *Les douze petits prophètes*, 355; Haupt, "The Book of Micah," 57; Steuernagel, *Lehrbuch*, 625; and Graham, "Some Suggestions," 256.

28. Beyerlin, *Die Kulttraditionen Israels*, 40–41.

6:1ff., or as the "heavens" and "earth" perform in Isa 1:2ff. In Mic 6 and Isa 1, the "mountains," etc., are not judges or jury who pass sentence on the accused,[29] nor are they *learning* witnesses who observe Yahweh's dealings with Israel in order to discover how he will deal with them, but they are *legal* witnesses who testify to the accuracy or truthfulness of the plaintiff's (Yahweh's) accusation against the defendant (Israel). "The witnesses serve as an indication or guarantee that an unfulfilled obligation exists, which justifies Yahweh in actually invoking the curses of the covenant."[30] But in Mic 1:2, the "peoples" and the "earth" are the accused, the defendants. That ויהי אדני יהוה בכם לעד[31] means "and let the Lord, Yahweh, be witness *against* you," is supported by compelling evidence. In v. 2, the peoples and the earth are addressed by the use of the second person of the verb: שמעו and הקשיבו, but in vv. 5–7, Israel is condemned in the third person, "dagegen zweifellos zu den übrigen Völkern, die in v. 2 zum Hören aufgefordert sind."[32] Also, עד . . . ב is used in Num 5:13; Deut 31:19; Josh 24:22; 1 Sam 12:5; Mal 3:5; and Prov 24:28, and עד . . . ב (the same construction which occurs in Mic 1:2) is used in Exod 20:16 (= Deut 5:20); Deut 31:26; Jer 42:5; and Prov 25:18 (cf. also Deut 17:7; 19:15, 16; and Ps 27:12) in contexts where the sense can hardly be anything but "witness against."[33] There is no exception to this

---

29. This is the view of Horton, *The Minor Prophets*, 257; Margolis, *Micah*, 59; J. M. P. Smith, *Critical and Exegetical Commentary*, 119–20; Schmidt, "Micha," 143, 144; Mowinckel, "Mikaboken," 21, 36; Goldman, *The Twelve Prophets*, 179; Ridderbos, *De Kleine Profeten*, 103; Weiser, *Das Buch der zwölf Kleinen Propheten*, 279; and others.

30. Huffmon, "The Covenant Lawsuit," 293. Cf. also 287, 292. This is the interpretation of Kuenen, *Historisch-Critisch Onderzoek*, 379 n. 12; Hylmö, *Kompositionen*, 253, 256; Sellin, *Das Zwölfprophetenbuch*, 342; Gemser, "The Rîb- or Controversy-Pattern," 130; George, *La Sainte Bible*, 39; Deissler, "Micha 6, 1–8," 229, 230; Deissler, *Les Petits Prophètes*, 341; and many others.

31. The Micah Pesher seems to have read here: י.[הוה [יהי אדני]בכם ה. Cf. מדבר מגילות יהודה, 151; Milik, "Fragments," 413–14; Barthélemy and Milik, *Qumran Cave I*, 77. In the last mentioned work, Milik argues that this represents the original text because the sequence יהוה אדני is so rare, occurring in only five other passages in the Old Testament: Hab 3:19; Pss 68:21; 109:21; 140:8; and 141:8. The Hebrew Scroll of the Twelve Minor Prophets discovered in 1955 near Wady Murabba'at agrees with the MT. Cf. Benoit et al., *Les Grottes*, 192.

32. Budde, "Das Rätsel," 85.

33. Wellhausen, *Die Kleinen Propheten*, 135; Marti, *Das Dodekapropheten*, 266; Hoonacker, *Les douze petits prophètes*, 355; J. M. P. Smith, *Critical and Exegetical Commentary*, 35; Cheyne, *Micah*, 17; Devescovi, "Camminare sulle alture," 237; Deissler, *Les Petits Prophètes*, 302, and several others, interpret ב . . . עד in Mic 1:2 to mean "witness against."

meaning for this idiom in the Old Testament! Furthermore, "peoples" most naturally refers to foreign nations, which is confirmed in this verse by the parallelism with "earth" in line b. "Since ארץ ומלאה is the usual expression for the whole earth..., עמים can hardly mean anything other than the nations in general."[34] Such a summons to the nations is quite appropriate in an oracle which announces impending doom on Israel, because the prophets considered Yahweh's punishment of Israel a model or pattern for Yahweh's future punishment of the nations. The nations are to see Yahweh's *witness against* (accusation of) them (vv. 2–4) in His punishment of His own people (vv. 5–7). If Yahweh does not spare His own people, the nations need not expect that He will spare them. "By his judgment of sinful Israel, Yahweh will even yet awaken the sleeping conscience of the sinful nations of the world."[35] The idea is: O peoples, O earth, "Be admonished by the horrible example of what has happened in Israel."[36] At the same time, the expression "Hear, O peoples, all of *them* (כלם),[37] give ear, O earth, and all that is in *it* (מלאה)," is rather curious. While the peoples and the earth are addressed, the prophet's audience is undoubtedly Israel. Thus this oracle *against* the nations may function in a specific way in this context. Perhaps Micah intentionally begins his oracle of doom concerning Samaria by imitating the popular prophets who regularly delivered oracles of doom against foreign nations. This would gain him a favorable hearing for the more immediate burden of his message, i.e., the impending doom of Samaria (and Jerusalem). If this is the case, Mic 1:2–7(16) bears the same general structure as Amos 1:3—2:8; Isa 3:13–15; and Zeph 1:2–6.[38]

---

34. Kolmodin, *Profeten Mika*, 2.

35. Hylmö, *Kompositionen*, 18.

36. Budde, "Das Rätsel," 85.

37. The Peshitta *klkwn* seems to imply בלכם, a reading which is adopted by Duhm, "Anmerkungen," 82; and Robinson, *Die zwölf Kleinen Propheten*, 130.

38. Thus similarly Hesse, "Wurzelt die prophetische Gerichtsrede?" 49.

7

On the Text of Micah 2,1aα-β[1]

THE TEXT AND INTERPRETATION of Mic 2,1aα-β have long posed serious difficulties for Old Testament scholars. The chief criticism of the present MT is that the phrase *ûpōʿălê rāʿ* describes those who *execute* plans which have already been *devised*, and therefore "and work evil" cannot describe what the wicked do "upon their beds." This has led scholars to suggest various means of removing the apparent illogicalness.

(a) Bruno reads *ṭōpĕlê* instead of *pōʿălê* in aβ in order to make the phrases in aα and aβ parallel:[2]

> Woe to those who devise iniquity
> And *conceive* evil upon their beds.

(b) Halévy,[3] T. H. Robinson,[4] and Scharbert[5] leave the consonantal text as it is, and change the pointing slightly to *pōʿŏlê rāʿ*, "evil works," thus making both "iniquity" and "evil works" direct objects of the verb "devise." *(c)* Similarly, Sellin,[6] Marty,[7] Nötscher,[8] and Deissler[9] read the singular *pōʿal rāʿ*, "evil work," in order to make it correspond to the singular

---

1. The numbering of scriptures throughout follows the MT.
2. Bruno, *Micha und der Herrscher*, 42, 55.
3. Halévy, "Le Livre de Michée," 110.
4. Robinson, *Die zwölf Kleinen Propheten*, 132.
5. Scharbert, *Die Propheten Israels*, 320.
6. Sellin, *Das Zwölfprophetenbuch*, 317.
7. Marty, *L'Ancien Testament*, 770.
8. Nötscher, *Zwölfprophetenbuch*, 92.
9. Deissler, *Les Petits Prophètes*, 309.

"iniquity" in aα. *(d)* Budde solves the difficulty by reversing the order of aβ and reading:

> Woe to those who devise iniquity
> Upon their beds, and work evil.[10]

(e) Because the metric length of line a is longer than line *b* as the MT now stands, and because "and work evil" must refer to the *execution* of plans (which is logically out of place before *bα*), many scholars consider פעלי רע to be a gloss on חשבי און, and thus conclude that it must be deleted.[11] In my opinion, this is a serious mistake because it obscures what is apparently an intentional play on words involving חשבי רע in v. 1 and חשבי רעה in v. 3, and thus destroys the principle of *jus talionis* which is not only characteristic of the doom sections of the book of Micah, but which is also clearly intended in 2:1–5 (as is demonstrated below). *(f)* Therefore, if the text demands emendation at all, it would seem best to delete ופעלי און in order to preserve the word play on חשב רע in vv. 1 and 3.[12]

But we must be very hesitant about emending the MT at the points under consideration because it is supported by the Versions: LXX, κόπους καὶ ἐργαζόμενοι κακά; Vulgate, *inutile et operamini malum*; Targum, מינם לסעב דביש; Peshitta, *'t' w'bryn byšt'*.[13] The "irregularity" of rhythm or meter does not necessitate a deletion, since it is by no means established that the meter in the Hebrew poetry of the Old Testament must conform to a rigid pattern. And yet, we are still faced with the problem of explaining the meaning of the MT as it now stands. Most commentators apparently assume that this verse means that the wicked meet together in the evening to plan their evil schemes against the innocent (line a), then the next morning put their plans into action (line b). This interpretation accounts for the compulsion of many exegetes to emend the

---

10. Budde, "Micha 2 and 3," 3.

11. Thus, Wellhausen, *Die Kleinen Propheten*, 137; Marti, *Das Dodekapropheten*, 272; J. M. P. Smith, *Critical and Exegetical Commentary*, 53–54, 56–57; Mowinckel, "Mikaboken," 8; Mowinckel, *Det Gamle Testamente*, 677; Lindblom, *Micha*, 56–57; to mention only a few.

12. Indeed, Duhm, "Anmerkungen," 84; and Leslie, *The Prophets*, 138.

13. Unfortunately, there is a lacuna in part of the pertinent section in the Hebrew Scroll of the Twelve Minor Prophets discovered in 1955 near Wadi Murabbaʿât, but nothing in this manuscript in any way casts suspicion on the MT. Cf. Benoit et al., *Les Grottes*, 192.

text. (g) It also accounts for the suggestion of Margolis[14] and Wade[15] that the verb "work" here does not necessarily refer to the execution of the plans, but may mean "mental work," and thus is parallel to "devise" in aα. However, the evidence does not support this solution. With one possible exception (Ps 58:3)[16], the root פעל always has to do with the *execution* of a deed or act, but never with its *conception*. It occurs twenty-four times with און, "trouble, wickedness, iniquity" (Job 31:3; 34:8, 22; Pss 5:6; 6:9; 14:4; 28:3; 36:13; 53:5; 59:3; 64:3; 92:8, 10; 94:4, 16; 101:8; 125:5; 141:4, 9; Prov 10:29; 21:15; 30:20; Isa 31:2; Hos 6:8); twice with עולה, "injustice, unrighteousness" (Job 34:32); שקר, "deception, falsehood" (Hos 7:1); המס, "violence, wrong" (Isa 59:6); and רע, "evil" (Mic 2:1). Thus פעל is commonly used in the Old Testament for the *execution* of evil deeds.

Now חשב (which is used with און in Mic 2:1) occurs sixteen times in the Old Testament with רעה (Gen 50:20; Jer 18:8; 26:3; 36:3; 48:2; Ezek 38:10; Mic 2:3; Nah 1:11; Zech 7:10; 8:17; Pss 35:4; 36:4; 41:8; 140:3; Esth 9:25; Neh 6:2; cf. מחשב להרע in Prov 24:8), and once with רע (Hos 7:15). Thus, the usual expressions in the Old Testament are "devise evil" and "work iniquity." One cannot help but wonder if the verbs in Mic 2:1aα–β were transposed at some stage in transmission. Yet, I think this also is unlikely for five reasons. First, none of the Versions indicates a text dif-

---

14. Margolis, *Micah*, 27.

15. Wade, *The Books of the Prophets*, 14.

16. There are two factors which preclude one's using Ps 58:3 as a conclusive argument favoring the interpretation of פעל as "mental work" in Mic 2:1. (a) The Text of Ps 58:3 is uncertain. The Peshitta *klkwn* suggests the reading *kulkem*, which is adopted by Cheyne, *The Book of Psalms*, 389; Kittel, *Die Psalmen*, 204; et al. Duhm, *Die Psalmen*, 158, reads *ballāṭ* "in secret," contending that this is a better antithesis to בארץ in line b than is בלבכם. The LXX ἐν καρδία, the Vulgate *in corde*, and the Targum *bĕlibbā'* agree with the MT, which provides an excellent antithesis to בארץ in line b. Thus Briggs, *The Book of Psalms*, II, 46; Kissane, *The Book of Psalms*, I, 249, 251; et al., defend the MT at this point. (b) But even if בלב is the correct text, two difficulties remain. First, some scholars doubt that the original verb with which it is connected in this verse was פעל. E.g., Buhl in the critical apparatus of BH³, suggests that the original text was תפללון, not תפעלון.

Second, even if בלב and פעל are retained, it is by no means certain that the text means to do wrongs mentally "in the heart." The LXX ἀνομίας and the Targum *'ila'* suggest a reading *'āvel* instead of the MT *'ōlōt*. Thus e.g., Kraus, *Psalmen*, 415, translates: "Nein, ihr entscheidet mit 'frevelerischem' Herzen auf Erden."

Consequently, it is impossible to deduce from Ps 58:3 alone that פעל can be used for "mental work," particularly in view of the fact that the overwhelming use of פעל in the OT points in a different direction.

ferent from the MT. Secondly, the apparently stereotyped expressions "devise evil" and "work iniquity" make it more probable that if a transposition had taken place in transmission, it would have been from the text represented in the present MT and Versions to the more frequently used phrases than vice versa. I.e., the principle of *lectio difficilior* argues in favor of accepting the MT. Thirdly, Isa 59:6 offers an interesting structural parallel to Mic 2:1 Line c speaks of מעשי און, "works of *iniquity*," and line d of פעלי המס, "deeds of violence." Here, as in Mic 2:1, און occurs in the former expression with a word other than פעל, and פעל occurs in the latter expression with a word other than און. Fourthly, Ps 21:12 and Prov 16:30 contain similar parallels to Mic 2:1. In the former, line a says נטו . . . כי רעה "if they plan *evil*," while line b reads לחשב מזמה "if they devise mischief." In the latter, line a refers to one who לחשב תהפכות[17], "devises perverse things," and line b to one who כלה רעה, "brings *evil* to pass." In both passages, one line uses חשב with a word other than רעה, and the other line uses רעה with a word other than חשב. Finally, the credibility of the present text of Mic 2:1 gains support from Ezek 11:2, אלה האנשים החשבים און והיעצים עצת רע. "These [are] the men who *devise iniquity* and who counsel wicked counsel . . ." Here חשב is used with און in the first phrase, and רע occurs in the following phrase. The order is the same as that found in Mic 2:1. The only thing missing is the verb פעל.

If "work evil" applies (almost?) exclusively to the *execution* of acts or deeds throughout the Old Testament, this must be its meaning in Mic 2:1. But if this is the case, how can the wicked possibly work evil על משכבותם, "upon their beds"? The use of this last expression in other Old Testament passages is very helpful in explaining how such is possible. The occurrence of the expression על משכב in the Aramaic section of Daniel (six times) may serve as a beginning. When Daniel is summoned to interpret Nebuchadnezzar's dream of the great image, he begins by saying to the king: "Thy dream חלמך and the visions of thy head upon thy bed על משכבך, are these: as for thee, O king, thy thoughts came upon thy bed על משכבך, what should come to pass hereafter" (2:28–29). Similar expressions are found in the story of Nebuchadnezzar's dream of the tree (Dan 4). The king recalls: "I saw a dream חלם which made me afraid; and the thoughts upon my bed על משכבי and the visions of my head troubled me" (4:2). He urges Daniel (Belteshazzar): "Tell me the visions of my dream חלמי that I have seen, and the interpretation

---

17. The point is still the same if we read יחשב following the LXX λογίζεται.

thereof. Thus were the visions of my head upon my bed על משכבי" (4:6-7). Shortly, he remarks: "I saw in the visions of my head upon my bed על משכבי," etc. (4:10). Once again, at the beginning of Daniel's dream of the four beasts it is said: "Daniel had a dream חלם and visions of his head upon his bed על משכבה: then he wrote the dream חלמא and told the sum of the matters" (7:1). The intimate relationship between the phrase "upon my (thy, his) bed" and "a dream" or dreams in these verses is obvious. Notice especially that "the visions of my dream" in 4:6 is parallel to "the visions of my head upon my bed" in 4:7.

A similar usage appears in Cant 3:1: "By night on my bed על משכבי, I sought him whom my soul loves." Most scholars agree that 3:1–5 has to do with a dream which the maiden is relating to the daughters of Jerusalem, but they interpret 3:1a differently. Budde, e.g., thinks that the maiden is telling how in her dream she awoke and felt for her lover whom she thought to be on the bed beside her, but he had gone. He writes: ". . . hat sie . . . geträumt, sie sei nachts erwacht und habe ihn vergeblich zuerst ihrer an Seite gesucht, dann weiter durch die Gassen der Stadt, immer vergeblich."[18] However, it seems more likely to me that Rudolph is correct in translating: "Nachtens auf meinem Lager (liegend), sucht' ich ihn," then in commenting (against Budde): "'Liegend' ist hinzugefügt, um deutlich zu machen, dass 'auf meinem Lager' zum Subjekt 'ich' gehört und nicht vom Verbum abhangt, *als ob der Geliebte vorher bei ihr im Bett gelegen habe*" (italics mine).[19] If this interpretation is correct, "upon my bed" apparently means "in my dream(s)."

The intimate relationship in OT thought between "the bed" and "dreams" is also reflected in the book of Job. 7:13–14 says:

> When I say, 'My bed will comfort me,
>   my couch משכבי will ease my complaint,'
> then thou dost scare me with dreams בחלמות
>   and terrify me with visions.

Again, we read in 33:14–15:

> For God speaks in one way,
>   and in two, though man does not perceive it.
> In a dream בחלום, in a vision of the night,
>   when deep sleep falls upon men,
>   while they slumber on their beds עלי משכב.

18. Budde, *Die Fünf Megillot*, 14.
19. Rudolph, *Das Buch Ruth*, 137, 138.

Finally, it may be noted that Isa 56:10 seems to use the participles חזים "dreaming" (a hapax legomenon) and שכבים "lying down" interchangeably. The cumulative evidence of these passages leads me to suggest that "upon their beds" in Mic 2:1 is an idiomatic expression equivalent to "in their dreams." I.e., the prophet does not describe the nocturnal meeting of wicked men to devise evil schemes against the innocent to be carried out the following day. Rather, he portrays the all-consuming passion for wickedness of individual evildoers—a passion which so dominates their lives that they cannot sleep and dream without thinking about "devising iniquity" and "working evil." These activities are as real to the wicked in their dreams as is the maiden's search for her lover in Cant 3:1. Thus in Mic 2:1, both "devise" and "work" can pertain to activities which take place *in reality* "when the morning is light," but, for the wicked, are as *real* in their dreams "upon their beds."[20]

Finally, the present MT must be retained in order to preserve the principle of *jus talionis* reflected in the phrase חשב רע in v. 1 and רעה חשב in v. 3, a principle which appears throughout the doom sections of the book of Micah (1:2—2:11; 3; and 6:1—7:6). The following examples may be cited as illustrations. *(a)* Israel had gathered riches for her temples from money received from sacred prostitution. As just retribution, the conqueror will carry these riches away to be used for sacred prostitution in a foreign land (1:7).[21] To be sure, scholars are not in agreement on the meaning of lines d and e, which are critical at this point. E.g., Riessler understands line e to mean that the silver and gold which had been gained through sacred prostitution for the temple would be returned to the prostitutes.[22] Others interpret these lines figuratively: Israel was rich in gold and silver, some of which she used for decorating her idols. She ascribed this material prosperity to the Baalim rather than to Yahweh. Therefore, Yahweh will leave Israel to the gods that she

---

20. Conceivably, "upon their beds" in Mic 2:1 might mean "interiorly" or "inwardly," thus agreeing with חשב, "to devise" in line aα, or (since the "bed" may be symbolic of one's privacy) "privately." However, the reference to the execution of evil plans when the morning dawns leads me to prefer the interpretation suggested in the text.

21. Several scholars have called attention to the principle of *jus talionis* in this verse. E.g., Weiser, *Das Buch der zwölf kleinen Propheten*, 238, writes: "Das Gesetz der Sünde, dass sie die Keime des Verderbens in suich selbst trägt, und der Sünder an ihr zugrunde geht, ist das Gesetz des göttlichen Gerichts."

22. Riessler, *Die Kleinen Propheten*, 107.

had chosen. Cf. Hos 2:5, 8–13.[23] However, it seems most likely that the reference is to the practice of purchasing silver and gold for decorating idols with the remuneration received from sacred prostitution practiced in the temples.[24] *(b)* The rich had driven the poor out of their houses, therefore Yahweh will send an enemy to drive them out of their land (2:9–10).[25] *(c)* Israel's rulers had not been merciful to the poor when they cried unto them for help in their distress, therefore Yahweh will not hear them when they cry unto him (3:2–4).[26] *(d)* The popular prophets had not used their gift of prophecy responsibly; therefore, Yahweh will take his gift away from them (3:5–6).[27] *(e)* The leaders of Judah had built up Zion with blood and iniquity, therefore Yahweh will bring upon Jerusalem the just desserts of her wickedness: Zion will be plowed as a field, Jerusalem will become heaps, and the temple mountain a forest sanctuary (3:10, 12).[28] *(f)* The rich had deprived the poor of the neces-

23. E.g., Orelli, *The Twelve Minor Prophets*, 192, argues that Israel "regarded her gain as gift of the gods, therefore it was a harlot's hire." Cf. more recently George, *La Sainte Bible*, 22.

24. Thus Elhorst, *De Prophetie van Micha*, 143; recently Deissler, *Les Petits Prophètes*, 304; Kraeling, *Commentary*, II, 207, et al.

25. Critics differ as to the identity of the speaker and audience in 2:10. (a) Schmidt, *Micha*, 138, thinks that a group representing the leading classes had come to Micah's home to rebuke him for his preaching, and that after Micah had replied to their charges (vv. 8–9), he commanded them to leave. (b) Hoonacker, *Les douze petits prophètes*, 372, 374 argues that Micah here is urging the oppressed (or possibly all the people) to flee from Palestine to avoid the approaching calamity which will be so great. (c) Scharbert, *Die Propheten Israels*, 321, understands the speaker to be in the land of Israel. He reads: "(und schreibt sie an): 'Auf macht euch davon; Hier durft ihr nicht Ruhen.'" (d) Several scholars regard "Arise and go, etc." as the harsh words of the rich to the poor as they drove them out of their houses. So Stade, "Bemerkungen," 165; Duhm, "Anmerkungen," 86; more recently Weiser, *Das Buch der zwölf kleinen Propheten*, 251; and Kraeling, *Commentary*, II, 211, etc. (e) In my opinion, Micah is ordering the Judean oppressors out of the land, a symbolic way of saying that the enemy will carry them into exile—a suitable retribution for those who had driven the innocent out of their homes. "Comme vous avez chasse des femmes et des enfants de leur demeure, vous serez chassés de votre pays qui ne sera plus le lieu de repos." Halévy, "Le Livre de Michée," 116. Many critics concur.

26. "Die Gottverlassenheit wird die rechte Strafe sein für ihr unverantwortliches Treiben, für ihre schnöde Missachtung jeglicher Grundrechte der Menschen." Schumpp, *Das Buch der Zwölf Propheten*, 200. Similarly many others.

27. "Weil die propheten ihre Sehergabe der Arment entzogen haben entzieht ihnen Gott diese Gabe." Bruno, *Micha und der Herrscher*, 69. Similarly many others.

28. Reading *lĕbāmat* instead of *lĕbāmôt*, following the LXX ἄλσος, Symmachus, Theodotion, and the Targum חרשא לחישת. Thus the majority of critics. In my opin-

sities of life; therefore, they will be deprived of prosperity, food, and security from the invader (6:10–15).[29] *(g)* The word play in 7:4 also seems to involve the *jus talionis* concept. The most upright of God's people are as a thorn hedge ממסוכה, therefore they will suffer perplexity סבוכתם.[30] *(h)* Also, it is significant that 7:9 assumes that indignation זעף is the natural consequence of sin חטא.[31]

Now if we leave the MT as it is in Mic 2:1, then 2:1–5 also exhibits the *jus talionis* principle. Apparently the structure is a (v. 1) *b* (v. 2)— *a'* (v. 3)—*b'* (vv. 4–5). The rich had "*devised* iniquity and worked *evil*" against the poor (v. 1), therefore Yahweh will "devise evil" against them (v. 3). "The phrase חשב רע [in v. 3] is emphatically repeated from v. 1, to set clearly before our eyes the *jus talionis* prevalent in God's providence."[32] The rich had wrested fields from the poor (v. 2), therefore Yahweh will send an enemy army to wrest the Promised Land from them (vv. 4–5).[33]

---

ion, יער לבמת does not mean an elevated height in the forest, as Haupt, "The Book of Micah," 220; Bruno, *Micha und der Herrscher*, 73; and others think, but a forest sanctuary. The prophet announces that the magnificent sanctuary of Yahweh in Jerusalem will be reduced to the level of a little frequented Canaanite high place. So Marti, *Das Dodekapropheton*, 280; Cheyne, *Critica Biblica*, 156; *Micah*, 34; Nielsen, *Oral Tradition*, 92; and others. Binns, "Micah," 586; and Ungern-Sternberg, *Der Rechtsstreit Gottes*, 64, 67, also interpret these verses as an example of *jus talionis*.

29. "Alwat zij anderen ontnamen, zal hun ontnomen worden door de vijand." Deden, *De Kleine Profeten*, 227. Several other scholars suggest a similar view.

30. Indeed, Beck, *Erklärung*, 192, argues that this is an intentional "alliteration zur Andeutung von talio."

31. It is true that 7:9 is part of a hope section in the book of Micah, but this verse is still relevant to the general proposition that the principle of *jus talionis* is characteristic of the prophetic work.

32. Kleinert, *The Minor Prophets*, 19. "God zal hen met gelijke munt betalen." Deden, *De Kleine Profeten*, 207. Similarly also many others.

33. "The punishment is in correspondence with the sin." Driver, *An Introduction*, 326–27. "Die Grossen haben einst den Kleinen ihre Güter und ihren Besitz genommen. Nun ist auch den Grossen, ja dem ganzen Lande und Volke der Besitz genommen worden" Schumpp, *Das Buch der Zwölf Propheten*, 200. "Die Folge der Ländergier der Machthaber des Volkes wird der gänzliche Verlust des Landes an fremde Eroberer sein" Weiser, *Das Buch der zwölf kleinen Propheten*, 247. Similarly also many others.

8

Micah 2:6–8 and the "People of God" in Micah

THE DIFFICULTIES CONNECTED WITH the interpretation of Mic 2:6–8 are many and complex, and there is little possibility that all the problems which these verses contain can be solved to the satisfaction of even a majority of critics. The purposes of this paper are to analyze the textual problems in vv. 6–8 offering a possible translation, to suggest a plausible function of these verses in their larger immediate context (i.e., 2:1–11), and to make some observations as to the concept of the "people of God" in this passage and in the book of Micah as a whole.

Textual Problems

"Le texte hébreu du livre de Michée nous est parvenu dans un état assez mauvais,"[1] and this is particularly true of 2:6–8. The MT and the Versions each have their own peculiar nuances of the thought in each of the verses involved in this passage. The Targum is not really a translation, but an explanation or interpretation, and therefore is of little value in attempting to understand mine the original text.

Verse 6.

The MT may be translated:

> You (plural) shall not speak, they (shall) speak,
> They shall not speak to (of) these,
> Reproaches shall not depart
> (or, He will not turn back reproaches).

---

1. George, *La Sainte Bible*, 18.

Micah 2:6-8 and the "People of God" in Micah

The structure of this verse, which is essentially the same in all the Versions, is important in determining the text and meaning. It is composed of three lines, each beginning with a negative (אל in line a and לא in lines b and c) and containing three words. Thus לא יטפו in line b should not be deleted as a dittograph on אל יטפו or יטפון in line a,[2] since this would destroy the symmetry. It also seems to favor an interpretation which would relate the three lines to each other in content in a synonymous or ascending pattern over one which would understand them as broken and poorly connected. This is especially true in light of the fact that the same kind of structure appears in v. 7. Thus, if Micah is the speaker in line a, it would seem logical that he is the speaker throughout vv. 6-7, but if Micah's opponents are the speakers in line a, they are the speakers throughout. The LXX μὴ κλαίετε δάκρυσι, μηδὲ δακρυέτωσαν ἐπὶ τούτοις, "Do not weep with tears (i.e., bitterly), nor are they to weep over these things," and very similarly the Syriac, "You shall not weep tears, and you shall not weep over these things" simply represent an interpretation of the verb נטף, i.e., "to drop (shed) tears," and do not suggest a different Hebrew text.[3] The Vulgate *Ne loquamini loquentes* and Targum לא תתנבון נבואה along with the context justify interpreting נטף in the sense of "prophesy, speak." However, the Vulgate pictures the prophet as apprehensively prohibiting a reply to his Woe Oracle in vv. 1-5 by anticipating his hearers' reply and refuting it.

In line b, the Versions differ as to the person of the subject. The Syriac (against the LXX, which it often follows!) and Targum read the second person plural, but this is probably due to the difficulty of the passage, a compulsion to create a more symmetrical parallelism, and the influence of תטפו in line a. The Vulgate reads the third singular *stillabit*, apparently referring to Micah. The first two lines of the Vulgate may be translated: (Micah) "And in speaking you shall not say: "He (i.e., Micah) shall not speak concerning these things." The singular is apparently due to the translator's interpretation of line a. The LXX agrees with the MT in reading the third person plural, which is supported by the principle of *lectio difficilior* and by the fact that the variant readings in the Versions can be better explained from this reading than from the other possibilities. לאלה is ambiguous and may be translated "to these people" or "of

---

2. J. M. P. Smith, *Critical and Exegetical Commentary*, 55; Budde, "Micha 2 und 3," 8.

3. Cf. Donat, "Mich. 2:6-9," 351.

these things." The Targum reads לעסא הדיה (You shall not teach) "this people," but this is not convincing because there is no basis for the word "people" in the MT or the Versions, and line c in the Targum bears no resemblance to the reading in the MT or the Versions. Furthermore, the reading "these people" would have to refer to the rich (cf. vv. 1–5) or to all Israel, in which case those who are forbidden to speak to them are "popular prophets," which is inconceivable in the Mican situation as 2:11; 3:5,11 make quite clear. The other Versions, the immediate context (cf. especially 2:11), and the larger context of the book of Micah agree in supporting the reading "of these things."[4]

The LXX and Syriac connect the last two lines of the verse by the preposition "for." The LXX οὐ γὰρ ἀπώσεται ὀνείδη, "for reproaches shall not drive (you, us?) away," has the prophet encouraging his hearers by assuring them that reproaches (of Micah and his followers) by opponents (the rich of vv. 1–5) will not drive them away. But the Syriac (And you shall not weep over these things), "for reproach shall not overtake you" (which is spoken concerning the house of Israel), has the prophet assuring his hearers that they will not be punished like the nation as a whole, and thus makes a contrast between Micah's audience in vv. 1–5 and his audience in v. 6. (Verse 7 begins with the last line of v. 6 in the Peshitta.)

The most difficult problem in v. 6 is that the feminine plural כלמות is used as the subject of the masculine singular verb יסג. The fact that the LXX has a plural subject ὀνείδη with a singular verb is insignificant, since it is grammatically correct in Greek for a neuter plural subject to be used with a singular verb. Weil solves the problem by arguing that the noun כלמות is to be taken adverbially ('shamefully'—connecting v. 7a to v. 6c as its subject): "Ne cedera pas honteusement celui qui est nommé le clan de Jacob!"[5]

But this destroys the symmetry of v. 7, the form of which is similar to v. 6. Appealing to the Syriac and the Vulgate *confusio* the majority of scholars emend *kĕlimmôt* to *kĕlimmût*,[6] which is attractive because it

---

4. Riessler, *Die Kleinen Propheten*, 110; Mowinckel, "Mikaboken," 9, 30; Mowinckel, *Det Gamle Testamente*, 3:578; and Schwantes, "A Critical Study," 65, suggest that *lĕʾelleh* should be emended to *lĕʾālāh*, "do not preach (prate) about a curse." But this is not supported by the Versions, and it depends on emending *heʾāmûr* to *heʾārûr* in v. 7.

5. Weil, "Le chapitre II de Michée," 147.

6. So Pont, "Micha Studiën, III," 347; Riessler, *Die Kleinen Propheten*, 110; Stave, *Israels Profeter*, 22; Budde, "Micha 2 und 3," 8; Nowack, *Die Kleinen Propheten*, 209;

Micah 2:6-8 and the "People of God" in Micah

retains the consonantal text, requires only a change in the pointing, and provides a singular subject for a singular verb. But *kĕlimmût* is feminine, and *yissag* is masculine, and the emendations *yaśśîg* ("reproach shall not overtake [us]"),[7] *yaśśîgenû* ("reproach shall not overtake us"),[8] or *yaśśîg kallānû* ("reproach shall overtake all of us"),[9] or connecting 7a with 6c ("shame shall not [never] reach the house of Jacob"),[10] do not alter this grammatical incongruity. Some scholars have solved the problem by making "reproaches" the object of the verb, which might be supported by the LXX. But if this is the case it is difficult to find the subject and a suitable meaning for the verb. A few scholars make "the house of Jacob" in v. 7a the subject and read: "The house of Jacob shall not encounter (meet with) reproaches."[11] But this disrupts the structure of vv. 6 and 7. Thus, it seems best to emend the masculine *yissag* to the feminine *taśśîg* to agree with the feminine singular noun *kĕlimmût*.[12]

In order to "translate" v. 6, it is necessary to analyze the "psychology" of the text, in spite of the fact this is ultimately subjective. A few critical views may be cited to call attention to the variety of possible interpretations. Van Hoonacker understands Micah to be the speaker throughout:

> Do not protest (speaking to his opponents in the audience)!
> When one (anyone) speaks, if he does not speak concerning these things (i.e., along the lines of Micah's preaching in vv. 1-5),
> He (i.e., Yahweh) will not turn away shame from him.[13]

Donat thinks that Micah is quoting the popular prophets who oppose him:

Sellin, *Das Zwölfprophetenbuch*, 319; Marty, *L'Ancien Testament II*, 771; George, *La Sainte Bible*, 28; Deissler, *Les Petits Prophètes*, 312.

7. Thus Pont, "Micha Studiën, III," 347; Marti, *Das Dodekapropheton*, 275; Donat, "Mich 6-9," 351; Stave, *Israels Profeter*, 22; Nowack, *Die Kleinen Propheten*, 209; Lindblom, *Micha*, 59; Sellin, *Das Zwölfprophetenbuch*, 319; Lippl, *Die zwölf kleinen Propheten*, 193; Nötscher, *Zwölfprophetenbuch*, 93; and Deden, *De Kleine Profeten*, 209, 232.

8. So Marty, *L'Ancien Testament II*, 771; George, *La Sainte Bible*, 28; Weiser, *Das Buch der zwölf Kleinen Propheten*, 248; Robinson, *Die Zwölf Kleinen Propheten*, 134.

9. Budde, "Micha 2 und 3," 8; and Nowack, *Die Kleinen Propheten*, 209.

10. Elhorst, *De Profetie va Micha*, 71, 119; J. M. P. Smith, *Critical and Exegetical Commentary*, 53; Stave, *Israels Profeter*, 22.

11. Marti, *Das Dodekapropheton*, 275; and Haupt, "The Book of Micah," 210-11.

12. Wade, *The Books of the Prophets*, 17, reads *lō' taśśîg kĕlimmāh*.

13. Hoonacker, *Les douze petits prophètes*, 368-69. See his comments.

Do not preach (Micah and sympathizers)! they (the false prophets) preach.
(Naturally) they (the false prophets) will not preach to these (their rich patrons):
"The calamity (which Micah announces) will not withdraw (i.e., be averted)."[14]

Mowinckel maintains that Micah's enemies are the speakers throughout:

"Do not desire this prophetic word!

Such words of curse (i.e., by Micah in vv. 1-5) shall not be prophesied!

Is there no end to his (i.e., Micah's) words of reproach?"[15]

These views make it clear that one must decide whether Micah is the speaker (and if he is, whether he is stating his own or that of his opponents), whether v. 6 is a dialogue between Micah and his opponents, or whether Micah's opponents are the speakers throughout. And what does line c mean? Are Micah's opponents complaining because the prophet's message constantly deals with Israel's destruction? Or is Micah complaining because the popular prophets would never preach to their wealthy patrons that Israel will be destroyed? Or are Micah's hearers affirming (against his oracle of doom in vv. 1-5) that calamity would not overtake them, as Micah had predicted? Or is Micah maintaining that no matter what his hearers say to the contrary, their calamity cannot be averted? The problem is complex and no "final and conclusive" solution can be given. But there are two guidelines which many interpretations have failed to consider, viz., *structure* and context. Verse 6 seems to be divided into three lines, each beginning with a negative particle. It is most natural, therefore, to believe that each line is intended to be somewhat parallel in thought and meaning, allowing for some progression or alteration of thought. Verse 7 is also composed of three lines, each in interrogative form (see below), and v. 6 of three lines, each beginning with a negative, so it is unlikely that v. 6c should be read as a question (if it is read as a question, it is most natural to interpret it as a question expecting an affirmative reply, "Shall not reproach overtake [us]?" which is inconceivable in the mouth of Micah or his opponents). It seems reason-

---

14. "Mich 6-9," 357. See Donat's line of reasoning, pp. 356-57. Thus similarly Schumpp, *Das Buch der zwölf Propheten*, 195.

15. Mowinckel, *Det Gamle Testamente*, 618.

able that (subconsciously, to be sure) the questions in v. 7 are responsible for understanding this line as a question (the syntax alone would not suggest this). "Reproach" may mean Yahweh's punishment or Micah's rebuke, since the former is the subject of the latter, i.e., Micah's (word of) reproach against the rich for mistreating the poor is inseparably connected with Yahweh's punishment of the rich according to the principle of *ius talionis* reflected in vv. 1–5.[16]

Using v. 6a for a standard, the whole verse makes good sense, retains a logical parallelism and progression of thought, and fits well into the general context, and may be read:

> "Do not speak," they (Micah's opponents) (shall) say,
> "Let them (Micah and those proclaiming his kind of message) not speak of these things (i.e., the things spoken in vv. 1–5),
> Let not reproach (i.e., the ignominy announced in Micah's message in vv.1–5) overtake [us] (prevail, overcome)."

Micah is either citing the words of his opponents (which he had heard on other occasions, or which are to be assumed between vv. 5 and 6—"they say") or apprehends what they are about to say or will say when they learn of his message in vv. 1–5 ("they shall say"). Their protest is twofold: they forbid Micah and those like him to preach such messages of doom as are found in vv. 1–5 (v. 6), and they seek to justify this censure by defending their understanding of Yahweh's nature (v. 7). All three lines of v. 6 are reprimands for the type of doom preaching found in vv. 1–5. The first is a direct address (in the plural) to the speaker(s). The second is a jussive directed against those who preach such oracles of doom. And the third is a jussive directed against the content of their message. The transition from the second person imperative to the third person jussive is quite natural. This translation requires only two slight changes in the consonantal text, viz., *yod* to *taw* in תשיע, and the *samek* to the *śin* in line c. The versions support the singular "reproach," and it is easy to see how the translator of the LXX and the Massoretic tradition confused the *-ût* with *-ôt*. The consistent singular of the verb in the MT and Versions indicates that a singular should be read here.

---

16. See my article: "On the Text of Micah 2, 1aα-β," 534–41.

Verse 7.

The MT may be translated:

> Shall it be said, O house of Jacob:
> Is the spirit of the Lord shortened?
> Are these his deeds?
> Do not my words do good for (to) the upright
> (with regard to) walking?

As in v. 6, the structure of v. 7 is important in deciding on the text and its interpretation. Leaving line a aside for the moment (whether it is read as a statement or a question, its function is to introduce what follows), v. 7 is composed of three lines, each in the form of a question, the first two expecting a negative and the last a positive reply. Like the negative commands in v. 6, these questions are essentially parallel. In light of this, the view that the prophet's opponents are the speakers in vv. 6–7c and that Micah's reply begins at v. 7d[17] is untenable, for the structure indicates that whoever the speaker is in line d (whether Micah or his opponents) must also be the speaker in lines b and c. Critics who understand the passage in this way explain the progress of thought in this manner: the prophet's opponents contend that if Yahweh acts as Micah proclaims, He is unjust, to which Micah ("his words") or Yahweh ("my words") replies that Yahweh blesses only the upright in Israel and not all Israel unconditionally.[18] They reason that after the prophet's scathing rebuke of his audience in vv. 1–5, they would hardly refer to themselves as "upright." And yet, it seems more logical to believe that this is precisely what they would do (cf. the pious "air" his audiences attempt to display in 3:11 and 6:6–7).

The LXX (ὁ λέγων), Syriac, and the Vulgate *(dicit)* apparently understood the *he* at the beginning of v. 7a as an article, while the Targum (הכרו) interpreted it as the *he* interrogative. There is no consensus on the meaning or even the correct reading of אמור. G. R. Driver and Schwantes

---

17. So Kleinert, *The Minor Prophets*, 20; Orelli, *The Twelve Minor Prophets*, 198; Beck, *Erklärung*, 120; Hoonacker, *Les douze petits prophètes*, 370; Margolis, *Micah*, 30–31; and Goldman, *The Twelve Prophets*, 163.

18. See e.g., Driver, "Notes on Difficult Texts," 263, who paraphrases the text this way: "*Shall it be said*, O house of Jacob, Is the ear of the Lord shortened?" etc., i.e., Will you accuse Jehovah of impatience? Will you charge Him with being the cause of your misfortunes? On the contrary, *His* words are always good with those who walk uprightly: if misfortunes come, the cause must lie in yourselves."

read הֲמוּאָר (hophal participle of אָרַר): "Will the house of Jacob be cursed?"[19] Many scholars arrive at a similar meaning by slightly emending the text to *he'ārûr*: "Is the house of Jacob cursed'?"[20] But the Versions unanimously agree with the MT in reading some form of אמר. Even though this is true, there are many possible interpretations. Haupt reads *ha'ōmar* "shall I say?" i.e., "Am I to think that Yahweh is impatient with them for their deeds?"[21] Taylor reads *hă'āmar* "does the house of Jacob say."[22] S. R. Driver and Margolis (claiming support from the Targum) read *he'āmôr* "shall one say, O house of Jacob."[23] G. A. Smith suggests the reading: "O thou that speakest to the house of Jacob" (assuming that the hearers are addressing the prophet) but does not make clear how he would read the Hebrew text.[24] Some scholars have suggested that Micah is denying that Israel is actually what she professes to be, and read: "O thou who art called (but actually are not in deeds) the house of Jacob."[25] It seems to me, however, that the original reading was probably *hā'ōmēr*,[26] which is supported by the LXX and Vulgate, and may explain

19. Driver, "Linguistic and Textual Problems," 266; Schwantes, "A Critical Study," 221 n. 30.

20. Thus Mowinckel, "Mikaboken," 678; Lindblom, *Micha*, 59–60, and 60 n. 1; Sellin, *Das Zwölfprophetenbuch*, 319; Lippl, *Die zwölf kleinen Propheten*, 193; Marty, *L'Ancien Testament II*, 771; Bloomhardt, *Old Testament Commentary*, 844; Nötscher, *Zwölfprophetenbuch*, 93; Deden, *De Kleine Profeten*, 209, 232; George, *La Sainte Bible*, 28; Deissler, *Les Petits Prophètes*, 312; Robinson, *Die Zwölf Kleinen Propheten*, 134; and Kraeling, *Commentary on the Prophets, II*, 211.

21. Haupt, "The Book of Micah," 4, 211.

22. Taylor, *The Massoretic Text*, 54.

23. Driver, "Notes on Difficult Texts," 263; Margolis, *Micah*, 30.

24. G. A. Smith, *The Book of the Twelve Prophets*, 538, note *.

25. On this point, see Driver, "Notes on Difficult Texts," 262.

26. Thus also J. M. P. Smith, *Critical and Exegetical Commentary*, 55. Very recently, Woude, "Micha II 7a," 388–92, has suggested *he'ămûr* that be emended to *he'ĕmîr*, and that either Yahweh or "the house of Jacob be understood as the subject of the verb. This same word occurs in Deut 26:17–18, where it seems to be a *terminus technicus* for a treaty between a king and his vassal. If the same term is the correct reading of Mic 2:7, this is one of several indications that treaty terminology was used in the preprophetic period between Yahweh and Israel. Van der Woude apparently intends that 2:7a be read either "He (Yahweh) has acknowledged the house of Jacob," or "The house of Jacob has acknowledged him (Yahweh)." While I agree that terminology from treaties between a king and his vassal lay behind the Old Testament concept of the covenant between Yahweh and Israel at a very early time, I am unable to accept van der Woude's emendation in Mic 2:7 because it destroys the symmetry of vv. 6–7 suggested in the present paper.

the plural participle in the Targum (which often interprets in a singular n the MT in a plural sense, cf. Hos 1). Something like this is required to preserve the symmetry of vv. 6 and 7. Assuming that this is the correct text, "the house of Jacob is the one saying:" in v. 7a corresponds to "they say," in v. 6a. Micah's opponents affirm that his message in vv. 1–5 is wrong because it is out of harmony with Yahweh's attitude toward his people.

They make three arguments: (a) "Is Yahweh's spirit shortened?" (expecting a negative reply). In other words, Yahweh does not become impatient with His people and bring great destruction on them, as the prophet had warned in vv. 3 and 5. Apparently a *he* has fallen out between the *resh* at the end of הקצר and the *resh* at the beginning of רוח, since רוח is feminine and requires the third person singular instead of the masculine.[27] (b) "Are these[28] his deeds?" (again expecting a negative answer). I.e., the calamities announced by Micah in vv. 3 and 5 are not the kind of deeds or acts which are compatible with Yahweh's nature and attitude toward Israel. (c) "Are not his words good to the one walking uprightly?" (expecting a positive reply). Micah's announcement of punishment for Israel is based on his assertion that the people were full of sin (vv. 1–2). But his hearers deny this, apparently on the assumption that because they are Yahweh's people and are diligent in offering sacrifices, he considers them "righteous" (cf. 3:11 and 6:6–7). The MT "*my* words" (supported by the Syriac, Vulgate, and Targum) is possible only if Yahweh or the prophet (as his spokesman) is the speaker, and scholars defend the MT on this ground.[29] Riessler reads *dibrê Yahwe*, "the words of Yahweh."[30] A few scholars read *dĕrākāyw*, "his ways."[31] But

---

27. So also Haupt, "The Book of Micah," 210–11; and Bruno, *Micha*, 49. The LXX οἶκος Ιακωβ παρώργισεν πνεῦμα κυρίου, "The house of Jacob has provoked the spirit of the Lord to anger," and somewhat similarly the Syriac (For reproach shall not overtake you which is spoken concerning the house of Jacob), "which has provoked the spirit of the Lord to anger," have apparently read הקציף or something similar instead of הקצר.

28. Instead of *ēleh*, Sellin, *Das Zwölfprophetenbuch*, 319; Lippl, *Die zwölf kleinen Propheten*, 193; Driver, "Linguistic and Textual Problems," 266; and Schwantes, "A Critical Study," 221 n. 33, read *ālāh*, "are his deeds a curse?" But this is unnecessary and is not supported by the Versions.

29. Thus Ewald, *Commentary on the Prophets*, II, 305; Beck, *Erklärung*, 120; Duhm, "Anmerkungen," 85; Driver, "Linguistic and Textual Problems," 266; and Schwantes, "A Critical Study," 67.

30. Riessler, *Die Kleinen Propheten*, 110.

31. Budde, "Micha 2 und 3," 9; Nowack, *Die Kleinen Propheten*, 210; and Lippl, *Die zwölf kleinen Propheten*, 193.

there is no reason to emend the MT more radically than necessary. The context calls for a third person singular (cf. lines b and c). The LXX has probably preserved the original text *děbārāyw*. The occurrence of three *yods* together here explains how it would have been possible for a copyist to accidentally omit a waw.

Several critics have expressed dissatisfaction with the *'im hayyāšār hôlēk*. Haupt changes *hôlēk* to אחריו, "Are not his words kind with him who walks upright and follows him?"[32] Bruno reads: *hăyāšār hôlēk 'im 'ammô* ("Are not his words good?) Does he not walk sincerely with his people?"[33] Pont emends *hôlēk* to *bělektô*, "Are not my words good to the upright in his walk?"[34] Taylor reads עם הישר הלכו, "with him that is upright in his walk."[35] Riessler inserts *'ammô* after *'im*, changes *hôlēk* to *hēlēk*, and reads: "Are not the words of Yahweh good to his people when they are upright in their walk?"[36] Sellin changes "him that walks uprightly" to *yiśrā'ēl kullōh*, "all Israel."[37] The most held emendation is *'im 'ammô yiśrā'ēl*, "Are not his words good to his people Israel?"[38] This is said to give rise to the response of the prophet (in the emended text!): *wě'attem lō' 'ammî*, "but you are not my people," in v. 8a. This reading assumes that after the prophet's scathing rebuke in 2:1-5, the rich oppressors would hardly refer to themselves as upright. But there is no reason to emend the MT here. The Versions tenaciously adhere to the idea and word order of the MT, and the idea expressed reflects the concept of uprightness held by Micah's opponents elsewhere in the book (cf. the use of *yāšār* in 3:9; 7:2, 4). G. R. Driver, Nötscher, and Schwantes (following the Targum) may be correct in transposing the last two words

---

32. Haupt, "The Book of Micah," 211.
33. Bruno, *Micha*, 50.
34. Pont, "Micha Studien III," 348.
35. Taylor, *The Massoretic Text*, 57.
36. Riessler, *Die Kleinen Propheten*, 110.
37. Sellin, *Das Zwölfprophetenbuch*, 319-20.
38. Thus Marti, *Das Dodekapropheton*, 275; Donat, "Mich 6–9," 352, 362 (possibly); J. M. P. Smith, *Critical and Exegetical Commentary*, 55; Schmidt, "Die großen Propheten," 138; Mowinckel, "Mikaboken," 678; Lindblom, *Micha*, 60, and 60 n. 2; Lippl, *Die zwölf kleinen Propheten*, 193; Marty, *L'Ancien Testament* II, 771; Deden, *De Kleine Profeten*, 209, 232-33; George, *La Sainte Bible*, 28; Brandenburg, *Die Kleine Propheten*, 1:78; Deissler, *Les Petits Prophètes*, 312; Robinson, *Die Zwölf Kleinen Propheten*, 134; and Kraeling, *Commentary on the Prophets*, II, 211; et al.

(ה)הולך ישרעם),[39] but there is no reason why the present text cannot be read intelligibly. It might be translated literally: "Are not his words good to the upright (with regard to?) walking," which in English idiom means: "the one walking uprightly."

Accordingly, v. 7 is a logical continuation of v. 6. In v. 6, the prophet cites his opponents' ("they") objections to his woe oracle in vv. 1–5, then in v. 7 he states their ("the house of Jacob") reasons for objecting. Thus v. 7 may be read this way:

The house of Jacob is the one saying:
"Is the spirit of the Lord shortened (i.e., impatient)? (– No.)
Are these (calamities announced by the prophet in vv. l–5) his (i.e., Yahweh's) deeds? (– No.)
Do not his (Yahweh's) words do good to him who walks uprightly?" (– Yes.)

The first two questions deny that Yahweh will punish his people as Micah has announced, and the last question asserts that He will be true to His nature and bless the upright (who are identified with Israel as God's chosen people).

Verse 8.

The MT may be translated:

> And (But) yesterday (already) my people rose up for an enemy,
> From the front of the garment you stripped off the mantle
> From those who pass by securely, those averse from war.

The structure of v. 8 is strikingly similar to that of vv. 6 and 7. It is composed of three lines, each of which contains a rebuke against the mistreatment of the helpless. The first two lines censure the *offence*, and the last line specifies the *offended*. This militates against emending *śalmāh* to *šōlĕmîm* (often also emending *mimmûl* to *mēʻal*, but hardly necessarily)[40] or *šālem*[41] "from peaceful people (a peaceful person) you

---

39. Driver, "Linguistic and Textual Problems," 266; Nötscher, *Zwölfproph-etenbuch*, 93; and Schwantes, "A Critical Study," 67.

40. So Wellhausen, *Die Kleinen Propheten*, 138; Marti, *Das Dodekapropheton*, 275; J. M. P. Smith, *Critical and Exegetical Commentary*, 53, 56; Stave, *Israels Profeter*, 22; Sellin, *Das Zwölfprophetenbuch*, 319; Lippl, *Die zwölf kleinen Propheten*, 193; Marty, *L'Ancien Testament II*, 771; Deden, *De Kleine Profeten*, 209, 233; and Weiser, *Das Buch der zwölf Kleinen Propheten*, 248 n. 4 (possibly).

41. Thus Pont, "Micha Studiën, III," 348; Nötscher, *Zwölfprophetenbuch*, 94; and

tear away the cloak" in v. 8b, or against positing the view that either of these was accidentally omitted by a copyist because of the similarity to שמלה. The LXX κατέναντι τῆς εἰρήνης αὐτοῦ τὴν δορὰν αὐτοῦ ἐξέδειραν, "Against his (my people's) peace they stripped off his skin," which is essentially followed by the Syriac: "My people rises up as a thief against his peace. You strip off his skin that you may pass over his hope," apparently confused שמלה with some form of שלום.[42] But the Vulgate *Desuper tunica pallium sustulistis*, "On top of the coat you have borne (!) the mantle," vindicates the MT. The offense condemned here is that of seizing a poor man's garment in pledge and failing to return it before sundown (cf. Exod 22:26-27). The reading "skin" in the LXX and Syriac is apparently due to interpreting אדר in its Aramaic sense instead of its Hebrew sense,[43] and may have been influenced by Mic 3:2-3. There is actually little reason to emend the text in line b.[44]

A recognition of the structure of v. 8 also alleviates the posed difficulties of שובי in line c. Many scholars, reasoning subconsciously that line c must correspond to a large extent with line b, assume that the last line of the verse must allude to an "offense" *as well* as to the "offended," and thus read שבי "(taking away) those who pass by securely as captives (not booty or spoils![45]) of war."[46] But there is no support for this in

---

Deissler, *Les Petits Prophètes*, 313; Hoonacker, *Les douze petits prophètes*, 371, emends שלמה אבד to שלמנאחר, and reads: Au-devant de Salmanasar vous arrachez a ceux qui vont leur chemin avec confiance, du butin de guerre." This is ingenious, but has no support in Versions and hardly needs refutation.

42. שלמו or perhaps שלמה, as G. A. Smith, *The Book of the Twelve Prophets*, 538 n.; and Haupt, "The Book of Micah," XXVI, 207; Haupt, "Micah's Capucinade," 93 and 108 n. 107, think.

43. Cf. Büchler, "אדר = Fell in LXX zu Micha 2, 8," 64.

44. It is possible that a *taw* has dropped out by haplography at the end of אדר, and that the text should be emended to אדרת as Wellhausen, *Die Kleinen Propheten*, 138-39; Pont, "Micha Studiën, III," 348; Lippl, *Die zwölf kleinen Propheten*, 193; and many other scholars think. It is less likely that the plural אדרות "mantles," suggested by Haupt, "The Book of Micah," 207; Riessler, *Die Kleinen Propheten*, 110; et al., is the correct text. However, אדר may be taken as a masculine noun with the same meaning as the feminine אדרת.

45. A translation suggested by Marti, *Das Dodekapropheton*, 275; Haupt, "The Book of Micah," 208; Donat, "Mich 6-9," 363, 365; J. M. P. Smith, *Critical and Exegetical Commentary*, 56; and Deden, *De Kleine Profeten*, 209, 233; but שבי does not mean "booty."

46. Taylor, *The Massoretic Text*, 62 (possibly); Wellhausen, *Die Kleinen Propheten*, 138; Hoonacker, *Les douze petits prophètes*, 371; Budde, "Micha 2 und 3," 10; Bruno,

the Versions. Verse 8c refers only to the offended; the offense has been defined in v. 8a–b.[47]

The first line of v. 8 is crucial to an understanding of the "people of God" in the book of Micah, and many interpretations have been suggested. As already mentioned, several scholars emend "him that walks uprightly" in v. 7d to *'im 'ammô yiśrāēl*, "Are not his words good to his people Israel?" and have Micah reply in v. 8a with ואתם לא עמי, "But you are not my people," often completing the line with *lĕ'ammî* (or *'al*) *lĕ'ôyēb tāqûmû*, "against my people you rise up as an enemy."[48] Similarly, several scholars begin this line with *wĕattem 'al*, and read: "But you, against my people you rise up as an enemy."[49] Scholars agree on the reading *tāqûmû*, Qal imperfect 2nd masc. pl., and on regarding "my people" in v. 8a as the oppressed (possibly because they connect this line with v. 7d). Van Hoonacker is somewhat unique in reading: "Mais vous, contre mon people, vous assistez son ennemi."[50] Kleinert thinks that "my people" in v. 8 refers to North Israel, and understands the passage to mean: But recently, when my people (the northern kingdom which already been attacked by Assyria) stood up (against Assyria), you (rich oppressors in Judah) stripped the robe off the garment from them that pass by securely (i.e., the North Israelites who fled to Judah for help against and protec-

---

Micha, 51; Mowinckel, "Mikaboken," 31; Sellin, *Das Zwölfprophetenbuch*, 319; Lippl, *Die zwölf kleinen Propheten*, 193; Nötscher, *Zwölfprophetenbuch*, 94; and Deissler, *Les Petits Prophètes*, 313.

47. Because of the LXX συντριμμὸν, Riessler, *Die Kleinen Propheten*, 110; Marty, *L'Ancien Testament II*, 771; and Weiser, *Das Buch der zwölf Kleinen Propheten*, 248 n. 6, read שבר. But all the other Versions favor some form of שוב. Wade, *The Books of the Prophets*, 19, is probably correct in interpreting "averse from war" as "not thinking of war," i.e., not having war (friction, antagonism, etc.) in mind.

48. Budde, "Micha 2 und 3," 9; Nowack, *Die Kleinen Propheten*, 210; Sellin, *Das Zwölfprophetenbuch*, 319, 321; Lippl, *Die zwölf kleinen Propheten*, 193; Bloomhardt, *Old Testament Commentary*, 845; Snaith, *Amos, Hosea, and Micah*, 87; Ungern-Sternberg, *Der Rechtsstreit Gottes*, 42; Brandenburg, *Die Kleine Propheten*, 78; and Weiser, *Das Buch der zwölf Kleinen Propheten*, 248.

49. Nötscher, *Zwölfprophetenbuch*, 94; Deden, *De Kleine Profeten*, 209, 233; Robinson, *Die Zwölf Kleinen Propheten*, 134; and Scharbert, *Die Propheten Israels*, 321. Emendations and translations which differ only very slightly from this have been suggested by W. R. Smith, *The Prophets of Israel*, 427–28 n. 4; Duhm, "Anmerkungen," 85; Riessler, *Die Kleinen Propheten*, 110; J. M. P. Smith, *Critical and Exegetical Commentary*, 53, 55; Schmidt, "Die großen Propheten," 138; and Bruno, *Das Buch der Zwölf*, 93, 215.

50. *Les douze petits prophètes*, 370–71.

tion from Assyria).⁵¹ Halévy maintains that Yahweh is the speaker in v. 8 and that Micah is the enemy. He reads: "Mon peuple considère son intermédiaire [i.e., Micah, as God's true prophet] comme un ennemi."⁵² In a rather extensive and important study. J. Reider⁵³ has sought to solve the problem by dividing *wĕ’ethmûl* into two words ואת מול and arguing that *mûl* is a noun of the *miktal* type from the doubly weak stem ולי, "to be near or adjacent," and means "friend, companion." He cites Exod 18:19; 1 Sam 17:30; Lev 5:8; and Num 8:2 in support of this, and translates Mic 2:8 in this way: "And the friend of my people it (namely my people) raiseth up into an enemy, off a friend ye strip garment and mantle, off those who pass by securely as if they were captives of war."⁵⁴ He contends that this interpretation restores the original force to the three lines of the verse, assuming that each of them speaks of turning a friend into an enemy.

On the basis of the Vulgate *e contraria*, the present follows Budde⁵⁵ in conjecturing that the MT *wĕ’ethmūl* is a scribal corruption of an original ואולם. This same word occurs in 3:8 to begin the prophet's contrast of himself with the popular prophets who are described in vv. 5–7. In 2:8 it is likely that he begins the contrast of his own message with that of the message of his opponents set forth in vv. 6–7. *yĕqômēm* may be regarded as the Pōʻlel imperfect 3rd masc. singular In this case, "my people" is the *subject* and refers to the *oppressors* rather than to the oppressed, and vv. 7d–8 may be read this way:

> (Micah's opponents): Do not his (Yahweh's) words do good to him that walks uprightly? (—Yes)
> (Micah): (This is true), however, my people has risen up as an enemy (against Yahweh, or against the poor),
> You (my people of line a) strip the mantle off the garment
> From those who pass by securely,
> i.e., those who are averse from war.

---

51. Kleinert, *The Minor Prophets*, 20 n. 4.
52. Halévy, "Le Livre de Michée," 109.
53. Reider, "Etymology," 89–96.
54. Ibid., 92.
55. Budde, "Micha 2 und 3," 10.

All the Versions understand "my people" as the subject of sentence in v. 8a and it is natural to equate this term with the subject (You) of the second line.[56]

The Coherence of Micah 2:1-11

This interpretation of Mic 2:6-8 has implications for determining the extent of the pericope beginning with 2:1. Many scholars consider vv. 1-5 and vv. 6-11 as two separate pericopes.[57] They argue that the allusion to prophecy (נטף) in vv. 6 and 11 shows that these two verses are the beginning and conclusion of the latter, and that v. 5 (or 4) is the natural conclusion of the former. But if vv. 6-7 are the reply of Micah's opponents to the prophet's reproach in vv. 1-5, this would hardly be a suitable beginning for a pericope in this prophetic book. It is unlikely that a pericope would begin with a *response* of the prophet's enemies. The provocation of this would be expected to precede the response itself, and vv. 1-5 is this provocation. Micah condemns the rich for oppressing the poor and announces the punishment which will come upon them. They retaliate by accusing Micah of being a false prophet because his message does not correspond to their understanding of the divine nature and requirements. Micah rejoinders by reinforcing his charges of sin against his opponents and by reiterating his announcement of punishment. Verse 5 may indeed be the "end" of Micah's oracle in the sense that vv. 1-5 reflect the entire message which the prophet intended to deliver on a certain occasion, but the vehement reply of his opponents in vv. 6-7 naturally gives rise to a repetition of the sins and punishment already mentioned in vv. 1-5 in light of this reply. This explains why captivity is threatened in vv. 4-5 as well as in v. 10, which indeed provides a strong argument for the coherence of vv. 1-11, which may best be understood if they are taken as a unit.[58]

56. Elhorst, *De Profetie va Micha*, 61, 119; Halévy, "Le Livre de Michée," 109. Horton, *The Minor Prophets*, 231, and Cheyne, *The Two Religions of Israel*, 367; and Cheyne, *Micah*, 27, are among those who consider "my people" to be the oppressors.

57. Verse 11 "enthält die Schlußantwort auf v. 6 und erweist sich damit als Abschluß der ganzen Strophe v. 6-11." Sellin, *Das Zwölfprophetenbuch*, 321. See also p. 319. So also Ewald, *Commentary on the Prophets*, II, 309 (vv. 1-5, 6-10); Marti, *Das Dodekapropheton*, 274; Lindblom, *Micha*, 59; Schwantes, "A Critical Study," 55-56; and Weiser, *Das Buch der zwölf Kleinen Propheten*, 245-49.

58. So Beck, *Erklärung*, 123, J. M. P. Smith, *Critical and Exegetical Commentary*, 52; Schmidt, "Die großen Propheten," 138; Cheyne, *Micah*, 23; Bruno, *Micha*, 41, 28;

The "People of God" in the Book of Micah

'am occurs eleven times in the doom sections of Micah (1:2—2:11; 3; 6:1—7:6). In 2:4, 11; 3:5; 6:2, 3, 5, 16, it is a comprehensive term for all Israel. In fact, "his people" and "Israel"[59] are used interchangeably in 6:2. In 1:9, "my people" refers to the Southern kingdom as distinguished from North Israel. The point is that the sin of the Northern kingdom had spread to Judah, and thus the punishment which North Israel had already suffered was to be expected in Judah. But the most significant use of "(God's) people" in the book of Micah is to be found in 2:8, where the expression "my people" is to be understood as the subject of the sentence and thus refers to the oppressors of the poor. Here "my people" refers to only a part of "Israel" (and this is true even if "my people" is taken as the oppressed in this verse), i.e., it divides Israel into two groups, viz., those who claim to be God's people but are not, and those who are genuinely God's people. A comparable distinction is made in v. 9, which seems to illuminate some the obscurities of v. 8a. The same phrase is used for the *oppressors* in v. 8 and for the *oppressed* in v. 9. Its use in v. 8 is derived from the claims made by Micah's opponents and therefore is ironical, while its use in v. 9 is straightforward and represents Micah's own position. The two verses vividly distinguish two groups in Israel, a distinction which also appears in 3:3, where "my people" is identical with the oppressed.[60]

It is significant that *gôy* occurs only in the hope sections of book of Micah (2:12-13; 4-5; 7:7-20), i.e., in 4:2, 3 (3 times), 7, 11; 5:7,14; 7:16), and that it refers to Israel only once, i.e., in 4:7. Speiser argues that *'am* is used in the Old Testament primarily in a subjective and personal sense, and is usually associated with a strong feeling of kinship, whereas *gôy* is used objectively and impersonally, and applies primarily to a loosely knit

---

Pfeiffer, *Introduction*, 590, Ridderbos, *De Kleine Profeten*, 70; Deden, *De Kleine Profeten*, 208; Wolfe, "The Book of Micah," 914 (vv. 1–10); and Deissler, *Les Petits Prophètes*, 314. Donat, "Mich 6–9," 350, 365, argues that the extent of the pericope is vv. 1–5 plus 10, and that vv. 6–9 are a parenthesis.

59. For discussions of the use of "Israel" and "Jacob" in the book of Micah, see Danell, *Studies*, 189-202; and my dissertation, Willis, "The Structure, Setting, and Inter-Relationships," 177–82.

60. Sellin, *Das Zwölfprophetenbuch*, 304, 324; and Deden, *De Kleine Profeten*, 200, interpret 3:5 in the same way. However, in this passage "my people" means all Israel. That the prophets make this people to err implies that they do err, and therefore are as guilty as those who lead them astray.

super-organization by which people are bound together externally.⁶¹ The deep concern of Yahweh for his "people" reflected in the book of Micah verifies this distinction in this prophetic book.⁶² The identification of "this people" in 2:11 with "this family" *(mišpāḥāh)* in 2:3 (incidentally, this is another indication that 2:1-11 should be taken as a unit) further substantiates the idea that "people" conveys the concept of intimate relationship between Yahweh and Israel.

With the exception of 7:14, *'am* occurs exclusively in the doom sections of the book of Micah. It means pan-Israel except in 2:8-9 and 3:3. But the purpose of the use of this word is not to assure Israel of her inviolability as God's people in spite of impending danger. This was the view of Micah's opponents, and is explicitly rejected in 2:6-9; 3:4, 11.⁶³ On the contrary, Micah called Israel "God's people" in order to condemn her for being unfaithful to Yahweh's covenant with his people. Therefore, it is most striking that this term figures so prominently in the lawsuit in ch. 6 (vv. 2, 3, 5, 16). At the same time, this lawsuit (and its companion piece in 1:2ff.) is crucial to an understanding of Micah's rather novel distinction between external Israel and genuine Israel. Apparently, Micah felt himself responsible to two types of people: Israel as a whole, which must be punished, and a handful of innocent sufferers whose cause Yahweh had espoused. Lindblom asserts that Micah's oracle which makes this differentiation is "das Originallste, das er . . . gesagt hat."⁶⁴ A number of scholars concur in this judgment.⁶⁵ The prophetic message, with its strong emphasis on approaching punishment, inevitably produced a division between those that rejected it and those who accepted it.⁶⁶ Thus,

---

61. Speiser, "'People' and 'Nation,'" 157-63, especially p. 159.

62. Note the use of "people" with possessives in the phrases "my people" (1:9; 2:4, 8:9; 3:3, 5; 6:3, 5, 16) and "his people" (6:2). See Speiser, "'People' and 'Nation,'" 158.

63. Cf. the way in which Amos uses the expression "the whole family" in Amos 3:1.

64. Lindblom, *Micha*, 147.

65. Weiser, *Das Buch der zwölf Kleinen Propheten*, 250, writes: "Die Erkenntnis, das der Begriff 'Gottesvolk' sich nicht deck mit der nationalen Zugehörigkeit zum Volk Israel, aus der Jesaja die letzten Folgerungen gezogen hat, ist für die Geschichte der alttestamentlichen Religion von weittragender Bedeutung geworden." See also especially Nowack, *Die Kleinen Propheten*, 210; Bruno, *Micha*, 3-5 (who considers this distinction to be "der Schlüssel zum rechten Verständnis des Micharätsels," 3); Deden, *De Kleine Profeten*, 200; and Deissler, *Les Petits Prophètes*, 313.

66. "The prophetic preaching created a split within the nation which separated membership of the true people of God from the mere fact of belonging to Israel." Eichrodt, *Theology*, I, 356.

the effect of the theophany in the cultic recitation was the purification of the community,[67] and in the book of Micah this theophany is a vital part of the lawsuit of Yahweh with his people.

---

67. So also Weiser, "Die Darstellung der Theophanie," 525.

9

A Note on ואמר in Micah 3:1

ואמר IN MIC 3:1 has been variously interpreted. (1) Rupprecht,[1] Steinmann,[2] and Kraeling[3] simply delete this word as a later addition. (2) Bruno[4] argues that the present Hebrew text is the remnant of an original כה אמר יהוה, which corresponds to the introduction to the oracles against the wicked leaders (Mic 2:3) and the false prophets (Mic 3:5). (3) In his earlier work on Micah, Mowinckel seeks to solve the difficulty by moving this word to its "original" position at the beginning of line c: "And I said, Is it not for you to know justice?"[5] In his later work, however, he leaves this word in its present position and emends the text to ויאמר, "and he said," "med tilbakeblikk tu 1:1."[6] The LXX καὶ ἐρεῖ (future!) and Syriac w'mr offer some support for this emendation, while the Targum ואמרית and Vulgate *et dixi* support the MT. (4) A number of scholars, including J. M. P. Smith,[7] Budde,[8] Nowack,[9] Wade,[10] Sellin,[11]

---

1. Rupprecht, *Wissenschaftliches Handbuch*, 268.
2. Steinmann and Hanon, *Michée*, 16.
3. Kraeling, *Commentary*, 212–13.
4. Bruno, *Micha und der Herrscher*, 58.
5. Mowinckel, "Mikaboken," 11, 33.
6. Mowinckel, *Det Gamle Testamente*, 680.
7. J. M. P. Smith, *Critical and Exegetical Commentary*, 67, 72.
8. Budde, "Micha 2 und 3," 17–19.
9. Nowack, *Die Kleinen Propheten*, 213.
10. Wade, *The Books of the Prophets*, 22.
11. Sellin, *Das Zwölfprophetenbuch*, 324.

Lippl,[12] Deden,[13] Schwantes,[14] and Weiser,[15] consider "And I said" to be the remnant of a narrative which originally preceded vv. 1–4, and which was omitted when the present form of the book of Micah was made. Eissfeldt says that this word "looks almost like the remnant of an autobiographical account."[16] Budde has offered the most elaborate defense of this solution to the problem. He maintains that an extensive redaction of the entire corpus of the Book of the Twelve Prophets was made by a group of editors in order to prepare these books for canonization.[17] This redaction was necessitated by a strong Jewish element[18] which (like the Samaritans) regarded only the Pentateuch as canonical. It consisted primarily of removing narrative sections from the prophetic books which contained words of those who opposed Yahweh and his prophets, leaving only divine oracles.[19] After such a redaction, the opposition could hardly deny the internal evidence for the canonicity of these books. Budde uses Mic 3 to illustrate the way in which these redactors worked. All three oracles in this chapter (vv. 1–4, 5–8, 9–12) seem to represent Micah's reply to opposition from his enemies. Originally there must have been a narrative passage before each of these oracles to serve as their background. Each was purposefully deleted by the redactors. But "then I said" in 3:1 preserves a fragment of the first of these narratives. Furthermore, Jer 26:17–19 seems to preserve the original narrative sequence of Mic 3:12, which describes Hezekiah's repentance as a result of Micah's preaching.[20]

12. Lippl, *Die zwölf Kleinen Propheten*, 182, 195.
13. Deden, *De Kleine Profeten*, 201, 210.
14. Schwantes, "A Critical Study," 83.
15. Weiser, *Das Buch der zwölf Kleinen Propheten*, 254.
16. Eissfeldt, *The Old Testament*, 408.
17. Budde, "Eine folgenschwere Redaktion," 218–29. Budde says two things which seem to contradict his theory. (a) He argues that this redaction was done "allgemach" (219). (b) He contends that this was not a redaction of already existing books, but an arrangement of traditional disparate materials into book form (226). The description given here adheres to the main thrust of Budde's argument.
18. According to Budde, this element continued to exist as late as the time of 2 Maccabees (2:13), and even as late as the time of Jerome and Origen. "Eine folgenschwere Redaktion," 225.
19. "Gott allein das Wort zu lassen, alles übrige, alles Menschliche, auszuschalten, das muß die Absicht gewesen sein" (Budde, "Eine folgenschwere Redaktion," Cf. also: "Micha 2 und 3," 19).
20. Ibid., 222–23.

Many critics regard "And I said" in Mic 3:1 as an attempt to connect the second and third chapters of this little prophetic book. (5) Beck,[21] Halévy,[22] Marti,[23] and Ungern-Sternberg[24] consider 3:1ff. to be a continuation of 2:11 or 2:13, and so translate, "Again I said" or "And I said (again)." (6) Stade[25] understands "Arise and go" in 2:10 to be the words of the rich addressed to the poor widows and orphans as they drove them out of their homes. Thus, he interprets 3:1ff. as Micah's reply to the rich, and reads "But I said." (7) Other scholars think that 3:1ff. is Micah's reply to the words of the false prophets in 2:11, and so read "And I said," or "But I said." Cornill writes: "The ואמר, 'and I said,' of iii 1 is just as much Micah's retort against the false prophets in ii 11 as iii 8 is to iii 7."[26] Similarly, Stave writes: "'Och (1. *men*) jag sade' förbinder det följande med den 2:11 afbrutna tråden" (italics mine).[27] Duhm,[28] George Adam Smith,[29] and Lindblom[30] take the same position. (8) Orelli[31] and Moulton[32] consider 3:1ff. to be Micah's reply to the false prophets who (according to their interpretation) speak in 2:12-13. Lindblom himself suggests the possibility that "and I said" could have been inserted by an editor who mistook 2:12-13 for an oracle of the false prophets.[33] These last four explanations are natural correlates to the widely held view that chs. l-3 form the first major division of the book of Micah.

However, in my opinion, the book of Micah falls naturally into an A (1-2)—B (3-5)—A (6-7) outline. Each major division begins with שמעו (1:2; 3:1; 6:1) and a doom section (1:2—2:11; 3; 6:1—7:6), and ends with a hope section (2:12-13; 4-5; 7:7-20).[34] To some extent, each of these

21. Beck, *Erklärung*, 134.
22. Halévy, "Le Livre de Michée," 195.
23. Marti, *Das Dodekapropheten*, 277.
24. Ungern-Sternberg, *Der Rechtsstreit Gottes*, 52.
25. Stade, "Bemerkungen," 164.
26. Cornill, *Introduction*, 340.
27. Stave, *De Mindre Profeterna*, 37.
28. Duhm, "Anmerkungen," 86.
29. Smith, *The Book of the Twelve Prophets*, 539.
30. Lindblom, *Micha*, 69.
31. Orelli, *The Twelve Minor Prophets*, 200.
32. Moulton, *Daniel*, 260.
33. Lindblom, *Micha*, 70.
34. Among the scholars who have arranged the book of Micah in three sections:

sections is independent of the other, so that in a sense we may agree with Ridderbos's judgment as to the interrelationship of the first two sections: "Het is volstrekt zo zeker niet, dat er zulk een nauw verband tussen h. 2 en h. 3 is te leggen."[35] But at the same time, there is evidence that an attempt has been made to connect the major divisions of the book by catchwords. Sections II and III are linked together by *šāmēʿû* in 5:14 and *šimʿû* in 6:1.[36] Sections I and II are connected by בראשם in 2:13 and ראשי יעקב in 3:1. This connection and the fact that sections I and III are each composed of a covenant lawsuit (1:2-7; 6:1-8); a lament (1:8-16; 7:1-6); an oracle giving the reasons for the impending doom (2:1-11; 6:9-16); and a relatively short hope oracle (2:12-13; 7:7-20)—whereas the middle division (II) is composed of a relatively short doom section (ch. 3) and a long hope section (chs. 4-5)—argues strongly against the view that 2:12-13 has been displaced from its original position and should be restored to it.[37] But this is another matter.

1-2, 3-5, 6-7, are: Farrar, *The Minor Prophets*, 129; Beck, *Erklärung*, 63; Rupprecht, *Wissenschaftliches Handbuch*, 269 (who remarks: "Verheißung ist das Ziel der Propheten. Drohung aber der Weg"); Kolmodin, *Profeten Mika*, 1, 16, 43; Halévy, "Le Livre de Michée," 291; Eiselen, *Prophecy and the Prophets*, 118; *The Prophetic Books*, 472; Farley, *Progress*, 100-101; McFadyen, "Micah," 792; and Ridderbos, *De Kleine Profeten*, 56-57. J. M. P. Smith, *Critical and Exegetical Commentary*, 72, who outlines the book according to a 1-3, 4-5, 6-7 arrangement, rejects the argument that "and I said" in 3:1 indicates an original connection between 2:10 and 3:1ff., and says: "Rather does a *new theme* present itself in ch. 3" (italics mine); Cheyne, *Micah*, 10, who follows Smith's outline of the book, admits that there are excellent reasons for following the 1-2, 3-5, 6-7 division.

35. Ridderbos, *De Kleine Profeten*, 57.

36. "An das 'höret,' mit dem die zweite Rede schließt, schließt sich das 'höret' der dritten Rede an." Rupprecht, *Wissenschaftliches Handbuch*, 270. "Le *šimʿû* (printing error for *šāmēʿû*) 'ont obéi' de v. 14, amorce le *šimʿû* 'écoutez' de vi 1." Renaud, *Structure*, 35. Thus similarly George, *La Sainte Bible*, 12; and Schwantes, "A Critical Study," 142.

37. Scholars are unable to agree on the original position of 2:12-18. Other than general attempts to solve the problem of the book of Micah by rearranging its pericopes, the following suggested solutions are worthy of note. (a) Bruno, *Micha und der Herrscher*, 60-63, who interprets 3:1-4 as an oracle against the priests, argues that 2:12-18 was originally an oracle of doom. For him, the order of the text should be: 3:1-2a, 3a, 2b; 2:12-13a. "Before them" in 2:18a and all of 2:18b are a late gloss. The הפרץ is a butcher, and 2:12-l3a describes the gathering of a flock or herd to be butchered. The idea is that just as the priests had done their part in butchering Israel's poor (3:l-2a, 3a, 2b), so they too would be butchered (2:12-13a), (b) Duhm, "Anmerkungen," 87, places 2:12-13 before 4:6-7 because of the striking similarity of meter and content between the two pericopes. He conjectures that this original order was disrupted by the insertion of 4:1-5 between the two passages. 2:12-13 was then moved to the margin, and a

Undoubtedly, Budde is correct in emphasizing that redactors purposefully deleted "original" material which might have become a part of the prophetic books. This should caution us against being too quick to limit what Micah, e.g., could or could not have said on the basis of the relatively few things which are ascribed to him in the book of Micah. But the reason for deletions, additions, alterations, etc., in this book is not to prepare it for canonization, but to arrange the oracles which had been handed down (in oral and/or written form) in such a way as to apply them to the redactor's contemporary situation. If Budde's explanation of "then I said" in Mic 3:1 were correct, surely the redactor would have removed the "narrative background" of 2:8–11 in 2:6–7 or of 6:8 in 6:6–7!

We would suggest, then, that ואמר in Mic 3:1 has another function. Amos 1:2, which begins with ויאמר without any "narrative background" preceding it, may be helpful in determining this function. If the third person singular of אמר can be used to introduce an oracle or (in this case) a major section of a prophetic book (Amos 1:2—2:16), there is no reason why the first person singular of the same verb cannot be used in the same way.[38] In my opinion, "And I said" may well be the redactor's way of indicating his own arrangement of the "Mican" oracles which had been handed down to him. If this is correct, it further substantiates the thesis that a major division is intended between chs. 2 and 3 rather than between chs. 3 and 4. Whether this word is the redactors' own insertion or a part of the "original" oracle (which, as Budde suggests, may have contained material preceding that which appears in the present text) cannot be decided with certainty. But the present writer feels that unless good arguments are given to the contrary, Koch's evaluation of the work of redactors points in the right direction. "Dabei setzt das Wort Redaktion einerseits voraus, daß der biblische Schriftsteller in der Regel nicht freischaffend gearbeitet hat, also kein eigentlicher Verfasser war,

---

later copyist put it in its present position. (A misprint on p. 86 of Duhm's essay seems to explain the statement of Lindblom, *Micha*, 67, that Duhm moves 2:12–13 to its original position before 4:5.) (c) König, *Einleitung*, 328, thinks that 2:12–13 belongs after 4:8. Deden, *De Kleine Profeten*, 216 admits this possibility. (d) But among those scholars who maintain that 2:12–13 must be transferred, the most widely held view is that they belong after 4:6–7. Thus Condamin, "Interpolations," 385–86; Sellin, *Introduction*, 176; *Das Zwölfprophetenbuch*, 322, 330; Clamer, "Michée," 1656; Lippl, *Die zwölf Kleinen Propheten*, 194; Deden, *De Kleine Profeten*, 210; and Renaud, *Structure*, 15 n. 1; 21, 22, 48.

38. This explanation agrees substantially with that of Margolis, *Micah*, 35; and Goldman, *The Twelve Prophets*, 165.

sondern bereits vorgeformte mündliche Überlieferung zusammenfaßt, ordnet, niederschreibt."³⁹ "Dieser formgeschichtliche Arbeitsgang wird bei der Bibel dadurch erleichtert, daß die Schriftsteller meist in großer Ehrfurcht an die überkommenen Einzelstücke herangetreten sind. Was sie an Eigenem hinzusetzen, besteht in der Regel nur im Rahmen, mit dem sie den weithin disparaten Stoff mündlicher Überlieferung zusammenfassen."⁴⁰

---

39. Koch, *Was ist Formgeschichte?* 62.
40. Ibid., 63.

10

ממך לי יצא in Micah 5:1

It is not uncommon for scholars to ignore the expression יצא לי ממך in Mic 5:1 in commentaries and other works. Those who attempt to reconcile the difficulty which it presents in its present context usually find it necessary to emend the text. Mowinckel[2] reads מלך instead of לי: "out of you shall come forth a king that is to be ruler in Israel." Fitzmyer[3] adopts the same reading. He argues that לי is out of place here because it never occurs before יצא anywhere else in the Old Testament. He drops the *yod* in לי and combines ל with יצא as a particle of emphasis. Bentzen[4] reads אל instead of לי, "out of you shall come forth *a deity (or God)*." Bruno,[5] Sellin,[6] and Schwantes (as a possible explanation)[7] read ילד instead of לי, "out of you shall come forth a child." On the basis of the Codex Alexandrinus of the LXX ἡγούμενος, Schwantes[8] also suggests that the reading may have been שר, "out of you shall come forth *a prince*." (cf. Matt 2:6.) Haupt[9] emends לי to לנו "from thee is come *to us*," and argues that this passage refers to the birth of Zerubbabel. T. H. Robinson[10] reads כי ממך instead of לי, "*for from you* shall come forth one

---

1. The versification of the MT is used throughout this article.
2. Mowinckel, "Mikaboken," 35; Mowinckel, *Det Gamle Testamente*, 686.
3. Fitzmyer, "ל as a Preposition," 12–13.
4. Bentzen, *King and Messiah*, 40.
5. Bruno, *Micha und der Herrscher*, 92.
6. Sellin, *Das Zwölfprophetenbuch*, 335–36.
7. Schwantes, "A Critical Study," 129.
8. Ibid.
9. Haupt, "The Book of Micah," 236.
10. Robinson, *Die zwölf Kleinen Propheten*, 142.

who shall be ruler." Lippl[11] regards the *yod* in לי as the remnant of the Tetragrammaton, and reads ליהוה, "for from you one shall come forth *to Yahweh* to be ruler." With come hesitation, Renaud[12] interprets the expression "come forth" as a description of physical birth, i.e., a going forth out of the bowels, and cites the use of יצא in 2 Sam 7:12 as evidence for this meaning.

It is true that the versions are not in exact agreement in their treatment of this difficult phrase, but they provide no compelling reason for emending the MT. The LXX ἐκ σοῦ μοι ἐξελεύσεται and the Vulgate *ex te mihi egradietur* agree with the MT. The Targum יפוק משיחא מנך קדמי, "from you the Messiah will go forth before me," probably represents an interpretation of that which was considered to be a difficult passage, and does not necessarily indicate that the Targum employed a different Vorlage at this point. The Syriac *mnky ypwq šlyṭ' dyhw' 'l yśryl*, "from you (fem.) will go out a ruler who will be over Israel," simply omits *lî*, "to me," and reverses "ruler" and the verb of being. The reason for the omission of "to me" is a matter of conjecture. It could have happened accidentally, or the translator may have thought that it was not necessary to retain this word to convey the meaning of the Hebrew into Syriac, or he may have had other reasons which cannot be ascertained. But in light of the other versions, the evidence for the retention of *lî* in the text is strong. Unfortunately, the "quotation" of Mic 5:1 in Matt 2:6 varies in many particulars from the MT and the versions, and so cannot be used with any degree of confidence to help determine the original text of Mic 5:1.

In light of this evidence, we need to re-examine the expression ממך לי יצא to try to find a possible meaning which meets the requirements both of the usage of the Hebrew expression in the Old Testament and of the context of Mic 5:1.

In my opinion, there is good reason for the word order in this phrase. The author apparently intends a type of polarity: "from ... to." The promised ruler will come forth from a certain town (Bethlehem) to a certain person (Yahweh). This polarity occurs before the verb for the sake of emphasis. As far as I know, יצא ל is not used anywhere else in the Old Testament in the precise sense which Mic 5:1 seems to require. The meaning of this phrase does not seem to be that the coming ruler will "come forth to meet" Yahweh. If so, we would expect יצא לקראת,

---

11. Lippl, *Die zwölf Kleinen Propheten*, 207.
12. Renaud, *Structure*, 52.

which occurs often in the Old Testament (Gen 14:17; Judg 4:18, 22; 1 Sam 13:10; 30:21; 2 Sam 6:20; Isa 7:3; Prov 7:15, etc.). To be sure, יצא often occurs with ל or אל to describe the "physical" act of one person approaching another, as Jehu going out to the servants (2 Kgs 4:11) or Moses going out to his brethren (Exod 2:11) or David longing to go to Absalom (2 Sam 13:39) etc.

But in Mic 5:1, the prophet is hardly announcing that the coming ruler will approach Yahweh "physically." Such an idea would be meaningless in this context. Therefore, it seems likely to me that ל יצא may have somewhat of a technical meaning in this verse.[13] It is used of an inferior king (the coming ruler) "going out" "from" a city "to" a superior king (Yahweh). As far as I know יצא is not used with ל anywhere else in the Old Testament to convey this idea. But there are several instances in which יצא is combined with אל or על in this sense. Now it is well known that ל, אל, and על can be used interchangeably.[14] Furthermore with verbs of motion, with persons, ל is not nearly so common as אל and על.[15] Therefore, we are justified in examining passages in the O.T. which use יצא with אל or על in cases where an inferior king is said to "come out to" a superior king in order to determine a possible meaning for the present MT of Mic 5:1. 1 Sam 11 offers an interesting example. When the people of Jabesh-gilead realize that they are unable to overcome Nahash and the Ammonites, they seek to avoid humiliation and surrender by suggesting an "honorable" covenant (v. 1). Nahash refuses to consent, desiring that Jabesh acknowledge his complete superiority. Thus he declares that Israel must be reproached by the men having their right eyes put out (v. 2). Jabesh is helpless and must submit unless she receives immediate help. The elders reply to Nahash: "Give us seven days respite that we may send messengers through all the territory of Israel. Then, if there is no one to save us, we will come out to you" (ויצאנו אליך), "We will give ourselves up to you" (v. 3, RSV). The messengers succeed in obtaining Saul to lead Israel against Nahash. But to make their attack as effective as possible, Jabesh sends a second message to Nahash: "Tomorrow we will

---

13. "To go out to war," an expression which occurs often in the Old Testament, e.g., in Num 26:2; 31:27; 1 Sam 17:20; 1 Chr 12:33, 36, etc., is, of course, out of the question.

14. Cf. BDB, 41 and 757 with passages cited there. "To give to" is נתן אל in Gen 21:14; 35:4, etc., but נתן ל in 1 Sam 10:4; 22:10, etc. "To go to a place" is הלך אל מקום in Deut 14:25; 26:2, etc. but הלך למקום in 1 Sam 2:20; 14:46, etc. Of course, many illustrations of the interchangeability of אל, על, and ל could be cited.

15. Cf. BDB, 511.

come out to you (נצא אליכם), and you may do to us whatever seems good to you" (v. 10). The terminology is similar to Mic 5:1. The seemingly inferior inhabitants of Jabesh must decide whether they will "go out to" Nahash. The context suggests that "to go out to" means to publicly acknowledge the superiority of and to submit to another.[16]

First Kings 20 seems to use the phrase "to go out to" in a similar way. Ahab soundly defeats Ben-hadad at Aphek, and the Syrian king takes refuge in the city. His life is in danger and there is no hope of escape. It is no longer a matter of preserving Syria's honor as a power comparable to Israel's. Thus, Ben-hadad's servants suggest: "Let us . . . put sackcloth on our loins, and ropes upon our heads, and *go out to* (ונצא אל) the king of Israel: perhaps he will spare your life" (v. 31). When the servants approach Ahab with this proposition, he accepts it, "then Ben-hadad *came forth to him*" (ויצא אליו, v. 33). Surely this means more than that Ben-hadad "went out of" Aphek "to" Ahab physically. Rather, Ben-hadad acknowledges that Ahab is superior and that he is inferior and thus ready to submit to him. But Ahab gives Ben-hadad much more than he asks. Instead of asserting his own superiority and Ben-hadad's inferiority, Ahab makes him an equal by acknowledging him as his brother (vv. 32–33) and by making a covenant with him (v. 34).

Second Kings 18 (= Isa 36) offers another example. The Rabshakeh comes to Jerusalem with a message from Sennacherib for the people under Hezekiah: "Thus says the king of Assyria, Make your peace with me, and *come out to me* (וצאו אלי, v. 31 = Isa 36:16) . . . and do not listen to Hezekiah when he misleads you, saying, The Lord will deliver us" (v. 32 = Isa 36:18). It seems unlikely that Sennacherib meant only for the Judeans to come out of the city of Jerusalem. Rather, he means for them to acknowledge Assyria's superiority and their own inferiority, i.e., to surrender to Assyria.

Second Kings 24 provides still another example. Nebuchadrezzar's army has besieged Jerusalem for some time, and the city is ready to fall. But it would not be proper for the king's servants to take the city themselves.[17] So Nebuchadrezzar appears, "and Jehoiachin the king of Judah

---

16. Driver, *Notes on the Hebrew Text*, 86, "of going out to surrender." He cites Isa 36:16 and 2 Kgs 24:12 in justification of this interpretation. Kleinert, *The Minor Prophets*, 33, and Deden, *De Kleine Profeten*, 218, understand תצאי in Mic 4:10 in the same way, and cite the same passages as Driver does to vindicate their position.

17. The same practice is demonstrated in Joab's defeating Rabbah, then summoning David to take the city himself (1 Sam 12:26–31).

went out to (עַל . . . וַיֵּצֵא) the king of Babylon . . . The king of Babylon took him . . .'" (v. 12). Again, "to go out to" does not merely describe the physical act of going out of the city, but is an expression meaning that Jehoiachin publicly acknowledged Nebuchadrezzar's superiority and his own inferiority.

Finally, Jer 38:21–23 may be cited. Like 2 Kgs 24, the historical situation is the siege of Jerusalem. The prophet declares: "But if you refuse *to surrender* (לָצֵאת) this is the vision which the Lord has shown to me: Behold, all the women left in the house of the king of Judah *were being led out to* (מוּצָאוֹת אֶל) the princes of the king of Babylon and were saying,

> Your trusted friends have deceived you and prevailed against you;
> now that your feet are sunk in the mire, they turn away from you.

"All your wives and your sons *shall be led out to* (מוּצָאִים אֶל) the Chaldeans, and you yourself shall not escape from their hand, but shall be seized by the king of Babylon; and this city shall be burned with fire."

Apparently, "to go out to" in this context means something more than a physical act. It is interesting that the RSV translates לָצֵאת by "surrender" in v. 21. In this context, it would be very difficult to avoid the idea of "submission" or "submissiveness" in the phrase under consideration.

In light of these passages, it seems to me that there is a reasonable interpretation of מִמְּךָ לִי יֵצֵא, in Mic 5:1 as the MT now stands. The present ruler of Israel (Judah) is governing in such a way as to obscure Yahweh's kingship as Israel's authentic ruler.[18] Thus, the prophet can envision only destruction for Israel in the immediate future (4:14). But after this, a ruler will arise who will "come forth to me (Yahweh)," i.e., who will fully surrender to or be completely submissive to Yahweh, the real king of Israel who governs the people through him. This interpretation agrees with Isa 11:1ff., which has several parallels to Mic 5:1ff. Among other things, Isaiah declares that the future ruler will come forth out of (מִ . . . יֵצֵא) the stock of Jesse,[19] and he will reign not in his own

---

18. Speaking of Isaiah and Micah, Rad, *Old Testament Theology*, II, 171, writes: "These prophets increasingly wrote off the reigning members of the house of David of their own day, and . . . they regarded the whole history of the Monarchy from the time of David as a false development. If they did not, what meaning could there be in their expectation that Yahweh would once again make an entirely new beginning?"

19. This is parallel to the announcement that the ruler will come forth out of Bethlehem-Ephrathah in Mic 5:1.

strength, but "his delight shall be in the fear of Yahweh" (v. 3).[20] That the complete submissiveness of the coming ruler to Yahweh is the intention of Mic 5:1 is further indicated by the statement: "And he shall stand, and shall feed his flock *in the strength of Yahweh, in the majesty of the name of Yahweh his God*" (Mic 5:3).

---

20. "When the prophet declares that the ideal prince will come from the family of Beth-Ephrath and not from the royal family which was then living in Jerusalem, he seems to be saying that the present dynasty will fall, and thus that the coming prince must come forth from a small beginning the same as David" (my trans.). Stave, *Israels Profeter*, 36. Ridderbos, *De Kleine Profeten*, 91, comments that "one shall come forth to me" in Mic 5:1 means that the ruler will come "to be at the service of his [Yahweh's] counsel, to do his work." (my translation). Similarly Marsh, *Amos and Micah*, 113, remarks: "The ruler was not to be, as Saul turned out to be, a self-seeking monarch, but one devoted to the will of God in all things."

11

The Authenticity and Meaning of Micah 5:9–14

IN A PREVIOUS ARTICLE, the present writer attempted to demonstrate the coherence of Mic 3–5 and to show the function of 5:9–14 in the final form of the book.[1] The task of this paper is to attempt to determine the meaning and origin of 5:9–14 and to trace the "history" of this oracle from its origin to its present position in the book. We may begin by analyzing the text of this passage. Unlike many pericopes in the book of Micah, the text of 5:9–14 is preserved very well. The symmetrical structure of this pericope is apparent from the recurrence of verbs in the perfect tense at the beginning of the lines,[2] the recurrence of מקרבך, and the repetition of the pronominal suffix -ekā in the middle of the line and -eykā at the end of the line. Here we submit an English translation of this pericope.

> V. 9 And it will be in that day, says Yahweh,
>   That I will cut off your horses from your midst,
>   And I will destroy your chariots.
> V. 10 And I will cut off the cities of your land,
>   And I will throw down all your fortresses.
> V. 11 And I will cut off sorceries from your hand,
>   And you will have no soothsayers.
> V. 12 And I will cut off your idols and your pillars from your midst,
>   And you will no longer worship the work of your hands.
> V. 13 And I will pluck up your Asherim from your midst,

---

1. Willis, "The Structure of Micah 3–5," 191–214.
2. Notice והכרתי in vv. 9, 10, 11, 12; והרסתי in v. 10; ונתשתי and והשמדתי in v. 13; and ועשיתי in v. 14.

The Authenticity and Meaning of Micah 5:9-14

And I will destroy your idols.
V. 14 And I myself will take vengeance in anger and wrath
On the nations that have not been obedient.

Actually, there are only two places in this passage where real textual problems exist.[3] In v. 13, עריך, "your cities," seems redundant and unnecessary after the reference to "cities" in v. 10. A variety of solutions have been suggested. (a) On the basis of the Targum בעלי דבבך some critics read צריך, "your enemies,"[4] which is very close to the present MT. (b) A few exegetes have suggested the reading בעליך, "your Baalim."[5] (c) Several scholars read ציריך, "your graven images."[6] (d) Van Hoonacker has suggested an emendation to עצרך, "your trees, pieces of wood,"[7] which apparently is to be related to idolatry. (e) Pont and (apparently) Kraeling suggest the possibility of reading עמודיך, "your pillars."[8] (f) The most widely accepted emendation is עצביך, "your idols, graven images."[9]

---

3. There are a few variant readings in the Versions and suggested emendations in this passage which are actually not worthy of examination because they are either unnecessary or are obviously careless copyist mistakes. (a) In v. 9, Hylmö, *Kompositionen*, 238 n. L, suggests that נאם be changed to אמר or אמר כה, as in Mic 2:3 and 3:5, because נאם does not occur elsewhere in the genuine oracles of Micah. (b) In v. 11, Riessler, *Die Kleinen Propheten*, 121, following the LXX ἐκ τῶν χειρῶν σου and the Peshitta *mn' ydk* replaces מידך with מידיך, "your hands," but the reading of the LXX and Peshitta does not necessarily indicate a different MT. Cf. the LXX of Num 22:7 and Taylor, *The Massoretic Text*, 125. (c) In v. 12, the reading of the Peshitta *'lwtk*, "your altars," apparently confused מצבותיך, "your pillars," of the present MT with מזבחותיך. Cf. Taylor, *The Massoretic Text*, 127, and Schwantes, "A Critical Study," 141. (d) In v. 12, the Targum reads ידך, "your hand," instead of the MT ידיך.

4. Thus Elhorst, *De Prophetie van Micha*, 167; Margolis, *Micah*, 58 (following Rashi, Ibn Ganah, and Kimhi); and Cheyne, *Micah*, 49.

5. This possibility has been suggested by Procksch in BH3 and Snaith, *Amos, Hosea and Micah*, 101.

6. So Wade, *The Books of the Prophets*, 47; Sellin, *Das Zwölfprophetenbuch*, 340; Lippl, *Die Zwölf Kleinen Propheten*, 211 (possibly); Nötscher, *Zwölfprophetenbuch*, 102; Deden, *De Kleine Profeten*, 223, 233; Bruno, *Das Buch der Zwölf*, 101, 217; and Deissler, *Les Petits Prophetes*, II, 339.

7. Hoonacker, *Les Douze Petits Prophètes*, 394.

8. Pont, "Micha Studiën, III," 355; and Kraeling, *Commentary*, II, 221.

9. Thus Procksch in BH3 (possibly); Pont, "Micha Studiën, III" (possibly); Kosters, "De Samenstelling," 268 n. 2 (following Hitzig); Orelli, *The Twelve Minor Prophets*, 210; Marti, *Das Dodekapropheton*, 290 (following Steiner); Duhm, *Die Zwölf Propheten*, 67 (apparently); "Anmerkungen," 90; Riessler, *Die Kleinen Propheten*, 121; Hylmö, *Kompositionen*, 240; Stave, *Israels Profeter, III*, 40; Nowack, *Die Kleinen Propheten*, 226; Mowinckel, "Mikaboken," 20, 36; Mowinckel, *Det Gamle Testamente, III*, 688; Lippl,

(g) The LXX τῆς πολεῖς σου, the Vulgate *civitates tuas*, and the Peshitta *mdyntk* support the MT. Several scholars explain the apparent discrepancy between v. 10 and 13 by contending that the "cities" of v. 10 are fortified cities, and those of v. 13 are centers of idolatry.[10] This may be the correct interpretation. (h) However, a cultic object would fit the context much better. Therefore, I am more inclined to follow Gaster[11] and Schwantes[12] in interpreting the Hebrew word here as a cognate to the Ugaritic *ʻr*, whose meaning is parallel to the Hebrew פסל.

"The nations" (v. 14) also seems out of place in this pericope because vv. 9–13 clearly seems to be directed against Israel. This has led most scholars to interpret the whole verse as a later addition by a rabid nationalist.[13] The general opinion is that v. 14 is "an addition by an editor who was unwilling that a prophecy denouncing Israel's idolatry should close without a word of condemnation upon the great idolatrous, heathen world."[14] However, a number of other explanations have been offered. (1) Haupt maintains that the speaker throughout vv. 9–14 is not Yahweh, but Judas Maccabaeus, who threatens to abolish Hellenistic practices and customs which had penetrated into Jewry (vv. 9–13), and then vows to punish the surrounding nations, such as the Edomites, Ammonites, etc. (v. 14).[15] (2) Some scholars solve the difficulty by deleting "the nations" in v. 14 and interpreting the whole pericope as an oracle of doom against

---

Die Zwölf Kleinen Propheten, 211 (possibly); Marty, *L'Ancien Testament*, II, 778; Snaith, *Amos, Hosea and Micah* (possibly); Wolfe, "The Book of Micah," 936; George, *La Sainte Bible*, 39; Brandenburg, *Die Kleinen Propheten*, I, 100 (apparently); Weiser, *Das Buch der zwölf Kleinen Propheten*, 277; Robinson, *Die zwölf Kleinen Propheten*, 144; and Scharbert, *Die Propheten Israels*, 330 (apparently).

10. Thus Ewald, *Commentary on the Prophets*, II, 322; Kleinert, *The Minor Prophets*, 38; and Beck, *Erklärung*, 173, 176.

11. Gaster, "Notes on the Minor Prophets," 163–64.

12. Schwantes, "A Critical Study," 142. Serra, "Una raiz," 161–76, especially 166–67; and Saydon, "The Maltese Translation," 4, have also adopted this explanation.

13. Thus Kosters, "De Samenstelling," 265, 268–69 (possibly); Baudissin, *Einleitung*, 529; Riessler, *Die Kleinen Propheten*, 121; Schmidt, *Die Grossen Propheten*, 152; Hylmö, *Kompositionen*, 242; Nowack, *Die Kleinen Propheten*, 226; Sellin, *Introduction*, 178; Wade, *The Books of the Prophets*, 47; Lippl, *Die Zwölf Kleinen Propheten*, 210; Pfeiffer, *Introduction*, 694; Snaith, "Micah," 309; Fichtner, *Obadja, Jona, Micha*, 49; George, *La Sainte Bible*, 13, 38; Meyer, "Michabuch," 931; Thomas, "Micah," 633; Weiser, *Das Buch der zwölf Kleinen Propheten*, 232, 278; Renaud, *Structure*, 14, 27; and Eissfeldt, *The Old Testament*, 411.

14. J. M. P. Smith, *Critical and Exegetical Commentary*, 116–17. Cf. also p. 113.

15. Haupt, "The Book of Micah," 45–48.

Israel.¹⁶ (3) Still others interpret the entire pericope as an oracle of doom against Israel by emending the text of v. 14 from "the nations" to הגוי, "the nation,"¹⁷ or ישראל, "Israel."¹⁸ (4) A few scholars solve the problem by changing "the nations" to הגאוים, "the insolent," and thus interpreting the whole passage as a threat against Israel.¹⁹ (6) Peiser suggests the possibility that vv. 9-13, like its counterpart Isa 2:6-8, originally may have been directed against some foreign nation—Assyria, Babylon, or Tyre—and that it was later emended so as to be directed against Israel.²⁰ (6) The Targum interprets the entire pericope as an oracle against foreign nations by adding עממיא to vv. 9, 10, 12, and 13. This may be one indication of the type of Jewish Community in which the Targum on Micah arose, as well as the way in which they applied the Old Testament to their situation. (7) A few scholars regard v. 14 as an integral part of Mic 5. Kleinert reasons that the writer announces that Israel will overthrow her enemies (vv. 4-5, 7), but first she must be purified (vv. 9-13), for only then can she overcome her adversaries (v. 14).²¹ Mowinckel suggests that a condemnation of horses, chariots, idols, etc., in Israel is ultimately a judgment on the nations whence these things came into Israel.²² Nötscher thinks that possibly v. 14 is integral to the context because Israel is one of the disobedient peoples that the writer has in mind.²³ T. H. Robinson preserves the connection between v. 14 and vv. 9-13 by arguing that "the nations" is a phrase which Judeans sometimes used for North Israel.²⁴ (8) It seems to me unnecessary to emend the text of v. 14. 5:9-14 is parallel in structure and thought to 4:9-10. An enemy army is attacking Israel, and Israel is retaliating with human power—both military and religious, thereby demonstrating her lack of faith in

16. Thus Sellin, *Das Zwölfprophetenbuch*, 341; Lippl, *Die Zwölf Kleinen Propheten*, 211; and Schwantes, "A Critical Study," 142.

17. Harrelson, *Interpreting*, 369.

18. Kosters, "De Samenstelling," 268 (possibly). Crook, "The Promise," 314 n. 5, argues that v. 14 "is probably the climax of an address against Israelite idolatry, than an editorial addition condemning the idolatrous heathen world."

19. Bewer, "Textkritische Bemerkungen," 68; and Scharbert, *Die Propheten Israels*, 329.

20. Peiser, "Micha 5," 367.

21. Kleinert, *The Minor Prophets*, 38.

22. Mowinckel, "Mikaboken," 20.

23. Nötscher, *Zwölfprophetenbuch*, 102.

24. Robinson, *Die zwölf Kleinen Propheten*, 146.

Yahweh. Yahweh declares that He Himself will remove these objects of faith, and will then give Israel the victory over her oppressors.

Now we look at Mic 5:9–14 from a traditio-historical point of view. This involves (among other things) a study of the authenticity of this pericope and of its "history" from its origin to its present position in the book of Micah. Over the past century, scholars have differed some six hundred years on the time when the book of Micah reached its "final form." Haupt dates it about 100 BCE or a little later.[25] But "this date is too late, for the prophetic books had been canonized by that time."[26] Several critics date the book about 200 BCE, when the prophetic corpus is supposed to have been canonized.[27] Others assign a date about 300 BCE or some time in the third century.[28] Still others are less specific and simply date it in the post-exilic period.[29] Those who attribute the whole book to Micah usually date the present form about 700 BCE or some time in the reign of Manasseh.[30] In relatively recent years, the fifth century BCE has been suggested as a possible date of the final form of the book.[31] However, in light of the historical situation which seems to be reflected in the book, the present writer agrees with Ungern-Sternberg and Harrelson in dating it in the exilic period.[32] In the wake of Nebuchadnezzar's first siege of Jerusalem (597) Judah would have been

---

25. Haupt, "The Book of Micah," 16.

26. Hyatt, "On the Meaning," 238 (Hyatt is reacting to Haupt's dating Mic 6:6–8 about 100 BCE). Hölscher, *Die Profeten*, 454, writes: "Damit wird m.E. jede Datierung größerer Abschnitte der Profetenschriften in die Makkabäerzeit durchaus unwahrscheinlich."

27. Marti, *Das Dodekapropheton*, 262, 264; Duhm, "Anmerkungen," 87; Nowack, *Die Kleinen Propheten*, 234; Pfeiffer, *Introduction*, 589, 593; Wolfe, "The Book of Micah," 900.

28. Gray, "Micah, Book of," 616; Steuernagel, *Lehrbuch*, 630; Hölscher, *Die Profeten*, 453; and L. P. Smith, "The Book of Micah," 210.

29. Pont, "Micha Studiën, I," 237; Elhorst, *De Prophetie van Micha*, 99; Baudissin, *Einleitung*, 532; Haller, "Michabuch," 368; Guthe, *Das Buch Jesaja*, 54; and Deissler, *Les Petits Prophetes*, 300.

30. Among those who hold the authenticity of the entire book are Nöldeke, Kleinert, von Orelli, Kolmodin, Beck, Rupprecht, Halévy, Margolis, Eiselen, Wiener, Clamer, Goldman, Ridderbos, Young, and Kapelrud.

31. Mowinckel, *Det Gamle Testamente*, 672 (shortly before the time of Nehemiah); Clarke, *Concise Bible Commentary*, 606; Tournay, "Review," 438; and Renaud, *Structure*, 64–65, 85, 93–94, 101, 111.

32. Ungern-Sternberg, *Der Rechtsstreit Gottes*, 9, 13, 48, 71, 78; and Harrelson, *Interpreting*, 362.

impressed with the hopelessness of thwarting the attack of her enemies. The fall of the city (586) would have been even more convincing. The popular understanding of Yahweh's relationship to Israel (Jer 7:3-4, etc.) indicates that many Jews would have interpreted this catastrophe as evidence of Yahweh's abandonment of His people. The book of Micah seems to reflect a crisis which the community had faced recently. This would partly explain the interest in hope oracles, the reflective character of 7:7-20, and some of the "radical" contrasts between the description of the present Situation and the glorious promises of the future in chs. 4-5. The fact that the Davidic tradition plays a vital role in this book may in part be due to the relatively recent fall of the Davidic dynasty. The period just after Jerusalem's fall would have been ideal for a writer to emphasize the futility of ruling without complete trust in Yahweh.

Now even though the final form of the book seems to come from the exilic period, the internal evidence supports a Palestinian provenance.[33] In the first place, the references to Zion and Jerusalem in the hope passages indicate that the writer is either in Jerusalem or near the city. In 4:8, 9, 10, 11, 13, 14; 7:11, 12, the speaker addresses the city as he would a person in close proximity. In 5:1 he addresses Bethlehem in the same way. 5:9-13 contains a similar type of address, which may be interpreted as an address to Jerusalem (as the representative of the whole land) or to all Judah. There are several references in the hope sections to the nations approaching Zion. These nations do not leave the speaker and go to Zion. They come from afar and assemble near Zion.[34] Similarly, the remnant comes from afar to assemble at Zion under Yahweh's leadership (2:12; 4:6-7; 7:12). 4:9-10 gives a vivid description of what is to take place. Zion[35] will go forth out of the city and dwell in the field, and shall come to Babylon, and "there" (*šām*) she shall be rescued, and "there" (*šām*) Yahweh will redeem her from the hand of her enemies.

Secondly, the destruction of the temple and the defeat of Jerusalem did not necessarily mean the cessation of the recital of the cultic traditions in Judah. After all, some of them had been recited in the amphictyonic cult before David ever made Jerusalem his capital. It is among

---

33. Contra Harrelson, *Interpreting*, 362-63, who attributes the final form of the book to exiles in Babylon.

34. 4:1, 3, 11, 12, 14 ("they have besieged *us*") 5:4-5 (the Assyrian comes into *our* land and treads on *our* soil and within *our* border).

35. *Here* (where the speaker is) and *not there*, as the address "you" shows.

such non-aristocratic groups as those which were left in Palestine by the Babylonians after 586 that one would expect to find cherished the type of promise expressed in the hope sections of the book of Micah. There are many striking similarities between this prophetic work and the book of Jeremiah.[36] Jeremiah 26 tells how Jeremiah was spared when certain of the eiders reminded his foes that Micah had made a similar declaration a century before and that not only was his life spared, but also King Hezekiah heeded his prophecy (vv. 16-19). But why did these eiders think of Micah? If the situation was as tense as the account seems to indicate, Micah and his oracle came to mind instantaneously and spontaneously. There may be two reasons for this. First, the Babylonian threat of Judah and Jerusalem forced the people to face a situation much like the Assyrian threats on Judah when Samaria fell in 721, when Sargon invaded in 711, and especially when Sennacherib besieged Jerusalem in 701. Prophecies uttered in this earlier period would tend to take on new and significant meaning for the later community. Furthermore, some of the Judean prophets of the sixth century (possibly including Jeremiah or some of his circle) may have considered themselves "disciples" of Isaiah and Micah—members of the Isaiah-Mican school. Possibly attention was called to the similarities between Micah and Jeremiah, between Micah's message and Jeremiah's message, so that it was only natural for the elders (who had heard Jeremiah on several occasions) to recognize immediately the parallel between his announcement of the destruction of the temple and Micah's threat (3:12). These similarities offer good reason to believe that it was a sixth century "circle of disciples" (possibly in some way connected with Jeremiah) which preserved the Micah corpus. It is recently been suggested that Isa 4:2-6; 13:1-22; 24-27 and 33-35 originated among "the disciples [of Isaiah] left in Judah after the city's fall in 586."[37] It is quite possible that a member of this circle of disciples is responsible for the arrangement and redaction of the final form of the book of Micah.

It is further significant that the references to a coming ruler in the hope sections of the book of Micah are somewhat vague. Even the statements which may appear to be specific only indicate that he will be a

---

36. I have listed thirty-one of the most important similarities in my dissertation, "The Structure, Setting, and Interrelationships," 307-10.

37. Harrelson, *Interpreting*, 245. See also p. 246. Only the leading classes were carried into Babylonian Captivity. Cf. Reicke, *Neutestamentliche Zeitgeschichte*, 7.

new David, that in contrast to the rulers who have brought Israel to ruin, he (like David) will give his people victory through Yahweh. This vagueness may point to a period before a concrete individual like Zerubbabel appeared as a possible fulfillment of Israelis messianic hopes. Such promises as are found in the hope sections of the book of Micah would have appealed to people who were dissatisfied with Judah's political policies, and who saw their position vindicated by the Babylonian invasions and the fall of Jerusalem. A member of the sixth century prophetic circle who considered himself to be in the Isaiah-Micah stream of tradition is the most likely candidate for redactor. But the message of the book of Micah in its final form seems to have in mind those who had not fully shared this view. The writer intends to take advantage of the disastrous circumstances which had arisen in order to convince these people that they must trust in Yahweh alone to give them ultimate victory over their enemies, and to restore them to their former status as the people of God.

But the date of the "final" arrangement of the pericopes in the book of Micah says nothing about the question of the authenticity of any pericope in the book. Micah 5:9–14 seems to have a specific function in the present form of the book. But now we must ask whether it is most likely that the compiler of the final form of the book created this oracle himself or whether he took it from the written or oral tradition to which he was heir, and if so, whether it may have originated from the prophet Micah. Methodologically, the present writer feels himself to be very near the traditio-historical stances of Engnell and Mowinckel in theory, possibly somewhere between them. Engnell defines the traditio-historical method as "*en analytisk metod*," and argues that its "närmaste uppgift är att *så vitt möjigt* arbeta fram traditionsverk, traditionssamlingar, traditionskomplex och enskilda traditionsenheter såväl som också eventuella skikt inom en muntlig Tradition."[38] And yet, he is very skeptical about the possibility of actually carrying this out, because the smaller individual units and complexes for the most part had already been fused in the oral transmission stage. "Samtidigt som detta betyder, att de muntliga traditionsenheterna och komplexen, deras sammansättning och utveckling, deras 'historia', i viss mån kunna spåras och följas även i de skriftligt fixerade textemas slutgiltiga form, förhåller det sig dock ofta så, att sammansmältningen och uniformeringen blivit så pass grundligt genomförd redan på det muntliga stadiet, att den analytiska uppgiften att

---

38. Engnell, "Traditionshistorisk metod," 1265.

utskilja enheterna och följa traditionens växt oftast ställer sig ytterst svår och att resultaten som nås blott kunna bli mer eller mindre hypotetiska."³⁹ Now while this possibility deserves serious consideration, it seems to me that Engnell is overly skeptical. I am somewhat more optimistic about the theoretical possibility of getting behind the final form of a book or complex to an earlier stage or even the original stage in the development of the tradition. One of the main reasons for this is that the very nature of the development and combination of traditions demands that we assume that the tradition which was handed down had a great influence on those who were responsible for the final form of the tradition. In fact, this influence must have been a primary motivation for their preserving the traditional material. If so, a genuine traditio-*historical* approach must trace the *history* of a tradition from its original inception through the various stages in which it functioned in Israelite life to the final stage which it assumed in the Old Testament book, whenever possible. Thus Mowinckel is correct when he says: "Traditio-historical point of view or method must either be an inquiry into the nature, the origin, the growth and the history of the tradition—or it is nothing at all."⁴⁰ "What is needed in O.T. research now is . . . to continue the work in a really historical investigation of the many traditions in the O.T. qua traditions. It is important to understand the nature of the separate traditions, their origin, growth, development, changes, etc., their collection to greater complexes and the joining together of the latter to 'books.'⁴¹ Now while this is true, it is unrealistic to think that from our vantage point we can *begin* the traditio-historical approach with the *original* stage of the tradition. Rather, the opposite is true. Subconsciously, we begin with the tradition in its *present final* context, complex, and book. Here Engnell's emphasis is important. Form critics from Gunkel⁴² to Koch⁴³ have con-

---

39. Engnell, "Traditionshistorisk metod," 1266–67. Cf. also Engnell, "Methodological Aspects," 22–23. See Mowinckel's criticism of this emphasis in *Prophecy and Tradition*, 18.

40. Mowinckel, *Prophecy and Tradition*, 30.

41. Ibid., 36.

42. ". . . muß es die erste Aufgabe der Wissenschaft sein, die einzelnen, ursprünglich selbständigen Stücke herauszuheben." Gunkel, "Die Propheten," xlii. Gunkel outlined four stages through which prophetic materials passed from their original to their final form: very brief ancient oracles (*Worte* or *Wortzusammenstellungen*), brief prophetic oracles in metric form (*Sprüchen*), longer oracles, approximately the length of a chapter (*Reden*), and whole books (*Bücher*). Gunkel, "Die Propheten," xlii–xliii.

43. "Erste Aufgabe jeder formgeschichtlichen Untersuchung ist die genaue

The Authenticity and Meaning of Micah 5:9-14

tended that the traditio-historical method *begins* with the original stage of the tradition. This is undoubtedly true of the actual growth of the tradition itself, and even of our systematic description of that growth, but the actual process by which we reach our conclusions and reconstruct the history of a tradition by its very nature works "backwards," i.e., from the final to the original form and stage of the tradition. Thus, in our previous essay, we attempted to determine the meaning and function of Mic 5:9-14 by analyzing it in the context of Mic 3-5, and by comparing it with its kindred "parallel" hope oracles which are similar to it in both structure and content. Now we move behind this "final form" to see if we can discover (with some degree of probability) its original stage.

The Major Scholarly Positions[44]

The critical judgments as to the authenticity of Mic 5:9-14 may be divided into four main categories: (a) the entire pericope is unauthentic;[45] (b) the nucleus of 5:9-14 (either 5:9-12a, 13a, or 5:9b-12a, 13a, or 5 9-12a, 13b, or all or portions of 5:9-12, etc.) is authentic, and the rest

---

Abgrenzung der literarischen Einheit." Koch, *Was ist Formgeschichte?* 127. Mowinckel, *Prophecy and Tradition*, 35, concurs: "In all tradition it is the separate narrative, the separate anecdote, the separate poem, the separate prophetic saying, etc., which is the original traditionary unit and the starting-point for the formation of the tradition."

44. In order to save space and avoid a multiplicity of footnotes, the next four notes present a rather extensive list of scholars who think that 5:9-14 is authentic or unauthentic in whole or in part. Then in the presentation of the arguments for and against the authenticity of this pericope, footnotes will be avoided unless a very significant point or quotation is made, since the scholars listed in Notes 46-48 offer the arguments discussed below.

45. Thus Stade, "Bemerkungen," 165; Kosters, "De Samenstelling," 265-66; Marti, *Das Dodekapropheton*, 262, 290; Seligsohn, "Micah, Book of," 535; Kent, *The Kings and Prophets*, 165; Haupt, "The Book of Micah," xxvi, 233; xxvii, 47-48, 55; Duhm, *Die Zwölf Propheten*, xxxvi; "Anmerkungen," 90; Riessler, *Die Kleinen Propheten*, 102; Hölscher, *Die Profeten*, 439, 457 n. 1; Lindblom, *Micha*, 98; Gautier, *Introduction*, 606; Mowinckel, "Mikaboken," 14, 20; Mowinckel, *Det Gamle Testamente*, 688; Pfeiffer, *Introduction*, 590, 593; Clarke, *Concise Bible Commentary*, 608; Snaith, "Micah," 309; Fohrer, "Micha," 1328; Robinson, "Micah," 407; Thomas, "Micah," 630, 632; Deissler, *Les Petits Prophetes*, 340; Robinson, *Die zwölf Kleinen Propheten*, 127; and Kraeling, *Commentary*, 221.

is secondary;[46] (c) 5:9–13 is authentic, and 5:14 is secondary;[47] and (d) the entire pericope is authentic.[48] Of course, (b) and (c) can be mixed. In the following paragraphs, the major arguments for and against the authenticity of this pericope are considered. It is readily admitted that the material presented here is to some extent an oversimplification of the complex problems involved.[49]

Arguments against Authenticity.

We may immediately dismiss several "stock" arguments which those who have denied the authenticity of this pericope have used, such as: (i) the style of this pericope is not like that of chs. 1–3; (ii) the meter or

---

46. Kuenen, *Historisch-Critisch Onderzoek*, 375; Skipwith, "On the Structure," 684; Ladame, "Les chapitres IV et V," 456–60 (460 n. 1); J. M. P. Smith, "Strophic Structure," 201; J. M. P. Smith, *Micah*, 12, 114; Peiser, "Micha 5," 367; Hylmö, *Kompositionen*, 241–42, 286, 288; and Berry, "Micah, Book of," 10.

47. Wellhausen, *Die Kleinen Propheten*, 146; Baudissin, *Einleitung*, 529–30; Cornill, *Introduction*, 342; Gray, "Micah, Book of," 615; Steuernagel, *Lehrbuch*, 620–27; Schmidt, *Die Grossen Propheten*, 152; Stave, *Israels Profeter, III*, 40; Nowack, *Die Kleinen Propheten*, 226; Sellin, *Introduction*, 177; Wade, *The Books of the Prophets*, 45, 47; Marty, *L'Ancien Testament, II*, 774, 778; Coppens, *Les douze petits prophètes*, 33 n. 1; George, "Michée (Le Livre de)," 1269; George, *La Sainte Bible*, 13; Fichtner, *Obadja, Jona, Micha*, 35, 49; Gottwald, *A Light to the Nations*, 307; Marsh, *Amos and Micah*, 118; Meyer, "Michabuch," 930; Pákozdy, "Michabuch," 1212; Weiser, *Das Buch der zwölf Kleinen Propheten*, 232, 278; Weiser, *The Old Testament*, 254; Renaud, *Structure*, 14; and Eissfeldt, *The Old Testament*, 411.

48. In addition to the scholars listed above under n. 30, the following may be mentioned. W. R. Smith, *The Prophets of Israel*, 290–91; Pont, "Micha Studiën, II," 444; Elhorst, *De Prophetie van Micha*, 103; König, *Einleitung*, 328; Sellery, "The Book of Micah," 14; Findlay, *The Books of the Prophets, I*, 247–48; G. A. Smith, *The Book of the Twelve Prophets*, 631; Horton, *The Minor Prophets*, 222, 255–56; Wildeboer, *Die Literatur*, 153–54 (but cf. 155); Hoonacker, *Les douze petits prophètes*, 346–47, 380, 393–94; Hoonacker, "Micheas," 278; Haller, "Michabuch," 368; Cheyne, *Micah*, 47; Farley, *The Progress*, 102; Binns, "Micah," 687; McFadyen, "Micah," 796; Sellin, *Das Zwölfprophetenbuch*, 307, 340–41; Lippl, *Die Zwölf Kleinen Propheten*, 183; Bewer, *Literature*, 120; Bewer, *Textkritische Bemerkungen*, 68; Bewer, *The Prophets*, 517; Bentzen, *Introduction, II*, 148; Paterson, *The Goodly Fellowship*, 86, 95; Crook, "The Promise," 314 n. 6; Buelow Shoot, "The Fertility Religions," 113–14; Deden, *De Kleine Profeten*, 222; Kühl, *The Prophets of Israel*, 89 n. 32; Gailey, "Micah . . . Malachi," 29–30; Schwantes, "A Critical Study," 142; Harrelson, *Interpreting*, 369; McKenzie, "Micah," 673; and Scharbert, *Die Propheten Israels*, 329.

49. The present writer has recorded thirty-one arguments against and thirty-nine arguments for the authenticity of 5:9–14. Certainly, the arguments on both sides are of varying weight. In this paper, I have selected the arguments which seem to me to be of greatest importance.

rhythm of 5:9–14 is not "Mican"; (iii) since the materials in Mic 4–5 are incoherent, they cannot be authentic, since chs. 1–3, which are authentic, are coherent. The book of Micah is so small that we are hardly in a position to label a "problem" passage "Mican" or "non-Mican" in style or rhythm. Even if it could be demonstrated to the satisfaction of all scholars that this pericope differs from the genuine oracles of Micah in style and rhythm, this would not be conclusive proof of the inauthentic nature of this passage, because there is no means of proving that this very oracle does not reflect a Mican style and rhythm in the circumstances under which he delivered it. And in light of the works of Ladame, Nielsen, and Renaud, as well as of the present essay, it should be clear that at least there is some doubt as to the accuracy of the contention that chs. 4–5 are incoherent.

In principle, there are two main strong arguments against the authenticity of 5:9–14. (1) It is inconceivable that a prophet of doom like Micah, who is very harsh in his condemnation of the capitals of Israel and Judah (chs. 1–3), could have spoken oracles of hope such as those which appear in Mic 4–5, where the future of Zion or Jerusalem is pictured so gloriously. However, it is becoming increasingly clear from a study of the Ras Shamra materials and from the form-critical understanding of the Psalms that the doom-hope motif was prominent very early in Israelite cult centers, and especially in Jerusalem.[50] Furthermore, the aversion to accepting hope oracles as authentic material from "doom" prophets fails to consider the possibility that the various oracles contained in a prophetic book may have been delivered at different times over a period of several years or even decades and under different circumstances.[51] It is clear that the prophets were not completely devoid of disciples even in their own lifetimes, else their genuine oracles would never have been preserved. By the very nature of this situation, it would be surprising if these men who so vehemently condemned the corruption among the leaders and the masses of Israel with oracles of doom had not balanced their messages with oracles of hope delivered to their own circles

---

50. Cf. Kapelrud, "Eschatology," 392–405. See also the interpretation of Mic 4:11–13 by Gottlieb, "Den taerskende Kvie," 167–71.

51. "Le discours des chs. IV–V ne peut avoir été composé par le prophète que dans des circonstances entièrement différentes de celles supposées aux chs. I–III." Hoonacker, *Les Douze Petits Prophètes*, 380. "It would be absurd to say that Micah could not have written, in the course of many years' ministry, a passage so different in tone and style as this [Mic 4–5] is from chs. i–iii." Horton, *The Minor Prophets*, 223.

of disciples, which those disciples cherished and handed down in the tradition.

(2) Another significant argument against the authenticity of 5:9–14 is that the ideas and terminology contained in this pericope originated much later than the time of Micah, or do not occur in the genuine oracles of Micah (by which 1:2—2:11 and 3 is often meant). (a) "In that day" in v. 9 is a late eschatological term. (b) "Saith Yahweh" in v. 9 does not occur in the genuine oracles of Micah. (c) "In anger and wrath" in v. 14 is a late expression. (d) In the pre-exilic period, the prophets referred to Israel's enemies specifically by name, and it was not until the post-exilic period that prophets began using the more general term "many nations" or "the nations," as in v. 14. (e) The condemnation of *pĕsîlîm*, *ʾăšērîm*, and *maṣṣēbôt* (vv. 12–13) did not originate until the Deuteronomic Reform under King Josiah in 621 BCE (cf. Jer 2:27; Deut 7:5; 12:3; 16:21–22). As a matter of fact, Isa 19:19 assumes that *maṣṣēbôt* were an accepted part of the Judean cult in Micah's day. (f) The idea of Yahweh coming to take vengeance on the nations is a late idea (cf. Isa 60:12; Zech 14:17–19).

With regard to (a)—(d), two observations are sufficient. First, even if it is true that the terms mentioned in v. 9 and 14 are late, this is scarcely a convincing argument against the authenticity of the entire pericope. As the oracle was handed down, these tiny additions may have been made for any number of reasons. Secondly, if the entire book of Micah were genuine, it is so small that we would hardly be justified in arguing that an expression or idea which is not to be found within it could not be Mican. Furthermore, Hos 10:10; Isa 2:2–4;[52] 8:9; and 29:7, which more and more scholars are coming to consider authentic, demonstrate that "many nations" was indeed an expression used by the eighth century prophets.[53] If Amos delivered the oracles against foreign nations

---

52. The authenticity of Isa 2:2ff. is still under sharp debate. It seems to me that von Rad, "Die Stadt auf dem Berge," 215–17; and Wildberger, "Die Völkerwallfahrt zum Zion," 66–76, have made a very strong case for its authenticity.

53. Stade, "Bemerkungen," 166, argues that the ideas expressed in Mic 4:1–5 arose first with Joel and the epigones of Ezekiel, and specifically states that they do not belong to the Assyrian period. But on p. 63 of the ZAW of the same year (1881), in discussing Zech 9:9—10:2, he contends that the concept of not having weapons of war in the Messianic Age is an idea which existed among the prophets of the Assyrian period, and cites Isa 2:2–4 and Mic 4:1–8 to support his argument. Stade also relegates Mic 4:1ff. to an early period on pp. 87 and 89 of the same issue of the ZAW. Pont, "Micha Studiën, I," 238 n. l, pointed out this inconsistency long ago.

ascribed to him in Amos 1:3–2:8, there is no reason why Micah could not have delivered oracles against "the nations."

The argument that "graven images," "pillars," and "Asherim" were condemned for the first time in the Deuteronomic Reform demands the late dating of a number of passages which many critics now consider genuine. Hosea 3:4; 8:4–6; 10:1–2; 13:2; 14:4; Isa 2:8; 10:10 and 31:7 (all of which are probably genuine) forbid Israel to worship idols and graven images. In spite of the fact that the present form of 2 Kgs 18:4 may be from the "Deuteronomic Compiler" or even from a post-exilic editor, there is no reason to doubt that it preserves a genuine tradition of the nature of Hezekiah's reform. "The most likely solution is that Hezekiah's reforms involved the destruction of all emblems used in the worship of the Lord which had any pagan association, especially those which were of Assyrian origin. This would involve the destruction of sacred pillars and sacred poles generally, and the suppression of heathen or semi-heathen cults wherever they happened to be."[54] If so, there is no reason why an announcement of the destruction of pillars and Asherim cannot go back to Micah, whose ministry was contemporary with Hezekiah. Again, the fact that the Deuteronomic Reform denounced graven images, pillars, and Asherim does not prove that this was the first time that they were denounced. "Altijd gaat er . . . aan een wet eene beweging vooraf; een wet is altijd *het resultaat* nooit *het begin* van eene reformatorische beweging . . . Juist omdat de אשרים in Deuteronomium zoo krachtig worden bestreden moet de bestrijding voor dien tijd aangevangen zijn."[55] "The Deuteronomic prohibition of *maṣṣēbôt* must have been prepared for by the teachings of the preceding prophets. Law is but the codification of an already existing sentiment or custom."[56] In Isa 19:19, *maṣṣēbāh* refers to a boundary stone which is to be erected at the border of Egypt (apparently) to symbolize the presence of Yahweh there. However, the *maṣṣēbôt* in Mic 5:12 are not boundary stones, but pillars which were placed alongside altars, and thus are clear indications of the influence of Canaanite Baalism on the Yahweh cult. It is for this

---

54. Snaith, "The First and Second Books of Kings," 289. Cf. also MacLean, "Hezekiah," 598.

55. Pont, "Micha Studiën, II," 447.

56. J. M. P. Smith, *Critical and Exegetical Commentary*, 114. "Bestimmte historische Ereignisse, durch die die Erkenntnis des Deut, gezeitigt und die nicht in ähnlicher Weise in der älteren Zeit vorhergegangen wären, lagen nicht vor." Nowack, "Bemerkungen," 284.

reason that Micah censured them. Actually, the argument against the authenticity of Mic 5:9-14 based on the attitude of this oracle toward the "pillars" and Asherim is weak because the Old Testament does not supply sufficient Information to enable us to reconstruct the different attitudes of Israel toward these cultic objects in the various periods of its religious history.[57]

Finally, in light of the numerous invasions into Palestine in the eighth century BCE, as well as the general unrest in Israel because of the constant threat of danger from foreign nations, prophetic oracles against foreign nations would hardly be unexpected, much less inconceivable. And if such oracles are understood to convey the same type of ideas as appear in Isaiah's announcement of Assyria's doom (Isa 10:5-19), it is not difficult to see the deep religious significance that they would have for prophetic figures such as Amos, Hosea, Isaiah and Micah. Thus, there are no compelling reasons to deny 5:9-14 to Micah.[58]

Arguments for Authenticity

At the same time, there are strong indications of the Mican authorship of this oracle. "Psychological" considerations such as (i) Micah was a man of the country and had negative attitudes toward urban life, or (ii) Micah was very emotional, quite capable of uttering oracles of doom at one moment and oracles of hope the next, etc., do not deserve a serious place beside these indications.

Five interrelated lines of reasoning offer compelling evidence favoring the Mican origin of 5:9-14. First, the denunciation of "pillars" and Asherim is less likely in the post-exilic period than in the pre-exilic period, since the problem was so much more acute in the earlier period. Even an oracle after the Deuteronomic Reform would condemn the high places in a different way than they are condemned here (apparently) as indications of the penetration of Canaanite religion into the Yahweh cult.[59]

---

57. "De getuigenissen van het O.T. aangaande de maççeba's en de asjéra's zijn niet talrijk genoeg, om er eene wel gewaarborgde geschiedenis van het gebruik dier voorwerpen op te bouwen." Kuenen, *Historisch-Critisch Onderzoek*, 376 n. 6.

58. "Rien n'empêche de faire remonter l'origine de ce morceau à l'époque de Michée." Ladame, "'Les chapitres IV et V," 459. "Gegen die Verfasserschaft des Micha ist nichts Durchschlagendes einzuwenden." Weiser, *Das Buch der zwölf Kleinen Propheten*, 277.

59. Even though the "high places" (*bamôt*) are not specifically mentioned here, they

Secondly, the ideas expressed in this pericope are parallel to those found in passages which the great majority of scholars attribute to the eighth century prophet. The censure against allowing Canaanite idolatry to penetrate into the Yahweh cult occurs in Mic 1:7. The warning against Israelis trusting in horses and chariots to deliver her from her enemies is found in 1:13. This oracle assumes that those addressed subscribe to the belief that since they are God's people, they are immune to punishment or destruction, just as do the prophet's audiences in 2:6-7 and 3:11.

Thirdly, the similarities in ideas between Mic 5:9-14 and Isa 2:6-8 are very striking. But most scholars attribute Isa 2:6-8 to Isaiah. Therefore, there is not valid reason to deny an oracle which exhibits similar ideas to Isaiah's contemporary. Micah undoubtedly prophesied in Jerusalem (cf. l:9, 12 and especially 3:9-12). It is inconceivable that he would not have known and generally shared the beliefs of his great contemporary. In fact, the close affinities between Mic 1:10-16 and Isa 10:28-32; Mic 2:1-5 and Isa 5:8-10; Mic 4:1-5 and Isa 2:2-5; Mic 5:2 and Isa 7:14; the concepts of the remnant, the covenant lawsuits, etc., which are common to both books in oracles which a majority of critics consider genuine, offer strong reasons to believe that Micah was a disciple of Isaiah, or at least a member of his prophetic circle.

Fourthly, 5:9-14 fits well historically in the time of Micah as an oracle delivered by an eighth-century prophet to stimulate or promote the religious reform of Hezekiah. Jeremiah 26:16-19 indicates that Micah's announcement of the destruction of Jerusalem and the temple (3:12) motivated Hezekiah to seek the favor of the Lord, which undoubtedly refers to the reform described in 2 Kgs 18:3-6. Micah 5:9-14 may well belong to the same period, and (if heeded) would naturally have educed the same results.[60]

Finally, it was characteristic of the eighth century prophets to censure trust in military power, prowess, and alliances (cf. Amos 2:13-16; Hos 8:14; Isa 31:1-3, etc.).

---

are certainly intended, because the "graven images," "pillars," and "Asherim" are cult objects connected with the high places. Cf., e.g., 1 Kgs 14:23. It is interesting that Reed, "Asherah," 252, sets the tenth century and the beginning of the sixth century BCE as the outer limits of the use of Asherim in cultic worship in Palestine. He writes: "Taking account of the date of the laws which refer to it, the object appears to have been known in Palestine from the tenth to the beginning of the sixth centuries B.C."

60. Micah 5:9-14 "is almost certainly Micah's and may have paved the way for the reformation of Hezekiah (cf. 2 Kgs 18:4)." McFadyen, "Micah," 796.

Conclusion

If the thoughts suggested in this paper are generally correct, we are in a position to reconstruct hypothetically the history of the tradition whose final form appears in Mic 5:9–14. The oracle originated with Micah as he attempted to inspire Hezekiah to reform Judean worship by removing those objects which betrayed the influence of Canaanite Baal worship on the Yahweh cult. It declared that in spite of the fact that Israel was constantly threatened by powerful foes, Yahweh would remove the objects of her trust, leaving her with no alternative but to trust in Him alone. This trust, intimately connected with the restoration of "pure" Yahwism, would be vindicated when *Yahweh Himself* delivered Israel from her oppressors. As the similarities between this oracle and Isa 2:6–8 indicate, this oracle was probably cherished and preserved through the long reign of Manasseh by the Isaian-Mican circle of disciples. Along with Mic 3:9–12 (and possibly several other oracles), it may have had a great influence on Jeremiah (a member of the Isaian-Mican circle) and on the Deuteronomic Reform in the reign of Josiah. A generation later, when Jerusalem fell to Babylon, non-aristocratic Israelites who were allowed to stay in or near Jerusalem and who had been influenced by Jeremiah recognized the obvious parallels between their own situation and that of Jerusalem in the days of Micah, and saw the relevance of Mic 5:9–14 and similar oracles purporting to be from him for their own generation. One of their number (or possibly the entire circle) arranged these "parallel" oracles roughly in the order that they have been handed down to us in the MT, connecting the originally independent pericopes by catchwords for use as cultic recitations in their worship.

PART TWO

The Book of Isaiah

12

The First Pericope in the Book of Isaiah

THE DETERMINATION OF THE extent of a pericope in any section of the Bible is vital to a proper analysis and understanding of the text. It is inseparably bound up with analyzing the structure of the passage, determining the various elements which may belong to a certain genre or *Gattung* represented by that passage, reconstructing the *Sitz im Leben* in which an oracle or literary piece was at home or out of which it was produced, and ascertaining the theological message intended by the speaker, writer, editor, or redactor. Frequently, scholars differ as to where pericopes begin and end, and accordingly they disagree on these related matters. This is the case with the pericope beginning at Isa 1:2. Scholarly views vary on the extent of this pericope, ranging from 1:2–3 to chapters 1–4, with several critics considering 1:2–31 as a unit. The purpose of this article is (a) to reexamine critically views which have been advocated as to the extent of the first pericope in the book of Isaiah, and to defend the view which seems to be supported by the best evidence; (b) to analyze the genre reflected in this pericope; (c) to suggest a possible *Sitz im Leben* for its emergence; and (d) to make a brief proposal concerning the relationship of its theological message to Isaiah's other oracles.

Apparently, one problem lying behind the attempt to determine the extent of a pericope is the definition of the word "pericope" itself. This English word is a transliteration of the Greek περικοπή, which meant "act of cutting around, section," and the Late Latin equivalent meant "section of a book." In some churches, it refers to a selection from the Bible appointed to be read in church or to be used as a text for a sermon. However, in scholarly usage it seems to refer to a (usually small) unit of scripture which is thought to have been what a prophet or some other speaker delivered at a specific time to a certain audience at a certain place, or to a literary unit which appears to form a complete whole because of either its poetic form, content, consistency of speaker or audience, and the like, or a combination of these. I think that either of these is helpful when one keeps in mind the nature of the material with which he is dealing. For example, Jer 29:4–23 preserves a "letter" which Jeremiah wrote to Jews who had been carried into Babylonian exile with Jehoiachin in 598/597 bce. On the other hand, Isa 1:2ff. contains an oracle the prophet uttered orally to some audience (note "hear," "give ear." and "has spoken" in v. 2). This is not to say that the entire oracle has been preserved, or that the MT preserves the prophet's *ipsissima verba*, or that this oracle has not passed through a history of its own, or that the present Hebrew text should be allowed to stand as it is without emendation. Instead, the intention is to affirm that there is good reason to believe that Isa 1:2ff. represents at least a part of an oracle Isaiah of Jerusalem delivered on some occasion, which the later editor of the complex to which chapter 1 originally belonged or the final editor of the book of Isaiah incorporated into his work because of its relevance to his own generation and circumstances, and thus adapted to his own theological purposes. This is just as likely (if not more so) as the view that this was a literary creation from the beginning, constructed perhaps to serve as an introduction to a literary complex on the entire book of Isaiah as a summary of Isaiah's message.

The Extent of the Pericope Beginning with Isaiah 1:2

1:1—4:6

Recently J. D. W. Watts suggested that Isa 1–4 forms the first "pericope" in the book.[1] Yet he does not mean Isaiah delivered this block of material to a single audience at one and the same gathering, but that chapters 1–4 compose the first literary unit in the book. Now this is questionable in the light of the new superscription in 2:1, the change of subject from chapter 1 to chapter 2, the inner coherence of chapters 2–4 apart from chapter 1, and other considerations.

---

1. Watts, "The Formation of Isaiah Ch 1," 109–19.

1:2—2:5

In three separate publications, P. R. Ackroyd argues that 1:2—2:5 is a coherent unit.[2] Just as Mic 4:1-3 forms an excellent conclusion to Mic 3, so Isa 2:2-4(5) provides an ideal conclusion to Isa 1. The doom-hope pattern in 1:2—2:5 corresponds to the same pattern in 3:1—4:6, and the thoughts expressed in 2:2-5 are very close to those found in 1:21-23, 26, 27-31. 2:1 was written by someone who knew that the same passage occurred in Mic 4 and Isa 2, and wanted to affirm it was genuinely Isaianic. However, 2:2-5 is more naturally connected with 4:2-6 as the introduction and conclusion of a prophetic complex following the pattern hope (2:2-5)—doom (2:6-22)—doom (3:1-15)—doom (3:16—4:1)—hope (4:2-6). Thus 2:2-5 and 4:2-6 form an *inclusio*. Also, Ackroyd seems to have in mind a literary unit, not an oral prophetic oracle.

1:2-31

An impressive number of scholars have regarded Isa 1:2-31 as a unit.[3] Some view it as a single oracle which the prophet delivered orally on the same occasion,[4] while others think of it as a literary unit.[5] This analysis is based on three fundamental arguments. First, these verses compose a coherent structure with a logical flow of thought. Zorell argues that this poem of thirty-six lines falls into two equal parts of eighteen lines each: in the first (vv. 2-15) the people are reproached for their sins, and in the second (vv. 16-31) they are called to repentance and threatened with destruction if they do not.[6] On the other hand, Mattioli finds a tripartite structure, each section beginning with the summons to "hear" (vv. 2, 10, 24). Since the hearers addressed in v. 24 are not specified, they must

---

2. Ackroyd, "A Note on Isaiah 2:1," 320-21; Ackroyd, "The Book of Isaiah," 332-33; Ackroyd, "Isaiah I-XII," 31.

3. Alexander, *Commentary on the Prophecies of Isaiah*, 80; Barnes, *Notes*, 73; Ley, "Metrische Analyse," 230-31; Feldmann, *Buch Isaías*, 24-25; Zorell, "Isaiae cohortatio," 69-70, Gemser, "The Rib- or Controversy-Pattern," 130; Rignell, "Isaiah Chapter I," 141; Penna, *Isaia*, 58-59; Ziegler, *Isaias*, 11-16; Mattioli, "Due Schemi letterari," 345-64; especially 349-60; North, "Angel-Prophet or Satan-Prophet?," 49.

4. Barnes, *Notes*, 73; Ley, "Metrische Analyse," 23.

5. "There is ground for a widespread conviction among exegetes that the *whole* of chapter 1 possesses a unity which even if it be coincidental can nevertheless be focused as 'a summary of the preaching of the First Isaiah'" (North, "Angel-Prophet or Satan-Prophet?," 49).

6. Zorell, "Isaiae cohortatio," 69-70.

be identical with those addressed in vv. 2 and 10, which suggests that the whole chapter is a unit.[7] Second, this chapter contains but a single genre, a covenant lawsuit. The lawsuit ordinarily consists of three essential parts, all of which are present in this chapter: an appeal to witnesses (vv. 2–9), an appeal to the guilty (vv. 10–23), and the pronouncing of the sentence (vv. 24–31). Everything in this section fits into a lawsuit.[8] Third, there are several connections of words and ideas throughout this chapter. For example, vv. 2–3 describe Yahweh's vexation over his unfaithful children, and v. 21 depicts his vexation over his unfaithful wife. The text speaks of Judah "revolting" (v. 5, Heb. סור) or "rebelling" (v. 23, Heb. סרר) against the Lord. "Zion" occurs three times throughout the chapter (vv. 8, 21 [LXX], 27). Three times the prophet comments on what Yahweh says (vv. 8–9, 21–23, 27–31). Several other examples might be cited.

While there is some validity to these observations, other factors need to be taken into consideration. First, v. 24 does not really contain the appeal to "Hear" as do vv. 2 and 10. In fact, a major division at v. 24 severs vv. 21–23 from vv. 24–26, thus destroying the chiastic structure of vv. 21–26. Second, it is questionable whether there is only one genre in Isa 1. איכה (at the beginning of v. 21) is the normal beginning of a lament (cf. Lam 1:1, 2:1, 4:1), and the content of vv. 21ff. reflects this genre. Third, the recurrence of words and themes does not necessarily demonstrate a single oracle delivered on the same occasion. Isaiah may have used the same words or spoken on the same subjects to different audiences on different occasions, and his oracles may have been arranged in their present order later because they contain the same words or ideas.

1:2–3 + 21–31

Recently S. Niditch has argued that Isa 1:2–31 consists of two originally independent pericopes: 1:2–3 + 21–31 and 1:4–20. The latter is personal; it is a sermon, following the structure of a woe oracle leading to a cultic polemic; its language is formulaic; and it follows a logical thematic development. On the other hand, the former is impersonal, and takes the form of a lawsuit.[9] However, this does not really explain why vv. 2–3

---

7. Mattioli, "Due Schemi litterari, 350–51.
8. Ibid., 351.
9. Niditch, "The Composition of Isaiah 1," 509–29.

were separated from their original sequel in vv. 21–31. Niditch herself admits that vv. 4–20 contain several elements which belong to the lawsuit form.¹⁰ Verses 21–31 conform to the genre of a lament, not to that of a lawsuit.

1:2–17

A few notable scholars in the early part of the twentieth century argued that the first pericope in the book of Isaiah is 1:2–17.¹¹ They reasoned that (a) the mention of Sodom and Gomorrah in v. 10 would not be understandable without v. 9; (b) vv. 2–17 seem to date from the same period; (c) the introductory formula in v. 18 sets off vv. 18–20 from that which precedes; and (d) the form and content of vv. 18–20 are different from that of vv. 2–17. While the first two arguments appear to be valid, the last two are not convincing (see the discussion of 1:2–20 below).

1:2–9

A widely held view is that 1:2–9 is the first pericope in the book of Isaiah.¹² This is based on the following arguments. (1) "Hear" (שמעו) and "give ear" (האזינו) in v. 10 point to a different audience from that addressed in vv. 2 (or 4)-9. (2) "Sodom and Gomorrah" are used of destruction in v. 9, but of sin in v. 10. (3) The theme of vv. 2–9 is different from that of vv. 10–17 (or 20): the former has to do with God's punishment of Judah and Jerusalem because of the sins of the people, whereas the latter contains a reproof against those who put their trust m external ritualistic acts of religion but whose hearts and daily lives are ungodly. (4) Verses 2–9

---

10. Ibid., 521–22. Here it may be mentioned in passing that Condamin, "Les Chapitres I et II," 10–14; Condamin, *Le Livre d'Isaie*, 1–7, divides Isa 1–2 into two pericopes, 1:1–27 and 1:28—2:22, but advances no arguments in support of this.

11. Marti, *Das Buch Jesaja*, 2; Whitehouse, *Isaiah I-XXXIX*, 88; Box, *Book of Isaiah*, 18; Viate, *Book of the Prophet Isaiah*, 5; Gray, *Isaiah I-XXVII*, 26–27; Duhm, *Buch Jesaia*, 23–24, 28, 31.

12. Cheyne, *Book of the Prophet Isaiah*, 17, 42–44; Dillmann, *Prophet Jesaja*, 1; Ruffenach, "Malitia," 145–49, 165–68; Procksch, *Jesaja I*, 37; Fischer, *Buch Isaias*, 28; Penna, *Isaia*, 46–59; Eichrodt, *Der Heilige*, 11–12, 30; Jones, "Isaiah Chapter One Verses One to Nine," 463–77; Jones, "Isaiah Chapter One Verses Ten to Seventeen," 457–71; Young, *Book of Isaiah*, 27–93; Auvray, *Isaie 1–39*, 38–39, 43; Frey, *Handkommentar*, 14, 39. Here may be mentioned also Robertson, "Isaiah Chapter I," 231, 233–34, who thinks that the first pericope is 1:2–7, and that vv. 8–9 are a later addition; and Vaccari, *Isaia-Geremia*, 21–26, who makes the first pericope 1:2–6.

come from a time of national collapse, while vv. 10–20 reflect a period of prosperity when external worship was being practiced regularly by those who could afford extravagant sacrifices. These arguments will be evaluated below.

1:2–4

Francis Brown argues that the first pericope in the book of Isaiah is 1:2–4, because the person of the verbs changes in v. 5 and the external state of the people is not mentioned until v. 5.[13] This raises the question whether a change of person or the presence of a word or an idea that has not been mentioned before is a valid criterion for determining the extent of a pericope.

1:2–3

Over the past thirty-five years or so, many scholars have adopted the view that the first pericope in the book of Isaiah consists of 1:2–3.[14] Several arguments have been advanced in defense of this position, (a) The meter or rhythm of vv. 2–3 is different from that of vv. 4–9. (b) The genres of vv. 2–3 and of vv. 4–9 are different. The former is an accusation, whereas the latter is a reproach giving way to a lament. (c) The tone of vv. 2–3 is different from that of vv. 4–9. (d) Yahweh is the speaker in vv. 2–3, but the prophet speaks concerning Yahweh in vv. 3–9. (e) הוי (v. 4) always stands at the beginning of a pericope. These arguments will be evaluated in the following section.

---

13. Brown, "The Measurements of Hebrew," 82.

14. Bentzen, *Jesaja*, 3; Mowinckel, "Jesajaboken I," 76–81; Slotki, *Isaiah*, 1–9; Steinmann, *Le Prophète Isaie*, 53–55, 65–66, 74–80, 107–10, 366–67, 369; Scott, "Book of Isaiah Chapters 1–39," 167; Auvray and Steinmann, *Isaie*, 21–27; Fohrer, "Jesaja 1 als Zusammenfassung der Verkündigung Jesajas," 253–55; Fohrer, *Buch Jesaja*, 23–46; Fohrer, *Propheten*, 100–1, 154–55; Fey, *Amos und Jesaja*, 62–77; Donner, *Israel unter den Völkern*, 119–21; Scharbert, *Propheten Israels*, 136, 197, 201, 204, 213, 216–17, 220–21, 285, 287–88, 313, 340–41; Wildberger, *Jesaja I*, 8; Loewenclau, "Zur Auslegung," 294; Childs, *Isaiah and the Assyrian Crisis*, 21; Osswald, "Zur Abgrenzung," 244; Claassen, "Linguistic Arguments," 9–10; Holladay, *Isaiah*, 6–8; Nielsen, *Yahweh as Prosecutor*, 27–28; Clements, *Isaiah 1–39*, 28–38, esp. p. 30.

1:2-20

A detailed study of Isa 1 has led the present writer to believe that the first pericope in this prophetic book is 1:2-20.[15] This is supported by the following considerations. First, contrary to what is often stated, the speaker in this section is the prophet throughout. While it is true that he relates the words of Yahweh in the first person singular in vv. 2c-3, 11-17, 18b-20b, in each case he introduces them by referring to Yahweh in the third person (cf. vv. 2b, 10, 18aß; cf. v. 20c). This fits well his references to Yahweh in the third person in vv. 4-9.[16]

Second, whereas הוי often stands at the beginning of a pericope, this is not always the case. הוי occurs toward the end of a pericope in Jer 50:27 and Zech 11:17 and in the middle of a pericope in Jer 47:6, and the closely related word אוי, in the middle of the pericope in Jer 48:46. Further, הוי is used in the middle of a pericope a second time in Isa 1 (i.e., in n. 24). The chiastic structure of vv. 21-26 with the repetition of words and ideas demonstrates that the pericope begun at v. 21 extends at least as far as v. 26,[17] thus negating the view that a new pericope begins at v. 24.

Third, vv. 2-3 lack a conclusion and vv. 4-9 lack an introduction. Verses 2-4 contain an accusation against Israel (Judah) for responding improperly (unnaturally) to God's love, then vv. 5-9 proclaim that this ingratitude is the reason for the recent calamities which have befallen the land.

Fourth, several words and ideas are repeated and intertwine in vv. 2-20. "Hear" (שמעו) and "give ear" (האזיני and האזינו respectively) occur in vv. 2 and 10. The use of the father-son relationship as a figure for the relationship between God and Israel appears in vv. 2 and 4 (note בנים in both verses, as well as the synonymous term זרע in v. 4). Four times reference is made to Israel's rebellion against Yahweh (vv. 2—פשע; 4—עזב; 5—סור; 20—מרה). The typical words for sin are found throughout the

---

15. This is the view of Betteridge, "Obedience and not Sacrifice," 45; Budde, "Zu Jesaja 1-5," 16-40; Kaiser, *Prophet Jesaja Kap 1-12*, 1-18 (ET *Isaiah 1-12* [London, 1972], 1-23).

16. Cf. Budde, "Zu Jesaja 1-5," 21.

17. See Marti, *Buch Jesaja*, 19; Box, *Book of Isaiah*, 28; Skinner, *Book of The Prophet Isaiah*, 11; Gray, *Commentary on the Book of Isaiah*, 31-32; Procksch, *Jesaja I*, 45; Bentzen, *Jesaja*, 13; Mowinckel, "Jesajaboken I," 80; Penna, *Isaia*, 57; Fohrer, *Jesaja 1*, 42 n. 13; Fey, *Amos und Jesaja*, 64; Wildberger, *Jesaja*, 57-58; Jones, "Exposition of Isaiah Chapter One," 320; Kaiser, *Prophet Jesaja*, 15 (ET, 19).

chapter (חטא in vv. 4, 18; עון in v. 4; רעע in vv. 4, 16 [twice]; און in v. 13). Israel is called a "people" (עם) three times (vv. 3, 4, 10). Verse 7 states that aliens "devour" the land of Israel, whereas in v. 19 Yahweh declares that if Israel is willing and obedient her people will "eat" the good of the land, and v. 20 warns that if the people rebel they shall be "devoured" by the sword. The Hebrew root used in all these passages is אכל תוסיפו occurs in both v. 5 and v. 13. "Blood" is used in a derogatory sense with reference to animal sacrifices in v. 11 and to various types of injustices in v. 15, explaining the figure of washing and making clean in v. 16, and of sins being "scarlet" or "crimson" in v. 18. Yahweh is depicted in highly anthropomorphic terms throughout. He has "nourished" and "brought up" children (v. 2), he has "had enough of" animal sacrifices (v. 11), his "soul hates" the appointed feasts of Judah, they are a "trouble" to him, he "is weary of bearing" them (v. 14), he "hides his eyes from" and refuses to "hear" those who pray to him (v. 15), his "eyes" are upon the people's evil (v. 17), and he asks his people to "reason together" with him (v. 18). Various parts of the human body are used throughout this pericope in a figurative sense referring to the people and to Yahweh. The prophet compares the afflicted condition of the people with an individual who is sick all over, including his "head," "heart," and "feet" (vv. 5–6). God denies that he requires animal sacrifices from the people's "hand" (v. 12), and declares their "hands" are full of blood (v. 15). God hides his "eyes" from those who pray (v. 15), and calls on sinners to put away their evil from before his "eyes" (v. 16).

Fifth, vv. 2–4 contain a general description of Judah's apostasy, vv. 11–17 make this description specific, and finally v. 20 returns to the general description.

Sixth, the address to "rulers of Sodom" and "people of Gomorrah" in v. 10 would not have made sense to a Judean audience at the beginning of an oracle without some prior context or background.[18] Verse 9 provides that background. So vv. 10ff. are not the beginning of a new oracle delivered by Isaiah to an audience at a different time and place from that found in vv. 2–9. Perhaps the prophet's words in vv. 2–9 caused an agitated stir and hubbub among his hearers, and he used the new address in v. 10 to get the audience quiet and to regain their atten-

---

18. Feldman, *Buch Isaias*, 11; Betteridge, "Obedience," 45; Marti, *Buch Jesaja*, 9; Wade, *Isaiah*, 5; Duhm, *Buch Jesaia*, 23–24, 28; Budde, "Zu Jesaja 1–5," 25; Kissane, *Book of Isaiah 1*, 3–4; Kaiser, *Prophet Jesaja*, 10–11 (ET, 12–14); Frey, *Handkommentar*, 34.

tion. Or possibly an angry hearer responded to or interrupted his oracle to challenge the validity of its message, and vv. 10ff. contain the prophet's response to that interruption.[19]

Seventh, there is no insurmountable reason why everything in vv. 2–20 cannot belong to a ריב or "lawsuit," given the *Sitz im Leben* in which Isaiah appears to have delivered this oracle (see below). The common procedure in attempting to ascertain the structure of a "lawsuit" is to compare passages in which the lawsuit is thought to exist and to deduce the probable original structure from the elements which the various passages have in common.[20] But this is precarious because of the paucity of texts at the scholar's disposal, the subjectivity of determining the extent of a pericope, and the fact that no "pure ריב" exists. In other words, even if we assume that there was a rigid "lawsuit" structure in Israelite society, a prophet could have adapted and reshaped that structure to suit his own message and purposes in almost any conceivable way. He could have expanded it, shortened it, or used a portion or all of it in the larger context of his own proclamation. It has long been recognized that vv. 2–3 and 18–20 reflect a legal suit. Since Yahweh the plaintiff at least begins his case as a father bringing charges against his own sons (vv. 2–4; cf. Deut. 21:18–21), the genuine concern of the speaker for his hearers (vv. 2, 5–6), his expressions of compassion (vv. 7–8), his plea for his audience to change their ways (vv. 16–17), and his offer of deliverance if they repent (vv. 18–19), are understandable. Admittedly, in a normal lawsuit a more legalistic, impersonal approach would be expected; but in the light of the personal relationship of the plaintiff and the defendant assumed here, these warmer, more personal touches are in order.

Eighth, the offer of forgiveness in v. 18 and the choice given the hearers in vv. 19–20 form a natural conclusion to the admonitions in vv. 16–17.[21] Without vv. 18–20, vv. 10–17 do not have a good conclusion, and without vv. 10–17, vv. 18–20 lack a specific, meaningful context. It is also conceivable (though not absolutely necessary) that a protest

---

19. Cf. Dillmann, *Prophet Jesaja*, 10; Marti, *Buch Jesaja*, 9; Wade, *Isaiah*, 5; Feldmann, *Buch Isaias*, 11; Fischer, *Buch Isaias*, 30. That Old Testament prophetic books preserve dialogues between a prophet and his hearers is well known. See Isa 28:7–13; Mic 2:6–8, 6:1–8; Jer 3:22–4:4; 14:2–12.

20. E.g., the analysis of Huffmon, "The Covenant Lawsuit," 285–95, especially 285–86.

21. So also Brown, "Measurements," 82; Betteridge, "Obedience," 43; Feldmann, *Buch Isaias*, 16; Kissane, *Book of Isaiah*, 4; Ward, *Amos and Isaiah*, 233 n. 9.

from the audience was expressed between vv. 17 and 18. A hearer may have declared that even if the people's sins were manifold and rebellious, they could be forgiven by the external acts of worship in spite of Isaiah's words. In this case, the reply in vv. 18-20 would mean that they could be forgiven only by God's grace and a genuine change of heart and life.[22] Or someone in the audience may have lamented that it would be impossible for the people to do what the prophet had demanded in vv. 16-17. In this case, the response in vv. 18-20 would mean that God's grace and forgiveness would empower them to do this.[23]

Ninth, vv. 2-20 may well reflect the same historical setting (see below).

Tenth, the statement כי יהוה דבר in v. 2aß and כי פי יהוה דבר in v. 20 are almost identical, and form an *inclusio* or envelope pattern around the material in between.

The Genre of Isaiah 1:2-20

Space prohibits a full discussion of the different scholarly positions on the genre of Isa 1:2-20 in the present study. The most prominent views of the various portions of this section are these: (1) vv. 2-3 are a lament,[24] a lawsuit,[25] or an accusation;[26] (2) vv. 4-9 are a punishment oracle in the form of a lament,[27] a woe oracle,[28] or a reproach;[29] (3) vv. 10-17 are a

---

22. So Fohrer, *Jesaja 1*, 39; *Die Propheten*, 114.

23. So Hertzberg, *Erste Jesaja*, 23.

24. Mowinckel, "Jesajaboken I," 76; Slotki, "Isaiah," 1; Loewenclau, "Auslegung," 297-98; Westermann, "Role of the Lament," 37; Dillmann, *Prophet Jesaja*, 4, labels vv. 2-9 an accusation beginning with a lament.

25. Wildberger, *Jesaja*, 9-16; Holladay, *Isaiah*, 46-48.

26. Bentzen, *Jesaja*, 2; Fohrer, "Jesaja 1," 255; *Jesaja 1*, 24; *Die Propheten 1*, 101; Fey, *Amos und Jesaja*, 119-20; Scharbert, *Propheten Israels*, 213, 220-21; Loewenclau, "Auslegung," 294-96.

27. Cf. Mowinckel, "Jesajaboken," 77; Fohrer, *Die Propheten*, 155.

28. Scharbert, *Propheten Israels*, 287.

29. Fohrer, "Jesaja 1," 257, calls it a "Scheltwort" (cf. *Jesaja 1*, 28); Wildberger, *Jesaja*, 20, designates it a "Weheruf"; and Childs, *Isaiah and the Assyrian Crisis*, 21, labels it "invective" or a "threat."

lawsuit,[30] a lament,[31] or a prophetic torah;[32] (4) vv. 18–20 are a lawsuit,[33] a discussion in a lawsuit,[34] or a threat of punishment and conditional promise.[35]

This overview indicates that scholars have been impressed with the legal elements throughout vv. 2–20. And, indeed, the term which appears to describe this pericope most accurately is "lawsuit." Yahweh is the plaintiff and judge (vv. 2aß, 10, 11aß, 18aß, 20c), the heavens and earth are witnesses of the veracity and appropriateness of Yahweh's accusations (v. 2aα), the prophet is Yahweh's spokesman or legal representative in the trial (vv. 2a, 4, 9, 10), the rulers and people of Judah are the defendants, and the (implied) defense of the accused is their present well-being (vv. 8–9) and the frequency and quantity of their ritualistic worship (vv. 11–15).

All the elements in vv. 2–20 may be regarded as vital aspects of a lawsuit, if it is kept in mind that the plaintiff is a father who feels compelled to bring accusation against his own son in order to turn him back from the path of destruction he has chosen to the care and security of his father. As the pericope progresses, the father-son figure is abandoned for a straightforward presentation of the actual situation in Judah. Accordingly, vv. 2–4 are not a "lament" in the normal sense of the word, like many psalms, but an expression of the father's deep regret over his son's rebellion against him. Verses 5–8 are not a reproach or a punishment oracle or a lament as usually understood, but a father's moving and pleading appeal to his son to turn away from his sinful course in order that the severe calamities he is presently experiencing might come to an end. Verse 9 emphasizes that the only explanation for Judah's survival is Yahweh's gracious mercy. Verses 10–15 express Yahweh's strong disapproval of his people's attempt to appease his anger by a mere external show of religion; then vv. 16–17 proclaim the ethical qualities which

---

30. Moriarty, "Isaiah 1–39," 267 (referring to vv. 10–20).

31. Penna, *Isaia*, 51.

32. Bentzen, *Jesaja*, 7; Fohrer, "Jesaja 1," 259–60; Jones, "Exposition of Isaiah Chapter One Verses One to Nine," 457, 459–60; Wildberger, *Jesaja*, 35–36; Reventlow, "Grammatical Solution," 52; Clements, *Isaiah 1–39*, 32.

33. Dillmann, 13; Jones, "Exposition of Isaiah," 319–27, especially 321–24.

34. Fohrer, "Jesaja 1," 262–65; Wildberger, *Jesaja*, 51, calls it an appellation for the introduction of a stipulation proceeding, while Clements, *Isaiah 1–39*, 34, labels it "a courtroom appeal."

35. Mowinckel, "Jesajaboken," 79.

Yahweh demands. Finally, vv. 18–20 contain a tender plea for the people to return to Yahweh with the assurance that he will then forgive them, followed by a clear statement of the alternative consequences of returning or rebelling.

This analysis suggests the possibility that a "lawsuit" may contain the following elements:

- A summons to the heavens and earth—v. 2a
- The regret of the plaintiff over the behavior of the defendant—vv. 2b–4
- The moving plea of the plaintiff that the defendant abandon such behavior, which is responsible for the present distressful conditions—vv. 5–8
- The observation that the only reason for the survival of the defendant is the mercy of the plaintiff—v. 9
- The plaintiff's disapproval of the defendant's insincere show of repentance—vv. 10–15
- The plaintiff's proclamation of conditions for the defendant's genuine repentance—vv. 16–17
- The plea for the defendant's return with a promise of subsequent forgiveness and declaration of alternative consequences of returning or rebelling—vv. 18–20.

This is not to affirm that all these elements are present in every lawsuit, or that they are all absolutely necessary to the lawsuit genre, but that in the right circumstances it is possible for them to be part of the lawsuit.

The Sitz im Leben of Isaiah 1:2–20

There has been a great deal of discussion concerning the "formal" *Sitz im Leben* of the "lawsuit," that is, the situation in the life of the people in which it was at home. Three major views have been defended: (1) it belongs to the sphere of international law and is to be connected with the Hittite suzerainty treaties;[36] (2) it is at home in the cult;[37] and (3) it is based on the court case at the gate of the city.[38] The third seems most

---

36. Harvey, "Le 'Rîb-Pattern'" 172–96; Limburg, "Root *ryb*," 291–304.

37. Würthwein, "Ursprung," 1–16.

38. Gemser, "Rîb- or Controversy-Pattern," 122; Huffmon, "Covenant Lawsuit," 293.

likely to the present writer, although Nielsen has a good point when she suggests that the ריב-pattern was an ancient Israelite frame of mind which could be expressed in any of the ways mentioned here. In other words, the forensic way of thinking was the Hebrew way of resolving a disagreement.[39]

Helpful as this concern may be, it is more important for a proper understanding of Isa 1:2–20 to attempt to determine the "actual" *Sitz im Leben* of this oracle, that is, the historical setting or kind of historical setting in which it was originally delivered and the mind-frame of the people for whom it was intended. Scholarly opinion is divided on this matter. Some critics connect this pericope (or portions of it) with the Syro-Ephraimite crisis in 735–732 BCE.[40] The following arguments are advanced in support of this date. First, the tone and teaching of chapter 1 closely resemble Isaiah's early oracles in chapters 2–5. Second, the "aliens" (זרים) mentioned in v. 7 could well be the Edomite, Philistine, and Syrian invaders allied with the Israelites in the Syro-Ephraimite crisis (cf. 2 Chr 28:5, 17–18). Third, Isa 1 appears at the beginning of the book. Fourth, the severe denunciations of this pericope fit the degenerate time of Ahaz much better than the reformation period of Hezekiah. Fifth, the abundance and frequency of sacrifice and ritualistic worship assumed in vv. 11–15 suggests a time of peace and great prosperity, which would have existed in Judah just before the Syro-Ephraimite invasion but not during the period of Sennacherib's invasion in 701 BCE Sixth, v. 8 does not state that Jerusalem was under siege at the time this oracle was delivered, but only that it was "*like* a besieged city."

---

39. Nielsen, *Yahweh as Prosecutor*, 24; "Bild des Gerichts," 310 n. 3.

40. Dillmann, *Prophet Jesaja*, 3; Skinner, *Book of the Prophet Isaiah*, 3; Ruffenach, "Malitia," 148; Fischer, *Buch Isaias*, 27, 29; and Ziegler, *Isaias*, 11, assign vv. 2–31 to 735–732 BCE; Condamin, "Les Chapitres I et II," 17–19, vv. 2–27; Kissane, *Book of Isaiah*, 4, 9, vv. 2–20; Whitehouse, *Isaiah I-XXXIX*, 89; Feldmann, *Buch Isaias*, 24, vv. 2–17; Robertson, "Isaiah Chapter 1," 232–34, vv. 2–7, 10–15, 18–20; Steinmann, *Le Prophète Isaïe*, 107, 108 n. *, 74–75 n. *, vv. 4–20; Auvray and Steinmann, *Isaie*, 22, vv. 4–9; Vaccari, *I Profeti*, 22, vv. 7–9; Procksch, *Jesaja I*, 37, 44; Bright, "Isaiah," 490; Moriarty, "Isaiah 1–39," 267, vv. 10–20; Scott, "Book of Isaiah," 171; Wildberger, *Jesaja*, 37. In addition, the following scholars cannot decide whether to date all or part of Isa 1 in 735 or 701 BCE: Penna, *Isaia*, 59, concerning vv. 2–31; Slotki, *Isaiah*, 1, concerning vv. 2–17; Scott, "Book of Isaiah," 167, concerning vv. 4–9; Rignell, "Isaiah Chapter I," 146, concerning vv. 5–9; Osswald, "Abgrenzung," 244, concerning vv. 18–20 (suggesting also 711 BCE as a third alternative).

However, the weight of evidence seems to favor the view that this oracle was originally delivered in connection with Sennacherib's invasion of Jerusalem in 701 BCE[41] This is supported by the following arguments. (1) The devastation described in vv. 5–8 is much more extensive than that resulting from the Syro-Ephraimite war, and fits Sennacherib's own statements concerning his invasion of Judah in 701 BCE.[42] (2) The aliens (זרים) of v. 7 could well be Assyrians, but hardly North Israelites, even if accompanied by Syrians. Neither North Israelites nor Judeans are ever called זרים in the Old Testament. (3) Ancient peoples, including the Israelites and Judeans, increased their external ritualistic practices in times of national or personal crisis in the hope of appeasing the deity and persuading him to intervene in their behalf in order to deliver them from their affliction (see e.g., Isa 22:12–13; Mic 6:6–8; Jer 34:8–22; Ps 78:34–37). Thus an intensification of ritualistic activity does not necessarily point to a time of peace and great prosperity. (4) The text and precise meaning of Isa 1:8c is widely debated. But even if one emends the text to כְּעִיר נְצוּרָה, as possibly suggested by the LXX and as adopted by many scholars,[43] this is not necessarily an argument against dating this oracle in 701 BCE Rather, it may reflect a time when Jerusalem was not actually under siege, but was cut off from the rest of the Jewish people by garrisons of enemy soldiers stationed at strategic places throughout the

---

41. Alexander, *Commentary on the Prophecies of Isaiah*, 80; Ley, "Metrische Analyse," 230; Smith, *Book of Isaiah I*, 3; Rogers, *Isaiah*, 640; and Frey, *Handkommentar*, 14, 19, date vv. 2–31 in 701 BCE; Betteridge, "Obedience," 46; Feldmann, *Buch Isaias*, 10; Budde, "Zu Jesaja 1–5," 25–26; Ackroyd, "Book of Isaiah," 332; and Kaiser, *Prophet Jesaja*, 10 n. 5 (ET, 13, n.c.), vv. 2–20; Box, *Book of Isaiah*, 21; Wade, *Isaiah*, 1; and Duhm, *Buch Jesaja*, 24, vv. 2–17; Hertzberg, *Erste Jesaja*, 20; Wildberger, *Jesaja*, 11, 20–1; Moriarty, "Isaiah 1–39," 267; Osswald, "Abgrenzung," 244; Auvray, *Isaïe 1–39*, 42, vv. 2–9; Gray, *Commentary on the Book of Isaiah*, 8–13; vv. 2–8 and possibly 2–17; Eichrodt, *Der Heilige*, 28–29, 34, vv. 4–9 and 18–20; Marti, *Buch Jesaja*, 7; Bentzen, *Jesaja*, 3; Mowinckel, "Jesajaboken I," 77; Fohrer, "Jesaja 1," 257–79; *Jesaja 1*, 28–29; *Die Propheten 1*, 155; Kilpatrick, "The Book of Isaiah," 168; Fey, *Amos und Jesaja*, 137; Donner, *Israel unter den Völkern*, 120–21; Jones, "Isaiah Chapter One Verses One to Nine," 468, 475–76; Scharbert, *Propheten Israels*, 285, 287; Childs, *Isaiah and the Assyrian Crisis*, 22; Ward, *Amos and Isaiah*, 238; Claassen, "Linguistic Arguments," 9–10, 13; Clements, *Isaiah 1–39*, 28, 30, vv. 4–9; Procksch, *Jesaja I*, 31, 35, vv. 5–9 and possibly 2–9.

42. See *ANET*, 288; *DOTT*, 67.

43. So e.g., Dillmann, *Prophet Jesaja*, 8–9; Feldmann, *Buch Isaias*, 10; Bentzen, *Jesaja*, 6; Penna, *Isaia*, 50; Donner, *Israel unter den Völkern*, 120.

country. In any case, the statement in v. 8c fits the events which occurred in connection with Sennacherib's invasion in 701 BCE.

There seem to be clues in the Bible which may shed light on the "actual" *Sitz im Leben* of this pericope more specially. Scholars have assigned it variously to the time just before, during, and just after Sennacherib's siege of Jerusalem.[44] In one sense, all these suggestions may point in the right direction. Isa 22:1–14 may indicate that Sennacherib lifted his initial siege of Jerusalem temporarily.[45] This led the people to rejoice and offer abundant sacrifices because the immediate threat to their survival was removed (vv. 1–2, 13). This temporary withdrawal of Assyria's troops may have been occasioned by the approach of Ethiopians and Egyptians from the south (2 Kgs 19:8–9; Isa 37:8–9a). A short time later, in an attempt to bluff Hezekiah and Jerusalem into surrender, Sennacherib sent a detachment of soldiers to Jerusalem with a threatening letter demanding that they submit immediately or suffer the consequences (2 Kgs 19:9b–13; Isa 37:9b–13). It is conceivable that, throughout the period when the siege was lifted but the Assyrians were still in the land and constantly loomed as a potential threat to return to the capital and resume the siege, the Judeans frequented the temple to engage in numerous ritualistic acts in order to persuade Yahweh to protect them from danger and to deliver them in case of renewed Assyrian attack, and that on one of these occasions Isaiah delivered the oracle now preserved in 1:2–20. If so, 22:1–14 and 1:2–20 are closely related. The former was proclaimed shortly after the siege was lifted, and the latter a short time later, but before the siege was resumed.

Isaiah 1:2–20 and Isaiah's Theology

It is a commonplace among scholars to refer to Isa 1:2–31 as a "programmatic introduction," "poetic concentrate," or "summarizing overview" of

---

44. Of the scholars mentioned in n. 30, Feldmann and Fohrer date it before the siege, Bentzen, Kaiser, Claassen, and Frey during the siege, and Ley, Mowinckel, Eichrodt, Donner, Wildberger, and Clements after the siege.

45. Over a hundred years later, during Nebuchadnezzar's siege of Jerusalem, the Babylonians withdrew from the city for a brief period to fight the Egyptians under Pharaoh-hopra who were advancing from the south During this time the Judeans, who had released their slaves as a sign of repentance in the hope of persuading Yahweh to deliver them from their enemies, re-enslaved them (Jer 37:6–11; 34:8–22). A short time later, the Egyptians returned to their homeland and the Babylonians resumed the siege of Jerusalem and captured it (Jer 39:2–10).

Isaiah's message.[46] This may be an overstatement. For example, vv. 11–15 contain a polemic against mere external ritualistic acts, but one would be hard pressed to find a similar emphasis elsewhere in the oracles of Isaiah (perhaps the most likely passages are 22:12–14 and 29:13–14). But, even if we assume for the moment that this is the case, the general scholarly view that this is to be explained by supposing a later redactor arranged Isaianic and non-Isaianic oracles to create this sort of introduction is not the only viable option. If the conclusions reached in the present article are correct, it may be that vv. 2–20 appear to be a summary of the prophet's message because he delivered this oracle near the end of his long career, when the various major emphases of his earlier oracles were paramount in his mind and seemed to be appropriate to the new situation with which the people were faced, a situation strikingly similar to several former ones experienced during his lifetime.

---

46. Fohrer is usually credited with this insight as a result of his article "Jesaja 1," 251–68. However, it goes back at least to Whitehouse, *Isaiah I-XXXIX*, 89, and Smith, *Book of Isaiah*, 4, if not earlier.

13

An Important Passage for Determining the Historical Setting of a Prophetic Oracle— Isaiah 1:7–8[1]

A MAJOR PROBLEM FACING the interpreter of a prophetic text is that of attempting to place it in its proper *Sitz im Leben*, whether cultic, sociological, or historical, or any combination of these. Since most, if not all, prophetic pericopes have a history of their own, it is likely that a text may have more than one *Sitz*. The first chapter of the book of Isaiah has been the subject of much discussion, and a number of interpretations have been advocated on a variety of subjects within this chapter. Verses 7 and 8 play a significant role in this chapter, particularly in the pericope which begins with v. 2 (or v. 4). These verses are worthy of a separate study in order to clarify certain basic issues and to suggest a possible way of understanding them in their original and present context. This

---

1. In the notes for this essay, the following frequently appearing works are cited by the author's last name only: Alexander, *Commentary on the Prophecies of Isaiah*; Barnes, *Notes*; Cheyne, *The Book of the Prophet Isaiah*; Dillmann and Kittel, *Der Prophet Jesaja*; Marti, *Das Buch Jesaja*; Condamin, *Le Livre d'Isaïe*; Whitehouse, *Isaiah I–XXXIX*; Box, *The Book of Isaiah*; Skinner, *The Book of the Prophet Isaiah Chapters I–XXXIX*; Ehrlich, *Jesaia, Jeremia*; Gray, *Commentary on the Book of Isaiah I–XXXIX* I; Duhm, *Das Buch Jesaia*; Feldmann, *Das Buch Isaias*; Rogers, *Isaiah*; Wade, *The Book of the Prophet Isaiah*; Procksch, *Jesaja I*; Fischer, *Buch Isaias*; Ridderbos, *De Profeet Jesaja I*; Bentzen, *Jesaja I*; Mowinckel, "Jesajaboken I"; *Isaiah*; Hertzberg, *Der Erste Jesaja*; Vaccari, *Isaia-Geremia*; Fitch, *Isaiah*; Scott, *The Book of Isaiah: Chapters 1–39*; Auvray and Steinmann, *Isaie*; Penna, *Isaia*; Eichrodt, *Der Heilige*; Kissane, *The Book of Isaiah I*; Ziegler, *Isaias*; Mauchline, *Isaiah 1–39*; Wildberger, *Jesaja*; Young, *The Book of Isaiah I*; Fohrer, *Das Buch Jesaja 1*; Bright, "Isaiah"; Moriarty, "Isaiah 1–39"; Snijders, *Jesaia I*; Kelley, "Isaiah"; Ackroyd, "The Book of Isaiah"; Auvray, *Isaie 1–39*; Frey, *Handkommentar zum Buch Jesaja*; Clements, *Isaiah 1–39*.

requires an examination of four specifics: the text and translation of vv. 7–8, the historical situation in which they were originally delivered, the circumstances which led to their preservation and ultimate incorporation into the present prophetic book, and their theological emphases.

Text and Translation

The MT has:

v. 7—
ארצכם שממה
עריכם שרפות אש
אדמתכם לנגדכם זרים אכלים אתה
ושממה כמהפכת זרים

v. 8—
ונותרה בת־ציון כסכה בכרם כמלונה במקשה
כעיר נצורה

This may be translated literally:

v 7—
Your land—a waste,
your cities—burned by fire,
your country[2]—before you foreigners are devouring it,
and (it is) a waste like an overthrow of foreigners.

v 8—
And maiden Zion remains like a booth in a vineyard,
like a hut in a field of cucumbers,
like a blockaded city.

In v. 7d the LXX says: καὶ ἠρήμωται κατεστραμμένη ὑπὸ λαῶν ἀλλοτρίων, that is, "and it has been laid waste, (having been) overthrown (destroyed) by foreign peoples." In other words: (a) the Hebrew noun "waste" is rendered by a passive verb "has been laid waste"; (b) the Hebrew preposition "like" is omitted and its accompanying noun "overthrow" translated by a passive participle "(having been) overthrown (destroyed)"; and (c) the Hebrew noun "foreigners" is explained or interpreted by understanding the noun as an adjective and adding a noun, "peoples," thus producing "foreign peoples." It is noteworthy that this line appears in LXX and that it has the word "foreigners." In v. 8 the

---

2. This is an example of *casus pendens*; see GKC §143a, 457.

LXX omits "and" at the beginning, reads the future ἐγκαταλειφθήσεται, "will remain," at the beginning of the verse, and inserts "and" before the second simile. In the final simile it has πολιορκουμένη, "blockaded," "besieged," which, according to several scholars, warrants a change in the vocalization of the MT (see the discussion on the point below).

The Vulgate, in v. 7a, substitutes the adjective *deserta*, "deserted, abandoned," for the noun "waste," and in v. 7d it has *et desolabitur sicut in vastitate hostili*, "and it will be forsaken as in a desolation by an enemy." So the verb is translated as a future (in contrast to the LXX) and the Vulgate has "foreigners" like the MT. In v. 8 it has the future passive *derelinquetur*, "will be left" (like the LXX), inserts "and" before the second and third similes, and for the third simile has *et sicut civitas quae vastatur*, "and as a city which is laid waste."

The Syriac Peshitta has the adjective *ḥarbā'*, "waste" (like the LXX) in v. 7a instead of the noun, begins v. 7b with "and," and contains v. 7d as the MT. It translates ארצכם in v. 7a and אדמתכם in v. 7c, both by the same word, *'ar'kôn*. On the other hand, it renders שממה in v. 7a by *ḥarbā'* but in v. 7d by *ṣedyā'*. In v. 8a it reads "and the daughter of Zion *has been left (remains)*," (*we'eštaḥrat*) (in contrast to the LXX and Vulgate), inserts "and" before the second and third similes, and understands the final simile to mean *'ayk medi(n)ta' ḥabištā'*, "like a besieged city" (cf. the LXX).

Finally, the Targum of Isa 1:7–8 strays farthest from a literal rendering of the Hebrew. It reads:

v. 7 —

ארעכון צדיא
קרויכון יקידת נור
ארעכון לקבל יכון עממיא מחסנין יתה
ובחו כיהון צדיאת

v. 8 —

ואשתארת פנשתא דציון כמטללתא במקשיא
כחר דאבעיוהי
כקרתא דצירין עלה

A literal translation would be:

v. 7 Your land is desolated,
your cities—a burning of fire,
your land—before you the Gentiles (peoples) are taking possession of it,
and by their sins it has been desolated.

v. 8 And the assembly of Zion has been left
like a booth in a cucumber field after its harvesting,
like a city of (under) siege.

Here in v. 7a the noun of the Hebrew text is translated by a passive participle, in v. 7b the Hebrew passive participle is rendered by a noun in the construct, in v. 7c "foreigners" is interpreted as "the Gentiles (peoples)" and "devouring" is replaced by "taking possession of," and v. 7 d is recast to say that the Gentiles have desolated the land by their sins. Like the Peshitta, the Targum translates both ארצכם and אדמתכם by the same word, ארעכון. In v. 8a "daughter of Zion" of the MT is understood as "assembly of Zion," then the first two similes are combined into one and expanded, and the third simile interpreted "like a city under siege."

This analysis shows that most of the variants in the ancient versions are incidental. Possibly the LXX and Vulgate rendered the beginning of v. 8a as a future because they took the *waw* + the perfect as representing the imperfect. However, this is not the case, since the *waw* here is evidently a *waw copulativum,* as in the Peshitta and Targum.[3] The text describes a present situation.

But in spite of the virtually unanimous agreement of the ancient versions with the MT, two lines or phrases have caused a great deal of discussion n among scholars: v. 7d and the third simile in v. 8. In v. 7d there are two matters of concern. First, many scholars believe that "like an overthrow of foreigners" is not suitable in the context, because it destroys the parallelism in lines a-c, the desolation of Jerusalem is not *like* an overthrow of foreigners – it *is* an overthrow of foreigners, and line d repeats the thoughts already expressed in lines a and c. They seek to solve the problem by emending the text or by deleting this line as a later insertion. Several emendations have been suggested. Slotki proposes that זרים here be understood as the plural of *zerem*, "flood," and the line be read, "like the overthrow of Floods."[4] Tur-Sinai suggests *zērim* "as the overthrowing of *the insolent* (men of Sodom)."[5] The most common emendation is to *sedōm*, "like the overthrow of Sodom."[6] Some

3. See in particular Davidson, *Hebrew Syntax,* §58b, 85.
4. Slotki.
5. Tur-Sinai, "A Contribution to the Understanding," 156.
6. In addition to Cheyne, Dillmann, Marti, Condamin, Whitehouse, Skinner, Gray, Duhm, Feldmann, Rogers, Wade, Fischer, Bentzen, Mowinckel, Hertzberg, Vaccari, Fitch, Scott, Auvray and Steinmann, Penna, Eichrodt, Kissane, Ziegler, Bright, Wildberger, Fohrer, Ackroyd, Auvray, Kaiser, Frey, and Clements, see Studer

scholars carry this a step further and contend that the next word at the beginning of v. 8, *we-nôtrâ* is a corruption of an original *wā-ʿămōrâ* "and Gomorrah," thus yielding the reading, "like the overthrow of Sodom and Gomorrah."[7] This is based on three arguments: (1) in all other passages in the OT in which *mahpēkat*, "overthrow," occurs, it is followed by "Sodom (and Gomorrah)" (i.e., Amos 4:11; Isa 13:19; Deut 29:22; Jer 49:18; 50:40); (2) it is easy to see how a copyist accidentally wrote *zārim* for *sedōm* as his eye fell on *zārim* in the previous line; and (3) this reading is suggested by the reference to the destruction of Sodom (and Gomorrah) in v. 9b.

However, these arguments are not compelling. In fact, there are considerations which make the retention of the MT here most likely. First, all the ancient versions support the MT. Apparently their translators found no insuperable problem with the Hebrew text. Second, while it is true that *mahpēkat* is always followed by "Sodom (and Gomorrah)" in the OT, this is not really as imposing as it seems at first. Outside Isa 1:7, the noun *mahpēkat zārim* occurs only five times in the entire OT, which is not a sufficient number of occurrences in such a large body of material to allow one to conclude that it was employed in only one way among the ancient Israelites. As voluminous as the OT is, that which has been preserved in it represents only a small fraction of the spoken and written Hebrew language of ancient times. The biblical texts cited above certainly warrant the conclusion that *mahpēkat sedōm wā-ʿămōrâ* was a widely used stereotyped expression, but not that this was the *only* way in which *mahpēkat* was used. As a matter of fact, the qal of the cognate verb הפך is used not only of the overthrow of Sodom and Gomorrah (Gen 19:21, 25, 29; Deut 29:22; Jer 20:16; Lam 4:6), but also of Rabbah (2 Sam 10:3 = 1 Chr 19:3), the mountains (Job 9:5; 28:9), the throne of foreign kingdoms, their chariots and their riders (Hag 2:22), the tent in the camp of Midian (Judg 7:13), the land (Job 12:15), and wicked mighty men (Job 34:25; Prov 12:7), and the niphal is used of the threatened overthrow of Nineveh (Jonah 3:4). If the verb of this root may be used in such a variety of ways, it follows that a noun from the same root may

---

in *Jahrbuch für Protestantische Theologie* 3, 714–15; Donner, *Israel unter den Völkern*, 120; Jones, "Isaiah Chapter One Verses One to Nine," 475–76; Childs, *Isaiah and the Assyrian Crisis*, 21; and Ward, *Amos and Isaiah*, 239.

7. So Procksch; Budde, "Zu Jesaja 1–5 (I)," 23; Vermeylen, *Du Prophète Isaïe à l'Apocalyptique*, 50–51.

have the same capability, even if there are no explicit examples of such in the OT. Thus *mahpēkat zārim* should be retained in Isa 1:7.⁸

But the meaning of this expression must be determined. Rignell interprets זרים as an objective genitive, and thinks the meaning is that the people of Judah have been smitten with a desolation which Yahweh lets befall those who are strangers to him, who are outside his covenant.⁹ However, this understanding is forced. זרים is undoubtedly a subjective genitive, and hence this expression means, "like an overthrow *by* foreigners," that is, a detached, disinterested, uncompassionate destruction.¹⁰ An example of the use of מהפכה in construct with a subjective genitive is found in Isa 13:19: כמהפכת אלהים את־סדם ואת־עמרה, which does not mean "the overthrow of God," but "God's overthrow" (of Sodom and Gomorrah).

A third argument favoring the MT in v. 7d is the repetition of שממה (cf. line a) and זרים (cf. line c) in v. 7. The Hebrew fondness for repetition is well-known. It is certainly characteristic of the book of Isaiah (cf. e.g., 2:7–8, 12–16; 3:24; 5:5–6, 19, 20). This line, then, may be viewed as a *summation* of what has been said in lines a–c.

> Your land—a *waste*,
> your cities—burned by fire,
> your country—(right) before you(r eyes)
>   *foreigners* are devouring it,
> yea, (it is)—a *waste*,
>   like an overthrow by *foreigners*.

Accordingly, the thought of lines c and d is that foreigners are in Judah eating the produce of the land from which the Judeans had been anticipating sustenance, and as a result the land is a waste, which has come to be accepted as typical of invasions by foreigners in the minds of the Judeans (cf. Jer 8:16).

A second issue connected with v. 7d is whether it is original or a secondary gloss or expansion. Several scholars regard this line as a later gloss on v. 7a (because of the repetition of שממה) or v. 9b (because of the repetition of *sedōm* [emended text]), because it offends the sense of rhythm and smoothness of thought expected or desired by the modern

---

8. So Alexander, Ehrlich, Mauchline, Young, Snijders.

9. Rignell, "Isaiah Chapter 1," 144–45. See Wade.

10. So correctly the LXX ὑπὸ λαῶν ἀλλοτρίων and Vulgate *hostili*; cf. Alexander, Dillmann, Condamin, Whitehouse, Skinner, Bentzen, Scott, Mauchline, Young, Auvray.

Western mind.¹¹ But the Hebrew text here and elsewhere *usually* does not conform to the strict rules of meter and logic that one would wish. Thus a decision must be made whether to follow the Hebrew text as it stands unless there are compelling reasons to do otherwise, or to emend the text to fit a sense of structural, rhythmical, and logical symmetry. The contention of this paper is that the Hebrew text deserves pride of place.¹² It is very doubtful that ancient Hebrew writers and speakers had guidelines governing their models of expression to which they sought to conform. And even if the nature of the language and thought patterns lent itself to certain predictable symmetrical structures, it is always possible that a speaker or writer did not conform to them because the thought or message which he wished to communicate did not fit the established mold.

Some scholars feel that the beginning of v. 7d is awkward. Indeed, 1QIsaa has ושממו עליה, instead of ושממה. This probably should be pointed as *wešāmēmû 'ālĕhā*, "and they will be appalled at (horrified by) it (this)," (as in an overthrow [destruction] by foreigners).¹³ But this probably does not point to a variant reading. Speier has suggested that it is a commentary on שממה derived from Lev 26:32.¹⁴ Others have proposed that one of the *mems* in שממה is a dittograph and that the original text had *wešāmûhā*, "and they (i.e., the foreigners of line c) have made (will make) it like an overthrow by foreigners (or of Sodom)."¹⁵ But none of these proposals is an improvement over the MT; understood in the sense suggested above, there is no reason why the MT should not be allowed to stand.

Now the prepositional phrase in the last simile of v. 8 poses two problems, viz., the meaning of the word modifying "city," and the intention of the whole phrase. Turning first to the text itself, (a) some scholars

---

11. So Studer, 714–15; Brown, "The Measurements of Hebrew Poetry," 84; Cheyne, Marti, Condamin, Box, Gray, Duhm, Feldmann, Budde, "Zu Jesaja 1–5 (I)," 23; Eichrodt, Ziegler, Donner, *Israel unter den Völkern*, 120; Wildberger, Fohrer, Kaiser, Vermeylen, *Du Prophète Isaïe à l'Apocalyptique*, 50; Clements.

12. This view is explicitly defended by Alexander, Dillmann, Ehrlich, Young, and Frey; and evidently accepted by several other scholars, who do not state that it is a later gloss.

13. This reading is adopted by Frey, who follows the emendation "Sodom" at the end of the line in place of "foreigners."

14. Speier, "Zu drei Jesajastellen," 310–11.

15. So Ehrlich, Kissane.

seek to solve the problem by deleting the expression as a gloss.[16] This is based on thee assumption that Jerusalem was under siege at the time this oracle was originally delivered, and therefore it would not make sense to say it was "*like* a besieged city," and/or on some specific interpretation of this line. But this explanation does not solve the problem, because apparently this phrase made sense to someone in its present context or else it would not have been incorporated into the text. Furthermore, there are several examples of triads in the early chapters of Isaiah (see e.g., 1:4e–g, 6d, 7a–c, 11c, 24a–c; 2:7–8), but the deletion of v. 8c would destroy the triad in this verse.[17] Ehrlich emends the text to *kaʿaḇôr bāṣîr*, "when the vintage is over,"[18] which in essence follows the Targum. (c) Wildberger suggests the reading *baṣṣîrâ ʿayir*, "like an ass's body in the fold." (d) Robertson proposes the niphal participle *niṣṣâ* or the niphal perfect third feminine singular *niṣṣeṭâ* from the III נצה toor, "to fall in ruins," and translates, "like a city which has fallen in ruins."[19] These proposals veer too far away from the consonantal text, and have little ancient testimony to support them. Rather, they represent attempts to make sense out of a difficult text. But emendation is probably unnecessary, since the consonantal text at least (if not the MT) may be understood so as to make good sense in the context. (e) Barnes (following Arnoldi of Marburg and Noyes), Rignell, and Kissane retain the MT *neṣûrâ* and interpret it in the sense of "delivered," or "protected," or "preserved."[20] Barnes opts for a slight emendation from *ke* to *kô*, "so (thus) is the delivered city," while Kissane says the comparison is with the "preservation" of the little city of Zoar in response to Lot's prayer when God destroyed the Cities of the Plain (Gen 19:20), indicating that Isa 1:8 refers to the fall of Jerusalem in 586 BCE and not to an Assyrian invasion in the days of Isaiah. This interpretation of *neṣûrâ* has little to commend it, however, because the entire surrounding context is emphasizing the destitute circumstances of Jerusalem, not that it has been preserved. When all the possibilities are taken into consideration, two basic understandings seem to be most likely. (f) עִיר in the present verse means "tower" (cf. 2 Kgs 17:9) rather than city," and *neṣûrâ* is a noun from נצר meaning "watch" here (cf. Isa

---

16. Thus Brown, "Measurements," 84; Budde, "Zu Jesaja 1–5 (I)," 23–24; Ziegler.
17. See Dillmann, Gray, Young.
18. Ehrlich.
19. Robertson, "Isaiah Chapter I," 233 n. 2.
20. Barnes; Rignell, "Isaiah Chapter 1," 145; Kissane.

65:4). Thus this third simile means "like a tower for the watch," "like a watch-tower," "like a lookout post."[21] Such a figure would be a striking parallel to the first two similes:

like a booth in a vineyard,

like a hut in a cucumber-field,

like a watch-tower.

(g) It is possible to interpret *neṣûrâ* as a qal passive participle from נצר, "to watch, guard, shut up, blockade."[22] In this case, the thought would be that Maiden Zion is "like a guarded (closely watched, blockaded, confined) city."[23] Or one might reconstrue the form *neṣûrâ* as a niphal participle from צור II, "to confine, shut in, besiege, enclose," which would suggest that Maiden Zion is "like a besieged city."[24] Those who adopt this last reading appeal to the LXX, Syriac Peshitta, and Targum, but these versions could indicate the understanding of *neṣûrâ* in the sense of "guarded" or "blockaded" as well. Now this figure can present a good parallel to the first two similes only if Jerusalem was not under siege when this oracle was delivered, but in a situation which might be compared with a siege. Alexander and Ehrlich try to solve the problem by arguing that in the period under consideration the whole nation of Judah was cut off from the surrounding world "like a besieged city."[25] However, the text specifically names "Maiden Zion," i.e., Jerusalem, as that which is "like a besieged city." This may be a clue as to the historical situation which existed when this, oracle was delivered (see below).

An examination of the text of Isa 1:7–8 reveals a type of subtle symmetry which demonstrates the fundamental dependability of the MT. Verse 7 contains three parallel expressions followed by a summation containing a simile using כ. Conversely, v. 8 begins with an all-encompassing statement followed by three similes each beginning with כ. There is a chiastic pattern here: A-B-B'-A'. Furthermore, v. 7 is addressed

---

21. This is the view of Marti, Box, Gray, Duhm, Wade, Eichrodt, Kaiser, Frey.

22. See the cautious comments in Brown-Driver-Briggs, *Hebrew Lexicon*, 666a.

23. This is the interpretation of Alexander, Bentzen, Slotki, Hertzberg, Tur-Sinai ("Contribution," 156); Young, Snijders.

24. This is the view of Dillmann, Condamin, Feldmann, Procksch, Ridderbos, Mowinckel, Penna, Ziegler, Donner (*Israel unter den Völkern*, 120). See also the guarded remarks in *KB*, 799a under צור.

25. Alexander, Ehrlich.

to the people of Judah individually in a group of hearers ("your" is plural throughout this verse) and deals with the desolate situation of the land of Judah which has come about as a result of a recent invasion by foreigners. By way of contrast, and in harmony with this description, v. 8 speaks to hearers *about* Maiden Zion in the third person and depicts her lonely, weak, and vulnerable position as a result of this invasion.

The Historical Situation

Whether the third simile in v. 8 is interpreted "like a watchtower" or "like a besieged city," it points to a time when Jerusalem was not actually under siege but alone, isolated, cut off from the outside world. Verse 7 further describes the situation as one in which an army of foreigners has recently invaded, leaving the land desolate and surrounding cities burned with fire; during the time the prophet is speaking, foreigners are devouring the produce of the countryside;[26] only Jerusalem remains standing, but she is cut off from outside relief because of the recent devastation and the continuing presence of foreign soldiers in the area, probably strategically, stationed at well-selected sites in garrisons.[27] This impression is supported further by the figurative language in vv. 5–6. Several scholars have correctly pointed out that the prophet moves from the figure in vv. 5–6 to the reality in vv. 7–8.[28] But the figure in vv. 5–6 is that of a father who has beaten his son repeatedly (cf. vv. 2, 4) for rebelling against him, and who desires to cease this if his son will only repent and turn back to him. It should be noted that the smiting is not the son's rebellion but the father's punishment for that rebellion, that at the moment the father is not smiting his son but has recently done so and will take it up again soon if his son does not turn back, and that there is still hope for the son to be cured if he will only repent.

The pericope to which vv. 7–8 belong is probably 1:2–20.[29] If so, the following data need to be taken into consideration in an attempt to determine the historical situation. First, the people's rebellion involves ingratitude (v. 2), unnatural (or inappropriate) response to God's loving

26. Cf. Gray.

27. See Feldmann, Procksch, Ridderbos, Slotki, Auvray.

28. Cf. Dillmann, Marti, Duhm, Feldmann, Procksch, Fischer, Bentzen, Penna, Ziegler, Auvray, Kaiser.

29. For an extensive survey of the various views on this matter, and a defense of this position, see my paper entitled, "The First Pericope," 63–77.

care (v. 3), forsaking Yahweh (v. 4), oppressing the weak and helpless (vv. 15e, 17b-e), and being unwilling to follow Yahweh and being disobedient to his will (v 19). The calamities which the Judeans have recently experienced at the hand of invading foreigners (v. 7) are Yahweh's punishment for this rebellion (vv. 5-6). Second, although the land and the cities round about have been devastated and burned down, Maiden Zion still survives (vv. 8-9). Third, in order to express appreciation to Yahweh for their deliverance and in order to secure themselves against further attacks and possible overthrow, the surviving Judeans in Jerusalem approach him with a great number of external religious rites including animal sacrifices, frequent attendance at the temple for public worship, faithful observance of a variety of feast days, and making many prayers (vv. 11-15d). Fourth, the prophet declares that the future of the destitute Judeans depends on their choice or decision in the present critical situation: if they are willing and obedient, Yahweh will drive away the foreigners from eating the produce of the land and the Judeans will be able to enjoy it (vv. 7, 19); but if they refuse and rebel, the foreigners will return and slay them with the sword (v. 20).

What historical situation most nearly fits all of these circumstances?[30] Scholars have proposed at least six possibilities. (1) Isaiah delivered this oracle near the end of the reign of Uzziah. The devastation of the country to which he refers in v. 7 alludes to the ravages of Judah by Israel and Syria during the reigns of Joash and Amaziah, the effects of which were still being felt in the days of Uzziah.[31] However, it is unlikely that Isaiah began his ministry during Uzziah's reign, the Judeans would hardly have called the Israelites "foreigners," and the texts describing the reign of Uzziah in 2 Kgs 15:1-7 and 2 Chr 26 give no indication of such severe destitution as that described in Isa 1:5-8. (2) Isaiah 1:2-7, 10-15, 18-20, 24-26, 29-31 are fragments of genuine Isaianic oracles originally delivered against North Israel, while vv. 8-9, 16-17, 21-23, 27-28 are post-exilic additions. "Israel" in the genuine oracles (vv. 3, 4, 24) indicates the northern kingdom, and the circumstances described in v. 7 fit the invasion of North Israel by Tiglath-pileser III at the end of the

---

30. In the article mentioned in the previous note, I have outlined the major views on this subject with the supporting arguments for each, and thus will not repeat that material here. In the present paper, only those points directly related to the argument being made are presented, along with additional considerations which seem to confirm the position adopted in the previous essay.

31. Barnes.

Syro-Ephraimitic War (734–732 bce). Verses 8–9 were added by a scribe after the fall of Jerusalem; his words here were prompted by his reading of the dissolution of the northern kingdom in v. 7.[32] But "Israel" is used frequently in the OT for Judah, especially after the fall of Samaria in 721 bce; this view breaks the continuity of structure and thought in vv. 7 and 8; and the application of vv. 7–8 to the fall of Jerusalem fails to take seriously the statement in v. 8 that "Maiden Zion *remains*." (3) Verses 2–20 were delivered before 735 BCE; vv. 7–8 do not contain a description of present conditions but a prediction, of the final destruction of Jerusalem which ultimately occurred in 586 BCE with Nebuchadnezzar's overthrow of the city and the temple.[33] Now, the crux of this position is the insistence that ו before נתורה at the beginning of v. 8 is a *waw conversivum,* but the discussion of the text of v. 8 above shows that this is not the case. The prophet *is* describing a *present* situation. (4) Verses 4–7c are from the eighth century BCE but not from the prophet Isaiah, v. 7d is a late gloss on v. 7a, and vv. 8–9 are a post-exilic addition referring to Nebuchadnezzar's destruction of Jerusalem and the temple in 586 BCE, as is shown by the diversity in rhythm, vocabulary, and content. The whole of Isa 1 has been composed and set in its present position by the Deuteronomic School which existed in Palestine after the fall of Jerusalem.[34] This viewpoint, recently advocated by Vermeylen, is based on an overly strict evaluation of rhythm, vocabulary, and content, and attempts to avoid or explain away the statement in v. 8 that "Maiden Zion *remains*," which could not be said after Jerusalem was destroyed by the Babylonians. (5) Isaiah 1:7–8 and the oracle of which it was originally a part were delivered during the period of the Syro-Ephraimitic crisis ca. 735–734 BCE in conjunction with the invasion (or threatened invasion) of Jerusalem by Syria and Israel; accordingly, the "foreigners" mentioned in v. 7 are the Syrians (and perhaps also the Edomites and Philistines, cf. 2 Chr 28:5, 17, 18), and v. 8c does not necessarily mean that Jerusalem was under siege when this oracle was delivered, even if the correct reading is "like a besieged city."[35] However, the term "foreigners" in v. 7 seems

32. Robertson, "Isaiah Chapter I," 232–34.
33. Kissane.
34. Vermeylen, *Du Prophète Isaie à l'Apocalyptique,* 50–56, 65–71.
35. For additional arguments in support of this view due to considerations other than those based on vv. 7–8, and for an enumeration of scholars who hold this view, see the article mentioned in n. 29.

to refer to the entire invading army, not merely a portion of it, and the devastation described in vv. 7–8 is much more extensive than that suffered by the Judeans as a result of the Syro-Ephraimitic invasion.

(6) Taking into consideration the overall thrust of Isa 1:2–20, and in particular the details in vv. 7–8 (and figuratively in vv. 5–6; cf. also vv. 19–20), it seems most likely that the oracle to which vv. 7–8 originally belonged was delivered in connection with Sennacherib's invasion of Jerusalem in 701 BCE Scholars have placed it variously before, during, and after this invasion.[36] Several factors indicate that it was delivered after Sennacherib's forces had besieged the city for a time, but had withdrawn temporarily to aid their comrades near Libnah against the approaching Egyptians, and shortly before they returned to resume the siege.

First, vv. 5–7 indicate that the Assyrians had already desolated the country and burned the fortified cities of Judah which had served as a protection to the capital, Jerusalem. The description here is strikingly similar to that found in Sennacherib's annals referring to this event.[37]

Second, the זרים, "foreigners," mentioned in v. 7 are probably Assyrians rather than Syrians and Israelites, since North Israelites and Judeans are never called זרים in the OT. When the prophet is speaking, they are devouring the produce of the land round about Jerusalem, but nothing is said about their being near the city engaged in a siege.

Third, the three similes in v. 8 suggest that Jerusalem juts up like a solitary, isolated, fragile structure in the midst of a desolate and foreboding terrain. She is cut off from the outside world by enemy forces stationed strategically throughout the land, and reminds the observer of a besieged city.

Fourth, texts like Isa 30:1–7 and 31:1–3 reveal that during Sennacherib's invasion of Jerusalem Hezekiah and his associates sent messengers to Egypt to make a league with that country so that she would send her army against the Assyrians in order to help the Judeans. Isaiah 37:8–9a (= 2 Kgs 19:8–9a) and Sennacherib's annals demonstrate that Tirhakah of Ethiopia, probably at the instruction of his brother Shebitku,

---

36. For details and discussion, see the essay mentioned in n. 29. On Sennacherib's invasion of Judah, see Luckenbill, *The Annals of Sennacherib*; Honor, *Sennacherib's Invasion of Palestine*; Haag, "La campagne de Sennacherib," 348–59; Leeuwen, "Sancherib devant Jerusalem," 245–72; and on the problem of the relationship of Isa 1:4–9 to that invasion, Claassen, "Linguistic Arguments," 1–18.

37. See *ANET*, 288; *DOTT*, 67.

King of Ethiopia and Egypt,[38] responded and led his army north along the Mediterranean coast to do battle with the Assyrians at Libnah. The Rabshakeh and his branch of the Assyrian army, who had been besieging Jerusalem, withdrew to Libnah to help their fellows against the Egyptians. This would have provided the kind of setting supposed in Isa 1:2-20.

Fifth, Isa 22:1-14 depicts a scene very similar to that assumed in 1:2-20, and probably comes from the same period. The following reconstruction seems plausible. The Assyrian troops under the Rabshakeh withdraw from Jerusalem to go to Libnah to help their fellows against the Egyptians (37:8-9a). As they depart, the Judeans watch from the housetops and wall, and burst into rejoicing because they have been delivered (22:1-2b, 13). Isaiah rebukes them for such rejoicing. He declares that it is a time to weep over the loss of their rulers who had tried to flee but had been captured (22:2c-4), over their attempts to save themselves when the Assyrians first invaded and put the city under siege instead of trusting in Yahweh (22:8b-11), and over their failure to repent when they were besieged, which had led to their present rejoicing and attempts to appease God's wrath by offering a multitude of animal sacrifices (22:12-13). Thus he announces that Yahweh will not forgive such a people, but will punish them even more (22:4-8a, 14). Soon after this, Isaiah appears again to declare to the people that their destitute condition is due to their continual rebellion against Yahweh (1:2-8), that the only reason their city is still standing is God's great mercy (1:9), that their reliance on the acceleration of external religious rites is vain (1:11-15d), and that Yahweh desires and requires in them a complete change of heart and life (1:15e-20).

Sixth, Isaiah's message in 1:2-20 is strikingly similar to that in Mic 3:9-12, where Micah condemns the rulers of Judah for practicing justice, for seeking only personal gain, and for assuming that they are free from the possibility of calamity because Yahweh is in their midst, and announces that Jerusalem and the temple will be destroyed as divine punishment for their infidelity. Apparently these oracles and others

---

38. It is true that Tirhakah (Taharka) did not become king of Egypt and Ethiopia until 690 BCE. The biblical writer called him "king" because he was writing after he became king; this practice is quite common in ancient Near Eastern writing. Contrary to a frequently repeated statement that Tirhakah was only nine years of age in 701 BCE, the evidence is that he was twenty or twenty-one at this time. See Kitchen, *Ancient Orient*, 82-84.

like them convinced Hezekiah and the Judeans to repent, because even though Sennacherib sent Hezekiah a threatening letter to surrender or suffer the consequences, and even though the Assyrians resumed the siege of Jerusalem shortly thereafter, Yahweh intervened, the Assyrians withdrew to Nineveh, and the city was spared (Isa 37:9b–37 = 2 Kgs 37:9–37; cf. 2 Chr 32:16–22). Approximately a century later, some of the Judean elders refer to Micah's oracle, the ensuing repentance of Hezekiah and the people of Judah, and the divine deliverance of the city Jer 26:17–19), indicating that the disciples of Micah and Isaiah preserved certain significant highlights of those critical days at least as late as the time of Jeremiah.

The Preservation of Isaiah 1:7–8

Several factors support the authenticity of Isa 1:7–8. (a) The description of the circumstances in Judah given in these verses is very similar to Sennacherib's report of his invasion of Judah and siege of Jerusalem in 701 BCE[39] (b) שממה is an integral part of the ancient blessings and curses of Israel's covenant tradition (cf. Exod 23:29; Lev 26:31–33), and thus would have been well known in this context in the eighth century BCE (c) שממה occurs in genuine Isaianic oracles (6:11; 17:9) with the same meaning which it has in 1:7. (d) The practice of burning cities with fire belongs to Israel's ancient Holy War tradition, particularly in conjunction with the conquest and settlement of Canaan (cf. Josh 6:24; 11:11, 13). (e) The personification of Zion as a maiden[40] is a favorite figure for Isaiah (cf. 10:32; 16:1; 37:22; and see Mic 1:13).[41]

While most scholars find no difficulty in assigning 1:4–9 (and, in fact, most of chapter 1) to the eighth century prophet, Kissane contends that vv. 7–8 are a prediction of the ultimate fall of Jerusalem in 586 BCE, and Vermeylen argues that only vv. 10–17 are authentic, that vv. 4–7c date from the eighth century BCE but are not Isaianic, and that vv. 8–9 are part of the Deuteronomic redaction of the book of Isaiah composed

---

39. See above.

40. It has long been recognized that בת in the construct followed by the name of a city does not mean "daughter of," but is an appositional genitive, so that בת ציון means "Daughter (or better, Maiden) Zion." See Dillmann, Marti, Whitehouse, Box, Skinner, Feldmann, Wade, Fischer, Slotki, Bright, Mauchline, Young, Kelley. See Stinespring, "No Daughter of Zion," 133–41; Steinspring, "Zion, Daughter of," 985.

41. See Wildberger and Moriarty.

by the exilic community of pious Jews left in Palestine after the fall of the city and the temple in 586 BCE (see above). According to Vermeylen, the redactors of the book of Isaiah placed 1:2-20 at the beginning in order to show that Yahweh himself had done away with animal sacrifices and other external religious rites by sending the Babylonians to destroy the temple as punishment for the rebellion of his people. Thus the fall of Jerusalem is not due to Yahweh's failure to be faithful to his chosen city, but to the infidelity of his people to the covenant with Yahweh. Vermeylen defends the late date of vv. 8-9 and of this redaction primarily by calling attention to the similarities in vocabulary and content between this passage and various texts in Jeremiah and Deuteronomy, and by dating passages in Isaiah and other eighth century prophets which are usually cited as evidence for the early date of 1:2 (or 4) through 9 to the time of Josiah or to the exilic or post-exilic period. His work is one of several relatively recent studies which tend to attribute the editing of OT books to the Deuteronomic school in the days of Josiah or shortly thereafter.[42]

However, there are certain subtle presuppositions in this approach which render it very questionable, if not wholly untenable. First, it assumes that the eighth century prophets were incapable of delivering oracles of the length and/or complexity of that represented in Isa 1:2-20. Redactors living a century later could compose such pieces, but speakers and writers a century earlier could not! The probability of such a distinction existing between two periods only one hundred years apart is very unlikely, and it becomes much less likely in light of the advanced literary development evidenced in the extant writings of Israel's neighbors dating several centuries earlier than the eighth century prophets (such as Ras Shamra, Mari, Nuzi, and various sites in Mesopotamia and Egypt).[43] Second, this view takes for granted that a sufficient bulk of literary remains from the various periods of Israel's history has been preserved (mainly in the OT) to allow the modern scholar to know the vocabulary,

---

42. See in particular the extensive work of Barth, *Die Jesaja-Worte*; on Isa 1, cf. pp. 52-54, 190-91, 217-20, 286-87, 292-94.

43. Niditch, "The Composition of Isaiah 1," 511, has well observed that "the student of traditional literature must ask whether the traditional author, the prophet-poet, may not have used such building blocks (referring here to the materials in Isa 1) himself in the composition of his work—particularly if the work was to be orally or extemporaneously delivered. Might not these blocks of material be provided by tradition-units which he could adapt and combine to fit his own particular needs?"

expressions, poetic rhythm, line of reasoning, etc., that Isaiah and the Deuteronomic school could or could not have used. Third, it presupposes that the so-called "Deuteronomic Theology" had no prehistory of its own, but sprang up suddenly and full-blown in the later years of the kingdom of Judah.

But in spite of these debatable features in the works of Kissane, Vermeylen, Barth, and others, there is an important kernel of truth in their positions which is helpful in seeking to reconstruct the traditio-historical stages in the development of certain OT books, including perhaps Isaiah and Micah. Using Isa 1:2-20 as a hypothetical model, the following history of this pericope seems plausible. (1) Isaiah delivered (the essence of) this oracle during the lifting of the Assyrian siege on Jerusalem in 701 BCE. (2) When Hezekiah and the people of Judah repented and the city was spared, some of Isaiah's associates or disciples preserved it because of the impact it had had on the hearers, and as a testimony to the efficacy of a word from Yahweh faithfully proclaimed in a time of crisis. Micah 3:9-12 was probably handed down by this same group. (3) The elders of Judah in the days of Jehoiakim, son of Josiah, were acquainted with the message which Micah (and Isaiah?) had delivered and with the repentance it evoked from Hezekiah and the Judeans, and used it as an argument to save Jeremiah from death at the hands of the priests and prophets of Judah at that time (Jer 26:16-19). (4) A few years later, this oracle took on new significance for the Jews during the last years of Zedekiah when the Babylonians besieged Jerusalem. In great fear, they ostensibly renewed their covenant fidelity to Yahweh by releasing their Hebrew slaves as the covenant required, and soon the Babylonians lifted the siege in order to go toward the Mediterranean coast to fight against the Egyptians as they approached from the south under Pharaoh Hophra. However, after the siege was lifted, the Jews re-enslaved the slaves they had released. Jeremiah condemns them for their mere external show of religion, and announces that the Babylonians will return and the city and temple will fall (cf. Jer 34:8-22; 37:11-15). These circumstances and Jeremiah's message are strikingly similar to those things reflected in Isa 1:2-20. (5) After the fall of Jerusalem, Jeremiah, Baruch, and the Jews left with them in the land of Palestine would have had a keen interest in preserving these oracles, whose truths were so obvious in the unfolding events which they were experiencing. Among other oracles, Isa 1:2-20, the essence of which had originally been delivered more than a century earlier, took on new relevance for their day.[44]

It is impossible to know whether it was *the* Deuteronomic School or Circle or Tradents who preserved this material. There may have been several closely or loosely related groups of Jews who handed down the various portions of the or in this period. In fact, certain "prophetic" circles may have preserved and handed on "Deuteronomic" material. But one thing seems clear: the theology which is often attached to the label "Deuteronomic" underwent a history of its own prior to the time of Josiah and the fall of Jerusalem. The prophets Isaiah and Micah (and even more, Jeremiah) undoubtedly played an important role in that process, and the oracles which now appear in the prophetic books attached to their names must be subjected to careful scrutiny in an attempt to discover what role, if any, each played. The present study of Isa 1:7-8 represents a modest attempt to see the place of vv. 2-20 in this development.

Theological Motifs

It is inconceivable that a full theology of the prophet Isaiah or the book of Isaiah could be derived from Isa 1:7-8 and its surrounding context. And yet, there are several important theological motifs which emerge if the conclusions reached in this study have basic validity.

God's people suffer great calamities when they rebel against Yahweh (vv. 5-7). Yahweh himself inflicts these calamities on his people as a father on a rebellious son (vv. 2, 4, 5-6).

As Lord of heaven and earth (v. 2) and as "the Lord of hosts" (v. 9), who is thus able to use all heavenly and earthly avenues to carry out his purposes, he does this by using "foreign" invaders to devastate the country in which his people live (v. 7; cf. 10:5-19).

Yahweh is very displeased that he is forced to bring such calamities on his people, and yearns for them to turn back to him so that he can cease punishing them (vv. 5a-b, 16-20).

Even though the Judeans deserve to be utterly destroyed, Yahweh has left a remnant of survivors in Jerusalem, only because of his merciful and compassionate heart, in the hope that the devastations which they

---

44. The present writer has argued in several places that the final redaction of the book of Micah was made by Jews in Palestine closely associated with Jeremiah after the fall of Jerusalem in 587 BCE. See "The Structure of the Book of Micah," 5-42, especially pp. 40-42; "A Reapplied Prophetic Hope Oracle," 64-76.

have already suffered will bring them to repentance (vv. 8–9). The use of נותרה in v. 8 and of היתיה in v. 9 (both from the root יתר, "to be left, to remain"), and of שריד, "survivors," in v. 9 indicates the presence of Isaiah's theme of the "remnant" in this pericope. Isaiah used the "remnant" concept in a variety of ways, depending on the circumstance, the composition of his audience, and the theological point he was trying to make.⁴⁵ Here the thought is not that a spiritual remnant has been spared from destruction because its members have repented and turned back to God. Just the opposite is true. The remnant is just as sinful and deserving of punishment as those who have already been overthrown. They are a remnant only in the sense that they have not suffered physical death or captivity like their brethren. By God's grace, they have another opportunity to repent; it is up to each of them individually as to whether he will become a spiritual remnant by ceasing to rebel and by beginning to obey Yahweh (cf. vv. 18–20).

---

45. On the concept of the "remnant" in the OT and in the book of Isaiah, see Heaton, "The Root שאר and the Doctrine of the Remnant," 27–39; Dreyfus, "La doctrine du reste d'Israël chez le prophète Isaïe," 361–86; Hasel, *The Remnant*.

14

On the Interpretation of Isaiah 1:18

THE MEANING OF ISA 1:18 has been widely debated. Three issues call for resolution in the process of doing an exegesis of this difficult verse: (1) the limits of the pericope to which it belongs; (2) the place, nature and import of the summons in line a; and (3) the precise nuance intended in lines b and c. Scholarly views differ because these issues are answered in a rather wide variety of ways. The purpose of this paper is to discuss the diverse positions in light of their respective supportive arguments, and to defend the viewpoint which seems most likely.

The Extent of the Pericope to which Isa 1:18 belongs

Karl Marti is the only author known to the present writer who regards v. 18 and vv. 19–20 as two separate pericopes.[1] He bases this on two arguments. First, Yahweh speaks in v. 18, but the prophet in vv. 19–20. However, this is not the case. The prophet is the speaker throughout, as the references to "the Lord" (*YHWH*) in the third person in vv. 18 and 20 show. Second, the contents of vv. 18 and 19–20 are not closely connected. Now such an affirmation is based on Marti's own subjective interpretation of these verses. In opposition to this is the fact that they can be viewed quite adequately as coherent both in form and in progression of thought. Verse 18 assumes the role of the consummation of restoration, and vv. 19 and 20 that of the blessing and the curse, in a covenant lawsuit.[2] Correspondingly, v. 18 contains Yahweh's offer of grace to his

---

1. Marti, *Buch Jesaja*, 15.
2. See Marshall, "Unity of Isaiah 1–12," 35–36.

people, then vv. 19-20 state the alternate responses open to them.³ The effect of Marti's position is to sever v. 18 from any contextual mooring, thus allowing a wide range of interpretations. Compelling arguments point in another direction.

"For the mouth of the Lord has spoken" at the end of v. 20 is a concluding formula,⁴ and איכה at the beginning of v. 21 is an introductory formula,⁵ indicating that v. 20 is the end of the pericope of which v. 18 is a part. But where does this pericope begin? There are three major views.

(i) Some scholars contend that it begins with v. 18. If this division is adopted, the interpretation of v. 18 must be determined in light of vv. 19-20 separate and apart from vv. 10-17. Again, the context would be so limited that a wide variety of understandings would be possible. Essentially this view is based on three arguments. First, v. 18 begins with an introductory formula, "Come now, let us reason together,"⁶ followed by a messenger formula, "says the Lord."⁷ But this is inconclusive, because "says the Lord" also occurs in v. 11, which is not at the beginning of the pericope, and v. 18a may be a response to a negative reaction to or a lament over the prophet's words in vv. 2 (or 10)-17, or the prophet's attempt to regain his hearers' attention after giving them a few moments to reflect on his sharp accusations, or after a disturbing hubbub in the crowd aroused by his charges, or the speaker's transition from accusations and admonitions to call to response. Second, the rhythm (meter) and structure of vv. 18-20 is different from that which precedes. For example, vv. 18-20 contain a figure followed by straightforward statements like vv. 4-9, whereas vv. 10-17 contain a mixture of rhetorical questions and straightforward statements.⁸ However, there are so many reasons why a speaker might change his style within the same oracle that

---

3. That vv. 18-20 belong together can virtually be regarded as the scholarly consensus.

4. So Dillmann, *Prophet Jesaja*, 13; Sjöberg, "Om edra synder aro blodroda," 301; Wildberger, *Jesaja*, 50; Jones, "Verses Eighteen to Twenty," 320.

5. איכה appears regularly at the beginning of laments; cf. Lam 1:1, 21, 41. See Bentzen, *Jesaja* 1, 11; Sjöberg, "Om edra synder," 301.

6. So Dillmann, *Prophet Jesaja*, 13; Bentzen, *Jesaja 1*, 9-10; Sjöberg, "Om edra synder," 300; Wildberger, *Jesaja*, 50.

7. Wildberger, *Jesaja*, 34. Note the comment of Auvray, *Isaïe 1-39*, 45, although apparently he rejects the validity of this argument.

8. See the remarks of Bentzen, *Jesaja 1*, 9-10, and Jones, "Verses Eighteen to Twenty," 320.

this argument is hardly compelling. Third, the content or subject matter of vv. 18–20 is different from the foregoing pericope.[9] While vv. 10–17 contain a condemnation of external religious practices, vv. 18–20 consist of a promise of forgiveness and a statement of the consequences of the people's response. On the contrary, vv. 18–20 fit together with vv. 10–17 quite nicely. For one thing, vv. 18–20 contain promises to come on those who respond to the admonitions in vv. 16–17, as well as a plea for the hearers to respond to the message of vv. 10–17.

(ii) Others suppose the pericope to be vv. 10–20. This rests on seven basic considerations. First, both vv. 10–17 and vv. 18–20 teach that man's obedience to God's will involves a change of heart and life rather than a mere correct performance of external religious rites.[10] Second, these verses are related to the covenant: vv. 10–17 recall covenant obligations, and vv. 18–20 contain certain elements characteristic of a covenant lawsuit.[11] Third, Isaiah's own call experience contains a mixture of condemnation (6:5, 9–13c) and hope through divine intervention, forgiveness, and promise (6:6–7, 13d-e); and one would expect both elements to be reflected in his message. Isaiah 1:10–17 is a rebuke and vv. 18–20 are required to round out the picture with an offer of forgiveness and an admonition to repent.[12] Fourth, the popular protest which must be assumed to lie behind vv. 18–20 can refer only to the instruction preserved in vv. 10–17. The thought is that mere external religious rites cannot bring salvation; this can only come through God's grace.[13] Fifth, vv. 10–17 lack a conclusion, and vv. 18–20 lack an introduction; but when these two units are combined, they complement each other very well.[14] Sixth, "Hear the word of the Lord" in v. 10 is a good

---

9. So Cheyne, *Book of the Prophet Isaiah*, 162; Gray, *Isaiah I-XXXIX*, 26–27; Duhm, *Buch Jesaia*, 31; Scott, "The Book of Isaiah," 174; Wildberger, *Jesaja*, 50.

10. So Fohrer, *Buch Jesaia I*, 40; Wildberger, *Jesaja*, 53, admits this affinity, but separates vv. 10–17 from 18–20 as two separate pericopes on other grounds; and Scott, "Book of Isaiah," 174, believes that vv. 18–20 are related to the same situation and probably come from the same period as vv. 10–17, even though he divides them into two pericopes.

11. See Jones, "Verses Eighteen to Twenty," 324, who nevertheless takes the view that vv. 10–17 and 18–20 are distinct pericopes. He suggests that the *Sitz im Leben* of the latter is the Covenant Renewal Festival in the Fall.

12. So Frey, *Handkommentar zum Buch Jesaja*, 45.

13. Fohrer, *Buch Jesaja*, 1, 39; Fohrer, *Die Propheten*, 114.

14. Ward, *Amos and Isaiah*, 233 n. 9. See also Brown, "Measurements of Hebrew Poetry," 82.

introduction for a pericope, and "for the mouth of the Lord has spoken" in v. 20 a good conclusion; and the two statements form corresponding external limits for a pericope.[15] Seventh, the theme of cleansing in v. 16 matches the same theme in v. 18.[16] One who accepts this analysis has a much richer context within which to explore the meaning of v. 18, and some of the interpretations which would be possible if the pericope were limited to vv. 18–20 are less likely in this case.[17]

(iii) Several scholars conclude that the pericope to which v. 18 belongs encompasses vv. 2–20. In another study, the present writer has attempted to defend this view with ten arguments.[18] In addition to the fifth argument stated in the previous paragraph, seven of the remaining nine are pertinent to the issue under consideration here,[19] and thus may be summarized briefly. First, the prophet is the speaker throughout vv. 2–20. Second, several words and ideas recur and intertwine in vv. 2–20. Third, Judah's apostasy is described *generally* in vv. 2–4, *specifically* in vv. 11–17, and again *generally* in v. 20. Fourth, the address to "rulers of Sodom" and "people of Gomorrah" in v. 10 calls for a prior context to make sense to the prophet's Judean hearers, and v. 9 provides that background. Fifth, everything in vv. 2–20 can be understood in the framework of a "covenant lawsuit." Sixth, it is possible to understand all of vv. 2–20 in the same historical setting, namely, during a temporary withdrawal of Sennacherib's troops from Jerusalem during the Assyrian siege of that city in 701 BCE Seventh, *kî YHWH dibbēr* in v. 2aß and *kî pî YHWH dibbēr* in v. 20c are almost identical, and form an *inclusio* or envelope pattern for the pericope in vv. 2–20. In view of these considerations, the contention of this essay is that Isa 1:18 should be interpreted as an integral and harmonious part of the pericope embracing vv. 2–20.

---

15. Ward, *Amos and Isaiah*, 233 n. 9.
16. Snijders, *Jesaja I*, 33.
17. The various interpretations of v. 18 are given in the third section of this paper.
18. Willis, "First Pericope," 63–77.
19. For a detailed defense of each argument, see the article cited in the previous note. The other two arguments pertain only to the internal coherence of vv. 2–9. One is that הוי (v. 4) does not always stand at the beginning of a pericope. The other is that whereas vv. 2–3 lack a conclusion and vv. 4–9 an introduction, the two taken together each supplements that which is lacking in the other.

The Place, Nature & Import of the Summons in Isa 1:18a

It is difficult to determine how Isa 1:18a fits into its surrounding context, and scholars have offered various explanations. These may be divided into two groups. On the one hand, there are those who deny that "let us reason together" (Hebrew ונוכחה) here is a legal term, and take it as an offer of conciliation. Alexander sees it as an invitation to the Jews to discuss whether Yahweh was willing to show them mercy; the rest of the verse affirms his power and willingness to forgive them, even though their sins are many and great.[20] Young interprets it as a command to the Jews to be judged in the light of God's law and repent.[21] Ehrlich translates: "Come, we will both receive a lesson," and explains that the thought is that Israel had been too wicked and Yahweh too unbending for the two to be reconciled, but now this will change.[22]

On the other hand, it is quite clear that this expression is a legal term, as is borne out by the use of the root יכח in the Old Testament (see especially Isa 2:4 [= Mic 4:3]; 11:3, 4; 29:21; 37:4; Amos 5:10; Hos 4:4; Mic 6:2).[23] Understood in this light, the following specific meanings have been suggested for Isa 1:18: "let us go to law," that is, "make yourselves right with me";[24] "let us come to an arrangement or decision";[25] "let us mutually establish what is right";[26] "let us together show the deciding court the cause of strife between us."[27] By assuming that this statement suggests a cold, legalistic tone, some scholars have difficulty fitting it into the context, especially with what follows in v. 18b-e. Box

---

20. Alexander, *Commentary*, 89.

21. Young, *Book of Isaiah I*, 76.

22. Ehrlich, *Jesaja, Jeremía*, 7.

23. For a complete list of the occurrences of this root in the OT, see *BDB* 406b-407a. Liedke, "יכח hi. feststellen, was recht ist," 730, states that "die Wurzel gehört ursprünglich wohl in den Bereich des Gerichtsverfahrens," and that its basic meaning is "to establish (show) what is right," "to put right, rectify." Mayer, "יכח, jkḥ," 621, agrees.

24. Dillmann, *Prophet Jesaja*, 13; cf. Marti, *Jesaja*, 15; Skinner, *Book of the Prophet Isaiah*, 9; Duhm, *Buch Jesaja*, 31, 32; Feldmann, *Buch Isaías*, 16; Fischer, *Buch Isaías*, 32; Bentzen, *Jesaja I*, 11; Scott, "Book of Isaiah," 174; Archer, "Isaiah," 611; Bright, "Isaiah -I," 491.

25. Gemser, "Rîb- or Controversy-Pattern," 125 n. 4.

26. See the explanation of Liedke, "יכח," 731.

27. See the explanation of Mayer, "יכח, jkḥ," 623; cf. Barnes, *Notes*, 94; Gray, *Isaiah I-XXXIX*, 28; Penna, *Isaia*, 54.

solves the problem by eliminating line a as a later addition.[28] Kissane, however, resolves the issue by contending that v. 18a is the conclusion of the pericope which began in v. 10, because (a) "says Yahweh" at the end of this line is a good conclusion for a pericope, and the prophet is the speaker in vv. 18b-20; (b) vv. 18b-20 are not argumentative as v. 18a requires, but vv. 10-17 are; and (c) the LXX has "and" at the beginning of v. 18.[29] Others interpret lines b-c as a threat (see the third section of this paper).

In contrast to these two positions, there appears to be no compelling reason why Isa 1:18a cannot be *both* a legal statement *and* a statement compatible with a gracious and loving appeal by the plaintiff to the defendants ("your" is plural in line b - חטאיכם) in lines b-e. Two considerations seem to favor this view. First, if vv. 2-20 compose a unit (as is argued in the first part of this study), then the plaintiff is a father, and the defendants are his "sons" (vv. 2, 4);[30] and even though Yahweh's accusations are pointed and severe, he still refers to his hearers as *"my* people" (v. 3). The situation here is similar to that in Hosea 11:1-9, where Yahweh describes Israel's sins (vv. 1-4), announces the severe punishment to come upon them (vv. 5-7), and then concludes with the agonizing, loving emotions of a distraught father who cannot bring himself to destroy his own son (vv. 8-9):

> How can I give you up, O Ephraim!
>   How can I hand you over, O Israel!
> How can I make you like Admah!
>   How can I treat you like Zeboiim!
> My heart recoils within me,
>   my compassion grows warm and tender.
> I will not execute my fierce anger,
> I will not again destroy Ephraim;
>   for I am God and not man,
> the Holy One in your midst,
>   and I will not come to destroy. (RSV)

Second, that Old Testament prophets borrowed elements from a legal *Sitz im Leben* common to their world does not mean they adhered rigidly to cold, hostile, impersonal feelings and attitudes (which must

---

28. Box, *Book of Isaiah*, 25.
29. Kissane, *Book of Isaiah I*, 12-13.
30. See Rad, *Old Testament Theology II*, 151.

have manifested themselves frequently in legal cases between people who had as their first concern the defense of their own interest) as they presented Yahweh's dissatisfactions with his people's behavior. An examination of lawsuits elsewhere in the Old Testament shows that this is the case. For example, in Jer 2:5 and Mic 6:3, Yahweh is introduced as plaintiff only to assume the role of defendant by asking his people to bring accusations against him so that he might know how he had wronged them and thus explain why they had turned away from him. Yahweh's words in Micah 6:3 are particularly striking:

> O my people, what have I done to you?
> In what have I wearied you? Answer me! (RSV)

Further it is noteworthy that in the lawsuits in Isa 3:13–15 and Psalm 50 (cf. vv. 4, 7) Yahweh addresses the defendants as "my people" or they are called "his people."

In view of these considerations, Isa 1:18a probably means "Come now, and let us settle our differences, says Yahweh," or something similar.[31]

The Precise Nuance of Isa 1:18b–c

It must be admitted at the outset that at the present state of knowledge, the precise nuance of Isa 1:18b–c will ultimately remain open to the subjective judgment of scholars for two reasons: (a) the Hebrew language is too imprecise in its verb forms to allow dogmatic conclusions as to the mode (mood) and emphasis intended; and (b) the way in which lines b and c fit best into the surrounding context is in the final analysis a subjective decision. Nevertheless, when the evidence is accumulated and each position is weighed, one position seems to be most likely. An analysis of the research done on this difficult passage indicates that at least seven interpretations have been proposed. Each of these deserves a fair hearing and warrants careful scrutiny.

---

31. So Burney, "Old Testament Notes," 437–39 ("let us enter into right relations"); Betteridge, "Obedience and Not Sacrifice," 42–43 ("Let us state the truth as to the basis of our mutual relations"); Gray, *Isaiah I–XXXIX*, 28; Feldmann, *Buch Isaias*, 16; Rignell, "Isaiah Chapter I," 152 ("Let us settle our accounts with each other"); Muckle, *Isaiah 1–39*, 8 ("Let us get the matter settled"); Kraeling, *Commentary*, 46–47; Kelley, "Isaiah," 189.

Option 1: These Lines Contain Rhetorical Questions[32]

Apparently this view was first espoused by J. D. Michaelis, and was adopted later by Koppe, Eichhorn, and Wellhausen.[33] Its advocates render the text:

> While your sins are as scarlet,
>   how can they be (considered to be) white as snow?
> While they are red like crimson,
>   how can they be as wool?[34]

Or,

> Wenn eure Sünden wie Karmesin sind,
>   Können sie (dann) als weiss gelten wie Schnee?
> Wenn sie rot sind wie Purpur,
>   Können sie (dann) wie Wolle sein?[35]

Three basic arguments have been advanced in support of this understanding. First, nowhere else in the genuine oracles of Isaiah is there such an unconditional offer of forgiveness to the people of Judah. However, in view of vv. 19–20, it may be questioned whether there is adequate warrant for assuming that if lines b and c were taken declaratively, they would have to be taken unconditionally. An offer of forgiveness and deliverance in v. 18 would fit well the appeals to repent in vv. 16–17. That the pre-exilic prophets called for repentance by their hearers indicates they believed in divine forgiveness.[36] Second, the whole context in which these lines are couched is that of a divine accusation brought against Judah in the tone of a threat, so that a promise or offer of forgiveness would be out of place here. On the contrary (as shown in the second section of this article), there are covenant lawsuits elsewhere in prophetic literature in which Yahweh demonstrates great compassion and a strong desire to forgive his people in the course of delivering his accusations against them. Third, it is not necessary for a sentence to have the so-

---

32. This is the view of Box, *Book of Isaiah*, 25; Bentzen, *Jesaja 1*, 10; Mowinckel, "Jesajaboken I"; Mowinckel, *Det Gamle Testament*, 79; Tur-Sinai, "A Contribution to the Understanding," 156; Napier, *Song of the Vineyard*, 225; Wildberger, *Jesaja*, 50, 52; Osswald, "Zur Abgrenzung," 245; Culver, "Isaiah 1 18," 133–41; Holladay, *Isaiah*.

33. According to Sjöberg, "Om edra synder," 295–96, and Jones, "Verses Eighteen to Twenty," 319. I regret that I have been unable to verify any of these.

34. Tur-Sinai, "Contribution," 156.

35. Wildberger, *Jesaja*, 50.

36. See Sjöberg, "Om edra Synder," 302, 305.

called "*He* interrogative" to be a question. Now it is true that Mitchell gives thirty-nine examples of this phenomenon in the Old Testament, twelve (or seventeen) of which he attributes to textual corruption,[37] and Gesenius lists thirty-two passages in which he supposes it to occur.[38] Several of their examples are questionable to say the least, but some of them appear well-founded. Thus, this affirmation may be accepted as possible. Still, the question remains as to whether this is the correct explanation of Isa 1:18b–c. If another explanation can be found which takes these two lines as statements, it seems most natural to interpret them in that way rather than as exceptions to the general rule that questions are introduced by the "*He* interrogative."

Option 2: These Lines Are Ironic[39]

Marti, who seems to have been one of the earliest advocates of this interpretation, translates:

> Wenn eure Sünden wie Scharlach sind,
> so werden sie natürlich schon schneeweiss werden!
> Wenn sie rot sind wie Purpur,
> so werden sie schon rein werden wie Wolle!

Blank adds words to the text in his attempt to communicate this idea:

> Though your sins are like scarlet,
> they shall be white as snow, *you say,*
> Though they are red like crimson,
> they shall become like wool, *you fondly imagine.*

This view is based on the same arguments as those advanced to support the position that Isa 1:18b–c are rhetorical questions, but has the advantage of reading these lines as statements rather than questions, thus avoiding the criticism that there is no "*He* interrogative" in the passage.

Option 3: These Lines Consist of the Objection of the Accused Quoted

---

37. Mitchell, "The Omission," 113ff.
38. GKC §150a, p. 473.
39. Marti, *Jesaja*, 15; Whitehouse, *Isaiah I–XXXIX I*, 94–95; Duhm, *Buch Jesaja*, 32; Bright, "Isaiah–I," 491 (who thinks these lines may contain sarcasm, indignant questions, or the judge's summation of the case as his opponents would have stated it); Good, *Irony*, 153–54; Blank, "Irony," 4.

by the Judge for the Purpose of Refutation[40]

Fohrer envisions the judge (Yahweh) couching his words in the form of a question:

> If your sins are fiery red,
>> can they be as white as snow?
> If they are red as dye-stuff,
>> can they be as wool?
> This points to the objection:
>> If our sins are fiery red,
>>> they can become as snow!

In other words, someone in Isaiah's audience, upon hearing his reproaches now recorded in vv. 10–17, shouted out that even if his charges were true and the people's sins were very bad, they could still be forgiven—to which Yahweh replies, "Oh, can they?" On the other hand, Scott pictures the judge as responding scornfully to the claim of the accused that even if they are guilty as the plaintiff asserts, they still can be forgiven. Accordingly, he translates:

> Though your sins are like scarlet
>> they shall be as white as snow [!]
> Though they are red like crimson,
>> they shall become like wool [!] Not so!

Once again, this interpretation grows out of the same type of reasoning as that used in connection with the first two views, and is supported by the same three reasons.

Option 4: These Lines Contain a Serious Exhortation.[41]

Consequently, they may be translated:

> Though your sins are as scarlet,
>> they *must* become white as snow,
> Though they are red as crimson,
>> they *must* become as wool.

Or one may read:

---

40. Scott, "Book of Isaiah," 174–75; Fohrer, "Jesaja I," 38–39.

41. Gates, "Notes on Isaiah 1," 16–17; Fullerton, "The Rhythmical Analysis," 61–62 n. 18; Kohler, "Ein verkannter," 196–97 (on 1 19); Procksch, *Jesaja I*, 36, 43–44; Kissane, *Book of Isaiah*, 7, 13; Ziegler, *Isaias*, 14; Kelley, 189.

> If your sins are like scarlet,
>   *let them* become white as snow;
> If they are as red as purple,
>   *let them* become like wool.

Fullerton thinks that Isaiah intends to stress the difficulty of Judah's repenting and returning to Yahweh. Procksch believes that Yahweh is calling on the people to do what is impossible, thus making severe punishment inevitable. Kissane and Kelley suggest that the prophet is giving the people a genuine option to return to Yahweh or be devastated. This interpretation is supported by three arguments. First, it preserves the declarative nature of the sentences. Second, it fits the alternatives set before the hearers in vv. 19-20. Third, it provides a viable element in a lawsuit Now all this must be admitted, and this understanding is very attractive, yet there is a different nuance which seems to this writer to fit the tone and context a little better (see g below).

Option 5: The protasis of these lines states the condition for forgiveness.
Snijders proposes uniquely that Isa 1:18b-c be understood in light of Ps 51:9 (MT) and the blood purification rite. In rites of cleansing of priests (Exod 29:20-21; Lev 8:30), of those contaminated by coming into contact with dead bodies (Num 19:16-19), and of lepers (Lev 14:1-9) and houses contaminated by lepers (Lev 14:48-53), the officiant dipped a bunch of hyssop in a *red* mixture of water and blood, and sprinkled it on the one to be cleansed. Isaiah spiritualizes this rite. His point is that before the sins of Judah can become white as snow, they must be cleansed from the bloodguilt described in vv. 15e-17. Verses 11-15d show that this cannot be done by mere external forms of religion. Instead, the sinners must be sprinkled (spiritually, in the heart) with the purifying red solution, that is, they must come to God with "a broken and contrite heart" (Ps 51:19 [MT]); and when this occurs, their sins will become white as snow, that is, God will forgive them. Thus Snijders translates:

> If your sins are (or shall become) as scarlet,
>   they are (or shall be) as snow;
> If they are (or become) red as crimson,
> They are (or shall be) white as wool.[42]

---

42. Snijders, *Jesaja*, 34-36. His translation in Dutch (p. 34) runs thus:

Indien uw zonden zijn (of zullen zijn of worden) als scharlaken,
  ze zijn (of zullen zijn) als sneeuw,

He suggests that the thought of this verse is much like that of Isa 64:6, which compares righteous deeds with "a bloody garment." Now while this explanation is intriguing and reflects Snijders' creativity, it is not the most natural interpretation of this passage and has the ring of forced exegesis.

Option 6: These lines form an assurance of Yahweh's forgiveness.
In this case, the verbs in the apodosis are translated "shall" or "will." This is the majority view. Yet, several scholars do not explain clearly what they mean by this rendering,[43] as though it were self-evident. On the contrary, this rendering itself may be understood in three ways.

(i) It may be an *unconditional* assurance that Yahweh will forgive his people no matter how sinful they are.[44] Such limitless and unselfish love and grace demand a response of submission to Yahweh's will and joyful obedience to him (v. 19a), while further rebellion against him would be intolerable ingratitude (v. 20a). The thought here appears often in scripture. Before and apart from any human act of righteousness, God saves man by his grace; such love, which is given with no strings attached, is so powerful and appealing that it is inconceivable that man could or would reject it (cf. Rom 5:6-11 4- 6:1-18; 2 Cor 5:14-21).

(ii) It may be a *conditional* offer of God's grace to the people, dependent on their being willing and obedient to God's will (v. 19a).[45] Most scholars who espouse this view do not believe that Isaiah was advocating "salvation dependent on human deeds of righteousness," yet at the same time, they stress that this is not an unconditional guarantee of forgive-

---

Indien ze rood zijn (of worden) als karmozijn,
ze zijn (of zullen zijn) als witte wol.

43. So Alexander, *Commentary*, 90; Barnes, *Notes*, 95; Condamin, "Les Chapitres I et II," 13; Feldmann, *Buch Isaias*, 17; Ruffenach, "Militia," 167; Steinmann, *Le Prophète Isaïe*, 75; Auvray and Steinmann, *Isaïe*, 25; Muckle, *Isaiah 1-39*, 9; Archer, "Isaiah," 611; Kraeling, *Commentary*, 47; Ward, *Amos and Isaiah*, 236; Ackroyd, "Book of Isaiah," 333.

44. So Ridderbos, *De Profeet Jesaja*, 8; Frey, *Handkommentar zum Buch Jesaja*, 46-47.

45. So Dillmann, *Prophet Jesaja*,13; Skinner, *Book of the Prophet Isaiah*, 9; Burney, "Old Testament Notes," 437-38; Betteridge, "Obedience and Not Sacrifice," 41-43, 47-48; Ehrlich, *Jesaja, Jeremia*, 7; Budde, "Zu Jesaja 1-5 (I)," 30; Fischer, *Buch Isaias*, 32-33; Slotki, *Isaiah*, 6; Hertzberg, *Erste Jesaja*, 23; Rignell, "Isaiah Chapter I," 152; Vriezen, *Outline*, 295-96; Jones, "Verses Eighteen through Twenty," 325-26; Clements, *Isaiah 1-39*, 34.

ness, but assurance that God can, will, and desires to forgive the people if they will return to him and accept his grace.

(iii) It may be an *encouragement* to the prophet's hearers that it is possible for them to be forgiven if they will repent and turn back to Yahweh.[46] This nuance is very close to g below, the difference being that those who espouse the present interpretation translate the imperfect forms of the verbs in the apodosis by "shall" or "will," whereas the view in the following section calls for the rendering "may" or "might." It should also be evident that the differences between the three understandings in the present section are based on differences in emphasis and in imagining the tone of voice of the speaker. The arguments which support these interpretations are the same as those which support the following view, and thus will be presented there.

g. *These lines contain an offer of the possibility of divine forgiveness.*[47] Cheyne translates:

> If your sins be scarlet,
>   they *may become* white as snow;
> Be they red as crimson,
>   they *may become* as wool

Similarly, Gray renders:

> Though your sins were like scarlet (robes),
>   they *might become* white like snow, etc.

Whether one reads "if," "even if" or "(al)though," the protasis of these two lines is clearly concessive.[48] There is no question as to whether the people are guilty of sin. The prophet declares that in spite of this it is possible for them to receive divine forgiveness if they will be willing and obedient. The imperfects here, then, have *potential* force. That Isa 1:18b-c is a sincere promise, assurance, or offer of the possibility of God's forgiveness is supported by five arguments. First, this is the oldest known interpretation of this verse, being attested in the LXX, Vulgate, early Jewish rabbis, early Church Fathers, and Luther.[49] Second, Yahweh's

---

46. So Penna, *Isaia*, 54; Eichrodt, *Der Heilige*, 32–33; Schoneveld, "Jesaja I 18–20," 343–44.

47. So Cheyne, *Book of the Prophet Isaiah*, 44, 163; Gray, *Isaiah I-XXXIX*, 26, 28; Vaccari, *I Isaia-Geremia*, 24; Young, *Book of Isaiah I*, 77; Mauchline, *Isaiah 1–39*, 55; Nielsen, "Das Bild des Gerichts," 316 n. 16; and the New English Bible.

48. See *GKC* §160a, p. 498; Burney, "Old Testament Notes," 435; Penna, *Isaia*, 54.

49. See the evidence collected by Sjöberg, "Om edra Synder," 293–95, who thinks

summons to the people of Judah to meet him in a lawsuit (v. 18a) does not necessarily require a threat or reproach or oracle of doom in what follows. In fact, in this pericope Yahweh appears as a loving father who is greatly distraught because his sons have rebelled against him (vv. 2–4). His desire is not to punish the guilty, but to restore the broken covenant relationship between himself and his sons (cf. Jer 2:5; Mic 6:3; and the discussion of v. 18a in the second major section of this paper). Third, since there is no *"He* interrogative" in these lines, it is best to read them as statements rather than questions.[50] Fourth, Isaiah's prophetic career spanned four decades, and thus it would be very precarious to affirm categorically that he *never* assured or promised his audience divine forgiveness during this entire period.[51] Fifth, both an attempt at reconciliation (v. 18) and a declaration of possible blessings and curses (vv. 19–20) belong to the covenant lawsuit pattern.[52]

In addition, there are two other considerations which favor the idea that Isa 1:18b–c contains an offer of the possibility of divine forgiveness. First, this fits the surrounding context. The staccato-like charges to repent and be converted in vv. 16–17 presuppose that (in the prophet's mind, at least) at the time these words were delivered there was a possibility that the hearers might turn back to Yahweh and that Yahweh would forgive them; and these verses most likely belong to the same pericope as v. 18 (see the first section of this paper). Likewise, vv. 19–20 set before the hearers the options of blessings or curses, depending on their response of repentance or rebellion. Such follows most naturally an

---

Rabbi Johanan ben Zakkai (after 70 CE) is the earliest known advocate of this view among Jewish scholars.

50. See the remarks of Burney, "Old Testament Notes," 433–34; Betteridge, "Obedience and Not Sacrifice," 42; Feldmann, *Buch Isaias*, 16.

51. Contra Duhm, *Buch Jesaja*, 32; cf. Jones, "Verses Eighteen through Twenty," 320. Sjöberg, "Om edra Synder," 306, writes: "It appears then not at all absurd that Isaiah, during his forty-year activity as a prophet, in spite of the call narrative, in certain situations spoke to the people concerning the necessity and possibility of conversion." [My translation—JTW. The Swedish runs: "Det ter sig da inte alls orimligt, att Jesaja under sin fyrtiôriga verksamhet somprofet trots kallesberâttel-sens ord i vissa situationer har talat till folket om omvändelsens nödvändighet och möjlighet."] The argument of Culver, "Isaiah 1 18," 137, that even if Isa 1:18b–c were read as a statement, it could not refer to forgiveness, because "sinners may become white but not their sins," takes the wording of the passage much too strictly and fails to allow for the possibility of metonymy here. See Gray, *Isaiah I–XXXIX*, 29; Ruffenach, "Malitia,"167.

52. See the article mentioned in n. 18 and Marshall, "Unity of Isaiah 1–12," 35–36.

offer of the possibility of Yahweh's forgiveness. Second, if the historical setting in which v. 18 was originally delivered was Sennacherib's invasion of Jerusalem in 701 BCE (cf. vv. 7-8 and the first part of this article), it is quite probable that the people felt that their misfortunes were proof either that Yahweh had abandoned them or that there was no way they could obtain his forgiveness. Over against such feelings, the most appropriate message the prophet could have offered would be that Yahweh was quite willing to forgive them in spite of the many heinous sins they had committed, but they must accept that forgiveness by renouncing their rebellion against him and returning to him in the attitude of willingness and obedience.[53]

The Theological Position of Isa 1:18

Ideally, an appraisal of the theological thrust of Isa 1:18 would entail a treatment of its meaning in the overall scope of Old Testament theology (with special attention to the texts which teach a similar message) at the three stages of its historical development, namely, in the present form of the book of Isaiah, in the complex or composition to which it belonged before its inclusion into the present book of Isaiah, and in the historical setting in which it was first delivered. Here only a few observations will be made.

Like the Old Testament as a whole, the book of Isaiah declares that Yahweh punishes the wicked, even among his own people. But his ultimate purpose in punishment is not to destroy but to redeem (10:5-7, 12).[54] Thus there is hope for those who repent and turn to God. Outside

---

53. Having adopted the widely held view that vv. 18-20 were delivered at the time of Sennacherib's invasion, Sjöberg, 305, says: "In this situation, when Isaiah uttered the command concerning the necessity—and possibility!—of conversion, and when, at the same time, he was convinced that Yahweh at this time would intervene for Jerusalem's salvation, the offer of conversion in Isa 1:18-20 can fit in a natural way." [My translation—JTW. The Swedish is: "I denna situation, då Jesaja latit budet om omvändelsens nödvändighet—och möjlighet!—gå ut, och da han samtidigt varit övertygad om att Jahve för denna gång skall ingripa till Jerusalems räddning, kan omvändelseerbjudanet i Jes. I:18-20 infogas på ett naturligt sätt."]

54. Jacob, *Theology*, 289, succinctly states the fundamental Old Testament teaching on punishment, repentance, and forgiveness when he writes: "What Yahweh seeks to obtain by punishment is the sinner's return and the possibility of a new life. Conversion is the indispensable condition of forgiveness; without it, all the means of forgiveness which God had made available run the risk of being inoperative." This appraisal agrees very well with the interpretation of Isa 1:18-20 advocated in the present paper.

Isa 1–12, there are several passages in the book of Isaiah in which the speaker appeals to his hearers to repent and/or offers them the possibility of divine forgiveness (see, e.g., 28:16–17; 30:19–22; 31:4–8; 38:17; 55:6–7; 57:14–19; 58:6–12). Isa 1:18–20 is quite in harmony with such passages.

It is difficult to determine the extent and precise content of the complex (oral or literary) to which Isa 1:18 belonged prior to its inclusion in the present prophetic book. Scholarly opinion ranges from chapter 1 by itself to chapters 1–5, 1–12, 1–27, 1–35, or 1–39 (or large portions thereof). Even if we adopt the smaller units (i.e., chs. 1–5 or 1–12), the motifs of divine punishment for the purpose of bringing repentance, and of the offer of divine forgiveness are attested. This is supported by at least three considerations, (i) These chapters hold out hope that a "remnant" will return to Yahweh and will survive beyond the present and imminent calamities (cf. 1:9; 4:2–3; 6:13; 7:3, 21–22; 10:20–21; 11:11, 16). (ii) Isa 8:16–18 speaks of "disciples" gathered about the prophet, to whom his message is entrusted. (iii) Several passages in these chapters distinguish between the destruction of the wicked and the redemption of the penitent among God's people (cf. 1:25–28; 3:9–11, 13–15; 8:12–15) and call for the hearers to repent and turn to Yahweh (cf. 2:5, 22; 7:4, 9).

Now when one attempts to get back to the message of the eighth century BCE prophet Isaiah, three matters relevant to an interpretation of Isa 1:18 must be taken into consideration. First, the way in which one understands the Call of the Prophet (ch. 6) has much to do with whether one thinks it was possible for Isaiah to extend the possibility of repentance and divine forgiveness to the people of Judah. G. von Rad places great importance on vv. 9ff. as being central to understanding Isaiah's message on this subject. Although he is very guarded in his statements, his basic interpretation seems to be: "The saying about hardening of heart in Is. VI sounds as if it shut the door on everyone, and it was intended to be understood in this way."[55] Now it must be agreed that Isaiah's Call is a key to understanding his message, but Isa 6:9ff. should be interpreted along with and in light of vv. 5–7 (where Isaiah himself repents and experiences Yahweh's forgiveness) and v. 13d-e (which an-

---

55. Rad, *Old Testament Theology II*, 154. For his entire discussion, see 151–75. Milgrom, "Repentance," 737b–738a, apparently follows von Rad's thinking when he writes, "Isaiah ... withdraws the offer of repentance at an early point in his career" and then invites the reader to compare Isa 1:16–20 with 6:9–13.

nounces that beyond Yahweh's punishment a holy remnant will survive).[56] Having turned to God himself, it most likely that the prophet retained the hope throughout his career that his fellows would do likewise.[57] And scholars generally agree that the "remnant" concept goes back to Isaiah himself, since he named one of his sons Shear-jashub ("A remnant shall return").[58]

Second, it is important to avoid interpreting an individual oracle in light of the subtle, unspoken assumption that Isaiah uttered basically the same message in all circumstances. On the contrary, over a forty-year period it should be expected that his thoughts and emphases would vary with changing general and specific situations. In Eichrodt's treatment of forgiveness in the prophets, he states this important principle exceptionally well:

> With them (i.e., the *prophets) forgiveness is increasingly viewed in an eschatological perspective* . . . Forgiveness, for all that they indeed reckon with such a thing as *an individual divine act at important crises in history* [italics mine—JTW; in a footnote at this point Eichrodt lists Isa 1:18 along with several other prophetic texts], strikes them overwhelmingly as God's concluding act, intimately bound up with the irruption of the new age. If this is sometimes overlooked, then the expressions for forgiveness which the prophets adopt from common usage are partly to blame for the mistake, in so far as their primary reference is to a *temporally limited and repeatable individual act*. Whether forgiveness is described as the wiping out of a record of guilt, the abolition and removal of a burden, the covering or taking away of a guilt that cries out accusingly for vengeance, or the passing

---

56. Ward, "Isaiah," 458b, correctly affirms that these lines are not a later addition, as has often been claimed. See also Cecily, "Concept of Sin," 115–16. Vriezen, "Essentials," 133, 137–38, believes that v. 13d-e is a later gloss, but one which correctly reflects Isaiah's message. He writes: "Yahweh never decided—even according to Isaiah—on a collective destruction without creating new life and without leaving a remnant to witness it" (ibid., 137).

57. "Isaiah's own experience in Ch 6 in which sin was expiated (*kipper*) at the altar, after his confession, must be allowed to interpret the promise of pardon in [Ch. 1] v 18." Thompson, *Penitence and Sacrifice*, 176. See also Burney, "Old Testament Notes," 437; Sjöberg, "Om edra Synder," 304–5.

58. Moriarty, "Isaiah 1–39," 266, says succinctly: "Isaiah never believed that the nation would be utterly destroyed and the divine promises cancelled out. There would be a remnant, cleansed in the fire of judgment, inheritors of the promise made to David. Isaiah's doctrine of the remnant gives a basic optimism to his work without clouding his vision of the inevitable judgment upon wickedness."

over of such, a ransom from slavery, or the healing of a mortal sickness, or whether it is rendered with *s-l-ḥ*, without the use of concrete imagery, as a passing over, an exercise of forbearance, all these are originally connected with the idea of the remission *on a particular occasion* [italics mine—JTW] of guilt that has accrued, and the restoration thereby of the earlier relationship until new guilt makes new forgiveness necessary.[59]

Third, an effort should be made to put oneself into the situation or type of situation in which Isa 1:18 was uttered.[60] The following reconstruction seems viable. Isaiah had preached in vain during the reigns of Jotham and Ahaz. It is likely that he saw in the ascension of Hezekiah to the throne a new hope for the conversion and restoration of Judah (Isa 8:23–9:6 [MT]; cf. 2 Kgs 18:1–18). Not long after Sennacherib came to the throne of Assyria in 705 BCE, a new crisis arose when many of the western states, including Judah, rebelled against their new suzerain. In 701 BCE, Sennacherib brought his army into Palestine. Isaiah 22:1–14 (especially vv. 1–2, 13) appears to come from a time shortly after an invading army had lifted its siege from around Jerusalem (cf. vv. 4, 8–10) and had withdrawn from the city. This probably has reference to Sennacherib's invasion in 701 BCE. When the Ethiopians and Egyptians approached from the south, the Assyrians withdrew from Jerusalem to meet them (cf. 2 Kgs 19:8–9a; Isa 37:8–9a). The Jews went up on the housetops to watch the soldiers retreat (Isa 22:1), and when they were out of sight rejoiced in a great celebration over their deliverance (vv. 2a-b, 13). Isaiah was incensed, and he delivered the oracle now recorded in vv. 1–14. He declared that it was not a time for rejoicing but for weeping (vv. 4, 12) because the Judean leaders had been slain or captured (vv. 2c-3), many of the houses in the city had been torn down to repair the breaches in the wall (vv. 9–10), the people had not genuinely repented but merely engaged in external ritual acts (vv. 11–13), and Yahweh would soon bring the enemy army back to besiege Jerusalem again (v. 5) because of this (v. 14).

This message received only negative response from the people. Shortly thereafter, word came to Jerusalem that the Assyrians might be returning to put the city under siege again (cf. 1:20). Just as the people

---

59. Eichrodt, *Theology of the Old Testament* 2, 457–58. See also Sjöberg, 301–2.

60. For further discussion of the material that follows, see my essay "The First Pericope in the Book of Isaiah," above.

had done shortly after the siege was lifted (22:13b-c), they feverishly engaged in numerous acts of external worship in the hope that they could persuade Yahweh to spare the city (1:11-15). At this time Isaiah delivered the oracle now preserved in 1:2-20. He reproved the people for rebelling against Yahweh, who had nurtured them as a father does his children (vv. 2-4). He asks them why they persist in the very sins which had brought the Assyrians and their allies into the land in the first place and had led to such a widespread desolation throughout the country and the isolation of Jerusalem from the outside world (vv. 5-9). He chides them for thinking that mere external acts of religion would persuade God to save them (vv. 10-15), and calls for a total change of heart and life (vv. 16-17). In response to their verbal or non-verbal feelings that Yahweh had deserted them or that they had become so wicked that there was no hope for their deliverance, Isaiah concludes his oracle by assuring them that they *could* be forgiven and spared (v. 18). They had the choice of being willing and obedient and thus receiving God's blessing, or of refusing and rebelling and thus being destroyed by the invading armies (vv. 19-20).

As a concluding postscript, it may be pointed out that Isa 35:9b-37 (= 2 Kgs 19:9b-37; cf. 2 Chr 32:17-23) and Jeremiah 26:17-19 (cf. Mic 3:9-12) state that Hezekiah and the Judeans did repent and thus Yahweh spared the city. In later times, however, the Judeans fell back to their old patterns of life and apostasy from Yahweh. Then oracles of Isaiah like those found in 22:1-14 and 1:2-20 took on renewed significance. Anonymous prophetic figures in the Isaianic tradition rehearsed, reapplied, and rearranged the earlier oracles of their master to suit new situations, until longer complexes of prophetic material were collected and ultimately the book of Isaiah emerged. Ward describes the process in this way:

> It is likely that older strata in the tradition were preserved, not for antiquarian reasons, but because they continued to be reapplied and reinterpreted in each new phase of the community's life. Thus the eighth-century oracles of judgment against Judah (1:2-26; 2:6—4:1; 5-8; 9:8—10:34; 22:1-14; 28:1—29:16; 30:1-8; 31:1-5) would have seemed painfully relevant to sensitive persons during the decades before and after the fall of the Judean kingdom (598-586 BCE). At each stage in the process of expansion, the older portions of the tradition would have been allowed to speak anew to the religious community, alongside, and partly

by means of, the new words which were formed in response to the demands of faith in changing circumstances.[61]

---

61. Ward, "Isaiah," 457a.

15

Lament Reversed—Isaiah 1:21ff

ISAIAH 1:21FF. CONTAINS AT least three problems which continue to challenge scholars and to evoke various conclusions. These are: (1) the form critical concerns for determining the extent of the pericope, the genre, and the *Sitz im Leben*; (2) the date of the original delivery of this oracle and its function in the present form of the Book of Isaiah; and (3) the religious teaching of this oracle and its place in Isaiah's theology and in that of the book of Isaiah. The purpose of the present paper is to set forth a certain position on these issues in the hope of eliciting reactions that might refute, further substantiate, or modify the positions taken here.

Form Critical Considerations

Extent of the Pericope

Some scholars regard Isa 1:2–31 as a single pericope because of repetition of words and ideas, the elements which belong to its genre, and the flow of thought.[1] Robert North writes: ". . . There is ground for a widespread conviction among exegetes that the *whole* of (Isaiah) chapter 1 possesses a unity which even if it be coincidental can nevertheless be focused as a 'summary of the preaching of First Isaiah.'"[2] However, an examination of the views held by exegetes shows that "widespread"

---

1. So Alexander, *Commentary on the Prophecies of Isaiah*, 80; Ley, "Metrische Analyse," 230–31; Feldmann, *Buch Isaias*, 14; Zorell, "Isaiae cohortatio," 69–70; Gemser, "Rîb- or Controversy-Pattern," 130; Rignell, "Isaiah Chapter I," 141, 146; Penna, *Isaia*, 58–59; Ziegler, *Isaias*, 11–16; Mattioli, "Due Schemi litterari," 345–64; and North, "Angel-Prophet," 49.

2. North, "Angel-Prophet," 49.

is an exaggerated term here, and furthermore it is obvious that North has in mind the final redactional stage of chapter 1 and not the original oracle delivered by the prophet orally. Condamin divides the pericopes in Isa 1-2 as 1:1-27 and 1:28-2:22;[3] Hertzberg makes 1:2-26 a single pericope;[4] Young thinks 1:10-31 is harmonious;[5] Mauchline views 1:18-31 as a unit;[6] Whitehouse combines 1:18-28;[7] and Scharbert groups 1:18-26 together.[8]

However, the most widely held view is that a new pericope begins at v. 21, and there can be little doubt that this is the case. Nevertheless, there is a serious problem as to the point at which this pericope should be terminated. Some carry it to the end of the chapter because of the similarity of theme, strophic arrangement by speakers (the prophet in vv. 21-23, Yahweh in vv. 24-26, and the prophet in vv. 27-31), chiastic structure—A (vv. 21-23)—B (vv. 24-26)—B' (vv. 27-28)—A' (vv. 29-31), and the connectives לכן (v. 24) and כי (vv. 29, 30).[9] But there is such a marked difference between vv. 21-28 and 29-31 that it is extremely difficult to believe that vv. 21-31 were spoken by the same person to the same audience on the same occasion. Loretz regards 1:21-27 as a unit in its present position in the text, but he thinks the present text is the end-product of a long history of development.[10] Others propose that

3. Condamin, "Les Chapitres 1 et 2," 10-14, 20-22.
4. Hertzberg, *Der Erste Jesaja*, 24.
5. Young, *The Book of Isaiah*, 1:27-93.
6. Mauchline, *Isaiah 1-39*, 44.
7. Whitehouse, *Isaiah I-XXXIX*, 88.
8. Scharbert, *Die Propheten Israels*, 340-41.
9. So Budde, "Zum hebräischen Klagelied," 245-47; Dillmann and Kittel, *Der Prophet Jesaja*, 1; Skinner, *The Book of the Prophet Isaiah*, 1-2; Feldmann, *Buch Isaias*, 21-22; Fischer, *Buch Isaias*; Ridderbos, *De Profeet Jesaja*, 1-12; Vaccari, *Isaiah-Geremia*, 21-22; Fitch, *Isaiah*, 563-64; Kissane, *Book of Isaiah I*, 14-15; Niditch, "The Composition of Isaiah 1," 513-29 (she considers vv. 2-3 + 21-31 a single pericope).

10 Loretz argues that vv. 21c-d and 27 are a commentary on the song in vv. 21a-b + 22-26. But then he reasons that v. 21e, 23e-f, 24d-25, and certain words and phrases in vv. 22, 24, 26 are later additions or glosses to the original poem. And he thinks vv. 21a-b, c-d + 22-26, 27 were incorporated into 1:1-2, 4 in the fourth stage of the growth of this chapter. Loretz, *Der Prolog*, 39, 42, 43, 48, 56, 113-14. However, these extensive emendations and omissions go beyond the bounds of what might be expected of ancient speakers and writers. The modern researcher is in no position to say what an ancient writer might compose. Certainly, Loretz's reconstructed text is smoother and more coherent according to the standards which have been developed in modern Western thought, where well-constructed symmetrical patterns are appealing.

vv. 21–23 should be separated from what follows because these verses contain a complete thought within themselves and vv. 24–28 paint an optimistic picture of the future in sharp contrast to the sinful state described in vv. 21–23.¹¹

The most prevalent scholarly position is that the pericope beginning at v. 21 extends to v. 26.¹² This is supported by the following considerations. (a) איכה, "How" (v. 21), is the usual beginning of a lament (cf. e.g., Lam 1:1; 2:1; 4:1; 1 Sam 1:19). (b) Verses 21–26 are arranged chiastically with several connecting terms and ideas. "The faithful city" and "righteousness" are lacking in v. 21 but are promised in v. 26. The "dross" plaguing the people now (v. 22) will be removed by God's intervention (v. 25). The "rebels," thieves, greedy lovers of bribes, and oppressors of the orphans and widows of v. 23 will be punished as God's "enemies" and "foes" by his wrath according to v. 24. The "judges" and "counselors" of v. 26 will replace the wicked "princes" of v. 23. (c) Verses 27–28 suggest a different background, terminology, theological perspective, rhythm, and parallelism from what precedes.

Now while these arguments are reasonable as far as they go, there are good grounds for including vv. 27–28 in the same pericope with vv. 21–26.¹³ First, these verses continue and deepen the thought of what precedes in a natural flow of ideas.¹⁴ Second, the contrast between the

---

However, one would be hard pressed to find many, if any, poetic pieces in the ancient Near Eastern world (Hebrew, Ugaritic, Akkadian, etc.) which would conform to the colometric criteria which Loretz demands of the text.

11. Thus Slotki, *Isaiah*, 1–9; Scott, "The Book of Isaiah," 165–79; Muckle, *Isaiah 1–39*, 6–10; Archer, *Isaiah*, 609–12; Kelley, *Isaiah*, 182–92; Kaiser, *Isaiah 1–12*, 40, 41.

12. So Cheyne, *The Book of the Prophet Isaiah*, 42–44, 17; Marti, *Das Buch Jesaja*, 2; Box, *The Book of Isaiah*, 18; Gray, *A Critical and Exegetical Commentary*, 1–40; Duhm, *Das Buch Jesaja*, 23–36; Budde, "Zu Jesaja 1–5 (I)," 34; Robertson, "Isaiah Chapter I," 233–34; Mowinckel, "Jesajaboken I," 80; Steinmann, *Le Prophète Isaïe*, 74–80, 369, 65–66; Bright, "Isaiah – I," 490–91; Fohrer, "Jesaja I," 253–54; *Das Buch Jesaja*, 41–46; *Die Propheten des 8. Jahrhunderts*, 112–15, 160–61; Fey, *Amos und Jesaja*, 62–77; Wildberger, *Jesaja*, 8; Jones, "Isaiah Chapter One Verses Twenty One to the End," 320 (see also "Isaiah Chapter One Verses Ten to Seventeen," 468); Snijders, *Jesaja, Deel I*, 15–43; Vermeylen, *Du Prophète Isaïe*, 71; Holladay, *Isaiah*, 6–8; Clements, *Isaiah 1–39*, 28–38.

13. This is the view of Brown, "The Measurements of Hebrew Poetry," 82; Procksch, *Jesaja*, 27–51; Bentzen, *Jesaja*, 1–14; Auvray and Steinmann, *Isaïe*, 21–27; Eichrodt, *Der Heilige*, 11–12, 25–43; Auvray, *Isaïe 1–39*, 38; Frey, *Handkommentar*, 14, 67.

14. Wildberger, *Jesaja*, 57, admits this, but still contends that only vv. 21–26 compose the pericope. Kaiser, *Isaiah 1–12*, 41, sees this as an argument that vv. 27–28 are a

redeemed and penitent and the rebels, sinners, and forsakers of the Lord within God's own chosen people in vv. 27–28 has a clear counterpart in the figure of Yahweh smelting away the dross and removing the alloy of the sinful city in v. 25. Third, "Zion" at the beginning of v. 27 connects with "the faithful city" in vv. 21 and 26 and with "the city of righteousness" in v. 26.[15] Fourth, while "righteousness" in v. 21 is repeated in v. 26, "justice" and "righteousness" of v. 21 in that same order recur in v. 27 (on the meaning of these two terms in these verses, see the section on theology below). Fifth, if vv. 27–28 are included in this pericope, then it follows the same general structure as vv. 2–20, namely, a description of Judah's sin and threat of punishment (vv. 2–15 and 21–25), a promise of redemption for the penitent (vv. 16–18 and 26), and a portrayal of a division between the penitent and the resolute sinners among God's people (vv. 19–20 and 27–28). Sixth, there are other passages in poetic literature in which the beginning is apparently "rounded off" or "complemented" at a certain point, only to be continued and completed a few lines or verses later (see Mic 3:9–11 + 12; 5:9–13 + 14; Jer 4:23–26b + 26c–28). Even though such a structure offends the strict demands of the contemporary logical mind, its recurrence in Old Testament literature suggests that it was quite acceptable to the ancient Semitic thought patterns. In light of these arguments, it seems best to regard Isa 1:21–28 as a single pericope.

Genre

Jones labels Isa 1:21–26 an "oracle of judgment which consists of three elements: the basis for the judgment (vv. 21–23), the messenger formula (vv. 24a–c), and the announcement of judgment (vv. 24d–26)."[16] Bentzen believes that in form (genre) vv. 21–28 are a lament, but actually they have the character of a "prophetic punishment oracle."[17] Similarly, Fohrer (in his 1966 commentary on Isaiah) states that in tone and meter, vv.

---

later addition to vv. 15–26 because they turn a "purificatory judgment" into a "selective judgment." See further n. 28 below.

15. This detail has had a strong influence on Loretz's reconstruction, although he does not reach the same conclusion as the present writer. Rather, he views vv. 21b and 27 as additions to the funeral song in vv. 21a + 22–26. Loretz, *Prolog*, 56.

16. Jones, "Verses Twenty One to the End," 323–25.

17. Bentzen, *Jesaja*, 11.

21–26 are a funeral lament, but in content a "reproach."[18] Kaiser thinks vv. 21–23 are a rebuke derived from the secular lament over the dead.[19]

However, the prevailing overwhelming scholarly view is that vv. 21–26 are a "lament" or "funeral elegy."[20] This is based on the following considerations. First, the oracle begins with איכה, "How," which is a common introduction for a lament (cf. Lam 1:1; 2:1; 4:1; 2 Sam 1:19). Second, it uses the (Hebrew) sounds uttered by hired mourners at funerals. Third, the meter or rhythm is *qinah* (3:2). Fourth, the tone of this whole pericope is similar to that of the book of Lamentations.

Now while all these observations are valid, they fail to take into consideration and/or do justice to vv. 25–26 (+ 27=28), which state that Yahweh's purpose in the impending judgment is not to destroy but to purify or refine, and announce the restoration of the city (Zion or Jerusalem) to her original "faithful" commitment to her divine husband and to the condition of being "righteous" in God's eyes because of godly leadership and just treatment of the poor and disadvantaged. If these verses are indeed a part of the pericope (and all the evidence suggests that they are; as a matter of fact, most scholars include vv. 25–26 in the pericope beginning with v. 21), they cannot be ignored in trying to determine its genre. Indeed, a few scholars have noted this in their analysis. Fohrer, in his article on Isaiah 1, pointed out that the oracle in vv. 21–26 proclaims a possible realization of salvation if the people will turn to God.[21] Mowinckel says that the prophet begins by imitating a lament, then turns it into an accusation or prophetic punishment oracle, but that, viewed as a whole, he exhibits a combination of threat and promise with an emphasis on promise.[22] Kraus says vv. 21–23 are

18. Fohrer, *Das Buch Jesaja I*, 42.

19. Kaiser, *Isaiah 1–12*, 40.

20. So Cheyne, *Book of the Prophet Isaiah*, 163; Dillmann, *Prophet Jesaja*, 14 (the lament appears in vv. 21–23, then the judgment begins with v 24); Marti, *Buch Jesaja*, 16–18 (vv. 21–23 are a lament, and vv. 24–26 a threat and mourning song); Skinner, *Book of the Prophet Isaiah*, 10; Duhm, *Buch Jesaia*, 32; Feldmann, *Buch Isaias*, 18; Budde, "Zu Jesaja 1–5 (I),"31; Slotki, *Isaiah*, 7; Steinmann, *Le Prophète Isaïe*, 78–79; Hertzberg, *Der Erste Jesaja*, 24; Scott, "The Book of Isaiah," 176; Ziegler, *Isaias*, 14; Bright, "Isaiah - I," 491 (vv. 21–23 are an elegy, and vv. 24–26 an oracle); Fey, *Amos und Jesaja*, 65–68; Wildberger, *Jesaja*, 57–58; Fohrer, *Das Buch Jesaja I*, 42 and 42 n. 13; *Die Propheten des 8. Jahrhunderts*, 115; Moriarty, "Isaiah 1–39," 267; Kelley, *Isaiah*, 190 ("lament" pertains only to vv. 21–23); Vermeylen, *Le Prophète Isaias*, 71.

21. Fohrer, "Jesaja 1," 265–66.

22. Mowinckel, "Jesajaboken I," 79–80.

a lament which stands in place of a reproach or reason for judgment, v. 24 contains Yahweh's affirmation that he will avenge himself, and vv. 25-26 announce hope for Jerusalem.[23] And Davies observes that it is composed of a rebuke in the form of a lament (vv. 21-23), a proclamation of judgment (vv. 24-25), and a promise of restoration (v. 26).[24] These synopses point in the right direction. The suggestion offered in the present study is that the expression which best describes Isa 1:21-28 is "Lament Reversed." In other words, the prophet begins his oracle in a way very similar to that in which many Old Testament laments begin; but before the oracle is concluded, he announces that Yahweh will intervene in behalf of his penitent, faithful people and transform their mourning into joy.

Admittedly this is a very delicate point, because the laments in the Psalter typically conclude with an acknowledgment of Yahweh's help and/or a bursting forth of grateful praise for his intervention in behalf of the speaker(s). Several scholars think that an unrecorded divine oracle uttered by a prophet or priest or some other cultic official is to be assumed between the actual "lamenting" or "complaining" and the "praise," and that the concluding section of "praise" is a vital part of the genre called "Lament."[25] This is certainly the case in some psalms. But with regard to Isa 1:21ff., three observations seem pertinent. First, not all psalms which may be categorized as belonging to the "Lament" genre conclude with praise, as Pss 25; 35; 39; 89; 120; 141 and 143 show. Second, the structure and content of Isa 1:21ff. is not the same as that of the Lament Psalms. The complaint in the Lament Psalms arises from distressful circumstances being experienced by the speaker(s), while that is Isa 1:21ff. is motivated by the present sinful condition of Jerusalem. There is no place for or indication of a favorable divine response to the complaint in Isa 1:21ff. In fact, Yahweh's response is resolution to avenge himself on his rebellious people (vv. 24-25). And too, the oracle in Isaiah ends with a divine promise, not with praise or a resolution to praise as in the Lament Psalms. Third, the "distress" described in Isa 1:24-25 is instigated by God for the express purpose of purifying and restoring

23. Kraus, "Die prophetische Botschaft," 131-32 (article first published in 1955).

24. Davies, *Prophecy and Ethics*, 91.

25. Descamps, "Pour un classement littéraire," 191-93; Hempel, "Psalms," 950-53; Sabourin, "Un classement littéraire," 23-58; and Westermann, "The Role of the Lament," 20-38.

his apostate people, whereas the "distress" in the Lament Psalms is the condition brought on by God or enemies or sin which was responsible for inducing the lament in the first place. Thus, one seems justified in regarding Isa 1:21ff. as a "Lament Reversed."

Sitz im Leben

But for whom and in what type of situation would a prophet in Isaiah's day offer such a message in this way? Surprisingly little scholarly discussion of this question has taken place, in spite of the fact that there are some clues which are suggestive. Wildberger and Jones think it was delivered at the annual Royal Zion Festival because of the similarities of language and thought with the Zion-, Enthronement-, and Royal-Psalms,[26] while Steinmann connects it with the more nebulous "Great Festival."[27]

The following data appear to be relevant in attempting to recover the *Sitz im Leben* of this passage. First, the direct speech and content of the oracle show that the Speaker and his audience are in Jerusalem (see especially vv. 21, 26, 27). Second, the prophet is addressing the common people, not their rulers, because he speaks to them *about* their rulers (vv. 23, 26). Third, the sins which Isaiah condemns (injustice, murder, theft, taking bribes, oppressing orphan and widow) assume that both he and his hearers are familiar with and respect long-established laws to which they have subscribed as members of a common community; it would seem most likely that these were laws known to us as portions of the Pentateuch.[28] Fourth, the figure of the "faithful" city which had become

---

26. Wildberger, *Jesaja*, 58; Jones, "Verses Twenty One to the End," 326–27.

27. Steinmann, *Le Prophète Isaïe*, 77 n. *.

28. Davies, *Prophecy and Ethics*, 93–109, is certainly correct to point out that the appeals of the eighth century prophets went far beyond mere legal observance of laws and were concerned with God's people treating persons as persons. However, it is unrealistic to attribute the source of the prophetic convictions to their total cultural milieu. This is too general, as opponents of the prophets could interpret the same milieu in a different way. Surely Isaiah drew heavily from Israel's legal heritage and from Amos, although it is very doubtful that he was dependent on wisdom traditions. The assessment of G. von Rad, *Old Testament Theology II*, 149, is convincing:

> Like Amos, Isaiah watches inexorably over the divine law of which he is spokesman. He carries forward Amos's indictments of every form of miscarriage of justice and of exploitation of the weak on so broad a front and with such passion that we may fairly assume that the eighth-century prophets must already have fallen heir to a certain tradition, a heritage which fur-

a "harlot," but could become "faithful" again by Yahweh's process of purification and repentance, assumes a prior understanding of the use of the marriage relationship as a fruitful way of describing the relationship between Yahweh and his people. Fifth, the expressions "Lord of hosts" and "Mighty One of Israel"[29] were well-known epithets of Yahweh when this oracle was first delivered (v. 24). Sixth, the speaker and his audience have a historical orientation; they can look back to the past and agree that there was a time when Jerusalem was faithful to Yahweh (v. 21); in addition, the prophet can contrast her fidelity of the past with her present apostasy and unfaithfulness (vv. 21–24, 28), and envision a future in which the former condition can be restored (vv. 25–27). Seventh, the very fact that the prophet begins with a reproaching lament (v. 21) presupposes that his hearers were in a joyful mood; and his accusations against them assume they were feeling secure in spite of their sins (vv. 21–23) because Yahweh had not intervened to punish them, apparently they were getting by with crimes of all sorts, and they took for granted that Yahweh regarded them as his friends (v. 24). All these details combine to suggest that Isaiah was attending a joyous festival at the Jerusalem temple during some period of his life when there appeared to be no threat of attack from enemy armies, so that the powerful rich among the Judeans were free to go about oppressing their poor brothers and neighbors to gain additional possessions for themselves. The Feast of Tabernacles, some festival celebrating Yahweh's protection of Zion, or the annual New Year's Festival seem to be the most likely candidates.

> nished them with the subjects on which prophets spoke. Isaiah's concern for the divine law cannot be stressed too strongly. It is society's attitude to this law which determines whether its relationship to God is in good order . . . In his [Isaiah's] eyes, the divine law is the greatest saving blessing.

A. Phillips, "Prophecy and Law," 222–24, thinks that the ultimate source of Isaiah's reproofs of oppressions of the poor and defenseless and of the perversion of justice is rulings on humaneness and righteousness, the principles of natural law, which were incorporated into the Book of the Covenant and disseminated to Israel from the royal court through its civil servants (a term more neutral than wisdom circles). Although Phillips's evaluation of the role of natural law and the importance of wisdom circles for the eighth century prophets lacks solid foundations, he is correct in stressing the influence of Israel's legal traditions on these prophets.

29. Kaiser, *Isaiah 1–12*, 44, however, who thinks Isa 1:21–26 originated in the fifth century BCE and later, contends that the divine epithet "the Mighty One of Israel" is an "archaizing" transformation of the earlier epithet, "the Mighty One of Jacob."

Date and Historical Background

Robertson, Vermeylen, Kaiser, and Loretz argue that Isa 1:21–26 is not authentic, but comes from the exilic period.[30] Vermeylen assigns it to Deuteronomistic circles in Palestine because the optimistic outlook of vv. 25–26 is characteristic of the Palestine Jews after the fall of Jerusalem, the vocabulary and linguistic features of this pericope are similar to Jeremiah and the Deuteronomistic school, and Isaiah taught the total destruction of Jerusalem, not that Yahweh would purify the city through affliction and save the righteous remnant. Robertson bases his case on the affirmation that Jerusalem was not corrupt in the days of Isaiah like 1:21–23 depicts it, the absence of any reference to the king in the allusions to leaders of the people in vv. 23 and 26, and the similarities of vocabulary and rhythm between this pericope and Lam 1, 2, and 4, which are of exilic origin. Kaiser draws his conclusion from his understanding of the context, and from the influence of Deuteronomistic theology on this passage. Loretz argues that the funeral song in vv. 21a + 22–26 reflects the situation after the fall of Jerusalem in 587 BCE, and that the additions in vv. 21b and 27 contain a "Zionistic" interpretation of this song from the post-exilic period. However, considerations in a different direction support the widely held scholarly position that this oracle is authentic.

A few commentators assign Isa 1:21–26 to the end of Isaiah's ministry near the time of Sennacherib's invasion of Judah and siege of Jerusalem, some time between 705 and 701 BCE[31] They advance the following arguments in support of this view. (1) Immediately after his call, Isaiah would have been a prophet of unconditional doom (cf. 6:9–13a); and only later would he have entertained the idea of a possibility of the

---

30. Robertson, "Isaiah Chapter I," 234–35; Vermeylen, *Le Prophète Isaïe*, 76–104; Kaiser, *Isaiah 1–12*, 1–2, 4, 5, 7–8, 40–45; Loretz, *Prolog*, 42–43, 48, 56, 58–61, 130, 152. Kaiser, *Isaiah 1–12*, 41, finds four stages in the growth of Isa 1:21–28. The nucleus is vv. 21–23a. To this vv. 24–25 were added to clarify the message of judgment in these verses. Later, v. 23b was added to balance the lines in the strophe, and v. 26 was added to guarantee that the purificatory judgment of vv. 24–25 was followed by a period of salvation. Finally, the last editor added vv. 27–28 as a declaration of principles he thought appropriate to the oracle in vv. 21–26. Loretz argues that 1:1 is the inscription for the entire Book of Isaiah, and that 1:2–2:4 is the prologue to the whole book, so that the whole of 1:1–2:4 is to be dated after the fall of Jerusalem in 587 BCE.

31. Marti, *Buch Jesaja*, 19–20; Budde, "Zu Jesaja 1–5," 35 (But Budde is uncertain about the date); Bentzen, *Jesaja*, 11; Frey, *Handkommentar*, 51–52.

deliverance of a remnant. (2) The "rebels" of v. 23 may have been those who made an alliance with Egypt in an attempt to thwart Sennacherib's invasion rather than trust in God (cf. 30:1-7; 31:1-3). (3) The change to good counselors announced in 1:26 is a similar thought to that of the change from Shebna to Eliakim in 22:15ff. (4) Verses 21-26 belong with vv. 2-20, which come from this period. Now, all of these arguments are based on a subjective impression of similarities of thought, and therefore this date is very tendentious and not compelling.

The historical situation assumed in Isa 1:21-26 and its content suggest that it comes from the early part of Isaiah's ministry, perhaps during the later years of Jotham (740-735 BCE) or at the beginning of the reign of Ahaz before the Syro-Ephraimitic invasion of Jerusalem (735-734 BCE).[32] Several considerations point to this period in Isaiah's ministry. First, the figure of the "faithful" city which had become a "harlot" seems to be connected with the terminology of the fertility aspect of Canaanite Baalism, which was very prominent in Judah in the days of Jotham (cf. 2 Kgs 15:35; 2 Chr 27:2) and Ahaz (2 Kgs 16:3-4; 2 Chr 28:2-4). Second, the concern for "justice" and "righteousness" (vv. 21, 26, 27) is identical with that of Amos in North Israel about 750 BCE (cf. Amos 5:7, 24; 6:12). Third, the sins of theft, taking bribes, and neglecting to defend the cause of the orphan and widow in legal cases (described in v. 23) are similar to those condemned in Amos 2:6-8; 4:1; 5:11-12; 8:4-6; Isa 3:12-15; 5:22-23; 10:1-4, passages which date to the time of Jeroboam II of North Israel and of Jotham and Ahaz of Judah. Fourth, the announcement of judgment in vv. 24-25 assumes that at the time this oracle was originally delivered, Judah was prospering without any fear of enemy attacks. Fifth, the idea that Yahweh will distinguish between the righteous and the wicked who constitute his chosen people, destroying the wicked and restoring the penitent (1:25, 27-28), is characteristic of the eighth century prophets (cf. Amos 9:8-10; Mic 2:6-8).[33]

The evidence, then, indicates that Isaiah delivered the oracle recorded in 1:21-28 at the temple in Jerusalem to common people who had gathered there to celebrate an important joyful festival some time

32. This is the view of Skinner, *Book of the Prophet Isaiah*, 11; Feldmann, *Buch Isaias*, 24; Procksch, *Jesaja*, 45; Steinmann, *Le Prophète Isaïe*, 77 n. *; Scott, "Book of Isaiah," 177; Eichrodt, *Der Heilige*, 37; Kissane, *Book of Isaiah I*, 14-15; Wildberger, *Jesaja*, 58; Kraeling, *Commentary on the Prophets I*, 48; Jones, "Verses Twenty One to the End," 320; Clements, *Isaiah 1-39*, 35.

33 See Willis, "Micah 2:6-8," 72-87.

during the latter years of Jotham or the early part of the reign of Ahaz. His purpose was to reprove his hearers of their heinous sins, announce the approach of divine punishment for these sins, and proclaim a day of destruction for the hard-hearted, and restoration and redemption for the penitent.

Religious Teaching

The religious message of Isa 1:21–28 is basically one of sin, punishment, and redemption. With these themes, it proved to be a message suitable not only to the worshipping Community of Yahweh in Jerusalem in the early years of Isaiah's prophetic ministry, but also to later generations of Jews in various periods, including the time of Sennacherib's invasion in 701 BCE (cf. Isa 22:3, 12–13; Mic 3:1–4, 9–11), Josiah's reform, the period after the fall of Jerusalem in 587 BCE, and the post-exilic age (see Zech 7:8–10; 8:14–17). Thus, in the complicated process which finally led to the production of the final form of the Book of Isaiah, the oracles now found in the first chapter naturally assumed a position at the beginning of the Isaianic collection, because their content continued to prove relevant to subsequent generations, and to incorporate some of the main themes of the entire book.

Sin is first and foremost against Yahweh. Yahweh had chosen or elected Israel when he brought her out of Egypt and entered into a covenant relationship with her (4:5–6; 11, 15–16). But by the days of Isaiah the people understood "covenant" as a legal system of good works and divine rewards, so Isaiah avoided the use of this word. At the same time, he preserved the idea of covenant by couching it in terms of daily intimate personal relationships such as that of a father and his sons (1:2–4) and that of a husband and his wife (1:21, 26).[34] Accordingly, sin is like a wife "forsaking" her husband (1:28) for other lovers, and thereby becoming a "harlot" (1:21) in place of a "faithful" wife (1:21, 26). Also by the time of Isaiah, the people assumed that their divine election was unconditional. Isaiah responded that, on the contrary, their continuation as God's elect depended on their fidelity to him and their attitude and behavior toward their fellowman in "justice" and "righteousness" (vv. 21, 23, 26). Those who had forsaken the Lord must repent (v. 27) or face destruction (v. 28). Hardened sinners who refuse to return are regarded

---

34. See Eichrodt, *Der Heilige*, 27–28.

as the "enemies" or "foes" of the Lord, who can expect his wrath and vengeance (v. 24).[35]

However, in the context of the pericope under consideration, apostasy from Yahweh consists of wrongs against one's fellowman.[36] Isaiah specified injustice, unrighteousness (vv. 21, 26), murder (v. 21), rebellion, theft, taking bribes, and neglecting the cause of the widow and orphan in legal cases (v. 23). "For Isaiah, there could be no explanation of Judah's crimes that was not a religious one. Its social crimes were only one aspect of its apostasy from Yahweh's law."[37]

Because of ("therefore") their sins, the people of Jerusalem and Judah will become the objects of God's wrath and vengeance (vv. 24-25a). The "rebels" and "sinners" of God's people will be "destroyed" and "consumed" (v. 28). As often in the prophetic literature (cf. Amos 4:12; Mic 3:12; Jer 9:6, 8), the text does not make clear the nature of the imminent devastation. Yet, the prevailing mood of Isaiah 1 would favor an invasion by an enemy army (cf. vv. 7-8, 19-20).

But Isaiah declares that the ultimate purpose of Yahweh's wrathful intervention is not to destroy but to "redeem" (v. 27). It is to "smelt away the dross" and "remove the alloy" (v. 25), so that the pure "silver" (cf. v. 22) can be "restored" (v. 26). Accordingly, Isaiah makes a distinction within God's elect people between the persistent sinners who refuse to return to Yahweh and the penitent who genuinely commit themselves to him again (vv. 25, 27-28).[38] This same distinction appears elsewhere in the eighth century prophets (Amos 9:8-10; Mic 2:6-8; Isa 8:14-15), and thus is not of exilic or post-exilic origin as some scholars have maintained.[39] Once Yahweh's purifying process is done, Isaiah envisions a return to conditions something like those which existed in the Golden Age

---

35. See Fey, *Amos und Jesaja*, 63-64.
36. See Marti, *Buch Jesaja*, 17; Wade, *Book of the Prophet Isaiah*, 9.
37. Vawter, *Conscience of Israel*, 195.
38. So Steinmann, *Le Prophète Isaïe*, 79-80; Fohrer, *Jesaja 1*, 265-67; *ZBK* 1 (1966): 44; Frey, *Handkommentar*, 65. The view taken here is based on the understanding that šābêhā in v. 27b means "her penitent ones" (see BDB, 997b) rather than "those who return to her," which would point to a post-exilic setting. For the contrary view, see Kaiser, *Isaiah 1-12*, 40 n. 10.
39. This is the view of Gray, *A Critical and Exegetical Commentary*, 37; Mowinckel, "Jesajaboken I," 80-81; Steinmann, *Le Prophète Isaïe*, 369; Bright, "Isaiah-I," 491; Fohrer, *Das Buch Jesaja I*, 45; Ward, *Amos and Isaiah*, 241.

of David and Solomon,[40] when the leaders of God's people will practice and promote justice and righteousness, and consequently Jerusalem will once again be called "the city of righteousness, the faithful city" (v. 26).

Yet, Isaiah makes it clear that all this cannot be accomplished by human determination and good works, but only through divine intervention and activity among his people. *He* (Yahweh) will vent his wrath on his enemies and avenge himself on his foes (v. 24); *he* will turn his hand against the sinful city and smelt away her dross and remove her alloy (v. 25); *he* will restore her judges and counselors as in the days of old (v. 26). In light of this emphasis, it is likely that משפט and צדקה in v. 27 refer to Yahweh's righteous judgments and purifying punishment[41] rather than to the qualities or characteristics of the penitent people of social justice and righteousness.[42] Even Vawter, who takes the latter view, is careful to insert the disclaimer that the righteousness of the people is "the work of Yahweh."[43]

Conclusions

The conclusions reached through the discussion in the various parts of this paper may be listed briefly as follows.

1. The pericope beginning at Isa 1:21 extends through v. 28.

2. This pericope begins as a lament, but it concludes with the promise of a bright future for the penitent. Therefore, it is best described as a "Lament Reversed."

---

40. So Dillmann, *Prophet Jesaja*, 14, 16; Marti, *Buch Jesaja*, 17, 19; Feldmann, *Buch Isaias*, 18, 20; Procksch, *Jesaja*, 48; Fischer, *Buch Isaias*, 35; Ridderbos, *De Profeet Jesaja*, 10; Bentzen, *Jesaja*, 13; Steinmann, *Le Prophète Isaïe*, 79–80; Auvray and Steinmann, *Isaïe*, 25; Kissane, *Book of Isaiah I*, 18; Ziegler, *Isaias*, 14–15; Archer, *Isaiah*, 611–12; Young, *Book of Isaiah*, 88; Snijders, *Jesaja*, 40–41; Kelley, *Isaiah*, 190; Ackroyd, "The Book of Isaiah," 333; Fohrer, *Die Propheten des 8. Jahrhunderts*, 116; Clements, *Isaiah 1–39*, 36. A return to this "Golden Age" is also reflected in Mic 4:8, on which see Kapelrud, "Eschatology," 398.

41. See also Alexander, *Commentary on the Prophecies of Isaiah*, 93; Dillmann, *Prophet Jesaja*, 16; Skinner, *Book of the Prophet Isaiah*, 11; Feldmann, *Buch Isaias*, 21; Ridderbos, *De Profeet Jesaja*, 11; Vaccari, *Isaiah-Geremia*, 25; Young, *Book of Isaiah*, 89; Kelley, *Isaiah*, 192.

42. Kissane, *Book of Isaiah I*, 19.

43. Vawter, *Conscience of Israel*, 200.

3. Originally this oracle was delivered in Jerusalem, probably at the temple during a joyous festival in the early years of Isaiah's ministry, to an audience of common people (not political or religious leaders) who felt secure from enemy attacks or other calamities and who assumed that they were acceptable to Yahweh because of their external religious acts.

4. Isaiah's message on this occasion charged his hearers with sin against Yahweh and their fellowman, announced the coming of divine judgment, yet not to destroy but to bring to repentance, and declared that Yahweh would redeem the penitent as pure silver is attained when it is separated from dross.

5. This prophetic message was central and programmatic in Isaiah's thought, and proved to be relevant to several similar subsequent situations in Jewish life and history, so that it was combined with other oracles (viz., vv. 2–20 and 29–31), which in time came to form the introduction to the present book of Isaiah.

16

The Genre of Isaiah 5:1–7

OVER A CENTURY OF scholarly research has produced a number of views as to the genre of Isa 5:1–7. Critical divergences on this issue are due basically to the interpretation of the biblical text and/or to the definition of a particular genre. The purpose of this essay is to discuss the various positions that have been proposed on this matter, to evaluate the arguments in support of each position, to defend a view which seems most natural and in keeping with the subject matter and setting of this pericope, and to make some general observations with regard to methodological problems in determining a genre growing out of this study.

An Uncle's Song

Jerome and Luther[1] translate the Hebrew דודי in Isa 5:1 as "my (paternal) cousin," while Aquila[2] and Ewald[3] render it by "my (paternal) uncle." Ehrlich, in his celebrated *Randglossen,* attempts to give a logical defense for the latter. He argues that the pronominal suffix with דוד (preferably *-ô* rather than *-î*) belongs to the whole phrase שירת דודי, and not to דודי alone. Accordingly, דוד serves to give a special meaning to the *nomen regens* שירת, viz., "eines Oheims Lied," which is an idiomatic expression meaning "eine oft wiederholte Moralpredigt." "To sing an uncle's song"

---

1. Jerome (Vulgate): *patruelis mei*; Luther ("Lectures on Isaiah Chapters 1–39," 57), "my cousin."

2. Aquila translated דודי by πατραδέλφου (Cod. gr. 5=710 πατραδέλφῳ) μου; see the critical apparatus in Zeigler, *Septuaginta Vetus Testamentum Graecum. XIV*, 137.

3. Ewald, *Commentary on the Prophets II,* 44, and 44 n. *, translating ידיד by *Vetter* and דוד by *Oheim.* The translator, J. F. Smith, renders the former by "dear friend" and the latter by "friend," in both instances obscuring the finer point of Ewald's meaning.

means something near the English phrase "to talk like a Dutch uncle." However, the Israelite expression is stronger because the uncle was also the father-in-law of the groom since one usually married his paternal cousin. It was customary for the uncle to subject his nephew's behavior to careful scrutiny and to reprove him when necessary.[4]

This ingenious view, however, must be rejected. (1) While it is true that דוד means "(paternal) uncle" in a number of passages (Lev 10:4; 20:20; 25:49 [twice]; Num 36:11; 1 Sam 10:14, 15, 16; 14:50; 2 Kgs 24:17; Amos 6:10; Jer 32:7, 8, 9, 12; 1 Chr 27:32; Esth 2:7, 15), it also means "beloved, darling, friend," in many passages in Canticles (1:13, 14, 16; 2:3, 8, 9, 10, 16, 17; 4:16; 5:2, 4, 5, 6 [twice], 8, 9 [twice], 10, 16; 6:1 [twice], 2, 3 [twice]; 7:10, 11, 12, 14 [Eng. 9, 10, 11, 13]; 8:5, 14), and this is the more natural meaning in Isa 5:1.[5] (2) Apparently there is no real support for Ehrlich's definition of "an uncle's song" (if there is, Ehrlich does not present the evidence, and no scholar since Ehrlich has attempted to do so, as far as the present writer knows). Instead, it appears that he invented this definition to make sense out of his translation. (3) The following line (Isa 5:1c) does not say, "My *uncle* had a vineyard, etc.," but "My *beloved* (ידידי) had a vineyard, etc."

A Satirical Polemic against Palestinian Fertility Cults

ידיד is used of God's love for man (Deut 33:12; Jer 11:15; Ps 60:7 [5]; 108:7 [6]; 127:2), of man's love for man (Ps 45:1 [heading of Ps 45]), and of man's love for God's dwelling place (Ps 84:2 [1]), and ידדות is used of God's love for man (Jer 12:7), but neither of these terms is used of man's love for God in the OT.[6] Graham points out that ידיד and the contexts in which it appears reflect a strong emphasis on God's special care and concern for his own people (Ps 60:7 [5]), on the physical blessings he has showered upon them (Ps 127:2), and on the minimal value of human works (Ps 127:2). They suggest that man has no moral responsibility in his relationship to God (Jer 11:13-15).[7] Under normal circumstances

---

4. Ehrlich, *Randglossen zur Hebräischen Bibel IV*, 19–20.

5. For a careful analysis of the use of דוד in the OT and in ancient Near Eastern literature, with an extensive bibliography, see Sanmartin-Ascaso, "דּוֹד *dôd*," 152–67. Unfortunately, Jenni, *Theologisches Handwörterbuch zum Alten Testament I*, does not have a treatment of דוד or ידיד.

6. Cf. Good, "Love in the OT," 165.

7. Graham, "Notes on the Interpretation of Isaiah 5:1–12," 167–68.

(he argues), Gray would be correct in insisting that Isaiah would not use ידיד in speaking of Yahweh, because of its irreverant connotations.[8] However, men in public often use terms and expressions that are not their own and that do not express their own views, as satirical polemics against positions and viewpoints that they oppose.[9]

At the same time, a number of scholars interpret דוד as a divine name on the basis of the Moabite Stone (Mesha Inscription), line 12,[10] Amos 8:14 (emended text),[11] Akkadian divine names like Dadi-ilu and personal names like Abu-dadi, Dadiya, and Dadanu,[12] and OT proper names like Dodai (1 Chr 27:4), Dodo (Judg 10:1; 2 Sam 23:9 [Qĕrê], 24; 1 Chr 11:12, 26), Dodavahu (2 Chr 20:37), Eldad (Num 11:26, 27), and Elidad (Num 34:21).[13] Dod has been identified with Adad (or Hadad), the Palestinian counterpart of the Babylonian god Tammuz, and it has been suggested that Isa 5:1–7 was modeled after Cant 8:11–12.[14] Many Israelites were drawn to the physical attractions of the fertility cults, and Isaiah satirizes the potentially harlotrous Yahwism that they were practicing by using the divine name Dod for Yahweh.[15]

Graham notes that several details in Isa 5:1–7 indicate that the prophet is attacking fertility cult practices, (a) He uses the figure of the vineyard (כרם), which is common in fertility rites, where the participants think of the land as a vineyard and of the deity as the one who fertilizes

---

8. Gray, *The Book of Isaiah I*, 84.

9. Graham, "Notes," 167.

10. So Fey, *Amos und Jesaja*, 142–43 n. 3; Wildberger, *Jesaja*, 167. However, Ollendorff, "The Moabite Stone," 197–98 reads "the altar-hearth of *David*"; Williams, "Moabite Stone," 420 renders: "Bringing Ariel [cf. II Sam. 23:20; or the altar hearth of (cf. Ezek. 43:15–16)] its DWD back from there"; and Albright, "Two Little Understood Amarna Letters from the Middle Jordan Valley," 16 n. 55; "The Moabite Stone," 320 reads *dawîdôh*, "its chief(tain)," comparing *dawîdum*, "chief of a tribe," in the Mari Letters, and translates: "I brought (back) thence (from there) (the man of) Arel (or Oriel), its chieftain." Against Albright, Tadmor, "Historical Implications of the Correct Rendering of Akkadian *dâku*," 130–31, has shown that *dawîdum* of Mari and Alalakh should be pronounced *daḥdûm* and translated "defeat."

11. See the LXX ὁ θεός σου and the critical apparatus in BHS.

12. Wildberger, *Jesaja*, 167.

13. See Winckler, *Altorientalische Forschungen I*, 341, who thinks *dyd* or *dwd* means *daimōn*; the brief discussion of Stade, "Zu Jes. 3,1. 17. 24. 5,1. 8, 11. 12–14. 16. 9,7–20. 10,26," 134–35; and Sanmartin-Ascaso, "דוֹד *dôd*," 159–60.

14. Graham, "Notes," 167–68.

15. Ibid., 169 n. 1.

that land for his darlings. (b) The reference to "pruning" *(zmr)* the vines in n 6 betrays fertility cult language, since *zmr* appears as a *terminus technicus* for a fertility cult ritual song in Cant 2:12. (c) In a fertility cult song, the *śōrēq* (v 2) would have been used of the people under the figure of weeds or plants that grew in the vineyard, rather than under the figure of the vineyard itself.

The prophet composed his song as a satirical polemic against the fertility cult tendencies in Israel's popular religion. He begins by saying, "Let me sing, I pray, . . . *my* Dod-song" (*šîrat dôdî*), which promises to be quite different from the popular Dod-song of his day. He dares to use *yādîd* in speaking of Yahweh, but satirically, in order to emphasize that Yahweh does not react magically or mechanically to the whims and fancies of his devotees. Instead, he seeks moral and ethical righteousness (v. 7), and it is this that differentiates true Yahwism from the fertility cults. The prophet first reveals this when he introduces the picture of the "wine vat" (*yeqeb*) (v. 2), emphasizing the vineyard's responsibility to produce fruit in keeping with the owner's arduous labor in its behalf, not the fruit of the soil or of the womb, but of right human relationships (v. 7).[16]

There are many particulars that make Graham's view plausible. Other genuine passages in the book of Isaiah show the prophet's concern with high moral and ethical standards and practices (1:16–17, 23; 3:14–15; 10:1–2). The only other place where *dôd* occurs in the sense of "beloved" outside Isa 5:1 is in Canticles, whose theme and language have strong affinities with ancient Near Eastern fertility cults. Dod could be a divine name. And the prophets use satirical polemics against their opponents (cf. Amos 4:4–5; Hos 4:13).

However, there are good reasons to reject Graham's explanation. Anyone familiar with Graham's works knows his strong disposition for finding allusions to the fertility cults in the OT, even in the most unlikely places![17] While Dod *could be* the name of a deity, it never has this meaning elsewhere in the OT (except, perhaps, in proper names), and its other occurrences in the OT suggest that it means "beloved, darling,

---

16. Ibid., 168–71.

17. See e.g., his article entitled "Some Suggestions toward the Interpretation of Micah 1:10–16," 237–58, where he argues that *yôšebet* in Mic 1:11 (twice), 12, 13, 15 is the prophet's sarcastic way of referring to the female goddess of the fertility cults (pp. 239–40).

friend," in Isa 5:1. And then, Graham's understanding is not the most natural explanation of Isa 5:1-7.

The Prophet's Song concerning His Own Vineyard

Unlike the MT and the other ancient versions, the LXX reads *tō ampelōni mou* ("my vineyard") at the end of Isa 5:1b, and the first person singular of the verbs in v 2 *(perietheka, echarakōsa, ephyteusa, ōkodomēsa, ōryxa, emeina)*. On the strength of this, Gray suggests that *yādîd* in v. 1a might be used of a lifeless object (something loved), that *dôdî* could be emended to *dôday* (my love), that *lĕkarmô* might be emended to *lĕkarmî* (my vineyard) following the LXX, and that the second *lîdîdî* could be a dittograph on the first *lîdîdî*, leaving the possibility that the original reading may have been *lî*. Accordingly, v. 1 can be translated:

> Let me sing of the thing that I love,
> the song of my love for my vineyard:
> I had a vineyard
> on a very fertile hill.

If one retains the MT and reads "the song of my beloved" in v. 1b, then v. 1a implies that the beloved is the subject of the prophet's song or the person to whom it is addressed, and 1b that the beloved is the author of the song and his vineyard the subject, which is awkward. Besides, the speaker's use of the third person in the MT of vv. 1b-2 shows that the beloved is not the author, but the subject. If the text is emended as suggested above, partly following the LXX, the prophet is able to conceal his real message from his hearers by pretending to describe the plight that he had had with his own vineyard, until he is ready to reveal that he had actually been talking about Yahweh and Israel all along. He does this suddenly when he speaks of commanding the clouds not to rain on his vineyard (v. 6d-e), and then explains the meaning of his song (v. 7).[18]

The weaknesses in this suggestion are obvious. Gray himself admits that no one has given a satisfactory explanation of vv. 1-2. His proposal is based on one ancient version, and requires an extraordinarily large number of emendations and interpretations. His misgivings about the MT as it stands are based on too limited a number of alternative explanations, as further views given below will make amply clear.

---

18. Gray, *Book of Isaiah I*, 84-85.

The Prophet's Song Expressing Sympathy for His Friend Yahweh

Almost eight decades ago, Cersoy contended that "en retraçant tous les soins que la vigne a reçus et toute l'ingratitude qu'elle a marquée, le poète [i.e., Isaiah] montre combien il partage les sentiments de son ami, combien il s'intéresse à lui."[19] It is true that in the course of his essay, Cersoy uses the words "parabole," "chant populaire," "procès" and "apologue" (an allegorical narrative usually intended to convey a moral) in referring to this pericope, but his whole line of argumentation shows that his primary view is that the prophet composed this song for the specific purpose of expressing his sympathy for and interest in his friend (Yahweh), who had worked so hard to provide his vineyard with the best opportunities for growth and fruitfulness, but who was greatly disappointed at its yield of inferior and useless grapes.

Cersoy insists that as the MT stands, vv. 1a ("Je vais chanter, au sujet de mon ami") and 1b ("le chant de mon ami sur sa vigne") are redundant. Moreover, the prophet's friend does not speak in v. 1e, as one would expect from the MT of lines a and b. It is not satisfactory to reason that in vv. 1c-2 the prophet is preparing his audience for the song that is to begin in v 3, because "and now" (*wĕʿattāh*) is dependent on what precedes and cannot be the beginning of a song, and because vv. 1b-2 are the only lines in vv. 1–7 that are in poetry or meter—the rest of the pericope is in prose!

Isaiah never says that God is the speaker in this passage. Indeed, he puts words into God's mouth by using the first person singular in vv. 3–6, but this is a literary device. The prophet does not use two different words (*yādîd* and *dôd*) simply to avoid monotony. According to the MT, *yādîd* and *dôd* are two different persons. However, all hypotheses built on the MT fail to establish the identity of *dôd* (the speaker is the prophet and the *yādîd* is Yahweh). Consequently, the text must be emended. But, if possible, this should be done without changing the consonantal text (thus the emendation to *dôdîm*, "love, affection," is not best). Accordingly, Cersoy reads *šîrat dôday* which means literally "le chant de mon amitié" or "mon chant d'amitié," and then resultantly "mon chant amical," since the pronominal suffix can be attached only to the *nomen rectum* in a construct expression. Cersoy explains that "my (Isaiah's)

---

19. Cersoy, "L'Apologue de la Vigne," 43.

friendly song" means a song "celui que j'ai composé pour lui (i.e., my friend [Yahweh]) et qui lui dit mon affection."[20]

In more recent times, de Orbiso has adopted basically the same position. He describes the whole pericope as a mixed parable with allegorical elements, recognizing that vv. 3–4 contain the characteristics of a lawsuit and that vv. 5–6 are composed of threats. And yet, his fundamental contention is that the prophet is showing his love for his beloved's (Yahweh's) vineyard in order to console him in his feeling of great disappointment.

Like Cersoy, de Orbiso insists that if one adopts the MT, three different people are introduced in v. 1: the prophet who announces his song, the beloved *(yādîd)* to or for *(lĕ)* whom he will sing, and the friend *(dôd)* whose song he is borrowing. Otherwise, the initial words would read:

> I will sing for my beloved
> his song for his vineyard.

If *yādîd* is Yahweh (as vv. 6–7 suggest), and *dôd* is a synonym for *yādîd*, then the prophet announces that he is about to sing *to* God the song *of* God, which does not make sense. This impossible interpretation can be avoided by emending the text very slightly to *dôday* or *dôdîm*. Unlike Cersoy, de Orbiso opts for the latter in deference to Vaccari, and reads:

> Quiero cantar para mi amado
> un cántico de amor a su viña.[21]

Troubled by the fact that outside Isa 5:1 *yādîd* is never used of God, de Orbiso rejoinders that the prophet intentionally employs a term commonly applied to God's people in speaking of God, because they had become unworthy of such an honorific name, and the prophet wanted to express his sincere love for God in this song. He also affirms that while *yâdîd* is not used of God outside Isa 5:1, Canticles uses *dôd* more than

---

20. Ibid., 41–44. Cf. Ruffenach, "Peccati malitia et punitio," 205, who translates "in honorem Dei, quemamo."

21. Orbiso, "El cántico ala viña de amado (Is 5,1–7)," 718–21, 725; cf. Vaccari, *I Profeti*, 33, who reads: "Voglio cantare per il mio diletto un cantico d'amore alla vigna di lui." See also Steinmann, *Le Prophète Isaïe*, 68, who reads: "Que je chante à mon ami le chant 'de son amour' pour sa vigne!" However, Steinmann identifies the friend with Yahweh, ibid., 69 n. 3.

thirty times in speaking of God and Christ [*sic*]²² in spite of the fact that the emendation of *dôdî* to *dôdîm* is a vital point in his position!

It has been intimated that Stade took virtually the same view as Cersoy,²³ without elaborating as extensively. Appealing to the meaning of *lĕ* in the expression *šîrû lānû*, "Sing to (for) us," in Ps 137:3, he contends that in the phrase *'āšîrâh . . . lîdîdî* in Isa 5:1, one must expect *lĕ* to introduce the person(s) for whom or to whom the song is to be sung - in this instance, Yahweh. He also emends the second *lîdîdî* in v. 1 to *lĕdôdî*, and argues that *lĕ* must have the same sense here as in *lĕkarmô* at the end of the following stich, viz., "concerning." At the same time, however, Stade believes that all along the prophet was actually communicating to his audience a song of Dod (Yahweh) concerning his vineyard. In vv. 5–6 Dod himself speaks. Prior to this (*sic*) the prophet transferred the song of Dod which he was singing from the first to the third person.²⁴

While many observations of Cersoy and de Orbiso are valid and helpful, their arguments are tenuous. "Au sujet de" = "para" is not the only way to translate the *le* in *lîdîdî*; it can also mean "concerning, on behalf of, in place of, etc."²⁵ In view of the Semitic fondness for word plays, there is no reason why the prophet could not have carefully chosen two words with similar sounds (*yādîd* and *dôd*) to speak of the same person, apart from any concern about using two different terms to avoid monotony (which, after all, may be more of a modern concern than an ancient one). This would be expected particularly in a passage like Isa 5:1–7, where there is an abundance of literary affinities, repetitions, and word plays.²⁶ The interchangeability between the first person and the third person in prophetic oracles is so frequent that the shift from the third person in vv. 1–2 to the first person in vv. 3–6 and then back to the third person in v 7 seems commonplace.²⁷ Cersoy's insistence that *šîrat dôdî* cannot contain the prophet's announcement that he is about

---

22. Orbiso, "El cántico," 722; 722 n. 37.

23. See the comment of Schottroff, "Das Weinberglied Jesajas," 78 n. 40.

24. Stade, "Zu Jes. 3, 1, etc.," 134–35.

25. Ironically, Lys ("La Vigne et le Double Je.," 10): translates the first *le* in v. 1 by "à la place de," and the second by "au sujet de." Laridon ("Carmen Allegoricum Isaiae de Vinea," 4): sharply opposes Cersoy's view.

26. The most thoroughgoing analysis of the interconnections of words and phrases in Isa 5:1–7 is that of Lys, "La Vigne," 1–16.

27. Orbiso, "El cántico," 719, compares the alternation of speakers in Ps 2 and in the Songs of the Servant in Isa 40–55.

to sing "the song of my friend (beloved)" because his friend does not speak in v. 1e, is not necessarily valid. The prophet may be relating his friend's sentiments in his own words in vv. 1c-2, and then continuing in his friend's words in vv. 3–6 to make a more vivid impression on his audience. Even when a prophet uses the first person singular in relating Yahweh's words, it is he and not Yahweh who is actually speaking. While it is not impossible that a prophet might express his sympathy for Yahweh to an Israelite or Judean audience, it is more in keeping with a prophet's role for him to proclaim Yahweh's message to them in his name or on his behalf. It is best to view Isa 5:1–7 in this way unless there is strong evidence in the context demanding a different understanding.[28]

A Drinking Song

Cheyne briefly suggested that Isa 5:1–7 might be a drinking song because of its spirited melody and dancing rhythm, but that the bitter irony at its end dispels this illusion.[29] Unfortunately, Cheyne does not explain the implications of this proposal. That drinking songs were sung at Israelite vintage festivals is quite likely (cf. Judg 9:27; 21:19–23; Isa 16:10; 22:13).[30] However, it is not clear whether Cheyne thinks Isaiah assumed the role of a drunkard singing a drinking song to get the people's attention, or whether he adapted a popular song that was normally sung at a celebration of a large grape harvest, or something else. What disappoints the husbandman in this text is not that he is deprived of the drinking of good wine, but that his well-kept vineyard has not produced good fruit (vv. 2, 4, 7).

A Bride's Love Song

Before continuing, it should be noted that most scholars find more than one genre in Isa 5:1–7.[31] In the present study, it is neither feasible nor necessary to note each term used by each critic in describing this literary

---

28. For the same reason, it is not possible to accept the translation of Guthe, *Das Buch Jesaia*, 596: "meinem Liebling." The prophet does not address his friend in the song, and Isa 5:1–7 is not a song of praise to God. Cf. Alexander, *Commentary on the Prophecies of Isaiah I*, 127.

29. Cheyne, *The Prophecies of Isaiah I*, 29.

30. See Eissfeldt, *The Old Testament*, 88–89.

31. Fohrer (*Die Propheten des Alten Testaments. Band I*, 107), points out that "das sogenannte Weinberglied weist eine merkwürdige Mischung von Redeformen auf."

piece. However, occasionally it will be necessary to discuss the views of the same scholar in conjunction with two different *Gattungen*. The concern in every case is to present the major view of each writer.

Most scholars understand Isa 5:1–7 as a song of love or friendship, and connect it in some way with the marital relationship. Specific views here may be divided into three general areas: Isa 5:1–7 is a bride's love song to her beloved, it is a groom's love song to his bride, or it is a song of the friend of the bridegroom.

Outside Isa 5:1, *dôd* in the sense of "beloved, darling," appears only in Canticles, where it is found exclusively on the lips of the young maiden speaking about or to the young man she loves.[32] Furthermore, the young maiden in Canticles is described in connection with or under the figure of the vineyard (Cant 1:6, 14; 2:15; 7:9 [8]; 8:11–12). Accordingly, Schmidt has suggested that in Isa 5:1 the prophet assumed the role of a young maiden or a new bride under the figure of a vineyard in order to get the attention of his hearers, as it was customary for a young maiden to sing such songs.[33] He has been followed, at least in part, by Budde (who contends that it is just as logical for Isaiah to assume this role as it is for him to appear as a Klageweib with a Leichenklage, as in Isa 1:21–26),[34] Fohrer,[35] Ziegler,[36] and Lys.[37]

Admittedly, in Canticles *dôd* is used only by the young woman in speaking of the man she loves. But Canticles is a unique book in the OT, and can hardly be regarded as the standard by which to determine the genre and terminology of a prophetic piece like Isa 5:1–7, even if it is the only book outside Isa 5:1 which uses the word *dôd* in the sense of "beloved, darling." Most of Isa 5:1–7 cannot be understood as a bride's love song to or about her beloved, irrespective of one's interpretation of v. 1a–b. The bride would not begin a song which has the express purpose of emphasizing her own sin and of announcing her own rejection and

---

32. For the passages, see sections 2 and 3 above.
33. Schmidt, *Die Grossen Propheten*, 40.
34. Budde, "Zu Jesaja 1–5," 52–53.
35. Fohrer, *Das Buch Jesaja I*, 75–76; Fohrer, *Die Propheten*, 107.
36. Ziegler, *Isaias*, 22–23.
37. Lys, "La Vigne," 8–9. Lys contends that Israel ("the vineyard") failed to recognize Yahweh as her true *dôd* or *yādîd*. Thus, the prophet discreetly identified himself with Israel in calling God "my beloved." The vineyard *never* speaks in the passage, but Isaiah speaks the words that one would expect Yahweh's vineyard, Israel, to speak, if they acknowledged him as their true *dôd*.

destruction. If the bride is the speaker in vv. 1–2, it is difficult to explain the sudden transition to the words of the groom in vv. 3–6.[38] At best, vv. 1–2 could be labeled a bride's love song, but not vv. 3–7; and vv. 1–2 can be explained in other ways that are more in harmony with the rest of the pericope.

A Groom's Love Song

In the OT and in ancient Near Eastern literature, the vineyard, the garden, and the field are used to describe erotic sexual relationships between two lovers. The vineyard is used for the arena of lovemaking in Cant 1:6; 7:13 [12], and for the young maiden who shares in the lovemaking in Cant 1:6; 2:15; 8:11–12. Advice given to a noble husband, supposedly by the Egyptian vizier Ptah-hotep (ca. 2450 BCE), contains these lines: "If thou art a man of standing, thou shouldst found thy household and love thy wife at home as is fitting. Fill her belly; clothe her back. Ointment is the prescription for her body. Make her heart glad as long as thou livest. She is a profitable *field* for her lord"[39] (italics added). Similarly, the satirical letter of Hori preserved in Papyrus Anastasi I (latter half of the thirteenth century BCE) states: "Thou art come into Joppa, and thou findest the meadow blossoming in its season. Thou breakest in to the inside and findest the fair maiden who is watching over the *gardens*. She takes thee to herself as a companion and gives thee the color of her lap"[40] (italics added). Again, an Egyptian love song found on Papyrus Harris 500 (1300–1100 BCE) has the words:

> "How good it would be
>   If thou wert there with me
> When I set a trap!
>   The best is to go to the *fields,*
>   To the one who is beloved!"[41] (italics added)

In an ancient Egyptian love song, the maiden sings:

---

38 Cf. Junker, "Die Literarische Art," 261; Schottroff, "Das Weinberglied," 79; and Wildberger, *Jesaja*, 165.

39. Translated in *ANET* by Wilson, "The Instruction of the Vizier Ptah-Hotep," 413b.

40. Translated in *ANET* by Wilson, "A Satirical Letter," 478a.

41. Translated in *ANET* by Wilson, "Love Songs," 468a.

"I am your beloved, the best.
  I belong to you like the *ground*,
which I have planted with flowers
  and with all sorts of sweet-smelling herbs.
Lovely is the canal therein,
  which your hand has digged,
to refresh us in the north wind,
  a beautiful place to wander."[42] (italics added)

Lambert has recently published a most interesting Late Babylonian cuneiform text of the Ritual Tablet (BM 41005) containing these relevant lines (obv. ii: lower portion of column ii, lines 9–20):

9. "You are the mother, Istar of Babylon." "To the *garden* of your lover when I /he /she []

10. "When Zarpanîtum became angry she went up to the ziggurat. [. . .]

11. At the side of the dais of the Anunnaki, in the district of the Street of Eturkalamma up to the *garden* [. . . .]

12. The Lady will pass through the Gate of My Lady and will. . . [.]

13. Zarpanîtum will go down to the *garden* and will keep crying to the gardener,

14. "Gardener, gardener, *building inspector* [. .]

15. What is the *plant* you have that belongs to *my friend?*" (mi-nu-u Sam-mu-ka sá ru-u$_8$-u-a) Zarpanîtum to the *garden*. . [ ] will stand,

16. "Gardener, gardener, be the *building inspector* of my city!"

17. the bed of my girl-friend. [. . .]

18. "Bring down and place." "Together with the pleasant breeze." At the side of the *garden*. .[. . .]

19. "The wifehood of happy women, the wifehood of slave-girls," and "I will go when the Lady

20. has crossed over the river [. . .]" (italics added except in lines 14 and 16).[43]

---

42. See Schottroff, "Das Weinberglied," 81–82.
43. Lambert, "The Problem of the Love Lyrics," 104–5.

Four times in the Tell el-Amarna tablets, Rib-addi, the prince of Byblos, quotes this statement: *"My field* (territory) is likened to a woman without a husband, because it is not ploughed"[44] (italics added).

In view of texts such as these, many scholars believe that when Israelites in the eighth century BCE heard someone speak of the relationship between a husbandman and his vineyard, their minds would immediately turn to erotic love between a young man and his sweetheart, a groom and his bride. In one of his earlier works, Mowinckel proposed that the speaker in Isa 5:1a-b is Yahweh, and that his "beloved" is his bride, Israel. However, the bride is described in a veiled manner under a masculine form *(dôd),* in keeping with ancient Near Eastern custom.[45] This interpretation allows one to avoid the offense of Isaiah using erotic terms in speaking of Yahweh.[46] At the same time, it presents two awkward (if not impossible) situations in the pericope itself: the bride does the work in the vineyard in v. 2, and the bride is the owner of the vineyard in vv. 1b-2 while Yahweh is its owner in vv. 3-6. For these reasons, Bentzen and Budde rejected Mowinckel's view,[47] and in a later work Mowinckel himself takes the position that in v. 1a–b the prophet is speaking of his "friend" Yahweh, who has a vineyard, Israel.[48]

Several scholars believe that Isa 5:1–7 is a lament or complaint of a disappointed lover (Yahweh). The prophet begins by singing, in behalf of or concerning his "friend" *(yādîd),* a love song concerning his "vineyard," i.e., sweetheart or bride, Israel. He describes the great effort and care that his friend had expended on his bride, and how she had not responded to his love, but had jilted him (vv. 1b-2). Then he rehearses his friend's own words of accusation and judgment on his unfaithful bride

---

44. Amarna Letters 74:17-19; 75:15-17; 81:37-38; 90:42-44; translated by Albright, "Some Canaanite-Phoenician Sources," 7.

45. Mowinckel, *Profeten Jesaja,* 35-37.

46. Gray, *The Book of Isaiah I,* 84; Steinmann, *Le Prophète Isaïe,* 69; and Scott, "The Book of Isaiah: Chapters 1–39," 197, insist that Isaiah would not use the erotic term *dôd* in speaking of Yahweh.

47. Bentzen, "Zur Erläuterung von Jesaja 5,1–7," 209 n. 1; Budde, "Zu Jesaja 1–5," 53.

48. Mowinckel, *De Senere Profeter,* 90. Junker ("Die Literarische Art," 261–62) and Schottroff ("Das Weinberglied," 79) follow Bentzen and Budde in rejecting Mowinckel's earlier work, apparently not having consulted this later publication.

in the first person singular (vv. 3–6). Finally, Isaiah explains the reason for his judgment in his own words (v. 7).[49]

Contrary to most scholars, Bentzen insists that the prophet does not *gradually* reveal the hidden meaning in his poem to his audience, but discloses it *suddenly* in v. 7. He would not have let his hearers know that he was speaking of them until they pronounced judgment on themselves, which they must have done by some sort of gesture of agreement in the supposed silence between vv. 6 and 7. It is not necessary to believe that God exposes his true identity in the statement, "I will also command the clouds that they rain no rain upon it," in v. 6d-e. 2 Sam 1:21 shows that man can pronounce a curse on the clouds. Furthermore, the meaning of this passage is that the unfaithful bride will not be able to conceive and bear children, which is just the opposite of the wedding blessing found in Gen 24:60 and Cant 7:3.[50] Some scholars emend the text to *dôdîm*, "a love song,"[51] or *dôday*, "my love song,"[52] which further supports the view that the prophet has in mind an amorous or erotic relationship between a groom and his bride.

Nevertheless, there are several compelling arguments against understanding Isa 5:1–7 as a song of a disappointed lover. (1) In other OT texts where Israel is compared with a vineyard or a vine (as in Hos 9:10, 16; 10:1; Isa 3:14; 27:2–6; Jer 12:10; Ps 80:9–17 [8–16]), there is no erotic connotation. (2) Isaiah would not have used erotic terms in speaking of God. (3) This interpretation does not explain why the prophet speaks of Yahweh as his *dôd* or *yādîd*, and not as the *dôd* or *yādîd* of the bride. (4) The meaning of specific elements in the erotic use of the vineyard in Canticles does not correspond to the meaning of those same elements in Isa 5:1–7. In Canticles, the grapes represent the maiden's breasts

---

49. Bentzen, "Zur Erläuterung," 210; Bentzen, *Jesaja*, 33–34; Mowinckel, *De Senere Profeter*, 90; Weiser, *The Old Testament*, 27, 49; Eichrodt, *Der Heilige in Israel*, 66; Scharbert, *Die Propheten Israels*, 222–23; Ackroyd, "The Book of Isaiah," 335; Kaiser, *Isaiah 1–12*, 60; Sanmartin-Ascaso, "דּוֹד *dôd*" 160, 164–65.

50. Bentzen, "Zur Erläuterung," 210; Bentzen, *Jesaja*, 36. Steinmann, *Le Prophète Isaïe*, 70 concurs that the statement in v 6d-e does not necessarily expose God as the speaker, but the reason he gives is that in the Orient "la colère n'y connaît point de limites à l'hyperbole." On 2 Sam 1:21, in addition to the commentaries, see Ginsberg, "A Ugaritic Parallel," 209–13; Speiser, "An Analogue to II Sam. i, 21," 377–78; Fenton, "Ugaritica-Biblica," 67–68.

51. Cheyne, *The Prophecies of Isaiah* 1:29–30, 2:138 (following Lowth). Cheyne argues that the small stroke (׳) in ׳דוֹדִי stands for the missing ם.

52. Marti, *Das Buch Jesaja*, 52; Budde, "Zu Jesaja 1–5," 54.

(Cant 7:9 [8]), but in Isa 5:2, 4, 7 they stand for justice and righteousness. It is difficult to see how phrases like "he digged it and cleared it of stones," and "hewed out a wine vat in it" (Isa 5:2) could be understood in an erotic sense.[53] (5) Isaiah, like his northern contemporary Hosea, frequently uses the relationship of a groom and bride or husband and wife in speaking of the relationship between Yahweh and Israel (cf. Isa 1:21, and the term "daughter of Zion" in 1:8; 10:32; 16:1; 22:4), and thus would have been quite capable of making it clear that this is what he had in mind in Isa 5:1–7, if that were indeed the case. Instead, he declares that the "men of Judah" (not the "daughter of Zion") are his vineyard (Isa 5:3, 7).[54] (6) The content of Isa 5:1–7 shows that this is not a love song.[55] (7) That this pericope has to do with a groom and bride is not the most natural interpretation.

A Song of the Friend of the Bridegroom

Troubled by the view that Isaiah refers to Yahweh as "my beloved" in an erotic sense in Isa 5:1, Junker has proposed that *yādîd* and *dôd* be interpreted as *ho philos tou nymphiou*, "the friend of the bridegroom" (cf. John 3:29).[56] The groom chose his most beloved and faithful friend to serve as *Vermittler* between him and his bride. The rabbis probably had this person in mind when they spoke of the *šôšĕbîn*. The friendship between the groom and his "friend" was so close that the friend could not appear as witness in a court case involving the bridegroom, because he would be prejudiced in his favor. The friend of the bridegroom had to make proper preparations for bringing the bride to the groom's home. The prophet used this figure in order to emphasize the intimate relationship between Yahweh and Israel, and his own function in that relationship.[57] If a groom had reason to bring a complaint against the bride, the friend of the bridegroom was authorized to break the wedding agree-

---

53. Cf. Wildberger, *Jesaja*, 169; Schottroff. "Das Weinberglied," 83.

54. Cf. Schottroff, "Das Weinberglied," 84; Pezzella, "La parabola della vigna (Is. 5,1–7)," 5.

55. See Gray, *The Book of Isaiah I*, 87; Scott, "The Book of Isaiah: Chapters 1–39," 197.

56. Junker, "Die Literarische Art," 264–65. Cf. *mērē'* (and the cognate verb *rē'āh*) in Judg 14:20; 15:2, 6, with the comments of BDB 946, and Moore, *A Critical and Exegetical Commentary on Judges*, 339.

57. Junker, "Die Literarische Art," 264–65, 264 n. 2.

ment and this is the role Isaiah is playing in Isa 5:1–7.[58] Junker's view has been adopted by Eichrodt, Wildberger, and Schedi,[59] and Schottroff concurs that if Isa 5:1–7 is to be interpreted in the context of love and marriage, this is the preferable understanding.[60]

But this explanation also has its weaknesses. It grows out of misgivings about a fairly widely held scholarly understanding of Isa 5:1–7 rather than out of the text itself. If Isaiah is depicting himself as the friend of the bridegroom Yahweh, this is the only passage in the OT where a prophet's relationship to Yahweh is described in this way. Besides, this is not the most natural interpretation of Isa 5:1–7.

A Lawsuit or Accusation

Several critics have suggested that Isa 5:1–7 (or at least vv. 3–7) is a lawsuit (procès,[61] Gerichtsrede,[62] Rechtsstreit[63]) or legal accusation (gerichtlichen Anklagerede).[64] Yahweh is the plaintiff, the prophet (conceivably as the friend of the bridegroom[65]) is the defender or advocate (Verfechter) of the rights of his jilted or rejected friend and beloved,[66] and the vineyard (the bride) is the defendant. Fohrer has given the

---

58. Wildberger, *Jesaja*, 165.

59. Eichrodt, *Der Heilige*, 66; Wildberger, *Jesaja*, 165, 166, 170; Schedi, *Rufer des Heils*, 110.

60. Schottroff, "Das Weinberglied," 79–80.

61. Cersoy, "L'Apologue," 46.

62. Schedi, *Rufer des Heils*, 115.

63. Budde, "Zu Jesaja 1–5," 56; Schedi, *Rufer des Heils*, 112–13.

64. Fohrer, *Die Propheten* 1, 107; cf. *Das Buch Jesaja I*, 75. Somewhat similarly, Scott ("The Book of Isaiah: Chapters 1–39," 196) labels the whole pericope a "reproach and threat." Cf. also his study entitled, "The Literary Structure of Isaiah's Oracles," 181. Scharbert (*Die Propheten*, 223) says it contains a "Prozessdisputation." In special studies on the "lawsuit" in the prophets, the following scholars briefly mention Isa 5:1–7 as a lawsuit: Gemser, "The Rîb- or Controversy-Pattern," 129–30; Weiser, *The Old Testament*, 63 ("The *parable* in Isaiah's *song* of the vineyard [Isa 5:1ff.] is based on the theme in a *fable* of a man's *lawsuit* against his vineyard" [italics added]); Westermann, *Basic Forms of Prophetic Speech*, 200; Limburg, "The Root *ryb*," 302 (following Westermann). But see below.

65. Eichrodt, *Der Heilige*, 66; Wildberger, *Jesaja*, 166.

66. Schedi, *Rufer des Heils*, 112.

most extensive treatment of this position,⁶⁷ and he has been followed by Eichrodt, Wildberger, Ackroyd, Kaiser, and Schedi.⁶⁸

This view may be supported by three arguments: (a) Verse 3 contains an appeal to the legal community to act as arbiters or judges (*šipṭû*) between the groom and the bride (or between the husbandman and his vineyard). The purpose of this legal maneuver is to establish that the guilty party is not the plaintiff (who had done everything within his power to provide for and care for the vineyard), but the defendant (the vineyard, because it had not produced good fruit).⁶⁹ (b) The concern for "justice" and "righteousness" (v. 7) is a legal concern, (c) The structure of this pericope follows that of a Speech of Accusation:

1. A binding relationship is established between plaintiff and defendant.

2. The plaintiff produces evidence that he has been faithful to this relationship.

3. The plaintiff complains because the defendant has not fulfilled his responsibility.

4. An appeal is made to the legal community to render a decision in the case.⁷⁰

The view that Isa 5:1–7 contains legal elements and has a legal thrust is compelling. However, this does not necessarily mean that it is best to categorize this passage *on the whole* as a lawsuit,⁷¹ since legal matters can also belong to genres other than a lawsuit, and there are other elements in the pericope that hardly belong to the lawsuit genre. It is strange to speak of a husbandman bringing a lawsuit against his vineyard (unless, of course, the vineyard represents a bride, and the husbandman, her

---

67. Fohrer, *Das Buch Jesaja I*, 75–77; Fohrer, *Die Propheten 1*, 107–8.

68. Eichrodt, *Der Heilige*, 66; Wildberger, *Jesaja*, 166; Ackroyd, "The Book of Isaiah," 335; Kaiser, *Isaiah 1–12*, 59; Schedi, *Rufer des Heils*, 112.

69. Budde, "Zu Jesaja 1–5," 56; Fohrer, *Das Buch Jesaja I*, 77–78; Fohrer, *Die Propheten 1*, 107–8; Ackroyd, "The Book of Isaiah," 335.

70. Fohrer, *Das Buch Jesaja I*, 75 and 75 n. 34; Wildberger, *Jesaja*, 166; Kaiser, *Isaiah 1–12*, 59.

71. In contrast to the scholars mentioned in n. 64 above, the following do not include Isa 5:1–7 in their treatments of the "lawsuit": Hesse, "Würzelt die prophetische Gerichtsrede," 45–53; Huffmon, "Covenant Lawsuit," 285–95; Harvey, "Le 'Rîb-Pattern,'" 172–96.

groom). Furthermore, the title "song" (v. 1) and the detailed description of the husbandman's care for (vv. 1b-2) and demolition of (vv. 5-6) his vineyard lie outside what is usually considered to be basic elements of a lawsuit. The present writer feels that the legal aspect should be emphasized, but placed within the framework of a larger genre, viz., the parable (see below).

A Fable

Much of the debate on the genre of Isa 5:1-7 has been due to a lack of agreement over the precise definition of crucial terms, especially the terms fable, allegory, and parable. Different scholars insist that elements which others assign to a fable are more basic to an allegory or a parable, and vice versa. At this point, it does not seem likely that universally acceptable definitions of these terms are possible. And even if such definitions could be attained for modern western literature, it appears extremely doubtful that the same criteria could be superimposed convincingly and satisfactorily on ancient Near Eastern texts. Perhaps the best each critic can do is to define the terms he uses as accurately and as comprehensively as possible.

In 1899, Cersoy spoke of Isa 5:1-7 as an "apologue,"[72] which is sometimes equated with a fable.[73] However, Cersoy made no attempt to demonstrate that this pericope is a fable. His main concern was to show that it contained a song of the prophet in which he was showing sympathy for his friend Yahweh. In 1926, Lesêtre published a rather lengthy article on the apologue, which he defined as "l'exposé d'une vérité morale sous une forme allégorique" (following Littré), and as "un récit allégorique qui contient une vérité morale facile a saisir sous la transparence du voile dont elle est couverte" (following Gerusez), and which he identified with a fable. He divided biblical apologues into four categories: (1) Apologues that attribute reason and speaking to things that do not have them (Judg 9:8-15; 2 Kgs 14:9-10; Ezek 19:2-9); (2) Apologues that are based on actions or affairs of ordinary life (2 Sam 12:1-4; Eccl 9:14-16; Prov 9:1-5; Isa 5:1-6; Ezek 19:2-9 [sic]; Prov 6:6-8; 23:5; Sir 11:4; 13:3); (3) Apologues in action (Hos 3:1; Ezek 23:2-49; Jer 13:1-7; 18:3-4; 19:1-10; 24:1-8; 27:2-6; Ezek 15:2-5; 17:3-10; 12:4-7; 24:3-12; 20:3-9; 47:1-7);

---

72. See Cersoy, "L'Apologue."
73. Lesêtre, "Apologue," 788.

and (4) Apologues in vision (Gen 27:7-9; 40:5-22; 41:1-24; Judg 7:13; Amos 7:1-9; 8:1-2; Dan 2:31-35; 4:2-13; 7:3-7; 8:3-26; Esth 11:2-11; Zech 1:8; 2:1,6 [1:18; 2:2]; 4:2, 3; 5:1, 6-7; 6:1-8; 11:4-10). Lesêtre says that it was the second group (which includes Isa 5:1-6) that served our Lord so well under the name of parables. He argues that while 2 Sam 12:1 -4 and Eccl 9:14-16 are developed apologues, the rest of the passages mentioned in the second group contain only sketches or indications of apologues, and thus he quotes with approval Herder's view that most oriental maxims are merely abridged fables.[74]

In 1928, E. Ebeling, A. Bertholet, and H. Gunkel published a rather brief article on the fable, in which Ebeling defined a fable as

> eine Abart der Parabel. . . , nennen wir eine erdichtete, einen Grundgedanken stark hervorkehrende Erzählung, die den Zweck hat, durch Aufweis dieses Grundgedankens eine bestimmte, gegebene Lage zu klären, und deren handelnde Personen— dies das Eigentümliche der F(abel) im Unterschied von anderen Parabeln aus dem Reiche der Tiere, Pflanzen und von andern personifizierten Wesen genommen sind,

and argued that the themes of the fable originally came from the legend or fairy-tale (Märchen), but differed from the latter by the teachings which they contained.[75] Gunkel thought that the fable was very popular in ancient Israel, where legends with their personification of creatures in nature played a prominent role in the popular tradition. Among the fables of the Bible, he mentions those of the trees in Judg 9:8ff., of the arrogance and fall of the world tree in Ezek 31, of the lawsuit (Rechtsstreit) of a man with his vineyard in Isa 5:1ff., of the quarrel of the ax with the arm in Isa 10:15, of the potter and the clay in Isa 29:16; 45:5; Jeremiah 18; Rom 9:19-21, and of the strife between the members of the human body in 1 Cor 12:14ff.[76] Weiser, Eissfeldt, and Fohrer[77] also use the term fable (along with other terms) in speaking of Isa 5:1-7, but without offering any substantial explanation for or defense of the preferability of this term above others. At the same time, Williams, Blank, and McKenzie[78]

---

74. Ibid., 788-81.
75. Ebeling, "Fabel," 489.
76. Gunkel, "Fabel," 490-91.
77. Weiser, *The Old Testament*, 63; Eissfeldt, *The Old Testament*, 37; Fohrer, "Fabel," 853-54; Fohrer, *Introduction to the Old Testament*, 314.
78. Williams, "The Fable in the Ancient Near East," 3-26; Blank, "Fable," 221;

find only two fables in the OT: Jotham's fable of the trees in Judg 9:8ff. and Jehoash's fable of the thistle in 2 Kgs 14:9.

The only extensive defense of the view that Isa 5:1–7 is a fable is that of Schottroff.[79] He takes his cue from Gunkel's dictum that a lawsuit between a man and his vineyard must be "märchenhaft."[80] Contrary to the assumption of many, he insists that the fable did not originate as a means of criticizing those in power. Sumerian fables were recited at court festivals to praise and extol the king and the court, not to reprimand or condemn them. This would explain why Isaiah aroused no contempt or suspicion when he began to sing about his friend and his vineyard on a festival occasion. As the fable was characteristically conflict poetry, it is doubtful that the prophet's hearers realized what he had in mind until he gave his explanation in v. 7. The abrupt transition from the third person (vv. 1–2) to the first person (vv. 3–6) would have aroused no suspicion, because such transitions were common in ancient Near Eastern fables.

Since the subject matter of a fable is inanimate natural objects, plants, and animals, a conflict between a man and his vineyard certainly fits this genre. Schottroff urges that the closest parallel to Isa 5:1–7 in ancient Near Eastern literature is the fable of the conflict between the fertility- or underworld-goddess Nisaba and the wheat, which follows the general three point structural pattern of Sumerian and Akkadian examples of this sort of poetry:

1. A mythological introduction, which gives the cosmological raison d'être of the conflicting parties.

2. A dispute, in which the opposing parties boast of their own superior functions and degrade each other.

3. An appeal to the deity, who renders a decision and reconciles the disputants.[81]

McKenzie, "Fable," 266 (who thinks fables can involve persons, animals, or inanimate objects); Jacobs, "Fable," 676 (who restricts fables mainly to animals); and Engnell, "Fabel," 593; Gadegård, "Fabel," 485 (who restricts OT fables to Judg 9:8–15 and 2 Kgs 14:9).

79. Schottroff, "Das Weinberglied," 68–91, esp. pp. 84–88.

80. Ibid., 75. To avoid an erotic term for Yahweh, and convinced that Isa 5:1–7 describes a lawsuit, Gunkel (*Das Märchen*, 26) and Hempel ("Jahwegleichnisse der israelitischen Propheten," 77 n. 2) emend *dôdî* to *rîbô*: "das Lied Von seinem Streit' mit seinem Weinberg," in v. 1b.

81. Schottroff, "Das Weinberglied," 86–87.

Isa 5:1–7 follows this pattern. Furthermore, the idea that the owner of the vineyard has the power to command the clouds to withhold the rain in v. 6d-e need not be an indication that the speaker is Yahweh or an imprecation by a human husbandman. "Vielmehr erscheint es als ein im Rahmen der Gattung 'Fabel' durchaus denkbarer Zug, dass ebenso, wie ein Weinberg als willentlich fehlhandelndes Wesen vermenschlicht und zur Rechenschaft gezogen werden kann, auch ein Weinbergbesitzer Wolken Befehle zu erteilen vermag."[82]

Now while Schottroff argues his case cogently, it must be asked whether the features which he attributes to a fable could not, with as much reason, be assigned to an allegory or a parable. To be specific about one case in point, the NT uses the word *parabolē* to describe the story that Jesus told about the vineyard that a husbandman entrusted to wicked tenants (Matt 21:33–41), which has many affinities with Isa 5:1–7, and may be based upon it.

An Allegory

Experts generally agree that there are two basic features which distinguish an allegory: (1) it differs from a parable in that each metaphorical element of the allegory represents a corresponding reality, whereas the parable conveys a single truth;[83] and (2) it reads into or finds in an ancient historical event, story, or literary production meanings that were not originally intended.[84]

Accordingly, the earliest allegorical interpretation of Isa 5:1–7 appears in the Targumic paraphrase of this passage. Here some of the crucial lines may be presented in English translation:

> v. 1 line a: The prophet said, I will now sing unto Israel, which is likened to a vineyard, the seed of Abraham my friend,

---

82. Ibid., 88.

83. The allegory "ist wohl zu unterscheiden von der Parabel, in der es allein oder vorwiegend auf Darstellung *eines einzelnen Gedankens ankommt*" (italics added), Gunkel, "Allegorie," 219; cf. McKenzie, "Allegory," 21; Gerhardsson, "Allegori, allegorisk utlaggning," 46; Wiberg, "Lignelser," 40. In many cases, however, it must be admitted that "the border line between parable and allegory is a very narrow one." Black, "The Parables as Allegory," 273–87; quote from 285.

84. "In allegorical interpretation an *entirely foreign subjective meaning* is read into the passage . . ." (italics added), Geffcken, "Allegory," 327. So similarly Mangenot, "Allégorie," 368; Mowry, "Allegory," 82. For Crossan's philosophical explanation of an allegory, see his article "Parable of the Wicked Husbandman."

> line b: A song of my friend concerning the vineyards of my people, the beloved ones of Israel,
>
> line c: I gave them an inheritance
>
> line d: In a lofty mountain, in a fat (fruitful) land,
>
> v. 2 line c: And I built my sanctuary among them,
>
> line d: And also I gave them my altar to make atonement for their sins,
>
> v. 3 inserted line before line a:
>
> O prophet, say to them, Behold, the house of Israel have rebelled against the law, and are not willing to return,
>
> v. 5 line c: I will take away my presence from them, and they shall be for a spoil,
>
> line d: I will break down their sanctuaries, and they shall be for a trampling,
>
> v. 6 line c: But they shall be cast out and forsaken,
>
> line d: And my prophets will I command not to utter a prophecy concerning them.[85]

Luther presents the kind of allegorical interpretation of Isa 5:1–7 typical of writers from the time of the church fathers until the modern critical period. In v. 1 he translates *dôdî* as "my cousin," interprets this as one's closest and dearest friend, and applies it to Christ; and reasons that *qeren* means the power and kingdom and dominion of the Jews, which through God's help was strong enough to crush all nations. In v. 2 the wall could be the protection of angels (following Jerome), but more probably is the law, which separated the Jews from all other nations (cf. Eph 2:14); the stones are the elect Gentiles; etc.[86]

---

85. My translation is from המקראות גדלות (New York: Pardes, 1951), ט-ח, and in places differs slightly from Stenning, *The Targum of Isaiah*, 16, because of a different text or because of word choice.

86. Luther, "Lectures," 57–61.

In the modern critical period, a few scholars have alluded to Isa 5:1–7 as an allegory[87] or a parable with allegorical elements,[88] without offering any extended defense of this position. Occasionally a modern commentator allegorizes a single element in the pericope, but not the whole. Young and Wildberger see in the hedge and wall of v. 5 an allusion to Yahweh's protection of Israel against enemies in the land of Canaan.[89]

The only attempts to defend at length the allegorical interpretation of Isa 5:1–7 in modern times (known to the present writer) are those of Ruffenach and Bentzen (in his Danish commentary on Isaiah). Ruffenach repeatedly calls this pericope an allegory, and his interpretation of individual statements throughout the paragraph indicates that he understands each phrase to convey a specific meaning. For him, the planting of the vine (v. 2) represents God bringing Israel into the land of Canaan, the protection around the vineyard (v. 5) stands for angels that guard God's people, the tower (v. 2) is the temple, the wine vat (v. 2) is the altar; the bad grapes (vv. 2, 4, 7) are all kinds of sin, especially idolatry, etc. Ruffenach repeatedly appeals to very ancient authorities such as Theodoret, Thomas Aquinas, Cornelius a Lapide, and particularly Jerome.[90]

By taking the vineyard as a symbolic figure for a bride on the basis of passages in Canticles (as 1:6, 14; 2:15; 8:12), Bentzen is able to view Isa 5:1–7 as an "erotiske allegori." He insists that the prophet does not gradually reveal the true identity of the vineyard and its owner, but preserves the allegory intact through v. 6, and then, suddenly and surprisingly for his hearers, reveals its true meaning in v. 7. Isaiah would not have played with fire and risked giving himself away before the condemnation was clear. Behind the allegory of a husbandman and his vineyard Isaiah intended to depict a defrauded husband's lament over his unfaithful wife, who had borne him illegitimate children, represented by the "forvildede baer" (vv. 2, 4). The statement "My beloved had a vineyard on a very fertile hill" (v. 1) means that the prophet's friend had a beautiful and fruit-

---

87. Mangenot, "Allégorie," 369; Laridon, "Carmen Allegoricum," 8; Vaccari, *I Profeti*, 33; Rad, *Old Testament Theology 2*, 151, 181; Scharbert, *Die Propheten*, 222–23; Sanmartin-Ascaso, "דוֹד *dôd*," 160, 164, 165.

88. Penna, *Isaia*, 75; Orbiso, "El cántico," 718, 721; Pezzella, "La parabola," 5 n. 2.

89. Young, *The Book of Isaiah I*, 194; Wildberger, *Jesaja*, 174.

90. Ruffenach, "Peccati," 206–9.

ful wife, whom he loved and expected to bear him many children. The husbandman's efforts (v. 2) are all figurative, indicating that the groom had done everything a wife could want according to law and morals (cf. Exod 21:10). The building of the watchtower represents the idea that the husband watched jealously over his wife's faithfulness. The legal statements (vv. 3–4) are intended to establish that the defrauded husband had done all he could for his wife, and thus had a right to be disappointed by her infidelity.[91] Bentzen complains that commentators have not understood the statement, "I will also command the clouds that they rain no rain upon it" (v. 6), which is the high point of the curse. Most have followed Ewald, who thinks that the prophet deliberately revealed the identity of his friend at this point. But if this is the case, Isaiah also allowed the people to see prematurely that they were trapped in their own judgment. Accordingly, Bentzen appeals to 2 Sam 1:21 to show that *man* can utter a curse over a piece of land that rain not fall on that land. The groom's meaning is: Would that my unfaithful wife no longer be able to bear children![92]

The allegorical interpretation of Isa 5:1–7 is subject to three major criticisms. (1) The alleged allegorical meanings of specific elements in the text do not come naturally from the text itself, but betray a great deal of ingenuity on the part of the interpreter. One senses that the commentator is *making an allegory* out of the biblical text rather than that the prophet himself presented an allegory. There are several passages in the OT that use the figure of a vine or a vineyard where it is clear that the writer has no intention of referring to the relationship between a groom and his bride (Isa 3:14; 27:2–5; Jer 2:21; Ps 80:9–17 [8–16]). (2) It is impossible to explain each element in Isa 5:1–7 allegorically without being fanciful. At the same time, that there is more than one detail in this pericope which obviously should be given a specific meaning argues neither against its conveying one major thought nor against its being considered a parable.[93] Jeremias has criticized Jülicher because, whereas he struggled "to free the [NT] parables from the fantastic and arbitrary allegorical interpretations of every detail," he contended that "the surest

---

91. Bentzen, *Jesaja*, 1:33–35.

92. Bentzen, *Jesaja*, 1:36; so earlier in Bentzen, "Zur Erläuterung," 210.

93. "Since an allegory [like a parable] is also an extension of a simile and since every metaphor presupposes a simile, confusion between the forms of parable and allegory has frequently . . . occurred." Mowry, "Parable," 649.

safeguard against such arbitrary treatment lay in regarding the parables as a piece of real life and in drawing from each of them a single idea (here lay the error) of the widest possible generality."[94] (3) Allegory in the true sense of the word is of Greek origin and thus later than the time of Isaiah. To be sure, Gunkel argued that the scribes must have learned the allegorical interpretation of scripture from the use of allegories in the OT.[95] However, experts now generally agree that the Jews took over the allegorical method from the Greeks, and that the allegorical method became established among Jewish interpreters between the Alexandrian Aristobulus (mid-second century BCE) and Philo (mid-first century CE).[96] Therefore, to speak of Isaiah as having delivered an allegory is anachronistic.

A Parable

It is generally agreed that a parable is an *extended simile* or metaphor. But beyond this, there is great disagreement among scholars as to its precise definition. This is partly due, no doubt, to the various speech and literary forms called *māšāl* and *parabolē* in the OT and NT respectively, and partly to the modern canons of definition to which each interpreter is willing to subscribe. Studies relevant to Isa 5:1-7 seem to have produced five definitional bounds within which a parable may be said to belong. (1) In contrast to an allegory, a parable intends to convey a single thought.[97] (2) In contrast to an allegory and a fable, a parable relates a realistic story intended to teach a lesson, and does not engage in fanciful,

---

94. Jeremias, *The Parables of Jesus*, 16 (who argues that Jesus' parables were allegorized prior to and by the Synoptists, pp. 52-70).

95. Gunkel, "Allegorie," 220.

96. Cf. Wiberg, "Allegori," 57; and the extensive discussions of Geffcken, "Allegory, Allegorical Interpretation," 327-30; Mowry, "Allegory," 82-83; and Büchsel, "ἀλληγορέω," 260-61. On this point, I am more traditional, and less philosophically inclined than Crossan, "Parable of the Wicked Husbandmen," 462; cf. McNeile, *The Gospel according to St. Matthew*, 186.

97. Alexander, *Commentary I*, 129; Nourse, "Parable (Introductory and Biblical)," 630; Lesêtre, "Parabole," 2107; Steinmann, *Le Prophète Isaïe*, 70; Engnell, "Liknelser," 1496; Mowry, "Parable," 649; Hauck, "παραβολή," 746; Stanley and Brown, "Aspects of New Testament Thought," 788. Nourse (629), Lesêtre (2109), and Hauck (749) consider Isa 5:1-7 to be a parable. Crossan ("Parable as Religious and Poetic Experience," 334) criticizes this distinction on philosophical grounds.

inappropriate, or unnatural analogies.⁹⁸ (3) In contrast to a similitude (*Gleichnis*), which has to do with *typical* conditions or events, a parable portrays a *specific* or *particular* situation.⁹⁹ (4) A parable contains an intentional decoy (*Köder*) or camouflage (*Tarnung*) so as to distract the hearers from, or (better) draw them into, the speaker's experience and resultant message (cf. Mark 4:10-12).¹⁰⁰ (5) A parable is presented in such a way as to make the hearers participants in the event being portrayed and empathizers with a certain character or characters in the plot, and to force them naturally to pass judgment on themselves. The parable intercepts the hearers where they are, but does not leave them there—it has the power to move them off dead center, either one way or the other. The hearers are either open or not open to the speaker's message;¹⁰¹ they participate in it or refuse to do so.¹⁰² If one accepts these last two stipulations, the following texts may be regarded as parables: Nathan's story of the rich man and the poor man who had only one little ewe lamb (2 Sam 12:1-4; cf. vv. 5-7), the story that the woman of Tekoa told David about the widow with two sons (2 Sam 14:5b-7; cf. vv. 1-24), the prophet's story of the escaped prisoner (1 Kgs 20:39-40a; cf. vv. 35-42), the oracles of Amos against foreign nations (Amos 1:3-2:3), and Isaiah's story of the vineyard (Isa 5:1-7).¹⁰³

---

98. Nourse, "Parable," 628; Bultmann, *The History of the Synoptic Tradition*, 198; Pezzella, "La parabola," 5 n. 2; Stanley and Brown, "Aspects of New Testament Thought," 788.

99. "Bultmann, *History*, 174; cf. Engnell, "Liknelser," 1496.

100. "Koder" and "Tarnung" are terms used by Junker, "Die Literarische Art," 259. Cf. also Marti, *Buch Jesaja*, 52; Bright, "Isaiah - I," 493; Hauck, "παραβολή," 749; Schottroff, "Das Weinberglied," 69, 74, 89. Funk (*Language, Hermeneutic, and Word of God*, 161) emphasizes the element of surprise in the parable.

101. "Freedom for the Word"—so Fuchs ("What is Interpreted in the Exegesis of the New Testament?," 89, 90, 98, 102, 103). Cf. the existential emphases of Funk, *Language*, 142-43, 150-51; and Crossan, "Parable of the Wicked Husbandmen," 462 n. 33.

102. Wilder, *The Language of the Gospel*, 92; Funk, *Language*, 133, 140, 143; Crossan, "Parable of the Wicked Husbandmen," 462, 464. In a more recent essay ("Parable as Religious and Poetic Experience," 340-44, 346, 349, 358), Crossan argues that an allegory cannot *create* participation in the experience, while a parable can. See also Carlston, "Changing Fashions," 231-33. Engdahl ("Jesu liknelser som språkhandelser," 90-108) has written an important critical evaluation of the views of Funk, Wilder, Crossan, Via, and Perrin.

103. Procksch, *Jesaja I*, 89; Mowinckel, *De Senere Profeter*, 90; Scott, "The Book of Isaiah: Chapters 1-39," 196; Muckle, *Isaiah 1-39*, 19, 20; Scharbert, *Die Propheten*, 223; Schottroff, "Das Weinberglied," 68-69, 71, 74, 89; Ackroyd, "The Book of Isaiah," 335.

Some of these guidelines require further discussion. On point (1), while it is basically valid that a parable teaches a single point, Jülicher has pressed this beyond the limits of actuality by superimposing more modern literary notions on ancient literature and by insisting on too rigid a definition. It is difficult to make a fine distinction between a parable that conveys one message but whose message has two or more secondary points or characters and an allegory. Many experts readily call Nathan's story of the ewe lamb (2 Sam 12:1–7) a parable. This story has a single immediate point (viz., the rich man's unjust treatment of the poor man is reprehensible and calls for severe punishment) and a single ultimate point (viz., David's treatment of Uriah is reprehensible and calls for severe punishment). At the same time, specific details in the story have a natural parallel to the real event: the rich man represents David, the poor man stands for Uriah, the ewe lamb is Bathsheba, and the death penalty is the just punishment.

> Jülicher claims that a parable has properly but one idea—it must illustrate but one thought; its figures are parts of one picture which represents but one truth. This really useful rule, which operates to do away with the abuse of the parables through excessive allegorizing, is, however, contrary both to the well-known use of the parable in Jewish circles and to the Gospel report of Jesus' own interpretation of His parables (e.g., Matt 13:18ff.). While it is true that the main purpose of a parable is to convey one general idea, subordinate ideas may easily be suggested. The fact is, the purpose of each parable must be ascertained by itself, without the application of theoretical rhetorical principles, with which Jesus had no concern.[104]

Accordingly, the prophet's explanation (Deutung) of the song of the vineyard in Isa 5:7 (viz., that the owner is Yahweh, the vineyard is Israel and Judah, the good grapes are justice and righteousness, and the bad grapes are bloodshed and a cry) in no way detracts from the single thrust of the whole passage, viz., the owner's (Yahweh's) disappointment in the failure of his vineyard (Israel, Judah) to produce good fruit. If Nathan's story of the ewe lamb is a parable, there is no reason why Isaiah's song of the vineyard cannot be a parable also. On points (4) and (5), it is true that frequently a parable camouflages the speaker's real message

---

[104] Nourse, "Parable," 630. Cf. Lesêtre, "Parable," 2114, 2116–17; Hauck, "παραβολή," 753; Funk, *Language*, 136; Stanley and Brown, "Aspects," 789; and Wiberg, "Lignelser," 42–43.

until just the right moment to reveal it, in order to retain the attention of the hearers, and to get them to pronounce judgment on themselves. However, this is not always true of a parable, nor is the parable the only means of achieving this effect.

A Suggested Solution

The present writer gets the distinct impression, from studying form critical and/or traditio-historical treatments of specific texts, that the genre of any given passage usually receives the least serious attention. We who deal with such matters seem to assume that the determination of the genre is obvious *prima facie,* and merits little careful analysis. This is not said to detract in the least from the importance of attempting to determine the extent of a pericope, or the *Sitz im Leben,* or the stages of transmission, etc., but to emphasize the importance of giving due attention to real issues pertaining to genre.

Reflection on the divergent views of Isa 5:1–7 suggests that some scholars determine the genre of a text by their interpretation of its content (the prophet's song concerning his own vineyard, a bride's love song, a groom's love song); others, by its occasion (a drinking song, a song of the friend of the bridegroom, a lawsuit or accusation); others, by its purpose (a satirical polemic against Palestinian fertility cults, the prophet's song expressing sympathy for his friend Yahweh, a bride's love song, a groom's love song, a lawsuit or accusation); and still others, by its literary type (an uncle's song, a fable, an allegory, a parable). And indeed, these four concerns are inseparably connected with the problem of genre. The scholar's primary goal should be to determine and define the genre of a text in such a way as to comprehend all that is in that text. To be sure, this undertaking is so complex that one may not be successful; and yet, with various scholars working on the same or similar texts, that which escapes one may be suggested by another, and that which is not clearly defined by one may be stated in a more polished form by another. In this endeavor, it is of utmost importance to define, as clearly as possible, the crucial terms which one uses. In doing so, he should strive to conform to generally accepted definitions as much as possible, while respecting the right of other scholars to use different terms for the same phenomenon, and to use the same terms with different shades of meaning, or more exclusively or inclusively.

Perhaps Isa 5:1–7 may be used as a test case to stimulate further discussion. It seems best to the present writer to classify the literary type of this pericope as *parable*, and to describe its contents as *a parabolic song of a disappointed husbandman*. These terms are not new. I have *deliberately* selected frequently used expressions in hope that widely accepted definitions may be utilized in the direction of a unified view.

The significant thing is to clarify what is intended by each term in this description, especially the term used for the literary type, viz., parable. The word *song* is chosen for three reasons. (1) The biblical text itself uses the verb *šîr* and the noun *šîrâ* (v. 1) in describing the prophet's words. Methodologically, it is the scholar's task to try to understand what would have been conveyed by these terms to the minds of Judeans in the eighth century BCE, and not to subject these words to modern standards. It would take us far afield to discuss *šîr* and its cognates here. But to say the least, Isa 5:1–7 should be studied in light of other OT poetic pieces that are entitled *šîr*, as e.g., Pss 45, 46, 48, 66, 67, 68, etc.; the critic should try to discover whether *šîr* demonstrates that the prophet sang, chanted, or poetically recited this oracle, or could have done any of these three; whether it would have been sung to the accompaniment of a musical instrument, and if so, which one; and the kind of setting in which such a song would have been accepted and expected by the hearers.[105] It is interesting to note the various ways scholars have envisioned the prophet's original presentation of this song (see the pertinent analyses above). The wide disparity on this point is due to a lack of description in Isa 5:1–7 and to a failure to analyze the nature of and *Sitzen im Leben* associated with the *šîr*. (2) The prophet's song consists of vv. 1c–7, and not merely vv. 1c–2[106] or 1c–5.[107] The structure and smooth flow of thought of the whole pericope bear strong witness to its coherence. (I do not feel that it is necessary to demonstrate this here, in view of Lys's excellent analysis).[108] In other words, the word *song* comprehends the whole piece. This is not to deny that Isaiah may have borrowed a few words or lines from a popular song to arrest his hearers' attention. But it is to affirm that if he did so, he incorporated these masterfully into his

---

105. Such issues raise the question of the nature and use of music in OT times. Cf. Werner, "Music," 457–69 with a rather extensive selected bibliography.

106. Cersoy, "L'Apologue," 46; Wildberger, *Jesaja*, 164.

107. Kosmala, "Form and Structure in Ancient Hebrew Poetry (Continued)," 168.

108. Lys, "La Vigne," 1–16.

own larger composition. (3) Verses 1–7 are poetic throughout, without prose interruption.[109]

The adjective *parabolic* has been chosen because it has these characteristics, (a) The prophet has a single lesson in mind in this pericope. This is demonstrated forcefully by the recurrence of *qwh . . . w* "(he/I) looked for . . . , but . . ." (vv. 2, 4, 7).[110] The point is that, in spite of the husbandman's (Yahweh's) untiring efforts in behalf of the vineyard (Israel/Judah), the vineyard did not produce the quality of grapes (justice and righteousness) that such effort normally warrants, but grapes of an inferior quality (bloodshed and a cry). The result is that the husbandman is greatly *disappointed* (necessitating the use of this work in classifying this paragraph), and resolves to expose the vineyard to man and beast to be reduced to a waste. The specific identifications of the husbandman, the vineyard, the good grapes, and the bad grapes do not detract from, but contribute to, the single thought. "A good parable is an organic whole in which each part is vital to the rest; it is the story of a complex and sometimes unique situation or event, so told that the outstanding features of the story contribute to the indication and nature of its point,"[111] and this is precisely the situation one encounters in Isa 5:1–7. (b) The similarities between Yahweh and the husbandman, Israel and the vineyard, etc., were appropriate and natural, not fanciful and inappropriate, to the ancient mind. This may be established from the frequency with which these parallels occur in the scriptures (cf. Hos 10:1; Isa 3:14; 27:2–5; Jer 2:21; Ps 80:9–17 [8–16]; Matt 21:33–41; John 15:1–8; etc.), and must not be discounted because such figures are offensive or unattractive to the modern mind of any culture. (c) Assuming that *parable* is the correct designation for texts like Nathan's story of the ewe lamb (2 Sam 12:1–7), the story of the widow with two sons (2 Sam 14:1–24), and the tale of the escaped prisoner (1 Kgs 20:35–42), a strong case can be made for the view that a parable often contained legal elements. Further, assuming that *parable* can justifiably be applied to the lost sheep (Luke 15:3–7; cf. v. 2) or to the mustard seed (Matt 13:31–32), it may be concluded

---

109. Contra Cersoy, "L'Apologue," 46.

110. So Wildberger (*Jesaja*, 173). Funk (*Language*, 146–47; and "Beyond Criticism in Quest of Literacy," 149–70) emphasizes the difficulty of determining the major point of a parable.

111. Cadoux, *The Parables of Jesus*, 52; cf. Funk, *Language*, 148–49, 151–52; Via, "The Relationship of Form to Content," 171–84.

that it could deal with inanimate objects and plants. In other words, to designate Isa 5:1–7 as *separable* is to affirm that it contains a lawsuit or an accusation, not to deny it. In this particular, one use of a parable is similar to one use of a fable. Furthermore, parables and fables can both deal with plants. Schottroff, who argues at length that Isa 5:1–6 is a fable, affirms that when the explanation in v. 7 is attached, it transforms the whole into a parable![112] Now the element "song" can be combined with the element "parable" (involving a "lawsuit" or an "accusation") since the prophet uses a "song" to arrest his hearers' attention and to draw them into participation in the event, so that they may deliver and be struck down by their own accusation of or lawsuit against themselves.

(d) Isaiah 5:1–7 depicts a *specific* situation and not a *typical* condition or event. Accordingly, it is preferable to label it a *parable* rather than a *similitude*, (e) The prophet's words in Isa 5:1–7 reflect his experience of God, simultaneously camouflage and reveal his real message, capture the interest of his hearers, and force them to participate in what he has experienced. Whether his audience began to realize gradually that they were condemning themselves after the statements made in v. 3, or v. 4, or v. 6d-e, or learned it suddenly from the unexpected explanation in v. 7, his message forced them to examine and pass sentence on themselves. While any one of these particulars might also be characteristic of another genre also, since all five appear in Isa 5:1–7, it seems best to classify this pericope as a parable.

Finally, the affirmation that the words in Isa 5:1–7 represent the song of a *husbandman* is intended to suggest four thoughts. (1) Admitting *dôd* is ordinarily used of a young man in erotic contexts, and that *vineyard* sometimes appears as a symbolic term for a bride or young maiden, the present proposal insists that our passage does not contain a bride's love song, or a groom's love song, or even a song of the friend of the bridegroom, but a husbandman's song describing his comprehensive labor, and his *disappointment* when the vineyard did not bear good fruit. It may be that some details in this paragraph *could* describe the relationship between a man and a woman figuratively, but many of them *cannot*, as e.g., digging the vineyard, clearing it of stones, building a watchtower in the midst of it, hewing out a wine vat in it (v. 2), removing its hedge, breaking down its wall, not pruning or hoeing it, and commanding the clouds not to rain on it (vv. 5–6). In other words, the most natural view

---

112. Schottroff, "Das Weinberglied," 89.

of Isa 5:1–7 is that it concerns a husbandman and his vineyard.[113] Then the MT of v. 1b may be retained. The idea that there is a *"love song"* here is more imaginary than factual.

(2) This expression indicates that *yādîd* and *dôd* refer to the same person: in v. 1b the vineyard is said to belong to the speaker's *dôd*, and in v. 1e to the speaker's *yādîd*.

(3) This phrase denotes that the song originated with the husbandman (Yahweh), who is the *prophet's friend (not lover)*, just as Abraham is said to be Yahweh's "friend" (*'ōhēb*) (Isa 41:8; 2 Chr 20:7).[114] The reason *dôd* was selected was to form a word play with *yādîd*. Such a choice is just as appropriate as the choice of *mšpḥ* (a hapax legomenon) in v. 7 to create a word play with *mšpṭ*. Yahweh is *yādîd* and *dôd* in his relationship to the *prophet, not* in his relationship to the *vineyard*. Isaiah claims to be reciting or repeating a song composed by his friend (Yahweh) concerning Yahweh's vineyard. I.e., *lîdîdî* in v. 1a does not mean *"to my beloved"* or even *"concerning, with regard to my beloved,"* but *"for, in the name of, in behalf of, in place of my beloved."*[115]

(4) This term places Isa 5:1–7 in a natural and suitable *Sitz im Leben*, viz., a vintage festival.[116] While others celebrate the harvest of good grapes, the prophet, nay, Yahweh himself, bemoans the *disappointing produce of his vineyard*, calls on his hearers to decide whether he is at fault or his vineyard, and announces his decision to abandon his vineyard because of its lack of response to his labor. The bringing of a legal case does not necessarily require that the vineyard represent a person, i.e., a bride. The focus is on that which is *represented by the vineyard*, and

---

113. Cf. Fey, *Amos und Jesaja*, 142–43 n. 3.

114. The qal participle *'ōhēb*, which means "friend" in several OT texts (as e.g., Jer 20:4, 6; Esth 5:10, 14; 6:13; Pss 38:12 [11]; 88:19 [18]; Prov 14:20; 18:24; 27:6), means "lover" in Lam 1:2; the piel participle means "lover" in a number of passages (Hos 2:7, 9, 12, 14, 15 [5, 7, 10, 12, 13]; Jer 22:20, 22; 30:14; Lam 1:19; Ezek 16:33, 36, 37; 23:5, 9, 22). Although *dôd* means "lover" in OT texts outside Isa 5:1, there is no reason why it cannot mean "friend" in this passage.

115. See especially Fischer, *Buch Isaias*, 51–52; and the definition of *lĕ* in BDB, 515.

116. It has often been suggested that Isaiah delivered this song when a large number of people from Jerusalem and the Judean countryside assembled in Jerusalem for a vintage or harvest festival. Cf. Skinner, *Book of the Prophet Isaiah*, 32; Gray, *The Book of Isaiah I*, 83; Procksch, *Jesaja I*, 87; Hertzberg, *Der Erste Jesaja*, 34–35; Scott, "The Book of Isaiah: Chapters 1–39," 196; Eichrodt, *Der Heilige*, 65–66; Fohrer, *Das Buch Jesaja I*, 75; Orbiso, "El cántico," 718–19; Bright, "Isaiah - I," 493; Moriarty, "Isaiah 1–39," 269; Wildberger, *Jesaja*, 166; Kaiser, *Isaiah 1–12*, 59.

not on the vineyards the symbolic figure, as is indicated by the fact that at the crucial moment of decision, Yahweh does not summon the vineyard, but the hearers (who are represented by the vineyard), and speaks of the vineyard in the third person (vv. 3–4).

17

Textual and Linguistic Issues in Isaiah 22:15-25

IN LIGHT OF THE comparative brevity of Isa 22:15-25, this text presents the interpreter with an extraordinary number of difficult textual and linguistic problems. The present study represents an attempt to define and describe these problems, to present and evaluate the various solutions scholars have proposed in dealing with them, and to defend the position which seems to be most likely in view of the textual evidence, linguistic considerations, and the context of this passage.

The Position of Verse 15c

The phrase על שבנא אשר על הבית, "against (concerning, to) Shebna, who (is) over the house" (v. 15c), has evoked much scholarly discussion. The manner in which one deals with this line is important to his/her interpretation of the entire pericope (vv. 15-25). On the one hand, if v. 15c is a later addition (gloss), it is virtually impossible to reconstruct the historical setting in which this oracle was originally delivered, since initially it was addressed to a Judean official whom the prophet did not name, because this was unnecessary for the hearers present on that occasion. On the other hand, if the oracle originally contained the name "Shebna," one is in a much better position to determine the circumstances in which the prophet first uttered these words.

Scholars have dealt with v. 15c in four different ways. First, Fohrer and Clements delete this line. Fohrer offers no rationale for this. However, Clements argues that this phrase was inserted secondarily from Isa 36:3 and 37:2 to link 22:15ff., with persons who were prominent in Hezekiah's realm at the time of his confrontation with Sennacherib. The original prophecy in 22:15ff. either had no name, or the name it had was deleted and replaced by "Shebna." Verse 15c was probably inserted at the same time that vv. 20-23 and the transition v. 19 were added.[1]

Second, several scholars maintain that the phrase, "Against Shebna, who is over the house," is a marginal gloss or the original superscription of the oracle in vv. 15ff. which later was inserted incorrectly into its present position.[2] Various ones have advanced three arguments in defense of this view. (a) עַל at the beginning of v. 15c cannot introduce a phrase which stands in apposition to the immediately preceding phrase in v. 15b beginning with עַל.[3] (b) Since Isaiah's hearers knew whom he was condemning, it was not necessary for him to call that person by name.[4] (c) Two titles, here "steward" and "he who is over the house," could not have stood in juxtaposition originally, as they do in this passage.[5]

Third, Hertzberg and Scott move the phrase "concerning Shebna" immediately after "Yahweh of hosts," without explanation.[6]

Fourth, the majority of scholars follow the MT, and thus leave v. 15c in its present position.[7] Six arguments support this position. (a) All

---

1. Fohrer, *Das Buch Jesaia*, 251; Fohrer, *Die Propheten des Alten Testaments*, 144; Clements, *Isaiah 1-39*, 188.

2. Among those critics who assert this view without offering any supporting argument are: Cheyne, *The Book of the Prophet Isaiah*, 40; Mowinckel, *Jesajaboken. 1. Kap. 1-39*, 139; Kraeling, *Commentary on the Prophets I*, 106 (who says that this line is a later addition, but may have been added on reliable information); Ackroyd, *The Book of Isaiah*, 345; Kaiser, *Isaiah 1-39*, 148, 150; and Jensen, *Isaiah 1-39*, 183; *Isaiah 1-39*, 243 (who states that originally the person condemned in this pericope was not named, but Shebna in the later addition may be correct historically).

3. Dillmann, *Prophet Jesaja*, 203 (possibly); Marti, *Buch Jesaja*, 174; Condamin, *Le Livre d'Isaïe*, 151; Fullerton, "A New Chapter," 623; Fullerton, "Shebna and Eliakim," 503 (where he states that v. 15c probably is not authentic, but is historically trustworthy); Gray, *A Critical and Exegetical Commentary*, 373, 377, 382; Duhm, *Buch Jesaja*, 163; Procksch, *Jesaja I*, 288; Bentzen, *Jesaja I*, 172-73; Penna, *Isaia*, 210; and Wildberger, *Jesaja*, 832.

4. Marti, *Buch Jesaja*, 174 (who says it is uncertain whether Shebna was the person addressed here historically); Duhm, *Buch Jesaja*, 163; and Procksch, *Jesaja*, 289 (who argues that "Shebna" is a correct, though later, insertion).

5. Marti, *Buch Jesaja*, 174; Procksch, *Jesaja*, 288; Martin-Achard, "L'oracle contre Shebna," 243.

6. Hertzberg, *Der Erste Jesaja*, 91; and Scott, "The Book of Isaiah," 292.

7. Many of these make no attempt to defend the correctness of the present position of v. 15c, but their concerns in interpreting vv. 15-25 and their line of reasoning make

the ancient versions have this phrase in the same place it appears in the MT. (b) אל and על are often used interchangeably in the Hebrew Bible.[8] For example, when Jonathan is telling his armor-bearer how they will know whether they ought to attack the Philistine garrison at the pass of Michmash, the decision rests entirely on whether the Philistines say to them, "Come up to us." If the Philistines say this, Jonathan and his armor-bearer will attack their garrison. This statement occurs three times in this context:

> Then said Jonathan, ". . . If they say to us, 'Wait until we come to you,' then we will stand still in our place, and *we will not go up to them* (לא נעלה אליהם). But if they say, 'Come up to us' (עלו עלינו), then we will go up . . ." And the men of the garrison hailed Jonathan and his armor-bearer, and said, 'Come up to us' (עלו אלינו) . . . (1 Sam 14:9–10, 12).

Again, the Hebrew expression meaning "to have sexual relations with" is בוא על in Gen 19:31 and Deut 25:5, but בוא אל in Gen 29:23, 30; 38:8–9; Deut 22:13; 2 Sam 12:24; Ezek 23:44; etc. Further, Isa 36:12 reports the Rabshakeh as saying to the embassy from Hezekiah, "Has my master sent me to speak these words *to your master and to you* (אל אדניך ואליך), and not *to the men* (על האנשים) sitting on the wall . . . ?" The parallel passage in 2 Kgs 18:27 has the same wording, except that in place of the first אל it has על. 1 Kings 16:7 uses על and אל interchangeably in the sense of "against." Especially when it expresses "direction towards" על is virtually a synonym of אל.[9] This is clear from comparing Isa 2:2 with Mic 4:1; 1 Kgs 1:33 with 1:38; 6:8b with 6:8c; Isa 29:11 with 29:12; 56:7 with 66:20 (the expression "bring . . . to my holy mountain"); Neh 6:17a with 6:17b; and several other texts. Accordingly, the use of אל and על in immediately succeeding phrases such as appears in Isa 22:15b and c is a well-established phenomenon in biblical Hebrew, and hardly supports the contention that the latter phrase must be a later addition because it begins with a different preposition than the former. (c) If the phrase

---

it quite clear they assume the MT is reliable at this point. A list of these scholars would be much too long to be practical. Some of them are mentioned in the following notes.

8. Alexander, *Commentary on the Prophecies of Isaiah*, 386; Dillmann, *Prophet Jesaja*, 2023 (possibly); Kamphausen, "Isaiah's Prophecy," 47–49; Koenig, "Shebna and Eliakim," 682–83; Feldmann, *Buch Isaias*, 269; Schoors, *Jesaja*, 135; and Watts, *Isaiah 1–33*, 286, 287.

9. ". . . In gen. על in such cases seems to be used merely as a syn.—perh. as a slightly more graphic syn.—of אל." BDB, 757a; cf. also 41a.

"Concerning (Against, To) Shebna, who is over the house" was originally the superscription of the pericope vv. 15–25, it is inconceivable that it would have been moved from that position to its present place in the text.[10] (d) If Isa 22:15c were a superscription, it would have read משא שבנא, "The oracle concerning Shebna," like the surrounding oracles (22:1; 23:1) and many other oracles in Isa 13–23 (see 13:1; 14:28; 15:1; 17:1; 19:1; 21:1, 11, 13), and not על שבנא.[11] (e) The phrase כה אמר יהוה, "Thus says Yahweh" (with its numerous variant forms) is a very common introduction to prophetic oracles in the Hebrew Bible (see e.g., Isa 7:7; 10:24; 28:16; 29:22; 30:15; 37:21, 33; 38:5; 43:14; 45:1, 18; 48:17; 49:7, 8; 50:1; 52:3; 56:1; 65:8, 13; 66:1, 12; as well as Amos 1:3, 6, 9, 11, 13; 2:1, 4, 6; 3:11, 12; 5:3, 4, 16; 7:17; Jer 4:27; Obad 1). The "messenger formula," כה אמר אדני יהוה צבאות, "Thus says the Lord Yahweh of hosts," in Isa 22:15a is identical to that in Isa 10:24, and very close to נאם אדיני יהוה צבאות, "utterance of (says) the Lord Yahweh of hosts," in Jer 49:5 and 50:31 (see the identical divine name in Amos 9:5; Jer 46:10; 50:25; Ps 69:7 [Eng. 69:6]),[12] and to כה אמר יהוה אלהי צבאות, "Thus says Yahweh the God of hosts," in Jer 5:14; 6:6; 7:21; 9:6, 16 (Eng. 9:7, 17); 11:22; 16:9; 19:3, 11, 15; 23:15, 16; 25:8, 32; 35:17; 38:17; 44:7; and very often.[13] (f) The reference to Shebna in Isa 22:15 could hardly have been inferred from the texts in Isa 36:3, 22; 37:2, where Shebna appears as Hezekiah's "secretary" or "scribe," not as his "steward" or "master of the palace."[14]

The evidence strongly favors the retention of the MT of Isa 22:15. Yahweh's mention by name of the individual to be addressed by a prophet, as well as a term (or terms) further identifying that individual, is not without analogy in the Hebrew Bible. For example, Yahweh instructed Nathan the prophet, "Go and tell my servant David" (2 Sam 7:5). He declared to Shemaiah the man of God, "Say to Rehoboam the son of Solomon, king of Judah, and to all the house of Judah and Benjamin,

---

10. Feldmann, *Buch Isaias*, 269.

11. Kissane, *Book of Isaiah I*, 244.

12. אדני in Isa 22:15a is omitted by two Hebrew mss, the LXX, Theodotion, and the Syriac, as well as by Marti, 174; and Procksch, *Jesaja*, 288. In light of usage in the Hebrew Bible as indicated by the passages cited above, however, there is no compelling reason to delete this word here.

13. On the messenger formula of the prophets, see Rendtorff, "Botenformel und Botenspruch," 165–77 = "Ges. Studien zum AT," 243–55; and Bjorndalen, "Zu den Zeitstufen der Zitatformel," 393–403.

14. Koenig, "Shebna and Eliakim," 683.

and to the rest of the people" (1 Kgs 12:23). He commanded Elijah the Tishbite, "Arise, go down to meet Ahab king of Israel. . . . And you shall say to him" (1 Kgs 21:18–19). The same phenomenon also appears in the book of Isaiah, "Go forth to meet Ahaz, . . . and say to him" (Isa 7:3–4). Similarly, Yahweh instructed Isaiah, "Go and say to Hezekiah" (Isa 38:5).

Kaiser argues that if one moves Isa 22:15c to the beginning of the pericope, it is unnecessary to add the phrase "and say to him" at the end of this verse.[15] This is not the case, however, since the instruction, "Come, go to his steward," still remains after the "messenger formula," "Thus says the Lord Yahweh of hosts," even when v. 15c is placed at the beginning of the oracle. In either case, one must either add the statement, "and say to him," following the LXX, Syriac, and Vulgate,[16] or imagine its presence while reading the text.

The evidence, then, favors accepting the MT of Isa 22:15 as it now stands. In this case, the mention of Shebna in line c is an important factor in an attempt to determine the historical setting of the pericope 22:15ff. This is further supported by the reference to "Eliakim the son of Hilkiah" in v. 20, since Shebna and Eliakim are mentioned together also in Isa 36:3, 11, 22; 37:2 = 2 Kgs 18:18, 26, 37; 19:2.

The Arrangement of the Lines in Verse 16

The present order of the four lines in Isa 22:16 has caused much discussion among scholars. The problem arises from the fact that lines a-b are in the second person singular, whereas lines c-d are in the third person singular. Scholars have offered five solutions to this problem.

First, lines c-d should be emended to the second person singular, following the LXX and Vulgate.[17] However, the reading of the LXX and

---

15. Kaiser, *Isaiah 1–39*, 148.

16. LXX: καὶ εἰπὸν αὐτῷ; Syriac: *w'mr lh*; Vulgate: *et dices ad eum*. So Wildberger, *Jesaja*, 831.

17. The LXX reads:
ἐποίησας σεαυτῷ ἐν ὑψηλῷ μνημεῖον
καὶ ἔγραψας σεαυτῷ ἐν πέτρᾳ σκηνήν
and the Vulgate has:
excidisti in excelso memoriale diligenter
in petra tabernaculum tibi.
Wade, *The Book of the Prophet Isaiah*, 147, proposes this emendation as a less likely, but possible, solution to the problem.

Vulgate probably does not reflect a different Hebrew text, but the grammatical and syntactical necessities of the Greek and Latin languages.

Second, Hayes and Irvine take the י which stands at the end of חצבי and חקקי as a first person singular pronominal suffix, and translate lines c–d:

> O my quarrier, an exalted position was his tomb,
> O my carver, in the rock is a habitation for him![18]

However, one can hardly doubt that the י in these two lines is a *ḥireq compaginis,* so that the present MT retains an old form of the participle, which is attested several times in the Hebrew Bible (as e.g., in Isa 1:21).[19]

Third, Schroeder removes the third person in lines c–d by dividing the words differently. He makes the ו at the end of קברו the copula before חקקי, and לו at the end of line d the first word in v. 17, pointing it לוּ, "certainly, indeed." Then he reads vv. 16–17aa:

> What do you have here and whom do you have here,
> that you have hewed out for yourself here a tomb,
> hewing out on a high place a tomb,
> and cutting out in the rock a habitation?
> Indeed, behold, . . .[20]

Admittedly this solution is ingenious, but it does not enjoy any support in the ancient versions, involves too many changes in the MT, and is unnecessary.

Fourth, the original order of vv. 15–16 was 15, 16c–d, 16a–b. In transmission, somehow 16c–d and a–b have been reversed. So they must be restored to their original order.[21] Five arguments have been advanced to support this view. (a) The use of the third person singular in lines c–d shows that these two lines are a continuation of Yahweh's command to Isaiah which begins in v. 15, since it refers to the steward in the third person.[22] (b) The rearrangement, lines cdab, makes the text clearer and

---

18. Hayes and Irvine, *Isaiah the Eighth-Century Prophet*, 285.

19. See Bentzen, *Jesaja I*, 173; and Oswalt, *Book of Isaiah Chapters 1–39*, 419.

20. Schroeder, "Miscelle. 3. לוּ = lû 'fürwahr,'" 302–3.

21. In addition to the scholars mentioned in notes 22–24, this is the solution proposed by Fischer, *Buch Isaias*, 158; Mowinckel, *Jesajaboken*, 139–40; Auvray and Steinmann, *Isaïe*, 101, n.e.; and Schökel, *Isaias*, 111.

22. Marti, *Buch Jesaja*, 174; Wade, *Book of the Prophet Isaiah*, 147 (likely); Vaccari, *I Profeti I. Isaia-Geremia*, 75; Penna, 210; Kissane, *Book of Isaiah I*, 243, 244; Ziegler, *Isaias*, 75; and Penna, *Isaiah*, 583.

more lively than the MT.²³ (c) In contrast to the ambiguity of the MT, it leaves no doubt that Isaiah is to meet the steward at the tomb he is hewing out. (d) It removes the present disturbing juxtaposition of "you have hewn" in line b and "hewing" in line c. (e) It makes the contrast between v. 16a–d (which describes what the steward is doing "here" [three times]) and v. 17 (where the prophet announces that Yahweh will "hurl him away violently," i.e., from his present abode) more striking.²⁴ Now a careful examination of these arguments reveals that this proposed rearrangement actually rests completely on the first argument. And yet, this argument has two compelling considerations against it: all the ancient versions agree with the order of lines in the Hebrew text, and this contention is based on grammatical principles of the languages into which the Hebrew text is translated rather than on grammatical principles of Hebrew (see below).

Fifth and finally, the lines in v. 16 are quite intelligible as they appear in the MT and all the ancient versions, and the grammar of the Hebrew syntactical construction found here is attested several times in the Old Testament and may be translated clearly when this construction is understood.²⁵ This is based on three considerations. (a) The transition from second person singular to third person singular appears a number of times throughout the Old Testament, sometimes in ancient poetic texts (see e.g., Gen 49:8–9; Num 21:19; 24:5–7; Deut 33:18–19; Judg 5:4–5; 1 Kgs 14:7–11; Amos 9:7–8; Hos 10:9–10; Mic 3:1–4), as does the transition from the third person singular to the second person

---

23. Feldmann, *Buch Isaias*, 268, 270.

24. Arguments (c), (d), and (e) are all from Marti, 174.

25. Some scholars have explained the shift from the second person in lines a–b to the third person in lines c–d by imagining that the prophet made some type of change in his speech or in his eye movements between the two. (a) Alexander, *Commentary on the Prophecies of Isaiah*, 387; and Young, *The Book of Isaiah*, 2:108, conjecture that after Isaiah uttered the questions in lines a–b, in lines c–d he expressed his own surprise at what he saw, or his eyes moved from the steward to the tomb he was hewing out. (b) Dillmann, *Prophet Jesaja*, 203, asserts that lines c–d are an exclamatory statement by the prophet. (c) Skinner, *Book of the Prophet Isaiah*, 169, suggests that Isaiah was addressing bystanders in lines c–d. (d) Oswalt, *Book of Isaiah Chapters 1–39*, 419, proposes that the prophet addressed lines c–d to the surrounding crowd, or to "the elements," calling on them to look on the outrageous behavior of Shebna (cf. Isa 1:2). In the opinion of the present writer, such explanations implicitly presuppose that there is something wrong with the Hebrew grammar in these lines, and thus are subject to the same criticisms as the "third solution" discussed above.

singular (1 Sam 2:1; 2 Sam 3:33–34; 1 Kgs 8:12–13).[26] In Isa 22:16, lines c–d function as an "extended vocative" completing the thought of lines a–b.[27] (b) Although the MT as it stands contains an acceptable Hebrew grammatical construction, its relative infrequency compared with the continuation of the second person singular or the third person singular suggests that this reading is the *lectio difficilior*,[28] and therefore more likely correct. (c) Moving lines c–d before lines a–b elevates a matter of secondary importance (i.e., the steward's constructing a tomb for himself on a rocky height near Jerusalem) above the main point,[29] namely, that the steward is arrogating to himself high recognition among the Jewish authorities for personal gain and glory.

The evidence seems to favor retaining the order of lines in v. 16 as they appear in the MT and the ancient versions. In this case, this verse may be translated:

> What do you (sing.) have here and whom do you have here,
>> that you have hewed out for yourself here a tomb,
> hewing out on a high place his tomb,
>> cutting in the rock a habitation for himself?

The Meaning and Flow of Thought in Verses 17–18b

Scholars agree in general that Isa 22:17–18b presents a coherent flow of thought. However, the precise meaning of these lines is very difficult to ascertain with precision and with certainty, because of the different meanings which may be assigned to the three verbs which occur in them.

Some commentators are disturbed by the apparent redundancy in vv.7a ("Behold, Yahweh is about to hurl you away violently,") and 18b ("and [he will] throw you like a ball into a wide land"). Certain ones have tried to solve this problem in one of three ways. (a) Some omit vv.17ag–18ba:

> O you strong man.
>> He will seize firm hold on you,

---

26. See the important study of Gilbert and Pisano, "Psalm 110 (109), 5–7," 343–56, esp. 346–47, who cite the passages listed above.

27. See Kamphausen, "Isaiah's Prophecy," 47; Young, *Book of Isaiah*, 108 n. 39; and Schoors, *Jesaja*, 136.

28. So Watts, *Isaiah 1–33*, 288.

29. Duhm, *Buch Jesaja*, 163–64.

and whirl you round and round,
and throw you,

contending that this disrupts the original smooth flow of thought:

Behold, Yahweh will hurl you away violently
like a ball into a wide land.³⁰

Clearly, this omission leaves a smooth text. But it does not explain how the present text came into existence; and the need for excising such a large amount of material is based on a particular understanding of that text (for other ways of interpreting this passage, see below).

(b) Some scholars emend v. 17aβ to read טלטל [כ]הבגד, "as one shakes out a garment," instead of טלטלה גבר, "a hurling, O mighty man." They reason that the *kaph* fell out by haplography, the *beth* and *gimel* were transposed (a scribe or copyist erred here according to the principle of metathesis), and the *daleth* and *resh* were confused.³¹ Then they read:

Behold, Yahweh will (is going to) shake you out
[as one shakes out a garment]
and rids oneself vigorously of lice
(or, and is going to pick the lice off you [cf. Jer 43:12]),³²
or something similar.

(c) Several scholars seek to solve this problem by interpreting the *pilpel* of טול as "throw down, cast down, knock down,"³³ or "stretch out,"³⁴ or "shake violently,"³⁵ because this yields a logical order in the announcement of what Yahweh will do to the steward:

---

30. Cheyne, *Book of the Prophet Isaiah*, 40; Marti, *Buch Jesaja*, 175; and Gray, *Critical and Exegetical Commentary*, 374, 379.

31. This emendation was first suggested by Ginsberg, "Some Emendations in Isaiah," 55–56 (possibly); and has been adopted by Driver, "Isaiah I–XXXIX," 48–49 (see the NEB); Herbert, *Book of the Prophet Isaiah. Chapters 1–39*, 137, 138; Kaiser, *Isaiah 1–39*, 148, 148 n. c, 154; Clements, *Isaiah 1–39*, 189 (possibly); Sawyer, *Isaiah*, 1:195–96; and Hayes and Irvine, *Isaiah the Eighth-Century Prophet*, 285.

32. For this meaning of עטה, see the study of A. von Gall, "Jeremia 43,12," 105–21.

33. So Alexander, *Commentary on the Prophecies of Isaiah*, 387–88; Procksch, *Jesaja*, 289; Hertzberg, *Der Erste Jesaja*, 92; and Wildberger, *Jesaja*, 831–33; and the JB.

34. So Ehrlich, *Randglossen zur hebräischen Bibel* 4, 79; Bentzen, *Jesaja I*, 174; and Vaccari, *I Profeti I. Isaia-Geremia*, 75.

35. Eitan, "Contribution to Isaiah Exegesis," 68. Ginsberg, "Some Emendations in Isaiah," 55–56, also understands טלטל to mean "shake out" *if* it comes from the root טול.

Behold, Yahweh will cast you down with all force
  [or, stretch you out lengthwise]
  [or, shake you violently],
O mighty man,[36] and will seize you firmly
  [or, grasp you forcibly][37]
  [or, throw you on the ground],[38]
he will wrap you up like a turban
  [or, whirl you round and round].
  [or, kick you off],[39]
[and throw you][40] like a ball into a wide land.

However, the use of the root טול in the Old Testament indicates that it does not mean "cast down" or "stretch out" or "shake," but "cast out, hurl," as most scholars recognize.[41] This has led to another explanation of vv. 17–18b. First, the prophet summarizes Shebna's fate (v. 17a); then, he expands upon that summary in three logical-stages (vv. 17b–18b).[42] Accordingly, one may translate:

Behold, Yahweh will hurl you away violently,[43]

However, he thinks the more reasonable meaning of טלטל in Isa 22:17 is "fold," from the root טלא, because of the near-synonym in the following line, צנף, "to fold." So the reading he apparently prefers is:

Behold YHWH is going to fold you
  as one folds a garment
and is going to wrap you up.

36. Kissane, *Book of Isaiah I*, 24–44, emends גבר, "mighty man," to גדר, "wall," and translates:

Behold, Jahweh will cast thee down headlong,
  as one casts down a wall,

pointing to the same figure in Isa 5:5 (he has 30:30, but this is clearly incorrect) and Ps 62:4 (Eng. 62:3). However, this proposal in not compelling, and no scholar known to the present writer has followed him.

37. So Dillmann, *Prophet Jesaja*, 203; Kamphausen, "Isaiah's Prophecy," 61; Skinner, *Book of the Prophet Isaiah*, 169; Gray, *Critical and Exegetical Commentary*, 379, 382; Wildberger, *Jesaja*, 832; Watts, *Isaiah 1–33*, 287; RSV; and NRSV.

38. Eitan, "Contribution to Isaiah Exegesis," 68.

39. See the discussion of the translation of v. 18a below.

40. See the discussion of the translation of v. 18b below.

41. See BDB 376b; and Holladay, *A Concise Hebrew and Aramaic Lexicon*, 123b.

42. See especially Kamphausen, "Isaiah's Prophecy," 61; and Schoors, *Jesaja*, 136.

43. The translations: "is about to cast thee a casting" (Young, *Book of Isaiah*, 105); "is hurling you a hurling" (Watts, *Isaiah 1–33*, 287); and "wird dich schleudern eine

O mighty man,[44]
Yea, he will roll you up tightly,[45]
  [or, he will seize you firmly,]
he will wrap you up like a turban,
  [or, whirl you round and round,][46]
[he will throw you][47] like a ball into a wide land.

Several particulars support this translation and interpretation. First, the hiphil of the root טול (v. 17a) is also used in Jer 22:26, 28 in Yahweh's announcement that he will "hurl" Coniah (Jehoiachin) and his mother "into another country," that is, Babylon. This is strikingly similar to Isa 22:17a and 18b, where Yahweh announces that he will "hurl" Shebna "into a wide land," that is, Assyria.[48] Second, it is not uncommon

---

Schleuderung" (Dillmann, *Prophet Jesaja*, 203) are too literal and wooden (see, similarly, the translation of Ziegler cited in the following note).

44. Several scholars emend טלטלה to טלטלת, which they interpret as being in construct with גבר. This has led to a variety of translations:

Siehe Jahve wird dich fortschleudern
  mit Manneswurf (Fischer, *Buch Isaias*, 158).
Behold, the Lord will hurl thee up and down
  with a man's throw (Slotki, *Isaiah*, 103);
Behold, the Lord is about to cast thee
  a casting of a man (Young, *Book of Isaiah*, 105, 109–10);
Siehe, Yahwe wird dich fortwerfen
  mit starkem Wurf (Ziegler, *Isaias*, 75).

The Vulgate reads: *sicut asportatur gallus gallinaceus*, "just as a poultry-cock might be carried away," which is, indeed, a curious rendering. The KJV and Barnes, *Notes on the Book of the Prophet Isaiah II*, 34, translate: "the Lord will carry thee away with a mighty captivity," which is hardly defensible.

45. It is difficult, if not impossible, to know whether עטה here means "roll up, wrap, wrap, envelop, fold together" or "seize." BDB, 741b–742a, list two different roots עטה, the one meaning "wrap, etc.," occurring 16 times in the Old Testament, and the one meaning "seize," occurring only once. Among those who opt for the meaning "wrap up, etc." are Condamin, *Le Livre d'Isaïe*, 151; Skinner, *Book of the Prophet Isaiah*, 169; Ehrlich, 79; Feldmann, *Buch Isaias*, 268; Wade, *Book of the Prophet Isaiah*, 147; Hoonacker, *Het Boek Isaias*, 124; Fischer, *Buch Isaias*, 158; Slotki, *Isaiah*, 103; Hertzberg, *Der Erste Jesaja*, 92; Vaccari, *I Profeti I. Isaia-Geremia*, 75; Kissane, *Book of Isaiah I*, 244; Ziegler, *Isaias*, 75; Penna, *Isaiah*, 210; and Young, *Book of Isaiah*, 105, 109–10 ("and to cover thee with a covering"). (For those who adopt the reading "seize," see above.)

46. See the discussion of the translation of v. 18a below.

47. See the discussion of the translation of v. 18b below.

48. The similarity here has already been pointed out by Gray, *Critical and Exegetical Commentary*, 374, 379; Penna, *Isaiah*, 211; Snijders, *Jesaja*, 219; Wildberger, *Jesaja*, 839; and Oswalt, *Book of Isaiah Chapters 1–39*, 420.

for a biblical writer to summarize what he wishes to say, *then* to expand upon it in detail (see e.g., Jos 7:1, *then* vv. 2-26; Judg 2:11-23, *then* 3:7-16, 31; 1 Sam 14:52, *then* 15:1-9; Isa 7:1-2, *then* vv. 3-17). Third, the idea of Yahweh's hurling Shebna away violently in the summary statement (Isa 22:17a) prepares the hearer or reader for the climactic idea of Yahweh's throwing Shebna into a wide land (v. 18b) in the more detailed elaboration. Fourth, the *athnach* under גבר in v. 17a suggests that the Massoretes understood this word to punctuate the flow of thought at this point in the text. Since the preceding Hebrew word, טלטלה, is in the absolute, גבר is to be interpreted as a vocative, "O man,"[49] and, because of the tone of Yahweh's speech and the context, is to be understood as ironical and sarcastic.[50]

---

49. "O man" (Cheyne, *Book of the Prophet Isaiah*, 137; Kamphausen, "Isaiah's Prophecy," 61; Hoonacker, *Het Boek Isaias*, 124 [in Dutch]; Bright, "Isaiah – I," 505 [meaning "Mister" or "Mr. Man"]), "O Mann" (Feldmann, *Buch Isaias*, 270; Procksch, *Jesaja*, 288 [suggesting, however, that one may read rbgh, "Herr Ritter," 290; "O thou man" (Slotki, *Isaiah*, 103 [possibly]); "du Mann" (Dillmann, *Prophet Jesaja*, 203; Wildberger, *Jesaja*, 831, 832); "du Kerl" (Hertzberg, *Der Erste Jesaja*, 92); "my fellow" (NRSV); "Big Man" (Herbert, *Book of the Prophet Isaiah. Chapters 1-39*, 138); "du storkar" (Mowinckel, *Jesajaboken*, 140); "O mighty one" (Whitehouse, *Isaiah I-XXXIX*, 257); "O grand homme" (Condamin, *Le Livre d'Isaïe*, l51); "O mighty man" (Gray, *Critical and Exegetical Commentary*, 374, 379; Watts, *Isaiah 1-33*, 287); "O you [thou] strong man" (Wade, *Book of the Prophet Isaiah*, 147; RSV; Clements, *Isaiah 1-39*, 189; Widyapranawa, *The Lord is Savior*, 128). Marti, 175; Condamin, *Le Livre d'Isaïe*, 151; Whitehouse, *Isaiah I-XXXIX*, 257; Duhm, *Buch Jesaja*, 164; Feldmann, *Buch Isaias*, 270; Wade, *Book of the Prophet Isaiah*, 147; Procksch, *Jesaja*, 288; Hoonacker, *Het Boek Isaias*, 124; Eitan, "Contribution to Isaiah Exegesis," 68; and Wildberger, *Jesaja*, 832, divide the Hebrew as טלטל הגבר to obtain the vocative. However, גבר without the article can function as a vocative. Barr, "'Determination' and the Definite," 319-22 demonstrates this. He writes (319-20) in response to Joüon:

> A person or thing addressed in the vocative, he [Joüon] says, is always determined and therefore ought always to have the article. In fact however the article is fairly often omitted, especially in poetry or in lofty prose. The article is generally present when it is a matter of persons who are present; when the persons are not present, or are more or less imaginary, the article is often lacking. In fact, Joüon admits there can be great freedom in the inclusion or absence of the article. The evidence makes very feeble the connection between vocative, determination, and article.

50. So Condamin, *Le Livre d'Isaïe*, 151; Whitehouse, *Isaiah I-XXXIX*, 257; Ehrlich, 79; Feldmann, *Buch Isaias*, 270; Wade, *Book of the Prophet Isaiah*, 147; Procksch, *Jesaja*, 288; Hertzberg, *Der Erste Jesaja*, 92; Bright, "Isaiah – I," 505; Wildberger, *Jesaja*, 831, 832; and Clements, *Isaiah 1-39*, 189. Alexander, *Commentary on the Prophecies of Isaiah*, 387-88, retains the MT, but reads, "like a man," and compares Job 38:3.

The meaning of the root צנף in Isa 22:18a is debated. A few scholars compare it with the Arabic *dafana,* "to kick," and read, "and he will send (catapult) you with a powerful kick,"[51] which apparently lies behind the interpretation reflected in the RSV and NRSV, "whirl you round and round."[52] Most scholars, however, think the meaning is "wrap up," "wind up," "roll up," "coil," or something similar. Rinaldi reasons that צנפה is a later addition inserted in imitation of טלטלה in v. 17a, and so should be deleted; and he contends that the Hebrew root צנף means "to move an arm in a circle with something in the hand." Accordingly, he translates v. 18a-b:

> Rotating (the arm) he will set you in motion [ ]
>   like a hoop toward a large land on every side.[53]

Some propose that the prophet has in mind the Egyptian practice of wrapping mummies.[54] Others suggest he is thinking of rolling up twine or string or yarn or thread or scraps of cloth into a ball or skein or wad or bundle or coil.[55] The evidence, however, indicates he has in view the

---

However, this is neither compelling nor necessary. Skinner, *Book of the Prophet Isaiah,* 169; Kamphausen, "Isaiah's Prophecy," 61; Slotki, *Isaiah,* 103; and Watts, *Isaiah 1–33,* 287 do not state whether they think this address is ironical or not. Dillmann, *Prophet Jesaja,* 203 thinks the prophet used this term to avoid attributing any dignity to this official and to emphasize his standing before God (he was a man and nothing more). Cheyne, *Book of the Prophet Isaiah,* 137 denies that this address is ironical, and Vaccari, *I Profeti I. Isaia-Geremia,* 75, translates "O valentuomo" (O worthy man), which is a title of respect.

51. This was first proposed by Eitan, "Contribution to Isaiah Exegesis," 68–69; and has been adopted by Wildberger, *Jesaja,* 831–33: "und schleudert dich mit machtigem Fusstritt"; and Watts, *Isaiah 1–33,* 287, 288: "Winding up, he will throw you a throw."

52. Barnes, *Notes on the Book of the Prophet Isaiah II,* 35, reads "sling round and round," and says the figure is that of throwing a stone with a sling. However, there does not seem to be any support for this view, and no other scholar has adopted it, as far as I know.

53. Girando (il braccio) ti mette in moto [ ]
    come un cerchio verso una terra larga
    da tutte le parti ("due mani").
    (Rinaldi, "Is. 22,18," 205).

54. Galling, *Biblisches Reallexikon,* 239; Snijders, *Jesaja,* 219; and Clements, *Isaiah 1–39,* 189 (possibly).

55. Alexander, *Commentary on the Prophecies of Isaiah,* 388; Dillmann, *Prophet Jesaja,* 203; Kamphausen, "Isaiah's Prophecy," 62; Skinner, *Book of the Prophet Isaiah,* 169; Wade, *Book of the Prophet Isaiah,* 147; Feldmann, *Buch Isaias,* 268, 270; Procksch, *Jesaja,* 290 (moving v. 18aα before v. 17b, yielding the sequence: Yahweh will strike

figure of wrapping a turban about the head, as is indicated by the use of this verb with the cognate noun מִצְנֶפֶת, "turban," in Lev 16:4, which may be read literally, "and with the linen turban he will wrap (his head)" (מִצְנֶפֶת also appears elsewhere in the Old Testament in the sense of "turban": Exod 28:4, 37 [twice], 39; 29:6 [twice]); 39:28, 31; Lev 8:9 [twice]; Ezek 21:31 [English 21:26]); and by the occurrence of the cognate noun צָנִיף, "turban," in Isa 3:23; 62:3 (qere); and Zech 3:5 (twice).[56]

In v. 18b, several of the ancient versions have a verb which does not appear in the MT. The LXX has καὶ ῥίψει σε, "and he will throw thee;" the Vulgate, *mittet te*, "he will send thee"; and the Targum, וְיַגְלוּנָךְ, "and he will banish thee (carry thee into captivity)." A few scholars have tried to connect v. 18b with v. 17a, reading:

> Behold, Yahweh will surely hurl you, O man
> having seized you
> and wadded you up like a ball,
> into a broad land.[57]

Some commentators think that the MT represents the original text, but that this is a pregnant construction and that "and he will throw you" must be supplied.[58] It seems most likely, however, that the LXX reflects the original text, probably וְיוֹרְךָ, and that this text should be restored.[59]

Shebna a long time, then form him into a ball, then seize him, then throw him away like a ball); Fischer, *Buch Isaias*, 159; Ridderbos, *De Profeet Jesaja*, 142, 144; Mowinckel, *Jesajaboken*, 140; Bentzen, *Jesaja I*, 174; Hertzberg, *Der Erste Jesaja*, 92; Vaccari, *I Profeti I. Isaia-Geremia*, 75; Scott, "The Book of Isaiah," 293; Ziegler, *Isaias*, 75; Fohrer, *Das Buch Jesaia I*, 252, 254; Penna, *Isaiah*, 210; Schoors, *Jesaja*, 135; Kaiser, *Isaiah 1–39*, 148, 154; and Oswalt, *Book of Isaiah Chapters 1–39*, 420.

56. So Whitehouse, *Isaiah I–XXXIX*, 257–58; Gray, *Critical and Exegetical Commentary*, 379, 382–83; Slotki, *Isaiah*, 103; Kissane, *Book of Isaiah I*, 242; Young, *Book of Isaiah*, 110; Clements, *Isaiah 1–39*, 189 (possibly); and Hayes and Irvine, *Isaiah the Eighth-Century Prophet*, 285.

57. Hoonacker, *Het Boek Isaias*, 124 (possibly); Wade, *Book of the Prophet Isaiah*, 148; and Oswalt, *Book of Isaiah Chapters 1–39*, 420.

58. Skinner, *Book of the Prophet Isaiah*, 169; and Slotki, *Isaiah*, 103.

59. Procksch, *Jesaja*, 290; Fischer, *Buch Isaias*, 159; Ridderbos, *De Profeet Jesaja*, 142, 144; Mowinckel, *Jesajaboken*, 140; Kissane, *Book of Isaiah I*, 242, 243, 245; Penna, *Isaiah*, 210; Snijders, *Jesaja, Deel I*, 219; Young, *Book of Isaiah*, 110 n. 42; Schoors, *Jesaja*, 135; Sawyer, *Isaiah*, 195; Watts, *Isaiah 1–33*, 287, 288; and Hayes and Irvine, *Isaiah the Eighth-Century Prophet*, 285.

The "Chariots" in Verse 18c

Scholars debate the meaning of the last half of Isa 22:18. Various critics have proposed four interpretations. (a) Some think a reference to the king's (or Shebna's) "chariots" is out of place here. The preceding, parallel, line says, "There you will die." And the context has to do with the tomb Shebna is hewing "on the height" "in the rock" (v. 16). Therefore, Condamin reasons that the original text here had קבר, "sepulchre, tomb," yielding the excellent parallelism:

> There you shall die,
>   and there your glorious tomb shall be;

and fitting into the context very nicely. A later copyist mistakenly moved the *resh* to the beginning of the word, and changed the *qoph* to the similarly sounding *kaph*, giving רכב "chariot" (singular, as in the LXX).[60] (He offers no explanation, however, as to how the plural מרכבות, "chariots," which is a distinctly longer word, arose.) Kissane agrees with Condamin in principle, but emends the text to read ושממה קברת כבודך, "and thy splendid tomb shall be desolate."[61] Gray arrives at basically the same meaning by conjecturing that possibly מרכבות, "chariots," is a copyist's error for an original משכב[ת], "dwellingplace(s)," here meaning "tomb(s)" (see Isa 57:2; Ezek 32:25).[62] However, these emendations are not necessary, and this view has not enjoyed scholarly acceptance.

(b) The Targum supplies the verb of being between lines c and d: "and there the chariots of thy glory shall be the shame of thy master's house." Similarly, Mauchline thinks that lines c and d should be closely united to emphasize the contrast between כבוד, "honor" ("glory"), in line c and קלון, "shame," in line d.[63]

(c) The LXX has τὸ ἅρμα σου τὸ καλόν, "thy beautiful chariot," which has led a few scholars to propose that the original Hebrew text had the singular construct מַרְכֶּבֶת.[64] However, there is no compelling reason to emend the MT at this point.

---

60. Condamin, *Le Livre d'Isaïe*, 151–52.
61. Kissane, *Book of Isaiah I*, 242, 243, 245.
62. Gray, *Critical and Exegetical Commentary*, 380, 383.
63. Mauchline, *Isaiah 1–39*, 173.
64. Duhm, *Buch Jesaja*, 164; Mowinckel, *Jesajaboken*, 140; and Herbert, *Book of the Prophet Isaiah. Chapters 1–39*, 137.

(d) The evidence favors the retention of the plural "chariots." The Syriac, Vulgate, and Targum have the plural. It was typical for a king or prince to flaunt his power and authority by riding in a retinue of chariots near or through large public gatherings (Gen 50:9; 1 Sam 8:11-12; 1 Kgs 1:5; 2 Kgs 5:9; Jer 17:25; 22:4), as well as in a single chariot specially designated in some way as the chariot of a high official (Gen 41:43; 46:29; Judg 4:15; 2 Sam 15:1; 1 Kgs 14:18). In Isa 22:18c, the prophet apparently denounces Shebna for boasting in the chariots of king Hezekiah which were under his control.[65]

The Subject in Verse 19

The MT of Isa 22:19 has the first person as subject of the first verb, and the third person as subject of the second:

> And I will thrust you from your office,
> and from your station he will cast you down.

Scholars have proposed four solutions to this problem. (a) Some contend that the third person should be read in both lines.[66] This would fit well the use of the third person in vv. 17-18, and make Yahweh the subject throughout vv. 17-19. Further, the LXX has only one verb in v. 19, and it is in the third person. However, the change from the third person (vv. 17-18) to the first person (v. 19a) is common in the prophetic literature (see e.g., Isa 10:12), as is the transition from the first person (v. 19a) to the third (v. 19b) (see e.g., Isa 14:30).[67] (b) Others think the third person in line b is an indefinite, equivalent to a passive, and thus read: "and you will be cast down."[68] But this is less likely, and most commentators

---

65. Skinner, *Book of the Prophet Isaiah*, 170; Wade, *Book of the Prophet Isaiah*, 148; Procksch, *Jesaja*, 290; Ridderbos, *De Profeet Jesaja*, 143, 144; Bentzen, *Jesaja I*, 174; Vaccari, *I Profeti I. Isaia-Geremia*, 75; Moriarty, "Isaiah 1-39," 276; Schoors, *Jesaja*, 136; Wildberger, *Jesaja*, 833; Watts, *Isaiah 1-33*, 287, 288; and Oswalt, *Book of Isaiah Chapters 1-39*, 416 n. 5.

66. Condamin, *Le Livre d'Isaïe*, 152; and Hertzberg, *Der Erste Jesaja*, 92.

67. Among the scholars who have emphasized this point with regard to this verse are Barnes, *Notes on the Book of the Prophet Isaiah II*, 35; Cheyne, *The Prophecies of Isaiah*, 138; Dillmann, *Prophet Jesaja*, 204; Kamphausen, "Isaiah's Prophecy," 63-64; Koenig, "Shebna and Eliakim," 676-77; Skinner, *Book of the Prophet Isaiah*, 170; Slotki, *Isaiah*, 103-4; Snijders, *Jesaja*, 219; Young, *Book of Isaiah*, 105, 111-12; and Oswalt, *Book of Isaiah Chapters 1-39*, 416, and 416 n. 6.

68. So Alexander, *Commentary on the Prophecies of Isaiah*, 389; and the RSV.

do not accept this explanation. (c) Some attempt to preserve the MT by suggesting that the subjects in lines a and b are different. So Watts says the king speaks in line a, declaring he will thrust Shebna from his office; then his courtiers speak in line b, referring to the king in the third person and echoing his statement in line a by repeating the warning that the king would cast Shebna down from his station.[69] Similarly, Hayes and Irvine believe that in line a Isaiah states that *he* ("I," i.e., Isaiah) is thrusting Shebna from his office; then in line b he declares that the king ("he") will cast him down from his station.[70] Yet, there is nothing in the text which suggests a change of speakers.

(d) The weight of evidence favors the view that originally the first person appeared in both lines.[71] The *aleph* and *yod* were often confused in the ancient Hebrew script. Also, the Syriac, Targum, and Vulgate read the first person in both lines. The prophet is reporting Yahweh's announcement (note v. 15a):

> I will thrust you from your office,
> and from your station I will cast you down.

In that case, the first person singular in vv. 20-23 follows naturally.

The Meaning of יתד in Verses 23 and 25

Scholars agree that יתד in Isa 22:25 means a "nail" which is driven into a wall to hold household utensils and other things, because the context (cf. v. 24) demands this interpretation. However, critics understand the meaning of יתד in v. 23 in different ways. Two major viewpoints have been proposed.

On the one hand, many commentators think יתד means "tent peg" in v. 23 and "nail" in v. 25. This is because יתד usually means "tent peg"

---

69. Watts, *Isaiah 1-33*, 287, 288.
70. Hayes and Irvine, *Isaiah the Eighth-Century Prophet*, 285, 286.
71. This is the view of the majority of scholars, including Cheyne, *The Book of the Prophet Isaiah*, 41; Marti, *Buch Jesaja*, 175-76; Fullerton, *A New Chapter*, 624-25; Box, *The Book of Isaiah*, 105 n. 1; Gray, *Critical and Exegetical Commentary*, 374, 380, 383; Duhm, *Buch Jesaja*, 164; Feldmann, *Buch Isaias*, 268, 271; Wade, *Book of the Prophet Isaiah*, 148; Procksch, *Jesaja*, 288, 290; Hoonacker, *Het Boek Isaias*, 124; Fischer, *Buch Isaias*, 159; Bentzen, *Jesaja I*, 174; Mowinckel, *Jesajaboken*, 140; Auvray and Steinmann, *Isaïe*, 102; Kissane, *Book of Isaiah I*, 242, 243; Ziegler, *Isaias*, 76; Schökel, 112; Penna, *Isaiah*, 210; Auvray, *Isaïe 1-39*, 210; Schoors, *Jesaja*, 136; Herbert, *Book of the Prophet Isaiah. Chapters 1-39*, 137; Wildberger, *Jesaja*, 833; and Clements, *Isaiah 1-39*, 189.

in the OT (cf. Judg 4:21 [twice], 22; 5:26; Isa 33:20; 54:2; Zech 10:4; Ezra 9:8).⁷² Several reason that vv. 24–25 are a later addition, and thus the meaning of v. 23 is to be determined apart from any consideration of the verses which follow. Procksch and a few others following him suggest that the figure in v. 23 is reflected in the modern practice of giving the most distinguished guest of a Bedouin tent the place at the corner-peg or angle-peg of the tent.⁷³

On the other hand, many scholars believe יתד means a "nail" or "peg" driven into a wall for the purpose of hanging vessels of various kinds upon it.⁷⁴ The custom mentioned by Procksch hardly suits the context of Isa 22:15–25. Apart from the question of whether vv. 24–25 are a later addition, the first responsibility of the exegete is to interpret that passage in the context in which it now stands. Verse 24 does not have any antecedent if it is separated from v. 23. By connecting it with v. 23, it becomes clear that that on which "they will hang the whole weight of his father's house" is the יתד of v. 23. Thus, in the present form of the text, יתד in v.23 must refer to a "nail" or "peg" driven into a wall. The context and weight of evidence favors the latter interpretation.

The Figures in the Last Half of Verse 24

Commentators agree that the last half of Isa 22:24 stands in apposition to "the whole weight of his father's house" in the first half of the verse, that it elucidates more specifically the meaning of that phrase, and that it alludes to a rather large number of Eliakim's relatives. However, they disagree on the precise meaning and referent in each of the three phrases.

72. Hertzberg, *Der Erste Jesaja*, 92, 93; Kissane, *Book of Isaiah I*, 245; Fohrer, *Das Buch Jesaia I*, 254–55; Alonso Schökel, *Isaias*, 112; Snijders, *Jesaja*, 221, 222; Herbert, *Book of the Prophet Isaiah. Chapters 1–39*, 137, 139; Kaiser, *Isaiah 1–39*, 158; Wildberger, *Jesaja*, 842–43, 849, 850; Clements, *Isaiah 1–39*, 190; Sawyer, *Isaiah*, 196; and Watts, *Isaiah 1–33*, 288.

73. Procksch, *Jesaja*, 291–92; Fischer, *Buch Isaias*, 160; and Ziegler, *Isaias*, 76. Procksch, *Jesaja*, 293, states that the "peg" in v. 25 is driven into a wall.

74. Alexander, *Commentary on the Prophecies of Isaiah*, 390; Barnes, *Notes on the Book of the Prophet Isaiah II*, 37–38; Cheyne, *The Prophecies of Isaiah I*, 138; *The Sacred Books of the Old Testament 10*, 41; Dillmann, *Prophet Jesaja*, 204; Marti, *Buch Jesaja*, 176; Skinner, *Book of the Prophet Isaiah*, 171; Gray, *Critical and Exegetical Commentary*, 381; Feldmann, *Buch Isaias*, 271–72; Hoonacker, *Het Boek Isaias*, 125; Ridderbos, *De Profeet Jesaja*, 145; Mowinckel, *Jesajaboken*, 140; Scott, "The Book of Isaiah," 293; Archer, *Isaiah*, 625; Kraeling, *Commentary on the Prophets I*, 107; Penna, *Isaiah*, 212; Young, *Book of Isaiah*, 116, and 116 n. 48; Schoors, *Jesaja*, 137; and Oswalt, *Book of Isaiah Chapters 1–39*, 422.

The first phrase is הצאצאים והצפעות. Many scholars interpret this as a figurative expression taken from the plant world, referring to Eliakim's relatives, and thus translate: "shoots and leaves," "scions and offshoots," "sprouts and wild (or water) shoots," "shoots and twigs," "shoots and outgrowths," "shoots and scions," "twigs and leaves," and so on.[75] The substantive צאצא is used twice in the OT with reference to plant life, both times in the book of Isaiah (34:1; 42:5). However, it is used predominantly of the offspring of human beings, as is indicated by the various contexts in which it appears, and by the words with which it stands in parallelism, namely, בן, "son" (Job 27:14), and זרע, "offspring, descendant" (Isa 44:3; 48:19; 61:9; 65:23; Job 5:25; 21:8; 31:8). The substantive צפיעה is not helpful in determining the meaning here, because it is a *hapax*. Usage in the OT, then, favors understanding these two words as literal terms for offspring, and translating: "offspring and issue," "offspring and descendants," "offspring and offshoot," or something similar.[76]

The second disputed phrase in the last half of v. 24 is כל כלי הקטן. Eitan contends that קטן may be connected with the Arabic *qatana*, which means both "to *reside* in a place" and "to *serve* someone," thus combining the ideas of "household" and "service," and translates: "all household vessels."[77] However, there is nothing in the OT which suggests that קטן means "household."[78] The usual understanding of this phrase, "all small vessels" or "every small vessel," fits the context well. It refers to the

---

75. Cheyne, *The Prophecies of Isaiah I*, 138; Dillmann, *Prophet Jesaja*, 205; Marti, 176; Duhm, *Buch Jesaja*, 165; Feldmann, *Buch Isaias*, 272; Procksch, *Jesaja*, 292; Hoonacker, *Het Boek Isaias*, 125 (referring to Eliakim's near and distant, noble and ignoble relatives); Fischer, *Buch Isaias*, 160; Ridderbos, *De Profeet Jesaja*, 145; Fohrer, *Das Buch Jesaia I*, 255; Penna, *Isaiah*, 212; Schoors, *Jesaja*, 137; Kaiser, *Isaiah 1–39*, 149; and Wildberger, *Jesaja*, 843, 850.

76. So Barnes, *Notes on the Book of the Prophet Isaiah II*, 38; Gray, *Critical and Exegetical Commentary*, 382, 383; Mowinckel, *Jesajaboken*, 140; Kissane, *Book of Isaiah I*, 245–46; Driver, 49; and Young, *Book of Isaiah*, 116, and 116 n. 49. Procksch, *Jesaja*, 292, omits this expression as a later gloss (so also Mowinckel, *Jesajaboken*, 140 [possibly]) because "every small vessel" fits the figure of hanging something on a wall, but "offspring" does not. However, this argument is not compelling, because the text here clearly intends a comparison: as small vessels hang on a nail, so ignoble and insignificant people hang on a successful relative. See Wildberger, *Jesaja*, 843.

77. Eitan, "Contribution to Isaiah Exegesis," 68–69.

78. See Wildberger, *Jesaja*, 843.

younger and unimportant relatives of Eliakim,[79] possibly even to worthless or mischievous members of his clan.[80]

Fischer thinks the three phrases in the last half of v. 24 belong together: "die Spößlinge und Schößlinge" are Eliakim's closest relatives, and "all die kleinen Gefäße, von den Waschbecken (angefangen) bis zum Kruggeschirr" are his most insignificant and most distant relatives.[81] Several exegetes have suggested that these three phrases are contemptuous, sarcastic, and derisive, some citing, in the first phrase, the similarity between the Arabic *waṣi'a*, "was soiled," the Hebrew צוֹאָה, "dung, filth, filthiness" (see 2 Kgs 18:27 = Isa 36:12; Prov 30:12; Isa 4:4; 28:8) and צֶאֱצָאִם, then translating the latter "droppings"; and between the Arabic *ḍafa'a*, "voided excrement and made water," the Hebrew צֹפִיעַ, "dung" (see Ezek 4:15), and צְפֻעוֹת, then translating the latter "excretions."[82]

The third disputed phrase in the last half of v. 24 is מִכְּלִי הָאַגָּנוֹת וְעַד כָּל־כְּלֵי הַנְּבָלִים. Barnes translates this: "from the vessels of cups to all the vessels of flagons." He reasons that the former are small vessels, and thus represent humble and poor members of Eliakim's household; while the latter are large vessels, and so typify influential and wealthy members.[83] Kissane suggests this phrase may be an interpolation.[84] However, he advances no argument to support this. The crucial words in this phrase are אַגָּנוֹת and נְבָלִים. The former root occurs in two other passages in the OT, viz., Exod 24:6 and Cant 7:3, in both cases meaning "basin"; so the expression of which it is a part in Isa 22:24 means "basin-shaped" or "basin-like" "vessels." The latter root is found in eleven other OT texts, viz., 1 Sam 1:24; 10:3, 5; 25:18; 2 Sam 16:1; Isa 30:14; Jer 13:12 (twice); 48:12; Lam 4:2; and Job 38:37, where it means "jar," "jug," "pot," "pitcher," "skin-bottle," 'leather jar," "amphora"; so the expression to which it belongs in Isa 22:24 means "jar-shaped vessels," "jug-like vessels," "leather" or "skin" "bottles," "pots," or something similar. Both expressions are

---

79. Ehrlich, *Jesaia, Jeremia*, 80; and Wade, *Book of the Prophet Isaiah*, 149.

80. Kissane, *Book of Isaiah I*, 246.

81. Fischer, *Buch Isaias*, 160.

82. Cheyne, *The Prophecies of Isaiah I*, 138; Dillmann, *Prophet Jesaja*, 205; Fullerton, *A New Chapter*, 628; Koenig, "Shebna and Eliakim," 679; Skinner, *Book of the Prophet Isaiah*, 171; Duhm, *Buch Jesaja*, 165; Feldmann, *Buch Isaias*, 272; Wade, *Book of the Prophet Isaiah*, 149; Driver, 49; and Wildberger, *Jesaja*, 843, 850.

83. Barnes, *Notes on the Book of the Prophet Isaiah II*, 38–39.

84. Kissane, *Book of Isaiah I*, 246.

probably contemptuous and refer to Eliakim's most distant, least illustrious, and most insignificant relatives.[85]

The Syntax and Meaning of Verses 24-25

Scholars do not agree on the meaning of Isa 22:24-25. This is due to two problems in the text, which various critics resolve in different ways. One problem is that Isa 22:15-25 declares that Shebna will be removed from his office as the king's steward and taken into exile, where he will die (vv. 15-19); Eliakim will replace him, bring great honor to his father's house by the way he serves the people, and be firmly established in his office (vv. 20-23); and Eliakim's relatives will take advantage of their relationship to him for their own aggrandizement, so that both he and they will fall (vv. 24-25). Now, it is hardly likely that in a "threat oracle" against the steward Shebna, Isaiah would have promised confidently that his successor will enjoy a permanent tenure in office *and* would have declared that his successor will use his office to show favoritism toward his relatives (nepotism) and thus lose his high position. A second problem affecting one's understanding of vv. 24-25 is that *grammatically* it is possible to read these verses in different ways.

Generally speaking, researchers have proposed four solutions to these problems. (1) Some assert that v. 25 refers to Shebna, not to Eliakim. It summarizes what Isaiah had said about Shebna in vv. 15-19. After comparing Eliakim with a nail fastened in a sure place (v. 23), the prophet uses the same simile to declare that another nail (Shebna) which, at the time he is uttering this oracle, appears to be securely fastened (in his office of royal steward) will soon fall under the weight of his relatives who have taken advantage of his powerful position to exalt themselves.[86]

---

85. Cf. Dillmann, *Prophet Jesaja*, 205; Whitehouse, *Isaiah I-XXXIX*, 258-59; Feldmann, *Buch Isaias*, 272; Wade, *Book of the Prophet Isaiah*, 149; Procksch, *Jesaja*, 292; Fischer, *Buch Isaias*, 160; Mowinckel, *Jesajaboken*, 140; Penna, *Isaiah*, 212; and Young, *Book of Isaiah*, 116-17.

86. Calvin (according to Fullerton, *A New Chapter*, 626 n. 10); Alexander, *Commentary on the Prophecies of Isaiah*, 391; Barnes, *Notes on the Book of the Prophet Isaiah II*, 39; Kamphausen, "Isaiah's Prophecy," 52, 55, 65, 67, 70; and Slotki, *Isaiah*, 105. According to Condamin, *Le Livre d'Isaïe*, 154, Knabenbauer held this view, and cited twenty-six scholars preceding him who did the same. I have not seen Knabenbauer's work, or his list of these scholars. Schoors, *Jesaja*, 137, cites Dillmann as holding this position. This must have been the case in one or more of the first five editions of his commentary on Isaiah, because in his sixth edition of 1898, 205, he specifically rejects this view. Archer, *Isaiah*, 625, tries to avoid the difficulty here by arguing that v. 25 refers

However, it is clear that this explanation does not arise from an exegesis of the text. Rather, it represents an effort to show how Isaiah could have delivered the entire oracle found in Isa 22:15–25 to the same audience on the same occasion. Fullerton is certainly correct in stating that this solution is absolutely impossible. On any sound principle of exegesis, the יתד in v. 25 must refer to the same person as the יתד in v. 23, viz., to Eliakim.[87] Furthermore, the question directed to Shebna in v. 16, "whom have you *here* (i.e., in Jerusalem)?" seems to deny that Shebna had a "father's house" in Jerusalem as vv. 24–25 assume of this individual.[88]

(2) Others propose that vv. 24–25 refer to Eliakim, but are to be read as a conditional sentence: v. 24 contains the protasis, and v. 25 the apodosis. Then one would translate: "If they hang on him the whole weight of his father's house, . . . in that day, . . . the peg that was fastened in a sure place will give way. . . ."[89] Admittedly, the OT has conditional sentences without the introductory אם.[90] However, in the context of Isa 22:20–25, it is unnatural to consider vv. 24–25 as a warning to Eliakim against playing favoritism toward his relatives in the high position he is to receive. Such a warning would be out of place after v. 23b, where the prophet announces that Eliakim will bring honor to his father's house.[91]

(3) Several scholars propose that vv. 24–25 do not refer to Shebna or Eliakim, but to an opponent of the redactor responsible for the later addition of these verses. Marti thinks they could allude to the death of

---

to others besides Eliakim, who wrongly assumed that they were as securely established as he, but had not committed themselves to Yahweh as he had done, and so some day must be cut off. However, nothing in the text suggests such an explanation.

87. Fullerton, *New Chapter*, 626.

88. This point was suggested by Skinner, *Book of the Prophet Isaiah*, 171, long ago, but apparently has been overlooked by most scholars.

89. Kuenen, *Historisch-Critisch Onderzoek* 2, 68 (*"indien* Eljakim de hem verleende macht misbruikt, om al de zijnen, groot en klein, te bevoordeelen, *dan enz."*); von Orelli (according to Kamphausen, "Isaiah's Prophecy," 72); Koenig, "Shebna and Eliakim," 677–80; Smith, *Book of Isaiah* 1 (1908 ed.), 318–19; Feldmann, *Buch Isaias*, 272–73; Hoonacker, *Het Boek Isaias*, 125; Joüon, *Grammaire de l'hébreu biblique*, 167 ab ("mais si on prétend y suspendre toute la gloire. . . . alors, le piquet cedera et tout tombera avec lui"); Ziegler, *Isaias*, 76; Young, *Book of Isaiah*, 116 n. 49; and Auvray, *Isaïe 1–39*, 213–14, who reasons: "il soit peu vraisemblable qu'un disciple d'Isaïe ait éprouvé le besoin de souligner une erreur de prévision de son maître" (213).

90. See the observations by Koenig, *Historisch-Kritisches Lehrgebäude*, 390q.

91. Fullerton, *A New Chapter*, 626; Shebna and Eliakim, 503–4; and Wade, *Book of the Prophet Isaiah*, 146.

the ungodly high-priest Alkimus in 160 BCE (see Josephus, *Antiq.*, XII 9.7), and to the removal of his family from the high-priestly office.[92] Vermeylen advances the view that a redactor who interpreted systematically all oracles in Isa 13-23 added Isa 22:24-25 in order to show his hostility toward wicked Jews. Verses 24-25, along with many other verses in the book of Isaiah, belong to the group entitled, "The Revenge of the Ungodly." The redactor thus identified Eliakim and his family with the unfaithful ones.[93] Kaiser thinks that a historicizing redactor added vv. 24-25 to oppose a hated contemporary, who was perhaps a Jewish tax official working for the Ptolemies and responsible for the finances of Judea and the temple.[94] Clements proposes that vv. 24-25 announce the removal of the prosperity and safety promised to Eliakim in vv. 19-23, as synonymous with the fall of the Davidic dynasty, and thus were added after the carrying away of Zedekiah in 587 BCE.[95] Now while any of these proposals *could be* correct, there is nothing in the text to suggest such interpretations, and therefore they must remain in the realm of conjecture.

(4) The most natural interpretation of Isa 22:24-25 in light of the MT and the ancient Versions is that these verses contain a prediction of the fall of Eliakim and his relatives, who have tried to elevate themselves politically, socially, and economically by putting pressure on Eliakim as a high official in Judah to show them special favors because they are his kinsmen (whether one understands this as a bona fide prediction, or as a *vaticinium ex eventu*). The use of the figure of the "peg" or "nail" in v. 25 indicates Eliakim was still functioning in his office as the king's steward when this announcement was uttered, and thus that this announcement was not directed against Eliakim's relatives *only*, at some time after his death.[96] Verse 24a suggests that when the oracle recorded in vv. 24-25 was first delivered, several of Eliakim's relatives had already put pressure on him to give them special favors and that he had yielded to that pressure. Thus the situation assumed in vv. 24-25 is that the hopes attached to Eliakim's leadership in vv. 20-23 have been dashed, and that the prophet

---

92. Marti, *Buch Jesaja*, 177.
93. Vermeylen, *Du Prophète Isaïe à l'Apocalyptique*, 342, 738.
94. Kaiser, *Isaiah 1-39*, 159.
95. Clements, *Isaiah 1-39*, 190-91. Clements writes: "The downfall of Eliakim has become synonymous with the downfall of the royal Davidic family of which he was a servant" (191).
96. Contra Marti, *Buch Jesaja*, 177; and Jensen, *Isaiah 1-39*, 184.

responsible for vv. 24–25 is aware of the pressure brought on Eliakim by his kinsmen, and of Eliakim's favoritism toward them (nepotism).⁹⁷ In light of this change of circumstances, the prophet announces that they will hang on him "the *whole* weight" of his father's house. In time, this will bring about his fall and that of his kinsmen who have sought to capitalize on their relationship to him for their own benefit. Verses 24–25 do not make sense as a separate oracle. Their author clearly is building on and making strategic connections with at least vv. 20–23 (whether he received this oracle orally or in written form). In v. 25, he uses the expression היתד התקועה במקים נאמן, "the peg (nail) that was fastened in a sure place," in order to connect his oracle with the expression ותקעתיו יתד במקום נאמן, "and I will fasten him like a peg in a sure place," in v. 23. There can be no doubt that he wants his readers to identify this person as Eliakim (cf. v. 20).⁹⁸ Referring to the same individual in v. 24, this redactor states that they will hang on him כל כבוד בית אביו, "the whole weight of his father's house." Here he is intentionally repeating the terminology at the end the v. 23, which declares that he (Eliakim, cf. v. 20) will become a throne כבוד לבית אביו, "of honor to his father's house," assigning a different meaning to כבוד, viz., "weight" (in the sense of "burden," as משא in v. 25 indicates), instead of "honor." His point to the readers of the present text, then, is that because Eliakim's family elevated themselves by attaching themselves to the "honor" he had brought to himself and them by attaining his high position, Eliakim will be "weighted down" with the pressures his relatives were bringing upon him.⁹⁹

---

97. Essentially this is the view of Alexander, *Commentary on the Prophecies of Isaiah*, 390; Barnes, *Notes on the Book of the Prophet Isaiah II*, 38; Whitehouse, *Isaiah I-XXXIX*, 256; Skinner, *Book of the Prophet Isaiah*, 171; Gray, *Critical and Exegetical Commentary*, 381–82; Rogers, *Isaiah*, 649; Wade, *Book of the Prophet Isaiah*, 146, 149; Procksch, *Jesaja*, 292–93; Fischer, *Buch Isaias*, 160–61; Ridderbos, *De Profeet Jesaja*, 145; Slotki, *Isaiah*, 104; Hertzberg, *Der Erste Jesaja*, 93; Vaccari, *I Profeti I. Isaia-Geremia*, 76; Scott, "The Book of Isaiah," 292, 294; Muckle, *Isaiah 1–39*, 78; Fohrer, *Das Buch Jesaia I*, 255; Kraeling, *Commentary on the Prophets I*, 107; Alonso Schökel, *Isaias*, 112; Martin-Achard, "L'oracle contra Shebnâ," 242–43; Moriarty, "Isaiah 1–39," 276; Penna, *Isaiah*, 212; Isaiah, *A New Catholic Commentary on Holy Scripture*, 583; Snijders, *Jesaja*, 222; Schoors, *Jesaja*, 137; Herbert, *Book of the Prophet Isaiah. Chapters 1–39*, 138 (possibly); Wildberger, *Jesaja*, 849–50; Sawyer, *Isaiah*, 194, 197; Watts, *Isaiah 1–33*, 287; and Widyapranawa, *The Lord is Savior*, 130.

98. So Dillmann, *Prophet Jesaja*, 205; Fullerton, *A New Chapter*, 626–27; Skinner, *Book of the Prophet Isaiah*, 171; Feldmann, *Buch Isaias*, 273; and Schoors, *Jesaja*, 137.

99. So Koenig, "Shebna and Eliakim," 679; Feldmann, *Buch Isaias*, 273; Kraeling,

In view of the conclusions drawn from the textual and linguistic discussions undertaken in this study, Isa 22:15–25 may be translated into English as follows:

V. 15: Thus says the Lord, Yahweh of hosts:
"Go forth (s.), go to this steward,
to Shebna, who is over the house, and say to him:
V. 16: What do you have here and whom do you have here
that you have hewed out for yourself here a tomb,
hewing out on a high place his tomb,
cutting in the rock a dwelling for himself?
V. 17: Behold, Yahweh will hurl you away violently,
O mighty man;
Yea, he will roll you up tightly,
V. 18: he will wrap you up like a turban,
he will throw you like a ball into a wide land.
There you will die,
and there your glorious chariots will be,
O disgrace of your master's house.
V. 19: Yea, I will thrust you from your office,
and from your station I will cast you down.
V. 20: And it shall come to pass in that day
that I will call for my servant, Eliakim the son of Hilkiah.
V. 21: And I will clothe him with your tunic,
and your girdle I will bind firmly about him,
and your rule I will give into his hand,
and he will be a father to the inhabitants of Jerusalem
and to the house of Judah.
V. 22: And I will put the key of the house of David on his shoulder,
and he will open and no one will shut,
and he will shut and no one will open.
V. 23: And I will drive him like a nail into a firm place,
and he will be a throne of honor to his father's house."
V. 24: "But they will hang on him
all the weight of his father's house,
the offspring and the descendants,
every small vessel,
from the basin-shaped vessels
even to the jar-shaped vessels.
V. 25: "In that day," says Yahweh of hosts,
"the nail which was driven into a firm place will be removed,

---

Commentary on the Prophets I, 107; Snijders, *Jesaja*, 222; Kelley, "Isaiah," 257; Schoors, *Jesaja*, 137; and Vermeylen, *Du Prophète Isaïe à l'Apocalyptique*, 342.

> yea, it will be hewn off, and it will fall,
> and the burden which is upon it will be cut off,
> for Yahweh has spoken."

Now if the textual and linguistic results deduced from this study are correct, they indicate three important conclusions for an exegesis of this pericope. First, Isa 22:15-25 is a prophetic oracle concerning specific, named leaders, not concerning anonymous officials. It consists of an announcement of Shebna's removal from office and exile, of his replacement by Eliakim the son of Hilkiah, and of the tragic fall of Eliakim. Second, the MT contains an introduction to this pericope in v. 15a which is quite common for prophetic oracles, and so there is no compelling reason to change it, as, e.g., by making v. 15c the beginning of this oracle. Third, it is hardly possible that the announcement found in vv. 24-25 was delivered on the same occasion to the same audience as that found in vv. 15-23. Whereas vv. 15-23 form a coherent and complete oracle apart from vv. 24-25, vv. 24-25 are not complete within themselves, and do not make sense apart from vv. 15-23. Accordingly, vv. 24-25 never existed alone as a separate pericope. It seems clear that they were added to vv. 15-23 after some of Eliakim's relatives had put pressure on him in his high position to give them special privileges, and the rest of his kinsmen (*"all* the weight of his father's house") were contemplating the same.

18

An Interpretation of Isaiah 22:15–25 and Its Function in the New Testament

THE PRIMARY PURPOSE OF this paper is to offer some suggestions as to the meaning of Rev 3:7 and Matt 16:19 in light of their use of Isa 22:22. In order to accomplish this, it is necessary first to set forth an interpretation of Isa 22:15–25 with a view to ascertaining the meaning of v. 22 in that pericope. Then one must examine Rev 3:7–13 and Matt 16:13–23 respectively as the two New Testament contexts in which Isa 22:22 is cited in order to attempt to determine how this Old Testament text functions in each of these contexts.

An Interpretation of Isaiah 22:15–25[1]

Isaiah 22:15 begins a prophetic oracle addressed to Shebna, who is "steward" and "master of the household." Since Isa 36:3, 11, 22; 37:2 indicate that Shebna functioned as an official under Hezekiah, this verse assumes that Hezekiah had made Shebna steward and master of his household some time between his succession to the throne (715 BCE) and the Assyrian siege of Jerusalem (701 BCE). *In its present form*, Isa 22:15–25 contains a doom oracle directed against Shebna (vv. 15–19), an announcement that Eliakim will receive the office Shebna now holds (vv. 20–23), and a doom oracle directed against Eliakim (vv. 24–25). Isaiah vehemently condemns Shebna (1) because he is hewing out a tomb for himself "on the height" "in the rock" (v. 16), that is, in that

---

[1]. For a recent discussion of the text of Isa 22:15–25, see Willis, "Textual and Linguistic Issues." A detailed explanation of the interpretation of Isa 22:15–25 sketched here appears in Willis, "Historical Issues in Isaiah 22:15–25," 60–70.

area of Jerusalem set aside for the burial of kings and other dignitaries; and (2) because he is very ostentatious, frequently appearing in public places riding in one of his "splendid chariots" of state (v. 18).[2] He declares that Shebna will be taken into Assyrian captivity, die there, and lose his splendid chariots to his captors (vv. 17-18). Eliakim will replace Shebna in his high official position (vv. 19-23). But Eliakim's relatives will pressure him to give them special favors, Eliakim will yield to this pressure, and eventually he will lose his office and both he and his relatives will fall (vv. 24-25).

However, these things did not turn out quite like Isaiah envisioned. When the Assyrian army of Sennacherib was besieging Jerusalem in 701 BCE, Hezekiah sent Eliakim who was over the house, Shebna the secretary (or scribe), and Joah the recorder to meet the Tartan, the Rab-saris, and the Rabshakeh, the Assyrian officials delegated by Sennacherib, to discuss the situation (2 Kgs 18:18, 37 = Isa 36:3, 22). This indicates that before this Assyrian invasion, Hezekiah had removed Shebna form the office of "steward" or the one "who is over the house" (Isa 22:15), had demoted him to the office of "secretary" or scribe (הסופר), and had elevated Eliakim to the office of "steward" which Shebna formerly held. There is nothing to indicate that the Assyrians carried Shebna into captivity with his splendid chariots, or that he died in a foreign land, as Isaiah had announced (Isa 22:17-18). The Rabshakeh tells that three-man delegation form Hezekiah to surrender or the Assyrians will overthrow Jerusalem and destroy its inhabitants (2 Kgs 18:28-35 = Isa 36:13-20). Hezekiah's

---

2. Skinner (*Book of the Prophet Isaiah Chapters I-XXXIX*, 168); Condamin (*Le Livre d'Isaïe*, 153); Hayes and Irvine (*Isaiah the Eighth-Century Prophet*, 284); Wessels ("Isaiah of Jerusalem," 1-13, esp. 5, 8-12); and others propose that a major reason Isaiah opposed Shebna is that he was a prominent member, if not the leader, of the pro-Egyptian and anti-Assyrian party in Jerusalem that Isaiah denounced (Isa 30:1-7; 31:1-3), whose rebellion led to Sennacherib's invasion of Judah and siege of Jerusalem in 701 BCE, or to Sargon II's invasion of the western states in ca. 713-711 BCE. Auret ("Different background for Isa 22:15-25," 46-56) thinks Eliakim was the one "who is over the house" under Hezekiah until Sennacherib conquered Hezekiah in 701 BCE. Then Sennacherib forced Hezekiah to demote the anti-Assyrian, Eliakim, and to put the pro-Assyrian, Shebna, in his place. Isaiah 22:15-23 preserves an oracle of Eliakim re-installed to his former position. While this is a different historical reconstruction than that proposed by most scholars, it still assumes that political issues are involved in the removal of Shebna and the appointment of Eliakim. Some connect Isa 22:15-25 with the previous pericope, 22:1-14, and suggest that Shebna was one of the rulers mentioned in v. 3. While these proposals are possible, nothing in the oracle in Isa 22:15-25 states or even implies them.

representatives return to the king and relate the Rabshakeh's threat. Fearful, Hezekiah sends Eliakim, Shebna, and Joah to Isaiah to ask him to pray that Yahweh will deliver the city from the invaders. Isaiah assures them that Yahweh will intervene and save Jerusalem (2 Kgs 19:1–7 = Isa 37:1–7), and this occurs (2 Kgs 19:8–36 = Isa 37:8–37). After the Assyrians leave Jerusalem, Eliakim's relatives put increasing pressure on him to use his high office to help them gain lucrative and enviable governmental positions, and he yields to this pressure. Isaiah or one of his disciples denounces this nepotism, and affirms that it will become worse and worse until Eliakim cannot bear the burdens his relatives are heaping upon him, and thus will fall, that is, lose his position as "steward" and he "who is over the house," or something worse; and his relatives will fall with him (Isa 22:24–25). The threefold repetition of כל in v. 24 indicates that when Isaiah or his disciple uttered this oracle, some members of his household were already bringing pressure on him to use his influence to elevate them; and now Isaiah foresees that his *whole* house will do the same: "And they will hang on him (Eliakim) *the whole weight* of his ancestral house, the offspring and issue, *every* small vessel, from the cups to *all* the flagons." Beyond this, there is no information as to what happened to Eliakim ultimately.

Isaiah 22:15–25 preserves an oracle which Yahweh instructed Isaiah to deliver to Shebna. Throughout the oracle, the speaker addresses Shebna in the second person singular and speaks of Eliakim in the third person. This pericope uses four terms to describe the מצב "office," or מעמד "station" (v. 19), held first by Shebna and then by Eliakim under Hezekiah king of Judah: סכן "steward"; אשר על הבית "(he) who is over the house" (v. 15); אב "father" (v. 21); and מפתח בית דוד "(bearer of) the key of the house of David" (v. 22).[3] While these terms originated in different milieux, and in the history of Israel and Judah only gradually were applied to the high government official under consideration here, their concurrence at this focal point apparently is due to the fact that there were striking similarities between the function of the person who bore each title originally and the function attached to the official discussed in the present context. That fact that all four terms are applied to the same official indicates that they were understood to be fundamentally synonymous, or at least to share a basic common core meaning. Hence,

---

3. A study of these four terms with extensive bibliography appears in Willis, "אב as an Official Term," 115–36.

methodologically one may use any one of these terms to understand the sense of any other of these terms.

The usages of the Akkadian *saknu(m)* in the Alalakh texts, the Nuzi tablets, the Amarna letters, and elsewhere, of the Ugaritic *skn*, of the Phoenician *skn*, of the Aramaic *skn*, and of the Hebrew סכן and סגן in the Old Testament indicate הסכן in Isa 22:15 means "substitute" (for the king), "prefect," "governor," "Steward," or "deputy," that is, the person responsible for the care of the royal palace and of the people, thus the highest official in the land under the king.[4] The nineteen occurrences of the title אשר על הבית, "(he) who (is) over the house(hold)" (sometimes without אשר) in the Old Testament (Gen 39:4, 16, 19; 41:40; 44:1, 4; 1 Kgs 4:6; 16:9; 18:3; 2 Kgs 10:5; 15:5 = 2 Chr 26:21; 2 Kgs 18:18, 37; 19:2 = Isa 36:3, 22; 37:2; Isa 22:15), and its eight occurrences in Hebrew inscriptions dating from the pre-exilic period, as well as the usage of synonymous terms in the Old Testament and in Akkadian texts, suggest that in the early period of the Israelite monarchy beginning with Solomon, it referred to a high governmental official who was in charge of the royal palace and its inhabitants, and later to one who held the highest post in the nation under the king and was over the entire royal estate. Accordingly, he held a governmental position similar to that of the "chief steward" in Egypt and a high official in Canaanite city-states.[5] The contexts in which the Hebrew word אב "father" (or its equivalent) appears as a term for a high governmental official in the Old Testament (five times: Gen 45:8; 1 Sam 24:12; 2 Kgs 5:13; Isa 9:6 [Heb. 5]; 22:21), the Ebla tablets (ca. 2500 BCE), an Egyptian text (early 15th century BCE), the Kilamuwa Inscription (9th century BCE, Phoenician), the Karatepe Inscriptions (9th-8th centuries BCE, two in Hittite, one in Phoenician), the Elephantine Papyri (Late 5th century BCE, Aramaic), and 1 Macc 11:32 indicate this individual was "second in command" under the king, with very widespread administrative responsibilities.[6] "The

---

4. See especially Alt, "Hohe Beamte in Ugarit," 1–11; Henshaw, "The Office of *Saknu* in Neo-Assyrian Times: I," 517–25; Henshaw, "The Office of *Saknu* in Neo-Assyrian Times: II," 461–83; Lipiński, "*Skn et Sgn* dans le sémitique occidental du nord," 191–207; Petit, "L'évolution sémantique," 53–67; and Stolper, "The *šaknu* of Nippur," 127–55.

5. See in particular Vaux, "Titres et fonctionnaires égyptiens," 196–98; Mettinger, *Solomonic State Officials*, 70–79, 109–10; and Layton, "Steward in Ancient Israel," 633–49.

6. See especially Ward, "The Egyptian Office of Joseph," 144–50.

key of the house of David" which Yahweh says he will place on Eliakim's shoulder (which, apparently, had been on Shebna's shoulder) evidently refers to an actual large wooden key which the royal "steward" carried on his shoulder to lock and unlock doors to various public buildings and offices, whose locks were large (cf. Judg 3:25; 1 Chr 9:27). Thus it signified his extensive authority in the Judean governmental administration. He was in charge of the governmental offices and royal chambers, and permitted or refused people to go in to the king. From the central governmental complex in the royal capital, he exercised supreme authority over the entire country. There are noteworthy similarities between Isa 22:22 and the Egyptian inscriptions on the tomb of the vizier Rekh-mi-Re (who lived during the reign of Thut-mose III, Eighteenth Dynasty, 1490–1436 BCE) in the report to the treasurer, and in the account of the daily opening of the king's house.

> Then the vizier, he shall report to the chief treasurer, saying, "All thy affairs are sound and prosperous; every seat of the court is sound and prosperous. There have been reported to me the sealing of the sealed chambers to this hour (and) the opening of them to (this) hour, by every responsible incumbent."
>
> Now, after each has reported to the other, of the two officials, then the vizier shall send to open every gate of the king's house, to cause to go in all that goes in, and to go out all that goes out likewise, by his messenger, who shall cause it to be put in writing.[7]

This suggests that when the Egyptian vizier opened the palace gates day officially began, and when he closed them the day officially ended. Hence, he was in complete control of the royal palace and the territory under its jurisdiction.[8] The other terms used for the official who carried the key of David on his shoulder in Isa 22:15–25 (discussed above) indicate he had a very high authoritative role in Israelite (Judean) government. A. S. Wood describes this official's function very well when he writes: "What Isaiah had in mind no doubt is the grand vizier as major domo, into whose hands I committed 'unlimited authority over the royal household, carrying with it a similar influence in all affairs of state.'"[9]

---

7. Breasted, *Ancient Records of Egypt*, 2:679–80, (pp. 274–75).
8. See in particular Martin-Achard, "L'oracle contra Shebnâ," 241–54.
9. Skinner, *Isaiah I*, 170; Wood, "Key," 10.

Isaiah 22:22 and Revelation 3:7-8

The figure of (Shebna and?) Eliakim carrying "the key of the house of David" on his shoulder, and opening so that none shall shut, and shutting so that none shall open (Isa 22:22) stands behind the statement about Jesus in Rev 3:7-8 and about Peter in Matt 16:16-19. C. H. Dodd, B. Lindars, and G. K. Beale have argued very persuasively that New Testament quotations of and references to Old Testament texts are intended to call the hearers' or readers' attention to whole Old Testament contexts in which those quotations or references appear, and not to those quotations or references in isolation from their Old Testament contexts.[10] Further, Lindars affirms that the same Old Testament texts may be used in more than one New Testament context, but that the logical sequence of applications of this Old Testament text may not correspond to the chronological sequence of the New Testament books in which it is quoted or mentioned. As an example, he cites the use of Isa 6:9-10 in John 12:39-40 (the oldest logical application in the New Testament); Acts 28:25-28; and Mark 4:11-12 (the latest logical application in the New

---

10. In describing the early Christian *method* of using the Old Testament, C. H. Dodd (*According to the Scripture*, 126), writes: "The method included, first the *selection* of certain large sections of the Old Testament scriptures . . . The sections were understood as *wholes*, and particular verses or sentences were quoted from them rather as pointers to the whole context than as constituting testimonies to and for themselves. At the same time, detached sentences form other parts of the Old Testament could be adduced to illustrate or elucidate the meaning of the main sections under consideration. But n the fundamental passages it is the *total context* that is in view, and is the basis of the argument." B. Lindars (*New Testament Apologetic*, 16-17) applauds Dodd's position on this point: "By drawing our attention to the blocks of material from which the testimonies have been drawn, Professor Dodd has shown that *the primary meaning must be ascertained by reference to the whole passage*. Generally quotations in the New Testament have not been selected with complete disregard of the original context. Their meaning has been already fixed by the process of working over whole passages which seem most relevant to the Church's fundamental doctrines" (emphasis mine—JTW). Lindars reasons that the early church used a somewhat limited group of Old Testament passages primarily for apologetic reasons, quoting certain lines form them under various circumstances to address particular issues. "But this is no arbitrary digging out of proof-texts, without taking the context into account. On the contrary, the context with its Christian interpretation has already defined the meaning of them. It is with this definite meaning that they are found to be useful at a particular stage in argument or discussion" (19).

G. K. Beale ("Revelation," 321-22) argues that in Revelation, John uses Old Testament texts in harmony with their broader contextual meaning, and cautions against confusing disregard for context with change of application.

Testament), where "the sequence of interpretation is the direct opposite of the presumed order in which the books themselves were written."[11] Both of these principles are at work in the use of Isa 22:22 in Rev 3:7 and Matt 16:19.

Although the book of Revelation apparently was written later than the Gospel of Matthew, it preserves an application of Isa 2:22 which is logically earlier than the application of this text in Matthew. Jesus' statement to Peter in Matt 16:19, "I will give you the keys of the kingdom of heaven," assumes that Jesus already possesses these keys and thus is in a position to give them to Peter. But Rev 3:7 describes Jesus as the one "who has the key of David." The traditions reflected in these two texts precede the books in which they are preserved. The origin of each tradition must be determined by considerations other than the dates of the books in which it is preserved.

The letter which the risen Christ instructs John to write to the church in Philadelphia begins by declaring:

> These are the words of the holy one, the true one,
> who has the key of David,
> who opens and no one will shut,
> who shuts and no one opens. (Rev 3:7)

Apparently Christ designates himself in this way because he begins his message to the church at Philadelphia by saying: "I know your works. Look, I have set before you an open door, which no one is able to shut" (v. 8). Scholars have understood the connection between this description of Christ and these initial words in various ways.

First, G. B. Caird argues that in v. 7 John echoes the language of Isa 22:22, where "the key of the house of David" symbolizes that Eliakim, the new steward under Hezekiah, has complete control over the royal household, and authority to grant or refuse access to the king's presence. Thus one might expect John to use this text to declare that Christ had the right to refuse access to God But John develops the imagery of the key in a different direction. In v. 8, Christ declares that he has opened a door of opportunity for the Philadelphian Christians to participate in the conversion of the Jews living in their region. Here he turns upside down the Jewish hope of converting the Gentiles to God, frequently expressed in the Old Testament, especially in the book of Isaiah (cf., for example, Isa

---

11. Lindars, *New Testament Apologetic*, 18.

43:4; 45:14; 60:14), and declares that it is not the Gentile oppressors of Israel, but the Jewish persecutors of the church, who must accept Christ as the true Holy One of Israel, and the church as the true Israel. Human beings cannot accomplish this conversion of Jews to Christ. However, since Christ has opened the door of opportunity for Christians to proclaim the gospel faithfully to the Jews, no one can shut the door, but God will supply the power for the gospel to realize success among the Jews.[12]

Second, several scholars contend that the statement Christ has the key of David is messianic (cf. Rev 5:5; 22:16), and that this means that he has complete authority to admit people to or to exclude people from the city of David, the New Jerusalem. In this context, admission pertains primarily to believing Gentiles and exclusion primarily to unbelieving Jews, but still the scope is universal. Christ has authority in the kingdom of God (Eph 1:22) essentially analogous to Eliakim's authority in the kingdom of Hezekiah. H. B. Swete refers to Eliakim as the "antitype" (*sic* Does he mean "type"?) of the exalted Christ. The "open door" of v. 8 calls to mind Paul's use of the same figure (1 Cor 16:19; 2 Cor 2:12; Col 4:3), and thus refers to the opportunity for Christian teachers at Philadelphia to preach the gospel, especially to unbelieving Jews (cf. v. 9). The Old Testament expectation that the Gentiles would be converted to God through the missionary efforts of the Jews (cf., for example, Isa 60:14) is reversed here, so that the expectation expressed in Rev 3:8–9 is that the Jews would play the role of the heathen and acknowledge Christians to be true Israel.[13]

Third, A. Farrer calls attention to several connections between the context of Isa 22:15–25 and the context of Rev 3:7–13. In Rev 3:7, John agrees with Matt 16:19 in taking the key to be the key of life and death, whose possessor has the authority to exclude from or to admit to the messianic kingdom or the New Jerusalem. Just as the unfaithful key-bearer Shebna is demoted and a worthy minister Eliakim put in his position (Isa 22:15–23), so the elders of the synagogue, who falsely claim they have the authority of David and use that authority to shut the door of access to God to Christians, will be humbled before those who faithfully follow Christ, who has the key of David and opens a door to Christians

---

12. Caird, *Commentary on the Revelation*, 51–53. On the "inverted use of the Old Testament" in Rev 3:9, see Beale, "Revelation," 330–31.

13. Scott, *Revelation*, 152; Swete, *Apocalypse of St John*, 53–54; Charles, *Revelation of St John I*, 86–89; and Ford, *Revelation*, 416.

which none can shut (cf. John 9:34–10:9). Christ's admonition, "hold fast what you have, so that no one may seize your crown" (Rev 3:11), places the Philadelphian Christians in bold contrast to Shebna, who, in forfeiting the keys, loses his crown (Isa 22:21, LXX) to faithful Eliakim. Also, just as the Lord promises the victorious Philadelphia Christian that he will make him a pillar in God's temple, and he will never leave it again (Rev 3:12).[14]

Fourth, several scholars reason that John uses the language of Isa 22:22 in Rev 3:7 to present Christ as the Davidic Messiah with absolute authority to admit persons to or to exclude them from the New Jerusalem, the heavenly kingdom. John's purpose may be to contrast Christ's admitting Jews into God's kingdom, as the only mediator between humanity and God, with the practice of the local synagogue in Philadelphia of excommunicating Christian Jews. Thus the "open door" refers to the opportunity which Christ has given Christian Jews, who have been excommunicated from the local synagogue (v. 9), to enter into the messianic kingdom, God's eternal kingdom; and not to a great opportunity for missionary activity by Christians at Philadelphia. Christ's announcement that those "who say that they are Jews and are not" will "come and bow down before your feet" (v. 9) suggests Christian vindication against Jewish opponents, not the conversion of Jews to Christ.[15] The use of Isa 22:15–25 here and the context of Rev 3:7 favor this interpretation.

These considerations yield four conclusions. First, Christ "has" the key of David (Rev 3:7) because God the Father has given it to him. Secondly, as a result of this, Christ functions as the major domo under God his Father. In this role, he is like Shebna and Eliakim, both of whom served as major domo under Hezekiah. John draws this analogy by borrowing language from Isa 22:22, the meaning of which was already well

---

14. Farrer, *Revelation of St John the Divine*, 80–81.

15. Preston and Hanson, *Revelation*, 66–67; Morris, *Revelation of St. John*, 78–79; Beasley-Murray, *Book of Revelation*, 100–101; Mounce, *Book of Revelation*, 116–17; Sweet, *Revelation*, 101–3; and Collins, "The Apocalypse (Revelation)," 1003.

The statements of E. H. Plumptre ("Epistles to the Seven Churches," 286–87) are confusing. On the one hand, he says that the open door of v. 8 refers to the admissions of the Gentiles into the church; but on the other hand, he says it refers to divinely-approved opportunities for mission work by the church. It is difficult to understand how the door Christ opens could be an opportunity for Christian preachers to proclaim the gospel to Gentiles and the admission of the Gentiles into the church at the same time.

known to his readers.¹⁶ Thirdly, as majordomo, Christ has complete authority over the King's (that is, God the Father's) household or kingdom, the church. He has total control over who is admitted into the King's presence and who is excluded from it, like Shebna and Eliakim did under Hezekiah (Isa 22:22). Fourthly, in contrast to the authorities in the local synagogue at Philadelphia who have excommunicated Christian Jews, the exalted Christ sets before these excommunicated individuals an open door into God's kingdom, where he will make them pillars in the temple of God so that they shall never go out of it (Rev 3:12). Those who pretend to be Jews, but in reality are of the synagogue of Satan, will then come and bow down before the feet of genuine Jewish Christians whom they had excommunicated, thereby conceding defeat at their hands because of Christ's power (Rev 3:9).

Isaiah 22:22 and Matthew 16:16–19

Matthew's description of Peter's great confession of Christ and then opposition to his announcement that he would go to Jerusalem and be crucified there (Matt 16:13–23) assumes that his readers knew the Old Testament passage concerning Shebna and Eliakim in Isa 22:15–25. There are three critical issues in this Matthean pericope, the solution to each of which may be illuminated by recognizing the way this Isaianic text provides a background for it.

First, it is important to attempt to determine precisely what Peter was confessing about Jesus' identity (Matt 16:16). Many scholars believe the expression, "You are . . . the Son of the Living God," means Peter was affirming Jesus' divine origin and nature.¹⁷ They cite Matt 2:15; 3:17; 4:3, 6; 8:29; 11:27; and 14:33, where Jesus is called the "Son of God," and interpret these texts to mean by this expression that Jesus is divine. Perhaps this meaning could be argued from John 5:18, according to which the Jews concluded that because Jesus called God his Father, he

---

16. G. von Rad (*Old Testament Theology*, 2:47–48, 373) explains the relationship between Isa 22:15–25 and Rev 3:7 typologically. First Shebna, then Eliakim, possessed "almost Messianic full powers," but both of them failed in their God-appointed task. "Thus, the office of 'the key of David' remained unprovided for until finally it could be laid down at the feet of Christ (Rev. III 7)" (373).

17. So Filson, *Commentary on the Gospel according to St Matthew*, 185; Sutcliffe, "St Peter's Double Confession," 31–41; McKenzie "Gospel according to Matthew," 91; Hill, *Gospel of Matthew*, 260; Brown, Donfried, and Reumann, *Peter in the New Testament*, 86 (citing John 20:31); and Viviano, "The Gospel according to Matthew," 659.

Isaiah 22:15 and Its Function in the New Testament

made himself equal with God. However, in the context of Matt 16:16, it seems clear that "the Son of the Living God" is equivalent to "the Christ" (Messiah).[18] "Messiah" (1 Sam 24:6; 26:9, 11; 2 Sam 1:14; Pss 20:6; 84:9 [Hebrew 10]; 89:38) and "Son of God" (2 Sam 7:14; 1 Chr 22:10; 28:6; Pss 2:7; 89:26–27) are two of several titles for the kings of Israel and Judah in the Old Testament. Accordingly, Peter's confession assumes the widely held Jewish belief of his day that God will raise up a king who will sit on David's throne in Jerusalem, and through him will bring about his ideal kingdom on earth, and affirms his personal conviction that Jesus is that king.

Secondly, it is necessary to attempt to determine the meaning of "binding" and "loosing" in Matt 16:19, and how Jesus' statement about Peter's binding and loosing is related to his promise that he would give Peter the keys of the kingdom of heaven. Scholars have interpreted δέω "bind," and λύω "loose," in Matt 16:19 in at least four ways.

(1) On the basis of the use of δέω and λύω in intertestamental Jewish sources and elsewhere in the New Testament (for example, Mark 3:20–27 = Matt 12:22–29 = Luke 11:14–22; Mark 7:31–37; Luke 13:10–17),[19] Hiers argues that the sayings of Jesus now preserved in Matt 16:19 and 18:18 originally had to do with Jesus authorizing or empowering Peter and the Twelve to exorcise demons, that is, to "bind" demons and to "loose" the demon-possessed in order to prepare them for their new life in the kingdom of God. But in their present Matthean contexts, these statements may refer to Jesus authorizing church leaders to make decisions with regard to congregational order or Christian morality. "Binding" and "loosing" suggest that Peter and the other apostles would have authority to deal with whatever problems might arise in the continuing years of the church, possibly including matters of doctrine, excommunication, and determining the ultimate destiny of members of the church.[20]

(2) Some argue that "bind" and "loose" are terms pertaining to discipline in the church, including the right to condemn ("bind") or acquit ("loose") (cf. Matt 18:18). The meaning of Matt 16:19 is stated

---

18. So also Albright and Mann, *Matthew*, 181, 194; Kee, "Gospel according to Matthew," 629.

19. On the use of this terminology in this passage, see Welzen, "Loosening and Binding," 175–87.

20. Hiers, "'Binding' and 'Loosing,'" 233–50.

in a different way in John 20:23, which speaks of the disciples forgiving and retaining sins, apparently by preaching the gospel. Thus, to "loose" refers to the divine power to forgive sins, and so to admit converts into and to restore penitent sinners to the church. To "bind" is to announce God's judgment on unbelievers and impenitent sinners, and to excommunicate offenders from the church.[21] "Binding" and "loosing" refer to the broad power of allowing or refusing entrance into the kingdom.[22]

(3) Others contend that "bind" and "loose" allude to teaching what is forbidden or permitted. In rabbinic literature, these terms are used of the verdict of the teacher of the law who declares an action "bound" (forbidden, wrong) or "loosed" (permitted, right), not of retaining sins or forgiving them.[23] Thus, Peter has the authority to declare what laws in the Mosaic Torah are "binding" on Christians, and what laws they are "loosed" from observing.[24] Stated somewhat more broadly, binding and loosing refers to "the interpretation of the scriptures and the determination of an appropriate Christian way of life."[25]

(4) It seems best to understand "binding and loosing" together as a unified concept equivalent to possessing the keys of the kingdom of heaven, and meaning the totality of power entrusted to Peter and the

---

21. So Cullmann, *Peter: Disciple, Apostle, Martyr*, 211; Emerton, "'Binding and Loosing,'" 325–31 (possibly); Menoud, "Binding and Loosing," 438; Bonnard, *L'Évangile selon Saint Matthieu*, 246; Basser, "Derrett's 'Binding' Reopened," 297–300; and Bromiley, "Keys, Power of the," 12. Hill (*Gospel of Matthew*, 262) argues that views (1) and (2) amount to the same thing, namely, Peter has authority to make pronouncements (legislative or disciplinary), and these will be ratified by God in the Last Judgment. Falk ("Binding and Loosing," 92–100) proposes that "binding" refers to holding a person to a vow, while "loosing" pertains to releasing a person from a vow. This is a type of retaining or forgiving sins, but seems much too limited for the contexts of Matt 16:19 and 18:18.

22. See Cullmann, *Peter: Disciple, Apostle, Martyr*, 209–10; and Brown, Donfried, and Reumann, *Peter in the New Testament*, 97.

23. McNeile, *Gospel according to St Matthew*, 243; Smith, *Gospel according to St Matthew*, 154; Cox, *Gospel according to St Matthew*, 111; Filson, *Commentary on the Gospel according to St Matthew*, 187; Tasker, *Gospel according to St Matthew*, 158; Emerton, "Binding and Loosing"—Forgiving and Retaining," 325–31 (possibly); Kee, "Gospel according to Matthew," 630; Derrett, "Binding Loosing," 172–77; and Kesich, "Peter's Primacy," 51–52.

24. Johnson, "Gospel according to St Matthew, 453; and Marcus, "Gates of Hades," 443–55, esp. 449–55.

25. Collins, "Binding and Loosing," 744. So also Bornkamm, "Authority to 'Bind' and 'Loose' in the Church," 37–50; Mantey, "Distorted Translations," 409–16; and Manns, "La Halakah dans l'évangile de Matthieu," 129–35.

other apostles without being more specific.[26] J. L. McKenzie writes: "The phrase certainly signifies the exercise of authority; but the nature and use of the authority are not specified."[27] Accordingly, "binding" and "loosing" are ultimately the same as "shutting" and "opening," which is the task of the majordomo of the palace or nation. In Matt 23:13, Jesus condemns the Pharisees, saying: "You lock people out of the kingdom of heaven. For you do not go in yourselves, and when others are going in, you stop them." They do this by portraying the Law as a heavy burden which is hard to bear (Matt 23:4), by not practicing what they teach (Matt 23:3), and by doing their deeds to be seen by men (Matt 23:5-7). In sharp contrast to this, Jesus instructs Peter to declare that God is anxious to forgive penitent sinners and grant them entrance into his kingdom, but turns away the self-righteous, who are quick to condemn and shut out others.[28] "Binding and loosing" in Matt 16:19 and 18:18 may very well be a case of merismus, a syntactical phenomenon in which two polar terms are used to express the whole reality.[29] I. Krasovec pairs פתח "to loose," with אסר "to bind."[30] But there is also good reason to pair פתח with סגר. In the piel, פתח means "to loose, loosen, set free."[31] And in the hiphil, סגר means "to deliver up to, shut up, imprison."[32] This calls to mind the merismus "bind ... loose" in Matt 16:19 and 18:18. In view of this, Matt 16:19 affirms that "Peter is ... the chief steward, the *major domus*, in the Kingdom; the 'keys' are the symbol of rule and authority, entrusted by the real Holder ... ; cf. Apoc. iii. 7 (based on Is. xxii.22)."[33]

> Isa xxii 15ff. undoubtedly lies behind this saying [i.e., Matt 16:19]. The keys are the symbol of authority, and Roland de Vaux

---

26. See Menoud, "Binding and Loosing," 439 (who does not accept this view).

27. McKenzie, "Gospel according to Matthew," 92.

28. See Luz, "Primacy Text," 41-55, esp. 46-47. M.A. Powell ("Do and Keep what Moses Says," 419-35, esp. 433-34) also calls attention to the contrast between Matt 16:19, 18:18, and 23:13, but thinks "binding and loosing" have to do with interpreting the words of Moses for the present day, which inevitably affects determination of membership in the community.

29. "Die einzelnen Termini besitzen nicht eine realistische Bedeutung, sondern stehen symbolisch-stellvertretend für die gesamte Realität oder Gattung einer gegebenen Ebene" (J. Krasovec, *Merismus*, 3).

30. Krasovec, *Der Merismus*, 134-35 (no. 202), citing Job 12:18 as an example.

31. BDB, 835.

32. BDB, 689.

33. McNeile, *Gospel according to St. Matthew*, 243.

> ... rightly sees here the same authority as that vested in the vizier, the master of the house, the chamberlain, of the royal household in ancient Israel ... The role of Peter as steward of the Kingdom is further explained as being the exercise of administrative authority, as was the case of the Old Testament chamberlain who held the "keys" ... Peter's initiative is well illustrated by the admission of a Gentile to the community in Acts x-xi, under the guidance of the Spirit.[34]

The Greek expressions ἔσται δεδεμένον (δεδεμένα) and ἔσται λελυμένον (λελυμένα) are future perfect periphrastics. Since this syntactical form is rare in the New Testament, the force of its meaning must be respected here. Hence, the statements in which these periphrastics appear in Matt 16:19 and 18:18 should be rendered: "Whatever you shall bind on earth *shall have been bound* in heaven, and whatever you shall loose on earth *shall have been loosed* in heaven" (so also the Vg). "It is the church on earth carrying out heaven's decisions, communicated by the spirit, and not heaven ratifying the church's decisions."[35]

Thirdly, it is somewhat disturbing that the pericope describing Peter's great confession (Matt 16:13-20) is followed immediately by the pericope in which Peter opposes Jesus when he announces that he must go to Jerusalem and suffer and die there, and Jesus responds by addressing Peter as Satan and by accusing Peter of being on the side of men rather than on the side of God (Matt 16:21-23). However, Peter is holding to the common Jewish messianic understanding of his day, and thus cannot accept the concept of a "suffering Messiah."[36] The sequence

---

34 Albright and Mann, *Matthew*, 196-97.

35. Ibid., 197. The advocates of all four of these views usually believe that the "rock" on which Jesus will build his church is Peter. However, Chilton ("Shebna, Eliakim, and the Promise to Peter," 311-26) argues that the "rock" here is Mount Zion, referring to the Temple. The overall framework of the *Targum of Isaiah* centers on the restoration of the house of Israel, at the center of which are the Temple and Jerusalem. This targum speaks to dispersed and disoriented Israel, who has no cult but expects a Messiah who will restore the Temple and the autonomy of Israel, but only for those who repent according to the Law. In Matt 23:16-22; 5:23-24; 17:24-27; 21:12-13; 24:1-25, Jesus is presented as developing halakoth in respect to the Temple. Similar to the targumic interpretation of Isa 22:22, in Matt 16:18-19 Jesus is establishing the mechanism for articulating the cultic halakah. While Chilton's argument is well-presented and worthy of serious consideration, it does not seem to come naturally from the context of Matt 16:13-20.

36. See McNeile, *Gospel according to St Matthew*, 244, 245-46; Cox, *Gospel according to St Matthew*, 113; Filson, *Commentary on the Gospel according to St Matthew*,

of Peter's God-revealed confession of Jesus (Matt 16:17) followed by Peter's Satan-motivated objection to Jesus' proclamation that he must suffer and die (Matt 16:21–23) corresponds strikingly to the sequence of God's elevation of Eliakim to Shebna's office (Isa 22:20–23) followed by a prophetic announcement that he and all his household will fall (Isa 22:24–25). The language of Jesus' promise to give Peter the keys of the kingdom of heaven calls to mind God's promise to Eliakim in Isa 22:22. And the sequence of Peter's confession of and opposition to Jesus calls to mind the sequence of Eliakim's rise and fall.

Conclusions

This study has led to the following conclusions.

First, Isa 22:15–23 was addressed to Shebna, the major domo of Hezekiah, some time between 715 and 701 BCE. The prophet condemns Shebna for his arrogance, announces that he will be removed from the office of steward or major domo and carried into exile, and declares that at Eliakim will replace him. Shebna was removed from being major domo and replaced by Eliakim, but instead of being carried into exile was demoted to secretary or scribe.

Second, Isa 22:24–25 is a later oracle by the prophet or one of his disciples when he learned that some of Eliakim's relatives were putting pressure on him to use his office to benefit them. The prophet declares that this problem of nepotism will increase until "all" of Eliakim's household will be involved; then Eliakim and his whole house will fall. However, vv. 24–25 do not make sense without statements to which they refer in vv. 15–23, so this later oracle could not have circulated independently of vv. 15–23, and is inseparably connected to this earlier oracle.

Third, accordingly, Isa 22:15–25 should be read as a whole. In this verse, four basically synonymous terms for the major domo emerge: "steward" (v. 15), "(he) who (is) over the house" (v. 15), "father" (v. 21), and "(he who carries) the key of the house of David" (v.22). Each of these terms may be used to illuminate the meaning of any of the other terms.

Fourth, Isa 22:22 provides the background for the description of Christ in Rev 3:7 as the one who has the key of David, who opens and no one will shut, who shuts and no one opens. In the context of Isa 22:15–25,

---

188–89; Bonnard, *L'évangile selon Saint Matthieu*, 248; Albright and Mann, *Matthew*, 200; and Hill, *Gospel of Matthew*, 263–64.

the king is Hezekiah and, first Shebna, then Eliakim is his major domo; and, essentially parallel to this, in Rev 3:7, God is the king and Christ is his major domo. Under God's appointment to this position, Christ has complete authority over God's kingdom; he has the key of David, and he allows or forbids people to enter that kingdom.

Fifth, Matt 16:13-23 assumes the reader knows the context of Isa 22:15-25, and in Matt 16:19 Jesus borrows the language of Isa 22:22. According to Matt 16:16, Peter confesses that Jesus is "the Christ," "the Son of the living God," that is, that Jesus is king. The expression "Son of God" is one of the common Old Testament titles for a king, and the context of Matt 16:16 shows Peter had that nuance in mind in his confession, not the idea that Jesus is divine as in other New Testament contexts. Jesus commends Peter for the words he used, but not for his understanding of those words. He tells Peter that he (Peter) will be the rock on which his (Jesus') church will be built. Then, in his role as king, Jesus gives Peter the keys of the kingdom of heaven, the authority and responsibility to bind and loose on earth what has already been bound and loosed in heaven, that is, Jesus makes Peter the major domo of his kingdom with all the privileges and responsibilities accruing to that function.

Sixth, the sequence of Peter's confession that Jesus is the Christ, the Son of the living God, that is, that Jesus is king (Matt 16:13-20), immediately followed by Peter's denunciation of Jesus for announcing that he will go to Jerusalem to suffer and die there, and Jesus' rebuke of Peter for setting his mind on human things rather than divine things (Matt 16:21-23), is strikingly similar to the sequence of Isaiah's announcement that Shebna will be removed from his position as major domo under Hezekiah and will be replaced by Eliakim (Isa 22:15-23), immediately followed by the prophet's declaration that Eliakim will fall along with his household because all his household will seek special favors from him as one who holds a high office in the Judean government (Isa 22:24-25).

Acknowledgments

THE AUTHOR AND PUBLISHER gratefully acknowledge the permission and cooperation of the journals and publishers that published the original editions of the chapters in this volume.

"The Structure of the Book of Micah." Previously published in *Svensk Exegetisk Årsbok* 34 (1969) 5–42.

"Thoughts on a Redactional Analysis of the Book of Micah." Previously published in *SBL Seminar Papers* 13 (1978) 87–107.

"Fundamental Issues in Contemporary Micah Studies." Previously published in *Restoration Quarterly* 13 (1970) 77–90.

"The Structure of Micah 3–5 and the Function of Micah 5 9–14 in the Book." Previously published in *Zeitschrift für die alttestamentliche Wissenschaft* 81 (1969) 191–214.

"Micah 4:14—5:5—A Unit." Previously published in *Vetus Testamentum* 18 (1968) 529–47.

"Some Suggestions on the Interpretation of Micah 1:2." Previously published in *Vetus Testamentum* 18 (1968) 372–79

"On the Text of Micah 2.1aα-β." Previously published in *Biblica* 48 (1967) 534–41.

"Micah 2.6–8 and the People of God in Micah." Previously published in *Biblische Zeitschrift* 14 (1970) 72–87.

"A Note on ואמר in Micah 3.1." Previously published in *Zeitschrift für die alttestamentliche Wissenschaft* 80 (1968) 50–54.

"ממך לי יצא in Micah 5:1." Previously published in *Jewish Quarterly Review* 58 (1968) 317–22.

"The Authenticity and meaning of Micah 5.9–14." Previously published in *Zeitschrift für die alttestamentliche Wissenschaft* 81 (1969) 191–214.

"The First Pericope in the Book of Isaiah." Previously published in *Vetus Testamentum* 34 (1984): 63–77.

"An Important Passage for Determining the Historical Setting of a Prophetic Oracle—Isaiah 1.7–8." Previously published in *Studia Theologica* 39 (1985): 151–69.

"On the Interpretation of Isaiah 1.18." Previously published in *Journal for the Study of the Old Testament* 25 (1983): 35–54.

"Lament Reversed—Isaiah 1.21ff." Previously published in *Zeitschrift für die alttestamentliche Wissenschaft* 98 (1986) 236–48.

"The Genre of Isaiah 5.1–7." Previously published in *Journal of Biblical Literature* 96 (1977) 337–62.

"Textual and Linguistic Issues in Isaiah 22,15–25." Previously published in *Zeitschrift für die alttestamentliche Wissenschaft* 105 (1994) 377–99.

"An Interpretation of Isaiah 22.15–25 and its Function in the New Testament." Previously published in *Early Christian Interpretation of the Scriptures of Israel*, edited by Craig A. Evans and James A. Sanders (Sheffield: Sheffield Academic, 1997), 334–51.

Bibliography

Ackroyd, P. R. "The Book of Isaiah." In *The Interpreter's One-Volume Commentary on the Bible*. Edited by Charles M. Laymon. London: William Collins, 1972.
———. "Isaiah I–XII: Presentation of a Prophet." In *Congress Volume: Göttingen 1977*, 16–48. VTSup 29. Leiden: Brill, 1978.
———. "A Note on Isaiah 2:1." *ZAW* 75 (1963) 320–21.
Ahlström, G. W. *Joel and the Temple Cult of Jerusalem*. VTSup 21. Leiden: Brill, 1971.
Albright, W. F. "Some Canaanite-Phoenician Sources of Hebrew Wisdom." In *Wisdom in Israel and in the Ancient Near East*, edited by M. Noth and D. Winton Thomas, 1–15. VTSup 3. Leiden: Brill, 1969.
———. "Two Little-Understood Amarna Letters from the Middle Jordan Valley." *BASOR* 89 (1943) 7–17.
Albright, W. F., and C. S. Mann. *Matthew*. AB 26. Garden City, NY: Doubleday, 1971.
Alexander, Joseph A. *Commentary on the Prophecies of Isaiah*. Grand Rapids: Zondervan, 1953.
Allegro, J. M. "Uses of the Semitic Demonstrative Element *z* in Hebrew." *VT* 5 (1955) 309–12.
Allen, Leslie C. *The Books of Joel, Obadiah, Jonah and Micah*. NICOT. Grand Rapids: Eerdmans, 1976.
Alonso Schökel, Luis. *Isaias*. Los Libros Sagrados 9. Madrid: Ediciones Cristiandad, 1968.
Alt, Albrecht. "Hohe Beamte in Ugarit." In *Studia Orientalia Ioanni Pedersen*, edited by Flemming Hvidberg, 1–11. Copenhagen: Einar Munksgaard, 1953.
Amit, Yairah. "'The Glory of Israel Does Not Deceive or Change His Mind': On the Reliability of Narrator and Speakers in Biblical Narrative." *Proof* 12 (1992) 201–12.
Andersen, Francis I., and David Noel Freedman. *Amos*. AB 24A. New York: Doubleday, 1989.
———. *Hosea*. AB 24. New York: Doubleday, 1980.
Anderson, Bernhard W. "Foreknow, Foreknowledge." In *The Interpreter's Dictionary of the Bible*, edited by G. A. Buttrick, 2:311–14. Nashville: Abingdon, 1962.
———. "God, OT View of." In *The Interpreter's Dictionary of the Bible*, edited by G. A. Buttrick, 2:417–30 Nashville: Abingdon, 1962.
———. "A Worldwide Pilgrimage to Jerusalem." *BRev* 8/3 (1992) 14, 16.
Anderson, G. W. *A Critical Introduction to the Old Testament*. London: Duckworth, 1959.
———. "A Study of Micah 6:1–8." *SJT* 4 (1951) 191–97.
Archer, Gleason L., Jr. *Isaiah*. Wycliffe Bible Commentary. Chicago: Moody, 1962.
Auret, A. "A Different Background for Isa 22:15–25 Presents an Alternative Paradigm: Disposing of Political and Religious Opposition?" *OTE* 6 (1993) 46–56.
Auvray, Paul. *Isaïe 1–39*. SB. Paris: Gabalda, 1972.
Auvray, Paul, and J. Steinmann. *Isaïe*. 2nd ed. La Sainte Bible. Paris: Cerf, 1957.

Baab, O. J. "Marriage." In *The Interpreter's Dictionary of the Bible*, edited by G. A. Buttrick, 3:278–87 Nashville: Abingdon, 1962.
Bach, R. ". . . Der Bogen zerbricht, spiesse zerschlägt und wagen mit Feuer verbrennt." In *Probleme biblischer Theologie: Gerhard von Rad zum 70. Geburtstag*, edited by Hans Walter Wolff, 13–26. Munich: Kaiser, 1971.
Barnes, Albert. *Notes, Critical, Explanatory, and Practical, on the Book of the Prophet Isaiah* 1. London: Routledge, 1852.
Barr, James. "'Determination' and the Definite Article in Biblical Hebrew." *JSS* 34 (1989) 307–35.
Barstad, Hans M. *The Religious Polemics of Amos: Studies in the Preaching of Am 2, 7B–8; 4, 1–13; 5, 1–27; 6, 4–7; 8, 14*. VTSup 34. Leiden: Brill, 1984.
Bartelt, Andrew H. *The Book around Immanuel: Style and Structure in Isaiah 2–12*. Biblical and Judaic Studies from the University of California, San Diego 4. Edited by W. H. Propp. Winona Lake, IN: Eisenbrauns, 1996.
Barth, Hermann. *Die Jesaja-Worte in der Josiazeit*. WMANT 48. Neukirchen-Vluyn: Neu-kirchener, 1977.
Barthélemy, D., and J. T. Milik. *Qumran Cave I*. Discoveries in the Judaean Desert 1. Oxford: Clarendon, 1964.
Basser, H. W. "Derrett's 'Binding' Reopened." *JBL* 104 (1985) 297–300.
Baudissin, W. W. Graf. *Einleitung in die Bücher des Alten Testaments*. Leipzig: S. Hirzel, 1901.
Beale, G. K. "Revelation." In *It Is Written: Scripture Citing Scripture: Essays in Honour of Barnabas Lindars*, edited by D. A. Carson and H. G. M. Williamson, 318–36. Cambridge: Cambridge University Press, 1988.
Beasley-Murray, G. R. *The Book of Revelation*. NCB. Grand Rapids: Eerdmans, 1981.
Beck, J. T. *Erklärung der Propheten Micha und Joel*. Gütersloh: Bertelsmann, 1898.
Becker, U. "Jesajaforschung (Jes 1–39)." *TRu* 64/1 (February 1999) 1–37; 64/2 (May 1999) 117–52.
Benoit, P., et al. *Les Grottes de Murabba'ât*. DJD 2. Oxford: Clarendon, 1961.
Bentzen, A. *Introduction to the Old Testament* 2. Copenhagen: G. E. C. Gad, 1948.
———. *Jesaja*, Band I. *Jes 1–39*. Copenhagen: G. E. C. Gad, 1944.
———. "Zur Erläuterung von Jesaja 5,1–7." *AfO* 4 (1927) 209–10.
Berry, G. R. "Micah, Book of." In *Encyclopedia Americana* 19:10. New York: Encyclopedia Americana, 1934.
Betteridge, W. R. "Obedience and not Sacrifice: An Exposition of Isa 1:18–20." *BW* 38 (1911) 41–49.
Beuken, W. A. M. "Isaiah Chapters LXV–LXVI: Trito-Isaiah and the Closure of the Book of Isaiah." In *Congress Volume: Leuven 1989*, edited by J. A. Emerton, 204–21. VTSup 43. Leiden: Brill, 1991.
———. *Jesaja Deel IIB*. De Prediking van het Oude Testament. Nijkerk: Callenbach, 1983.
———. "The Main Theme of Trito-Isaiah: 'The Servants of Yahweh.'" *JSOT* 47 (1990) 67–87.
Bewer, Julius A. *The Literature of the Old Testament*. New York: Columbia University Press, 1938.
———. *The Prophets*. New York: Harper, 1965.
———. "Textkritische Bemerkungen zum Alten Testament." In *Festschrift für Alfred Bertholet*, edited by Walter Baumgartner et al., 65–76. Tübingen: Mohr/Siebeck, 1950.

Beyerlin, Walter. *Die Kulttraditionen Israels in der Verkündigung des Propheten Micha.* FRLANT 72. Göttingen: Vandenhoeck & Ruprecht, 1959.

———, ed. *Near Eastern Religious Texts Relating to the Old Testament.* Translated by John Bowden. London: SCM, 1978.

Binns, L. E. "Micah." In *A New Commentary on Holy Scripture, including the Apocrypha.* Edited by Charles Gore, Henry Leighton Goudge, and Alfred Guillaume. New York, 1928.

Bjorndalen, A. J. "Zu den Zeitstufen der Zitatformel . . . אמר כה im Botenverkehr." *ZAW* 86 (1974) 393–403.

Black, Matthew. "The Parables as Allegory." *BJRL* 42 (1960) 273–87.

Blank, Sheldon H. "Fable." In *The Interpreter's Dictionary of the Bible*, edited by G. A. Buttrick, 2:221. Nashville: Abingdon, 1962.

———. "Irony by Way of Attribution." *Semitics* 1 (1970) 1–6.

Blenkinsopp, Joseph. *Opening the Sealed Book: Interpretations of the Book of Isaiah in Late Antiquity.* Grand Rapids: Eerdmans, 2006.

———. "The Servant and the Servants in Isaiah and the Formation of the Book." In *Writing and Reading the Scroll of Isaiah: Studies of an Interpretive Tradition*, edited by C. C. Broyles and C. A. Evans, 155–75. VTSup 70/71. Leiden: Brill, 1997.

Bonnard, P. *L'Évangile selon Saint Matthieu.* Commentaire du Nouveau Testament 1. Neuchâtel: Delachaux & Niestlé, 1963.

Born, A. van den. *Samuel.* Roermond: Romen & Zonen, 1956.

Bornkamm, G. "The Authority to 'Bind' and 'Loose' in the Church in Matthew's Gospel." *Perspective* 11 (1970) 37–50.

Bourke, J. "Le jour de Yahvé dans Joël." *RB* 66 (1959) 5–31, 191–212.

Box, G. H. *The Book of Isaiah.* London: Pitman, 1908.

Brandenburg, Hans. *Das Lebendige Wort. Band 9. Die Kleinen Propheten.* Giessen: Brunnen, 1963.

Breasted, James H. *Ancient Records of Egypt.* Chicago: University of Chicago Press, 1906.

Briggs, Charles Augustus. *A Critical and Exegetical Commentary on the Book of Psalms.* ICC. 2 vols. New York: Scribner, 1906 and 1909.

Bright, John. "Isaiah–I." *Peake's Commentary on the Bible.* Reprint. London: Nelson, 1967.

———. *Jeremiah.* AB 21. Garden City, NY: Doubleday, 1965.

Bromiley, Geoffrey W. "Keys, Power of the." In *International Standard Bible Encyclopedia*, edited by G. W. Bromiley, 3:11–12. Grand Rapids: Eerdmans, 1986.

Brown, Francis. "The Measurements of Hebrew Poetry as an Aid to Literary Analysis." *JBL* 9 (1890) 71–106.

Brown, Francis, Samuel Rolles Driver, and Charles Augustus Briggs, eds. *A Hebrew and English Lexicon of the Old Testament.* Oxford: Clarendon, 1907/1951.

Brown, Raymond E., et al., eds. *Peter in the New Testament: A Collaborative Assessment by Protestant and Roman Catholic Scholars.* Minneapolis: Augsburg, 1973.

Brueggemann, Walter. *First and Second Samuel.* Interpretation. Louisville: John Knox, 1990.

———. "Jeremiah's Use of Rhetorical Questions." *JBL* 92 (1973) 358–74.

———. *Tradition for Crisis: A Study in Hosea.* Richmond, VA: John Knox, 1968.

———. "Unity and Dynamic in the Isaiah Tradition." *JSOT* 29 (1984) 89–107.

———. "'Vine and Fig Tree': A Case Study in Imagination and Criticism." In *A Social Reading of the Old Testament: Prophetic Approaches to Israel's Communal Life*, edited by Patrick D. Miller, 188–204. Minneapolis: Fortress, 1994.

Bruno, D. A. *Das Buch der Zwölf: eine rhythmische und textkritische Untersuchung.* Stockholm: Almqvist & Wiksell, 1957.

Bruno, A. *Micha und der Herrscher aus der Vorzeit.* Leipzig: Deichert, 1923.

Büchsel, F. "ἀλληγορέω." In *Theological Dictionary of the New Testament*, edited by G. Kittel, 1:260-63. Translated by G. W. Bromiley. Grand Rapids: Eerdmans, 1964.

Budde, Karl. "Eine folgenschwere Redaktion des Zwölfprophetenbuchs." *ZAW* 39 (1921) 218-29.

———. *Die Fünf Megillot.* KHC 17. Tübingen: Mohr/Siebeck, 1898.

———. "Zum hebräischen Klagelied. 2. Das Klagelied Jes. 1,21ff." *ZAW* 11 (1891) 234-47.

———. "Zu Jesaja 1-5 (I)." *ZAW* 49 (1931) 16-40; "

———. "Zu Jesaja 1-5: Kapitel 2-4." *ZAW* 49 (1931) 182-211.

———. "Micha 2 und 3." *ZAW* 38 (1919) 2-22.

———. "Verfasser und Stelle von Micha IV 1-4 (Jes. 2, 2-4)." *ZDMG* 81 (1927) 152-58.

Bultmann, Rudolf. *The History of the Synoptic Tradition.* Translated by John Marsh. Oxford: Blackwell, 1963.

Burkitt, F. C. "Micah 6 and 7 a Northern Prophecy." *JBL* 45 (1926) 159-61.

Burney, Charles Fox. "Old Testament Notes: I. The Interpretation of Isaiah I 18." *JTS* 11 (1910) 433-47.

Cadoux, A. T. *The Parables of Jesus: Their Art and Use.* London: James Clarke, 1930.

Caird, G. B. *A Commentary on the Revelation of St. John the Divine.* New York: Harper & Row, 1966.

Campbell, J. C. "God's People and the Remnant." *SJT* 3 (1950) 78-85.

Cannawurf, E. "The Authenticity of Micah IV 1-4." *VT* 13 (1963) 26-33.

Cannon, W. "The Disarmament Passage in Isaiah II and Micah IV." *Theology* 24 (1932) 2-8.

Carlston, Charles E. "Changing Fashions in Interpreting the Parables." *ANQ* 14 (1974) 227-33.

Carniti, C. "L'espressione 'Il Giorno di JHWH': Origine ed Evoluzione Semantic." *BeO* 12 (1970) 11-25.

Carr, David. "Reaching for Unity in Isaiah." *JSOT* 57 (1993) 61-80.

———. "Reading Isaiah from Beginning (Isaiah 1) to End (Isaiah 65-66). Multiple Modern Possibilities." In *New Visions of Isaiah*, edited by R. F. Melugin and M. A. Sweeney, 188-218. JSOTSup 214. Sheffield: Sheffield Academic, 1996.

Carroll, Robert P. *Jeremiah: A Commentary.* OTL. Philadelphia: Westminster, 1986.

Castellino, G. R. "Observations on the Literary Structure of Some Passages in Jeremiah." *VT* 30 (1980) 398-408.

Cathcart, Kevin J. "Day of Yahweh." In *Anchor Bible Dictionary*, edited by D. N. Freedman, 2:84-85. New York: Doubleday, 1992.

Cazelles, Henri. "Histoire et géographie en Michée IV 6-13." In *Fourth World Congress of Jewish Studies, Papers*, edited by Shaul Shaked, 1:87-89. Jerusalem: World Union of Jewish Studies, 1967.

Cecily, Mary. "The Concept of Sin and Holiness in the Book of Emmanuel (Is. 1-12)." *Scr* 18 (1966) 112-16.

Černý, Ladislav. *The Day of Yahweh and Some Relevant Problems.* Prace z Vedeckyon Ustavu LIII. V Prace: Nakladem Filosoficke Fakulty University Karlovy, 1948.

Cersoy, P. "L'Apologue de la Vigne: Au Chapitre Ve d'Isaie (versets 1-7)." *RB* 8 (1899) 40-49.

Charles, R. H. *A Critical and Exegetical Commentary on the Revelation of St. John* 1. ICC. New York: Scribner, 1920.

Cheyne, Thomas Kelly. *The Book of the Prophet Isaiah*. SBOT 10. New York: Dodd, Mead, 1898.

———. *The Book of Psalms, or the Praises of Israel*. London: Kegan Paul, 1888.

———. *Critica Biblica, or Critical Notes on the Text of the Old Testament Writings—Part I. Isaiah and Jeremiah*. London: A. & C. Black, 1904.

———. "Gleanings in Biblical Criticism and Geography." *JQR* 11 (1898) 565–83.

———. *Micah*. Cambridge Bible for Schools and Colleges. Cambridge: Cambridge University Press, 1921.

———. "Micah (Book)." In *Encyclopedia Biblica*, vol. 3, cols. 3072–73. New York: Macmillan, 1902.

———. *The Prophecies of Isaiah*. 2 vols. 3rd ed. rev. New York: Whittaker, 1884.

———. *The Two Religions of Israel: with Re-Examination of the Prophetic Narratives and Utterances*. London: A. & C. Clark, 1911.

Childs, Brevard S. *Introduction to the Old Testament as Scripture*. Philadelphia: Fortress, 1979.

———. *Isaiah and the Assyrian Crisis*. SBT 2/3. London: SCM, 1967.

———. *The Struggle to Understand Isaiah as Christian Scripture*. Grand Rapids: Eerdmans, 2004.

Chilton, Bruce D. "Shebna, Eliakim, and the Promise to Peter." In *The Social World of Formative Christianity and Judaism: Essays in Tribute to Howard Clark Kee*, edited by Jacob Neusner et al., 311–26. Philadelphia: Fortress, 1988.

Claassen, W. T. "Linguistic Arguments and the Dating of Isaiah 1 4–9." *JNSL* 3 (1974) 1–18.

Clamer, A. "Michée." In *Dictionnaire de Théologie Catholique*, edited by E. Mangenot, 10:1653–55. Paris: Letouzey et Ané, 1929.

Clarke, W. K. Lowther. *Concise Bible Commentary*. New York: Macmillan, 1953.

Clements, Ronald E. "'Arise, Shine; for Your Light Has Come': A Basic Theme of the Isaianic Tradition." In *Writing and Reading the Scroll of Isaiah: Studies of an Interpretive Tradition*, edited by C. C. Broyles and C. A. Evans, 441–54. VTSup 70/1. Leiden: Brill, 1997.

———. "Beyond Tradition-History: Deutero-Isaianic Development of First Isaiah's Themes." *JSOT* 31 (1985) 95–113.

———. *Isaiah 1–39*. NCB. London: Marshall, Morgan & Scott, 1980.

———. "Patterns in the Prophetic Canon: Healing the Blind and the Lame." In *Canon, Theology, and Old Testament Interpretation*, edited by G. M. Tucker et al., 189–200. Philadelphia: Fortress, 1988.

———. "The Prophecies of Isaiah to Hezekiah concerning Sennacherib: 2 Kings 19.21–34 // Isa 37.22–35." In *Prophetie und geschichtliche Wirklichkeit im alten Israel: Festschrift für Siegfried Herrmann zum 65. Geburtstag*, edited by R. Liwak and S. Wagner, 65–78. Stuttgart: Kohlhammer, 1991.

———. "The Prophecies of Isaiah and the Fall of Jerusalem in 587 B.C." *VT* 30 (1980) 421–36.

———. "The Unity of the Book of Isaiah." *Int* 36 (1982) 117–29.

———. "'Who Is Blind but My Servant?' (Isaiah 42:19) How Then Shall We Read Isaiah?" In *God in the Fray: A Tribute to Walter Brueggemann*, edited by T. Linafelt and T. K. Beal, 143–56. Minneapolis: Fortress, 1998.

Collins, Adela Yarbro. "The Apocalypse (Revelation)." In *The New Jerome Biblical Commentary*, edited by R. E. Brown et al., 99-111. Englewood Cliffs, NJ: Prentice-Hall, 1990.

Collins, Raymond F. "Binding and Loosing." In *Anchor Bible Dictionary*, edited by D. N. Freedman, 1:743-45. New York: Doubleday, 1992.

Condamin, A. "Les Chapitres I et II du Livre d'Isaie." *RB* 13 (1904) 10-14.

———. *Le Livre d'Isaie*. EBib. Paris: Lecoffre, 1905.

Conrad, Edgar W. "The Community as King in Second Isaiah." In *Understanding the Word: Essays in Honor of Bernhard W. Anderson*, edited by J. T. Butler et al., 99-111. JSOTSup 37. Sheffield: JSOT, 1985.

———. *Reading Isaiah*. OBT. Minneapolis: Fortress, 1991.

———. "The Royal Narratives and the Structure of the Book of Isaiah." *JSOT* 41 (1988) 67-81.

Coppens, J. *Les douze petits prophètes: bréviaire du prophétisme*. Paris: Desclee de Brower, 1950.

Cornill, Carl H. *Das Buch Jeremia*. Leipzig: Tauchnitz, 1905.

———. *Introduction to the Canonical Books of the Old Testament*. Translated by G. H. Box. New York: Putnam's, 1907.

Couturier, Guy P. "Jeremiah." *The Jerome Biblical Commentary*. Edited by R. E. Brown et al. Englewood Cliffs, NJ: Prentice-Hall, 1968.

Cox, G. E. P. *The Gospel according to St. Matthew*. TBC. London: SCM, 1956.

Crook, Margaret B. "The Promise in Micah 5." *JBL* 70 (1951) 313-20.

Cross, Frank Moore, Jr. "The Divine Warrior in Israel's Early Cult." In *Biblical Motifs: Origins and Transformations*, edited by A. Altmann, 11-30. Cambridge: Harvard University Press, 1966.

Crossan, John Dominic. "Parable as Religious and Poetic Experience." *JR* 53 (1973) 330-58.

———. "The Parable of the Wicked Husbandmen." *JBL* 90 (1971) 451-65.

Cullmann, Oscar. *Peter: Disciple, Apostle, Martyr*. 2nd ed. Translated by Floyd V. Filson. Library of History and Doctrine. Philadelphia: Westminster, 1962.

Culver, R. D. "Isaiah 1 18—Declaration, Exclamation or Interrogation." *JETS* 12 (1969) 133-41.

Cunliffe-Jones, H. *The Book of Jeremiah: Introduction and Commentary*. TBC. London: SCM, 1960.

Danell, G. A. *Studies in the Name Israel in the Old Testament*. Translated by Sydney Linton. Uppsala: Appelbergs boktrykeriaktiebolag, 1946.

Davidson, A. B. *Hebrew Syntax*. 3rd ed. Edinburgh: T. & T. Clark, 1901.

Davies, Eryl W. *Prophecy and Ethics: Isaiah and the Ethical Traditions of Israel*. JSOTSup 16. Sheffield: JSOT, 1981.

Davis, M. S. "An Investigation of the Concept of the Repentance of God in the Old Testament." ThD diss., New Orleans Baptist Theological Seminary, 1983.

Deden, D. *De Kleine Profeten*. Roermond: Romen & Zonen, 1953.

Deissler, Alfons. "Die Völkerwallfahrt zum Zion: Meditation über Jes 2,2-4." *BibLeb* 11 (1970) 295-99.

———. *Les Petits Prophètes 2*. La Sainte Bible 8/2. Paris: Letouzey et Ané, 1964.

———. "Micha 6, 1-8: Der Rechtsstreit Jahwes mit Israel um das rechte Bundesverhältnis." *TTZ* 68 (1959) 229-34.

Deissler, Alfons, and M. Delcor. *Les Petits Prophètes 1*. La Sainte Bible 8/1. Paris: Letouzey et Ané, 1961.

Deist, F. E. "Notes on the Structure of Isa. 2:2-22." *ThEv* 10 (1977) 1-6.

———. "Parallels and Reinterpretation in the Book of Joel: A Theology of the Yom Yahweh?" In *Text and Context. Old Testament and Semitic Studies for F. C. Fensham*, edited by Walter Claassen, 63-79. JSOTSup 48. Sheffield: JSOT, 1988.

Delcor, M. "Sion, centre universel: Is 2,1-5." In *Études Bibliques et orientales de Religions compares*, 92-97. Leiden: Brill, 1979.

Derrett, J. D. M. "Binding Loosing (Matt 16:19; and 18:18; John 20:23)." *JBL* 102 (1983) 172-77.

Descamps, A. "Pour un classement littéraire des Psaumes." In *Melanges Bibliques rédigés en l'honneur de André Robert*, 187-96. Travaux de l'Institut Catholique de Paris 4. Paris: Bloud et Gay, 1958.

Devescovi, U. "Camminare sulle alture." *Rivista Biblica* 9 (1961) 235-42.

Dietrich, Walter, and Milton Schwantes, eds. *Der Tag wird kommen. Ein interkontextuelles Gesprach über das Buch des Propheten Zefanja*. SBS 170. Stuttgart: Katholisches Bibelwerk, 1996.

Dillmann, A. *Der Prophet Jesaja*. 6th ed. Edited by Rudolf Kittel. KHAT 5. Leipzig: Hirzel, 1898.

Dodd, C. H. *According to the Scripture: The Substructure of New Testament Theology*. New York: Scribner, 1953.

Donat, H. "Mich. 2:6-9." *BZ* 9 (1911) 350-66.

Donner, Herbert. *Israel unter den Völkern: Die Stellung der klassischen Propheten des Jahrhunderts v. Chr. Zur Aussenpolitik der Könige von Israel und Juda*. VTSup 11. Leiden: Brill, 1964.

Dozeman, Thomas B. "Inner-Biblical Interpretation of Yahweh's Gracious and Compassionate Character." *JBL* 108 (1989) 207-23.

Dreyfus, F. "La Doctrine du Reste d'Israël chez le Prophète Isaïe." *RSPT* 39 (1955) 361-86.

Driver, G. R. "Isaiah I-XXXIX: Textual and Linguistic Problems." *JSS* 13 (1968) 36-57.

———. "Linguistic and Textual Problems: Minor Prophets II." *JTS* 39 (1938) 206-73.

Driver, Samuel Rolles. "Notes on Difficult Texts." *The Expositor* 3rd ser. 5 (1887) 259-69.

———. *Notes on the Hebrew Text of the Books of Samuel*. 1913. Reprinted, Eugene, OR: Wipf & Stock, 2004.

Duhm, Bernhard. "Anmerkungen zu den Zwölf Propheten, III. Buch Micha." *ZAW* 31 (1911) 81-110.

———. *Das Buch Jesaia übersetzt und erklärt*. 5th ed. HKAT. Göttingen: Vandenhoeck & Ruprecht, 1968.

———. *Die Psalmen*. KHC 14. Tübingen: Mohr/Siebeck, 1899.

———. *Die Zwölf Propheten in den Versmaßen der Urschrift übersetzt*. Tübingen: Mohr/Siebeck, 1910. [English translation: *The Twelve Prophets: A Version in the Various Poetical Measures of the Original Writings*. Translated by Archibald Duff. London: A. & C. Black, 1912.]

Dus, J. "Weiteres zum nordisraelitischen Psalm Micha 7, 7-20." *ZDMG* 115 (1965) 14-22.

Ebeling, E. "Fabel." In *Religion in Geschichte und Gegenwart*, edited by Hermann Gunkel and Leopold Zscharnack, 2:489-90. 2nd ed. Tübingen: Mohr/Siebeck, 1929.

Ehrlich, A. B. *Jesaia, Jeremia.* Randglossen zur hebräischen Bibel 4. Leipzig: Hinrichs, 1912.

Eichhorn, Johann G. *Einleitung in das Alte Testament.* Vol. 3. 3rd ed. Leipzig: Weidmann, 1803.

Eichrodt, Walter. *Der Heilige in Israel Jesaja 1–12.* BAT 17/1. Stuttgart: Calwer, 1960.

———. *Theology of the Old Testament.* 2 vols. Translated by J. A. Baker. OTL. Philadelphia: Westminster, 1967.

Eiselen, Frederick Carl. *Prophecy and the Prophets in Their Historical Relations.* New York: Eaton & Mains, 1909.

———. *The Prophetic Books of the Old Testament: Their Origin, Contents, and Significance.* Vol. 2. New York: Methodist Book Concern, 1923.

Eissfeldt, Otto. "Ein Psalm aus Nord-Israel, Micha 7, 7–20." *ZDMG* 112 (1962) 259–68.

———. *The Old Testament: An Introduction.* New York: Harper, 1965.

———. "Zur Überlieferungsgeschichte der Prophetenbücher des Alten Testaments." *TLZ* 72 (1948) cols. 529–34.

Eitan, I. "A Contribution to Isaiah Exegesis." *HUCA* 12/13 (1937–1938) 55–88.

Elhorst, Hendrik Jan. *De Prophetie van Micha.* Arnhem: K. van der Zande, 1891.

Elliger, Karl. "Die Heimat des Propheten Micha." *ZDPV* 57 (1934) 81–152.

Emerton, J. A. "Binding and Loosing—Forgiving and Retaining." *JTS* 13 (1962) 325–31.

Emmerson, Grace I. *Hosea: An Israelite Prophet in Judean Perspective.* JSOTSup 28. Sheffield: JSOT, 1984.

Engdahl, Elisabet. "Jesu liknelser som språkhandelser." *SEÅ* 39 (1974) 90–108.

Engnell, Ivan. "Fabel." In *Svenskt Bibliskt Uppslagsverk,* vol. 1, column 59. Stockholm: Nordiska Uppslagsböcker, 1962.

———. "Liknelser." In *Svenskt Bibliskt Uppslagsverk,* vol. 1, columns 1495–97. Stockholm: Nordiska Uppslagsböcker, 1962.

———. "Methodological Aspects of Old Testament Study." In *Congress Volume 1959,* 13–30. VTSup 7. Leiden: Brill, 1960.

———. "Traditionshistorisk metod." In *Svenskt Bibliskt Uppslagsverk,* vol. 2, columns 1265–67. Stockholm: Nordiska Uppslagsböcker, 1963.

Everson, A. J. "The Days of Yahweh." *JBL* 93 (1974) 329–37.

Ewald, H. G. A. von. *Commentary on the Prophets of the Old Testament 2.* Translated by J. F. Smith. London: Williams and Norgate, 1876.

Falk, Z. W. "Binding and Loosing." *JJS* 25 (1974) 92–100.

Farley, W. J. *The Progress of Old Testament Prophecy in the Light of Modern Scholarship.* New York: Revell, 1925.

Farrer, A. *The Revelation of St. John the Divine.* Oxford: Clarendon, 1954.

Feldmann, F. *Das Buch Isaías übersetzt und erklärt.* EHAT 14. Münster: Aschendorff, 1925.

Fensham, F. C. "A Possible Origin of the Concept of the Day of the Lord." In *Biblical Essays 1966: Proceedings of the Ninth Meeting of "Die Ou-Testamentiese Werkgemeenskap in Suid Afrika" Held at the University of Stellenbosch 26th–29th July 1966,* 90–97. Pretoria: Pro Rege-Pers, 1966.

Fenton, T. L. "Ugaritica-Biblica." *UF* 1 (1969) 65–70.

Fey, R. *Amos und Jesaja.* WMANT 12. Neukirchen-Vluyn: Neukirchener, 1963.

Fichtner, J. *Obadja, Jona, Micha.* Stuttgart: Stuttgarter Bibelhefte, 1957.

Fiddes, Paul S. *The Creative Suffering of God.* Oxford: Clarendon, 1992.

Filson, Floyd V. *A Commentary on the Gospel according to St Matthew.* London: A. & C. Black, 1960.

Findlay, G. G. *The Books of the Prophets in Their Historical Succession, I.* London: C. H. Kelly, 1900.
Fischer, J. *Das Buch Isaias übersetzt und erklärt I.* HSAT 7/1. Bonn: Peter Hanstein, 1937.
Fitch, W. *Isaiah.* NCB. Grand Rapids: Eerdmans, 1953.
Fohrer, Georg. *Das Buch Jesaja I.* 1st ed. ZBK. Zürich: Zwingli, 1960; 2nd ed, 1966.
―――. "Fabel." In *Religion in Geschichte und Gegenwart 2,* edited by Kurt Galling et al., columns 853-54. 3rd ed. Tübingen: J. C. B. Mohr, 1958.
―――. *Introduction to the Old Testament.* Nashville: Abingdon, 1968.
―――. "Jesaja 1 als Zusammenfassung der Verkündigung Jesajas." *ZAW* 74 (1962) 251-68.
―――. "Micha." In *Evangelisches Kirchenlexikon 2,* edited by Heinz Brunotte and Otto Weber, columns 1327-28. Göttingen: Vandenhoeck & Ruprecht, 1956.
―――. "Micha 1." In *Das Ferne und Nahe Wort: Festschrift Leonhard Rost,* edited by Fritz Maass, 65-80. BZAW 105. Berlin: de Gruyter, 1967.
―――. *Die Propheten des Alten Testaments. Band I. Die Propheten des 8. Jahrhunderts.* Gütersloh: Gerd Mohn, 1974.
―――. "Der Tag JHWHs." *EI* 16 (1982) 43-50.
Ford, J. M. *Revelation.* AB 38. Garden City: Doubleday, 1975.
Fox, Michael. "The Identification of Quotations in Biblical Literature." *ZAW* 92 (1980) 416-31.
Fretheim, Terence E. "Divine Foreknowledge, Divine Constancy, and the Rejection of Saul's Kingship." *CBQ* 47 (1985) 595-602.
―――. "The Repentance of God: A Key to Evaluating Old Testament God-Talk." *HBT* 10 (1988) 47-70.
―――. "The Repentance of God: A Study of Jeremiah 18:7-10." *HAR* 11 (1987) 81-92.
―――. *The Suffering of God: An Old Testament Perspective.* OBT. Philadelphia: Fortress, 1984.
Frey, H. *Handkommentar zum Buch Jesaja Der Zusammenstoss des heiligen Gottes mit der Vermessenheit seiner Gemeinde (Jesaja Kapitel 1-5).* Bad Liebenzell: Liebenzeller Mission, 1975.
Fuchs, E. "What Is Interpreted in the Exegesis of the New Testament?" In *Studies of the Historical Jesus,* 84-103. SBT 1/42. London: SCM, 1964.
Fullerton, K. "A New Chapter out of the Life of Isaiah." *AJT* 9 (1905) 621-42.
―――. "The Rhythmical Analysis of Is 1 10-20." *JBL* 38 (1919) 53-63.
―――. "Shebna and Eliakim: A Reply." *AJT* 11 (1907) 675-86.
―――. "Studies in Isaiah." *JBL* 35 (1916) 134-42.
Funk, Robert W. "Beyond Criticism in Quest of Literacy: The Parable of the Leaven." *Int* 25 (1971) 149-70.
―――. *Language, Hermeneutic, and Word of God: The Problem of Language in the New Testament and Contemporary Theology.* New York: Harper, 1966.
Gadegård, N. H. "Fabel." In *Gads Danske Bibel Leksikon,* edited by Eduard Nielsen and Bent Noack, vol. 1, column 485. Copenhagen: Gad, 1965.
Gailey, J. H. "Micah . . . Malachi." *The Layman's Bible Commentary* 15. Richmond, VA: John Knox, 1962.
Gall, A. von. "Jeremia 43,12 und das Zeitwort עטה." *ZAW* 24 (1904) 105-21.
Galling, Kurt. *Biblisches Reallexikon.* HAT. Tübingen: Mohr, 1937.
Galling, Kurt, et al., eds. *Die Religion in Geschichte und Gegenwart.* 6 vols. 3rd ed. Tübingen: Mohr/Siebeck, 1957-62.

Gaster, Theodor H. "Notes on the Minor Prophets." *JTS* 38 (1937) 163–65.
Gates, O. H. "Notes on Isaiah 1:18b and 7:14b–16." *AJSL* 17 (1900–1901) 16–21.
Gautier, L. *Introduction à l'Ancien Testament 1*. 3rd ed. Lausanne: Payot, 1939.
Geffcken, Johannes. "Allegory, Allegorical Interpretation." In *Encyclopaedia of Religion and Ethics*, edited by James Hastings, 1:327–31. New York: Scribner, 1908.
Gemser, B. "The Rîb- or Controversy-Pattern in Hebrew Mentality." In *Wisdom in Israel and in the Ancient Near East*, 120–37. VTSup 3. Leiden: Brill, 1955.
George, Augustin. "Michée (Le Livre de)." *Dictionnaire de la Bible: Supplément* 5. Edited by L. Pirot and A. Robert. Paris: Letouzey et Ané, 1952.
———. *La Sainte Bible*. Paris: Cerf, 1958.
Gerhardsson, B. "Allegori, allegorisk utlaggning." In *Svenskt Bibliskt Uppslagsverk*, 1:46–47. Stockholm: Nordiska Uppslagsböcker, 1962.
Gesenius, Wilhelm. *Philologisch-kritischer und historischer Commentar über den Jesaia*. Vol. 1. Leipzig: Vogel, 1821.
Giesebrecht, F. *Das Buch Jeremia übersetzt und erklärt*. HKAT 3/2. 2nd ed. Göttingen: Vandenhoeck & Ruprecht, 1907.
———. Review of B. Stade's "Bemerkungen über das Buch Micha in *ZAW*." *TLZ* 6 (1881) 444.
Gilbert, M., and S. Pisano. "Psalm 110 (109), 5–7." *Bib* 61 (1980) 343–56.
Ginsberg, H. L. "Some Emendations in Isaiah." *JBL* 69 (1950) 51–60.
———. "A Ugaritic Parallel to 2 Sam 1:21." *JBL* 57 (1938) 209–13.
Glück, J. J. "Nagid-Shepherd." *VT* 13 (1963) 144–50.
Goeje, Michael Jan de. "Ter verklaring vau Micha III–V. Proeve van verklaring van Micha IV:1–V:2." *ThT* 6 (1872) 279–84.
Good, Edwin M. *Irony in the Old Testament*. 2nd ed. Bible and Literature Series 3. Sheffield: Almond, 1981.
———. "Love in the OT." In *The Interpreter's Dictionary of the Bible*, edited by G. A. Buttrick, 3:164–68. Nashville: Abingdon, 1962.
Gordis, Robert. *The Book of Job: Commentary, New Translation and Special Studies*. New York: The Jewish Theological Seminary of America, 1978.
———. *Koheleth—The Man and His World: A Study of Ecclesiastes*. 3rd ed. New York: Schocken, 1968.
———. "Micah's Vision of the End-Time." In *Poets, Prophets, and Sages: Essays in Biblical Interpretation*, 268–79. Bloomington: Indiana University Press, 1971.
———. "Quotations as a Literary Usage in Biblical, Rabbinic and Oriental Literature." *HUCA* 22 (1949) 157–219.
———. "Quotations in Wisdom Literature." *JQR* n.s. 30 (1939) 123–47.
———. "The Use of Quotations in Job." In *The Book of God and Man—A Study of Job*, 174–87. Chicago: University of Chicago Press, 1965.
———. "Virtual Quotations in Job, Sumer and Qumran." *FT* 31 (1981) 410–27.
Goslinga, C. J. *De Boeken van Samuel*. KVHS. Kampen: Kok, 1948.
Gottlieb, H. "Den taerskende Kvie, Mi. 4:11–13 (Die dreschende Färse - ugar. Material)." *DTT* 26 (1963) 167–71.
Gottwald, Norman K. *A Light to the Nations: An Introduction to the Old Testament*. New York: Harper, 1959.
Goulder, M. D. *The Psalms of the Sons of Korah*. JSOTSup 20. Sheffield: JSOT, 1982.
Gowan, Donald W. *When Man Becomes God: Humanism and Hubris in the Old Testament*. PTMS 6. Pittsburgh: Pickwick, 1975.

Graham, W. C. "Notes on the Interpretation of Isaiah 5:1–12." *AJSL* 25 (1928–29) 167–69.

———. "Some Suggestions toward the Interpretation of Micah 1:10–16." *AJSL* 27 (1931) 237–58.

Gray, George Buchanan. *A Critical and Exegetical Commentary on the Book of Isaiah I–XXXIX* I. *Isaiah I–XXVII*. ICC. Edinburgh: T. & T. Clark, 1912.

———. "Micah, Book of." In *Dictionary of the Bible*, edited by James Hastings, 1:614–15. New York: Scribner, 1909.

Gray, John. "The Day of Yahweh in Cultic Experience and Eschatological Prospect." *SEÅ* 39 (1974) 5–37.

Greenberg, Moshe. *Ezekiel 21–37*. AB 22A. New York: Doubleday, 1997.

Gressmann, Hugo. *Der Ursprung der israelitisch-jüdischen Eschatologie*. FRLANT 6. Göttingen: Vandenhoeck & Ruprecht, 1905.

Groot, Johannes de. *1 Samuel*. TeU. Groningen: Wolters, 1934.

Gross, Karl. "Hoseas Einfluss auf Jeremías Anschauung." *NKZ* 42 (1931) 241–56, 327–43.

Gunkel, Hermann. "Allegorie im A. T. und Judentum." In *Religion in Geschichte und Gegenwart*, edited by Kurt Galling, 1:354–55. 2nd ed. Tübingen: Mohr/Siebeck, 1909.

———. "Fabel." In *Religion in Geschichte und Gegenwart*, edited by Hermann Gunkel and Leopold Zscharnack, 2:490–91. Tübingen: Mohr/Siebeck, 1929.

———. *Das Märchen im Alten Testament*. Religionsgeschichtliche Volksbücher für die deutsche christliche Gegenwart. Tübingen: Mohr/Siebeck, 1917. [English translation: *The Folktale in the Old Testament*. Translated by Michael D. Rutter. Historic Texts and Interpreters in Biblical Scholarship. Sheffield: Almond, 1987.]

———. "Die Propheten als Schriftsteller und Dichter." In *Die Schriften des Alten Testaments*, edited by Hans Schmidt 2:36–72. Göttingen: Vandenhoeck & Ruprecht, 1915.

Gunkel, Hermann, and Leopold Zscharnack, eds. *Die Religion in Geschichte und Gegenwart*. 6 vols. 2nd ed. Tübingen: Mohr/Siebeck, 1927–31.

Gutbrod, K. *Das Buch vom König. Das erste Buch Samuel*. 3rd ed. BAT 11. Stuttgart: Calwer, 1970.

Guthe, Hermann. *Das Buch Jesaja (1–35)*. HSAT. Bonn: Hanstein, 1922.

Haag, E. "Der Tag Jahwes im Alten Testament." *BibLeb* 13 (1972) 238–48.

Haag, H. "La campagne de Sennacherib contre Jerusalem en 701." *RB* 58 (1951) 348–359.

Habermann, A. M. *Megillot Midbar Yehuda*. Tel Aviv: Machbarot Lesifrut, 1959.

Hagstrom, David G. *The Coherence of the Book of Micah: A Literary Analysis*. SBLDS 89. Decatur, GA: Scholars, 1988.

Hahn, Herbert F. *The Old Testament in Modern Research*. Philadelphia: Muhlenburg, 1954.

Halévy, J. "Le Livre de Michée." *RSém* 12 (1904) 97–117, 193–216, 289–312; *RSém* 13 (1905) 1–22.

Hall, Gary Harlan. "The Marriage Imagery of Jeremiah 2–3: A Study of Antecedents and Innovations in a Prophetic Metaphor." PhD diss., Union Theological Seminary, 1980.

Haller, Max. "Micha und Michabuch." In *Religion in Geschichte und Gegenwart*, edited by Hermann Gunkel and Leopold Zscharnack, vol. 4, columns 1–2. 2nd ed. Tübingen: Mohr/Siebeck, 1930.

Hamlin, E. J. "Nations." In *The Interpreter's Dictionary of the Bible*, edited by G. A. Buttrick, 3:517–22. Nashville: Abingdon, 1962.

Hammershaimb, E. "Einige Hauptgedanken in der Schrift des Propheten Micha." *ST* 15 (1961) 11–34. [English translation: "Some Leading Ideas in the Book of Micah." In *Some Aspects of Old Testament Prophecy from Isaiah to Malachi*, 29–50. Kopenhagen: Rosenkilde og Bagger, 1966.]

Harper, W. R. *Amos and Hosea*. ICC. New York: Scribner, 1905.

Harrelson, Walter J. *Interpreting the Old Testament*. New York: Holt, Rinehart & Winston, 1964.

———. "Non-Royal Motifs in the Prophetic Eschatology." In *Israel's Prophetic Heritage: Essays in Honor of James Muilenberg*, edited by B. W. Anderson and W. Harrelson, 147–65. New York: Harper & Row, 1962.

Harrison, Roland K. *Jeremiah and Lamentations: An Introduction and Commentary*. TOTC. Downers Grove, IL.: InterVarsity, 1975.

Harvey, J. "Le 'Rîb-Pattern,' réquisitoire prophétique sur la Rupture de l'Alliance." *Bib* 23 (1962) 172–96.

Hasel, Gerhard F. *Old Testament Theology: Basic Issues in the Current Debate*. 4th ed. Grand Rapids: Eerdmans, 1991.

———. *The Remnant: The History and Theology of the Remnant Idea from Genesis to Isaiah*. Andrews University Monographs 5. Berrien Springs, MI: Andrews University Press, 1972.

Hauck, F. "παραβολή." In *Theological Dictionary of the New Testament*, 5:744–61. Edited by G. Kittel and G. Friedrich. Translated by G. W. Bromiley. Grand Rapids: Eerdmans, 1967.

Haupt, Paul. "The Book of Micah." *AJSL* 26 (1909) 201–52; 27 (1910) 1–62.

———. "Micha's Capucinade." *JBL* 29 (1910) 85–112.

Hayes, John H. "The Tradition of Zion's Inviolability." *JBL* 82 (1963) 419–26.

Hayes, John H., and Stuart A. Irvine. *Isaiah the Eighth-Century Prophet: His Times and His Preaching*. Nashville: Abingdon, 1987.

Heaton, E. W. "The Root *sh'r* and the Doctrine of the Remnant." *JTS* n.s. 3 (1952) 27–39.

Heintz, J.-G. "Aux Origenes d'use Expression Biblique: ūmūšu qerbū, in A.R.M. X/6, 8?" *VT* 21 (1971) 528–40.

Helewa, F. J. "L'origine du concept prophétique du 'Jour de Yahvé.'" *Ephemerides Carmeliticae* 15 (1964) 3–36.

Hempel, J. "Jahwegleichnisse der israelitischen Propheten." *ZAW* 42 (1924) 74–104.

———. "Psalms, Book of." In *The Interpreter's Dictionary of the Bible*, edited by G. A. Buttrick, 3:942–58 Nashville: Abingdon, 1962.

Henshaw, R. A. "The Office of *Saknu* in Neo-Assyrian Times." *JAOS* 87 (1967) 517–25; *JAOS* 88 (1968) 461–83.

Herbert, A. S. *The Book of the Prophet Isaiah: Chapters 1–39*. CBC. Cambridge: Cambridge University Press, 1973.

Hertzberg, Hans Wilhelm. *Der Erste Jesaja übersetzt und ausgelegt Bibelhilfe für die Gemeinde*. Bibelhilfe für die Gemeinde. 2nd ed. Kassel: Oncken, 1952.

Hesse, Franz. "Würzelt die prophetische Gerichtsrede im israelitischen Kult?" *ZAW* 65 (1953) 45–53.

Hiebert, Theodore. "Theophany in the OT." In *Anchor Bible Dictionary*, edited by D. N. Freedman, 6:505–11. New York: Doubleday, 1992.

Hiers, Richard H. "'Binding' and 'Loosing': The Matthean Authorizations." *JBL* 104 (1985) 233–50.

———. "Day of the Lord." In *Anchor Bible Dictionary*, edited by D. N. Freedman, 2:82–83. New York: Doubleday, 1992.

Hill, David. *The Gospel of Matthew*. NCB. Grand Rapids: Eerdmans, 1981.
Hillers, Delbert R. *Covenant: The History of a Biblical Idea*. Seminars in the History of Ideas. Baltimore: Johns Hopkins University Press, 1969.
Hoffmann, Yair. "The Day of the Lord as a Concept and a Term in the Prophetic Literature." *ZAW* 93 (1981) 37–50.
Holladay, William L. *The Architecture of Jeremiah 1–20*. Lewisburg, PA: Bucknell University, 1976.
———. *A Concise Hebrew and Aramaic Lexicon of the Old Testament*. Leiden: Brill, 1971.
———. *Isaiah: Scroll of a Prophetic Heritage*. Grand Rapids: Eerdmans, 1978.
———. *Jeremiah 1*. Hermeneia. Philadelphia: Fortress, 1986.
———. *Jeremiah 2*. Hermeneia. Minneapolis: Fortress, 1989.
Hölscher, Gustav. *Die Profeten: Untersuchungen zur Religionsgeschichte Israels*. Leipzig: J. C. Hinrichs, 1914.
Honor, Leo L. *Sennacherib's Invasion of Palestine*. New York: Columbia University Press, 1926.
Hoonacker, Albin van. *Les Douze Petits Prophètes*. Paris: Gabalda, 1908.
———. "Micheas." In *The Catholic Encyclopedia*, 10:277–78. New York: Appleton, 1911.
Horton, Robert F. *The Minor Prophets*. The Century Bible. Edinburgh: T. C. & E. C. Jack, 1905.
Horwitz, William J. "Audience Reaction to Jeremiah." *CBQ* 32 (1970) 555–64.
Huddle, A. "Isaiah ii. 2–4." *ExpTim* 3 (1892) 272–73.
Huffmon, Herbert B. "The Covenant Lawsuit in the Prophets." *JBL* 78 (1959) 285–95.
———. "The Treaty Background of Hebrew *Yada'*." *BASOR* 181 (February 1966) 31–37.
Hyatt, James Philip. "The Book of Jeremiah: Introduction and Exegesis." In *The Interpreter's Bible*, edited by G. A. Buttrick, 5:776–1142. Nashville: Abingdon, 1956.
———. "On the Meaning and Origin of Micah 6:8." *ATR* 34 (1952) 232–39.
Hylmö, Gunnar. *Kompositionen av Mikas Bok*. Lund: Gleerup, 1919.
Jacob, E. *Theology of the Old Testament*. Translated by A. W. Heathcote and P. J. Allcock. New York: Harper, 1958.
Jacob, E., C.-A. Keller, and Samuel Amsler. *Osée, Joël, Amos, Abdias, Jonas*. CAT 11A. Neuchatel, Switzerland: Éditions Delachaux & Niestlé, 1965.
Jacobs, J. "Fable." In *Encyclopaedia of Religion and Ethics*, edited by James Hastings, 5:676. New York: Scribner, 1920.
Jacobs, Mignon R. *The Conceptual Coherence of the Book of Micah*. JSOTSup 322. Sheffield: Sheffield Academic, 2001.
Jenni, Ernst. "יוֹם *jōm* Tag." *Theologisches Handwörterbuch zum Alten Testament* 1. Edited by E. Jenni, with assistance from C. Westermann. 2 vols. Stuttgart: Chr. Kaiser, 1971.
Jenson, Philip Peter. *Obadiah, Jonah, Micah: A Theological Commentary*. Library of Hebrew Bible/Old Testament Studies 496. London: T. & T. Clark, 2008.
Jeremias, Joachim. *The Parables of Jesus*. Translated by S. H. Hooke. London: SCM, 1954.
Jeremias, Jörg. "Lade und Zion: Zur Entstehung der Ziontradition." In *Probleme biblischer Theologie. Gerhard von Rad zum 70. Geburtstag*, edited by H. W. Wolff, 183–98. Munich: Kaiser, 1971.
———. *Die Reue Gottes. Aspekte alttestamentlicher Gottesvorstellung*. BibS(N) 65. Neukirchen-Vluyn: Neukirchener, 1975.

Johnson, A. R. "The Role of the King in the Jerusalem Cult." In *The Labyrinth*, edited by S. H. Hooke, 71–111. London: Macmillan, 1935.

———. *Sacral Kingship in Ancient Israel*. Cardiff: University of Wales Press, 1955.

Johnson, S. E. "The Gospel according to St Matthew: Introduction and Exegesis." *The Interpreter's Bible* 7. Nashville: Abingdon-Cokesbury, 1951.

Jones, D. R. "Exposition of Isaiah Chapter One Verses One to Nine." *SJT* 17 (1964) 463–77.

———. "Exposition of Isaiah Chapter One Verses Ten to Seventeen." *SJT* 18 (1965) 457–71.

———. "Exposition of Isaiah Chapter One Verses Eighteen to Twenty." *SJT* 19 (1966) 319–27.

———. "Exposition of Isaiah Chapter One Verses Twenty One to the End." *SJT* 21 (1968) 320–29.

Joüon, Paul. *Grammaire de l'hébreu biblique*. 2nd ed. Rome: Pontifical Biblical Institute, 1947.

Junker, H. "Die Literarische Art von Is 5,1–7." *Bib* 40 (1959) 259–66.

———. "Sancta Civitas, Jerusalem Nova: Eine formkritische und überlieferungsgeschichtliche Studie zu Is 2." In *Ekklesia: Festschrift für Matthias Wehr*, 29–35. TThST 15. Trier: Paulinus, 1962.

Kahle, Paul, ed. *Biblia Hebraica 3*. Stuttgart: Württemberg Bibelanstalt, 1937.

Kaiser, Otto. *Der Prophet Jesaja Kapital 1–12*. ATD 17. Göttingen: Vandenhoeck & Ruprecht, 1963. [English Translation: *Isaiah 1–12*. Translated by John Bowden. OTL. London: SCM, 1972; 2nd ed. Philadelphia: Westminster, 1983.]

Kamphausen, A. "Isaiah's Prophecy concerning the Major-Domo of King Hezekiah." *AJT* 5 (1901) 43–74.

Kapelrud, A. S. "Eschatology in the Book of Micah." *VT* 11 (1961) 392–405.

———. "Mikas bok." In *Svenskt Bibliskt Uppsalagsverk*, 2:105–7. 2nd ed. Stockholm: Nordiska Uppslagsböcker, 1963.

Kee, Howard Clark. "The Gospel according to Matthew." In *The Interpreter's One-Volume Commentary on the Bible*, edited by C. M. Laymon. London: Collins, 1971.

Kelley, P. H. "Isaiah." The Broadman Bible Commentary 5. Nashville: Broadman, 1971.

Kelly, Brian. "Aquinas on Redemption and Change in God." *ITQ* 58 (1992) 249–63.

Kent, Charles Foster. *The Kings and Prophets of Israel and Judah*. Historical Bible. New York: Scribner, 1909.

Kesich, V. "Peter's Primacy in the New Testament and the Early Tradition." In *The Primacy of Peter: Essays in Ecclesiology and the Early Church*, edited by J. Meyendorff, 35–66. Crestwood, NY: St. Vladimir's Seminary, 1992.

Kessler, Martin. "From Drought to Exile: A Morphological Study of Jer 14:1–15:4." *SBLSP* 2 (1972) 519–23.

Kilpatrick, G. G. D. "The Book of Isaiah: Chapters 1–39, Exposition." In *The Interpreter's Bible*, edited by G. A. Buttrick, 5:149–381. Nashville: Abingdon, 1956.

Kissane, E. J. *The Book of Isaiah I*. Rev. ed. Dublin: Richview, 1960.

Kitchen, Kenneth A. *Ancient Orient and Old Testament*. Downers Grove, IL: InterVarsity, 1966.

Kittel, Rudolf. *Die Psalmen übersetzt und erklärt*. KAT 13. Leipzig: Deichert, 1922.

Klein, Ralph W. "The Day of the Lord." *CTQ* 39 (1968) 517–25.

———. *I Samuel*. WBC 10. Waco, TX: Word, 1983.

Kleinert, P. *The Minor Prophets*. Translated by George R. Bliss. New York: Scribner, 1874.

Koch, Klaus. *Was ist Formgeschichte?* Neukirchen-Vluyn: Neukirchener Verlag, 1964. [English translation: *The Growth of the Biblical Tradition: The Form-Critical Method*. Translated by S. M. Cupitt. New York: Scribner, 1969.]
Köhler, L. "Ein verkannter hebräischen irrealen Bedingungssatz." *ZS* 4 (1926) 196–97.
Kolmodin, A. *Profeten Mika*. Stockholm: Ev. Fosterlandsstiftelsens Förlagsexpedition, 1894.
König, E. *Einleitung in das Alte Testament*. Bonn: E. Weber, 1893.
———. "Shebna and Eliakim." *AJT* 10 (1906) 675–86.
Kosmala, H. "Form and Structure in Ancient Hebrew Poetry (Continued)." *VT* 16 (1966) 152–80.
Kosters, W. H. "De Samenstelling van het Boek Micha." *ThT* 27 (1893) 249–74.
Kraeling, Emil G. *Commentary on the Prophets, II*. Camden, NJ: Thomas Nelson, 1966.
Krasovec, J. *Der Merismus im Biblisch-Hebräischen und Nordwestsemitischen*. BibOr 33. Rome: Biblical Institute, 1977.
Kraus, Hans-Joachim. "Die prophetische Botschaft gegen das soziale Unrecht Israels." In *Biblisch-theologische Aufsätze*, 120–33. Neukirchen-Vluyn: Neukirchener, 1972.
———. *Psalms 1–59: A Commentary*. Minneapolis: Augsburg, 1988.
———. *Psalms 60–150: A Commentary*. Minneapolis: Augsburg, 1989.
———. "Zur Geschichte des Überlieferungsbegriffs in der alttestamentlichen Wissenschaft." *EvT* 16 (1956) 371–87.
Kruger, Paul A. "The Marriage Metaphor in Hosea 2:4–17 against Its Ancient Near Eastern Background." *OTE* 5 (1992) 7–25.
Kuenen, Abraham. *Historisch-Kritisch Onderzoek naar het Ontstaan en de Verzameling van de Boeken des Ouden Verbonds*. 2nd ed. Leiden: Engels, 1889.
———. "De Koning uit Beth-Ephrath." *Theologisch tijdschrift* 6 (1872) 45–66.
Kugel, James. *The Idea of Biblical Poetry: Parallelism and Its History*. New Haven: Yale University Press, 1981.
Kühl, Curt. *The Prophets of Israel*. Translated by Rudolf J. Ehrlich and J. P. Smith. Edinburgh: Oliver & Boyd, 1960.
Kutsch, Ernst. "Heuschreckenplage und Tag Jahwes in Joel 1 und 2." In *Kleine Schriften zum Alten Testament*, edited by Ludwig Schmidt and Karl Eberlein, 231–44. BZAW 168. Berlin: de Gruyter, 1986.
Kuyper, Lester J. "The Suffering and the Repentance of God." *SJT* 22 (1969) 257–77.
Ladame, F. "Les chapitres IV et V du livre de Michée." *RTP* 36 (1902) 449–60.
Laetsch, T. *The Minor Prophets*. St. Louis: Concordia, 1956.
Lambert, W. G. "The Problem of the Love Lyrics." In *Unity and Diversity*, edited by H. Goedicke and J. J. M. Roberts, 98–135. Baltimore: Johns Hopkins University Press, 1975.
Largement, R., and H. Lemaitre. "Le Jour de Yahweh dans le Contexte Oriental." In *Sacra Pagina: Miscellanea Biblica Congressus Internationalis Catholici de re Biblica*, 1:259–66. Paris: Gabalda, 1959.
Laridon, V. "Carmen Allegoricum Isaiae de Vinea." *Collationes Brugenses* 46 (1950) 3–9.
Layton, S. C. "The Steward in Ancient Israel: A Study of Hebrew (*'ašer*) *'al-habbayit* in its Near Eastern Setting." *JBL* 109 (1990) 633–49.
Leeuwen, C. van. "The Prophecy of the *Yom YHWH* in Amos V 18–20." In *Language and Meaning: Studies in Hebrew Language and Biblical Exegesis*, edited by James Barr et al., 113–34. Old Testament Studies 19. Leiden: Brill, 1974.
———. "Sancherib devant Jerusalem." *OtSt* 14 (1965) 245–72.

Lescow, Theodore. *Micha 6, 6–8: Studien zu Sprache, Form und Auslegung.* Stuttgart: Calwer, 1966.

Lesêtre, H. "Apologue." In *Dictionnaire de la Bible*, edited by F. Vigouroux, vol. 1/1, columns 778–81. Paris: Librairie Letouzey et Ané, 1926.

———. "Parabole." In *Dictionnaire de la Bible*, edited by F. Vigouroux, vol. 4/2, columns 2106–18. Paris: Librairie Letouzey et Ané, 1928.

Levenson, Jon D. "Zion Traditions." In *Anchor Bible Dictionary*, edited by D. N. Freedman 6:1098–102. New York: Doubleday, 1992.

Ley, J. "Metrische Analyse von Jesaia K I." *ZAW* 22 (1902) 229–37.

Liedke, Gerhard. "יכח hi. feststellen, was recht ist." In *Theologisches Handwörterbuch zum Alten Testament 1*, edited by E. Jenni and C. Westermann. 2 vols. Munich: Chr. Kaiser, 1971.

Limburg, James. *Jonah: A Commentary.* OTL. Louisville: Westminster John Knox, 1993.

———. "The Root *ryb* and the Prophetic Lawsuit Speeches." *JBL* 88 (1969) 291–304.

Lindars, Barnabas. *New Testament Apologetic: The Doctrinal Significance of the Old Testament Quotations.* Philadelphia: Westminster, 1961.

———. "'Rachel Weeping for Her Children'—Jeremiah 31:15–22." *JSOT* 12 (1979) 47–62.

Lindblom, J. *Micha literarisch untersucht.* Acta Academiae Aboensis. Humaniora 6:2. Åbo: Åbo Akademi, 1929.

———. *A Study on the Immanuel Section in Isaiah.* Scripta Minora Regiae Societatis Humaniorum Litterarum Lundensis 4. Lund: Gleerup, 1958.

Lipiński, E. "North Semitic Texts from the First Millennium BC." In *Near Eastern Religious Texts Relating to the Old Testament*, edited by Walter Beyerlin, 237–40. Translated by John Bowden. London: SCM, 1978.

———. "*Skn* et *Sgn* dans le sémitique occidental du nord." *UF* 5 (1973) 191–207.

Lippl, J. *Die Zwölf Kleinen Propheten.* HSAT 7/3/1. Bonn: Hanstein, 1937.

Loewenclau, Ilse von. "Zur Auslegung von Jesaia 1, 2–3." *EvT* 26 (1966) 294–308.

Lohfink, Gerhard. "'Schwerter zu Pflugscharen.' Die Rezeption von Jes 2,1–5 par Mi 4,1–5 in der Alten Kirche und im Neuen Testament." *TQ* 166 (1986) 184–209.

Long, Burke O. "Two Question and Answer Schemata in the Prophets." *JBL* 90 (1971) 129–39.

Loretz, Otto. *Der Prolog des Jesaja Buches (1,1–2,5). Ugaritologische und kolometrische Studien zum Jesaja-Buch I.* UBL 1. Altenberge: CIS, 1984.

Luckenbill, Daniel David. *The Annals of Sennacherib.* OIP 2. Chicago: University of Chicago Press, 1924. Reprinted, Ancient Texts and Translation. Eugene, OR: Wipf & Stock, 2005.

Lundbom, Jack R. *Jeremiah: A Study in Ancient Hebrew Rhetoric.* SBLDS 18. Missoula: Scholars, 1975.

Luther, Martin. "Lectures on Isaiah Chapters 1–39." In *Luther's Works*, edited by Jaroslav Pelikan. St. Louis: Concordia, 1969.

Lutz, Hanns-Martin. *Jahwe, Jerusalem und die Volker, Zur Vorgeschichte von Sach 12,1–8 und 14,1–5.* WMANT 27. Neukirchen-Vluyn: Neukirchener, 1968.

Luz, Ulrich. "The Primacy Text (Matt 16:18)." *PSB* n.s. 12 (1991) 41–55.

Lys, D. "La Vigne et le Double Je. Exercise de style sur Esaïe V 1–7." In *Studies on Prophecy*, 1–16. VTSup 26. Leiden: Brill, 1974.

MacLean, H. B. "Hezekiah." In *The Interpreter's Dictionary of the Bible*, edited by G. A. Buttrick, 2:598–600. Nashville: Abingdon, 1962.

Mangenot, E. "Allégorie, Sens Allégorique de l'Écriture." In *Dictionnaire de la Bible*, edited by F. Vigouroux, vol. 1, columns 368–69. Paris: Librairie Letouzey et Ané, 1912.

Manns, F. "La Halakah dans l'évangile de Matthieu: note sur Mt. 16:16–19." *BeO* 25 (1983) 129–35.

Mantey, J. R. "Distorted Translations in John 20:23; Matthew 16:18–19 and 18:18." *RevExp* 78 (1981) 409–16.

Marcus, J. "The Gates of Hades and the Keys of the Kingdom (Matt 16:18–19)." *CBQ* 50 (1988) 443–55.

Margolis, Max L. *Micah*. Philadelphia: Jewish Publication Society of America, 1908.

Marsh, John. *Amos and Micah*. London: SCM, 1959.

Marshall, R. J. "The Structure of Isaiah 1–12." *BR* 7 (1962) 19–32.

———. "The Unity of Isaiah 1–12." *LQ* 14 (1962) 21–38.

Marti, Karl. *Das Buch Jesaja*. KHAT 10. Tübingen: Mohr/Siebeck, 1900.

———. *Das Dodekapropheton*. Tübingen: Mohr, 1904.

Martin-Achard, R. "L'oracle contra Shebnâ et la pouvoir de clefs, Es. 22,15–25." *TZ* 24 (1968) 241–54.

Marty, J. *L'Ancien Testament. Tome II. Les Prophétes*. Paris: Rombaldi, 1947.

Mattioli, A. "Due Schemi letterari negli Oracoli d'Introduzione al Libro d'Isaia Is 1 1–31." *RivB* 14 (1966) 345–64.

Mauchline, J. *1 and 2 Samuel*. NCB. London: Oliphants, 1971.

———. *Isaiah 1–39*. TBC. 3rd ed. London: SCM, 1970.

Mayer, G. "יכה, *ykh*." *Theologisches Wörterbuch zum Alten Testament* III 4/5. Edited by G. J. Botterweck and H. Ringgren. Stuttgart: Kohlhammer, 1980.

Mays, James Luther. *Micah*. OTL. Philadelphia: Westminster, 1976.

———. "The Theological Purpose of the Book of Micah." In *Beiträge zur alttestamentliche Theologie: Festschrift für Walther Zimmerli*, edited by H. Donner et al, 276–87. Göttingen: Vandenhoeck & Ruprecht, 1977.

McCarter, P. Kyle, Jr. *I Samuel*. AB 8. New York: Doubleday, 1980.

McCarthy, Dennis, J. "Notes on the Love of God in Deuteronomy and the Father-Son Relationship Between Israel and Yahweh." *CBQ* 27 (1965) 144–47.

———. *Old Testament Covenant: A Survey of Current Opinions*. Richmond, VA: John Knox, 1972.

McFadyen, J. E. "Micah." In *The Abingdon Bible Commentary*, edited by F. C. Eiselen et al. Nashville: Abingdon, 1929.

McKane, William. *The Book of Micah: Introduction and Commentary*. ICC. Edinburgh: T. & T. Clark, 1998.

———. *I and II Samuel*. TBC. London: SCM, 1963.

McKenzie, John L. *Dictionary of the Bible*. New York: Bruce, 1965.

———. "The Gospel according to Matthew." In *The Jerome Biblical Commentary*, edited by R. E. Brown et al. Englewood Cliffs, NJ: Prentice-Hall, 1968.

McNeile, A. H. *The Gospel according to St. Matthew*. London: MacMillan, 1952.

Mendenhall, George E. "Covenant." In *The Interpreter's Dictionary of the Bible*, edited by G. A. Buttrick, 1:714–23. Nashville: Abingdon, 1962.

Menoud, P. H. "Binding and Loosing." *The Interpreter's Dictionary of the Bible*, edited by G. A. Buttrick, 1:438–39. Nashville: Abingdon, 1962.

Mettinger, T. N. D. *Solomonic State Officials: A Study of the Civil Government Officials of the Israelite monarchy*. ConBOT 5. Lund: Gleerup, 1971.

Meyer, R. "Michabuch." In *Religion in Geschichte und Gegenwart*, edited by Kurt Galling, 4:929–31. 3rd ed. Tübingen: Mohr/Siebeck, 1960.

Meyers, Carol L., and Eric M. Meyers. *Zechariah 9–14*. AB 25C. Garden City, NY: Doubleday, 1993.

Milgrom, Jacob. "Repentance in the OT." In *The Interpreter's Dictionary of the Bible: Supplementary Volume*, edited by K. Crim, 736–38. Nashville: Abingdon, 1976.

Milik, J. T. "Fragments d'un Midrash de Michée dans les manuscrits de Qumran." *Revue Biblique* 59 (1952) 412–18.

Mitchell, H. G. "The Omission of the Interrogative Particle." In *Old Testament and Semitic Studies in Memory of William Rainey Harper*, edited by R. F. Harper and G. F. Moore, 1:113–30. Chicago: University of Chicago Press, 1907.

Moore, George Foote. *A Critical and Exegetical Commentary on Judges*. ICC. New York: Scribner's, 1903.

Moriarty, F. L. "Isaiah 1–39." In *The Jerome Biblical Commentary*, edited by R. E. Brown et al. Englewood Cliffs, NJ: Prentice-Hall, 1968.

Morris, Leon. *The Revelation of St. John*. TNTC. Grand Rapids: Eerdmans, 1969.

Mounce, R. H. *The Book of Revelation*. Grand Rapids: Eerdmans, 1977.

Mowinckel, Sigmund. *Det Gamle Testamente, oversatt av S. Michelet, S. Mowinckel, og N. Messel, III. De senere Profeter*. Oslo: Aschehoug, 1944.

———. "Jahves dag." *NTT* 59 (1958) 1–56, 209–29.

———. "Mikaboken: Oversettelse med noter og tekstkritisk kommentar." *NTT* 29 (1928) 3–42.

———. *Profeten Jesaja: En Bibelstudiebok*. Oslo: Aschehoug, 1925.

———. *Prophecy and Tradition: The Prophetic Books in the Light of Growth and History of the Tradition*. Oslo: Dybwad, 1946. [Re-edited as parts I & II of Mowinckel, *The Spirit and the Word: Prophecy and Tradition in Ancient Israel*, edited by K. C. Hanson, 1–80. Fortress Classics in Biblical Studies. Minneapolis: Fortress, 2002.]

Mowry, L. "Allegory." In *The Interpreter's Dictionary of the Bible*, edited by G. A. Buttrick, 1:82–84. Nashville: Abingdon, 1962.

———. "Parable." In *The Interpreter's Dictionary of the Bible*, edited by G. A. Buttrick, 3:649–54. Nashville: Abingdon, 1962.

Muckle, J. Y. *Isaiah 1–39*. Epworth Preacher's Commentaries. London: Epworth, 1960.

Napier, Davie. *Song of the Vineyard: A Guide through the Old Testament*. New York: Harper & Row, 1962.

Neve, Lloyd. "The Common Use of Traditions by the Author of Psalm 46 and Isaiah." *ExpTim* 86 (1975) 243–46.

Niditch, Susan. "The Composition of Isaiah 1." *Bib* 61 (1980) 509–29.

Nielsen, Eduard. *Oral Tradition: A Modern Problem in Old Testament Introduction*. SBT 1/11. Chicago: Allenson, 1954.

Nielsen, Kirsten. "Das Bild des Gerichts (*rîb*-pattern) in Jes. i–xii: Eine Analyse der Beziehungen zwischen Bildsprache und dem Anliegen der Verkündigung." *VT* 29 (1979) 309–24.

———. *Yahweh as Prosecutor and Judge: An Investigation of the Prophetic Lawsuit*. JSOTSup 9. Sheffield: JSOT Press, 1978.

Nogalski, James D. "The Day(s) of YHWH in the Book of the Twelve." *SBLSP* 38 (1999) 617–42.

North, Robert. "Angel-Prophet or Satan-Prophet?" *ZAW* 82 (1970) 31–67.

Noth, Martin. "God, King, Nation in the Old Testament: A Methodological Debate with a Contemporary School of Thought." *Journal for Theology and the Church* 1 (1965) 20-48. [Reprinted in *Laws in the Pentateuch and Other Studies*, 145-78. Translated by D. R. Ap-Thomas. Philadelphia: Fortress, 1967.]

Nötscher, Friedrich. *Das Buch Jeremias übersetzt und erklärt.* HSAT 7/2. Bonn: Hanstein, 1934.

———. *Zwölfprophetenbuch.* EB 4. Würzburg: Echter, 1948.

Nourse, E. E. "Parable (Introductory and Biblical)." In *Encyclopaedia of Religion and Ethics*, edited by James Hastings, 9:628-31. New York: Scribner, 1922.

Nowack, W. *Die Kleinen Propheten.* HKAT 3/4. Göttingen: Vandenhoeck & Ruprecht, 1922.

Ollenburger, Ben C. *Zion: The City of the Great King.* JSOTSup 41. Sheffield: JSOT Press, 1987.

Ollendorff, E. "The Moabite Stone." In *Documents from Old Testament Times*, edited by D. W. Thomas, 197-98. New York: Harper & Row, 1958.

Orbiso, T. de. "El cántico ala viña de amado (Is 5,1-7)." *EstEcl* 34 (1960) 715-31.

Orelli, Conrad von. "Micah." In *International Standard Bible Encyclopedia*, edited by James Orr, 3:2046-47. Grand Rapids: Eerdmans, 1952.

———. *The Twelve Minor Prophets.* Translated by J. S. Banks. Edinburgh: T. & T. Clark, 1893.

Osswald, E. "Zur Abgrenzung alttestamentlicher Predigtperikopen." In *Wort und Welt: Festschrift für E. Hertzsch*, 243-50. Berlin: Evangelische Verlagsanstalt, 1968.

Oswalt, J. N. "Righteousness in Isaiah: A Study of the Function of Chapters 56-66 in the Present Structure of the Book." In *Writing and Reading the Scroll of Isaiah: Studies of an Interpretive Tradition*, edited by C. C. Broyles and C. A. Evans, 177-91. VTSup 70/1. Leiden: Brill, 1997.

Overholt, Thomas W. "Jeremiah 2 and the Problem of 'Audience Reaction.'" *CBQ* 41 (1979) 262-73.

Page, T. E., ed. *The Apostolic Fathers I.* Loeb Classical Library. Cambridge: Harvard University Press, 1952.

Pákozdy, L. M. "Michabuch." In *Biblisch-Historisches Handwörterbuch.* edited by L. Rost and Bo Reicke vol. 2, columns 1211-12. Göttingen: Vandenhoeck & Ruprecht, 1962.

Parunak, H. Van Dyke. "A Semantic Survey of NḤM." *Bib* 56 (1975) 512-32.

Paterson, John. *The Goodly Fellowship of the Prophets: Studies Historical, Religious, and Expository in the Hebrew Prophets.* New York: Scribner's, 1948.

———. "Jeremiah." In *Peake's Commentary on the Bible*, edited by Matthew Black et al. London: Thomas Nelson, 1962.

Patrick, Dale. "Election." In *The Anchor Bible Dictionary*, edited by D. N. Freedman, 2:434-41. New York: Doubleday, 1992.

Paul, Shalom M. *Amos: A Commentary on the Book of Amos.* Hermeneia. Minneapolis: Fortress, 1991.

Peake, Arthur S. *Jeremiah I.* The Century Bible. Edinburgh: T. C. & E. C. Jack, 1910.

Peiser, F. E. "Micha 5." *OLZ* 20 (1917) 363-67.

Penna, S. *Isaia.* La Sacra Bibbia. Vecchio Testamento. Rome: Marietta, 1958.

Perrin, Norman. *What is Redaction Criticism?* Guides to Biblical Scholarship. Philadelphia: Fortress, 1969.

Petersen, David L. "Eschatology (OT)." In *The Anchor Bible Dictionary*, edited by D. N. Freedman, 2:575–79. New York: Doubleday, 1992.
Petit, T. "L'évolution sémantique des termes hébreux et araméens *phh* et *sgn* et accadiens *pahatu* et *saknu*." *JBL* 107 (1988) 53–67.
Pezzella, S. "La parabola della vigna (Is. 5,1–7)." *BeO* 5 (1963) 5–8.
Pfeiffer, Egon. "Die Disputationsworte in Buche Maleachi." *EvT* 19 (1959) 546–68.
Pfeiffer, Robert H. *Introduction to the Old Testament*. New York: Harper, 1948.
Phillips, Anthony "Prophecy and Law." In *Israel's Prophetic Tradition: Essays in Honour of Peter R. Ackroyd*, edited by R. Coggins et al., 217–32. Cambridge: Cambridge University Press, 1982.
Piper, Otto A. "Knowledge." In *The Interpreter's Dictionary of the Bible*, edited by G. A. Buttrick, 3:42–48. Nashville: Abingdon, 1962.
Plumptre, E. H. "The Epistles to the Seven Churches of Asia. VI.—Philadelphia. (Rev. iii.7–13)." *Expositor* 1st ser. 3 (1876) 286–87.
Pont, J. W. "Micha Studiën, I." *TS* 6 (1888) 235–46.
———. "Micha Studiën, II." *TS* 7 (1889) 436–53.
———. "Micha Studiën, III." *TS* 10 (1892) 329–60.
Porteous, N. W. "Jerusalem–Zion: The Growth of a Symbol." In *Verbannung und Heimkehr: Festschrift für Wilhelm Rudolph*, edited by A. Kuschke, 235–52. Tübingen: Mohr/Siebeck, 1961.
Powell, Mark Allan. "Do and Keep What Moses Says [Matthew 23:2–7]." *JBL* 114 (1995) 419–35.
Preston, R. H., and A. T. Hanson. *The Revelation of Saint John the Divine*. TBC. London: SCM, 1949.
Pritchard, James B., ed. *Ancient Near Eastern Texts Relating to the Old Testament*. 3rd ed. Princeton: Princeton University Press, 1969.
Procksch, Otto. *Jesaja I*. KAT 9. Leipzig: Deichertsche, 1930.
Rad, Gerhard von. *Genesis*. Transslated by John H. Marks. OTL. Philadelphia: Westminster, 1966.
———. *Old Testament Theology* Vol. 2. Translated by D. M. G. Stalker. Edinburgh: Oliver & Boyd, 1967.
———. "The Origin of the Concept of the Day of Yahweh." *JSS* 4 (1959) 97–108.
———. "Die Stadt auf dem Berge." In *Gesammelte Studien zum Alten Testament*, 214–24. Munich: Kaiser 1958.
Reed, W. L. "Asherah." In *The Interpreter's Dictionary of the Bible*, edited by G. A. Buttrick, 1:250–52. Nashville: Abingdon, 1962.
Reicke, Bo. "Liturgical Traditions in Mic 7." Translated by J. T. Willis. *HTR* 60 (1967) 349–67.
———. *Neutestamentliche Zeitgeschichte*. Berlin: Töpelmann, 1965. [English translation *The New Testament Era: The World of the Bible from 500 B.C. to A.D. 100*. Translated by David E. Green. Philadelphia: Fortress, 1968.]
Reid, W. S. "Election." In *International Standard Bible Encyclopedia*, edited by G. W. Bromiley, 2:56–57. Grand Rapids: Eerdmans, 1982.
Renaud, B. *La Formation du Livre de Michée: Tradition et Actualisation*. EBib. Paris: Gabalda, 1977.
———. *Structure et attaches littéraires de Michée IV–V*. Cahiers de la Revue biblique 2. Paris: Gabalda, 1964.

Rendtorff, Rolf. "Alas for the Day! The 'Day of the Lord' in the Book of the Twelve." In *God in the Fray: A Tribute to Walter Brueggemann*, edited by T. Linafelt and T. K. Beal, 186–97. Minneapolis: Fortress, 1998.

———. "The Book of Isaiah: A Complex Unity. Synchronic and Diachronic Reading." *SBLSP* 30 (1991) 8–20. [Revised in *New Visions of Isaiah*, edited by R. F. Melugin and M. A. Sweeney, 32–49. JSOTSup 214. Sheffield: Sheffield Academic, 1996.]

———. "Botenformel und Botenspruch." *ZAW* 74 (1962) 165–77.

———. "The Composition of the Book of Isaiah." In *Canon and Theology: Overtures to an Old Testament Theology*, edited and translated by M. Kohl, 146–69. OBT. Minneapolis: Fortress, 1993.

———. "Litterarkritik und Traditionsgeschichte." *EvT* 27 (1967) 138–53.

Reventlow, Henning Graf. "A Grammatical Solution of the Cultus Question in Is 1." In *Proceedings of the Twenty-Sixth International Congress of Orientalists*, 2:52–53 New Delhi: International Congress of Orientalists, 1968.

Ridderbos, J. *De Kleine Profeten*. 2nd ed. Kampen: Kok, 1932.

———. *De Profeet Jesaja, opnieuw uit den Grontekst vertaald en verklaard I*. Derde Druk. KVHS. Kampen: Kok, 1940.

Riessler, P. *Die Kleinen Propheten*. Rottenburg: Bader, 1911.

Rignell, L. G. "Isaiah Chapter I: Some Exegetical Remarks with Special Reference to the Relationship between the Text and the Book of Deuteronomy." *ST* 11 (1957) 140–58.

Rinaldi, G. "Is. 22,18." *BeO* 5 (1963) 205.

Ringgren, Helmer. "Litterärkritik, formhistoria, traditionshistoria—eller vad?" *Religion och Bibel* 25 (1966) 45–56.

———. "Oral and Written Transmission in the Old Testament." *ST* 3 (1950) 34–59.

Roberts, J. J. M. "The Davidic Origin of the Zion Tradition." *JBL* 92 (1973) 329–44.

———. "Isaiah 2 and the Prophet's Message to the North." *JQR* 75 (1985) 290–308.

———. "The Motif of the Weeping God in Jeremiah and Its Background in the Lament Tradition of the Ancient Near East." *OTE* 5 (1992) 361–74.

———. "Zaphon, Mount." In *The Interpreter's Dictionary of the Bible: Supplementary Volume*, edited by K. Crim, 977. Nashville: Abingdon, 1976.

———. "Zion in the Theology of the Davidic–Solomonic Empire." In *Studies in the Period of David and Solomon and Other Essays*, edited by Tomoo Ishida, 93–108. Winona Lake, IN: Eisenbrauns, 1982.

Robertson, E. "Isaiah Chapter I." *ZAW* 52 (1934) 231–36.

Robinson, A. "Zion and *Saphon* in Psalm XLVIII 3." *VT* 24 (1974) 118–23.

Robinson, H. W. "Micah." In *Encyclopedia Britannica*, 15:407. Chicago: Encyclopedia Britannica, 1960.

Robinson, T. H. *Die zwölf Kleinen Propheten*. 3rd ed. Translated by Otto Eissfeldt. Tübingen: Mohr/Siebeck, 1964.

Rogers, R. W. *Isaiah*. Abingdon Bible Commentary. Nashville: Abingdon, 1929.

Rohland, E. "Die Bedeutung der Erwählungstraditionen Israels für die Eschatologie der alttestamentlichen Propheten." PhD diss., University of Heidelberg, 1956.

Roth, W. M. W. "The Numerical Sequence X/X + l in the Old Testament." *VT* 12 (1962) 300–311.

Rowley, H. H. "The Prophet Jeremiah and the Book of Deuteronomy." In *Studies in Old Testament Prophecy Presented to Professor Theodore H. Robinson*, edited by H. H. Rowley, 157–74. Edinburgh: T. & T. Clark, 1950.

Rudolph, Wilhelm. *Das Buch Ruth, Das Hohe Lied, Die Klagelieder*. KAT 17. Stuttgart: Gütersloh, 1962.

———. *Jeremiah*. HAT 12. 3rd ed. Tübingen: Mohr, 1968.

———. *Micha–Nahum–Habakuk–Zephanja*. Edited by Wilhelm Rudolph et al. KAT 13. 3rd ed. Stuttgart: Gütersloh, 1975.

Ruffenach, F. "Malitia et Remissio Peccati (Is. 1, 1–20)." *VD* 7 (1927) 145–49, 165–68.

———. "Peccati malitia et punitio (Is. 5, 1–7)." *VD* 7 (1927) 204–10.

Rupprecht, Eduard. *Wissenschaftliches Handbuch der Einleitung in das Alte Testament*. Gütersloh: Bertelsmann, 1898.

Sabourin, L. "Un classement littéraire des Psaumes." *Sciences Ecclésiastiques* 16 (1964) 23–58.

Saebø, M. "יוֹם *yôm*; יוֹמָם *yômām*; יוֹם יהוה *yôm YHWH*." In *Theological Dictionary of the Old Testament*, edited by G. J. Botterweck and H. Ringgren, 6:7–32. 15 vols. Grand Rapids: Eerdmans, 1990.

Sanmartin-Ascaso, Joachin. "דּוֹד *dôd*." In *Theologisches Wörterbuch zum Alten Testament*, edited by G. J. Botterweck and H. Ringgren, 2:152–67. 11th ed. Stuttgart: Kohlhammer, 1974.

Sawyer, J. F. A. *Isaiah*. The Daily Study Bible (Old Testament). Vol. 1. Louisville: Westminster John Knox, 1984.

Saydon, P. P. "The Maltese Translation of the Bible." *MelT* 16 (1964) 1–22.

Scharbert, J. *Die Propheten Israels bis 700 v. Chr.* Cologne: Bachern, 1965.

Schedi, C. *Rufer des Heils in Heilloser Zeit. Der Prophet Jesaja Kapitel I–XII*. Paderborn: Schöningh, 1973.

Schmidt, Hans. *Die Grossen Propheten übersetzt und erklärt*. Die Schriften des Alten Testaments 11/2. 2nd ed. Göttingen: Vandenhoeck & Ruprecht, 1923.

Schmuttermayr, Georg. "Beobachtungen zu Jer 5,13." *BZ* 9 (1965) 215–32.

Schoneveld, Jacobus. "Jesaja i 18–20." *VT* 13 (1963) 342–44.

Schoors, A. *Jesaja*. De Boeken van het Oude Testament 9A. Roermond: J. J. Romen & Zonen, 1972.

Schottroff, Willy. "Die Friedensfeier. Das Prophetenwort von der Umwandlung von Schwertern zu Pflugscharen (Jes 2:2–5; Mi 4:1–5)." In *Die Parteilichkeit Gottes: Biblische Orientierungen auf der Suche nach Frieden und Gerechtigkeit*, Luise Schottroff and Willy Schottroff, 78–12. Kaiser Traktate 80. Munich: Kaiser, 1984.

———. "Das Weinberglied Jesajas (Jes 5 1–7). Ein Beitrag zur Geschichte der Parabel." *ZAW* 82 (1970) 68–91.

Schroeder, O. "Miscellen. 3. לֻ = lú 'fürwahr'." *ZAW* 32 (1912) 302–3.

Schulz, Alfons. *Die Bücher Samuel übersetzt und erklärt I*. EHAT 8. Münster: Aschendorff, 1919.

Schumpp, Mainrad. *Das Buch der Zwölf Propheten übersetzt und erklärt*. Herders Bibelkommentar. Freiburg: Herder, 1950.

Schunck, Klaus-Dietrich. "Der 'Tag Jahwes' in der Verkündigung der Propheten." *Kairos* 11 (1969) 14–21.

Schwantes, Siegfried J. "Critical Notes on Micah I 10–16." *VT* 14 (1964) 454–61.

———. "A Critical Study of the Text of Micah." PhD diss., Johns Hopkins University, 1962.

Scott, C. A. *Revelation*. Century Bible. Edinburgh: T. C. & E. C. Jack, 1904.

Scott, R. B. Y. "The Book of Isaiah: Chapters 1–39, Introduction and Exegesis." In *Interpreter's Bible*, edited by G. A. Buttrick, 5:149–381. Nashville: Abingdon, 1956.

———. "The Literary Structure of Isaiah's Oracles." In *Studies in Old Testament Prophecy Presented to T. H. Robinson*, edited by H. H. Rowley, 175–86. Edinburgh: T. & T. Clark, 1946.

Seitz, Christopher R. "Isaiah 1–66: Making Sense of the Whole." In *Reading and Preaching the Book of Isaiah*, edited by Christopher R. Seitz, 105–26. Philadelphia: Fortress, 1988.

———. *Zion's Final Destiny: The Development of the Book of Isaiah—A Reassessment of Isaiah 36–39*. Minneapolis: Fortress, 1991.

Seligsohn, M. "Micah, Book of." In *The Jewish Encyclopedia*, edited by I. Singer, 8:636. 12 vols. New York: Funk & Wagnalls, 1904.

Sellery, Samuel. "The Book of Micah." *CMQ* 6 (1893) 10–29.

Sellin, Ernst. *Introduction to the Old Testament*. Translated by W. Montgomery. London: Hodder & Stoughton, 1923.

———. *Das Zwölfprophetenbuch übersetzt und erklärt*. 3rd ed. KAT 12. Leipzig: Deichert, 1929.

Seow, C. Leong. "Hosea, Book of." In *The Anchor Bible Dictionary*, edited by D. N. Freedman, 3:291–97. New York: Doubleday, 1992.

Serra, R. M. "Una raiz, afin a la raiz ugaritica ǵyr 'guardar,' en algunos textos biblicos." *Claretianum* 4 (1964) 161–76.

Shoot, Frederick von Buelow. "The Fertility Religions in the Thought of Amos and Micah." PhD diss., University of Southern California, 1961.

Simkins, Ronald A. "God, History, and the Natural World of the Book of Joel." *CBQ* 55 (1993) 435–52.

Sjöberg, E. "'Om edra synder äro blodröda ...' Till tolkningen av Jes 1,18." *SEÅ* 12 (1947) 309–26.

Skinner, John. *The Book of the Prophet Isaiah Chapters I–XXXIX*. The Cambridge Bible for Schools and Colleges. Cambridge: Cambridge University Press, 1896.

Skipwith, G. H. "On the Structure of the Book of Micah and on Isaiah ii. 2–5." *JQR* 6 (1894) 583–86.

Slotki, I. W. *Isaiah*. Soncino Books of the Bible. London: Soncino, 1949.

Smal, P. J. N. *Die Universalisme in die Psalms*. Kampen: Kok, 1956.

Smelik, K. A. D. "The Meaning of Amos 5:18–20." *VT* 36 (1986) 129–45.

Smith, B. T. D. *The Gospel according to St. Matthew*. CGTC. Cambridge: Cambridge University Press, 1950.

Smith, G. A. *The Book of Isaiah*. Vol. 1. New York: Armstrong, 1888.

———. *An Exposition of the Bible*. Vol. 4. Hartford, CT: S. S. Scranton, 1904.

Smith, H. P. *A Critical and Exegetical Commentary on the Books of Samuel*. ICC. New York: Scribner's, 1904.

Smith, J. M. P. *A Critical and Exegetical Commentary on Micah, Zephaniah, Nahum, Habakkuk, Obadiah, and Joel*. ICC. New York: Scribner, 1911.

———. "The Day of Yahweh." *AJT* 5 (1901) 505–33.

———. "The Strophic Structure of the Book of Micah." *AJSL* 24 (1908) 187–208.

Smith, Louise Pettibone. "The Book of Micah." *Int* 6 (1952) 210–27.

Smith, W. R. *The Prophets of Israel and their Place in History to the Close of the Eighth Century*. New York: Appleton, 1882.

Snaith, N. H. *Amos, Hosea and Micah*. Epworth Preacher's Commentaries. London: Epworth, 1956.

———. "The First and Second Books of Kings." In *The Interpreter's Bible*, edited by G. A. Buttrick, 3:2–18. Nashville: Abingdon, 1954.

———. "Micah." In *The Teacher's Commentary*, edited by G. Henton Davies and Alan Richardson. London: SCM, 1955.

Snijders, L. A. *Jesaia I*. POut. Nijkerk: Callenbach, 1969.

Sohn, Seock-Tae. *The Divine Election of Israel*. Grand Rapids: Eerdmans, 1991.

Souza, B. de. "The Coming of the Lord." *LASBF* 20 (1970) 166–208.

Speier, Salomon. "Zu drei Jesajastellen: Jes. 1,7; 5,24; 10,7." *TZ* 21 (1965) 310–13.

Speiser, E. A. "An Analogue to 2 Sam. i, 21, Aqht I, 44–45." *JBL* 69 (1950) 377–78.

———. *Genesis*. AB 1. Garden City, NY: Doubleday, 1964.

———. "'People' and 'Nation' of Israel." *JBL* 19 (1960) 157–63.

Spieckermann, Hermann. "Barmherzig und gnädig ist der Herr . . ." *ZAW* 102 (1990) 1–18.

———. "*Dies Irae*: Der alttestamentliche Befund und seine Vorgeschichte." *VT* 39 (1980) 194–208.

Stade, Bernhard. "Bemerkungen über das Buch Micha." *ZAW* 1 (1881) 161–72.

———. "Zu Jes. 3,1. 17. 24. 5,1. 8, 11. 12–14. 16. 9,7–20. 10,26." *ZAW* 26 (1906) 129–41.

Stanley, D. M., and R. E. Brown. "Aspects of New Testament Thought." In *The Jerome Biblical Commentary*, edited by R. E. Brown et al., 2:768–99 Englewood Cliffs, NJ: Prentice-Hall, 1968.

Stansell, Gary. "Isaiah 28–33: Blest be the Tie that Binds (Isaiah Together)." In *New Visions of Isaiah*, edited by R. F. Melugin and M. A. Sweeney, 68–103. JSOTSup 214. Sheffield: Sheffield Academic, 1996.

Stave, Erik. *Inledning till Gamla Testamentets Kanoniska Skrifter*. Stockholm: Norstedt, 1912.

———. *Israels Profeter, III. Mika, Sefanja, Nahum, Den Profetiska Lagboken Habackuk*. Stockholm: Norstedt, 1919.

Steck, Odil Hannes. "Autor und / oder Redaktor in Jesaja 56–66." In *Writing and Reading the Scroll of Isaiah: Studies of an Interpretive Tradition*, edited by C. C. Broyles and C. A. Evans, 219–59. VTSup 70/1. Leiden: Brill, 1997.

———. "Tritojesaja im Jesajabuch." In *Studien zu Tritojesaja*, 3–45. BZAW 203. Berlin: De Gruyter, 1991.

Steinmann, J. *Le Prophète Isaïe: sa vie, son oeuvre et son temps*. LD 5. Paris: Editions du Cerf, 1950.

Steinmann, J., and Abbé Hanon. *Connaître la Bible*. Bruges: de Brouwer, 1962.

Stenning, J. F. *The Targum of Isaiah*. Oxford: Clarendon, 1949.

Steuernagel, Carl. *Lehrbuch der Einleitung in das Alte Testament*. Sammlung theologischer Lehrbücher. Tübingen: Mohr/Siebeck, 1912.

Stinespring, W. F. "No Daughter of Zion." *Enc* 26 (1965) 133–41.

———. "Zion, Daughter of." In *The Interpreter's Dictionary of the Bible: Supplementary Volume*, edited by K. Crim, 985. Nashville: Abingdon, 1976.

Stoebe, H. J. "*nḥm*." In *Theologisches Handwörterbuch zum Alten Testament*, edited by E. Jenni and C. Westermann, 2:60–61. Stuttgart: Kaiser, 1976.

———. "Und demütig sein vor deinem Gott." *WD* 6 (1959) 180–94.

Stolper, Matthew W. "The *šaknu* of Nippur." *JCS* 40 (1988) 127–55.

Streane, A. W. *The Book of the Prophet Jeremiah, Together with the Lamentations*. Cambridge Bible for Schools. Cambridge: Cambridge University Press, 1882.

Strydom, J. G. "Micah 4:1–5 and Isaiah 2:2–5: Who Said It First? A Critical Discussion of A. S. van der Woude's View." *OTE* 2 (1989) 25–28.

Studer, G. "Zur Textkritik des Jesaja." *JPT* 3 (1877) 706–30.

Sutcliffe, Edmund F. "A Note on לא הוא Jer 5,12." *Bib* 41 (1960) 287–90.

———. "St. Peter's Double Confession in Mt 16:16–19." *HeyJ* 3 (1962) 31–41.

Sweeney, Marvin A. "The Book of Isaiah as Prophetic Torah." In *New Visions of Isaiah*. edited by R. F. Melugin and M. A. Sweeney, 50–67. JSOTSup 214. Sheffield: Sheffield Academic, 1996.

———. *Isaiah 1–4 and the Post-Exilic Understanding of the Isaianic Tradition*. BZAW 171. Berlin: de Gruyter, 1988.

———. "Prophetic Exegesis in Isaiah 65–66." In *Writing and Reading the Scroll of Isaiah: Studies in an Interpretive Tradition*, edited by C. C. Broyles and C. A. Evans, 455–74. VTSup 70/1. Leiden: Brill, 1997.

———. "Structure and Redaction in Isaiah 2–4." *HAR* 11 (1988) 407–22.

Sweet, J. *Revelation*. TPI New Testament Commentaries. Philadelphia: Trinity, 1979.

Swete, H. B. *The Apocalypse of St. John*. 3rd ed. London: MacMillan, 1911.

Tadmor, Hayim. "Historical Implications of the Correct Rendering of Akkadian *dâku*." *JNES* 17 (1958) 129–41.

Tasker, R. V. G. *The Gospel according to St Matthew*. TNTC. Grand Rapids: Eerdmans, 1961.

Taylor, John. *The Massoretic Text and the Ancient Versions of the Book of Micah*. London: Williams & Norgate, 1890.

Thomas, D. Winton, ed. *Documents from Old Testament Times*. 1961. Reprinted, Ancient Texts and Translations. Eugene, OR: Wipf & Stock, 2006.

———. "Micah." In *Peake's Commentary on the Bible*, edited by M. Black and H. H. Rowley. Edinburgh: Thomas Nelson, 1962.

Thompson, R. J. *Penitence and Sacrifice in Early Israel Outside the Levitical Law*. Leiden: Brill, 1963.

Thordarson, Thorir K. "Notes on the Semiotic Context of the Verb *niḥam* in the Book of Jonah." *SEÅ* 54 (1989) 226–35.

Tomasino, Anthony J. "Isaiah 1.1–2.4 and 63–66, and the Composition of the Isaianic Corpus." *JSOT* 57 (1993) 81–98.

Tournay, R. "Review of *Die Kulttraditionen Israels in der Verkündigung des Propheten Micha* by W. Beyerlin." *RB* 67 (1960) 438.

Tur-Sinai, N. H. "A Contribution to the Understanding of Isaiah i–xii." In *Studies in the Bible*, edited by Chaim Rabin and Moshe Goshen-Gottstein, 154–241. Scripta Hierosolymitana 9. Jerusalem: Magnes, 1961.

Ungern-Sternberg, Rolf Freiherr von. *Der Rechtsstreit Gottes mit seiner Gemeinde: Der Prophet Micha*. Die Botschaft des Alten Testaments, Erläuterungen alttestamentlicher Schriften 23. Stuttgart: Calwer, 1958.

Vaccari, P. A. *I Profeti-1 Isaia-Geremia*. La Sacra Bibbia 6/1. Florence: Salani, 1952.

Vancil, Jack W. "Sheep, Shepherd." In *Anchor Bible Dictionary*, edited by D. N. Freedman, 5:1187–90. New York: Doubleday, 1992.

Vaux, Roland de. *Les Livres de Samuel*. La Sainte Bible. 2nd ed. Paris: Cerf, 1961.

———. "Le 'Reste d'Israël' d'après les prophètes." *RB* 42 (1933) 526–39.

———. "Titres et fonctionnaires égyptiens à la cour de David et de Sàlomon." In *Bible et Orient*, 189–201. Paris: Cerf, 1967.

Vawter, Bruce. *The Conscience of Israel: Pre-Exilic Prophets and Prophecy*. New York: Sheed & Ward, 1961.

Vermeylen, J. *Du Prophète Isaïe à l'Apocalyptique. Isaïe, I–XXXV, miroir d'un demi-millénaire d'experience religieuse en Israël* I. EBib. Paris: Gabalada, 1977.

———. "L'unité du livre d'Isaïe." In *The Book of Isaiah / Le livre d'Isaïe. Les oracles et leurs relectures, unité et complexité de l'ouvrage*, edited by J. Vermeylen, 11–53. BETL 81. Leuven: Leuven University Press, 1989.

Via, Dan O., Jr. "The Relationship of Form to Content in the Parables: The Wedding Feast." *Int* 25 (1971) 171–84.

Viviano, Benedict T. "The Gospel according to Matthew." *The New Jerome Biblical Commentary*, edited by R. E. Brown et al. Englewood Cliffs, NJ: Prentice-Hall, 1990.

Volz, Paul. *Der Prophet Jeremia übersetzt und erklärt*. KAT 10. 2nd ed. Leipzig: Deichert, 1928.

Vriezen, Th. C. "Essentials of the Theology of Isaiah." In *Israel's Prophetic Heritage*, edited by B. W. Anderson and W. Harrelson, 128–46. New York: Harper, 1962.

———. *An Outline of Old Testament Theology*. Translated by S. Neuijen. Oxford: Blackwell, 1958.

Wade, G. W. *The Book of the Prophet Isaiah with Introduction and Notes*. Edited by Walter Lock. Westminster Commentaries. 2nd ed. rev. London: Methuen, 1929.

———. *The Books of the Prophets Micah, Obadiah, Joel and Jonah, with Introduction and Notes*. London: Methuen, 1925.

Waltke, Bruce K. *A Commentary on Micah*. Grand Rapids: Eerdmans, 2007.

Wanke, Gunther. *Die Zionstheologie der Korachiten in ihrem traditionsgeschichtlichen Zusammenhang*. BZAW 97. Berlin: Töpelmann, 1966.

Ward, James M. *Amos and Isaiah: Prophets of the Word of God*. Nashville: Abingdon, 1969.

———. *Hosea: A Theological Commentary*. New York: Harper & Row, 1966.

——— "Isaiah." In *The Interpreter's Dictionary of the Bible: Supplementary Volume*, edited by K. Crim, 456–61. Nashville: Abingdon, 1976.

Ward, W. A. "The Egyptian Office of Joseph." *JSS* 5 (1960) 144–50.

Watts, John D. W. "The Formation of Isaiah Ch 1: Its Context in Chs 1–4." *SBLSP* 1 (1978) 109–19.

———. *Isaiah 1–33*. WBC 24. Waco, TX: Word, 1985.

Watson, Paul. "Form Criticism and an Exegesis of Micah 6:1–8." *ResQ* 7 (1963) 61–72.

Weil, Hermann M. "Le chapitre II de Michée expliqué par le Premier Livre Rois, chapitres XX–XXII." *RHR* 121 (1940) 146–61.

Weinfeld, Moshe. "The Day of the Lord: Aspirations for the Kingdom of God in the Bible and Jewish Liturgy." In *Studies in Bible*, edited by Sara Japhet, 341–72. Scripta Hierosolymitana 31. Jerusalem: Magnes, 1986

Weiser, Artur. *Das Buch der zwölf Kleinen Propheten*. 4th ed. ATD 24–25. Göttingen: Vandenhoeck & Ruprecht, 1963.

———. *Das Buch Jeremia übersetzt und erklärt*. ATD 20/21. 5th ed. Göttingen: Vandenhoeck & Ruprecht, 1966.

———. "Die Darstellung der Theophanie in den Psalmen und im Festkult." In *Festschrift, Alfred Bertholet zum 80: Geburtstag*, edited by W. Baumgartner, 513–31. Tübingen: Mohr, 1950.

———. *The Old Testament: Its Formation and Development*. Translated by D. M. Barton. New York: Association, 1961.
———. *The Psalms: A Commentary*. OTL. Philadelphia: Westminster, 1962.
Weiss, M. "The Origin of the 'Day of the Lord'—Reconsidered." *HUCA* 37 (1966) 29–60.
Wellhausen, Julius. *Geschichte Israels, I*. Berlin: Reimer, 1878.
———. *Die Kleinen Propheten übersetzt und erklärt*. 4th ed. Berlin: de Gruyter, 1963.
———. *Prolegomena zur Geschichte Israels*. 2nd ed. Berlin: G. Reimer, 1883. [English translation of the second edition: *Prolegomena to the History of Ancient Israel*. Translated by J. S. Black and A. Menzies. Cleveland: World, 1961.]
Welzen, H. "Loosening and Binding: Lk. 13.10–21 as Programme and Anti-Programme of the Gospel of Luke." In *Intertextuality in Biblical Writings: Essays in Honour of Bas van Iersel*, edited by S. Draisma, 175–87. Kampen: Kok, 1989.
Wendland, E. R. "Obadiah's Vision of 'The Day of the Lord': On the Importance of Rhetoric in the Biblical Text and in Bible Translation." *JOTT* 7 (1996) 54–86.
Werner, E. "Music." In *The Interpreter's Dictionary of the Bible*, edited by G. A. Buttrick, 3:457–69. Nashville: Abingdon, 1962.
Wessels, W. J. "Isaiah of Jerusalem and the Royal Court: Isaiah 22:15–25, a Paradigm for Restoring Just Officials?" *OTE* 2 (1989) 1–13.
Westermann, Claus. *Basic Forms of Prophetic Speech*. Translated by Hugh Clayton White. Philadelphia: Westminster, 1967.
———. "The Role of the Lament in the Theology of the Old Testament." *Int* 28 (1974) 20–38.
Whitehouse, Owen C. *Isaiah I–XXXIX*. Century Bible. Edinburgh: T. C. & E. C. Jack, 1905.
Wiberg, B. "Allegori." In *Gads Danske Bibel Leksikon*, 1:56–57. Copenhagen: Gad, 1965.
———. "Lignelser." In *Gads Danske Bibel Leksikon*, vol. 2, columns 39–43. Copenhagen: Gad, 1965.
Widyapranawa, S. H. *The Lord is Savior: Faith in National Crisis. A Commentary on the Book of Isaiah 1–39*. ITC. Grand Rapids: Eerdmans, 1990.
Wiklander, Bertil. *Prophecy as Literature: A Text-Linguistic and Rhetorical Approach to Isaiah 2–4*. ConBOT 22. Stockholm: Gleerup, 1984.
Wildberger, Hans. *Isaiah 1–12: A Commentary*. Translated by Thomas W. Trapp. Continental Commentaries. Minneapolis: Fortress, 1991.
———. *Jesaja*. BKAT 10/1–2. Neukirchen-Vluyn: Neukirchener, 1965, 1972.
———. "Die Völkerwallfahrt zum Zion." *VT* 7 (1967) 62–81.
Wildeboer, G. *Die Litteratur des Alten Testaments nach der Zeitfolge ihrer Entstehung*. 2nd ed. Translated by F. Risch. Göttingen: Vandenhoeck & Ruprecht, 1905.
Wilder, Amos N. *The Language of the Gospel: Early Christian Rhetoric*. New York: Harper, 1964.
Williams, Ronald J. "The Fable in the Ancient Near East." In *A Stubborn Faith: Papers on Old Testament and Related Subjects Presented to William Andrew Irwin*, edited by E. C. Hobbs, 3–26. Dallas: Southern Methodist University Press, 1956.
———. "Moabite Stone." In *The Interpreter's Dictionary of the Bible*, edited by G. A. Buttrick, 3:419–20. Nashville: Abingdon, 1962.
Williamson, H. G. M. *The Book Called Isaiah: Deutero-Isaiah's Role in Composition and Redaction*. Oxford: Clarendon, 1994.
Willis, John T. "אב as an Official Term." *SJOT* 10 (1996) 115–36.
———. "The Authenticity and Meaning of Micah 5:9–14." *ZAW* 81 (1969) 353–68.

———. "The First Pericope in the Book of Isaiah." *VT* 34 (1984) 63–77.
———. "Historical Issues in Isaiah 22:15–25." *Bib* 74 (1993) 60–70.
———. *Isaiah*. Living Word. Austin, TX: Sweet, 1980.
———. "Micah 2:6–8 and the 'People of God' in Micah." *BZ* 14 (1970) 72–87.
———. "Micah IV 14—V 5—A Unit." *VT* 18 (1968) 529–47.
———. "*mimmekhā lî yēṣē* in Micah 5, 1." *JQR* 58 (1968) 317–22.
———. "A Note on *w'mr* in Micah 3:1." *ZAW* 80 (1968) 50–54.
———. "On the Text of Micah 2,1aα-β." *Bib* 48 (1967) 534–41.
———. "A Reapplied Prophetic Hope Oracle." In *Studies on Prophecy: A Collection of Twelve Papers*, 64–76. VTSup 26. Leiden: Brill, 1974.
———. "Review of *Micha 6,6–8. Studien zu Sprache, Form und Auslegung*, by Theodor Lescow." *VT* 18 (1968) 273–78.
———. "Review of *Structure et attaches littéraires de Michée IV–V*, by B. Renaud." *Vetus Testamentum* 15 (1965) 400–403.
———. "Some Suggestions on the Interpretation of Micah I 2." *VT* 18 (1968) 372–79.
———. "The Structure of the Book of Micah." *SEÅ* 34 (1969) 5–42.
———. "The Structure of Micah 3–5 and the Function of Micah 5 9–14 in the Book." *ZAW* 81 (1969) 191–214.
———. "The Structure, Setting, and Interrelationships of the Pericopes in the Book of Micah." PhD diss., Vanderbilt Divinity School, 1966.
———. "Textual and Linguistic Issues in Isaiah 22:15–25." *ZAW* 105 (1993) 377–99.
Winckler, H. "Griechen und Assyrer." *AoF* 1 (1896) 305–7.
Wolfe, R. E. "The Book of Micah." In *The Interpreter's Bible*, edited by G. A. Buttrick, 6:895–949. Nashville: Abingdon, 1956.
———. "The Editing of the Book of the Twelve." *ZAW* 53 (1935) 90–129.
Wolff, Hans Walter. *Hosea*. Translated by Gary Stansell. Hermeneia. Philadelphia: Fortress, 1974.
———. *Joel and Amos: A Commentary on the Books of the Prophets Joel and Amos*. Translated by Waldemar Janzen et al. Hermeneia. Philadelphia: Fortress, 1977.
———. *Micah: A Commentary*. Translated by Gary Stansell. Minneapolis: Augsburg, 1990.
Wood, A. S. "Key." In *International Standard Bible Encyclopedia*, edited by G. W. Bromiley, 3:10–11. Grand Rapids: Eerdmans, 1986.
Woude, A. S. van der. "Micah in Dispute with the Pseudo-Prophets." *VT* 19 (1969) 244–60.
———. "Micah IV 1–5: An Instance of the Pseudo-Prophets Quoting Isaiah." In *Symbolae Biblicae et Mesopotamicae Francisco Mario Theodoro de Liagre Böhl Dedicatae*, edited by M. A. Beek et al., 396–402. Leiden: Brill, 1973.
———. *Micha*. POut. Nijkerk: Callenbach, 1976.
———. "Micha II 7a und der Bund Jahwes mit Israel." *VT* 18 (1968) 388–99.
Würthwein, Ernst. "Der Ursprung der prophetischen Gerichtsrede." *ZTK* 49 (1952) 1–16.
Young, Edward J. *The Book of Isaiah I: Chapters 1 to 18*. NICOT. Grand Rapids: Eerdmans, 1965.
———. *The Book of Isaiah II: Chapters 19–39*. NICOT. Grand Rapids: Eerdmans, 1969.
Ziegler, J. *Isaias*. EB. Würzburg: Echter, 1960.
Zimmerli, Walther. *Ezekiel 2*. Translated by James D. Martin. Hermeneia. Philadelphia: Fortress, 1983.
Zorrell, F. "Isaiae cohortatio ad paementitiam (Caput 1)." *VD* 6 (1926) 65–79.

www.ingramcontent.com/pod-product-compliance
Lightning Source LLC
Chambersburg PA
CBHW071149300426
44113CB00009B/1135